THE BEST OF ENEMIES

For Fiona, Oliver, Kate and Isobel, who lived through it all.

NORMAN FOWLER

THE

BEST

OF

ENEMIES

DIARIES 1980–1997

Biteback Publishing

First published in Great Britain in 2023 by
Biteback Publishing Ltd, London
Copyright © Norman Fowler 2023

ISBN 978-1-78590-815-6

10 9 8 7 6 5 4 3 2 1

A CIP catalogue record for this book is available from the British Library.

Set in Adobe Garamond Pro and Gill Sans

Printed and bound in Great Britain by
CPI Group (UK) Ltd, Croydon CR0 4YY

FSC
www.fsc.org
MIX
Paper | Supporting
responsible forestry
FSC® C171272

CONTENTS

Introduction: Two Prime Ministers   vii

PART I: THE THATCHER SUPREMACY   1
1. A Cabinet Divided: January 1980–January 1981   3
2. A 'No Hope' Budget: January–September 1981   25
3. The Biggest Spender in Whitehall: September 1981–March 1982   53
4. Her Finest Hours: April–June 1982   69
5. The Bloody Politics of Health: June–December 1982   87
6. Triumph and Tragedy: April 1983–October 1984   105
7. At War with the Chancellor: October 1984–September 1985   131
8. The Scapegoat: January 1986   151
9. At Odds with the Prime Minister: February 1986–February 1987   163
10. After the Victory: March–December 1987   191
11. A Rich Man's Budget: January–December 1988   215
12. Ten Years On: January–July 1989   245
13. Goodbye to All That: September 1989–January 1990   277
14. Fall of a Giant: June–November 1990   301

PART II: THE MAJOR INHERITANCE   321
15. The New Man: November 1990–December 1991   323
16. A Very Personal Victory: January–April 1992   351
17. The Party is Bust: April–August 1992   373
18. Black Autumn: September 1992   391
19. Disunited We Stand: October 1992–April 1993   405
20. The Fall of the Chancellor: April–May 1993   429
21. 'In Office But Not in Power': May–October 1993   441
22. Back to Basics: October 1993–February 1994   467
23. The Death of John Smith: February–July 1994   487
24. 'Back Me or Sack Me': October 1994–December 1995   517
25. From Government to Irrelevance: February 1996–May 1997   533

Key Players   551
Acknowledgements   557
Index   559

INTRODUCTION

TWO PRIME MINISTERS

These diaries are a tale of two Prime Ministers. The first dominated the political landscape for over a decade, winning three general elections before losing the confidence of her colleagues and being forced to resign. The second was her anointed successor who took up the baton and against all expectations won another election, before seeing his party mired in a bitter civil war over Europe and falling to a landslide defeat at the polls. Meanwhile, the relationship between the two suffered a spectacular breakdown, with the current and past occupants of No. 10 eventually coming to regard the other with barely concealed hostility.

I had the rare experience of observing both of these figures at close quarters, during a career that spanned almost three decades. In the 1970s I was appointed to Margaret Thatcher's first shadow Cabinet, serving under her in opposition until we won the 1979 general election. I was then a member of her Cabinet throughout the 1980s, standing down just months before she herself fell from office. In the 1990s her successor, John Major, recalled me to frontline politics, first to accompany him on the campaign trail in the 1992 general election, then afterwards to become Chairman of the Conservative Party. In the latter role I saw on a daily basis how Thatcher's behaviour after leaving office impacted negatively upon her successor.

It is perhaps inevitable that she should have cast such a long shadow. Margaret Thatcher was one of the most significant and consequential politicians of the postwar period, and despite it being more than thirty years since she left office, her legacy continues to exert a significant influence on the Conservative Party and on wider British politics. Whether she is revered or reviled, she cannot be ignored by students of politics or history.

The fascination which surrounds her is of course primarily due to her political achievements as Prime Minister, and the way that her governments reshaped the terms of political debate after the unrest of the 1970s. It is also in large part a result of her personal attributes. She was Britain's first female Prime Minister, which would have granted her a place in the history books regardless of how she had performed in office. But it was her character, relentlessly combative and fiercely determined, that marked her out as someone quite different to the previous occupants of No. 10.

The Greek tragedy of November 1990 is another factor in the enduring Thatcher mythology. The nature of her departure from office was a trauma from which she herself never recovered, and sections of the Conservative Party took many years to get over it, if indeed they ever have. As a fallen heroine, her achievements and political views were sanctified by her devout followers, who were reluctant to concede that her own mistakes and hubris had contributed to her downfall.

While my record of those years underlines the significance of Margaret Thatcher's time in office, her role in the years following her resignation tends to be overlooked. This is the part of the story on which I hope these diaries cast a new light. What is clear on re-reading them is how her bitterness at her ejection from office manifested itself as a quite unwarranted and personal campaign to undermine the leadership of John Major, the man she had previously promoted and endorsed as her successor. She allied herself with his Eurosceptic critics in open defiance of his policy on Europe and directly encouraged Conservative MPs to vote against his government. Major himself has since described her behaviour as 'intolerable', and as I saw at the time, his anger towards her frequently boiled over. As Party Chairman it was my job to mediate between them on a number of occasions, and this became ever more tricky as their relationship soured.

John Major was, and is, a good man, whose talents were evident when he was appointed as a junior minister under me in the DHSS. He later confided to me that his ultimate ambition was to be Chancellor of the Exchequer, not Prime Minister. Events propelled him into No. 10 but in retrospect, I think he might have been happier to have indeed remained next door at No. 11, although it is to his immense credit that he persevered while consolidating so many of the gains of the 1980s. In 1992 he won a great personal victory but the slow (or not so slow) disintegration of the Conservative Party in the years afterwards put him in an impossible situation. He was sensitive to criticism, and spent more time than was healthy obsessing over the press's opinion of him. Previously a well-adjusted and down-to-earth personality, the pressures of the premiership, not surprisingly, made him tense and frustrated. It is testament to his innate character that once out of office he returned to his previous equanimity, in stark contrast to his predecessor.

Although these diaries are indeed the tale of two Prime Ministers, it is Margaret Thatcher who looms largest. What I hope they demonstrate is how her influence, for good or ill, permeated the politics of the Conservative Party over a prolonged period of time. The diaries begin in January 1980, seven months into the new Thatcher government, but before embarking upon the day-to-day narrative, it might be helpful if I provide a brief prelude, casting my mind back to the real start of the Thatcher years, five years earlier.

* * *

In February 1975, three young Conservative backbenchers met in a small office high up in the main building of the House of Commons to consider the Conservative Party's future prospects in the wake of the dramatic leadership election. The three were Ken Clarke, Leon Brittan and myself. All three of us were very much at the beginning of our political careers – and all three of us were not impressed by the decision that the parliamentary party had just made to replace Edward Heath with Margaret Thatcher.

None of us had the traditional public school background of a Tory MP. I had progressed via the eleven-plus examination to a grammar school in Essex, King Edward VI, Chelmsford; Ken had won a scholarship to Nottingham High School; whilst Leon went to Haberdashers in North London. We had all been to university at Cambridge where differences in school, let alone religion, counted for little and then gone our separate ways. Ken married his life-long love, Gillian, based himself in Birmingham and practised at the Midlands Bar. Leon, who by common consent was the brightest of our Cambridge generation, had begun to build up his career as a defamation barrister. He had been told by the clerk in his chambers that if he persisted in politics he would get no more work from him. He persisted. As for myself, I had spent almost nine years on *The Times*, when for much of that period there were advertisements on the front page and all the reporters were anonymous. I became the paper's first home affairs correspondent, covering the area presided over by first, Roy Jenkins and then, Jim Callaghan. In the best traditions of Fleet Street my lack of knowledge did not prevent me from being sent off to cover the 1967 Middle East War.

Our concern after Mrs Thatcher's victory was about her capacity to beat Harold Wilson in a general election and reverse the downward spiral. Ken Clarke was typically the most outspoken. 'The counter-revolution starts here' he said, in words which I remember clearly from those long-ago years. His worry was that the developing Conservative policies of monetarism and non-intervention (espoused most prominently by Keith Joseph whose withdrawal from the leadership contest had given Margaret Thatcher her opportunity) would be neither popular nor effective. Leon Brittan's position was slightly different. By this time, he had progressed to the marginal seat of Cleveland and Whitby and feared that the appeal of an archetypal middle-class woman from London would not translate easily to the north east. I did not have a marginal constituency but my fears were similar. My South Nottingham seat had disappeared in redistribution so I was in search of a new seat. My worst experience was being defeated at a selection conference by the diarist Alan Clark, who had managed to see the questions in advance. Before that I had been runner-up to Michael Heseltine in Henley-on-Thames where the agent kindly told me that several members had doubts that I was rich enough to afford Henley. A few weeks later I was selected for the super safe Tory seat of Sutton Coldfield on the outskirts of Birmingham and served there happily for the next thirty years.

I was utterly amazed that shortly after the leadership election I received a call to go to the new leader's office and was there appointed as the youngest member of Margaret Thatcher's first shadow Cabinet. My job was to oppose the redoubtable Barbara Castle, the social services secretary, who headed the enormous double department covering both health and social security. She had been a leading Labour politician while I was still at school. I had no background in either health or social security and only three months as a lowly number three spokesman on the front bench. So why was I appointed?

I suspect much of the blame must go to Keith Joseph. He had been Ted Heath's reluctant shadow Home Secretary; well away from the economic and industrial areas that he loved. After four years of covering the Home Office I had just the knowledge and enthusiasm he needed and I came strongly recommended by him and supported by Airey Neave, the Colditz veteran and close friend of Margaret Thatcher, with whom I shared innumerable cups of coffee in the Commons tea room as he sought to persuade me to the Thatcher cause, only stopping when a whip or well-known opponent joined our table. Airey regarded them as the equivalent of prison camp guards where confidentiality had to be maintained.

For me, shadow Cabinet was a hell of a jump and for the first part of the interview I still expected Mrs Thatcher to tell me who my boss would be. When it became clear that I was the boss, I half mumbled words along the lines of 'I hope I can do it' to which her reply was to the effect of 'you should worry': she had to master foreign affairs where she had no experience whatsoever. For the next twelve months I worked as hard as I have ever worked, trying to learn the details of everything from mental health policy to pensions and getting to know the superior beings in the British Medical Association. But it was an ability to make reasonably workmanlike speeches that held me in good stead in those early months, culminating in only one of three standing ovations at the

1976 Conservative Party conference – the other two were for Michael Heseltine and the leader herself. I was beginning to find my feet and the commentators who were now predicting a reshuffle (a signature of the Thatcher years) did not expect me to feature. They could not have been more wrong – in politics, things are never as good (or as bad) as you think.

Eighteen months after my appointment to the shadow Cabinet I was called to the leader's office in the Commons. Margaret Thatcher came quickly to the point. 'I have something difficult to ask you to do', she said. 'I want you to move to transport.' I was to give my place to John Biffen, an early monetarist and follower of Enoch Powell, who ironically was to become one of her bitterest critics. She would do everything to preserve my position with the press but admitted it would be seen as a demotion. I was anything but convinced I should continue in her employment but agreed to take advice. My first interview was with the Chief Whip, Humphrey Atkins. Referring to my original appointment, he said 'You were lucky to be appointed' 'and if it had been up to me you wouldn't have been'. Managing human relations was not high on Atkins's list of attributes.

The news spread swiftly. Most people were surprised, including the lobby. Leon sent an immediate note and there followed a succession of encouraging messages. In the gents toilets, I met the Labour MP Dennis Skinner. He obviously regarded the move as part of some 'plot'. He said that I had established myself in the last three or four months – ever since my party conference speech. 'They can't say you were no good because the party saw for themselves at the conference'. Michael Heseltine said that I was right to stay, 'You may not be Chancellor by forty but you're years younger than the rest of us. I don't know why I should worry about your future'. Edward du Cann met me in the tea room. 'Old boy, everyone gets kicked in the balls once in this game. When it happened to me I didn't recover for two months'. He was sacked as Party Chairman by Ted Heath.

As it happened, the transfer was the best possible thing that could have happened to me. Being the opposition spokesman on health and social security under strict instructions not to promise an extra penny of spending and simultaneously look for every opportunity for cuts was a thankless task; rather like being defence spokesman under Jeremy Corbyn. Added to which, any new ideas, particularly in health, had the potential to provoke fierce attack and intense nerves from the shadow Cabinet and back benches alike. Once I had recovered from my disgruntlement, I slowly began to recognise my potential good fortune. In policy terms, transport was wide open. No Conservative had made any serious changes since Ernest Marples, the transport minister under Harold Macmillan. Transport was a sacred monument to public ownership and regulation stretching back to the 1940s and covering all kinds of activities. If you believed that deregulation and privatisation could benefit the public, and the companies themselves, then the opportunities were immense.

For two years I was left to my own devices to develop policy, but with regular and productive meetings with Margaret Thatcher. I also took advantage of overseas trips to the United States and Europe to see how they ran transport. Greyhound coaches in the US were an obvious guide for our new intercity coach services and the totting-up process for traffic offences was a European import.

With the 1979 election won the question, at least for me, was whether I, who had never even been a junior minister, would have the opportunity to put my plans into action. As she offered me the minister of transport job, Margaret Thatcher warned 'Don't be too quick to say yes ... we only have authority to pay in full twenty-two Cabinet ministers'. As a minister in charge of a department my pay would be the same as the Chief Whip, Michael Jopling, but with a full say in Cabinet, so in 1979 I became number twenty-three in the first Thatcher Cabinet.

And what of the other two in the trio who had discussed the future under Margaret Thatcher? Leon Brittan was recognised as a star intellect and became number two to the Home Secretary, Willie Whitelaw, who was the second most important man in the Cabinet. It required few powers of prediction to forecast that it was only a matter of time before Leon was promoted to the Cabinet. The outcome for Ken Clarke, however, was very different. He had laboured for three years as deputy to Keith Joseph at industry. The assumption was that he would be next promoted as Minister of State to Joseph in the new government; but that was not to be. The two men were not natural bedfellows, with Ken unable to repress his disagreements with his boss.

I could scarcely believe it when Ken was one of five possible candidates offered to me as my junior minister at transport. He became my parliamentary secretary. It was not what he wanted, nor expected, and for the first weeks of our partnership relations were strained. But soon enough his good humour broke through and for the next five years we worked together in the best partnership I ever had in government. Our first campaign was to plot a revolution in transport policy and move away from the dominance of government control.

In 1979 our concern was the position we had inherited after the winter of discontent: the high inflation, the strikes and the all-powerful unions, together with some conspicuously weak management. The need in 1979 was for fundamental reform. It was not a time for endless compromise. That was the essential battleground and it was this battle in which I thought that Margaret Thatcher deserved support. It was not so much 'wets' versus 'dries' – it was much more of a battle between the modernisers, not content to go on as before and those who thought that we should continue to manage the country as best we could, and had done so notably unsuccessfully since the end of the Second World War.

*   *   *

My diaries were mostly written in the shorthand reporters' notebooks I used when on *The Times*. They are not intended as a complete history of the time. They recount my experience working closely with two Prime Ministers. They stretch from what I persist in regarding as my political salad days in the years following the 1979 election. They take in the struggles to achieve economic recovery inside the Thatcher Cabinet, the fall of Thatcher herself and then the election of John Major – who was almost immediately undermined by his predecessor. This is not the well-scrubbed and edited view from No. 10. It is the view of a Cabinet minister who ran three, more accurately four, government departments in that period and later became Party Chairman while most of the party was in revolt over Europe. It is a story of a period that opened so hopefully, saw undoubted success, but was brought to an inglorious end by internal and open dispute – encouraged by the actions of the former leader who had relied on party loyalty to remain in power for over a decade.

I had, to all intents and purposes, given up diary writing after my change from social services to transport in 1976. In retrospect that was a vast pity, because it missed out the most important step of my life – my marriage to Fiona in 1979. My wife tells me to leave it at that – so I will only add that I could not have managed without her love, encouragement and friendship.

PART I

THE THATCHER SUPREMACY

I

A CABINET DIVIDED

JANUARY 1980–JANUARY 1981

Margaret *Thatcher's first Cabinet was anything but a united team with several Cabinet members like Jim Prior, Francis Pym and Norman St John-Stevas opposed to the scale of the Treasury's proposed spending cuts. There were others who suspended judgement but were careful not to be too closely identified with the Chancellor's policy. As for myself, I was free to implement the policies I had set out in opposition. I entered a world of nationalised industry. We had nationalised road haulage under the banner of the National Freight Corporation (NFC) to move our goods and deliver our parcels. There was even a nationalised removals company, Pickfords, ready to move our furniture. Bus and coach transport was dominated by the nationalised National Bus Company and surrounded by regulation. Any private-sector company brave enough to propose a new, cheap coach service from, say, Birmingham to London, had to apply to quasi-judicial traffic commissioners. They would invariably be opposed by the nationalised British Rail on the grounds that as they already ran such a service, there was no need for another. British Rail itself had a series of subsidiary companies, which were scarcely profitable and woefully underinvested. Their hotels were an outstanding example. The most famous hotel of all, Gleneagles, was at the time only open for six months a year. To complete the list of public ownership, there was the anonymous sleeping giant, the British Transport Docks Board, which owned ports like Southampton, Cardiff and Hull. The result of our work was three transport bills in three years; including the first privatisations under the Thatcher government.*

SUNDAY 13 JANUARY 1980

I am back after a week in the USA. The American way of life is one I admire and enjoy. The enthusiasm of the nation compares starkly with our own lethargy. Margaret Thatcher's visit there went down extremely well. If she was available, the Republicans would take her as their presidential candidate. As it is they are left with a choice between the uninspiring, like Baker and Bush; the alarming, like Reagan; or the appalling, like Connally. At this stage, Carter will win but that could change if something happens in Iran or Afghanistan. Feelings run high on both these subjects.[1]

MONDAY 14 JANUARY

Back to the department. Car at 8.30 and the normal grind of a day which ends after two Scottish votes at 1 a.m. In between I get the traces of transport back. Problems ahead include Horace Cutler's plans to build a vastly expensive Jubilee line extension – which we will stop.[2]

Even the Americans cannot afford these kind of expensive prestige projects anymore.

TUESDAY 15 JANUARY

The transport bill is in committee.[3] We are on our fifth session and we have reached clause 2. Goodness knows there's enough in the bill to debate: the denationalisation of the National Freight Corporation and the first reform of the traffic commissioners for fifty years. But the opposition choose to debate silly points like whether we should sit on Tuesday and Thursday as every committee has done since the year dot.

WEDNESDAY 23 JANUARY

My first appearance before the Transport Select Committee.[4] I arrive a

---

1   In the event, Ronald Reagan saw off his Republican competitors and easily defeated the incumbent, President Jimmy Carter.
2   The Jubilee line was finally opened in 1999 and provided an invaluable London link.
3   The bill introduced a major reform of bus licensing. it deregulated long-distance bus services and allowed authorities to deregulate local services on a trial basis. It privatised the NFC, a conglomerate of road haulage and other businesses, some similar, some not.
4   Departmental select committees had only been set up in 1979 following the election. They had wide terms of reference, could appoint specialist advisers and were supposed to operate regardless of party allegiances.

few minutes early to find a great crowd waiting in the corridor. The doors then open and we are all ushered in. Questioning goes on for two hours. We talk about everything from my position in Cabinet to energy policy. Sydney Chapman, my genial and loyal parliamentary private secretary, thinks it was 'a great triumph'. I thought it went well but was intrigued by the reaction of one *Tory* member of the committee afterwards. 'Fine', he said, 'we will have to sharpen up'. The select committee could be a remarkable new weapon against government with members putting their first loyalty to it rather than their party. The whips won't like this development and nor will ministers.

THURSDAY 31 JANUARY

Cabinet. There is a second-reading debate on public spending with the usual people arguing against more cuts: Jim Prior, Norman St John-Stevas, Ian Gilmour, Peter Carrington; a formidable group. The argument is that we are basically creating two nations because by going for social security and health we are hitting the poor. I argue that if we want to cut public expenditure – and it is what the Cabinet say they want – then we have to cut social security as that is the budget which has grown the most – £14 billion to £20 billion from 1974 to 1980. Norman St John-Stevas protests that only 'some' of the party want more cuts. John Biffen intervenes to say that if he wants to help the poor then we should stop aid to the arts (like Covent Garden opera), most of which went to the rich. Norman says that this is a thoroughly trivial argument and then sits fuming saying 'disgraceful', 'despicable' while even Nick Edwards shouts 'cheap'. Margaret restores order and finally we go to the specifics. Keith Joseph suggests that the Christmas bonus should go (a £10 bonus to all pensioners). I eagerly support. It was the first proposal I had ever made at Cabinet and Margaret had jumped down my throat. This time, Margaret is more responsive but won't accept. It was an election pledge. Had we taken a vote the Christmas bonus would have gone but Cabinets don't vote. In the last analysis the PM decides. She decided against. So we don't help the children. We help the middle class by giving them £10 for Christmas. Next in the firing line is Michael Heseltine. He has prepared an elaborate defence of his housing programme and suggests cutting mortgage tax relief. He is immediately told by Margaret that as long as she is PM that would not happen. After various other diversionary tactics he is roundly told by Margaret that she spends longer listening to him than any other minister. She believes that the housing programme should be cut – and cut it will be. By this time we are all pretty exhausted. It has lasted from 10 a.m. until well after 1 p.m. It had not been that bad but the tensions are obvious enough. There are a number of ministers who plainly don't believe in what we are doing on public spending. There are others who have doubts but keep their own counsel. This leaves Margaret Thatcher pretty isolated. No real problems yet – but if the going gets really rough…

SATURDAY 2 FEBRUARY

I am forty-two today. Fiona and I have a great row on my attitude to abortion. My view up to now has been to accept the views of my Roman Catholic constituents, not with any great enthusiasm but recognising the strength of *their* feeling. To be honest I have not given the issue a great deal of thought. It is not an issue which has touched me. Fiona says that it only really touches women in any event. It is not the greatest birthday but F's onslaught at least means I will make up my own mind and not simply jog along with the mass view. What is the mass view in any event? Most of the people who come to see me don't want abortions at all. It is not an argument on degree as far as they are concerned.

THURSDAY 7 FEBRUARY

The first Cabinet for a very long time where no one raises public expenditure. We talk instead about parliamentary allowances and the latest report from the Top Salaries Review Board. The report will probably go through untouched, but everyone is concerned that there are quite a number of MPs 'fiddling' their expenses. The favourite allegation (among Conservative MPs) was that four MPs (Labour) would share a car to drive north and then each claim the mileage allowance. Another charge (bipartisan) was that one or two MPs from far-flung constituencies claimed so much in mileage allowance that they must be in perpetual motion. While the charge from Labour was that too many Tories had outside interests, some undeclared. It is the kind of anecdotal discussion that politicians love and we meander happily on.

From Cabinet to the Transport Bill Committee. We are still going slow. We take them through the night. I slip away at 3 a.m. and come back reasonably fresh at 8.00. Still no real progress, so we decide to move a motion to sit on Friday afternoon and go on to midnight. Albert Booth almost blows a gasket at the prospect of a Friday night sitting and becomes almost speechless. He makes quite possibly the shortest speech he has ever made and sits down. Prescott is much better and a deal is done.[5] I withdraw the sittings motion and everyone retires more or less happy, but very tired. No one but a lunatic likes all-night sittings.[6]

WEDNESDAY 13 FEBRUARY

An early morning meeting with Keith Joseph on nationalised industry policy. Not a happy meeting. I find Keith a very difficult chairman. He has tramlines that he keeps to and if you are not on the same ones he clearly believes you are very eccentric if not rather stupid. I seek him out later to explain our 'great achievement'; that we were preparing to privatise the subsidiary companies of British Rail. 'But surely that's small beer?' he says. 'No', I reply, 'it would be one of the top 100 companies in Britain'. 'Is that so?' Keith is surprised.[7] Keith then moves onto another part of British Rail. 'But look hasn't Peter Hall[8] got something in what he says. I get the impression you don't take him seriously.' Hall believes that we should start replacing railway lines with roads. It is about the

---

5   Albert Booth, Labour MP for Barrow-in-Furness, was Labour's chief transport spokesman. Absolutely straight. Labour's number two transport spokesman, John Prescott, became an MP in 1970, and for a time we uneasily shared a room – Prescott, myself, Ken Clarke and Cyril Smith. In 1983 he joined the shadow Cabinet and later became Deputy Leader of the Labour Party. A powerful voice in the Labour Party.

6   Frankly the threat of a Friday night sitting was a bluff. We could not have carried out our threat. I cannot remember a Friday evening meeting of a Commons' bill committee. MPs would have wanted to be in their constituencies; the Hansard writers would not have reported the debates; and the Commons staff would probably have gone on strike.

7   I might have over-egged the claim – but not by much!

8   Transport economist and town planner.

least attractive political plan I have ever heard and it doesn't make economic sense either. Keith has been on about this for some years now. He obviously believes I am totally lacking in imagination on the point. He never noticed the awful row we had in November on closing rural rail lines. But there is no stopping him. He will never give up nor appreciate the political daftness of his plan. What reaction does he expect from the public, the unions, the industry in the drawn-out process of closures? Doubtless these are all rather plodding questions but he has not even considered them. I hope he runs his own show with a little more common sense.

SATURDAY 16 FEBRUARY

Dinner with friends in Putney. One of the guests was Maurice Oldfield, now in Ulster.[9] He was brought out of retirement to coordinate security and intelligence in Northern Ireland and now spends most of his time there. Unlike ministers he doesn't just go over for a few days and then come back. He is obviously committed to the job and to the province. He believes that we should take some 'symbolic' action to help the morale of the RUC and security services – like abolish the rule of silence. I think we should do that in any event so find no difficulty in agreeing. Alec Guinness apparently modelled 'Smiley' on Oldfield before doing *Tinker, Tailor, Soldier, Spy* – even down to the thick rimmed glasses. What a life he leads. Everywhere he goes, he goes with two guards and presumably will for evermore.

MONDAY 18 FEBRUARY

Lunch with Peter Parker.[10] My officials are concerned that I am not getting on with him well enough. I was surprised to hear this view and both Ken Clarke and Genie Flanagan[11] think it's rubbish. Nevertheless, Peter needs a little courting from time to time. He's something of an industrial

---

9   Director of MI6 1973–1978

10   Chairman of British Rail 1976–1983. A frustrated politician who should have been appointed to the House of Lords.

11   Civil servant and very able head of my private office.

prima donna but he's also the best chairman that BR have had in years. I like him and he's much better without an audience. Just the two of us, no playing to the gallery; an enjoyable and constructive lunch. Parker is an enthusiast. Thank God for enthusiasts. There are enough people telling you that 'it can never be done'.

THURSDAY 28 FEBRUARY

In the afternoon there is an opposition censure debate. Jim Callaghan is quite good and Margaret not so good. There is a marvellous moment when Margaret quotes from Barbara Castle's diaries about the weakness of 'our Jim' meaning Callaghan – which the opposition hilariously take to mean Jim Prior.

WEDNESDAY 12 MARCH

A thirty-minute meeting with Margaret at No. 10. It is the first time we have been alone since the election. We take tea upstairs with a private secretary sitting in. So not quite as in opposition when no one sat in. For thirty minutes I tell her what we are doing. It is evident that she has taken in a great deal, like the privatisation policies. The important point comes at the end. I ask her about the Channel Tunnel, which I want but which I feared she would be against. Not a bit of it. As long as there's no public money she thinks it would be a first-class plan. I bear the good news back to Marsham Street, which helps us considerably with our promised statement next week.

TUESDAY 17 MARCH

A big majority in the House for boycotting the Moscow Olympic games 315 to 147 but frankly I doubt if it will have any effect. The athletes will do their own thing and go.[12] They don't give a damn about the invasion

---

12   The Olympics were due to be held in Moscow in July 1980 but in December 1979 Russian troops invaded Afghanistan. There were widespread calls for the Games to be moved or boycotted. Most of the UK athletes did go but some, like the sailors and horse riders, did not. They were doubly punished when it came to the Olympic Games in London in 2012 when they were refused permission to parade with the Olympic athletes who had ignored the immorality of the Russian invasion.

by one country of another. As Michael Heseltine says, there are nasty echoes of the Nazi Olympics in Berlin in 1936.

WEDNESDAY 18 MARCH

Transport Questions and I announce our decision on the Channel Tunnel – that there is no public money, but if there was a viable privately financed scheme we would support it. In the main this is supported by the House. The railway MPs are glad to hear that at least the tunnel idea has not been rejected. Albert Booth says why don't we put public money into it – which was precisely the option rejected by the last Labour government. Media reaction is good. The Tunnel is still a long way off – late 1980s at the earliest – even if we get the right scheme. Then what will the French say? I would love to see the plan succeed but after all the false starts over the last 150 years there must be doubts about whether we will pull it off. Nevertheless the Tunnel is back on the agenda.

In November 1979 the Chinese rail minister Guo Weicheng (a veteran of the Great March) came to the UK as a guest of the British government. Our point of personal contact was football. We had both been goalkeepers in our youth and for him the undoubted highlight of his trip was watching an Arsenal match. In April 1980 I led a return railway industry delegation to China. It was only forty years ago, but the contrast between China today and China then speaks volumes for the speed of Chinese development.

TUESDAY 8 APRIL

Up at 7 a.m. for an early breakfast at the Peking Hotel. Fiona and I have been given a vast suite of three rooms and a bathroom.[13] At first, the view is obscured by fog but it soon lifts to a sunny spring day. From our room you look down onto a wide avenue. There are three lanes each way but two in both directions are taken up by bicycles. It is said there are 2.5

---

13   The Chinese invited me as transport minister and Fiona, who had helped me entertain the Chinese minister when in London. The department would not pay for her to travel to Hong Kong. They did, however, find enough money to enable three officials to travel there first class while I paid for Fiona to go by a cheaper airline.

million cycles in Peking. I believe it. We leave in our black limousine, which sweeps to one side everything in front. We pass by the television tower which was built by the Russians in the 1950s and is pointed out to us as a particularly bad piece of architecture. At the Ministry of Railways we have talks with the minister which are notably friendly. We know there is no prospect of instant business but he is encouraging on the prospects of the various companies that are with me. In the evening, a 'banquet' at the hotel. Very formal. Speeches between courses and translated paragraph by paragraph. The usual struggle to master our chopsticks.

WEDNESDAY 9 APRIL

The weather has deteriorated. It is now grey, overcast and with a cold wind. We make another early start and travel north to the Great Wall. The rush hour is at its peak. We pass lorries, trucks, tractors, buses, jeeps, three wheelers. The predominant colour is khaki, giving the impression of a city under military rule. All the vehicles seem to come from the 1950s. The lorries are snub nosed and basic and have soldiers and workers packed into the back. The buses are utilitarian and are all full to overflowing. The road itself is narrow, just a single lane, and our driver obviously believes that we have priority over everything.

THURSDAY 10 APRIL

Railways all day. First a visit to the main Peking marshalling yard which deals with, it is claimed, 400,000 tons of goods a day. This is probably an exaggeration. Nevertheless, the long lines of wagons full of coal, timber and assorted freight show just how much does go by rail. There is also no doubt that Dowty's retarders would be a considerable improvement on the outdated models they have.[14] It is unromantic but it is the kind of export we should be able to sell. Next, onto a locomotive works employing over 6,000 workers. The workers applaud us as we go past and there are chalk notices saying: 'Welcome our British Colleagues'.

---

14 A retarder slows down the speed of wagons being shunted. Without them, the life expectation of wagons is substantially reduced as they crash into each other.

It is impressive just how many women engineers there are – completely different to the British Rail works at Derby. I ask one of the women who has worked here for twenty years about her life. 'How do you like it?' She is not used to the glad-handing ways of British politicians. 'It is for the good of the party', she replies.

Our visit to Peking ends with a dinner at the embassy. Percy Craddock (who I think is very good and much better for us than 'Nicko' Henderson, our ambassador in Washington), presides over a reasonably typical English-style dinner: soup, fish, chicken, pudding. 'No concessions to the Chinese' says Craddock.[15] It is an enjoyable end to a successful trip. We have taken relations forward and the Chinese are, in their words, moving 'step by step' towards some contracts. The minister even says that he is interested in the Advanced Passenger Train – but not just yet.[16]

FRIDAY 11 APRIL

Back to the border by train. Another banquet has been prepared for us. A slight groan from the officials who have been eating one banquet after another. Two memories remain with me. The first was on the lake of the Summer Palace. One of our women guides bursts into song. She had an exceptional voice. It was explained to us that she had been an opera singer, but during the Cultural Revolution she had been forced out of the city to work in the fields. The second came right at the end of the trip. One of the industry party came up to say that he had just seen a perfect copy of the patented device he was trying to sell.

SATURDAY 19 APRIL

---

15 Sir Percy Craddock was our ambassador to China from 1978 to 1983. He played a major role in the Sino-British Joint Declaration in 1984 and became a foreign policy adviser to Thatcher, and briefly to John Major. After he retired, he became one of the most prominent critics of the Hong Kong Governor, Chris Patten.

16 Just as well. The APT never came into service. It broke down during a demonstration for my benefit. It remains a commentary on British Rail that they were unable to establish any major position in the overseas market and now we buy from overseas when once, prior to nationalisation, we were one of the major suppliers in the world.

Back in Britain and a wedding near Oxford. A real Poole family occasion. Oliver (Jr) was a page boy in yellow breeches and a white shirt. Oliver (Sr) arrived in a wheelchair pushed by his wife – a patch over one eye. A rather sad figure.[17]

SATURDAY 24 MAY

We have now been in power twelve months. What are the pluses – what are the minuses? The big plus is the way Margaret has developed as PM. She has imposed her authority and backed her judgement. We have cut public spending and we will cut the civil service. Ministers like Geoffrey Howe, John Nott and Peter Carrington have asserted themselves and no longer is there the jibe that we have no men of ability on our front bench. All told, things have gone much more smoothly than we might have expected. The big minus is inflation. It has bounded up to over 20 per cent and pay demands show no sign of slowing down. Added to this, we are self-evidently entering a recession. The real battles and tensions are still to come. As a government we are still too strident. The public want action but the action needs to be justified in words that seek to unite the nation, not divide it. Jim Prior and the others are winning on that. We haven't found the language or the style.

MONDAY 2 JUNE

Cabinet on the EEC Budget settlement.[18] Most people think that Margaret Thatcher has done wonders. There is no doubt that we would not have got anything like it without her determination. In conventional terms it is a triumph. But it is clear that is not the way she sees it at all. She says little and has obviously accepted that it is all that she will

---

17 Oliver is my stepson. His grandfather, also Oliver Poole, was Party Chairman for Harold Macmillan together with Quintin Hogg (later Lord Hailsham). Hogg rang the bell and rallied the troops. Oliver ensured that the organisation was up to scratch. There was no doubt that on the organisational level the Conservatives massively out-boxed Labour. It is one of my great regrets that because of his disabling stroke we were never able to compare notes.

18 The government had been negotiating the size of the UK's contribution to the European Community Budget since it took office. Britain's net contribution had risen from £150 million in 1976 to £1,100 million in 1980.

get. Peter Carrington and others talk of the achievement. John Nott and John Biffen accept but point out that nothing is altered; nothing is changed. The common agricultural policy marches on. The next time we fight it will be worse and nearer an election. There is also the unspoken belief (fear) that Labour will play the anti-Common Market card when the election comes.[19] Nevertheless, the deal goes through. The only memorable feature being Margaret's total lack of enthusiasm.

FRIDAY 6 JUNE

To Lucas in Birmingham to see the electric van, car and cycle. I gather we are ahead in development at the moment – but for how long? The potential is exciting but I fear the Americans, Japanese or Germans will get there first.

TUESDAY 10 JUNE

To Bournemouth for the Institute of Mechanical Engineers. I lecture them on the need for economy. The paper after mine literally starts with the sentiment that 'efficiency and competition has little relevance in the world of local government.'

TUESDAY 8 JULY

An important week for my second transport bill. The first battle is on drink driving: the accident toll is indefensible by any measure. I put the case before H committee.[20] I simply do not see why preventing drunken drivers killing themselves and anyone else who happens to get in the way should be seen as a question of civil liberties or 'a threat to the social life of the countryside'. I have given up the prospect of random tests to get

---

19   Labour did campaign on coming out of the EEC in the 1983 general election but the pledge was mixed up with so many others in the manifesto ('the longest political suicide note in history') that it failed to have any impact.

20   Many government decisions are delegated to Cabinet committees. The committees are usually referred to by a letter, e.g. E committee oversees economic affairs or H committee on home affairs. It is impractical for every decision to go to full Cabinet but the downside is that Cabinet ministers not on the relevant committee can find themselves excluded from some of the most important decisions. The theory is that any Cabinet minister who disagreed with a committee's decision or simply wanted all ministers to be involved could take it to full Cabinet – but this was undermined later in the Westland dispute.

the rest of the proposals through, although personally I would go for them. What the proposals amount to are the introduction of breathalysers, the elimination of procedural and technical defences, new action against the hit and run drivers and a reformed 'totting-up' system.[21] I am notably supported by Norman St John-Stevas but opposed by Christopher Soames and Michael Jopling. Michael reports that the Agricultural Committee was 'concerned'. Soames just doesn't like the idea. His argument is basically that 'you can't tell when someone is unfit to drive. Some can drive on a lot of drink.' Real saloon bar stuff. Willie Whitelaw is in the chair and agrees the proposals. We have the first drink drive legislation since 1968 and there is no reason why it can't be toughened up on its way through Parliament.

The point not mentioned is seat belts. If road safety is included in the bill what is to prevent an amendment on making the wearing of seat belts compulsory? The answer is nothing. An amendment all depends on the scope of the bill – compulsory seat belts obviously come under road safety. Personally, I would welcome this. I think the question should be settled once and for all. I am also at a loss to suggest any alternative. Going the American way and requiring manufacturers to put in automatic restraints is not possible. I would need all the EEC countries to agree! I have asked the lawyers to check and double check but they say that is the position. So the choice is, do nothing or act. Persuasion only works to a limited extent. I will, of course, be attacked for changing my mind but better that than make the wrong decision. We all know there is a majority both in the Commons and the Lords for compulsory seat belts. It is a scandal that they are being prevented from making a decision. My main aim is to get a bill so that the House can then decide: that I will fight for.

My plan to privatise British Rail subsidiaries (the hotels, the docks, Sealink) is before a different committee and much easier. The chairman is Keith Joseph. He congratulates me on taking the plans forward but

---

21 The proposals were based on the Blennerhassett report, *Drinking and Driving* – Department of the Environment report, HMSO 1976.

thinks there should be a statement in the House. I am not so sure. Why provoke a row prior to the bill? We leave it open.

MONDAY 14 JULY

Word comes through from the PM that she would like me to make a statement on privatising British Rail's hotels, Sealink and the rest. In her view, this is good news for the party and has the advantage of coming before yet another debate on unemployment. I duly appear at 3.30 p.m. The opposition is furious. There is a great deal about robbing the 'seed corn' although neither Sealink nor British Rail's hotels can conceivably be described as goldmines. Stephen Ross for the Liberals obviously thinks I have applied untold pressure to Peter Parker, and Donald Stewart for the SNP compares me to Dick Turpin. I enjoy the afternoon more as they continue.

THURSDAY 17 JULY

Cabinet. The opposition has chosen to debate the public sector next week. They are fielding Peter Shore and David Owen.[22] The PM chooses David Howell on our side but then who? John Nott declines. Then Jim Prior suggests me as having done well on Monday. The PM asks my view. I say 'fine'. She is so surprised to have someone who assents that she immediately agrees.[23] 'If they have an odd team' Margaret adds to laughter, 'so can we'. Angus Maude comes up to me afterwards and says he doesn't know why I 'volunteered'. He spoke at the wind-up on Monday. The noise was so great that not only could no one hear him, he couldn't hear himself.

MONDAY 21 JULY

The debate on the public sector opens amiably with reasonably effective speeches from David Owen and David Howell. No emotions stirred and

---

22 Peter Shore was a former member of Harold Wilson's Cabinet and very anti the European Community. Owen became one of the youngest foreign secretaries under Callaghan. He left the party in 1981 to form the Social Democratic Party (SDP) and led it from 1983 to 1987.

23 Excuses by ministers and shadow ministers to avoid speaking in debates of this kind were legion: 'Not quite ready', 'unbreakable commitment that day'.

the debate goes pleasantly on. Peter Shore starts his wind-up at 9 p.m. It is a good speech. I get up just after 9.30. I first announce our plans for the privatisation of the docks. Great protests from the Labour side: 'It should have been done in a statement etc'. Little do they know it would have been done otherwise in a written answer. I survive their protests and the House listens almost to the end. Then, at 9.57 Jim Callaghan gets to his feet and tries to intervene. No minister in his right mind gives way at this stage so I don't.[24] Great uproar. Callaghan tries to get in again. He seems to be asking (although I can scarcely hear in the noise) about the steel position in South Wales. More uproar as I refuse to give way. The Speaker intervenes. Callaghan comes back yet again. Again, I refuse to give way and end the debate by asking for the support of the House. Our side is delighted that I did not give way. Keith Joseph did two or three weeks ago just before 10 p.m. and was devastated. Clinton Davis[25] comes up from the Labour side to protest at my 'cowardice' in the most pompous way. I fear after listening to him twice I threaten to biff him. He looks surprised and goes away. Callaghan must be under very great pressure to want to interrupt me. I am, after all, only number twenty-three in the government. He is Leader of the Opposition – but for how much longer?

TUESDAY 22 JULY

The *Financial Times* interprets Callaghan's attempt to intervene as meaning I had stung him by a remark about the leadership and his possible retirement. An incredible number of colleagues have come up to say how good it was that I didn't give way. I have obviously had more impact with two minutes of inaudible toing and froing than with quite a number of my entirely audible speeches.

---

24 If the minister fails to move the closure motion at 10 p.m. the opposition can continue debating. To do this he has to be on his feet. If he allows the opposition speaker to take over and it goes past 10 p.m. then no closure can be moved for at least an hour. This is much to the chagrin of government supporters who have to hang around until the vote is finally called.

25 Stanley Clinton Davis, Labour MP and European Commissioner. Went to the Lords in 1990 and later became quite a friend – as so many of my former political opponents did.

THURSDAY 31 JULY

A Cabinet which shows all the strains of the coalition between the radicals and the gradualists. What becomes very clear is just how on edge Jim Prior now is. Margaret Thatcher makes a remark about the importance of 'sound money'. Jim replies, 'I don't give a damn for sound money.' He is more concerned about the unemployment figures. Margaret replies that anyone who feels he cannot support the government's economic policy should let her know. Silence from Jim and embarrassed silence all round. It's the last week in July but we all know it goes much deeper. It would be dangerous for the government to see Jim on the back benches. Nevertheless, the kind of economic policy he wants (expansionist, interventionist) he will certainly never get with Margaret. Relations are also pretty tense between the PM and Norman St John-Stevas. Margaret scarcely listens to his advice and Norman makes it worse by making his case in a rather petulant way.

TUESDAY 7 OCTOBER

To Brighton for the party conference. I am speaking today and I have one piece of luck. Today is the day that the 1980 Transport Act comes into operation. In spite of all the reservations that the bus industry had they have jumped into coach competition. Fares have come down and coach services have increased. I am on just after Norman St John-Stevas who wins a standing ovation. You forget how good Norman can be.

WEDNESDAY 8 OCTOBER

Transport gets a very full press. I am announcing policy and few of the other speakers have done that. The sketch writers are kind. Michael White in *The Guardian* says that I tried to get a libertarian theme out of transport and failed. 'You try', he says.[26] Quite so! Dinner with Will Camp of British Rail public relations. He does his job very well. He runs rings around our lot but he is not someone I warm to. There is

---

26   Michael White was my favourite sketch writer in a strong field.

something forever conspiratorial about him. His number two, Richard Faulkner, is in my view better.[27]

SUNDAY 12 OCTOBER

Back to Cambridge, twenty years after I was Chairman of the Conservative Association there. A very docile audience. The most hostile questions came from Patrick Jenkin's son, Bernard.[28]

MONDAY 20 OCTOBER

Talk with Peter Parker to say I would like him to stay on as Chairman. He says he is delighted to be asked but …' He is split. On one side he wants to finish the job. On the other, it is a job which is totally demanding. His wife Jilly doesn't want him to continue – and that makes a big difference. I say there is no rush. If he wants three years rather than five that would be fine. We will talk again later.

THURSDAY 23 OCTOBER

Splits in the Cabinet on view. The real tensions come when we move on to our plans to reduce the strength of the civil service. Francis Pym leads the doubters. He does not think that he can reach the savings target and he may be driven into 'doctrinaire' measures of privatisation. He is unhappy. Jim Prior chimes in to say that although industrialists are making a lot of noise about the public sector we should not worry so much about that but about the morale of the civil service. Anyone who confessed to being a civil servant at the party conference was hissed, he says. There is an element of truth in what Jim says, but only an element. He snorts when I say I am more concerned about the industrialists. It's not a good meeting as we agree to use our best endeavours to reach a minus 630,000 total.[29]

---

27 Now a Labour member of the House of Lords and a deputy Lord Speaker.
28 Bernard Jenkin later became a MP himself and was a nuisance to ministers from then on.
29 In December 2022, the size of the civil service was 483,450 (ONS March 2023).

THURSDAY 30 OCTOBER

The much-heralded Cabinet on public spending. Geoffrey Howe reveals that talks between Patrick Jenkin and the Treasury have resulted in agreement between them that benefits should be uprated by 3 per cent less than inflation.[30] Previous Cabinets, he says, have run away from decisions on the grounds that we have 'reached the limits of what is politically possible' or we must 'postpone the decision'. If we postpone the decision, then taxes will inevitably go up. Willie supports and says the message should go out that the Cabinet is united and committed to this strategy. He doesn't want to see newspaper stories in the next few days saying, 'senior Cabinet ministers say this or say that.' Margaret sums up to very much the same effect and emphasises that we must seek to get the reductions that the Chancellor is talking about. The only option will be further increases in tax and this is something that no one wants.

I say that if the Chancellor's policies are overturned, that would be a fundamental defeat for the whole government. Later in the division lobby Margaret comes up to me and says how very much she agrees with this last point. The PM has called an additional Cabinet meeting in the morning. This means I have to cancel a conference that I am opening in the Midlands. You might have thought that an industry organisation would appreciate that a Cabinet meeting might come before their own conference. Not a bit of it. The chairman sends a telegram to 10 Downing Street protesting to the Prime Minister.

THURSDAY 13 NOVEMBER

Cabinet begins with a sobering report from Humphrey Atkins on the hunger strike in the Maze prison which is now leading to demonstrations in Northern Ireland.

WEDNESDAY 19 NOVEMBER

Back to Cabinet for what we all fervently hope is to be the last stage of the public expenditure discussion. We begin with defence. Margaret

---

30   Inflation then was 15.4 per cent.

announces that the agreement has now been made. Francis Pym has agreed to contribute £200 million, which is £300 million below what the Chancellor was asking for. There is no discussion. It is quite obvious that Francis has won although I am not sure that he sees it that way. Apparently, he still believes that defence should be the exception to every conceivable rule.

That more or less brings the public spending discussions to an end. It has not been a pleasant two weeks. Even today, it is clear that relations are strained. Keith Joseph made an entirely innocuous point and was countered by Jim Prior who had brought Keith's election address along to Cabinet and proceeded to quote what he had said. In fact, it didn't have a great deal of relevance to what we were talking about, but it was a clear indication of the division that is now apparent in the Cabinet room. It is ridiculous that a minister comes along to a Cabinet meeting with the election address of one of his colleagues and quotes it against him.

SUNDAY 30 NOVEMBER

The position is depressing. We are not remotely a united Cabinet. Some ministers, like Francis Pym, have got away with a great deal, others, like Jim Prior, clearly don't like the ship that they are serving in but prefer nevertheless to serve in it rather than follow a course of their own on the back benches. The government crucially depends upon the force and upon the conviction of Margaret herself. She is helped considerably by Willie Whitelaw, although Willie is no one's idea of an economics minister. Around her in Cabinet she has a number of colleagues who, to put it at its most charitable, appear to be suspending judgement. In the end of course, Margaret, and all of us, are going to be judged on performance. Inflation is coming down – and coming down dramatically. If the recession bottoms out during the course of next year, industry starts investing again and unemployment starts to come down, then things could look very different by this time next year.

THURSDAY 3 AND FRIDAY 4 DECEMBER

To a Transport Council meeting in Brussels. A complete waste of time.

We are discussing the question of lorry permits – it is the only thing of any consequence we ever discuss. The Germans have a new transport minister, Volker Hauff, who both Norman Tebbit and I take an instant dislike to. Young, pushy and arrogant – but rated highly in West Germany. He simply says that he is not prepared to contemplate any increase in quotas. He refuses to budge and so too does the Italian minister – the appropriately named Signor Formica – so that is that. No permits. A wasted twenty-four hours. It is somehow symbolised when at lunch an interpreter is placed between Norman Tebbit and myself. I have never yet been to a European meeting that has produced anything worthwhile. If the Common Market were to be judged on Transport Council meetings it would be a total flop.

THURSDAY 18 DECEMBER

Lunch at Harold Lever's sumptuous flat in Eaton Square[31], where with Christopher Soames we discuss Philippe de Rothschild's views on a channel *bridge*. Ian MacGregor is also there.[32] His interest is that a bridge requires a formidable amount of steel. Rothschild's view is that a bridge is the modern solution. People drive cars – they want that kind of mobility. There is something in what he says – though the French government don't agree. He visualises a mini town in the middle of the Channel with a casino etc. and sees no problem in finance. A strange eccentric figure – but the wine he brought over is delicious – a couple of bottles of some rare vintage, which both Lever and Soames lust over and look at me resentfully when I venture to have a single glass.

THURSDAY I JANUARY 1981

A break in Casablanca. No bar with a piano, no Humphrey Bogart and

---

31 Harold Lever was elected as a Labour MP in 1945 and served in the Cabinets of Harold Wilson and James Callaghan chiefly as an economic adviser to the Prime Minister. In 1979 he went to the House of Lords.

32 Ian MacGregor, a Scottish-American metallurgist and industrialist, was appointed Chairman of the British Steel Corporation by Keith Joseph in 1980. In 1983, he moved to head the National Coal Board and was there for the 1984–85 miners' strike.

no Lauren Bacall. A modern Air France hotel with a view of an oil re-
finery. But not to complain. Long walks along a wide stretch of sandy
beach and a visit to the Mamounia in Marrakesh to see Frank and Nicole
Law.[33] To get there, we hire a small ancient Renault, which breaks down
halfway but fortunately outside a garage. Finally, we arrive at this very
upmarket hotel. The imposing doorman, who has probably never seen
such a modest car making an entrance to his hotel, takes it entirely in his
stride. 'Welcome to the Mamounia, *minister*', he says, swinging open the
door which almost comes off its hinges.

MONDAY 5 JANUARY

Back in Casablanca, the phone rings in the hotel bedroom at 8 a.m. It is
Tony Mayer, head of my private office, from London. He tells me that
the Cabinet Office had rung him at 11.20 last night to say that the PM
would like to speak to me. The only guidance is: 'you'll probably know
the reason'. The obvious meaning is that there is a reshuffle. But does
this mean I am involved? Where to? Our guess is education – with social
services a possibility. Another guess is that I am simply being promoted
in the job. We don't have long to wait. At 10 a.m. Downing Street is on
the phone – not the PM but the Chief Whip, Michael Jopling. He explains that there are one or two changes being made. I am only involved
to a small extent. Margaret would like me to stay with transport – but
on full pay. Our conversation is very short. Michael says that he doesn't
expect it will take me long to decide to have a pay increase.

MONDAY EVENING

When we land still no one knows the details of the shuffle. Len[34] picks
us up at Gatwick and we tune into the news. The news of a reshuffle is
just coming through but no details. A few minutes later, the car phone
goes. Tony Mayer comes through and then the Permanent Secretary,

---

33   Frank Law had become a very great friend. He had been sent by the NFC board to persuade me to
       cancel the privatisation but was entirely converted to it.
34   Len Wenham, my long-serving and loyal driver.

Peter Baldwin, who says how delighted he is to be the first to say 'Secretary of State'. It is of course enormously good for the department to be restored to their rightful Cabinet status. Tony then tells me the rest of the news. The big change is that Norman St John-Stevas is out. He was offered the job of Minister for the Arts but refused the demotion. I fear his execution was inevitable but I for one will miss him. He is somehow out of his age in this modern Cabinet but there is no more civilised man than Norman. The best news is that in comes Leon as Chief Secretary to the Treasury. It is a notable promotion. He will be working with his friend Geoffrey Howe. I suspect the Chancellor did not find John Biffen the toughest Chief Secretary. For Leon it is just the start. The only missing piece is Ken. He remains firmly where he is as parliamentary secretary for transport. She can't keep him at that level for ever. Fiona and I decide to go (very late) to Leon and Diana's wedding reception at No. 11. The whole place is buzzing with excitement. What a wedding present for Leon – richly deserved. Intellectually, he is the best of our generation. He is not a natural presenter of policy or even very much of an innovator. But give him a brief and he will come up with the best advice going. That could be his long-term problem. He is seen more as a brilliant adviser than a performer.

There are many old pals at the reception and we pick up Ken Clarke and John Gummer for dinner. After John and Penny have left, I say to Ken that I will go to the PM and talk about *his* position. It may not do any good, but it should avoid him being overlooked at the next shuffle round. Ken's growth potential is as good as Leon's. I think I can help in that. So this is really the end of 1980 – albeit six days into 1981.

2

A 'NO HOPE' BUDGET

JANUARY–SEPTEMBER 1981

*B y this stage the government was running into serious difficulties. Unem-
ployment was over two million and looked likely to go over three million.
The winter of discontent may have been behind us but strikes still scarred the
economy. Nationalised industries like steel and coal needed ever more subsidy
with the miners delivering a devastating blow to the government in February
1981. Politically, the government was in deep trouble, with some Tory MPs
already in a state of unrest. It made a singularly unpromising background for
the Chancellor, Geoffrey Howe, who was due to deliver his annual Budget to
the Commons in March. For Conservatives, reducing taxes was an article of
faith. On present policies there was certainly no prospect of that. This was the
prelude to the most important Budget of the early Thatcher years.*

THURSDAY 8 JANUARY 1981

The first Cabinet I have attended as a fully paid-up member. Christopher Soames says that at last she has made 'an honest man' of me. In the
afternoon we travel to Windsor to receive the seals of office. There is a
slight delay before going in for Norman St John-Stevas to surrender his
seals. The Palace is extremely good at organising these things and there
is absolutely no question that Norman would be left talking uncomfortably to us outside. He is dealt with first and quite separately, and it is
only when that was done that we move on to the more cheerful occasion
of new arrivals. When I was first made a member of the Privy Council
back in May 1979, it was the first time that I had come anywhere near

the Queen. I found the whole process nerve-wracking, as Leon obviously does today. This time it is easier. You go forward, kneel on the first kneeling stool with a testament in your right hand, read the oath and then move forward to the second stool. You kiss hands with the Queen, stand up, receive the box with the seals of office in it and retreat to the waiting line of privy counsellors without turning your back on the Queen herself. Upon examination, the seals themselves prove to be exactly that and doubtless with a plentiful supply of melted red wax would come up very well.

TUESDAY 13 JANUARY

The second reading of my new transport bill. The speech goes remarkably well. There is quite a full house. Enoch Powell is there and so too are some of the brightest of the various nationalised industry supporters. However, I am allowed to go through the introduction of private capital into British Rail and the denationalisation of the docks without any interruption whatsoever. The interest is in road safety. A whole range of speeches from both sides of the House suggest that random tests for drink should be introduced, and also that seat belts should be made compulsory. The most effective Labour speech comes from John Prescott in his wind-up but he speaks so fast that no one really has the opportunity to fully take in the points that he is making.

THURSDAY 15 JANUARY

A longish Cabinet. The most important question is the Scott report on inflation-proof pensions in the public sector.[35] From our point of view it is disappointing. The public sector unions will jump on the fact that provision of inflation-proof pensions is better in France and Germany than it is in the United Kingdom. We remit to Geoffrey the task of thinking of some response. Outside Cabinet, someone says that Bernard Scott has earned for himself a long retirement from public life without the benefit of an inflation-proof pension.

---

35   The inquiry into the value of pensions (Chairman Sir Bernard Scott). Report published 5 February 1981 – Cmnd 8147.

THURSDAY 22 JANUARY

I have a twenty-minute meeting with Margaret at my request. The main purpose is to say that transport is a small department and that Ken is doing the job not only of a parliamentary secretary but Minister of State as well. The implication, which I hope she would take, is that he should not be overlooked in the promotion stakes. She takes the point very quickly and asks me to make that plain to Ken. It is clear that Margaret regards transport as an area where there is much going on and the news is often good. She also regards it as a department which does not forever bring its problems to Cabinet. I suppose if I was Prime Minister that is the way I would want a department to run. I thank her for my new position in Cabinet. She cuts me off in midstream, saying that no thanks are due at all and that she was very embarrassed by the previous position. She also says that if from time to time I would like to just come in and talk, then she would like that.

FRIDAY 23 JANUARY

To Sutton Coldfield to do an advice bureau. I try to get to the constituency once a week. Nothing would be worse if it was said that, now I had become a Cabinet minister, I am never seen. This was the criticism of my predecessor Geoffrey Lloyd.[36] Coming back on the train, I meet Roy Hattersley who had been addressing a Fabian meeting in Coventry.[37] For once, he is quite affable. He says that he does not know what is going to happen at the Labour Party conference tomorrow. Mr Hattersley is not an endearing personality. Richard Crossman once said that he was like a Dickensian villain, and like all Dickensian villains he would be unmasked in the final chapter.

SATURDAY 24 JANUARY

The Labour Party conference at Wembley. The result for the moderates is even worse than they can have expected. The party is now dominated by

---

36 A distinguished former Cabinet minister who was rather out of his time. He had once been private secretary to Stanley Baldwin in an age before community politics.
37 Labour MP and journalist, deputy leader 1983–92.

the trade unions. Michael Foot is in hock to the unions and the Labour Party have now allied themselves to one of the most unpopular institutions in the country.[38] I do not see how men like David Owen and Bill Rodgers can continue to serve in a Labour Party of this kind.

MONDAY 26 JANUARY

Today we have the British Leyland decision. By any stretch of the imagination, an important decision affecting the Midlands particularly and the production of a range of cars including Rover, Triumph and the much-vaunted Metro as well as Land Rover. Extraordinarily, the issue has not come to full Cabinet, although as Keith Joseph's awkward statement reveals we are talking of well over £1 billion aid over the next few years. Labour support, and take delight in Keith's obvious discomfort. The party's reaction is more complicated. MPs with constituency interests are relieved but quite a number of others take the position of John Stokes who asks 'are we year by year to fill the bath with the plug out?'[39]

THURSDAY 29 JANUARY

A meeting with the rail union leaders, Sid Weighell (NUR), Ray Buckton (ASLEF) and Tom Jenkins (TSSA). They are all responsible and reasonable about the prospects for the railways. It is after meetings like this that you wonder why we cannot do better in this country in getting cooperation between government and unions.[40] The one symbol for the future which is agreed upon is electrification. My next task is to try to

---

38 After the Labour Party's defeat in 1979, relations between the left- and right-wing factions had become increasingly acrimonious. At Wembley, the left wing successfully reduced MPs' influence over the party's choice of leader. The following day, four senior Labour politicians, all MPs or former MPs and Cabinet ministers on the right of the party: Roy Jenkins, David Owen, Bill Rodgers and Shirley Williams, signalled their intent to leave the Labour Party and went on to form the Social Democratic Party (SDP).

39 My personal involvement was limited to buying one of the new Metros, which was billed as an example of what British engineering could do. It was a perfectly good car but the trouble was that the 'new' technology that built it was years behind its German and Italian equivalents.

40 Ray Buckton and Sid Weighell may not have much cared for me but this was as nothing compared to their enmity for each other. In meetings they always sat at opposite ends of the table. You still have echoes of these divisions between skilled drivers of ASLEF taking different views to the general railway workers of the NUR.

persuade colleagues to commit themselves to it. I have no illusions. This is going to be a tough battle. Margaret is no natural supporter of electrification – nor indeed of the railways.

MONDAY 16 FEBRUARY

This week is entirely dominated by coal. The rumbles of the approaching dispute were apparent last week, but everyone is surprised by the way the crisis has suddenly developed. The scene was set in a minute I read at the weekend from David Howell. It said that the executive of the NUM had decided at their meeting on 12 February to recommend industrial action in a ballot of members if the coal board did not withdraw its plans for closures. But the minute also said the plans for closure could be negotiated at a local level and there really was no need for alarm.

TUESDAY 17 FEBRUARY

It is clear that the strategy on coal is not working. The unions are not only threatening strike action, but strike action is being taken. It looks as though we are in for some kind of replay of 1974.

WEDNESDAY 18 FEBRUARY

David Howell meets with the unions and the message comes through that they have got everything that they wanted. In other words, the pit closures are off and the government will provide the money.

THURSDAY 19 FEBRUARY

The press is unanimously dreadful. It is considered a surrender and the government is blamed for not knowing what was going on. The whole thing does look like the most dreadful muddle. At Cabinet, everyone takes the view that it could have been handled better but everyone, without exception, also agrees that by Tuesday Margaret had no alternative but to concede as gracefully as she could. The alternative would have been a long, drawn-out strike. Keith Joseph and I both point out that the outcome of the union action has implications way beyond coal.

Keith is concerned about steel and says that MacGregor has already been on the phone. I am concerned about the railways where Peter Parker is trying to shed about 14,000 jobs. The comparison is painfully close to the National Coal Board who were trying to shed about 13,000. The press, of course, is now full of inquest stories. The two men reckoned to be most to blame are Derek Ezra, the chairman of the coal board, and David Howell. My view is that any minister must rely upon the chairman of his nationalised industry. Government ministers do not run the nationalised industries and that is why you have people like Ezra. To put it at its mildest, Ezra's antennae appear to have been remarkably insensitive. Margaret talks optimistically about next time choosing our ground.[41]

TUESDAY 24 FEBRUARY

I go over to the House of Commons to listen to Prime Minister's Questions and the steel statement by Keith Joseph.[42] Margaret had a very rough ride last Thursday and looks nervous. Nevertheless, she manages perfectly well. Keith Joseph's statement on steel is a different thing again. It is a truly agonised Joseph performance. He obviously does not like what he is doing and communicates that admirably to everyone. He is greeted with ironic cheers from the Labour side and has very little support from our side. It is an amazingly generous deal for the steel industry – £2 billion of aid – and it speaks volumes for the ability of Ian MacGregor. It is also another indicator of how Cabinet government is being conducted. At no stage has this enormous rescue programme come to full Cabinet. It has all been decided in E committee. It means effectively that anything from between one half to one quarter of the Cabinet can be excluded from some of the most major decisions that we have in front of us.

---

41   This was the prelude to the miners' strike of 1984–85, one of the bitterest strikes in Britain. Margaret Thatcher had no intention of being caught unprepared again.

42   When MacGregor was appointed Chairman of the British Steel Corporation, he was expected to deal with its low productivity and initiated a major reorganisation but needed government support for his corporate plan. This was given reluctantly.

TUESDAY 10 MARCH

Cabinet meets at 10.30 a.m. to hear the Chancellor's proposals on the Budget. It is a tense and unhappy meeting. Although most of us have had some idea of what was to be in the Budget, none of us knew its full extent. It soon becomes clear that it is going to be highly unpopular. Geoffrey introduces it in a very sober manner. He says that he is looking for a borrowing requirement of somewhere between £10.5 and £11.5 billion. However, as at the present forecast, the PSBR for next year is likely to be between £14 and £15 billion. National Insurance will raise him £1 billion and revenue from the North Sea another £1 billion. Excess profits tax upon the banks gives him a further £0.5 billion. He then comes to the area which will be most unpopular – his proposals to increase taxes. He will not implement the Rooker–Wise amendment on tax allowances;[43] petrol will go up by 20p per gallon; and there will be big tax increases on drinks and cigarettes.[44] He reckons that he can raise £2 billion in this way.

The attack soon starts. Jim Prior is first in saying that he thinks that this is a disastrous Budget which will do nothing for growth and will make the employment position even worse than it is already. Keith Joseph comes next and defends the Budget, but says that there should be more help for investment. His proposal is that private investment should come into some of the public sector industries – like telecommunications. I agree with this last point. This is exactly the kind of policy I have been arguing for the last couple of months. I want to see new ways of getting private investment into our public industries. In the debate which follows, virtually every member of the Cabinet takes part. We are all limited by the fact that Geoffrey has only got a few hours before he goes into battle with his Budget speech. Whatever we say at

---

43 In 1977 Labour MPs Jeff Rooker and Audrey Wise ensured legislation was passed so that the personal tax allowance would be linked to inflation. Primary legislation is needed if it is not to rise with inflation.

44 It was a period which left a permanent mark on the Chancellor. Years later when we were discussing John Major as the successor to Mrs Thatcher, Howe protested to me that Major had never had to increase taxes. His political virility had never been tested.

this stage can make absolutely no difference to the Budget statement in the afternoon. It is a deeply unhappy meeting and when I see Geoffrey afterwards he appears taken aback. In the afternoon, Geoffrey's speech gets an extremely hostile reception from the Labour side and a very cold one from our own side. For once, Michael Foot captures the mood of the public by calling it a 'no hope' Budget.

MONDAY 16 MARCH

What is clear from the weekend press is just how low morale in the Conservative Party now is. There have been some quite extraordinary leaks. There was a leak in *The Times* on Friday which set out the position of all the Cabinet on the Budget and their reactions to it. This went into such detail that it even mentioned the two members – Humphrey Atkins and the Chief Secretary – who did not make any contribution at all. These kinds of leaks are making Cabinet totally impossible, but more than that they are having a devastating effect upon morale outside of Westminster. It is unhappy and uncertain, reading day-to-day leaks about divisions inside the Cabinet. The so-called 'wets' normally lose around the Cabinet table, but when it comes to the press comment it is the wets who appear in the role of heroes. Anyone who supports the government's economic policy is regarded as an eccentric. We have either got to come together or go down to defeat.

FRIDAY 27 MARCH

For once, a day not dominated by politics. Fiona and I go out to dinner at a little Italian restaurant down by the river in Chelsea. I know that something is up. Even I know that. It is just over three years ago that we first went out to dinner. The restaurant is where I proposed a year later. Fiona breaks the news to me by giving me a present, a small bronze of a youth carrying a baby. We have been waiting a long time for this and were getting rather worried. We are both excited – and just a little apprehensive. Fiona loves children and will be a tremendous mother. But what about me? It is the first time. I have been broken into children by Oliver and that has been a great experience. My only fear is that I am a rather distant figure. I hustle off to work in the early morning and crawl back late at night. At weekends I am often away, and on Sunday I am normally trying to catch up on the boxes. But this life cannot go on forever. My resolution is to make time. Children have an unqualified right for time to be spent on them. I cannot quite get used to the idea yet.

TUESDAY 31 MARCH

A bad meeting with the Prime Minister on nationalised industries. She lectures everyone in sight. She lectures Keith Joseph and she treats Geoffrey Howe in a manner which can be most charitably described as patronising, and probably more accurately as contemptuous. She also has a go at me. She starts by calling me 'dear', which does not go down at all well. Having heard a few of her views on the transport nationalised industries, I point out that she has got it wrong. If she looks at the four nationalised industries in transport, we are denationalising two of them. We have introduced competition into another for the first time in half a century, and as for railways, which is her hate, we are denationalising the subsidiary companies and achieving more in terms of manpower reductions than at any stage for a decade. To be fair, she does not disagree and also to be fair, Keith Joseph puts up a good fight for his corner. Geoffrey, on the other hand, gives the impression that he has seen all this before and does not intend to get involved in a slanging match. There are some marvellous moments. She accuses all government ministers of not having the first idea about what is going on in their nationalised industries. She says that when she showed the accounts to Denis, he could not make head or tail of them. It is real 'Dear Bill' stuff. Even when there is good news she wants to find the bad news.

THURSDAY 2 APRIL

One of those dreadful all-night sessions. It is on the British Telecommunications bill and it drags on throughout the night and into the next morning. We have Cabinet at 10.30 on Thursday morning, huddled into the Prime Minister's office in the House of Commons. We all look bleary eyed and unshaven. At least when I say 'all', some have managed to avoid the night's torture. Margaret typically has led us into every division. I am not sure if I think it is the wisest course for the Prime Minister to take. Those like myself who have been up all night look enviously at those who have not.

FRIDAY 3 APRIL

To Liverpool to speak to Conservative industrialists. A curious hotel full of people waiting for the Grand National on the morrow. Irish voices and big men with outsize field glasses. The speech is good enough. Indeed, the chairman says that it is the best thing he has heard in years. I think that is slightly overstating it. I ask for cheese and biscuits rather than the ghastly chocolate gateau which is provided. I am certainly provided with cheese and biscuits – an enormous chunk of cheddar together with some custard creams.

SATURDAY 4 APRIL–SUNDAY 5 APRIL

I spend the weekend poring over the railway papers for the long-awaited meeting of E committee on electrification to be presided over by the Prime Minister. She has already made it totally clear that she wants nothing to do with it. Indeed, of all the conversations I have had with her in the last couple of weeks she has mentioned it on each occasion. She has sent in Alan Walters[45] to do a demolition job on the electrification report[46] and the Walters paper is in my box. The only thing Walters suggests is that we should look more carefully at the option of reducing the rail network. He says that 'many experts' believe that this would be a good idea. Who are these experts? Anyone with any political nous whatsoever would understand that this would be about the most disastrous policy to pursue as we are entering year three of our government.

---

45   British economist who was best known as the chief economic adviser to the Prime Minister from 1981 to 1983, and again for five months in 1989 when he played a prominent part in Nigel Lawson's resignation.

46   A joint review of rail electrification by the department and the industry, February 1981. It concluded that electrification was a sound investment and could offer real gains in efficiency and productivity.

I really do not think that the man understands what he is suggesting. The prospect of putting this kind of policy forward in our rural constituencies where we will be clobbered in any event during the next council elections makes the blood run cold. It may well be that Mr Walters is employed for his economic judgement but you have to temper economics with common sense. All this does not bode well. The tactics for the next few days must be to fight a holding action and certainly to avoid being committed to some lunatic political proposal such as the Walters alternative.

TUESDAY 14 APRIL

E committee and the railways. Margaret's mood has changed dramatically. I have two objectives. The first is to get colleagues to confirm our attitude to the rail system itself. I point out that I have given commitments both in opposition and in government that the railway system will be substantially maintained. I also point out that if we were to change it, then the consequences would be coming through in time for the general election. My position is agreed. No one mentions the Alan Walters paper. Willie Whitelaw says that in a previous election he reckons that he lost about 5,000 votes on this issue in his constituency, and other colleagues like George Younger make the same point. Margaret shows absolutely no disposition to argue with this political judgement.

The second objective is to get the electrification issue remitted to the CPRS[47] so that they can study it and at the same time study the prospects of the commercial railway. That is the inter-city services and freight. Again, this is agreed with surprisingly little comment. After a strikingly short meeting, no more than thirty minutes, I leave with my objectives secured. It is a remarkable change in climate.

WEDNESDAY 15 APRIL

I must have a masochistic streak. At 4.30 in the afternoon I am arguing

---

47   The Central Policy Review Staff (CPRS) was an independent unit within the Cabinet Office tasked with developing long-term strategy. It was established by Edward Heath in February 1971 but was later disbanded by Margaret Thatcher following the 1983 general election.

at H committee for approval for my plans to change to a points system for traffic offences like speeding.[48] This would save both police time and court time. My proposal is that I should now have authority to go away and draft a transport bill for 1982. The proposals go through and my third transport bill is on the launch pad – three in three years.

EASTER

The whole weekend at Grounds Cottage, our house in Sutton Coldfield. No one from the press and no one from the office rings up. It is absolutely marvellous. Oliver and I make the most enormous bonfire of old papers which Fiona and I have gone through. We sort out packing cases which have not been disturbed since 1974. We burn old carpet and other things that have been lying around in the outhouse for year after year. We play not only swing ball but football too. After two days of this open-air life I feel quite exhausted, but in a totally different way. It is good to be back in real life again. I am actually happier now than I have ever been. I hope that I am sensible enough to realise that politics, and certainly power in politics, is a transient thing. Of course I like the excitement and the ability to put ideas into practice, but I also love my wife and regard it as important that I should manage the not-always-easy relationship between stepfather and stepson. Oliver certainly seems very happy. We will soon have to tell him about the new arrival.

THURSDAY 30 APRIL

Cabinet. Humphrey Atkins arrives to tell us that Bobby Sands, who is on hunger strike, is likely to die at any stage. The crisis could well come over the forthcoming weekend. And his fear is that this will be the signal for the IRA to carry out a new campaign of violence. Atkins says that there are about 380 foreign journalists in Belfast waiting to see what will happen, and that the IRA will be anxious to give them something to

---

48   A simple totting-up system was introduced in 1972. The trouble with that was that it did not distinguish between minor speeding offences and potentially more dangerous ones. My proposal was to replace it with a points system where offences should be graded according to severity and allotted a number of points. When twelve points are accumulated within a three-year period, disqualification for at least six months would follow.

write about. It sounds very ominous. The violence could well stretch onto the mainland as well as in Northern Ireland.[49]

SATURDAY 9 MAY

I go back to Cambridge for a small dinner of old Chelmsfordians who are at Cambridge and I meet my old headmaster, Nigel Fanshawe, who must now be in his late sixties and still teaching.[50] One of the undergraduates, a bright man called Simon Heffer, is very active in Conservative politics. He is concerned that even now there is a gulf between the public schools and the grammar schools. I have to admit that the Cabinet is made up of predominantly public school men. The only two who are not public school are myself and Margaret.[51]

TUESDAY 2 JUNE

We only have two ministers in transport and Ken is away in Latin America, so tomorrow I have to do the 45-minute parliamentary question session alone. I have one piece of luck and that is that British Rail come to see me and tell me that their plans for privatising three of their Scottish hotels, including Gleneagles, are now near completion. The hotel business of British Rail has suffered from lack of investment over many years. There can be no justification for a government or a nationalised industry deciding to make investment in luxury hotels its priority. I say that they should go ahead and that I will announce it tomorrow.

WEDNESDAY 3 JUNE

Questions go well, although forty-five minutes is a long time as a solo act. Predictably, most excitement is generated by the privatisation of Gleneagles. The British Rail man who said that I should make a low-key

---

49 Sands died a few days later on 5 May. All told, ten republican prisoners died in the 1981 hunger strike and around sixty civilians, police and soldiers died in the seven-month campaign that followed.

50 My old school was King Edward VI Grammar School in Chelmsford. I owe Nigel Fanshawe a big debt. He pushed some of us into the sixth form early to concentrate on A-levels. For the first time, I had to work hard and won a place at Trinity Hall, Cambridge. If I had not gone to university, my father (with the best possible motives) had plotted that I be articled to either a chartered accountant or a solicitor; neither career appealed.

51 A slight exaggeration. John Biffen was also a grammar school boy.

statement was extremely optimistic. There is no way that you can make a low-key statement on privatisation in the House of Commons given that across the Chamber you have people like Cryer, Skinner and all the rail unions.

WEDNESDAY 10 JUNE

A meeting of EDL committee (the Cabinet committee dealing with disposals) and I tell them about the plans of the NFC management. It has been one of the most exciting turnarounds of all time. A few years ago the NFC was anything but enthusiastic about the prospect of privatisation. The first time I met my friend Frank Law, he had been sent by the board to dissuade me from my privatisation plans. Now in 1981 they have put together a deal which amounts to a management buy-out of the business, but a management takeover which is financed by their own money. Both Keith Joseph and Nigel Lawson obviously think that this is an exciting prospect. I only hope that when it comes to it the Treasury will not put too many obstacles in the way.[52]

FRIDAY 12 JUNE

Yesterday, the Lords voted for compulsory seat belts – 132 to 92. It is a foregone conclusion that the Commons will accept this. The debate is over.

WEDNESDAY 17 JUNE

The day begins with the long-heralded economic Cabinet. Geoffrey sets out his familiar position. His case is that inflation has come down, that we are on the right course, but that there are no obvious instant solutions available for unemployment. His central point is that on present spending plans, the government will go into the next general election with a tax burden which is higher than what was inherited in 1979. He clearly views this as neither politically nor economically tolerable.

---

52 The NFC became more than a management buy-out. Shares were distributed at all levels of the company with the result that AGMs were exceptionally well attended with 2–3,000 there – and the lorry drivers were not shy in putting their concerns direct to the chairman.

Geoffrey is immediately followed by Jim Prior, who sees unemployment rising to over three million later this year when the school leavers come on to the market, and that position repeats in the early autumn of 1982 and 1983. Jim basically wants some reflation and some public-investment projects. He takes the view, reasonably enough, that unemployment is the key issue. Following the two set pieces, almost every member of Cabinet takes part in the discussion that follows. It is clear that people like Francis Pym and Peter Walker are opposed to the general strategy, and people like John Nott and John Biffen are in favour. Very rarely do their arguments even touch each other. The most senior members of the Cabinet point to the political dimension. Peter Carrington, Christopher Soames and Willie Whitelaw all comment that the time to start thinking about the next general election is now.

In the afternoon it is back to No. 10 for railway electrification. This is the decisive meeting as far as the electrification project is concerned. George Younger told me after Cabinet this morning that Margaret is still pretty determined against it. However, when it comes to the meeting itself, the mood is not as hostile as it could have been. I start with a five-minute presentation of the case. I want electrification to be the instrument by which I can achieve the improvements in productivity that British Rail should make. There follows a brief and rather scrappy discussion. I am opposed by the Treasury. Leon argues that electrification is 'OK' in the future, but what he wants to see first are the improvements in productivity. I am supported in the argument by Jim Prior; not particularly effectively. He has an extremely curious argument about level crossings on his Suffolk line. No one is totally clear about the point he is trying to make but one thing is beyond doubt, that wherever else we electrify, there is no question of electrifying his Suffolk line. Margaret then sums up and slightly to my surprise, given her previous views, she says that she is prepared to consider the principle of electrification, but there is no question of us giving it unconditional support. So the meeting breaks up with agreement to electrification in principle, on the condition that the railway industry makes improvements in productivity. As far as I am concerned that is first class, and we have certainly managed to come back from the first meeting when electrification had been dismissed almost out of hand.

THURSDAY 18 JUNE

I see Margaret just before Cabinet. She is obviously extremely upset about the leaks from yesterday. No more than I am. When I woke the first headline I saw on *The Times* was 'Thatcher defeated by Cabinet critics on electrification'. Given the way that she had changed her position to be helpful, it was about the worst conceivable headline that I could imagine. Happily, it was only the first edition. The second edition is considerably better thanks to a talk I had with Julian Havilland,[53] who rang me at home at midnight, clearly at the behest of Harry Evans[54] to try and find out what had actually happened. I told him enough to make sure that the conditionality of electrification got over. Cabinet begins with an inquest about the stories in the morning's press. There follows one of the periodic inquests we have on press coverage when all kinds of solutions are put forward, including that Cabinet ministers should stop briefing their junior ministers on what happens in Cabinet. This is objected to by Michael Heseltine on the grounds that he had to reassure all his junior ministers this morning that I had not scooped the financial pool for electrification. My comment was that if they believed that then they would believe anything.

MONDAY 22 JUNE

In the morning I see Peter Parker about electrification. His reaction is very positive. He says that it gives the railways a fighting chance. From my point of view, his reaction is absolutely crucial. Later, in the House, the reaction of the Labour side is much more hostile. All the NUR-sponsored boys say that we are not going remotely far enough. On

---

53 A respected journalist. He was a lobby correspondent at Westminster for many years, political editor of Independent Television News, 1975–81 and *The Times*, 1981–86.

54 A legendary figure of post-war journalism. He was editor of the *Sunday Times*, 1967–1981, then *The Times* for a year from 1981 before being forced out by Rupert Murdoch.

the other hand, the reaction on our side is almost universally favourable. People are concerned that nationalised industries are running away with resources and the idea of conditionality is one that appeals. There follows a series of radio and television interviews and at six o'clock I meet the rail unions. They all bitterly criticise the announcement but Peter Parker sticks to his guns and says that in his view, this is not a defeat for the railway industry but a declaration of faith in very difficult times. By the end of the two-hour meeting, it would be an exaggeration to say that the unions had shifted their position but their opposition was much modified at any rate. It is in a situation like this that you see Peter at his best. In his heart of hearts he does not believe in privatisation and denationalisation. He sees British Rail rather like Mitsubishi: he cannot quite understand why silly Treasury rules get in the way of him expanding into other areas. But his handling of industrial and personal relations are, I think, first class and it is for reasons like that I think we should seek to keep him.

SATURDAY 4–SUNDAY 5 JULY

Extraordinary scenes in Liverpool. Buildings set on fire, petrol bombs thrown and policemen attacked. Only the use of CS gas restores some kind of order. It is concentrated in the Toxteth area, which is a classic run-down inner area. Already the debate has begun whether this is a law -and-order issue or a sign of social deprivation. The answer is both.

THURSDAY 9 JULY

Cabinet is dominated by the riots in Liverpool. Willie makes a comparison with what he first saw in Northern Ireland. There are, he says, a variety of reasons for what has happened. There is the feeling that nobody cares; there is the question of youth unemployment; there is the criticism of the police. He doubts (and I am sure that he is right) whether it is possible to isolate one particular reason. There follows a long and thoughtful discussion, which starts with a debate about what can be done in terms of law and order, about strengthening the law, about improving the Riot

Act, about special courts. Clearly this is important if we are to reassure people who have lost their livelihoods in the riots, but we also have to tackle the position in the cities, which will be identified as one of the causes of the riots whether we like it or not. My suggestion is that we should have one minister to coordinate all our efforts. Having talked to him before the meeting, I use the example of Quintin Hailsham who was given just such a role in Macmillan's government. Slightly surprisingly, I find this suggestion taken up first by Margaret and then by people like John Biffen. I imagined John would be opposed to a move of this kind but in fact he says that the situation we have marks a watershed and that what is required is political leadership. Most people appear to agree. The next stage is for a small group of ministers to meet and consider what can be done in hard practical terms. I hope that something more will result than simply a concentration upon law and order measures.

MONDAY 13 JULY

For the first time the Speaker gives a dinner for the Cabinet. Margaret is of course the guest of honour and she again shows her enormous stamina. She has been to Liverpool under the most strenuous and testing circumstances and yet, as most of us leave at around 11 p.m. for a vote, Margaret is still deep in conversation. Willie says she will now go back and do a few more hours' work before she finally goes to bed for a couple of hours. It is not something that Willie obviously faces with equanimity. I agree. Like him, I need my sleep.

THURSDAY 16 JULY

At Cabinet, Willie Whitelaw gives an update on the riots. The night before in Brixton the police went into the area and carried out a search for petrol bombs on information they had received. He says that an inquiry will be conducted, but he doubts whether the tactics were justified. He also pays great tribute to Lord Scarman,[55] who apparently went to

---

[55] The Law Lord who chaired the public inquiry into the causes of the 1981 race riots in Brixton. He had previously chaired inquiries into the August 1969 riots in Northern Ireland, the Red Lion Square disorders and the Grunwick dispute.

Brixton, talked with everyone and according to Willie, helped defuse a very explosive situation. Margaret announces that Michael Heseltine is going to go to Liverpool to carry out what she calls a pilot scheme of coordination. Her view is that a great deal of aid already goes to Liverpool and what is needed is some coordination of it – exactly what I was arguing last week. Michael has a very difficult job to put it mildly, but at last we are being seen to respond; not just to the law and order aspect but also to the social aspect. In the afternoon, Willie opens the debate in the House on the riots. The speech is an enormous success. It is not a particularly good speech in the sense of style. Willie takes almost no interruptions, but what is impressive, and particularly impressive to the other side, is that he talks about and acknowledges the social problems that exist in the cities. He is congratulated by Hattersley, who in return also makes a good speech. The House is attentive, silent and at its best.

In the evening I go to Television Centre to take part in a programme with Neil Kinnock and David Owen on the Warrington by-election. The result is much better for the Social Democrats than anyone had expected. It is not good for Labour but it is a pretty disastrous result for us as well. Our vote is down to a pathetic 7 per cent.[56] The SDP is a new force and above all, a force with political leaders whom the public have heard of, and in some cases like, politicians like Shirley Williams, David Owen and of course, Roy Jenkins.

MONDAY 20 JULY

Peter Parker comes in to see me about rail pay and I then talk privately with him about his own position. I set out a further variation on the offer that we are making. Peter's reaction is quite extraordinary. He says words virtually to the effect – 'thank you very much I will let you know in twenty-four hours' – and is haring out of the door before anyone

---

56 The Social Democratic Party (SDP) was formed in March 1981 by Shirley Williams, Roy Jenkins, David Owen and Bill Rodgers. Williams and Jenkins lacked parliamentary seats and with Liberal support, Jenkins became the SDP's first parliamentary candidate in Warrington. It was regarded as a safe Labour seat but Doug Hoyle only narrowly held it. Roy Jenkins was a close second, taking votes from both the Conservatives and Labour. The result was: Labour 14,280, SDP 12,521, Conservative 2,102.

has the chance to move. Peter Baldwin and I talk over what has taken place. My guess is that he has made up his mind to go. Peter says that we should not be quite so sure, but I think this is just optimism on his part. I suggest a bottle of champagne on it. I bet Peter Parker will not stay. Peter bets that he will.

WEDNESDAY 22 JULY

News comes through from British Rail that Peter Parker is to stay. I have lost a bottle of champagne but kept a chairman.

THURSDAY 23 JULY

The worst Cabinet that we have had in our period of government by a mile. There is only one good side to the discussion – as I write this on the Saturday, the details have not yet leaked; an altogether untypical stroke of luck. The Cabinet has before it a particularly gloomy paper from the Chancellor. Geoffrey's fear is that far from reducing taxation if we go on like this, we will be increasing taxation even further in the remaining Budgets of the parliament. He says that to go down that road would be economically damaging and politically impossible. Introducing his paper, he says that if the market takes the view that our determination to control public spending is weakening, we could find ourselves increasingly exposed to a reduced exchange rate with all the pressure that means for inflation. Quite exceptionally, Humphrey Atkins starts the discussion. I have never heard Humphrey talk about economics before and he does not really talk about it this time. But what he does say has some truth to it. In Northern Ireland he says they are rather more worried about unemployment than they are about reducing taxation. Humphrey is followed by Michael Heseltine, fresh back from Liverpool, who speaks emotionally about the position he has found there. He says that there is a sense of hopelessness and that this particularly affects the young. John Nott is one of the supporters of the general economic strategy and pays some tribute to it but is then entirely scathing. He says that it is a hopeless paper, there is nothing about the PSBR or about the GDP, that there are no figures to make any decent decisions on. Basically, the Chancellor should come back with a different and better paper. We all make set speeches and there is no real cut and thrust of debate. I come out in favour of the broad Heseltine argument – firm action on pay but an expanding capital programme. The most impressive intervention comes from Jim Prior. He does not make the kind of economically illiterate speech that we have had from one or two colleagues. He does not regard tax increases as being a disaster and is in favour of some kind of pay freeze, plus a deal on capital investment. Willie makes a pretty emotional speech. He says that the tolerance point of society (a phrase which he uses on a number of occasions) has been reached and he therefore does not believe that economies are possible. He does not see how he can make economies in his own areas like prisons and the police.

Margaret then sums up. She makes no concessions to any of the debate, which has obviously gone extremely badly. She says that all people are arguing for is the kind of reflation that we had in the Heath period of government and the last thing she wants to preside over is the kind of property boom that we saw then. Inflation, she says, is still one of the chief enemies of the country but then adds gratuitously that the only people who can face inflation with any kind of equanimity are those workers with industrial muscle, those on inflation-proof pensions and those with land and property. The last is directed particularly at Francis who has argued that inflation is not the issue. It really could not have been worse. It leaves the PM and the Chancellor isolated. Everyone has argued for change of one kind or another. The wisest words spoken were from Willie Whitelaw, who advised that the last week in July was not a time to make decisions. That is right, but I fear that there is no avoiding the fact that the party is probably in more disarray now than it has been at any stage since May 1979.

TUESDAY 28 JULY
The final stage of the current transport bill and the consideration of the amendments from the Lords. We come to the seat belt debate. My aim has been to ensure that the House has the opportunity to decide the

issue. It has become a parliamentary scandal that the House keeps on voting for it but nothing happens. There is of course considerable irony that I, as an original opponent of compulsion, should succeed in getting the House to a decision when my predecessors, who were consistent supporters of compulsion, failed dismally. I make it clear that if the principle is carried then the government will put the law into effect. When it comes to the vote, it comes as no surprise that compulsion is carried with a majority of seventy-seven. I say that the government will bring in the regulation as soon as possible and that the new law should come into effect by the middle of next year. The seat belt saga is over.

EVENING

Earlier, Ian Gow[57] had asked whether we could have dinner once the debate was over. He said he would fix up a table somewhere at 11.15. I was anything but clear what would be open at that hour, but in typically efficient Gow manner he managed to find the only place in town which is not only open but is serving food readily, willingly and well: The Savoy. We talk about the state of the Cabinet. Ian is particularly concerned about the party chairmanship. He makes it quite clear that he thinks that Peter Thorneycroft has come to the end of the road. Although he has done stalwart duty it would be a mistake for him to take the party through to the next election. Morale at Conservative Central Office is low and we need a new person at the helm. The difficulty is who to put in his place. I say one of the obvious choices would be Michael Heseltine, who seems to me to have the right appeal for a party chairman. Ian is obviously not convinced and he mentions two other names – Norman Tebbit and Cecil Parkinson. This is going to a different generation. The difficulty is that neither are in the Cabinet at the moment. Ian obviously thinks that there is some difficulty with Margaret on this issue. The obvious Cabinet appointment would be as Paymaster General, but Margaret characteristically does not like having people being paid for

---

57 Conservative MP for Eastbourne, exceptional PPS to Thatcher. He was assassinated by the Provisional IRA in 1990 when a bomb under his car exploded outside his home in East Sussex.

nominal jobs. He then turns to me and asks if I would be prepared to do the job. It is not an offer – it is a question of whether in principle I would be prepared to be considered. Nevertheless, it was a question that I was not expecting, nor did I have any adequate reply. I mumbled something to the effect that it would be a job which anybody from my generation would want to do, but that Margaret was in a better position than anyone to make a choice.

We then gossip about the changes which are obviously going to come. There is little doubt that they would like to get rid of Peter Walker but there is the question about whether it is better having him in the government than on the back benches. The energy department, according to Ian, is regarded as a great disaster area but equally, they do not want to get rid of David Howell who is a loyal supporter of the Prime Minister's general economic approach. Quintin Hailsham is regarded as too old and rather too eccentric at this stage. Quintin is a genuinely great man, much greater than the vast majority of us sitting around the Cabinet table at the moment. I would be very sorry to see Quintin go: he is still capable of making some of the most telling and indeed some of the most amusing points in Cabinet. All in all, the most interesting dinner I have had in months.

WEDNESDAY 29 JULY
The royal wedding of Charles and Diana. Quite exceptional. Amazing weather. The beautiful princess with an extraordinarily long train, and the small page boys. Members of the royal families from all over Europe; world leaders like Trudeau and Mitterrand; the immaculate wife of the American President. But for me the most moving part of it all is the re-action of the crowds along the route. Fiona and I set off about 9 o'clock from Hurlingham Road and by the time we reach Trafalgar Square, the crowds are thick on the pavements and they cheer anything. You only have to wave to get an answering cheer. They are good humoured and enthusiastic. It is an enormous contrast to the bleak reports coming from the cities over the last few weeks. The ceremony is clearly being

watched on television by the crowds outside the cathedral. Every crucial move between the bride and groom is followed a second or two later by the most enormous cheer from outside. It is a great occasion. After the wedding, we walk to the Bank of England where Margaret Thatcher is giving lunch for the assembled heads of state. We drink champagne in the courtyard and then go to our tables. On mine, I have Mrs Gandhi's son, Rajiv,[58] and the Lord Chief Justice, Lord Lane who is notably good news. A quite outstanding day and I suspect a much needed fillip for the whole nation.

WEDNESDAY 2 SEPTEMBER

Whitehall is now humming with rumours of a reshuffle. Downing Street appear to be doing nothing to deny them and so I assume that the shuffle will come, probably next week.

SATURDAY 12 SEPTEMBER

I am doing my advice bureau in Sutton Coldfield when Fiona takes a phone call from Adam Raphael.[59] Basically, his message is that Jim Prior is going to dig in and won't be making his much-predicted move to Northern Ireland.[60] Adam tells Fiona that that leaves me in line to go to Northern Ireland. I'm not sure that I totally believe this last part of the story – nor what my reaction to it is. In some ways Northern Ireland would be the most fascinating job in government. It spreads over all the departments and would be tremendous experience from that point of view. Against that there are the obvious security difficulties. What would worry me most would be the need for a guard for Fiona, Oliver and the new baby. Nevertheless, both Fiona and I agree that if an offer is made then I would accept, even given the difficulties. The major lesson we learn from Adam's telephone call is that probably the best place to be for the rest of the weekend is London.

---

58 Rajiv Gandhi served as the sixth Prime Minister of India from 1984 to 1989 after the assassination of his mother. He himself was assassinated by a suicide bomber during the election of 1991.

59 *The Observer* journalist, one of the best political reporters of the time.

60 When written that part of the story was certainly correct: Jim later changed his mind, much to the frustration of those journalists who had been told of his original intent.

SUNDAY 13 SEPTEMBER

I work on my boxes during the day without interruption. My guess had been that No. 10 would set up the reshuffle interviews during Sunday but the phone is entirely silent. It is not until 8 o'clock in the evening that I understand why. While I am upstairs, Fiona answers a ring on the bell. It is Stephen Sherbourne,[61] who used to work for Ted Heath and lives just down the road. He has been asked to come round and knock on my door by Tony Mayer who knows that I am in London. Apparently, No. 10 have been trying to get through for some time but our phone has developed a curious fault. For the person ringing from outside, the ringing tone continues but we don't hear it, so it simply sounds to the caller as though we are out. I rapidly ring No. 10 and ask for Clive Whitmore.[62] He asks whether I'm in London on Monday and could I come in to see the Prime Minister at 10.20 a.m.? He tells me it's about changes in the government and I press him a little harder to see if I can get some more information. Clive is much more forthcoming than the Chief Whip was when I was in Casablanca. He tells me that he hopes it will be good news as far as I am concerned, that he would expect me to be offered a job that I had done in opposition. I say that sounds fine and ring off. What that means of course is that I will be offered the job of social services. It is not a job that I expected in the least to be offered. It is a very major department. Frankly, for me, there is a feeling of anti-climax. It certainly wasn't the department that I was looking for and the prospects of making political runs in social services don't immediately seem great.

MONDAY 14 SEPTEMBER

I arrive at Downing Street at about 10.15 a.m. It's the first time that I've been involved in a reshuffle in person and turned up in Downing Street. The entrance is thronged with photographers and cameramen. I smile pleasantly, I hope, say good morning and go into No. 10. As no one

---

61 Political secretary to Margaret Thatcher and later Chief of Staff to Michael Howard when he was Conservative leader. Created a life peer in 2013.
62 Civil servant, Margaret Thatcher's principal private secretary 1979–1982.

is there to meet me, I make my way to the Cabinet room. One of the attendants asks if I would mind waiting in the waiting room. This I do. I must be in there about twenty minutes when David Howell also comes in. We murmur pleasantries to each other. Eventually, in comes Clive Whitmore. He jokes about the arrangements going wrong. In other words, ministers are not expected to meet each other as they go in to see the Prime Minister. He leads me up to the Prime Minister's drawing room and says that the delay has been because she has had a difficult meeting prior to mine. This has been with Jim Prior, whom I meet on the stairs. Jim is red-faced and flanked by the Chief Whip. The meeting has gone on for much longer than planned. Margaret clearly wants to make progress when it comes to me. She offers me social services which, given the conversation of last night, hardly comes as a surprise. She then goes on to describe the junior ministers whom she would like to go with me. She wants Geoffrey Finsberg to take George Young's place. George has fallen out of favour in this job because of his espousal of the anti-smoking cause (he is the minister for health!) and his opposition to sponsorship. Margaret says that if he doesn't lay off soon there won't be any tobacco firms prepared to sponsor any sport in the country. I say I would like Ken to join me as a Minister of State. Margaret obviously thinks there is something in this, but can't see how she can move both of us. She confirms that David Howell will be taking over at transport but she doesn't tell me where Patrick Jenkin will be moving to. It is a very friendly chat.

Leaving, I meet Nigel Lawson coming up the stairs. If David has got transport, I suppose then Nigel must have energy. The crowd of photographers and cameramen outside has grown even thicker. Clearly the word has got out that today is the day. I walk as briskly as possible to my car and make my getaway. Someone calls out my name and I give a wave of my hand. From No. 10 I go back to the Department of Transport, tell Ken what has happened and say that I don't think that I'm going to be successful in getting him over. I will have another go, but I fear that it looks as though he is going to be stuck where he is for the present. He is obviously disappointed, but not, I suspect, as put out as he would be if Nigel Lawson was to be his number one. I spend the next few hours with Chris and Patrick from the private office, packing my pictures and belongings and files into packing cases. Just after lunch, a call comes through from David Howell asking when he can come round to have a chat with Peter Baldwin. Apparently, David has already packed up his office and has simply left. At about 3 o'clock I decide that the best thing to do is to make an approach to the DHSS and Patrick Jenkin's private office to see what the position is. Tony Mayer rings up to find that no one in the DHSS knows what's happening. This of course could mean anything. It could mean that Patrick is going to be told what will happen once Jim Prior's fate is decided. Eventually, at about 5.30, the news comes through that Patrick is moving to industry.

Driving over to the DHSS, I become aware for the first time of just how far away it is. The office is at the Elephant and Castle and we enter by some extraordinary back route, which takes us to what is called the ministerial lift. It is rather like entering some enormous warehouse. My immediate concern is that there is a paper at Cabinet tomorrow morning which has been put in by Patrick Jenkin about pay in the National Health Service; a subject upon which I am not notably well briefed and the biggest by far of what Peter Baldwin calls the smouldering fires. I go to bed unelated. I am very conscious of the new knowledge that I need to acquire very quickly indeed.

COMMENT

The result of the reshuffle was that I returned to all the problems that I left behind in 1976, but with the obvious difference that I was now responsible for sorting them out. A triumphant return? That was not remotely my feeling at the time. The immediate problem was the pay of the vast workforce of doctors, nurses and support staff. I do not know how many of my predecessors felt as I did that working with the health unions was often more constructive than with the spokesmen of the British Medical Association (BMA) and the consultants. But health was only half of my job: pensions and social security caused even more challenges. Facing the need that existed among the poor and providing them and everyone else with a decent pension were issues that had faced a succession of commissions and inquiries – the most famous of which was that of Lord Beveridge, whose report was implemented just after the Second World War. The whole system was now beginning to show its age.

3

THE BIGGEST SPENDER
IN WHITEHALL

SEPTEMBER 1981–MARCH 1982

This was a period when the battles over public spending dominated the headlines. Handling the annual public spending round was to become a major part of my life. I spent two or three months a year doing virtually nothing else but negotiating with the Treasury – putting me in direct conflict with Leon Brittan, one of our original 'gang' of three. Leon was a friend for over twenty years, but it made no difference to either side. We both had a job to do and it was totally inevitable that the minister in charge of controlling public spending as Chief Secretary should come into conflict with the minister with the biggest budget. It would be nice to say that because of our long association and in spite of our differences, our discussions were conducted in a perfectly friendly way. It would be nice; but it wouldn't be true. We fought so strongly that after one confrontation, Ken Clarke half-jokingly (but only half) said he doubted if we would ever speak to each other again.

TUESDAY 15 SEPTEMBER 1981

Our first new Cabinet. We are given a plan of where we are all now seated. I have gone to Mark Carlisle's old seat, flanked by Michael Heseltine on one side and Leon Brittan on the other, facing the Prime Minister. There is no question that this is a better class of seat. You can get into a debate without having to go into contortions to attract attention. The Prime Minister welcomes the new arrivals and we get used to everyone's new titles.[63] It's a desultory meeting and I'm soon back in the department. I say 'soon' but it takes about twenty minutes to get back from Downing Street to the Elephant and Castle and for me that means a completely new lifestyle.

WEDNESDAY 16 SEPTEMBER

The DHSS is two separate departments put together by Harold Wilson to give Dick Crossman a major job. There are plenty of people who say that it should now be divided again. What of the occupants of the DHSS? It's very early days. We're all feeling our way. They regard me with caution. All the publicity says that I have come in to cut their budgets and put all their programmes under a Thatcherite gaze. I also regard them with caution. Not so much because I suspect that they want to preserve their programmes – I haven't yet met a civil servant in any department who doesn't – but more because no one appears to be talking about new ideas. I have two permanent secretaries. The number one, Ken Stowe, is on holiday. He has a big reputation and used to work at No. 10 with Jim Callaghan. The story is that had Labour won the 1979 election he would have become head of the civil service.[64] My second Permanent Secretary is Geoffrey Otton who used to be in the Home Office.[65] Today, Otton gives me a presentation about his social security side, which concentrates entirely upon the department's managerial and administrative role. What I search for in vain are any ideas that they've been keeping up their sleeve; waiting for a new arrival.

MONDAY 5 OCTOBER

I am now seriously getting down to work. The most immediate problem

63   Leon Brittan (Chief Secretary to the Treasury), Nigel Lawson (energy), Cecil Parkinson (Party Chairman) and Norman Tebbit (employment).

64   Sir Kenneth Stowe was the very bright, very political, Permanent Secretary at the DHSS. He had previously been principal private secretary to three very different Prime Ministers: Harold Wilson, Jim Callaghan and Margaret Thatcher. I was very fortunate. He was the best civil servant I ever worked with.

65   Not in the same class. A rocky relationship throughout.

is public spending. The difficulties are immense. I am now responsible for almost half of all public spending – almost a half![66] – but the vast majority of my spending is protected by various pledges that have previously been made. The Prime Minister has, time and time again, pledged herself to retain the value of pensions and, just as firmly, to maintain spending on the health service in line with what the last Labour government planned.

WEDNESDAY 7 OCTOBER

I go to the Treasury for a meeting with Leon on public spending. It is not a formal bilateral but rather an hour's meeting with the Chief Secretary over a cup of tea. We both agree that social security and health are bound by a great number of commitments. Leon then suggests that the way through is for us to go to the Prime Minister and explain that if she wants the size of cuts that he has in mind then she will have to say quite openly that we are breaking the pledges that have been made. I think that the politics of doing it are absurd and that the Prime Minister's own position would be seriously, if not fatally, undermined. I am not prepared to do this. Leon hums and haws but makes it quite clear that he is going to minute the Prime Minister to say that if she needs more than he is proposing, then the only way this can be done is by breaking the pledges on indexing pensions. I make it clear that if that is the decision then it is not a decision which I would support or indeed go along with.

SATURDAY 17–SUNDAY 18 OCTOBER

Leon has sent round a Cabinet paper that sets out his aim to cut over £3 billion from all planned spending. For me, he has advocated hotel charges for patients in hospitals and General Practitioner charges, although both have been publicly rejected by the Prime Minister. He

---

66   Total central government expenditure was £58,435 million (HM Government, *The Government's Expenditure Plans: 1981–82 and 1983–84*). Of this, £7,794 million was on health and personal social services and £19,775 million on social security. Total DHSS expenditure was therefore about 47 per cent of all central government expenditure.

has also advocated 5 per cent off supplementary benefit which I cannot support. The paper gives him his figures, that is true, but it is not real politics to suggest that this is a group of proposals which the government could carry through. By coincidence, Peter Baldwin rings up on Sunday to tell me that the final stage of the privatisation of the NFC has been agreed and the management can go ahead and buy it. That is enormously good news, and I then ask Peter what his public spending proposals look like. Apparently, they look as bad to him as Leon's proposals look to me.

TUESDAY 20 OCTOBER

Cabinet, and our first discussion on public spending since the appalling one last July. The Cabinet is much more restrained than the July fiasco. The newcomers, Tebbit, Lawson, Parkinson, all dutifully come in on the side of the Chief Secretary and the Chancellor. But the consensus is not for the scale of cuts which the Treasury is proposing. I do not think that anyone who has been here before really thinks that it is realistic to get to £3 billion plus. The most interesting observation by quite a long way comes from John Biffen, now Leader of the House. He says quite unequivocally that he is concerned about the SDP and their onward march. If the prospect is reducing spending on the scale proposed with catastrophic political repercussions, then he would prefer to increase taxes.

I put my own position like this. Clearly, I am the biggest-spending department. In any cuts that I carry out there are some criteria that I need to meet. First, the cuts have to be honest. In other words, we are pledged in certain areas and I would not want to go back on those. Notably, I would not want to go back on the pledge on pensions, nor would I want to go back on the pledge on the health service. Second, the cuts should be socially justifiable. In particular, I am concerned that we should not interfere with the safety net of supplementary benefit. And third, I say that it is important that what we decide to do should be politically possible. The proposals should be politically literate as well as economically literate. I don't think that Leon is very amused by this observation. I say I have been asked by the Treasury to introduce 'hotel' charges for hospital patients and charges for people who visit their GPs. These have both been specifically and personally rejected by the Prime Minister in statements not only before the election but since the election and on the floor of the House of Commons. It reduces the whole exercise to farce if those are going to be put down as realistic options.

In the afternoon, I have my first parliamentary questions in the new department. They are very unexciting but one point comes through loud and clear. Whereas transport questions were rather a friendly occasion, social services is a battlefield. Norman Buchan politely welcomes me to my job, only to get two or three people on his side making comments to the effect of 'what are you welcoming him for?' Later, I meet Norman Tebbit to talk about the unemployed. I have not seen Norman before at close quarters in a person-to-person situation. I thought he was good, forceful, even impressive, but there is something in the political 'skinhead' description. He certainly has an unfortunate phrase for every situation. Talking about the position of one group he agrees that we might have to pay to keep them quiet – the only question is 'how many millions of pounds per squeal?'

FRIDAY 23 OCTOBER
To Sutton Coldfield for our annual dinner with Nigel Lawson. The real drama comes before the dinner. My MGB would not start; a strange mush rather than the engine struggling to start. So, following safety instructions, I ring the police. Two men arrive and are as nervous as I am on this particularly black night in the middle of the country. The car had been left a week or so in a very insecure outside garage but in the end, we decide that the likely culprit is not a terrorist but a field mouse who has chewed through the distributor.

Fiona was coming to the dinner but her consultant has told her to stay in London and not to travel. The date of birth is approaching rapidly – 20 November, we think – in spite of all the politics I really must find time to enjoy and take part in the good things of life.

TUESDAY 27 OCTOBER

A session with the Chief Secretary is a fair disaster. Leon lines up with his officials and I line up with mine. Leon has no arguments for any of the changes that he wants in the health programme, except that he has got to make cuts. From then on it is very rugged stuff and relations entirely break down. I think I win, if anyone wins a contest of this kind but it is a real slog with not much joy for anyone.

TUESDAY 3 NOVEMBER

I am now before the hanging jury chaired by Willie Whitelaw.[67] It meets in a small conference room in the Cabinet Office and next to Willie are George Younger and Patrick Jenkin, with Leon sitting next to me, facing them. Various Treasury officials sit on the end of the square table, keeping the score. Leon appears very much as the prosecuting counsel.

We don't agree on a great deal. I manage to dispose of some of Leon's more lunatic ideas on health, like hotel charges for hospitals which are, for some extraordinary reason, still on the table and for a charge to be levied to visit your GP. I only have to repeat what Margaret has said on these two issues for both proposals to be disposed of. The trouble is that although I think I won the argument on most of the issues, we are still a very long way from Leon's original figures. The committee apparently think that I can get a prescription charge of £1.50 through. If that is the price for getting growth in the National Health Service then I am prepared to pay it.

WEDNESDAY 4 NOVEMBER

The meeting resumes at 9.45 a.m., just before the state opening of Parliament, and this time we go through the social security budget. Again, there is very little agreement. I am trying to fight off the prospect of reducing benefits like supplementary benefit, unemployment benefit and child benefit even further. Leon doesn't have an argument but simply

---

67   The Chief Secretary to the Treasury has ministerial responsibility for controlling public spending. He has a meeting with each department to discuss their budget – 'bilaterals'. Those departments that cannot agree then go before the Star Chamber or hanging jury, at this time under the chairmanship of Willie Whitelaw. The final stage is to go to Cabinet if there is still no agreement.

says that it is necessary for his figures. The trouble with the debate on social security is that, with the exception of Patrick Jenkin, I am not at all sure that there are many people around the Cabinet table who fully understand the issues involved. With the public and, particularly, with pressure groups, the decisions will be highly contentious. I reserve entirely my position on the abatement of benefits – but I am not confident about the outcome when we come to Cabinet.[68]

SUNDAY 8 NOVEMBER

In Sutton Coldfield for the Remembrance Day service. At 8 o'clock there is a phone call from Fiona. She says that there had been some bleeding, and she has rung the hospital and they have asked her to come in. She says, however, that there is nothing to worry about. She thinks it is a false alarm. She is going to ask her father to drive her to St Thomas'. She doesn't think that it is necessary for me to come back and I should go ahead and read the lesson at the church. About 10 o'clock another phone call comes through. This time from Fiona's father, John, who says that they are at the hospital and that Fiona is going to stay for a while, but no one is very worried about her condition. Fiona also comes onto the telephone and repeats the same message. So I go off to the service, reassured that nothing much is afoot, and saying that I will get back to London as soon as the service is over. This proved very easy. For once, the Remembrance Day service runs ahead of time and I am able to get a train from Birmingham International at just before 1.00 p.m. Len picks me up at Euston (we are scheduled to go down to Leeds Castle that evening to speak at an International Year of Disabled Persons conference) and takes me to St Thomas'. I go up to the seventh floor and immediately find that things are very much more advanced than I had thought. The sister I meet says that Fiona will be very pleased to see me, and when I go to the delivery room she immediately bursts into tears! At 6.30 p.m., our daughter is born and immediately gives a cry. Nurses came hither

---

68 Abatement is the reduction in what otherwise would be paid to keep a benefit in line with inflation. Thus if inflation is at 10 per cent, the benefit should be increased by 10 per cent to keep pace but the government may decide to abate it to pay, say 5 per cent.

and thither, and the little creature is given back to Fiona as we devoted parents gaze at her in admiration.

TUESDAY 10 NOVEMBER

Had she been a boy, we had the names already worked out – Edward George. But on girls we were not as decided. Fiona very much wanted the name Kate, and I rather wanted the name Genevieve. In the end, we do a marvellous politician's compromise and call her Kate Genevieve. I hope she likes it in later life. Although Fiona is an NHS patient at St Thomas', I am able to ignore the visiting rules and manage to pop in and out between my various trips over from the Elephant and Castle to Whitehall. For once, the office's position at the Elephant is an advantage. As the news gets round, flowers and cards appear in a great flood. Everyone is enormously kind, and soon the tiny room looks rather like a greenhouse, there are so many flowers and plants. The lady at the centre of attention appears blissfully ignorant of everything that is going on around her. I can see that I'm going to be a doting father. I had never considered myself as someone who was very taken with small babies who, by nature, cry and make a lot of noise. There's nothing like having a baby of your own to change your prejudices.

WEDNESDAY 11 NOVEMBER

I have dinner with Ken Clarke at La Poule au Pot. It's very good to see him again. It reminds me exactly what I lack at the department and that is a minister who I can take into my confidence and get sound and good advice from. To be able to talk not only principles, but tactics. How I wish that he was at the Department of Health! And how I intend to fight like hell to ensure that he gets into my team.

SUNDAY 15 NOVEMBER

Fiona and Kate come home. St Thomas' has been marvellous. We invite in a few photographers as we leave, but Kate sleeps solidly through all the photographs. Even now as I work on the boxes I want to go into her bedroom and stroke her head or carry her in my arms.

MONDAY 16 NOVEMBER

To my surprise the photographs of Kate and Fiona are included in virtually every newspaper. Colleagues come up to me throughout the day to congratulate me. They obviously regard it as about the best piece of news that's come out of my department for quite some time.

THURSDAY 19 NOVEMBER

After Cabinet, a group of us go upstairs to Margaret Thatcher's study to talk about my public-spending plans. We sit round in an informal circle: Margaret Thatcher, Willie, the Chancellor, Leon and Robert Armstrong[69] at the side. It soon becomes clear that the Treasury tactic of bringing in Margaret at this stage is not necessarily going to bring them success. We first go through the health spending plans. I have agreed to a £1.50 prescription charge, but Margaret reopens the agreement and says that it is too expensive. I say that my original choice had been £1.30. She says that seems about right to her and Leon goes down to total defeat. She then looks at the other charges. After a long wrangle, she asks me which of the two items I am bidding for I would prefer: £100 million to ensure growth in the National Health Service; or £100 million for the coming pay round. I say that I want £100 million for growth – that is what we have pledged to do, and what we must continue to do. So, to all intents and purposes, the health budget is now settled. From my point of view it has been settled very satisfactorily indeed. As I go out, Robert Armstrong whispers to me, 'well done'. All told, it is much, much more successful than I had ever thought it would be.

MONDAY 23 NOVEMBER

Following the 10 o'clock division, I go to Margaret Thatcher's room behind the Speaker's chair in the Commons to continue the discussion, this time on social security. The cast is Margaret, the Chancellor, the Chief Secretary and the senior official is Clive Whitmore. We gather around the fireplace with Margaret still suffering from the after-effects

---

69   Top civil servant, principal private secretary to Prime Ministers Ted Heath and Harold Wilson 1970–1975, Cabinet Secretary under Margaret Thatcher 1979–1987.

of her cold, staring contemplatively into the fire. I gather that the immediate problem is John Nott. He has proved, according to all accounts, impossible to deal with. Apparently, the Treasury and the defence department are something like £600 million apart. The question is, how do we deal with Nott? I don't feel either qualified or much inclined to advise on that. I have, after all, half a billion pounds' worth of problems of my own, so after about ten minutes we get round to the social security package. I face most difficulty on the safety net of supplementary benefit to protect the poorest. Leon continues to press. If not a 5 per cent reduction then a 3 per cent? Would I be prepared to do 2 per cent? Or even 1 per cent? I say I would not, that I have gone as far as I am prepared to go. A hurried consultation between Geoffrey and Leon results in Geoffrey saying that he is prepared, reluctantly, to accept my position, but that he must point out that we are now half a billion pounds adrift as far as the savings are concerned. I point out that we still have to talk about the National Insurance Contributions Bill. Geoffrey is proposing a 0.85 per cent increase. I see no reason why that increase should not go up to 1 per cent. After a lot of further discussion that is also agreed. As I leave, the conversation goes back to John Nott and how they can handle him. The discussion has gone far better than I had any reason to expect.

THURSDAY 26 NOVEMBER

The vast majority of budgets have been settled but there are some items that have to come to Cabinet. All of mine go through successfully. The only flack I get is when we come to abatement. Keith Joseph intervenes to say that the fact that I am not abating unemployment benefit will make work incentives even worse. He is very concerned.[70] I notice that Nigel Lawson is looking suitably hawkish on the question so I take it head-on and say that Keith is out of date. Later, I pass him a note saying I'm sorry that I was so passionate about it, and he passes me a note back saying that he was sorry that he'd forgotten about the earnings-related

---

70 The theory was to cut the benefit and thus 'incentivise' the unemployed to go back to work – even though there was a shortage of jobs.

supplement. As we end, Cecil Parkinson passes me a note which says that he didn't realise that I was so tigerish on these occasions. He asks: 'whatever's happened to that nice Norman Fowler that we used to know?'

FRIDAY 27 NOVEMBER

The morning brings depressing news from Crosby. Shirley Williams has won the by-election, the first seat won by the SDP.[71] Thank goodness we didn't move any further down the public spending cuts road. We're going to have all our work cut out to stem the SDP tide. They are now so much the opposition.

THURSDAY 7 JANUARY 1982

The whole family are at Grounds Cottage after the Christmas break. I go into the city to look at the Birmingham Children's Hospital. The wards are overcrowded and the facilities are too spread out so that sometimes a sick child has to be wheeled into the open air to get from one part of the hospital to another. But my most lasting impression is of the intensive care unit where there are three babies all about the same age as Kate, all suffering from whooping cough. There is no way that the babies could have been inoculated against whooping cough. They are too young but they have caught the disease from older brothers and sisters who have not been inoculated as a result of all the publicity in the mid-1970s about the dangers of the vaccination. The BBC's *Panorama* programme played a discreditable part here, but all too little has been done since to point out the dangers of *not* being vaccinated.[72]

FRIDAY 8 JANUARY

The snow is now coming down. I go into Sutton Coldfield to visit a day nursery for mentally handicapped children. Thank goodness for voluntary

---

71 Crosby was regarded as a very safe seat for the Conservatives but Shirley Williams won the election on 26 November, taking almost half the votes cast and becoming the first MP to be elected for the SDP.

72 In the mid-1970s, some doctors questioned the safety of the pertussis (whooping cough) vaccine, claiming that it could cause brain damage in young children. Despite protests from the majority of the medical community, public confidence in the vaccine dropped significantly.

organisations. Some of the people have worked here as volunteers for ten, fifteen, or even twenty years. By lunchtime the snow is falling so heavily and lying so thick that the rest of the day has to be abandoned. We shut up shop and watch the television news and traffic reports from around the country.

SATURDAY 9 JANUARY

All the fields around here are covered in a foot of snow. There is no way to make journeys in and out of Wishaw. The night is fantastic. It is a full moon and a clear sky. The shadows from the trees can be seen quite clearly on the snow in the surrounding countryside, even at 11 o'clock at night. We will be lucky to see a sight quite as beautiful as this again.

SUNDAY 10 JANUARY

We dig out the car and are able to make the main road and the motorway without incident – and then back to London.

MONDAY 11 JANUARY

A visit to the Rampton Special Hospital. The hospital stands isolated from any major population centre. The result is that the nurses at Rampton are all local and the sons and daughters, and even the grandsons and granddaughters of people who served at Rampton previously. You have a position in which an enclosed community is guarding and caring for an enclosed community. I am not certain that everyone has made the transition from the old ways of prison warders and turnkeys to nurses yet. Some have, but I doubt if it is general. The shadow of police investigation still hangs very heavily over the hospital and it will be a great relief all round when the investigations finally come to an end.[73]

---

73   Rampton was a high-security psychiatric hospital. On 22 May 1979, Yorkshire Television broadcast an exposé programme called *Rampton: The Secret Hospital*, alleging serious instances of patients being ill-treated by members of the staff. The documentary led to an inquiry by Sir John Boynton, *The Review of Rampton Hospital*, December 1980, Cmnd 8073. The report found serious problems relating to the hospital's geographical and professional isolation, its management structure and its difficulty in recruiting staff. He was also highly critical of the internal complaints procedure. At this time the DPP was still investigating possible crimes.

MONDAY 22 FEBRUARY

A statement on charges for overseas visitors, which will raise about £6 million for the health service. Labour rage away that it is the destruction of the National Health Service as we know it. I find this an extremely difficult argument to understand. I doubt even Nye Bevan believed that we should provide a free health service for anyone who happens to be in this country at the time that he falls ill or who comes to this country specifically for treatment – particularly as, if they take out medical insurance before they come, the cost can be covered. This is precisely what happens if *we* go to America or Australia or Canada.

TUESDAY 2 MARCH

I have a meeting on health service pay at No. 10. The PM is sympathetic to the idea of a preferential offer for nurses, but much less sympathetic to the other groups. I say that even with extra money for nurses, I cannot guarantee success. It is going to be an extremely difficult wages round and of course we do not do the negotiating. Margaret obviously has her doubts about how far the preferential treatment should go but supports my bid on the grounds that I am the minister responsible and that if I believe this is what is required, then I must be backed.

WEDNESDAY 3 MARCH

There have been rumbles all week that at long last my ministerial changes are on their way. I am due to meet the PM at 4.30 about housing benefit and I receive a message to be there fifteen minutes early. Margaret gives me a cup of tea and tells me that Ken will be Minister of Health, replacing Gerry Vaughan, and Tony Newton will replace Lynda who is moving to transport.[74] This is the best conceivable outcome of all my efforts. Both Ken and Tony are undoubted candidates for Cabinet and I now have two people that I can actually talk to about the politics of the DHSS.

---

74 Lynda Chalker was very good but had been in the job too long. She started in social security when I was doing it in opposition, six years earlier, and she had done nothing else since. She was the world's expert but needed a change.

THURSDAY 4 MARCH

Cabinet. Trident is raised without papers and without warning. It is difficult for Cabinet members to take a decision of this importance without the analysis that our departments usually give to this kind of paper and the claims that are made. We are talking about costs modestly estimated at £7.5 billion. But I suppose this is all fairly theoretical, for as far as I can see there is no one who wants to mount an argument against. If the Treasury believe that the cost can be afforded – and they seem to – then Trident is quite clearly a more effective means of maintaining an independent nuclear deterrent than any other available option.

Later in the evening, both Ken and Tony come round to dinner. We celebrate with champagne, enjoy ourselves and talk politics. How marvellous after six months to get two people who are on the same wavelength, whom I can speak to and consult, and are also good company.

FRIDAY 12 MARCH

I meet the management side of the Whitley council. These are the people who, in their various areas, negotiate with the trade unions on health service pay. There is a Whitley council for nurses and midwives, a Whitley council for the administrative and clerical workers and a Whitley council for ancillaries. They make the offer and we provide them with the money. But they have a kind of independence which they very much value and cherish. Most of them are extremely put out that we have made it clear that a differential offer was going to be made to the nurses. It is a curious machine. There is no sense of leadership, although my officials tell me that when they get into negotiation they are much better. I only hope that's right. We are entrusting negotiations on a pay bill of about £6.5 billion to these people and they are all entirely voluntary. We don't even pay them for the work that they do. All we do is pay their travel expenses.

FRIDAY 26 MARCH

Roy Jenkins has won the Hillhead by-election for the SDP by 2,000 votes. A big victory for them and a big defeat for us. As John Biffen said, the

SDP are now making big advances which should make all of us consider. There will be increasing calls in the party for us to change our policies.

COMMENT

Margaret Thatcher, like her Chancellor, was determined to find economies and social security came under particular scrutiny. Her attitude to social security was highly influenced by her period in the Ministry of Pensions in the early 1960s as a junior minister to John Boyd Carpenter. Throughout that period, the concern was the elderly and retired, but by the 1980s the caravan had moved on. Many elderly were still in need but many, thanks to occupational pensions, were comparatively better off. The group who were now indisputably in need were the families with children, the single parents, and those at the very bottom of the income scale and reliant on supplementary benefit and housing benefit. These were too often seen by the Treasury and No. 10 alike as promising targets for spending cuts. With one or two exceptions, Cabinet ministers were all too willing to see social security not as protection for the poorest but as an obvious target for public spending cuts – which of course had the effect of relieving pressure on their own budgets.

4

HER FINEST HOURS

APRIL–JUNE 1982

The Falklands transformed Margaret Thatcher's reputation. She was rightly praised for the courage of her leadership and her refusal to be persuaded into a compromise solution by the Americans and some round the Cabinet table. What was clear was that if the operation failed then she, if not the whole government, would have fallen.

FRIDAY 2 APRIL 1982

A telephone call comes through at home from No. 10 just before 8.30 a.m. saying that there will be a special Cabinet meeting at 9.45 to discuss the position in the Falkland Islands.[75] I drive in very rapidly and make the meeting with about two minutes to spare. There is only one television cameraman outside but I suspect the interest of the press and television will change. Inside the Cabinet room, John Nott is accompanied by Field Marshal Bramall, Chief of the General Staff and Admiral Sir Henry Leach, Chief of the Naval Staff. There were some absentees, like Leon, Peter Walker and George Younger but most of the Cabinet have made it, Quintin Hailsham typically on his bicycle. We are quickly told about the situation that has developed. This is that not only have the Argentinian fleet continued their route to the Falklands, but that there was now every

---

75 The previous day, the Foreign Secretary had reported that the Argentinian fleet was steaming towards the Falkland Islands. The issue had evidently been discussed in committee but not in full Cabinet, where the Falklands had not figured much in our discussions. There was the curious tale of the scrap metal merchants who had landed in South Georgia but that was regarded as rather a joke. What was now clear was that it was anything but a joke.

reason to believe that troops had landed. This is not confirmed from Port Stanley for the good reason that we have lost communication with them. Humphrey Atkins is to give a statement in the House at 11 o'clock and the immediate problem is, what does he say?[76] After some discussion, it is agreed that he can say that a task force is standing by and could set sail at any time. But the discussion is a very scrappy affair with little hard information to go on. Quintin lectures us on this being a time to stand together as if anyone was going to do anything else. The only discordant note comes from Norman Tebbit, who says that if he was a backbencher he would be asking a number of questions. He would be asking why had we been caught unawares? What had our intelligence services been doing? What methods were open to us in retaliation on trade? Norman rather overstates his criticism of the intelligence services but he is right. Those will be the questions asked. We break up after about an hour and go over to the House. Humphrey makes a statement, probably the best statement I have heard him make. He keeps his replies very short and does not get into any serious trouble – but of course the House is also in the dark about what is happening.

During the afternoon a further call comes through from No. 10. There is to be another Cabinet meeting: this time at 7.30 that evening. On the Cabinet table we find an intelligence report. Confirmation has now been received that Argentinian troops have landed and have occupied Port Stanley. In its final paragraph, it says that the best assessment is that the Argentinians will reinforce the troops already there and it will be very difficult, if not impossible, to dislodge them. It then becomes clear that the report has not been seen by either John Nott or the Chief of the Defence Staff, or indeed, anyone else in the Ministry of Defence. It is a joint intelligence report and defence only has a certain input. There is to be a debate in the House of Commons on Saturday for the first time since Suez. Margaret then asks the *crucial* question, and that is whether colleagues are prepared for her to announce in her speech that the

---

76   The Foreign Secretary, Peter Carrington, was in the House of Lords. Humphrey Atkins, as the Lord Privy Seal, acted as Foreign Affairs Spokesman in the Commons.

British naval task force will set sail. Given the time that it will take to get from Britain to the Falkland Islands (between two and three weeks), this still leaves open the option to change course. The decision is effectively to take military action to recover the Falkland Islands. For the first and only time, Margaret goes round the Cabinet table asking each of us to state his position. There is almost total unanimity that the fleet must sail. There is really no option and to do anything less would be unacceptable to the public and the party, although we all believe that the maximum diplomatic pressure must be exerted to try and resolve the matter. The one dissident voice is John Biffen. He has already warned of the trade consequences as far as the Argentine is concerned. Although we are obviously going to freeze their assets in London, the trade balance is heavily in our favour and there are many British assets (and debts) in Argentina. John questions what we are going to do once we have taken the Falkland Islands – a very relevant question.[77] I think that not only do we have no choice but that the international implications if we were not to act could also be very grave, in Gibraltar for example. The meeting then is over very quickly and we troop out to find Downing Street thronged with television cameras. It is now more like a television studio. I go out with Quintin. A brave reporter asks him whether he has any comment, to which Quintin replies: 'I wish you a very good evening'.

SATURDAY 3 APRIL

The press is appalling. We are attacked universally. The trouble is of course that everyone has been caught unawares. There has been no sense of impending crisis. Very few newspapers were prominently featuring the Falkland Islands story twenty-four hours ago. Everyone is angry and frustrated and that mood is fully reflected in the House of Commons debate. Margaret rises to rather half-hearted shouts of 'resign' from the other side but makes a reasonable speech in the circumstances. She is followed by Michael Foot who makes a devastating speech that ends with

---

[77] A similar question was asked by at least one senior military commander at the time of the 1956 Suez invasion. 'Fine I can take the canal – but what do we do next?'

an attack on the government in which he says that we have betrayed the country. From then on the debate goes from bad to worse. Edward du Cann protests his loyalty to the government but then in his customary manner puts the boot in and says that the whole thing has been handled in an incompetent way. Nigel Fisher also has a go at the government but happily destroys his own case by saying that one action which is open to us is to ban Argentina from the World Cup. Ray Whitney attempts a defence of the government line, which is more a defence of the Foreign Office and is virtually howled down by our own side. Bernard Braine is his usual pugnacious self while on the other side, David Owen is impressive in his denunciation of government policy, and even John Silkin manages to put together quite a reasonable speech. But the real disaster is John Nott's summing-up. It is not altogether fair to blame John for that. He is one of the better debaters that we have but his case sounds weak and certainly does not convince our side at all. He speaks against a barrage of noise and cries of 'resign' from the Labour side, while our side sit in solid and stony silence. It is one of the unappetising parts of politics, and particularly Conservative politics: when a man is in trouble all too rarely does the Conservative Party rally to him. They would just about rally to Margaret but there is no prospect of them rallying to John. Suddenly, the proceedings end with the Speaker saying that the House stands adjourned, and the agony comes to a close.

Labour, the SDP and the Liberals are far more bellicose and far more jingoistic than any Conservative. They have been attacking defence spending year after year, but as John Nott proves fairly disastrously, there is no way that you can tell them that just at the moment. Far more worrying is the state of the Conservative Party. It is an issue that has managed to combine both the right of the party and the wets, and the professional dissidents like Cormack into a pretty united front against the front bench. From John's point of view, the events cannot really have come at a worse time. He has staked everything on Trident and because the defence budget has been so overstretched he has had to make economies elsewhere. The economies have fallen on the navy and on the surface fleet, and there are a whole range of people who do not like that.

No one is jumping to his defence. I think he will survive but it is going to be a close-run thing. There is a great deal of backbench criticism of the Foreign Office and of Carrington in particular. It is fair to say that Peter has never really brought the Cabinet up against the prospect of an invasion of the Falkland Islands. Certainly, the Falklands have figured in the reports that he has given to Cabinet. No one can doubt that but whether he has managed to communicate the potential seriousness of the situation is another matter again. Perhaps one of the problems is that Peter rather majors in producing well-rounded reports for Cabinet on what is going on overseas. These reports are often very amusingly done, in the rather cynical world-weary way that Peter manages; whether he has alerted all his colleagues to the danger is, I fear, another matter. I do not know what he has said at the overseas committee but certainly in full Cabinet, the message did not come through.

SUNDAY 4 APRIL

The press is again appalling. Television and radio programmes are full of Conservative politicians putting the knife into the government with varying degrees of enthusiasm.

MONDAY 5 APRIL

Tony Newton and I settle down to a meeting in the department, but after about five minutes a note is passed to me that Peter Carrington has resigned. I show this to Tony and we continue talking about child benefit. A few minutes later another note comes through saying that not only has Peter Carrington resigned but other resignations are expected. At this stage we decide to abandon the meeting. It soon transpires that all the foreign office ministers – Peter Carrington, Humphrey Atkins and Richard Luce – have resigned. The difficulty with resignations is that they are basically an admission of guilt. It appears to establish that not only have we been caught unawares, but we have been culpable in not foreseeing what was happening. It is an honourable thing for Peter to have done but it weakens the government's overall position. Humphrey Atkins appears to have loyally gone with his chief and Richard Luce likewise. Over at the House, colleagues are pretty stunned by the affair. By the late afternoon the news comes that Francis Pym is taking over as Foreign Secretary. He is probably about the only man with the experience and stature who could step into Peter Carrington's shoes. At the same time, John Biffen is going to become Leader of the House. That will be a popular appointment in House of Commons terms. Another more surprising piece of news, which I pick up from Leon, is that the new trade secretary is to be Arthur Cockfield. I have always regarded Cockfield as a grey, slightly eccentric figure with a decidedly odd speaking style. He is certainly extremely fortunate to find himself in the Cabinet. I gather that the reason is that it is considered essential that we have three lords in the Cabinet. It is a very odd way to make appointments in the 1980s but there we are.[78]

TUESDAY 6 APRIL

Margaret begins Cabinet by saying how very much she regrets the resignation of Peter Carrington. Francis Pym reports on the diplomatic situation but the whole meeting is a very low-key affair. We all have our eyes on the debate tomorrow. Certainly, we cannot afford a repetition of Saturday. I have a note from Ken Stowe, which says that he had a talk with the Permanent Secretary at the Treasury, Douglas Wass, who says the Chancellor is concerned about how we are going to finance the cost of the present exercise – never mind the cost of a continuing commitment in the South Atlantic. Ken says ominously that it was his view that the Chancellor is bound to look for some cutbacks in civil programmes later this year.

WEDNESDAY 7 APRIL

Debate on the Falklands. Francis Pym opens and from the beginning it is quite clear that the House's mood has changed. Francis speaks with force and authority and altogether, makes an extremely good speech. It

---

78 David Cameron went to the other extreme and for a time had no one from the Lords as a full member of the Cabinet. Mrs May had one – the Leader of the Lords – and Rishi Sunak currently only has one.

goes down very well on our side. Patrick Cormack is even to be seen waving his order paper. Denis Healey, on the other hand, makes a pretty poor speech. The content is fine but there is no animation and at times it appears that he is going to dry up altogether. When it comes to the wind-ups, John Nott fully redeems himself and establishes what many of us already knew, that he is a tough character and a very good debater. He has the advantage of being able to announce something new and that is the 200-mile exclusion zone around the Falklands. He is never in trouble and the overall effect is that the government are once more in control.

WEDNESDAY 14 APRIL

The House is recalled from the Easter break and we have a Cabinet meeting in the morning. Margaret reports on Alexander Haig's visit.[79] Haig had started the negotiations believing that all that was required was some compromise. Margaret has dug in, saying that it was crucial that Argentina should not be seen to gain because of its aggression. Haig had then come forward with a plan: Argentinian troops should withdraw from the Islands; a commission should be set up to include representatives from Britain, Argentina and the United States; all three flags should fly on the Islands; their day-to-day running should be in the hands of the local councils made up of the Islands' inhabitants; and that this should be regarded as an interim period. Reaction to these proposals is mixed. Francis obviously believes that they represent a good deal as far as Britain is concerned and that there is no prospect of returning to the position directly before the invasion. The most outspoken opposition to compromise comes from Quintin. He sees it entirely in terms of black and white. He says that Argentina has been guilty of aggression and that

---

79   President Reagan's administration was divided over the conflict. American Secretary of State Alexander Haig, believing equivocation could undermine the NATO alliance, favoured backing the British. Thomas Enders, the Assistant Secretary of State for Inter-American affairs, feared that would undermine US anti-communist efforts in Latin America. US Ambassador to the UN Jeane Kirkpatrick sided with Enders and was the guest of honour at a dinner held by the Argentine Ambassador on the day the Argentine military landed on the Islands. Reagan said he couldn't understand why two US allies were arguing over 'that little ice-cold bunch of land down there.' In the end Haig's shuttle diplomacy failed and Reagan blamed Argentina, declared US support for Britain and imposed economic sanctions against Argentina.

there should be no prospect at all of compromising with the aggressor. If we do that, then we are lost internationally. To this, Willie Whitelaw replies that the public mood is likely to change and although it is true that public opinion is very much on our side at the moment, what public opinion basically wants is for us to be successful, but without any fighting and without any casualties. I don't think that Willie is correct in this. My own belief is that British public opinion is rather more sturdy than he indicates. The leader in today's *Times* shows our action is supported. It would also appear from what the Defence Secretary says that our military strength is superior. At any rate, Haig is now going to Buenos Aires. Frankly, there is nothing much more to do but wait and see what happens.

The debate during the afternoon is a pretty low-key affair. The Prime Minister is listened to virtually without interruption, apart from Tam Dalyell.[80] Michael Foot puts in another extremely good performance. It is one of the intriguing aspects of the whole Falklands position that a number of politicians have really come into their own. One of these is undoubtedly Michael Foot and another is David Owen.

MONDAY 19 APRIL

I was due to be in the United States this week to try and bring in some inward investment from American pharmaceutical companies, but have cancelled the trip. The postponed lunch at No. 10 takes place but it is rather fraught. Margaret is very much on edge and makes it clear that she believes that the Foreign Office has let the government down by not foreseeing what was taking place in Argentina. She believes that the advent of Galtieri as President and the coming together of Argentina and Russia on grain sales should have been seen as indications that there could be a new and serious threat to the Falkland Islands. Willie tries very hard to persuade her off this line. He says that the last thing that we should do is to give the impression to the outside world that we have been at fault in this. There is then a discussion in which Margaret is

---

80   Labour MP for West Lothian, then for Linlithgow who was a leading critic of the Falklands War and
      in particular the sinking of the *General Belgrano*.

arguing one point and Willie, John Biffen and myself are arguing another without anyone really listening to the arguments. Margaret is making a perfectly defensible point, although it is not one I would agree with. Willie is also making a perfectly defensible point and Margaret is not listening to that. My argument is that four-fifths of the nation supports the action that we are now taking, but four-fifths of the nation also believes that we were culpable in being caught unawares. It would be very foolish for us to add credence to that last view by in any way suggesting that we were ill-prepared and caught by surprise.

In the evening the news comes from Buenos Aires that Haig has finished his talks. Late-night guidance from No. 10 appears to be that the deal which the junta would accept is unacceptable to this country. Well, we will find out in a very few hours' time. A Cabinet has been arranged for tomorrow. Both Denis Healey[81] and David Steel have been on television talking about the importance of compromise and keeping negotiations open. It is pretty easy for oppositions to take this position. They have to do very little but stand back, observe and not irrevocably commit themselves to any course of action. However helpful Michael Foot's speeches may appear, their case will always be that we should have foreseen the invasion as the last Labour government did in 1977.[82]

TUESDAY 20 APRIL

Cabinet had been fixed for 10 o'clock in the morning but finally takes place at 5.15 in the afternoon. For once, we are provided with some papers concerning the dispute. There are three documents. The first is a document which sets out what Haig believes the Argentinians are prepared to agree to; the second is a commentary of his own; and the third sets out the kind of proposals that we ourselves consider acceptable.

81 Deputy leader of the Labour Party and shadow Foreign Secretary.
82 In 1977, James Callaghan's Labour government ordered a small flotilla, led by the nuclear-powered submarine *HMS Dreadnought*, to the South Atlantic after a party of fifty Argentine 'scientists' landed on the island of South Thule. Codenamed Operation Journeyman, it was carried out in the utmost secrecy. The then Foreign Secretary, David Owen, insisted that not even the crews were to be told where they going until they were at sea. While the Argentinian government was privately warned by the British that there was a nuclear submarine in the area, the rest of the world was unaware of what was going on.

There is no way that the government could agree to the proposals which the Argentinians find acceptable. They will withdraw their troops but not before we have withdrawn our naval fleet and sent it back to its 'normal' position. They are not prepared to be ruled by the wishes of the islanders. The most they would do is to take note of them. Overall, their proposals are unacceptable and no one around the table seeks to dispute that. Nevertheless, it is agreed that Francis should go to Washington rather than make Haig take yet another transatlantic trip and see if there is anything further that can be gained by negotiation. The most revealing information coming back from Haig's trips to Buenos Aires is his impression of the junta there. It is quite clear that he feels that there is no one that he can really do a deal with. Galtieri is looking over his shoulder: there are something like fifty corps commanders whom he has to consult and he is in no position to deliver. Other information also suggests that the man is an alcoholic and with the best will in the world it is extremely difficult to see how Haig, or indeed anyone else, is going to find a solution which is capable of sticking. Nevertheless, the negotiations will go on.

THURSDAY 22 APRIL

Another Cabinet with Francis Pym still in Washington and Douglas Hurd deputising. John Nott has not been saying a great deal, if anything, at full Cabinet meetings, but on this occasion he does report. He repeats what Haig has already set out, namely that it is extremely difficult to know how any kind of deal can be struck with the kind of junta that is in power in Argentina. More than that, he says, we now have the task force rapidly approaching the Falklands and we simply cannot leave them bobbing about on the rough seas of the South Atlantic week after week as the negotiations go on. There are two things therefore that have been decided. He reveals that there are some troops already on South Georgia who are making a reconnaissance of the ground. If that reconnaissance is satisfactory, the next stage will be to take South Georgia. Second, he says, is to set an air limit in addition to the maritime exclusion zone. This will mean that the Argentinians will not be able to bring supplies through to the Falklands or at least if they try, they will be liable to be shot down. His information on the Argentinian force on the island is that morale is low and that the men there are predominantly conscripts who are ill-equipped and ill-trained to be fighting in these kinds of conditions. In contrast, we will be able to deploy some very highly trained people who have been trained in Arctic warfare and are very much equipped for this kind of operation. There is a discussion about the wisdom of taking South Georgia. The Cabinet is predominantly in favour but there are two exceptions – Jim Prior and Peter Walker. Both have very serious doubts about it. Their position is that the most important thing to do is to keep world opinion, and particularly American opinion, with us and that it is likely to disappear if it is seen that we are attacking South Georgia when negotiations have not run their course. However, the majority view is that with the fleet there and given the options, there is little alternative but to take South Georgia if that can be done, and all the intelligence appears to suggest that it can. It is certainly my view that we should go ahead.

Everything else in Cabinet rather pales into insignificance. I give a report on the impending crisis in the National Health Service with virtually every union threatening to take industrial action in pursuit of their pay claim.

SUNDAY 25 APRIL

At 6 o'clock the news comes through that British troops have landed on South Georgia. There is very little information. Helicopters have apparently fired on an Argentinian submarine but I imagine that the landing is now in full operation and our hope must be that the action will be short, sharp and successful. The radio is already saying that there will be a statement in the House of Commons tomorrow. I imagine, and I certainly hope, that there will be a Cabinet meeting in the morning. Yesterday, I received a phone call from No. 10 asking whether I could make a Cabinet meeting at 6 o'clock. Later, I received a phone call saying it was cancelled but there might be one on Sunday. The television shows that there was a meeting of the inner group on Saturday at 6 o'clock which went on for three hours and apparently, there has been a further meeting of the inner group today at Chequers and Margaret has been to see the Queen. I make no real complaint about it, but at some stage the Cabinet should also be brought into these decisions. I hope tomorrow.

MONDAY 26 APRIL

The news that comes in from South Georgia is all good. We have recaptured the island and what is more, we have done it without any loss of life. The Argentinians on the island have surrendered. There is a mood of quiet elation in the country plus, it has to be admitted, some self-congratulation. People begin to tell you that Britain has always been good at this kind of thing. We have the experience which other countries simply do not match. The admiral in charge of the task force, Sandy Woodward, adds a rather discordant note by describing the taking of South Georgia rather like a football match and predicting a walkover when it comes to the Falklands. I am sure that urgent public relations advice from Neville Taylor and Co.[83] will now be winging its way to the South Atlantic. However, so far, the news is good. The military efficiency of the task force is beyond question but there have not yet been casualties and the public mood could just as easily change.

WEDNESDAY 28 APRIL

The day begins with Cabinet. The Prime Minister says that the Americans have now circulated proposals for an end to the conflict. These are being put to the Argentinians. There is no question of us having accepted or endorsed the proposals. She is going to send them round to Cabinet because they present difficulties as far as we are concerned. John Nott says that with effect from Friday there would be a total exclusion zone established around the Falkland Islands. That would apply to air as well as to sea.

---

83   My former head of public relations and later, head of the Government Information Service.

THURSDAY 29 APRIL

Another Cabinet. We consider the American suggestions for ending the conflict in the South Atlantic. There are many things wrong with the proposals from our point of view, but it is not in the British interest that we should be seen to be responsible for the breakdown of the talks. It is equally important that the Americans should be under no illusion that we have serious reservations about a number of the details. Most of us take the view that our reservations should be sent to Haig and the President. Everyone is concerned that the Argentinians are simply going to string the negotiations along as they consolidate their position. In the afternoon there is another debate. Michael Foot's position has become 'negotiate, negotiate'. Do everything you can to avoid armed conflict. Margaret's response is that the aim is still a negotiated settlement but that it would be totally inconsistent to support sending the task force but then oppose its use.

SATURDAY I MAY

The weekend is dominated by news of the sinking by a British submarine of the Argentinian cruiser, the *General Belgrano*. The elation of the previous week disappears in a puff of smoke. At last it is clear to everyone that this is war. There is an undeniably uneasy feeling about the sinking. The ship was outside the total exclusion zone. The impression is that Britain was going beyond what was absolutely necessary. The loss of life is on a horrific scale.[84]

TUESDAY 4 MAY

Cabinet. John Nott says that the overriding concern must be the protection of British forces. He had warned Argentina on 23 April that any approach by Argentine warships or military aircraft which could amount to a threat to interfere with the mission of British forces in the South

---

84   Three hundred and twenty-five people were killed in the attack; the largest casualties in any one day of the war. In 1985, a senior civil servant, Clive Ponting, leaked documents to Labour MP Tam Dalyell revealing that the *Belgrano* had not only been outside the exclusion zone, but had also been sailing away from it when it was fired upon. Ponting was prosecuted under the Official Secrets Act. In spite of the judge's summing-up, the jury upheld Ponting's defence that his disclosure was in the public interest.

Atlantic would encounter the appropriate response. That was the threat which had been posed by the *Belgrano* and it had been countered. It was believed that the destroyers accompanying the *General Belgrano* carried Exocet missiles. Why the two destroyers left the *General Belgrano* to its fate was not clear. At Prime Minister's Questions, Margaret makes it clear that she very much regretted the loss of life that had taken place and the same message came through in the succeeding statement from John Nott. For perhaps the first time, the opposition were on the attack. They obviously regarded the loss of life as not only regrettable, but many of them believed it was also avoidable. A few hours later the whole mood of the House changes. The news comes through, first as a rumour but then confirmed, that a British ship had gone down and has been sunk. As I hurry to my room on the Cabinet floor to see the 9 o'clock news, I meet John Nott. He tells me that the news is bad, that we have lost a ship, a Type 42 destroyer, *HMS Sheffield*, and also two Harriers. This was all too quickly confirmed on the news bulletins. Down below in the Chamber the House is debating a Scottish local government bill but soon, the points of order begin to come up on the screen and the inevitable demand for a statement takes place. John Nott makes the statement and gives as much information as he can – which is not very much. He puts the casualty figures at thirty. From our side, the worst intervention is from John Wells who (without justification) accuses Michael Foot of being a 'prize hypocrite' and from their side, Leo Abse makes a rambling intervention suggesting that we should end operations. Cecil Parkinson, who I was sitting next to, says that there is no way he is going to grow old in the service of this House.

THURSDAY 13 MAY

In the afternoon, another debate on the Falklands – the fifth. Francis Pym runs into some flack from our side. People like Julian Amery, Stephen Hastings and Bernard Braine distrust the United Nations negotiations and fear we will be sold a pup. Ted Heath (in his first speech) simply adds to their fears. His position is that we should listen to the views of the islanders but that they do not have the right to veto any agreement.

WEDNESDAY 19 MAY

The first of the health unions' one-day strikes. It must be extremely frustrating for the unions who are battling to get some coverage for their dispute. Having said that, I do not think that our luck will hold for ever.

THURSDAY 20 MAY

Margaret says negotiations are at an end. In the House she is emphatic. The proposals put forward by Britain have been rejected by Argentina and they have therefore been withdrawn. Britain has a responsibility to restore the islanders' democratic way of life and she bluntly tells us that we will do. Not much room for doubt there. Foot wants more discussion and for Margaret to go to the United Nations herself and David Owen, for the first time, gets himself into a muddle by arguing for the terms to stay on the table as hostilities take place.

WEDNESDAY 26 MAY

John Nott announces that there has been a major increase in operational activity in the South Atlantic. Successful raids were made from the task force on the Port Stanley airfield and all our aircraft returned safely. However, *HMS Coventry*, there to provide early warning of air attack and an air-defence screen for the supply ships unloading water in San Carlos was hit by several bombs and suffered severe damage. She later capsized. Initial casualty figures are that twenty members of her crew died in the attack. Also, *Atlantic Conveyor*, a Merchant Navy ship, was hit by Exocets and set on fire. Four of those on board were killed.

THURSDAY 27 MAY

In spite of the Falklands the health dispute now dominates my life. I make a statement on NHS pay which is fairly rough stuff. The House merrily gets back to all-out hostilities and a hail of abuse is heaped on me from the other side. Willie Hamilton simply says the Falklands venture should be called off and the money should be diverted to the NHS.[85]

TUESDAY 8 JUNE

We have another 24-hour health strike. Again, the Falkland Islands obscures what is taking place. The House is more interested in what the Prime Minister has to say about the Falklands and the reason that she vetoed a United Nations resolution that was supported by Foot. Margaret gives a one-sentence reply to the effect that there is no obstacle in the way of Argentinian withdrawal – except the Argentinians.

THURSDAY 10 JUNE

A supply day from the opposition on health pay but again overshadowed by the Falklands. Good and bad news. John Nott goes on before me to say that British forces are now surrounding Port Stanley. Earlier, Darwin and Goose Green had been captured. But on 8 June an air attack had been launched against two landing ships, *Sir Galahad* and *Sir Tristram*. Both ships were hit. The *Sir Tristram* had virtually completed offloading and she was not severely damaged. The *Sir Galahad* had started offloading but still had men on board when it was bombed and set on fire.[86]

On the health dispute, Gwyneth Dunwoody calls on me to refer the whole matter to ACAS.[87] I am able to trump her call by announcing during my speech that I have asked Pat Lowry[88] to act as a go-between but that this does not mean that we are prepared to go to arbitration. We are not prepared to sub-contract the decision on what national resources should be made available to health to some outside body, but I do say that Lowry will see if there is common ground.

---

85   A left-wing MP for a Scottish constituency 1950–1987. Well known for his republican views.

86   The fireball that engulfed the *Sir Galahad* was caught by the BBC and was one of the defining images of the war. It cost the lives of thirty-two Welsh Guards, eleven other soldiers and five civilian crew. One of the most seriously injured soldiers, Simon Weston, became a nationally recognised figure after documenting his recovery from severe burns and for his decades of charity work.

87   Gwyneth was a Labour MP from February 1974 to her death in 2008 and a front bench spokesman.

88   An industrial relations expert who became Chairman of ACAS in 1981.

MONDAY 14 JUNE

A crucial week for negotiating what more we can give to the health service. Our first hurdle is the Treasury. What we would like to achieve is a settlement of about 6 per cent for the ancillaries, 6.5 per cent for the ambulance men and 7.5 per cent for the nurses. We have a great deal of internal discussion about how this offer should be presented. Of course, the conventional wisdom is that you should always keep something back because I don't think any of us believe that the unions are going to accept 6 per cent although clearly our hope is that the nurses will take away the 7.5. But the conventional wisdom is all very well if you in fact have something in your back pocket which you can give away. We have not. Leon is not unreasonable on the issue. After a lot of argument, he says that the limit he is prepared to go to is £45 million from the Treasury and the contingency reserve, but at the same time what he wants to see is some kind of manpower control system introduced. This is in fact, very much what both Ken and I would like to see as well.

MONDAY EVENING

A dramatic short statement in the Commons by Margaret just after 10 p.m. British forces have advanced, she says. Large numbers of Argentine soldiers have thrown down their weapons. They are reported to be flying white flags over Port Stanley. Enormous cheers in the House and Michael Foot, David Steel and David Owen unite in their congratulations. It looks as though the war is over. As Jeremy Moore, the commander of the land forces, says in a message to the commander in chief of the fleet, 'The Falkland Islands are once more under the government desired by their inhabitants. God Save the Queen'.

COMMENT

It has often been said that if only Margaret Thatcher had been more collegiate, more consensual, more ready to listen, then her government would have been both happier and more successful. Geoffrey Howe made very much this point to me at a later stage in the government and no one can doubt that he deserved to be treated better by a Prime Minister he served both well and, almost to the end, loyally. But the Falklands show the other side of the argument. She was under vast pressure to accept the argument of the American Secretary of State, Al Haig, that there must be a compromise solution without going to war. I suspect several members of the Cabinet would have been happy enough had she taken this course. Her refusal to back down marked her out as a leader apart. That very quality of determination and a refusal to accept convenient retreats for the sake of looking consensual explains not only much of the Falklands success but also her determination to right the economy and reform industrial relations law. On the other side of the argument, it also explains why, after her third victory, she ignored advice and pursued her longstanding ambition to reform the rates and ensure that an elderly widow did not pay the same as a working family living next door. It was of course her alternative to the community charge – the poll tax – that did much to eventually bring her down. But that was all in the future. In 1982 she triumphed as a war leader, exhibiting all the qualities of certainty and belief that a war leader requires. Another quality was her sheer stamina. There was no question of clearing the table and celebrating. Twenty-four hours later, she was back in action overseeing my plans to counter the impending health strike.

5

THE BLOODY POLITICS
OF HEALTH

JUNE–DECEMBER 1982

After I left the government, a surprising number of people came up to me whenever there was a new 'health crisis' saying: 'you never had these problems in your time'. As Mr Salter in Evelyn Waugh's Scoop *would have put it: 'Up to a point, Lord Copper'. The 1982 health dispute was one of the longest public sector disputes since the Second World War – and a very rough dispute at that. The campaign was accompanied by days of action, demonstrations, one of which brought 60,000 on to the streets, and resulted in tens of thousands of delayed operations.*

WEDNESDAY 16 JUNE 1982

The Prime Minister has called a meeting this evening to discuss tactics in the health dispute. The meeting takes place in her drawing room at No. 10. Margaret has just won the Falklands War and is still very much in that mood. She is combative on every conceivable point and the meeting lasts two hours when frankly, it could all have been over in thirty minutes. Margaret wants to put all her views on the NHS, which are only marginally more benign than her views on British Rail. She obviously believes the health service is totally over-staffed. It is all very well me talking about a ceiling on manpower, what she wants is manpower being reduced. The conversation tends to be a debate between myself and Margaret with Ken coming in from time to time and with the Treasury ministers, Geoffrey and Leon, as onlookers. I think Ken is genuinely rather shocked by the style of the whole meeting. Personally, having done electrification with the Prime Minister, it doesn't seem to me that extraordinary. There is no question that the style is combative. There is also no question that general blame is apportioned around the room. If the health service think that I am hawk-like, they should meet Margaret in one of these moods. She tells me that if the nurses get all this money this year, they can't expect to come back next year for even more. In other words, they are a very special case. I am not quite sure how this argument can be sustained given that 7.5 per cent is only marginally ahead of people like local authority manuals but that is the leader's view.[89] Still, when all the rhetoric has been taken away, the result is not too unsatisfactory. Margaret agrees that I can offer talks on new pay arrangements although she is not happy about this. Her point is that no one had consulted her before the prospect of new pay arrangements was offered. I say that I had told the Chancellor of the Exchequer what I was doing but I was under the impression that she was fighting a war and didn't want to be disturbed with all the other decisions of government at that stage. Her response to that was that she had taken the chair of every Cabinet economic committee throughout the Falklands dispute.[90]

MONDAY 21 JUNE

The pay negotiations start again. I call in the chairmen of the Whitley councils who do the negotiating for us. Some of the chairmen are good; some are pretty awful. I still find it extraordinary that we put the handling of something like £6.5 billion of wages in the hands of unpaid, part-time and not particularly professional negotiators. The chairman who deals with the crucially important Nurses' and Midwives' Council is a manufacturer of garden gnomes – which I am sure he does extremely well – but whether it qualifies him to handle pay negotiations with some very professional negotiators on the other side of the table is another matter.

---

89 The health unions' claim was for 12 per cent. We moved to 6 per cent for the ancillaries and 7.5 per cent for the nurses.

90 This meeting, it should be emphasised, came only twenty-four hours after the victory in the Falklands – the most dramatic achievement of her first term. There was no question of her taking a day or two off to relax.

FRIDAY 9 JULY

I visit St Thomas' Hospital in Lambeth. The last time I had been there was when Fiona was having Kate. This time it is all very different. A strike by about twenty-five people in the central sterile supplies store has drastically reduced the hospital's activities. The other problem is caused by the unions trying to distinguish between emergency and urgent cases in who is admitted. The result is that about 1,000 operations have been postponed and now, even cancer patients are being delayed. There is no doubt that the strikers believe that St Thomas' is a good target being just over the road from Westminster.

FRIDAY 23 JULY

I go to Bristol and arrive at the regional health headquarters to be met by what is now the ritual demonstration. They try to block the path to the car but are so surprised when I jump out and ask them to let the car through that they very quietly and politely move to one side. I then go in, have a talk with their leaders and get on with the meeting. At this stage there is no real venom in the dispute.

THURSDAY 29 JULY

Cabinet. We are now getting into injury time as far as this parliamentary session is concerned. Everyone is tired, tempers are frayed and the sooner we go down the better. The rail strike is out of the way and there is no doubt at all that everyone would like the health dispute to be out of the way as well. No such luck. I tell them that the Royal College of Nursing (RCN) has decided to ballot their members and it will take them five weeks to complete the process. I also warn them that the ballot form itself contains no recommendation from their negotiating committee and that all the nurses are being asked to do is to say whether they think 7.5 per cent is sufficient. They are almost bound to say 'no' because it is a ridiculous and empty question.

MONDAY 9 AUGUST

A week of action begins. I don't think I can remember a day on which I have given so many interviews to so many people. It starts with the *Today* programme in the morning and goes on to virtually every known radio station and television outlet. In the afternoon I fly to Manchester by helicopter, courtesy of Granada Television, to do *World in Action*. The programme is an illustration of the kind of thing that we are up against. John Humphreys is the interviewer and has what looks to the viewer like a jury of six people. Humphreys questions them in turn about the state of the health service and the dispute. There is no one among the six who is remotely in favour of the government's stand. If your six consist of Rodney Bickerstaffe of NUPE, Ian Hargreaves of the Royal College of Nursing, an articulate and militant nurse, an ancillary worker, Sir Sidney Hamburger, who has just resigned as regional health chairman in the north west, and a consultant from Guy's who is trying to get some money out of us to continue his pet project, then you can hardly expect a very well-rounded picture. But this is precisely the programme that Granada Television put together. Fortunately it is done in a cack-handed way. All of the panellists are fairly nervous and I am then given ten minutes or so to answer the points that have been raised. The programme ends with a summing-up. The producers of *World in Action* obviously feel that my part of the programme hasn't ended with the degree of controversy that they would like. They suggest that we should retake the last part of the programme. I decline.

Low cloud and rain have come in and the helicopter can't take off. We therefore have to go back by train but this has one advantage: Rodney Bickerstaffe is on the same train.[91] We spend about thirty minutes talking quite privately without notes and with no one else present. He is an interesting man. There is no common ground in the way that we approach things. He believes that his predecessor, Alan Fisher, achieved absolutely nothing for the low-paid. The low-paid are still low-paid. He also believes that the government deserves no credit for having brought inflation down because that is an inevitable consequence of unemployment. He looks faintly surprised when I say that the first aim of the health service is to look after the patient. And the staff, he adds. Of course, I say, no service can fail to have the morale of the staff in mind but nevertheless, the first aim is to

---

91   General Secretary of the National Union of Public Employees (NUPE) from 1981.

look after patients or there is no other justification for it. He believes in the need for a fundamental change in society and I think he is entirely genuine in his concern for the low-paid. He obviously views us Tories as figures from the 1930s intent upon depressing the living standards of the poor. And yet the people he is talking about would not be in the Conservative Party if that was what it stood for. My generation at Cambridge – Ken, Leon, John Gummer – would not have joined the Conservative Party and remained members of it if we thought that was our role. There is this fundamental gulf between us and I do not think that there is a great deal that I can ever say to Rodney Bickerstaffe which would persuade him that there were men of goodwill in the Conservative Party.

TUESDAY 10 AUGUST
Caroline, who is not notable for her praise, thought my interview with *World in Action* went fantastically well.[92]

THURSDAY 12 AUGUST
A copy of *The Lancet* appears on the desks of Fleet Street. In it there is a leading article by the Editor which is highly critical of the government. It is mostly critical of what he says is the Thatcher philosophy but what really goes beyond the pale is his assertion that the government is simply waiting for a death to take place as an essential part of their tactics. *The Lancet* says that I should offer my resignation.

FRIDAY 13 AUGUST
I am interviewed about *The Lancet* article on the *Today* programme and say that it is beneath contempt. To my slight surprise, I find that my comments are leading the *Evening Standard*. The whole affair illustrates another aspect of this dispute. From all I understand, the editor of *The Lancet* is devoted to the health service. I assume he believes in a well-meaning way that if he makes comments of this kind, then it will in some way influence the outcome of proceedings. What he appears not to understand is that

---

92   Caroline Bell, my invaluable parliamentary secretary.

it will give the unions exactly the kind of moral support that they need. What he is succeeding in doing is being yet another of those generous well-meaning men who, by their own ineptitude, prolong the dispute.

TUESDAY 17 AUGUST

Ken, who has been on holiday, returns to the country today. We get him on the radio pretty rapidly so that it is established he is back in the country. This is for his sake as much as for anyone else's. A tour of some of the more critical spots has been organised and Ken, after two weeks away, is of course fresh and raring to go.[93]

WEDNESDAY 25 AUGUST

I have managed to have a week in France with Fiona, Kate and Oliver. Today, we drive to Bordeaux airport and meet Ken Clarke who is flying in. Untypically, Ken looks quite rattled. He has given an interview to the *Daily Telegraph* which has led to the most extraordinarily misleading headline – that we are on the point of calling in the troops. Not good news. Our whole purpose is to cool the issue not to raise the temperature. But the thing that has really unnerved him is that his private office booked him through VIP facilities at Heathrow three or four days in advance so that even the doziest journalist based at the airport knew that 'K. Clarke, Minister of Health' was about to go on holiday. Fortunately, they didn't manage to get a photograph of him but that was not for lack of trying. He was literally chased onto the tarmac by six photographers and it was only because the captain refused to allow the cameramen on to the plane that he avoided a photograph altogether. Frankly this was just as well, for Ken was wearing undoubted holiday gear and with his rather cherubic expression he only needed a Brownie camera around his neck to be the typical tourist off to Spain.

I am back in the department by about 4 o'clock and no sooner back

---

93 Ken Clarke's holidays (sometimes taken in the middle of disputes) proved a consistent source of complaint both inside and outside of government. Margaret Thatcher, who never took holidays herself, thought him self-indulgent. At times I admit I grumbled but in retrospect, I think the Clarke view on life was entirely sensible.

than am on the air giving interviews on Ken's supposed statement about troops. The obvious point to make is that there is no intention of using troops and the only areas in which troops might be used would be if military ambulances were needed.

THURSDAY 26 AUGUST

The long-awaited nurses' ballot. It comes out two-to-one against us, which was predictable from the beginning. Radio and television are running strongly with the RCN ballot story.

FRIDAY 27 AUGUST

The press brings a hostile reaction. *The Guardian* is the worst. If there's one thing worse than Fowler, it says, it's Clarke and if there's one thing worse than Clarke, it's Thatcher. More seriously the *Daily Mail* comes out strongly against us. There is notably sensible comment in *The Times* and the *Telegraph* and papers like the *Express* and *The Sun*.

WEDNESDAY 1 SEPTEMBER

I have invited Albert Spanswick and Peter Jacques home to Hurlingham Road.[94] The meeting, which is notably friendly, is held on the basis that no one is to know about it and it is entirely without commitment. In fact, Albert has much more to lose if the meeting was to leak out than I have. He has his militants to try to keep in order. We will meet again after the TUC Congress. If there is one thing that we are agreed on it is that the Royal College of Nursing's protracted handling of the whole affair has loused up everything. Albert says that it has extended the dispute. There is only one problem left over from the meeting: Albert has left his trilby hat hanging up in our house. What would his members think of that?!

---

94   Albert Spanswick became General Secretary of COHSE in 1974 and was elected to the general council of the Trades Union Congress (TUC) in 1977. He was Chair of its Health Services Committee. Peter Jacques worked at the TUC for twenty-five years, most of that time as head of the social insurance and industrial welfare department and was Secretary to the Health Services Committee.

WEDNESDAY 8 SEPTEMBER

The early part of the day and early afternoon is dominated by preparations for a whooping cough vaccination for Kate. Fiona and I decided some time ago that Kate should be vaccinated and this is her third dose coming up. We've also decided that it would be a good idea to have the press and television there, and of course they make quite a thing of it. Both main channels turn up and so do the photographers. Kate is fantastic. She gives one surprised yelp as she is punctured by the needle and then calms down immediately, fascinated by all the cameras. She couldn't be better and later in the evening, we are rewarded by some very good photographs on television. Let's hope it has some effect and encourages other parents to inoculate. At 5.30 p.m. I go to see Jim Prior and talk to him about a two-year deal for the health workers. He is entirely in favour of us trying to find a way through the dispute.

THURSDAY 9 SEPTEMBER

Cabinet. There is a short discussion about the health dispute and both John Nott and Michael Heseltine say that all the press reports about how it is being mishandled are extremely stupid. As far as they are concerned, the dispute is being handled very well indeed. Nick Edwards says the same and adds that it is about time that the rest of the Cabinet came in and gave some support. There is no critical comment. If there are ministers who are 'unhappy' about the handling of the dispute, they certainly don't raise their heads over the parapet at this meeting.

We next go onto what is the real issue of the day – the CPRS report on the long-term options for public spending. This has been pressed for by Geoffrey Howe and we have the report before us, which in Margaret's words 'thinks the unthinkable' and contains some pretty hairy ideas. They have obviously identified the DHSS, defence and education as the big spenders. As far as we are concerned they want to see studies of new health charges and new ways of financing the service, such as through a system of private health insurance, not to mention deindexing pensions and social security.

In no way am I against looking at new ideas but frankly it is political madness to think about them right in the middle of the longest health dispute since the year dot. There would be revolution if you tried to do that at this moment. As the discussion goes on, others rally to my side. We can certainly look at how we expand private health insurance but let us be political about it.

FRIDAY 10 SEPTEMBER

The media response to the Cabinet meeting or more properly, the briefing by Bernard Ingham was dramatic. It is all about the health dispute. Nothing about the CPRS! The *Express* has a front-page headline saying, 'No more pay for nurses: No surrender to the unions: No recall of Parliament'. The *Mail* says, 'Not a penny more – Maggie'. They say that the Prime Minister and her colleagues rallied to the Health Secretary and said 'No' to any extra cash, 'No' to any new government initiative and 'No' to recalling Parliament to discuss the issue as demanded by Michael Foot yesterday. *The Sun* had a leader which said, 'No surrender' and generally the message to the TUC at Brighton was that there was no chance of the government simply caving in.

TUESDAY 14 SEPTEMBER

After Cabinet, Ken Stowe and I prepare for our next meeting with Albert and Peter, codenamed Janswick. They present themselves at Hurlingham Road soon after 5 o'clock. We put a new plan to break the deadlock to them. A two-year deal. It has advantages for both sides. We are now months into the financial year. The advantage would be that health workers would get back pay and an increase – and in a few months' time would get another increase. The advantage for us would be that we would have settled the pay issue for eighteen months.

THURSDAY 16 SEPTEMBER

The proposals are sent over to Peter Jacques at the TUC headquarters first thing in the morning and almost simultaneously to the Royal College of Nursing. So far so good. But just before 2 p.m. we have a message from the TUC that they want us to receive a small delegation for exploratory talks. This delegation was apparently to consist of Albert, Peter Jacques and a press officer from the TUC whom no one had ever heard of before. Obviously, things have gone wrong and soon it became clear just how wrong they have gone. The conversation is perfectly polite but it is absolutely clear that Albert is having great difficulty in carrying his people with him. We have negotiated with the chairman and the secretary of the Health Services Committee but it looks as though our worst fears are going to be confirmed and they are unable to deliver the goods.

The first news came through at 6 o'clock, not from a message from the TUC headquarters but from a press conference; that the Health Services Committee was not even prepared to come and negotiate. By this stage I was extremely angry. We had been let down by Spanswick and Jacques. There was absolutely no question about it. Yet, here they were issuing statements which were saying words to the effect that the government's offer was a sham and it was all a public relations gimmick. The angriest interview I give was to some Labour correspondent from the BBC who took himself extremely seriously. It was unbelievable to get the kind of hostile questioning from this particular jerk when if he only knew half the truth he should have been putting the questions to Spanswick and Jacques. But I suspect that even had he known the truth he wouldn't have done that. One of my abiding impressions of this dispute has been the abysmal standard of the vast majority of Labour correspondents who simply live on trade union handouts. There are one or two exceptions like *The Observer*'s man and the *Sunday Times* man, but God preserve us from the BBC. Back upstairs there was not a great deal more that we could do. We adjourn for the evening with Trevor Clay of the RCN still in play and behaving very honourably in the media, saying that he thought the unions had been far too hasty in rejecting our proposals.

FRIDAY 17 SEPTEMBER

The press strangely enough goes rather well. Most of them communicate the anger that I felt and in a curious way this was no bad thing.

Certainly, I don't think anyone was under any impression that I was playacting. Ken and I spend the whole day seeking to brief leader writers and correspondents.

WEDNESDAY 22 SEPTEMBER

Day of action by the unions. I start very early. I get into the office at about 7.30 a.m., do an obligatory interview with Brian Redhead on *Today* and then the rest of the day is spent doing one interview after another. Television reporters come in for the lunchtime programmes, the afternoon programmes, the evening programmes. From our point of view there isn't much to be done. One military ambulance has to be used in an emergency case but that's about it and it's not until the evening that I see the big demonstration on television. It's quite impressive to get 60,000 people marching. It obviously takes some organising but reports also show that the vast majority of the health service has gone on working.

THURSDAY 23 SEPTEMBER

A mixed press for the day of action. Most are fairly critical and the *Mail* uses the phrase that it has altered nothing. Indeed, it is only BBC television who take a dewy-eyed view of the whole proceedings. I do think that they just get carried away by their own pictures at times.

THURSDAY 30 SEPTEMBER

I give a report in Cabinet on the dispute which recounts what happened with Spanswick and Jacques but also reports that we are still in negotiations with the Royal College of Nursing and other professions. I also say that the resurrection of the CPRS report has added a new dimension to the whole dispute and that this is an issue which is likely to haunt us until the next general election. I first get support from Willie who says that he has been round the country and that there is general admiration for my stand personally (which is kind of him to say in full Cabinet) and that there is great apprehension about the CPRS report. Quintin intervenes and says that when he first read the CPRS report it made his hair stand on end, and at his age that takes some doing.

WEDNESDAY 6 OCTOBER

Party conference. Such is my translation from transport to health, that for this conference I have two Special Branch men attached to me throughout.[95] The debate proves to be one of the best of the day. The proposer does his job very well and the last speaker from the floor, a consultant from Addenbrooke's, really gets the conference moving. The hall is packed and Margaret is next to me on the platform; so too is the Chancellor and Norman Tebbit. It is the kind of fighting speech that the conference like and they generously give me a warm and rather pro-longed standing ovation. Ken says it is the best speech I have done so far and we both agree that we needed a speech and a reaction like that.

FRIDAY 8 OCTOBER

Today is the Prime Minister's speech. The demonstrators are fewer on the ground than they were two years ago but immediately when they see me coming out of the hotel there is an enormous chant of 'Fowler out'. Margaret's speech is good, crisper than usual and from my point of view, first class because it sets out the government's commitment to the health service – the health service is safe with us.

SATURDAY 9 OCTOBER

Frank Johnson in *The Times* says that last year I was 'an ordinary hard-working citizen living quietly in the Cabinet'. Today, I am one of the well-known hate figures of the left.

THURSDAY 14 OCTOBER

A meeting of the public sector pay committee under the Chancellor of the Exchequer. I report on the health dispute and the desire of the nurses and the other professional bodies to have some kind of inde-pendent inquiry into their pay structure. This is not greeted with any enthusiasm at all. The argument – particularly from the Treasury – is that independent inquiries can lead to any kind of conclusion, which is

---

95   One of them commented that two ministers had been given protection, myself and Norman Tebbit. The difference was that my men were armed and his were not!

perfectly true. Leon then suggests that a review body might be a better solution. Needless to say, I accept the suggestion with alacrity although Leon immediately qualifies the proposal. As far as I am concerned, if we can get a review body for nurses and the other professional bodies, then I am quite sure that the RCN would regard this as a great step forward and it should certainly clinch their support. I go back to the department to get officials to prepare suggestions on how a review body can work. All told, this week could go down as the turning point.

MONDAY 18 OCTOBER

Parliament resumes and I tell the House that the dispute in the health service means about 110,000 operations have been cancelled and about 105,000 outpatient appointments postponed. It is also estimated that hospital waiting lists have increased by 115,000. What is more interesting however, is what is now taking place outside – or to be more accurate, what is *not* taking place outside. The regional days of action are now seen to be a failure on the part of the TUC. The mood is summed up by a cartoon in *The Guardian* with one civil servant saying to another that the regional days of action are so badly organised that Len Murray has to ring up Norman Fowler to ask where they are being held.[96]

THURSDAY 21 OCTOBER

The papers all show that the opposition's attack in yesterday's debate failed. Gwyneth comes in for particular stick from *The Guardian* and Michael White is scathing about the whole opposition performance. He says that they gave vent to their natural genius for opposition and by the look and sound of them yesterday, they may have many happy years ahead of them. At Cabinet, Margaret says that the debate yesterday had gone extremely well. In the afternoon I go to open a newly renovated hospital in Wimbledon. The police have taken elaborate precautions, and with some cause. There are about 100 demonstrators outside the hospital with a rather touching British faith in how things should be conducted. There is a horseshoe drive in front

---

96   Len Murray was General Secretary of the TUC 1973–1984. He became a life peer in 1985.

of the hospital with 'In' and 'Out' marked very clearly. The demonstrators gather around the legal entrance to the drive – while the police promptly guide my car through the exit and against the one-way system.

FRIDAY 5 NOVEMBER

The most exciting development today is the news that the TUC's Health Services Committee has called off Monday's transport workers' day of solidarity and agreed to start talks with the department again. It comes after the London bus leaders decided to call off the 24-hour sympathy strike and continue normal working. There are also reports of votes against strike action from other transport workers. The TUC try to put the best face on it and say that they have been strongly urged by Pat Lowry to suspend Monday's strike to provide the right atmosphere for new talks, but there is no disguising the significance of the step that the unions have taken.

SATURDAY 6 NOVEMBER

'Hospitals all set for peace,' says the *Daily Mail* and all the papers predict that the dispute is now near its end. In fact, it is too early to make predictions of that kind but clearly it has run out of steam.

MONDAY 8 NOVEMBER

In the Commons we debate the welfare state. It is a day which has been chosen by the opposition but it is a lacklustre performance. The debate gives me the opportunity of spelling out the extra £80 million that we have won for the National Health Service and the ways in which it will be spent. It is always the danger when the opposition choose a day for a debate that the government will simply use that day to make a major announcement. From my point of view, the debate could hardly be better chosen. Once I was able to get away, I go and see Margaret. My aim is to persuade her I need an extra £12 million. That would be a fig leaf as far as the union leaders were concerned. Margaret saw the point, although she still wanted me, when presenting it, to refer to the inquiry on health service manpower so that I could underline the message that manpower reductions were necessary and stress the link between pay and jobs.

TUESDAY 9 NOVEMBER

My statement on a new pay review body for nurses goes ahead. I suppose I had fought so hard that we should give some special treatment to nurses on the grounds that they did not take industrial action that I had forgotten how it might look to the outside world. When I announce it there is more or less silence on our side: not particularly hostile, but gently puzzled. They haven't been prepared for it; they didn't really know what to think. Some are opposed. John Patten said, in a notably unhelpful intervention, that the term 'review body' is not one to set the heart racing or a cause for great enthusiasm. I would have thought that he would recognise that people who do not take strike action do deserve some credit and some kind of special treatment.[97]

WEDNESDAY 10 NOVEMBER

The *Daily Mail* say, 'Fowler Splits Health Unions' and the *Daily Mirror* say that I have offered 50p to clinch the deal and that it was all a hollow victory. It is the first time the word 'victory' has been used. The *Telegraph* lead on the pay review body for nurses. No one regards the two-year deal as being some kind of giveaway. Those colleagues who had argued otherwise have been proven completely wrong.

THURSDAY 11 NOVEMBER

I report to Cabinet that in the case of the nurses, the revised two-year pay offer and the proposal to consult on a review body have been taken away and it is hoped that the RCN council would decide to recommend acceptance of the settlement package later that day. I also report that the annual conference of the RCN had voted against affiliation to the TUC and in favour of retaining their rule against industrial action. In the case of the health unions, they have now entered into negotiations with the government after calling off the national day of action. I had indicated that the government might be prepared to increase its offer in respect of 1983–4 by 0.5 per cent for these groups, provided that the unions were prepared to

---

97   In fact, a little later, John Patten joined the health department as parliamentary secretary and became a very effective Health Minister.

conclude a settlement on the two-year basis. So far, however, NUPE has remained intransigent. The trade unions were holding further discussions that morning with ACAS, who were likely to reaffirm the government's position; that no more money would be available in respect of 1982/3 and that there would be a differential pay increase in that year in favour of the nurses. The Prime Minister sums up by saying that negotiations are at a critical stage.

MONDAY 15 NOVEMBER

I go to the Cambridge Union to debate a motion on private health. Albert Spanswick was due to appear on the other side but the local COHSE organiser has put a picket round the Cambridge Union and Albert decides not to cross the picket lines. The police tell me that they are going to take me in through the back entrance of the Union. I say that's all right as long as some of the demonstrators are to be found there. I certainly don't intend to skulk in the back way to the Cambridge Union. Two Special Branch men say there is absolutely no danger of that. They are as anxious as I am that I should not be seen to be skulking in. Apparently, they had some trouble over Norman Tebbit the week before. They hadn't 'shown' him to the demonstrators. Well, they showed me all right. It was a typical event. Television lights so that you couldn't see, a rather more hostile group of pickets than usual, a few eggs, none of which hit me, and a lot of shouting. It was all over in a few minutes and they went away apparently happy. It is now becoming commonplace for tomatoes and eggs to be thrown at any political opponent. Michael Heseltine got the same treatment in Liverpool.

The motion basically says that private health has no part to play in Britain today. I am surprised at the size of our majority. We win with almost 400 votes to 150. That's not a bad majority for an undergraduate audience – but of course television, radio and the press will be far more interested in the demo that preceded the debate rather than the debate itself.

THURSDAY 18 NOVEMBER

I report to Cabinet that the council of the Royal College of Nursing has recommended the government's latest pay offer to the membership on the basis that it is the best that can be achieved and that a two-year pay agreement will allow it to concentrate its resources on securing satisfactory arrangements for the review body. The health unions are now consulting their members but industrial action has already been considerably reduced and mainly confined to a few trouble spots.

THURSDAY 25 NOVEMBER

Cabinet. I report that industrial action in the health service is continuing to decline. Action has been called off at Addenbrooke's and St Thomas', which were both notorious trouble spots. A few districts are still affected but the great majority of districts are now back to normal or near-normal service. COHSE and NALGO probably want a settlement, but there is no question that NUPE does not.

SATURDAY 27 NOVEMBER

I take Oliver to watch Fulham play Sheffield Wednesday down the road at Craven Cottage. The chairman of Fulham, Ernest Clay, heard that I was coming and invites us into the directors' box. Just after the game starts, who should arrive but George Best. The chairman asks me to pass down Oliver's programme, which Best duly signs and passes back. Oliver at his politest says thank you but a few minutes later asks quietly, 'who is George Best?' Although George Best is a very familiar name to people of my generation, ten and eleven year olds today think more about Kevin Keegan. Keegan, I think, probably plays his career rather well and will end up financially sound. I very much doubt whether that will be the end result for George Best.

MONDAY 29 NOVEMBER

Albert Spanswick writes a piece for *The Star* in which he says, 'be fair – how could we say yes to this pay offer?' But when it comes to it he knows perfectly well that he may have to say 'yes'. The unions know that they could not go on if the nurses vote for acceptance.

WEDNESDAY 15 DECEMBER

It's all over. The Royal College of Nursing say that its 200,000 members have voted six to one to follow the advice of their council and accept the government's offer. There's a 50-per-cent poll and therefore there's no dispute. A few hours later, the TUC Health Services Committee take only ninety minutes to end the dispute.

THURSDAY 16 DECEMBER

The morning's press spell out the result: 'The health service dispute collapses,' says the *Financial Times*. 'Surrender in health pay fight,' says *The Star*. 'NHS dispute collapses in 90 minutes of talks,' says *The Times*. At Cabinet, Margaret calls out 'NHS dispute', pauses and adds: 'What dispute?' There is a growl of approval from around the table. I say that the ballot by the RCN had shown a majority of 84 per cent in favour of accepting the two-year pay offer. The Health Services Committee of the TUC has also decided in favour of a two-year settlement. The pay negotiations have been formally concluded at meetings of the various Whitley councils, and the dispute was therefore at an end. I add that although the industrial action has undoubtedly damaged the health service, the settlements reached on the basis of pay increases of 6–7.5 per cent for 1982/3 and 4.5 per cent for 1983/4 were important in the national context. They were a radical reduction on the 12-per-cent claims and would obviously be taken as a signal elsewhere. A two-year deal is obviously good and best of all, the nurses have a review body which at last recognises their refusal to take strike action.

FRIDAY 17 DECEMBER

The Cabinet minutes say: 'The cabinet congratulated the Secretary of State for social services on bringing the National Health Service dispute to such a satisfactory conclusion.'

6

TRIUMPH AND TRAGEDY

APRIL 1983–OCTOBER 1984

*M*argaret Thatcher won the general election of June 1983 with ease. She *faced the most inept Labour Party since the war. Leading Labour figures like Roy Jenkins, David Owen and Shirley Williams had already split from the party to form the Social Democratic Party. Responding to this challenge from the centre, Michael Foot countered with a set of unquestionably left-wing policies designed to please party members, which Gerald Kaufman memorably called the 'longest political suicide note in history'. Margaret Thatcher, fresh from her triumph in the Falklands, could hardly have asked for more. That part of the story is well known. What is less well documented is the response of the newly elected Conservative government and particularly that of the new Chancellor of the Exchequer, Nigel Lawson, to make fresh spending cuts.*

THURSDAY 14 APRIL 1983

Margaret has arranged for me to stay behind after Cabinet, ostensibly to talk about the review body report on doctors' and dentists' pay that has just arrived. In fact, she wants to talk about the election. Michael Heseltine and Nigel Lawson also stay. The problem, she says, is that October might be a good time but two sets of bad unemployment figures will come out in September. If we then go a little later – say late October – then the other parties will have just had their party conferences and their support always goes up as a result. In addition, inflation will be rising not falling. June looks a better bet. Nigel disagrees. He says that the recovery has only just started. People need time to believe in it. June is therefore too early. My view is I do not see how we can argue that the recovery is booming at the same time as bad unemployment figures are being published. I also don't like the idea of fighting an election with bad figures being published during the campaign. There will be unexpected bad news in any campaign but at least we can avoid the predictable. Michael is not very helpful. He says that Margaret will win whenever she goes, but he agrees it is one of the more difficult decisions she will have to make. There will be no decision until the results of the local elections are known and the choice appears to be between June and the (risky) option of 1984.

The Conservatives won the local elections on 5 May but not by the land-slide that some were predicting. Arguably, the main victors were the Liberal Democrat alliance who won 329 council seats and now had 3,200 councillors. Nevertheless, the decision was taken to opt for a June election and a long campaign.

MONDAY 16 MAY

Labour publishes its general election manifesto: an incredibly long list of aspirations and prejudices. In the press it gets taken apart, even by those who are usually sympathetic like *The Guardian*. It is an albatross around their neck. Our tactics are obvious: to make *their* plans the issue. Withdrawal from the Common Market; more nationalisation; ever and ever more public spending. It is an impossible mixture. It has been put together to keep the Labour Party united but not to fight an election.

TUESDAY 24 MAY

A press conference at Central Office and briefing with Margaret is at 8 a.m. Today, she is on one of her highs. She asks questions but does not listen to the answers. For half an hour acolytes rush hither and thither. After her briefing session the press conference is a piece of cake.

FRIDAY 3 JUNE

Margaret comes to the West Midlands and does well. She speaks at the

National Exhibition Centre and despite a bad hall where the voice disappears, succeeds in bringing the audience to their feet. Much better than at the Town Hall in 1979. She could not have been kinder about me, mentioning my 'contribution' on at least six occasions and ascribing the whole of the pension increases in the last four years to my efforts! How the lady changes. Things are obviously going our way and she is more relaxed. She waves a small Union Jack flag back at the audience who are a sea of Union Jacks. She improvises in her speech. She insists on all the candidates following her out through the hall. Margaret at her best.

THURSDAY 9 JUNE

Election day. The early results show that we have won a landslide victory. Our vote is marginally down but Labour's has dropped catastrophically. We are winning all kinds of seats we didn't expect – and doubtless getting all kinds of MPs who we were not expecting either. In Birmingham however, the position is not as good. Next door in Erdington, we fail to overturn a 600 Labour majority. My own majority goes down from 26,000 to 19,000 – although that looks worse than it is. Nationally, the poll is just over 70 per cent compared to almost 80 per cent in 1979. My result is, in fact, pretty typical.

FRIDAY 10 JUNE

It looks as though we will have almost double the number of seats in the Commons than Labour. Foot's campaign has been a disaster and he has lost over fifty MPs. Even worse, he now finds the SDP/Liberal Alliance breathing down his neck, although the first past the post system understates their success – almost eight million votes and a quarter of the electorate. I spend a couple of hours during the afternoon going round Sutton Coldfield with the loudspeaker thanking electors for their support. During the evening, a call comes through from Robin Butler at No. 10.[98] Robin tells me that he has been asked by the Prime Minister

---

98   Civil servant from 1961 to 1998, served as private secretary to five Prime Ministers, secretary of the Cabinet and head of the Home civil service 1988–1998.

to ring up those ministers who she intends to keep where they are. That part of the conversation is disposed of in thirty seconds. He then asks me what my views on the rest of the team are. I say that I want to retain Ken Clarke and Tony Newton but I think that Geoffrey Finsberg is probably due for retirement and Hugh Rossi deserves a change to somewhere like environment; housing is his first love.

SATURDAY 11 JUNE

The Prime Minister herself comes on the phone. She wants me to take Rhodes Boyson as social security minister. She hardly allows me to get a word in edgeways before she launches into a defence of Rhodes. She has obviously had difficulty placing him. In fact, I think it is a good idea. Rhodes has a rather fierce reputation with the public but is no one's fool, and would be the kind of original thinker that we need at social security. So, I say as far as I am concerned that it is fine. I go off to an event at my local army barracks and come back to hear the news coming through of the Cabinet appointments. The big news is that Francis Pym has been fired and has not, apparently, been offered any other job. Geoffrey Howe has become Foreign Secretary, Nigel Lawson is Chancellor and the very good news is that Leon has a notable promotion to Home Secretary. I don't think Leon was on many people's list as the man most likely to become Home Secretary; that was being pencilled in for Norman Tebbit. But they are appointments very much in character with Margaret's own personality. She genuinely likes people with first-class minds around her and no one can deny the credentials here of either Leon or Nigel. She obviously prefers loyalists in those crucial posts and again, Nigel and Leon fit the bill. Norman Tebbit must be a little miffed, but had he become Home Secretary then he would have become heir apparent to the leadership. Margaret has enough political nous not to put Norman into such an overwhelmingly strong position at this stage. As it is, she has left the power struggle in the future very much open. One casualty is David Howell. It was much predicted but I am sad to see David go. I think he had a rough time from Margaret but he never recovered from the handling of the energy department. It is quite difficult to see where he goes now.[99]

MONDAY 13 JUNE

I go to No. 10 for lunch with the Prime Minister. One of Margaret's preoccupations is who is to become the next Speaker. She does not want Jack Weatherill and makes this completely clear.[100] She clearly does not understand why Francis Pym does not want the job. Jim Prior tells her in no mean terms that he thought it very unlikely that Francis Pym would change his mind. Peter Walker cannot understand why anyone should want to become Speaker.

TUESDAY 5 JULY

News is coming through that the new Chancellor is about to embark on a fresh cuts exercise. He wants an immediate cut of £450 million across government. This means making a cut in health service spending during *this* financial year on a budget which has already been agreed. It is obviously going to be difficult for either Ken or myself to defend cuts to the NHS, particularly after the statements we made during the campaign. On the other hand, what would be the realistic chances of winning such a battle against the Chancellor? This is his first proposal to Cabinet. It is inconceivable that he will not be backed by the Prime Minister and fairly unlikely that other colleagues won't back him.

THURSDAY 7 JULY

The paper goes through Cabinet without much difficulty. As far as we are concerned the news is bad, but not as bad as it might be. It means approximately a cut of about £80 million in hospital budgets, and that

---

99   David had a deserved and successful new life in the Lords. He became Deputy Leader and then formed the very successful International Relations Select Committee. An object lesson in what ex-Cabinet ministers should do after Cabinet.

100   Bernard (Jack) Weatherill was elected Speaker and continued in the role until 1992. He was the first Speaker to be televised and he was the last to wear a wig. He tried to enforce the right of Parliament to be publicly told about government policies before they were announced to the press or elsewhere.

should not be impossible on a budget of about £8 billion. We manage to reduce the bill to the health service by including the pharmaceutical industry in the spending cuts. The industry is not happy about this new turn of events, but I think they realise that their turn has been coming for some time.

MONDAY 18 JULY

The Treasury papers on the long term come today. There are two papers: one from the Chancellor of the Exchequer on economic prospects and the second from the new Chief Secretary, Peter Rees. Together, they are probably the most important papers that we are likely to consider over the lifetime of this government.

Nigel is entirely frank about his aim. Lower taxation is the overriding priority. The aim is to reduce the basic rate of income tax to 25 per cent. Peter Rees then spells out what this means for public spending. Departments have proposed increases in spending totalling £6 billion. It is impossible to accept that figure but £2.5 billion of that is unavoidable. For example, pension spending has to be increased because people are living longer. The Chief Secretary's solution is that this £2.5 billion will need to be provided by cuts to existing programmes, including social security and health. In other words, the Chancellor is saying that we must work flat out to achieve reductions in taxation.

THURSDAY 21 JULY

Cabinet. It never ceases to amaze me at times like this that one or two of the minsters who are most affected have quite clearly not read the Cabinet paper in detail. Michael Heseltine makes it quite clear in his opening comment that he really has not gone into the detail. Nevertheless, his message is clear: if we are to cut then it means that we have to attack social spending. How precisely this squares with his view of Liverpool I am not altogether sure. I come after Michael and put my case. I share the Chancellor's wish to reduce the burden of taxation and in particular, I would like to see the tax on industry reduced. It is not part of my case that the social programme should be ring-fenced from the rest of the economy but there has to be a balance. Reducing taxation is not our only objective. We have other manifesto commitments and it is vital that we keep them. The public feel strongly about good schools and adequate provision for the elderly. It would be disastrous for this party if we acquire a reputation for damaging the health service. Following me, no one really challenges the paper at all. Patrick Jenkin says that we must keep our promises to the pensioners but he accepts the general paper so one way or another it is a pretty bad day. The only bit of sympathy that I have had throughout the discussion has come from Cecil Parkinson as Chairman of the party. Neither Peter Walker nor Jim Prior bark at all.

We have agreed, virtually unanimously, on a strategy to reduce taxation at a time of high unemployment and undoubted social need. The only way that can be achieved is by cutting social spending. There is no alternative to that. Furthermore, there is no time to sensibly reduce it. I am certainly in favour of having a fundamental new look at social security. It is absurd that we should regard ourselves as debarred from looking at the kind of system that has grown from the Beveridge report. Many of the assumptions of the Beveridge report have proved false. We also have an enormously complex social security system. There are far too many staff employed in the department working out the complexities of supplementary benefit, for example. But the fact remains: if we are going to reform the system then we are not going to be able to reform it overnight. There is also a very major political question. We risk losing our reputation for honesty. We have not remotely prepared the public for the kind of changes which are likely to be necessary. We went through the general election defending the Conservative government's record in health and social security over the last four years.

FRIDAY 22 JULY

There is a gathering crisis as a result of yesterday's Cabinet. *The Guardian* carries a story that I argued against the public expenditure proposals in Cabinet and that both Ken Clarke and I might resign if pushed too hard. This is in fact precisely the kind of story that I do not want to have at this stage. I don't see any point in being seen to be pushed reluctantly down a particular road. It carries no conviction with the public and it carries no conviction with colleagues.

TUESDAY 26 JULY

I decide that the best thing to do is to have a word with Margaret. I go in the evening. We have a long and rather rambling talk. She is obviously quite concerned about the stories of resignation and we speculate upon the source of these rumours and then have a long talk about social security. When I mention to her that we will have to postpone the abolition of the earnings rule[101] she says that she would not do that, and equally on the death grant[102] she says that she would allow that to wither on the branch. This is all very well but these are two of the easier savings that I could make. I suspect she feels that something should be done on unemployment benefit, which personally, I believe would be disastrous. All told then, it looks as though it is going to be a very difficult autumn.

WEDNESDAY 31 AUGUST

France. We are at the end of an almost three-week break. I have been pounding up and down the beach at La Baule and spending the time reading Beveridge and other assorted social security reports. Beveridge, and the assumptions of Beveridge, need a thorough revision. He planned on full employment and the government putting money into 'public works' to create employment. Hardly our position. He planned on his new social security system being insurance-based with entitlements building up over a twenty-year period. That didn't happen either and what we have now is pay-as-you-go, meaning that tomorrow's generation is given the burden of paying for this generation's retirement. I would like to try and reshape the system. That could save money. I do not run away from that, but it will take time. We cannot reshape the system overnight.

---

101 Under this rule, once a pensioner's earnings exceeded a certain amount deductions were made progressively from their state pension.

102 This was a single payment of £30 made to the family of anyone who died regardless of wealth and had become meaningless as a contribution to funeral costs.

WEDNESDAY 14 SEPTEMBER

Our long-planned pensions conference on the rights of early leavers. The present position cannot be justified. Anyone who leaves his job and takes another loses out – unless of course he is transferring within the public sector, where special provisions apply. It is one more example of a disgraceful two-nations position on pensions. My officials tell me that the pensions industry is now prepared to accept change or, to put it another way, to give up defending the indefensible. They are now much more worried about the prospect of portable pensions: people not joining their schemes but creating their own small portable funds.[103]

FRIDAY 16 SEPTEMBER

For the last two weeks I have been preoccupied with preparations for the 'seminar' on both health and social security that I had agreed to have with the Prime Minister. We duly turn up at No. 10 with ministers, officials and a collection of thick briefing folders. It becomes clear from the start that Margaret is not going to keep to any agenda and indeed, I doubt whether she has read the papers. She is still recovering from her eye operation, and although the public relations message is that she is back to full work, this is obviously not the case. The result is that her agenda is a letter that she has received from a consultant she met who happens to be extremely critical of the NHS and its administration. Fortunately, some of the specific suggestions he makes are foolish, but Margaret keeps going on for around half an hour about the inefficiency of the health service while Ken Clarke and I seek to play out the storm. Strangely, it helps. Neither the Chancellor nor the Chief Secretary can get a word in, although Peter Rees does begin a sentence several times, which seems to

---

103   I wanted to expand the provision of pensions and favoured a review in which we would take evidence in public and allow all interested parties to have their say. My interest was personal. When my father died in 1963, my mother was able to go back to teaching and buy back her years of service to the point where she was able to qualify for a pension. This contrasted strongly with my father's treatment in the private sector. He died four years before retirement age. There was no widow's benefit and all my mother received for his thirty years of loyal service to one company was a payment of about £9,000, mostly made up by the return of his own contributions.

indicate that he would favour higher health service charges. As he never gets to the end of the sentence we never find out.

Over lunch, Margaret was at her courteous and hospitable best. She has obviously quite enjoyed the morning, and remarks that it is much better when Parliament is not sitting. She doesn't say so, but like most of her predecessors she finds the twice-weekly grind of Prime Minister's Questions a strain and a distraction from serious policymaking. After lunch, we get on to social security. We win one notable victory. Margaret agrees that I should chair a social security inquiry. This keeps the review out of the hands of the Treasury.[104]

WEDNESDAY 21 SEPTEMBER

The first of the public spending talks with the Chief Secretary on health. Peter Rees's style is very different from Leon's. Leon would never dream of admitting that he was not an expert on a particular part of the DHSS budget. It would be a matter of pride that he knew the subject – and all too often he did. Peter adopts a simpler approach. 'Of course you're the expert', 'I don't know the details of this but…'. When, at one stage, I asked how he proposed to present a particular change he advocated, he replied, 'my dear Norman, I don't know that – I'm only interested in getting the money.' The result of this slightly disarming approach was that the meeting was notably more courteous than meetings with Leon used to be, and shorter. There seemed to be little point in extending the meeting if the Chief Secretary was not going to join any meaningful debate.

FRIDAY 23 SEPTEMBER

I am due to speak to an Age Concern conference in Sheffield. At the station I am met by Special Branch who tell me there is a demonstration at the university. 'What about?' I ask. 'It seems to be against Norman Tebbit's bill,' was the reply. By the time I arrive on the campus, the

---

104   That was a very significant victory. It meant that not only did we have more time but we could now conduct the most fundamental examination of pensions and social security since Beveridge. The Treasury showed little interest in reform, only in how much money could be saved. My view was to make sensible economies where they were available, but above all to reform the system. It should not just be a cutting exercise. That became the battleground over the next two years.

issue and the mood have changed. They are demonstrating, not against Tebbit, but 'Norman Fowler's manpower cuts.' The posters have been changed to make clear which Norman they were aiming for. They would have demonstrated against anything, but manpower is the flavour of the day following *The Guardian* piece.[105]

SUNDAY 25 SEPTEMBER

I leave for Germany to see social security officials there. Margaret has come back from her European trip with the idea that the Germans are doing much more than us in cutting the social security budget. I had organised the trip previously, but it should serve as a good way to check the story. At the airport I am met by the ambassador, Jock Taylor, whom I knew in the Hague. His story is that the Prime Minister has been sold a social security pup. Apparently, the Germans had been piqued by some remarks that Margaret had made about the way the Dutch were successfully tackling their social security overspending problem. Their answer was basically 'not as well as us' but according to the ambassador, they are not doing much compared to what we have already done.

MONDAY 26 SEPTEMBER

How right Jock Taylor is. The cuts that the German government has in mind are tiny compared with what we have done. A comparison between us and the Germans is like a comparison between a Mini and a Mercedes: meaningless.

WEDNESDAY 28 SEPTEMBER

Back to London and more problems with the health service. A new element is beginning to creep into the discussion. 'The party is worried.' The presentation is beginning to be criticised.

---

105   A story in *The Guardian* that morning said that I had ordered the first manpower cuts in the NHS for thirty years. In fact, for the past few weeks we had been conducting a long-overdue review of manpower. The aim was to achieve a reduction of, say 5,000 – 0.5 per cent of the manpower employed.

FRIDAY 30 SEPTEMBER

We announce the final manpower figures today – a reduction of 4,800 out of 820,000.

SATURDAY 1 OCTOBER

The press goes quite well and an interview with the *Express* pays off with a reasonable piece, albeit with the headline, 'The Axeman Strikes Back'.

SUNDAY 2 OCTOBER

The papers are not good. The *Sunday Telegraph* does a crude hatchet job, which simply takes anything that can be used critically in my past career; some of it almost unbelievable undergraduate trivia. The *Sunday Times* constructs an article which claims I have 'forged a pact of fury' between everyone in the health service, private and public. We have a family council of war. I explain my reservations about public expenditure to Fiona and John [Donald, my father-in-law]. I am in a very gloomy mood after the Sunday press. We all agree there is no joy in staying on to defend policies I don't agree with. I should fight my corner, but if I lose I should go. That settled, I feel rather more cheerful about the immediate future.

TUESDAY 4 OCTOBER

The immediate hurdle is the party conference next week. In theory, it provides an unparalleled opportunity to answer the critics both outside and inside the party. What I need to do is enthuse Conservatives who yet again are being told that the manpower policy spells the destruction of the NHS as we know it. Nick True and I get down to work.

THURSDAY 13 OCTOBER

The speech goes well in a good debate. One of the speakers catches the mood of 'fight back' by appearing in boxing gloves. At the end I get a long standing ovation and Norman Tebbit comes up to say it was the best speech of the conference.

FRIDAY 14 OCTOBER

The press is good. In the afternoon it is the lady's turn and from our point of view it could not have been better. She is kind about my speech yesterday but most importantly, repeats the pledge that we will keep to our health spending commitments, which disposes of some of the Treasury's wilder ideas. On social security however, she is more restrained and there is a great deal about limiting public spending. There remain battles ahead and probably big ones. But the big news of the day is the resignation of Cecil Parkinson. He would have been Foreign Secretary and the undoubted heir to Margaret Thatcher. A political tragedy.[106]

1984

Nineteen eighty-four was dominated by my reviews on pensions and social security. For nine months ministers (Tony Newton, Rhodes Boyson and myself), civil servants and external experts whom we had recruited to help, went round the country inviting people and organisations to give evidence, in effect acting as a select committee asking questions of the public.

Although social security is often written off by politicians as too complicated to understand, it has more impact upon the poorest people in the country than any other spending. It also raises basic questions about spending in general. An outstanding example was the state earnings related scheme.[107] On the face of it, this sounds like an insurance scheme. It was anything but: there

---

106   Cecil resigned following revelations that his former secretary, Sara Keays, was pregnant with his child. Had it not been for his affair, Cecil would in all likelihood have been appointed Foreign Secretary. All these prospects sadly came crashing down. When the affair was first reported, I cannot pretend it came as an entire surprise to me. Some years before I had gone quite late after a vote to an Islington restaurant. There were only three couples in the restaurant: myself and Linda, my then wife, a well-known Tory MP dining without his wife, and Cecil with Sarah Keays.

107   For most employees then, pension provision above the minimal basic state pension was through one of two routes. Half of the workforce made contributions to an occupational scheme, the other half was in the state earnings-related state pension scheme (SERPS). This unfunded, pay-as-you-go state scheme had been introduced in 1978 by Barbara Castle. SERPS allowed people to increase their state pension income by building up an 'additional state pension', based on their level of earnings over their working life.

was no invested fund, only promises about how much future contributors would be prepared to pay. The public spending bill, which could be massive, came in the future. For the Treasury in 1984, this had its advantages. The cost was kicked further down the road and the tax relief of an alternative pension was avoided. In social security the system needed to be simplified and we needed to be sure that help was being directed to the right people. A number of outdated benefits needed to be abolished, notably the death grant, which at the time was a universal amount paid irrespective of the financial position of the family receiving it.

FRIDAY 13 JANUARY

I have a long advice bureau and then back to London. Fiona is really not very well at the moment. She has a cough which she cannot get rid of and it would be good if she could just do nothing for a few days. No one apart from John and Eileen and my mother know that she is pregnant, but it will soon become pretty obvious. Even more reason to take things a little easy.

TUESDAY 24 JANUARY

The first public meeting of our pensions inquiry. It is well attended, about sixty or seventy people, plus press and even a television company. They are not accustomed to our procedure of ministers putting points to witnesses. Frankly, it is much more relaxing asking the questions than answering them.

FRIDAY 27 JANUARY

In Sutton Coldfield to visit the Good Hope Hospital. The unions have organised a 'grim-faced protest', in other words they are all under orders not to smile. Batteries of cameramen come to watch this epic event. I smile throughout and the general impression seems to be that the unions have rather made chumps of themselves.

SATURDAY 18 FEBRUARY

We do not have a dog's chance of winning the Chesterfield by-election and we will be lucky to remain in second place. It depends how truly awful the Liberal candidate is. Tony Benn is basically not holding press conferences and simply relying on photo calls, which is quite a sensible piece of tactical campaigning from his point of view.[108]

TUESDAY 28 FEBRUARY

Parliamentary questions. They are very low-key, perhaps because the Labour leadership have just fired Frank Field and Max Madden for voting with the SDP on the GCHQ affair. Whereas I do not think anyone will lose much by the absence of Mr Madden, Frank Field is a very different kettle of fish. He is an impressive performer with a formidable knowledge in this area. It can only be good news from our point of view that he has now stepped down but personally, I think it is a great pity.

THURSDAY 1 MARCH

Cabinet. An interminable wrangle on the legislative programme for next year. Willie Whitelaw and John Biffen are, needless to say, trying to keep the legislative programme in some kind of check. Others are trying to get their bills into the programme: Norman Tebbit succeeds in getting his films bill into the programme; Patrick Jenkin singularly fails to get his housing bill, which in fact would have all kinds of implications for housing benefit, into the same programme; Michael Heseltine remains uncharacteristically quiet throughout – apparently defence do not have legislation. This is very different from the days when he was at the Department of Environment when these meetings could go on for an extra hour as Michael sought to get all kinds of bills in. Fortunately, no one comes round to my two bills: fluoridation[109] and parliamentary pensions. Adopting the only sensible tactic on occasions like this when sacrifices are being sought, I remain quiet throughout.

---

108 Tony Benn was the Labour candidate. His Bristol seat had been redistributed and although he stood in Bristol East, he lost to the Conservative candidate. Benn won Chesterfield on 1 March with 24,633 votes, the Liberals came second with 18,369 votes and the Conservatives came third with 8,028 votes.

109 The Water (Fluoridation) Bill was very simple, stating that water authorities may add fluoride to the water supply following an application from the local health authority.

FRIDAY 8 JUNE

Out campaigning in the West Midlands for the European elections. So far, apathy reigns. The public view them on a par with county council contests. I read the approved script served up to me. I am required to say: 'We are participating in the world's only true election. We are participating in an exercise in democracy in which 200 million can share'. As I move around Sutton Coldfield I can see no sign of this enthusiasm being shared.

SUNDAY 17 JUNE

The early results of the Euro elections show that we are losing seats but not catastrophically. Ted Heath says that we were apathetic and didn't try. 'How many members of the Cabinet were out campaigning?' If I search my conscience, I did not exert myself massively.

TUESDAY 19 JUNE

The final results of the elections are now in. We have lost fifteen seats but as the press suggests are quite relieved that it was not worse. To my mind, the really significant result was that the turnout was 32 per cent – barely half of the European average. The doyen of psephologists, David Butler, sums it up in *The Times*: 'Britain voted reluctantly for a Parliament in which it did not believe.'

THURSDAY 19 JULY

The birth of my second daughter. We go to St Thomas' Hospital early in the morning. She is the 'wrong' way round and so Fiona is being induced early. We are warned that it may take some time and Fiona says I should go to Cabinet over the road. It proves to be bad advice. A message comes in after a few minutes summoning me 'urgently' back to the hospital. I pass the note to Willie who, slightly nonplussed, then passes it to Margaret, who nods and I leave. I am soon back at St Thomas' to find Fiona stating very firmly that she does not want a caesarean. Fortunately, her consultant appears at that moment and says there is no need.

And about 1.30, the baby girl makes her entrance. At once, it is obvious that she is very different to Kate, much smaller and more delicate but all is well with both mother and baby.

MONDAY 23 JULY

The press is on to the story. She becomes the baby who interrupted a Cabinet meeting. Flowers and cards are filling the room. The baby Helen has been renamed Isobel Geraldine (Fiona decided she was not a Helen!). They were due to come home but the hospital think the baby is jaundiced so worry she may be dehydrated and have put her in an incubator under lights for twenty-four hours. She looks extremely tiny and vulnerable. Now I have two daughters to worry about, not to mention a stepson. Life is becoming more joyful but also more serious. I need to plan ahead, which I have never done before.

SUNDAY 9 SEPTEMBER

Back from the Isle of Wight after a holiday which was a resounding success. Kate has been temperamental since Isobel's arrival but is now restored to her more normal, cheerful self. Isobel was less than exemplary at night but she is forgiven a great deal by her mother on account of her red hair. She is now almost eight weeks old and is beginning to show an interest in her surroundings.

In Hurlingham Road the phone is ringing. 'It is Downing Street,' the voice said. 'Could the Chief Whip have a word?' There was then silence. No one could find the Chief Whip: he'd gone out to lunch. Eventually, John Wakeham rings back to tell me what is proposed in the long-awaited shuffle: Ken Clarke, against my expectations (and advice) is to stay and Rhodes Boyson (surprisingly) is to move to Northern Ireland. Tony Newton is promoted to Minister of State and Ray Whitney is to come from the luxury of the Foreign Office to the salt mines of the DHSS. I had already told John my views and he has done me proud by keeping Tony in the department in the middle of the reviews. His departure would have been a major blow. I was surprised and sorry to see Rhodes go. We had worked well together. He was not the man for the detail of the social security department, but everyone liked him. I was most surprised by the decision not to move Ken. I had strongly supported his promotion and I think he would have been ideal for the job of beefing up the environment team. Instead, Ken Baker is to get the job.

THURSDAY 13 SEPTEMBER

The new Cabinet meets.[110] The discussion is dominated by the coal dispute. Forty-five pits are working normally and eighty-three are on strike. Coal production is high and stocks at the power stations have gone up. Peter Walker gives an optimistic report. He has been optimistic throughout. The big fly in the ointment is the decision by the colliery managers to ballot on whether to strike. Their president is a close friend of Scargill.[111] Most of the concern in Cabinet is about the number of police injured and the apparent inability of the court system to deal speedily with the arrested pickets.

Nigel Lawson and Margaret Thatcher suggest that we should leave Ian MacGregor[112] in no doubt that he should not give in on the right to close uneconomic pits. It all sounds rather academic – after all, if he doesn't know that by now he shouldn't be running a toy train set, let alone a major nationalised industry. However, outside in the street, Peter Walker says that MacGregor was all for settling last night and he had to intervene. Peter's view is that MacGregor is 'hopeless' – an impression shared by the television public who saw the extraordinary spectacle of the chairman arriving for talks with a plastic carrier bag hiding his face.

WEDNESDAY 19 SEPTEMBER

Public spending. The Chief Secretary's opening bid is horrific. Just from

---

110 Prior was replaced in Northern Ireland by Douglas Hurd and David Young entered the Cabinet as Minister without Portfolio.

111 A walkout at Cortonwood Colliery in March 1984 had led to the NUM's Yorkshire Area sanctioning a strike. The NUM president, Arthur Scargill, made the strike official across Britain although there had been no national ballot beforehand. In September, the strike was therefore ruled illegal.

112 Now Chairman of the National Coal Board.

my budget, he wants cuts of £750 million next year, £800 million the year after and £2 billion in 1987–88.

THURSDAY 20 SEPTEMBER

A long Cabinet. The coal dispute dominates the proceedings. It is quite clear that Margaret – and others like Norman Tebbit – believe that the public pressure is for 'something else' to be done. We fly around trying to find that 'something else', but without success. Most, I think, accept that we are likely to have a long struggle and frankly, it is a question of endurance. The most difficult thing to do is stay patient – or more accurately to prevent the public and the press losing patience. In passing, Peter Rees says to me that if the government is to make its figures on public spending, 'we will need something pretty heroic from you.'

SATURDAY 22 SEPTEMBER

The Bishop of Durham makes a stupefyingly silly intervention into the miners' dispute. He is interpreted as backing Scargill and the nitwit calls for the dismissal of MacGregor.

WEDNESDAY 26 SEPTEMBER

Another meeting of the pensions review. They have proved an outstanding team. The government input has been good – particularly Barney [Hayhoe] and his officials from the Treasury. John Redwood from No. 10[113] has done very well, as have the independent members, but the real star is Mark Weinberg.[114] He is tough, intelligent and above all, able to express his ideas with imagination. I think the group recognise that SERPS is doomed. The question is, what do you put in its place? Do you need to put anything in its place? There is no unanimity here.

---

113 At this time John Redwood headed Margaret Thatcher's Policy Unit in Downing Street. He became MP for Wokingham in June 1987.

114 Mark Weinberg had a long and successful career in the life insurance and wealth-management industry. He began his career as a barrister and later on, founded three successful life insurance businesses.

FRIDAY 28 SEPTEMBER

Norman Tebbit comes to Sutton Coldfield. I meet him at the station and we arrive at the dinner just in time to sit down. His speech does not have the content of John Biffen's last year, but he holds the audience throughout. They watch him spellbound and afterwards there is general agreement that it is a very good speech. We leave just before midnight and go home. Fiona goes to bed – her first night off from the children for three months! Norman and I talk. He obviously realises that he is in line for the succession but points out that everything depends on how long Margaret Thatcher continues. He says that he is now fifty-three and he wouldn't expect to be in politics when he is sixty-five. A slight, and I think genuine, feeling that he won't be mortally wounded if he doesn't become Prime Minister. The next step? I suggest he will be Party Chairman in twelve months' time. He doesn't dissent. By no measure is Norman an extravagant character. He talks most readily about work in hand (regional policy) and more cautiously about ambitions and personalities. Although he makes it quite clear that he has no time for Peter Walker who he thinks has given consistently over-optimistic advice throughout the coal dispute, and will not accept advice himself.

THURSDAY 4 OCTOBER

To No. 10 for a seminar on social security. On this occasion – unlike last year – we keep to the agenda I have set out. The importance of the meeting lies in discovering what Margaret is in favour of and what she is against. That does not determine the reviews, but it is a road block we should take into account. Margaret is typically cautious. In summary, she supports the idea of insurance, opposes the abolition of child benefit, considers housing benefit too generous (also some parts of supplementary benefit), could be persuaded to abolish SERPS, does not think that we should touch inflation-proofing of pensions – and sees the point of the reviews. Nigel Lawson, who is also there, has only one purpose: to save money. As for the social arguments, he doesn't understand them, and the political arguments, he ignores. He should have been Chief

Secretary – that's what chief secretaries are there for. A useful meeting leaving everything to play for.

MONDAY 8 OCTOBER

To Brighton for the party conference. I spend most of the day working on my speech for Wednesday. I have a difficulty. For the last two years, I have been in the middle of a health crisis. In terms of the speech however, this has an advantage. The audience is expectant. The atmosphere is right for a 'fighting speech'. This year there is no immediate crisis – just the usual grumbles about the health service's lack of resources. I travel to Brighton with Tony Newton and Nick True.[115] Tony is speaking on social security on Tuesday morning. We meet Malcolm Rutherford (*Financial Times*) on the train and he joins us. He is one of the best of the political writers. He says that we should make more of the reviews, make it clear that they are going ahead with the intention of important reform. People – and the media – forget, he says.

WEDNESDAY 10 OCTOBER

I am on the platform to hear Ken Clarke reply to the debate on drugs. He does it well, and has worked up a good package of announcements. Fiona comes down at lunchtime and we go over to the conference hall for the health debate. The debate itself is quite good and includes one outstanding conference performance from a nurse. My speech goes well – a standing ovation – which I think is worth rather more than the two previous ones. It is a relief to have it over – but I remember the advice, 'the next speech is always the worst.' If you have done badly you have to recover. If you have done well you have to keep it up.

THURSDAY 11 OCTOBER

Fiona breakfasts with Roberta Wakeham while I talk to Age Concern over a modest coffee and toast. In social services we start with sparse

---

115 My excellent special adviser for five years. Later, he went to the Policy Unit and in 2010 was appointed to the House of Lords. He is currently Leader of the Lords.

breakfasts with the pressure groups, whereas in transport we ended the day with expensive dinners. Lunch is with Charlie Douglas-Home of *The Times* and others like Geoffrey Smith and Julian Haviland.

After lunch I went to my room at the Grand and managed to catch most of Norman Tebbit's speech. It was good, but for my money, not up to Michael Heseltine's standard. Nevertheless, there was no doubt what the conference thought. The reception was ecstatic. He could have read the telephone directory and they would have cheered. What is the Tebbit magic? First, he expresses the views they want to hear, not because he calculates their expectations, but because his views are the views of the majority of the conference. Second, he has a sharpness of response and of phrase, which effortlessly puts him in the first division.

In the evening I go to the Metropole and dinner with Brian Wenham of the BBC, together with John and Sarah Biffen. Biffen is in good form as we run over who may lead and what may happen. With Fiona back in London, I decide to miss the conference ball and get off to an earlyish bed.

FRIDAY 12 OCTOBER

A few hours later I am woken by an enormous cracking bang that is followed by what seems to be the sound of stones or bricks falling. Then there is silence. I grope for the light. It is just before 3 a.m. I go to the door, open it and look out. Our small corridor is exactly the same: the lights are on and seeing another door is open on the opposite side, I call out: 'what's going on?' No one has any idea. The door is on a tight hinge. It is an effort to keep it open. I decide to put some clothes on and go and look. As I close the door the fire alarm starts ringing. Now I realise *something is* wrong. It is probably a bomb, and although this part of the hotel seems alright, there must be the possibility of fire. I go into the corridor and turn right through the swing doors to the main staircase.

The scene there is very different. It reminds me, irresistibly, of a stage play of the First World War. There is smoke and dust everywhere. In the grey murk a line of people is moving down the staircase. No one is hurrying and few are talking. I join the line. Jock Bruce-Gardyne confirms that it is a bomb. Jock is fully dressed and carrying two suitcases, but Keith Joseph is in his dressing gown and carrying his red box in one of the sacks in which they're delivered. Another member of the group is Patrick Jenkin, who is in literally nothing more than his dressing gown – 'I always sleep like this', he says.

At the bottom of the staircase we are directed to the back of the hotel and are soon out in the road. We move round the side and to the front. It is still dark but even so, looking up at the Grand Hotel it is possible to see what has happened. The explosion (everyone believes it is a bomb) has caused a partial collapse of the hotel's façade on the fourth and fifth floors. There is a U-shaped cut out of the building. As Michael Jopling remarks, 'with damage like that it is difficult to see how injuries, and even deaths, can have been avoided.'

In a few minutes we are pushed back along the front by the police. By this time I am joined by Nigel Lawson, who has appeared in an old sweater. None of us think much of the invitation to go to the Metropole. Having just escaped from one hotel, there is no particular appeal in setting up in the one next door. Sure enough, about a quarter of an hour later, the order comes to evacuate the Metropole. On the front there is now a collection of refugees from the Grand, reporters and others who have heard the explosion. The number of reporters seems to be growing by the minute. It is next to impossible to move without being asked for an account of what has happened. Dimly we are all becoming aware that something has.

It is an interesting commentary on security precautions that we have half the Cabinet wandering about on the Brighton seafront. Not even the Chancellor of the Exchequer rates protection. That must be wrong. It is one thing for the Social Services Secretary, the Education Secretary, the Agriculture Secretary not to be protected. It is impractical to protect everyone, but the Chancellor of the Exchequer should rate protection and I'm sure they would in any other country. We decide to try our luck at the Bedford. We find a settee and settle down. Coffee is provided by the hotel and they are even prepared to give away rooms. Personally, I am going to stay up. In another armchair is a man in jeans who says his company owns the Grand. We politely inquire about the insurance. After about an hour I make my way back to the Metropole. Rumours are rife. It is believed that the Prime Minister was evacuated safely and is back in London but there are a number missing: George Younger is mentioned, as is Norman Tebbit, and no one has seen John Wakeham. I meet Keith Joseph, still in his pyjamas, and we sit down to have a cup of coffee. He refuses point blank to be photographed by the press – with one exception – a woman from the *Sunday Times* who is obviously upset by the events of the night and persuades him to sit down and be photographed. I ask her if she is alright. She says she is not a news photographer, but a portrait one.

The Metropole announce that Grand Hotel refugees can have breakfast with them in a special room. I phone Fiona about 6 a.m. to tell her what has happened before she hears it on the radio. She says she will ring my mother who will be very worried. Breakfast is a rather touching sight. Not only are there all the Grand Hotel residents, still clothed exactly as when they left, but the early shift of the Grand Hotel has come to serve us. There are about five waiters for each table. A message next comes through about clothes. Marks & Spencer are opening their doors early to allow those without clothes to be kitted out while another, grimmer, message concerns the Tebbits. Eric Ward, who has been at the hospital, says that Margaret is particularly badly injured. There is still no news of either John or Roberta Wakeham.

The decision has been taken that the conference will go on. One of the agents shepherding ministers to the conference centre takes me down via a modest little 'gents outfitters' to buy a tie. We go in through the back of the conference centre and up to the speakers' room behind the stage. Willie Whitelaw is there, so too are Leon and Geoffrey Howe. Willie is furious about the BBC television pictures of Norman Tebbit being rescued from the rubble, which he says was photographed in very close detail. The stories of the night are interrupted by the news that the Prime Minister has arrived and is sitting on the platform. We hurry down – a rather depleted Cabinet. The audience is also smaller than usual and many are still coming into the hall, past what I imagine are new security checks. The audience rises to its feet, however, as they see some familiar faces. We then have a short service – a period of silence – and go straight on to the debate on Northern Ireland. The conference is subdued and people listen with one ear to the predictable contributions on Northern Ireland which have overspilled so violently into Brighton.

LATER

I drove back to London that night but the following day I returned as Health Secretary to visit the hospital. I intentionally did not include an account in my diary. I only wanted to pay tribute to the courage and fortitude of the men and women in that hospital ward, some of whom were both injured and had lost husbands or wives in the attack.

Five people were killed:
Anthony Berry (Deputy Chief Whip)
Roberta Wakeham (wife of Chief Whip John Wakeham)
Eric Taylor (NW Area Chairman of the Conservative Party)
Muriel Maclean (wife of Sir Donald Maclean, president of the Scottish Conservatives)
Jeanne Shattock (wife of Sir Gordon Shattock, Western Area Chairman)

Over thirty others were injured, some, like Margaret Tebbit, very severely injured indeed. Others badly injured included Norman Tebbit, John Wakeham and Walter Clegg. It was an utterly unjustified terrorist attack by the IRA which achieved nothing except suffering for those affected.

7

AT WAR WITH THE CHANCELLOR

OCTOBER 1984–SEPTEMBER 1985

My longstanding struggle with the Treasury came to a head in the first months of 1985. Nigel Lawson continued to pursue savings to reduce taxation. He saw social security as an obvious target. Partly in response to his attacks, I had announced the reviews of social security and pensions. The battle lines were drawn. I wanted to ensure that the social security budget was being used effectively and went to those people who needed help.

WEDNESDAY 31 OCTOBER 1984

Meeting with Margaret. She says that Margaret Tebbit is in better spirits but still paralysed. As for Norman, he is very concerned that things are going on which he does not know about. She therefore says a trip by me to Stoke Mandeville would be very welcome.[116]

THURSDAY 1 NOVEMBER

Cabinet. Geoffrey Howe starts a rather gloomy report on the succession to Mrs Gandhi.[117] His message is that her son Rajiv will be no substitute. At this, Margaret intervenes and says that Geoffrey really has got to remember that all this is being recorded and in thirty years' time the Cabinet papers will be published. The message is that Rajiv is an outstanding

---

116   I went to Stoke Mandeville several times. On each occasion I was touched by Margaret Tebbit's quiet courage and the consistent support she received from Norman.

117   Indian Prime Minister Indira Gandhi was assassinated by her bodyguards on 31 October 1984 at her residence in New Delhi.

new leader and – amid laughter – Robert Armstrong quickly scribbles away to get the words down accurately. Next, the BBC comes in for criticism for its coverage of the Southall Sikh community rejoicing at Mrs Gandhi's death. Margaret says, in effect, that the BBC is a disaster – both in its television reporting and on radio. Something should be done, but no one has any idea what.

WEDNESDAY 21 NOVEMBER

At 10 p.m., an extraordinary scene in the House of Commons. I am called back 'urgently' from a function in the City to make a statement in the House on supplementary benefit for strikers' wives in the coal dispute, but the need for a statement is soon forgotten. Instead, there is a demonstration supporting the miners. A group of left-wing MPs led by Dave Nellist occupy the floor of the House just as I am about to speak.[118] At issue is the deduction in benefit payable to strikers' dependents in a trade dispute. The aim of the existing legislation is to prevent a strike being entirely supported by public funds. In this case the deduction is small – a £1 deduction from the benefit. I don't get past my opening sentence before I am interrupted by Eric Heffer, Terry Fields and of course, Dave Nellist, and the debate goes no further. Instead, Nellist advances on the government front bench, seizes my statement and tears it up. The Speaker attempts to restore order again and when that fails, adjourns the House for 'grave disorder having arisen'.

THURSDAY 22 NOVEMBER

The press gives last night's events full play. The *Daily Mail* lead the paper with a heavy black headline: 'Uproar in Commons' while the *Express* talk of 'Mob picket in the House'. The press is firmly against the demonstrators. Even David Hencke of *The Guardian* points out that under the 1980 legislation which governs all this, I had no option but to reduce the taxpayers' contribution and rely on strike pay to make up the difference

---

118   Dave Nellist, left-wing Labour MP for Coventry South East. His support for the Militant Tendency led to his eventual expulsion from the Labour Party.

– that is the £1. Not that this verdict will worry Nellist and co. – they have achieved their goal of showing their unity with Arthur Scargill.

WEDNESDAY 2 JANUARY 1985

Tony Newton and I drive to Wilton Park, an impressive country house used by the Foreign Office as a conference centre. Meals are taken in a dining room, complete with minstrels' gallery and our talks are in the library in front of a blazing log fire. The weather outside is awful – snow and ice – but everyone turns up on time: Ken Stowe, Strachan Heppell, Anne Bowtel, Geoffrey Otton, Nick Montagu, Clive Smee from the department and John Redwood from No. 10. The idea is that outsiders like Mark Weinberg will come down for their sessions and David Willetts[119] will take over later from John. The plan is to start our report on reforming social security. Discussions begin after dinner and start with an outburst from Geoffrey Otton, who says that ministers do not understand what a good service he is running. Having got that off his chest we start in earnest.[120]

I want a system that encourages employment. Nothing is more important than that we remove the barriers that stand in the way of new employment and job mobility. I want to eliminate some of the complexity. Above all, I want to tackle real need. Our diagnosis of want shows that it is low-income families with children – the unemployed and low-wage earners – who are worst off. Pensioners are comparatively better off and their position has improved considerably in the last fifteen years because of improvements in pensions. This is not a popular message for colleagues.

As regards retirement, my judgement (and belief) is that we must provide a proper alternative if and when SERPS goes. I would dearly love to introduce a compulsory occupational scheme like that in Switzerland, but I judge that my chances of getting it past the employment and industry ministers are slight. They will be concerned at the increase in

---

119 David was also in Margaret Thatcher's Policy Unit, having worked as Nigel Lawson's private researcher and in the Treasury's monetary policy division. He entered Parliament in 1992 as MP for Havant.

120 Looking back, I am amazed at my moderation. Otton was an unimaginative defender of the status quo. He was pretty irrelevant to the review.

costs for industry.[121] Nigel Lawson has already made his opposition clear, but that is not conclusive as he seems to believe that supplementary benefit will pick up the uncovered, just as it always has done.[122]

FRIDAY 11 JANUARY

Summing-up the week. The discussion has been good and the opportunity of six or seven full, virtually uninterrupted, days is a rare thing in government. We would not have covered a quarter of the ground had we stayed in the office and been interrupted by the usual everyday crises requiring immediate ministerial action or comment. For the next stage, I have asked Anne Bowtell and the officials to put together a paper for the Cabinet committee that has been set up to consider our proposals.[123] I will write the green paper itself with help from Steve Godber.[124] The second volume of the green paper will consist of the individual reports on retirement, supplementary benefit and housing benefit. The last report will be our diagnosis of need: an objective analysis of where help should go. The aim for the first draft is next Friday!

TUESDAY 15 JANUARY

I meet about six representatives of the American pharmaceutical industry to hear their protests about the limited list of drugs. The campaign against the limited list of drugs is one of the most discreditable campaigns against the government. In effect, the BMA and the drugs industry are combining to oppose more money going to the health service. My plan is to reduce the drugs bill by substituting generic drugs for a range of branded drugs, which by no stretch of the imagination are at the cutting edge of science. They include ordinary painkillers and sedatives, not to mention Beechams pills, Alka Seltzer and Andrews Liver Salts. The BMA

---

121 In fact I had no opposition from Patrick Jenkin who had taken over at the DTI.

122 To the argument that the Swiss ran a good compulsory scheme Nigel Lawson used the Harry Lime put-down that the only thing that had ever come out of Switzerland was the cuckoo clock. Financially, however, it would have been better to have invested in the Swiss franc rather than the Lawson pound.

123 Anne Bowtell was an outstanding Deputy Secretary. In 1997 she became Permanent Secretary at the DSS.

124 New head of the private office, very able.

say the policy interferes with the doctors' absolute right to prescribe and the industry object to having these nice little earners cut back.

WEDNESDAY 16 JANUARY

H committee and commercial surrogacy. The case of the surrogate baby, Baby Cotton, born over Christmas has aroused public anxiety. Our proposal is that there should be a short bill introduced this session to deal with the problem. Ken and I are opposed by the business managers, the lawyers and above all, Quintin Hailsham. He believes that there are many things to be settled about the baby's status. I agree, but under Quintin's course, the position just becomes worse and even more babies will be born into legal limbo. We can at least prevent that by acting now, but the majority is against me, including Nick Edwards and Keith Joseph. I say it must go to Cabinet.[125]

THURSDAY 24 JANUARY

Following Cabinet, lunch with Theo Constantine at Bucks.[126] An engaging man. At one stage, Theo was Chairman of the Harrow Conservative Association when Commander Anthony Courtney was his Member of Parliament. Courtney was well and truly fixed by the KGB and lost both the seat and his nomination by the party.[127] He sued Theo for some remarks he had made and won. Theo still remembers the case clearly: it was expensive. The junior council for Courtney was one Leon Brittan.

125　Kim Cotton became Britain's first surrogate mother. She was paid £6,500 to carry a child for an anonymous Swedish couple through an American agency. She never met or knew the identity of the parents. There was intense media coverage and much criticism of those involved due to the thought of babies being 'bought and sold'. Ken and I wanted a quick bill to prohibit the operation of commercial surrogacy agencies and the advertising of surrogacy services in the UK. We did not intend that it should cover the complex issues in the Warnock report published the previous year (the *Report of the Committee of Inquiry into Human Fertilisation and Embryology*, chaired by Mary Warnock). Later, in 2008, non-profit-making surrogacy agencies were officially legalised.

126　Theo Constantine was a businessman and Conservative political activist who served as both the chairman and president of the National Union.

127　The KGB had become seriously irritated by Commander Courtney's campaign against their activities. On a trip to Moscow, Courtney was caught in a classic 'honey trap' when he was photographed through the keyhole with a Russian Intourist guide. The photograph was then circulated in his constituency and he was finally deselected. His protestations that he was innocent were met with scepticism by his wife when she recognised the underpants she had given him at Christmas. To his credit, Courtney continued to do battle with the KGB – and with Theo Constantine.

THURSDAY 31 JANUARY

Cabinet photograph with Norman Tebbit and John Wakeham, both back after Brighton. Just before we go upstairs, Nigel comes up and says he wants a word. He's seen the proposed Cabinet document on social security. 'It won't do,' he says. 'You've made proposals on National Insurance. That is a Budget matter. You have no authority to make proposals on National Insurance'. Furthermore, he says that I am making proposals on tax and the family allowance and he cannot allow this either. His reaction is extraordinary. As far as I'm concerned, if colleagues agree with him he can forget about the whole review. In between these exchanges we smile at the cameras, but the argument continues down the staircase to the Cabinet room. I say we must talk afterwards. He and the Prime Minister are answering a vote of censure in the afternoon and the Prime Minister wants a quick Cabinet so she can concentrate on her speech. She looks set to close the meeting, but I pass her a note saying that the issue of commercial surrogacy is urgent. She takes it and simply rides roughshod over all objections to a quick, short bill. She will not defend inaction, she warns. The Cabinet are dragooned into agreeing that if we can draft legislation then it will be introduced. Doubtless the obstructions will now begin. I cannot complain. I have managed to get the Prime Minister to bounce Cabinet into instant action, which is smack against the judgement of many of them.

WEDNESDAY 6 FEBRUARY

The first meeting of the Cabinet committee (christened Misc. III) set up to consider my proposals.[128] Margaret is in the chair. I introduce my paper and end by emphasising the tight timetable. Nigel comes in next. He congratulates me on an excellent and thorough piece of work, even saying it was well-written. He wants savings however. Willie Whitelaw is next. I

---

128 *Inter alia* to reform pensions, introduce a new family credit for low-income families in work and introduce a simpler, more easily understood system. Child benefit (a favourite target of some on the right) would stay. The problem was savings. I wanted as near to a cost-neutral system as possible. Public spending savings mostly came from abolishing SERPS and some small reductions in housing benefit, but the major savings were for the 1990s and later.

suppose I might have expected some support here, but it is not forthcoming. Willie says that if the pain of legislation is to be sustained, then the party must see that substantial savings are being found. In other words, he says that there is no case for reform for its own sake. He equates 'radical reform' with savings. That is altogether unhelpful and I cannot help feeling that he has not spent very long reading the report. Margaret says that this is basically a second-reading debate. It must be extremely unhelpful, she concedes, for me to hear individual criticisms, but these are made against the background of congratulation on the general thrust and quality of the paper. She is concerned about the family credit and supplementary benefit proposals. She doesn't want supplementary benefit to become a way of life. There is general agreement that SERPS should go, with Margaret making the suggestion that there should be a compulsory occupational scheme as a replacement. Nigel Lawson and Peter Rees are against this. They fear an increase in tax relief on contributions but I think we can win this battle. The meeting breaks up after almost two hours. It has been amicable and the green paper remains on the road, to the delight of some touchingly concerned officials, but the big battles are still to come.

WEDNESDAY 13 FEBRUARY

The second meeting of Misc. III. We agree to both abolish SERPS and to introduce a compulsory occupational scheme over the protests of Nigel Lawson and Peter Rees that it will mean a bigger tax relief bill. Nigel Lawson accepts defeat but hopes that any alternative pensions scheme will be as 'mean' as possible. Laughter – but he means it. One of the more bizarre parts of the discussion was on my proposal to abolish the 25p a week pension payment for the over eighties, which has remained unchanged since the 1970s. In spite of all the talk about savings, the overwhelming view (led by Margaret herself) was that this would be politically damaging, so the 25p addition remains! I don't much care one way or another, but it is a strange decision for a committee bent on savings.[129]

---

129   Even more extraordinary is that the extra 25p per week – the equivalent of £13 a year – for the over eighties is still paid today. It was first introduced in 1971 and has never been uprated.

THURSDAY 14 FEBRUARY

Pre-Budget Cabinet. Led by Margaret, almost everyone supports savings in social security. There is depressing unanimity, broken only by Peter Walker and, in a more cautious way, by Keith Joseph who in effect says that there must be justice – the middle class must take their share. My major point is that if our aim is to help the low earner then we need to find new ways of bringing help to families with children through the tax system. Margaret listens to this but comments at the end that we should not forget the interests of the middle class. Frankly, I don't think there is much chance of that. The Chancellor must have been very happy at how the meeting went.

MONDAY 25 FEBRUARY

Margaret has been in the United States and has returned determined to move us to a more self-help community. At the colleagues lunch at No. 10 Margaret herself is in no doubt: social security benefits are standing in the way of recovery. She has been shown a chart in Washington which, in a pretty simplistic way, relates new jobs to the length of unemployment benefit. In the United States it lasts for only six months and thus, people are 'encouraged' to get jobs. She puts this argument forward vigorously and is back to what I would call her 'British Rail' mood.[130] She will brook no argument and there are of course some colleagues who broadly agree with her. The message is that we are just tinkering with social security. She wants real action. I defend almost alone and at one stage warn her that an indiscriminate attack on the welfare state will put us in opposition for a decade. It is an awful lunch.

Misc. 111 follows lunch and by ill chance supplementary benefit is next for consideration. Our case for reform is that supplementary benefit is too complex for claimants to understand and for staff to administer.

---

130   This description came from a lunch Margaret Thatcher and I had in the days of opposition with Peter Parker and his British Rail board. One board member made the mistake of saying that the only thing wrong with the railways was that they did not have enough money devoted to them. Margaret took off vertically and no one else got a word in edgeways for the rest of the lunch. I made the mistake of thinking her performance was partly for effect and at one stage gave her a friendly wink. It was not a good idea. Returning to the Commons I was lectured on the task ahead.

Instead, we propose a basic income support scheme, plus a discretionary social fund for emergencies. The basic Treasury point put (again) by the Chief Secretary is to the effect that the savings envisaged are modest and that the proposals will not receive support unless the savings are greater. In other words, make controversial proposals really controversial and we will win the public battle!

TUESDAY 26 FEBRUARY

A potentially disastrous strike from the Chancellor. Today, we receive a minute dated 22 February from Peter Rees to the Prime Minister, which unaccountably appears to have been delayed in the post! This sets out Nigel Lawson's new ambitions. Encouraged by the pre-Budget discussion, and doubtless by the Prime Minister's mood, he has upped his aim for savings from the DHSS from £750 million by 1988–89 to £2 billion by 1987–88. The Chief Secretary's minute says that 'the Chancellor and I have been thinking further about what our objectives should be in Misc. III.' It makes clear that they really do believe that a bigger savings package would be easier to present. 'Controversy would focus on the one or two "big" measures needed to save £2 billion and there might be scope to defuse any really difficult situations that arose on the smaller economies.'[131]

What of course this establishes once and for all is that Nigel Lawson is not interested in social security reform. He wants all the money he can lay his hands on to enable him to reduce taxation. Nothing – but nothing – is going to interfere with that aim. I most certainly am not going to preside over cuts of that magnitude – nor, from what he says entirely unprompted, is Tony Newton. The immediate question is how we proceed with another meeting of the Cabinet committee coming up in a couple of days' time. After a talk with Tony and Ken Stowe I decide to get the meeting called off. Fortunately, the Treasury has been clumsy: as well as not sending the minute to me, they have not sent it to anyone else, including the secretariat of Misc. III. We have no difficulty in getting the meeting postponed on

---

131   Peter Rees suggested possible areas that were not uprating the unpledged benefits in 1986/87; biennial upratings for all benefits; and means testing child benefit.

the grounds that the minute creates a new situation – as indeed it does. An increase in the savings total of £1.25 billion in a matter of a few weeks.[132]

MONDAY 4 MARCH

The social security debate in government is now beginning to feature in the press. The *Sunday Times* had a piece at the weekend entitled 'Welfare battle rocks Cabinet.' In fact, Michael Jones has not got very much of the true battle – yet. So far, we've been relatively lucky with the press. There have been plenty of predictions, but some have been self-cancelling. The *Telegraph*, for example, has predicted both the end of SERPS and its continuation.

WEDNESDAY 6 MARCH

The meeting on social security at No. 10. Margaret's mood has changed. She listens to me with some sympathy as Andrew Turnbull takes notes. I make it clear that I feel strongly on this issue and that I could not achieve the target of £2 billion savings. There was no way we could contend that the review was a reform of social security – it would rightly be seen as simply a cutting exercise. All our work from the last eighteen months would be destroyed. Margaret says the reviews had to be considered against the background of increasing, and increased, spending on social security, although most significantly she had not identified a savings figure. The rather lame conclusion is that she asks me to find the 'greatest savings I can' – a notoriously unsatisfactory outcome for any self-respecting Treasury minister. The significance of our meeting is twofold. Misc. III is back on the road but Margaret Thatcher's common sense was of greater significance. I had not used the word 'resignation' but we both realised that that would be the result if no agreement could be reached. Margaret says, in a slightly hurt way, that she had supposed I shared her aspiration of bringing down taxes. The answer to that is 'yes – but at what price?' In the end, as is usually the case, Margaret Thatcher the politician triumphed over Margaret Thatcher the ideologue.

---

132   The total cut requested in social security was £2 billion, the equivalent to £5.8 billion today.

THURSDAY 7 MARCH

The announcement on Baby Cotton has a good reception on both sides of the House. For the first time I can remember, the official Labour opposition welcomes a step that we are taking. As John Patten remarks, it may not be so easy with next week's announcement on prescription charges.

MONDAY 11 MARCH

Prescription charges remain one of the most emotive issues in health politics. It is foolish that they do because 70 per cent of prescriptions are dispensed for free thanks to the generous exemption system. Nevertheless, it is an article of faith on the Labour side that they should be abolished for everyone (in particular the middle class) and although this aim is never quite carried out in government, they become strident when in opposition. On this occasion we are seeking to increase the charges from £1.60 to £2.00.

MONDAY 25 MARCH

Misc. III and the Chief Secretary goes back to his £2 billion target. With family support on the agenda he sets out ways to reduce child benefit. Fortunately, it received little support. I point out that there was a whole range of pledges and public statements which precluded the introduction of means testing. In contrast, my proposals for family credit are well received, with Patrick Jenkin in particular thinking it was a much better way of bringing help to low-income families. I argue that although the position of the elderly had improved substantially over the last twenty years, there had not been comparable improvements in the position of low-income families with children.

WEDNESDAY 27 MARCH

The sixth meeting of Misc. III at 9 a.m. We are running out of time and the Cabinet secretariat are helping me substantially to make progress. An assortment of proposals for colleagues today. It is ludicrous that university students should start their lives drawing housing benefit and supplementary benefit. In principle, there is a strong case for abolition and the obvious way of recompensing them is through the grant system.

Everyone agrees with me in principle but they also agree that action will have to be coordinated with Keith Joseph's student grants review. I doubt whether there will be much action this side of an election. Then there is the death grant. Some of my officials regard this as the acid test of our seriousness. Successive governments have avoided action and simply hoped that the problem would go away. Everybody is entitled to a grant of £30 – a fraction of the cost of a funeral. We are now paying £12 million to administer the payment of £17 million. Our proposal is that families who need help should be given it in full through the social fund and those who do not will receive nothing. I am glad to say that the proposal is accepted without demur – except that one or two people are concerned about 'presentation'!

THURSDAY 18 APRIL

Steve Godber rings to tell me that a minute has just come from Nigel Lawson which basically challenges my paper for the Cabinet meeting on Thursday. What is worse is that the Chancellor is also challenging the figures. From a purely practical point of view, this is likely to cause chaos on Thursday. Colleagues (understandably) will be confused and the meeting will not make progress. From a constitutional point of view, Nigel Lawson's action is indefensible. The financial implications of every Cabinet paper have to be cleared by the Treasury. If issues cannot be settled then they are brought to Cabinet with the issues of disagreement made plain. Nigel had agreed to the paper and it has been circulated. He is now re-opening the whole issue and the pensions issue in particular. I am speaking at a dinner but I have a chance to read the minute afterwards. It is to the Prime Minister with a copy to Willie Whitelaw alone and is clearly designed to make Willie Whitelaw as nervous as possible. The logic of what the Chancellor is saying is either to scrap SERPS but put nothing in its place; or to leave the decision until after the next election, which the Chancellor finds 'politically attractive.' The whole minute is breathtaking. Any one of his points could have been raised at any stage over the last few months. It is, for example, clear that the tax relief bill goes up if you have more private pensions and you give tax relief. It is a monstrous bounce – an attempt to defeat the pensions proposals at the last minute, and this from the man who confided to me at the outset of the review that he didn't mind what else happened as long as I got rid of SERPS.

WEDNESDAY 24 APRIL

First to the department to meet Ken Stowe and Tony Newton. We are in no doubt that the Cabinet meeting tomorrow should *not* go ahead. Ken Stowe agrees with me that it is a sure recipe for chaos to proceed with a paper that the Treasury is challenging on the grounds that the figures have not been worked out. I then go over to the Treasury to see Lawson. On this occasion I am angry and even Lawson senses it. I say it is a very serious setback, that constitutionally, the papers submitted are agreed and that our agreement on the policy goes back to 12 February. His minute goes to the heart of the debate and we cannot go ahead to Cabinet on this basis. I have therefore asked the Prime Minister to take the paper off the agenda.

Lawson looks surprised at this but soon bounces back on the grounds that it would be irresponsible for him not to put forward these objections on the first occasion that he could. This, of course, is part of the trouble. He works to last-minute schedules. What makes me most angry is that he is changing his mind. SERPS, the great burden, is still the great burden – but as it is for the future he is basically not interested. His solutions are indefensible. You cannot abolish SERPS and leave a vacuum for the good reason that it would not be filled. As for leaving it until after the next election – how? Back at the department, Ken Stowe tells me that Robert Armstrong strongly agrees that the item should come off. He is as put out as everyone else as no one in the Treasury had sent him a copy of the minute.

THURSDAY 25 APRIL

Cabinet is over quickly! Most colleagues don't know what is happening and the position is not explained in any depth. The Prime Minister says something to the effect that there are still a few loose ends to tie up. Everyone looks blank. Nigel and I keep quiet and the meeting ends. Regrettably, there are more inquisitive souls outside. It has been known for some time that the review is due to be taken this Thursday. Bernard Ingham tells the morning lobby that it's off the agenda and by lunch the *Standard* has its newspaper boards out, talking of 'Cabinet in chaos'. There is puzzlement in the party and in the press, but Julian Haviland of *The Times* gets it about right – the tactic of the Treasury bounce.

FRIDAY 26 APRIL

The press is thick with stories of the Lawson/Fowler row. No one buys the line of a few loose ends to be tied up. *The Guardian* – conspiracy theorists as always – wonders whether it isn't all a synthetic duel to establish that the eventual position is not quite as awful as it might seem. If only they were right. The Prime Minister has asked for figures agreed between the departments to be sent to her today. A meeting has been arranged for next Monday and social security is back on the agenda for next Thursday. It would be disastrous if we missed another Cabinet.

MONDAY 29 APRIL

In preparation for our meeting, Nigel Lawson has sent round another tendentious minute. We meet in the drawing room of No. 10. Present are Willie Whitelaw, John Wakeham, Nigel Lawson, Peter Rees, Tony Newton and myself. I admit that I was concerned at the way the meeting might go – Willie Whitelaw in particular might get nervous. I need not have worried. Margaret is loyal to decisions taken. She is not one for agonised second thoughts. That is the difference between her and Willie and explains why she is Prime Minister and he is not. She listens to Nigel argue that his preferred course is that SERPS should be abolished with 'voluntary' provision for private pensions, or if that was not possible then a modified SERPS. Again, a change of emphasis on his minute twenty-four hours earlier. Margaret Thatcher did not like this argument at all and for the next ten minutes went for her Chancellor. She pummelled him like a boxer who has got an opponent on the ropes. In particular, she attacked his political judgement. How can you abolish SERPS and put nothing in its place? Did he not see the importance of going from public to private in pension provision? She looked almost despairingly at him. To be fair to Nigel, he stands up to the battery quite well. A number of colleagues would have been laid flat out on the canvas by this barrage. To the outsider not immersed in the detail of the case, two facts are clear: that Nigel has left it very late and is in danger of overturning the work of several months and that he has a conflict of principle with the Prime Minister – not the way to win your Cabinet battles.

THURSDAY 2 MAY

Cabinet. Much press interest outside No. 10 while colleagues inside the Cabinet room await my presentation with a mixture of interest and amusement, amusement because I'm taking them through an explanatory slideshow. The nightmare is that the machine will break down or that the slides will get mixed up. In fact, everything goes very smoothly. Colleagues look and listen in a darkened room. No one interrupts. I bring it to an end. At 9.15 we go to the main Cabinet agenda, next week's business, foreign affairs and then back to us. The social security benefits were agreed.[133] Pensions next week.

MONDAY 6 MAY

The result of our weekend's labours has been circulated and we meet again at No. 10. We are all dressed in weekend clothes as a passing nod to the bank holiday. We wait in uncomfortable hostility in John Wakeham's room at No. 12. If any Downing Street watcher should notice our arrival the story is that we are having a party and, to add to the slight cloak-and-dagger nature

---

133   Family credit was introduced to help low-income working families with children. Later, this was replaced with tax credits by Gordon Brown, but with the same aim of helping people in work on low incomes. Child benefit was retained as the only recognition in either the social security or tax system for the extra expense of having children. The social fund introduced a discretionary form of emergency help for people in need, rather than the indiscriminate and costly single payments regime. Supplementary benefit was replaced by the simpler income support and young people in training were eventually taken off it. A whole series of special grants and payments which had been introduced years before, like the inadequate death grant, went. Housing benefit was to be reformed so it did not discriminate against the low-paid in work, and the whole system was to be simplified.

of the meeting, we all arrive through the rear of Downing Street, rather than the main entrance. In fact, the meeting goes off without incident.

THURSDAY 9 MAY

Cabinet. Pensions agreed![134] The aim now is to publish the green paper. My aim is Monday 3 June. The House will have just returned and Monday is a good day to make a controversial statement. On Tuesdays and Thursdays they are 'hyped up' by Prime Minister's Questions.

13 MAY ONWARDS

The next days are indistinguishable. We have about ten days to clear three volumes. Tony Newton and I divide up the work. He is invaluable as he has been throughout. We work with officials late into every evening; too often finishing with McDonald's hamburgers.

FRIDAY 24 MAY

We are now right up against time. I am due to go to the Isle of Wight today with Oliver. He is collected from school and waits and waits. He is sent out with Len to buy more McDonald's. In spite of the fact that it is a civil service holiday my team is in the office. Finally, I leave just before ten, leaving Tony to tidy up a few more paragraphs and taking a copy with me to check on the train. We arrive in Ryde just before midnight and get a taxi out to Seaview. I feel like I don't want to see another social security paper ever again.

SUNDAY 26 MAY

The final, final deadline is to have it with the printers in Derby on Monday night – also a holiday. Two of my best people are going there to ensure that there are no last-minute hitches. On Sunday morning I dictate my very final corrections from the public phone box in Seaview

---

134   SERPS was to be abolished and the second pension to be replaced by various occupational schemes provided by the private sector. The proposals were not popular with the industry and by the time the white paper was published eighteen months later, opinion had moved on, SERPS was reduced rather than abolished; companies could set up their own schemes and individuals could set up their own private pensions.

to Brian Walmsley, one of my officials who is staying near Blackpool. Now, there is no turning back.

WEDNESDAY 29 MAY

It will be a major battle of that there is no doubt and the whole process has been made immeasurably more difficult by all the press coverage. There have been any number of leaks and speculation. The message is coming back that the party is 'nervous'. The party is nervous about most things just now and will need winning over. Ken Clarke's view is that 'this is the most difficult battle you've been in.' I agree.

MONDAY 3 JUNE

Statement on the inquiry. A full House with most of the social security experts, like Frank Field and Gordon Brown, in attendance. They are deeply suspicious of my intentions. Who has ever heard of a Thatcher minister producing anything other than a hostile welfare report? Needless to say, Michael Meacher describes it as 'a return to the Victorian poor law' but his comments appear to persuade very few on either side of the House. Family credit, which brings extra help to low-income families in work, is long overdue and welcomed on our benches and I suspect, more widely. The same is true of our pension proposals and the aim to move to a system whereby everybody in work has a pension of their own in addition to the basic state pension. The sticky point for us is that we have quite deliberately not put in illustrative figures. We will obviously include estimates in the white paper and Tony and I are getting down to these. But the whole aim of the statement is to describe the new structure so that hopefully the public and the press understand the new changes we are making. We shall see how successful we are.

TUESDAY 4 JUNE

The green paper is now established. The major problem is the absence of figures but in the main, the reaction to it has been good and incomparably better than was feared in May.

SUNDAY 1 SEPTEMBER

Another reshuffle is looming. Downing Street is soon on the line. The Prime Minister wants to talk to me. That is a pretty sure sign that I am staying in place. My guess is that it is going to be a nice talk about my indispensability at the DHSS, and so it proves. She says, 'I know you must be disappointed, that is why I have rung but quite frankly, there was no one else who could do the job at this stage.' She added that I had done a superb job. I repeat my feelings that I want to move to an industrial department. She says she understands but adds, 'I must tell you I have much worse things to do tonight.'

MONDAY 2 SEPTEMBER

Ken rings. He has been asked to get to Downing Street by 2.30. I tell him what I know – namely that the news was good, but how good I did not know. At lunchtime, BBC radio is suggesting that Leon is to move. No one knows where and no one knows who is to take his place. Later, Ken rings again and tells me he is in the Cabinet but still in a number-two role – as the Commons spokesman on employment with David Young doing the number one job. We both agree that the good news is qualified. He obviously wants to be more than a number two but he is in the Cabinet. We talk of the other changes. For once he is nearer the news. Leon is being transferred to trade and industry and is to be replaced by Douglas Hurd, and Tom King is to go to Northern Ireland. I must say that I find those changes extraordinary. I know that there has been criticism of Leon's television manner but I cannot imagine that Douglas will be tremendously better, while Leon, in my view, has proved a good Home Secretary, making changes that are both sensible and reforming. He must be furious.

TUESDAY 3 SEPTEMBER

John Major is waiting for me in the department.[135] He is the new

---

135   John Major's first ministerial appointment. Having been a whip he was moved to the most junior ministerial role and one of the least desired by those wishing to make their way – parliamentary under-secretary for social security.

parliamentary secretary but at the moment does not know which side of the department he is going to. His only guidance from the Prime Minister was to 'ask Norman,' which he does. I say 'I *want* you on the social security side' but admit there is confusion about Ray Whitney's position. Ray is presently doing social security but is he going or staying? In the end we decide that the best thing to do is for John to go home armed with all the files on social security.

WEDNESDAY 11 SEPTEMBER

Ken Clarke sends me a long letter of support, which is good of him. Now Ken has properly launched, I think he has enormous potential. The question is not whether he will rise, but how far? I have lunch with John Major. He is an excellent addition to the department.

MONDAY 16 SEPTEMBER

The day starts with a *Today* interview in the radio car on the social security reviews to mark the end of the consultation period. Returning to the kitchen the phone goes – it is Jeffrey Archer.[136] He congratulates me on the way the interview went: 'It is just how I want my ministers to do it.' I hope he doesn't try his '*my* ministers' bit on Willie.

Lunch with Leon. He has recovered well from the batterings of the previous week but is not pleased with the way he has been treated. He was called to Chequers on Sunday afternoon and apparently thought, as well he might, that he was being asked for his advice. This impression did not change even when he met John Wakeham and Willie Whitelaw, or even when he was alone with Margaret Thatcher. She started a long speech on the importance of industry before getting round to the point that she wanted him to move there. Margaret has lost a natural supporter.

COMMENT

One obvious lesson from the whole exercise is that you cannot reform social

---

136   He had just been made Deputy Chairman of the party to Norman Tebbit.

security without the cooperation of the Chancellor of the Exchequer. Chancellors like Ken Clarke and George Osborne were sympathetic to this cause. Strangely, for such an intelligent man, Nigel Lawson was content to play a one-club game of cutting the headline rate of tax as if this was the only thing that incentivised the public. Anything that conflicted with that aim was vetoed.

Ten years previously, Brittan, Clarke and Fowler had met to consider their future under Margaret Thatcher. The obvious change today was that we were now all Cabinet ministers and many of our early doubts (although not all) had been dispelled. By any objective standard, both Ken and I had done well enough but our good fortune was tinged with some disappointment. Ken had had enough of being a number two and after a record period in health and social security, I wanted a change. But these were pinpricks compared to the treatment meted out to Leon Brittan. Leon had originally done best in the promotion stakes. From Treasury Chief Secretary he had been a surprise appointment to Home Secretary, one of the youngest in the twentieth century, and was beginning to show his potential. His misfortune had been that his period of office coincided with the miners' strike and Arthur Scargill's rabble-rousing oratory. In the Tory Party a popular theory became that we were losing the publicity battle because neither the Home Secretary nor the Chancellor were natural communicators. We could afford one minister in such a leading position but not two. Of course, dwarfing all this in its eventual importance was a largely unnoticed promotion to the ministerial ranks. It was not considered the most glamorous of appointments that day but five years later, he was Prime Minister.

8

THE SCAPEGOAT

JANUARY 1986

After the Westland dispute was all over, Margaret Thatcher and her advisers tried to pretend that the takeover of Britain's only helicopter company was a matter of no great consequence and did not deserve the attention it received at the time. But this was to substantially downplay the importance of a dispute within government that led to the resignation of two Cabinet ministers, raised a series of questions on how government was being conducted, challenged the right of a Cabinet minister to take his case to the whole Cabinet and very nearly led to the fall of the Prime Minister herself. Mrs Thatcher narrowly avoided that fate but one minister, Leon Brittan, the Industry Secretary, was not so fortunate. He did No. 10's bidding – and became the scapegoat.

THURSDAY 2 JANUARY 1986

Thank goodness for Michael Heseltine. The Westland helicopter saga dominates the front pages. The debate on my social security reforms has gone quiet over Christmas. As a government we are beginning to look pretty silly but from a narrow departmental point of view, the longer he keeps the affair going the better. By far Michael's best point is the lack of serious Cabinet discussion about the issue. There's been no discussion with papers, thus half the Cabinet are excluded from a proper consideration of the issues. The dispute itself however shows every sign of getting out of hand, with the Department of Defence and the DTI engaging in vigorous counter-briefing.

SATURDAY 4 JANUARY–WEDNESDAY 8 JANUARY

New York. A truncated trip to the United States to look at the progress of their personal pension schemes, which have the unfortunate initials IRA – Independent Retirement Accounts. It is truncated because Cabinet is to meet on Thursday, despite it being the recess, in the hope of resolving the row. Concorde means the journey is easy enough and while here we fit in a tight schedule of meetings in New York and Washington. At dinner at the Residence it becomes clear that the Americans are much more interested in talking about my pension plans than their own. One or two think we might be going too far! I have noticed before that in spite of the reputation that the Americans have for the free market, this is not always shown in Washington, where a mixture of protectionism and paternalism often rules supreme.

WEDNESDAY 8 JANUARY

I arrive back at Heathrow at 10 p.m. and ring Ken Stowe, whom I have asked to keep me in touch with Westland. He tells me the position is very confused and changing from minute to minute. Michael Heseltine has the bit between his teeth and is fighting for a European option. Leon is also active, briefing broadly on the lines that it is up to the shareholders.

THURSDAY 9 JANUARY

Cabinet opens with parliamentary business. We then move on to Westland. Michael is sitting next to me on my right. The atmosphere in the room is tense. Margaret opens by saying that the Cabinet has already decided that the future of the company is a matter for the shareholders: that means that no minister should lobby one way or the other. The events of the last few weeks have done great damage to the government, she says, and then reads out some of the headlines there have been over the last few days, all of which speak of division between ministers. If it goes on like this the Cabinet will have no reputation. Collective responsibility must be restored. Leon then comes in to say that Westland's emergency general meeting is on Tuesday. There were revised proposals from both the Americans and the Europeans. The Westland directors had approved the American offer, but the decision was up to the shareholders. The reconstruction proposals, he says, require a two-thirds majority.

Next is Michael Heseltine. He starts very quietly in a deliberately low-key way. He says he has very little to add. He has put the issues to his colleagues and it is now up to the shareholders. He has no intention of putting one view or another. It is important that after Cabinet nothing should be said to the media that indicates the government favours one course or another. We should maintain a neutral stance and distance ourselves from the controversy. No attempt should be made to guide the media. There were one or two half-smiles at this – given Michael's record of guidance. Nevertheless, it was a conciliatory statement.

There is some short general discussion with Norman Tebbit saying that he was sympathetic to the European option and Nick Ridley (aggressively and unhelpfully) saying he was not. The real trouble comes when Margaret suggests (reading from a brief in front of her) that the next days are going to be sensitive and she would like to see all statements and answers to questions cleared through the Cabinet Office to ensure consistency. Michael says quite reasonably that although he has no objection to clearing new statements it was practically impossible to clear every reply through the Cabinet Office. If he was asked to confirm a statement that he had made already, he would be in an impossible position if he was not able to do this. Others however, disagree: Norman Tebbit, George Younger, Tom King and Leon all say that Margaret's proposal is perfectly acceptable.

At one stage, Margaret looks as though she might waver on her insistence but in the end comes back to it. It seemed to me that this was the breaking point. Quite calmly, Michael closes his folder while she is still speaking. When she has finished, and before anyone else has a chance to intervene, he says he cannot accept this decision. There had been no collective discussion of the matter and he must leave. Margaret says that she is 'very sorry', but Michael takes his file and walks to the door. It is all over very quickly. There is silence in the room. It all seems unreal. Once

Michael has left, Margaret takes control again. We will continue but it would be 'a good idea' to have a break for coffee in about twenty minutes. Geoffrey Howe drones his way through foreign affairs – although frankly no one is listening – and eventually we adjourn for our break.

I speak with Peter Walker who is aghast at what has happened.[137] I ask him if Michael had said anything to him before the Cabinet meeting but the answer is 'no.' Michael had given no warning that he had reached this stage. Michael walks by himself. He seeks no allies, discusses no tactics.

Over coffee, I talk to Leon. Leon thinks the Welsh temperament has taken over but it is obviously more than that. I have scribbled on my pad 'Heseltine silenced.' That means that had he agreed to the Prime Minister's proposal, the press would have reported it as a victory for her and a crushing defeat for him. When we go back into the Cabinet room, George Younger is appointed Defence Secretary on the spot and Malcolm Rifkind is to become Scotland Secretary; proof that contingency plans had been made. We then proceed to do less than justice to Ken Baker's rates paper.[138] The heart has gone out of the meeting. It is allowed through as a green paper, in spite of the reservations of Treasury ministers past and present. In its way, it could well be as important a political event as Michael Heseltine's abrupt departure.

Outside No. 10 the photographers and reporters have now gathered. Leon is finding himself the centre of attention. He is as unprepared as the rest of us but the cameras flash as soon as he enters the street. 'Have you any comments, Mr Brittan?' they ask. Leon keeps his head down and goes straight to his car. Later on television, I see him saying that he does not regard it as a victory and that he was sorry Michael had left. I go back to the department and call in my ministers. We chew over the resignation. Everyone agrees it is bad news and Tony Newton says that it will not be made any better by the party personalising it as a contest

---

137 A close friend of Heseltine.
138 A green paper proposing the abolition of domestic rating in favour of a uniform 'community charge' on all resident adults that was later known as the poll tax.

between Michael and Leon – with most instinctively taking the side of the more glamorous Heseltine. Later that night I see the events of the day on television. Michael Heseltine is dominating the evening media. As far as I can recollect, *News at Ten* has a more or less verbatim account of what has taken place.

FRIDAY 10 JANUARY

To Birmingham for a meeting with the chairmen of all the Birmingham constituencies. They are concerned at what has happened, but not over-concerned. The affairs of Westland seem like pretty small beer and there is a lack of real comprehension of the events. What is self-evident is that the battles between defence and the DTI over Christmas could not continue. On this, Margaret was right. She had to intervene to prevent the government looking silly. The trouble is that the end result is the resignation of one of the best communicators and best ministers in the government. It is a very high price to pay.

MONDAY 13 JANUARY

The press over the weekend has been dreadful. Heseltine has been having a whale of a time appearing on every programme known to man. At one stage, No. 10 suggested I might do *The World This Weekend* but I decline, on the basis that I had not been on the committee that looked at Westland. Although true, it is a weak excuse in front of the cameras. I had heard John Biffen using it on another television programme and saying very feebly that as he wasn't on the committee he couldn't comment on a whole series of questions. Another reason for declining is that I have no desire to join in what looks like an orchestrated attack on Heseltine.

Parliament returns and Leon is put up to make a statement on Westland. The House is both full and tense, but Leon does well. I say to him in the corridor afterwards that 'it was a good Geoffrey Boycott innings.' However, an hour or two later it becomes clear that Leon is in difficulty. During his statement Heseltine had asked him if he had received a letter from the chairman of British Aerospace. Leon had replied that he had not, and what is more, he knew of no such letter. It now transpires that such a letter had come, not from the chairman, but from Raymond Lygo, F. There is no doubt that Leon's declared ignorance of the letter – in effect, 'I don't know what you are talking about' – had substantially defused the position. Leon is to make a statement at 10 p.m. As the last person to make a statement at 10 p.m. in the House I can vouch for the difficulty. By that time the place is overheated: not everyone would survive a breathalyser test. My statement had been brought to an end by Dave Nellist, who snatched my statement and tore it up. That had effectively let me off the hook. On this occasion, the opposition were not going to spoil it that way.

Leon makes the best of a pretty awful job. His explanation that because the letter was marked 'Private and Confidential' he could neither reveal its contents nor even its existence satisfied no one. Roy Jenkins captures the mood best by saying that when Thatcher and Leon are together again 'we shall count our spoons quickly' when they leave. I fear that Leon is now in deep trouble, although it is obvious that the opposition are really after Margaret's blood, not his.

TUESDAY 14 JANUARY

One of the results of this concentration on Westland is that the government's other business is entirely overshadowed. I go to L committee to get approval for the introduction of the social security bill. It is given in a few minutes. None of the correspondents who were writing so anxiously before Christmas about the 'political consequences' of the reforms have asked me about the subject for weeks. Westland dominates everything.

WEDNESDAY 15 JANUARY

The House is packed to hear the debate on Westland. Kinnock makes a good speech. Thatcher is not particularly impressive, while Heseltine makes a strong defence of his position. Heseltine's speech is immediately hailed by Jim Callaghan as one of the most impressive resignation speeches he has ever heard. 'We all know', he says, 'what the pressures are that lead up to a resignation.' Quite how Jim knows this is unclear, as he successfully resisted the temptation to do anything so foolhardy throughout his career. It is not clear that there was any issue which would have driven him to resignation. His failure as Chancellor and his boundary redistribution tactics in 1969 did not seem to have caused him too much of a crisis of confidence. Yet all this is now forgotten – Jim is the elder statesman, above the hurly-burly of politics and, it has to be conceded, very effective.

THURSDAY 16 JANUARY

What we will do for our friends! I start the day at some ludicrously early hour talking with Norman St John-Stevas on breakfast television. My message is simple: Leon's performance last night was very good and he is a man of great integrity. Norman is also very helpful. I think the crisis is over for the time being.

Cabinet is notable for the fact that Westland is not mentioned. Most of the time is spent on the Channel Tunnel. We have a number of bidders to choose from and Margaret Thatcher wants it to be announced when she meets President Mitterrand on Monday. The rail option is chosen: a historic decision, regrettably made at a time when the nation has its mind elsewhere.

FRIDAY 17 JANUARY

A press conference on the social security bill.[139] It is low-key. Some radio interviews, but not a television camera in sight. During the afternoon, I hear that Raymond Lygo is now saying that his account of the meeting with Leon Brittan might have been 'misstated'. That is good news for Leon and the government. I go to Birmingham to talk to 300 life insurance men about my personal pension plans and get a surprisingly warm reception. It is important that we enthuse them if the new plans are to be successful.

---

139 The bill gave effect to the proposals set out in the white paper on social security published in December.

SATURDAY 18 JANUARY–SUNDAY 19 JANUARY

The press is still full of Westland but *Britannia*'s operations off Aden are now making the main headlines. Westland could be behind us. There is one difficulty, however, the Solicitor General's letter.[140] Robert Armstrong is holding his inquiry but everyone I know assumes that the letter (which accused Heseltine of misstating the position) was leaked by the DTI. Either it was leaked without permission or with ministerial (that is Leon's) say so. Either way, the opposition must be on to a good thing. Meanwhile, I actually *do* have departmental business: a difficult statement and an appearance before the select committee.

MONDAY 20 JANUARY

I meet Michael Heseltine in the lobby for the first time since his resignation. He playfully warns me against being seen with him. I said I hope all this would not become a conflict between him and Leon. He says grimly that he isn't interested in Leon. His target is Thatcher. When she refused his Friday meeting, which she had previously promised, then his resignation was inevitable. It would not have made any difference had I or anyone else intervened at Cabinet to find another way of clearing government statements. Michael is still talking Westland non-stop. By chance I immediately run into Leon, who is cheerful and hoping that it will calm down.

THURSDAY 23 JANUARY

Cabinet is very short. I go in with Willie Whitelaw. There are photographers by the dozen. Leon suddenly appears at our shoulder. I break off to talk to him but Willie keeps right on. Leon tells me that the inquiry will say that he authorised the disclosure of the Solicitor General's letter but this had only been done *after* consultation with No. 10. Leon says that

---

140   The advice of the Solicitor General, Sir Paddy Mayhew, in which he effectively said that Heseltine had misstated the position had been leaked to the press. It was clearly to the government's advantage but the leaking of a law officer's advice was strictly out of bounds. The problem became, who was responsible for the leak?

neither he nor his officials would agree to this last piece of information being kept out.

Margaret sets out what she will say in her statement on the leak inquiry this afternoon. This is that it was necessary for the information in the Solicitor General's letter to be released that day as a press conference affecting the company was being held. Apparently, she has nothing much else to say as an excuse. It is all desperately thin. Willie Whitelaw says it is important that the statement is made, otherwise it will simply 'drag on.' Margaret says that she will do her best to clear the matter up this afternoon. Leaving No. 10 we are all too early for our cars. Ken Clarke and I wander off down Whitehall on foot. We agree that Leon is now in a perilous position. The obvious question is why had he authorised the leak and said nothing when the inquiry was set up? We are joined at the underpass going over to Westminster by Nick Ridley and David Young. Ridley wants us to form up to Leon and say he should do the 'honourable thing' and resign, thus protecting the Prime Minister. I say I am not prepared to do that. The afternoon is just as dreadful as we had all imagined. Margaret is severely mauled by the opposition – 'wasting police time' etc. – but the party is remarkably loyal to her. Leon is dangerously exposed. In the evening there is the 1922 Committee. Charles Wardle[141] tells me that there were a number of calls for Leon's resignation.

FRIDAY 24 JANUARY

Ironically, I am in Nottingham. Ironically, because it was here that almost twenty years previously Leon and I had fought it out for the nomination of the South Nottingham constituency. The final was between us two. My victory had delayed his entry into the Commons until 1974 and for a time had substantially put back what had been a developing friendship. On this visit the subject was once again Leon's future. I gave a number of interviews backing Leon and saying that he should not resign. I arrive in Sutton Coldfield for an advice bureau by 4.30 p.m. During the advice bureau the news comes through that Leon has resigned. This amazingly

---

141 Conservative MP for Bexhill and Battle 1983–2001. He became my PPS.

talented man's career had ended in an astonishingly bizarre way. There are few of my contemporaries who can match Leon's intellect and judgement. He was constantly being asked his advice on this problem or that both at university and later in London when we had all come down. It is a stark tragedy.

SATURDAY 25–SUNDAY 26 JANUARY

Coming back to London I buy all the papers. There is still an air of unreality about the whole affair. It almost defies belief that someone as sensible as Leon could have perished in this way. But the papers quite clearly set out his political obituary. He is perceived as too loyal to the Prime Minister. Rebellion does not come easily to him, even when his own future is at stake.

SUNDAY 26 JANUARY

I stonewall on David Dimbleby's Sunday television show while Douglas Hurd does the same with Brian Walden. We both have one advantage in these interviews. We were not on the Westland committee and can truthfully say that they must wait for the Prime Minister's reply to the debate tomorrow.

MONDAY 27 JANUARY

The debate. We are lucky. Neil Kinnock makes an awful speech, Margaret Thatcher quite a good one. The party want to forget about Westland and greet her speech with a waving of order papers. Heseltine completes the story with a mini party-conference speech appealing for political unity. Apparently, John Wakeham called him over the weekend about speaking. Heseltine is now rather nervous at the effect that his resignation has had. From the party manager's point of view he did everything that could be expected. From his own point of view, rather less. He gives the impression that the great constitutional issue is now forgotten. Foot (in a really good speech) was able to make quite a lot out of 'ratting' and 're-ratting.' The result is that once again the Westland affair is off the boil but it will be a brave man who believes that this is the end of it.

TUESDAY 28 JANUARY

After the dramas of the last week I get a second reading of the social security bill. The bill, which was to be the most controversial piece of legislation of the session, gets through with only about thirty or forty attending the opening speeches.

WEDNESDAY 29 JANUARY

I meet Michael Heseltine in the corridor. He says he has just written to me and we promise to have lunch. 'I have all the time in the world', he adds.

COMMENT

Far from being a matter of little consequence, Westland was one of the most personal and bitter disputes between ministers in the history of the Thatcher government. What my diary indicates is the very direct part that the Prime Minister played, using not only her influence but also her position to defeat the plans of the defence secretary she herself had appointed. In this she was supported by Charles Powell,[142] who progressively took over running the campaign against Heseltine, although it can be taken for granted that Mrs Thatcher knew of the moves that were being made. She also had the advantage of having the support of the whole government machine, including that of Bernard Ingham, the No. 10 head of public relations. Against this array, Heseltine seemed a lonely and isolated figure.

Indeed, that is exactly the picture that the Thatcher camp tried to paint. Heseltine was portrayed as the exception to a picture of Cabinet consensus. That picture would have had substantially more credibility had Cabinet had more opportunity to discuss the issues on which total agreement was claimed. Even the final position that it was a matter for the shareholders would have been improved by knowing just who some of the shareholders were and how many were hiding behind nominee companies holding their shares.

These issues came to a climax over the leak of a letter from one of the law officers, Sir Patrick Mayhew, the widely trusted Solicitor General. Mayhew

---

142   Civil servant, her chief adviser on foreign affairs and who became her private secretary in 1984.

thought that some statements previously made by Heseltine were inaccurate and wrote a letter to that effect. The letter became public and the question then became who leaked the information?

The Attorney General returned from his sick bed and demanded an inquiry. With reluctance, No. 10 concurred and the Cabinet Secretary Robert Armstrong was asked to do it. On one point everyone was agreed – the leak had taken place with the agreement of the Secretary of State, Leon Brittan, and had been carried out by his head of press relations, Colette Bowe. But no one seriously believed that either Brittan or Bowe would have acted on their own initiative. Leon insisted that No. 10's role should be made public and it became clear that the leak had been authorised by officials at No. 10. He took the view that if that was what the Prime Minister wanted he would agree. Mrs Thatcher claimed later that no one had told her that the information was going to be published by leaking the letter to the press.

It was not enough to deflect the attack on Brittan. Prominent members of the Conservative backbench 1922 Committee wanted the head of someone who could be called responsible. They did not want Thatcher, and Powell's part was largely unknown to the outside world. Brittan was the obvious fall guy. Leon Brittan was thrown to the wolves. There was no defence campaign organised for him by No. 10 and he was forced to resign. The campaign was to save the Prime Minister: the loss of a Cabinet minister was collateral damage. The price was the loss to British politics of one of the most outstanding members of my generation.

9

AT ODDS WITH THE
PRIME MINISTER

FEBRUARY 1986–FEBRUARY 1987

Ninety eighty-six saw me at personal odds with the Prime Minister. Our most fundamental division was over the new public health threat of HIV/Aids and how it could be countered. In February I had written to the Home Affairs Committee warning that the previous twelve months had seen 275 cases of Aids with 144 deaths. Even worse, there were an estimated 20,000 people already infected with the virus and the figure was expected to double annually unless action was taken. There was no treatment or drugs or vaccine and the bleak message was that those who contracted HIV were almost certain to die. It was about as profound a challenge as any Health Secretary or government was likely to face. In spite of this, Mrs Thatcher resisted attempts to spread knowledge of the disease making use of all forms of communications.

I freely admit that at the time I knew little about the gay population. My first reaction to the prejudice that I saw in the 1980s was the oldest of all political motivators – it was not fair. It was not fair that gay men should be demonised in so much of the press or that utterly false solutions should be peddled, like the proposal popular on both sides of the Atlantic that those with HIV should be compulsorily isolated. They deserved protection in the same way as anyone else threatened by illness and disease. I could not understand the hostility to warning the public about the dangers of contracting HIV. It seemed obvious to me that as there were no drugs to treat those who already had the virus, our priority should be to warn those who were unaffected of *the dangers while at the same time caring for those who were already infected and dying. But giving public health warnings plunged me into fresh controversy with those who believed that it was a 'moral' issue.*

We were clashing not only with outright opponents but also with those (like many in the churches) who took the view that we should not conduct a campaign that endorsed or even recognised homosexuality (it had been legalised in 1967). Some went even further and advocated that government ministers should put the case for chastity although such action was against the history of two world wars which clearly showed that straightforward public health messages were the most effective. The omens for what was to become the biggest public health campaign in the forty years since the Second World War were not good.

The second issue that confronted me in 1986 (this time as a Midlands MP) was an attempt by two giant American corporations to take over the British motor industry centred around Birmingham. After years of decline in the industry (a product of strikes, union intransigence and weak management) there were at last signs of some recovery. Tough managers like Michael Edwardes were bringing the workforce to its senses and brands like Land Rover remained world leaders. The question was whether the government, who financially supported Leyland, would continue in its efforts or whether the prospect of outright sale would persuade ministers to throw in the towel.

MONDAY 3 FEBRUARY 1986

The *Daily Mail* has a story that two giant American corporations, Ford and General Motors, are to take over both Leyland cars and Leyland trucks.[143] The sale is to include Land Rover and Range Rover and the lesser-known, but profitable, Freight Rover. Peter Walker had previously told me that the Ford proposal was in the wind, backed by Nigel Lawson but with Margaret Thatcher and Geoffrey Howe on the fence. This is the

---

143 British Leyland was the result of a series of mergers between different British motor-vehicle manufacturers. In 1975, it went bankrupt and was partly nationalised by the government. The industry became a byword for strikes and the power of the shop stewards but the management was also at fault, too often weak and unwilling to challenge the unions. A new managing director, Michael Edwardes, was appointed in 1977.

first time that anyone, other than Peter Walker, has even contacted me about this, even given my West Midlands connection.

WEDNESDAY 5 FEBRUARY

John Wakeham tells me that the press has a story that two Cabinet ministers are about to ride to Leyland's rescue. This, he takes to be Peter Walker and me. He complains that he needs another row involving Cabinet ministers like a hole in the head.

THURSDAY 6 FEBRUARY

An early morning call from No. 10 inviting me to EA committee on Leyland after Cabinet. Papers are on their way. I say that I want all the papers, not just the meeting papers, and that I still intend to raise the issue at Cabinet. This I do, pointing out that it would be a good idea if Cabinet members with strong regional interests were at least kept in touch with plans of this kind. Margaret agrees and is at pains to apologise and say that we must find ways of avoiding this situation in future.

MONDAY 10 FEBRUARY

I go into the House before the department. On the Cabinet corridor, I run into Leon who is coming in to clear up. He tells me that he has been flooded with letters since his resignation. He doesn't really want to go back to the Bar and is clearly determined to stay in politics and to come back onto the front line. I think he has quite a mountain to climb and I wonder if he realises that even now.

MONDAY 17 FEBRUARY

Dinner with Leon and Diana at La Poule au Pot. Leon is in a remarkably cheerful mood. He sees his resignation as a setback but not irrevocable. We all, Diana included, advise him not to wait around for an offer to return. My advice is that Leon should do something away from politics for the next year or so. On the Westland affair itself, Leon makes it clear that he was under constant pressure from Margaret to counter the

Heseltine propaganda, regular phone calls pointing out what was in the morning newspapers. Leon has well and truly been left holding the baby. Margaret is very lucky to have survived. Westland managed to bring out some of the worst aspects of her style of leadership: decisions in small groups, the hectoring of senior ministers. Leon was particularly vulnerable having just been demoted.

TUESDAY 25 FEBRUARY

A new dispute on Aids. The Prime Minister writes to me objecting to the 'risky sex' part of our proposed advertisements. They set out a warning on the dangers of sexual intercourse with an infected person and the importance of using a condom. 'Anal (back passage) intercourse involves the highest risk and should be avoided', the advertisement says. 'Obviously any act that damages the penis, vagina, anus or mouth is dangerous particularly if it causes bleeding. Even wet kissing with an infected person may be risky'. Margaret has read my paper and, writing through her principal private secretary, Nigel Wicks, asks 'Do we have to have the section on risky sex? I should have thought that it could do immense harm if teenagers were to read it'. She asks Whitelaw to present her view to the members of H committee and report back on their conclusions. Despite her attempt to influence the conclusion, her intervention does not persuade the committee. They not only agree with my approach but say that it should be extended to other media.

WEDNESDAY 26 FEBRUARY

The committee meeting minutes quote the summing-up of Willie Whitelaw, together with a tactful reference to the Prime Minister's objection: 'The committee agreed that the campaign should proceed as planned and thought that the explicit references to sexual practices were a regrettable necessity'.

I arrive at the department just in time to stand in for the Queen in presenting a British Empire medal to one of the messengers who is about to retire. As is the wont of the civil service, a party has been arranged with wine and crackers. I think they overdo this at times, but on this occasion it is just right for a modest, conscientious man who has done a humdrum job well for many years.

Even the rejection of her argument by the Home Affairs Committee did not stop the Prime Minister's action against the advertisements. Extraordinarily, she went above her Cabinet committee (not to mention her Secretary of State) and sought to persuade the Advertising Standards Authority to intervene but this was roundly rejected. The Authority said 'they consider that given the purpose of the advertisement and the fact that the advice in it is given by the Chief Medical Officer, the text shows a reasonable respect for commonly held standards of decency and propriety'. Even more extraordinary the PM also asked for a check on whether the advertisements could be prevented under the Obscene Publications Act. This was also swiftly rejected on the Home Office advice that there was an overwhelming public interest requirement to provide factual information to the public to prevent the spread of Aids.

THURSDAY 6 MARCH

The decisions on the Aids advertisements do not satisfy the Prime Minister. She is now seeking to reopen the whole issue. A letter to my office from Nigel Wicks says:

The Prime Minister has emphasised that she remains against certain parts of the advertisement. She thinks that the anxiety on the part of parents and many teenagers, who would never be in danger from Aids, would exceed the good which the advertisement might do. In her view it would be better to follow the 'VD' precedent of putting notices in doctors' surgeries, public lavatories etc. But to place advertisements in newspapers which every young person could read and learn of practices they never knew about would, in her view, do harm.

Wicks says that these were the Prime Minister's 'firmly held views' and I am told that I 'might wish to consider showing the Prime Minister an amended advertisement that omits the parts which, in the Prime Minister's view, would be likely to offend'. I am not prepared to do that.[144]

TUESDAY 25 MARCH

A scrappy Cabinet. We come to Leyland. Paul Channon reports. Margaret says that the takeover is a great opportunity missed but that the political factors are too great. I say that it is not just a question of political judgement – the position on Freight Rover shows that the commercial arguments don't all run the same way. We would be closing down a business in the West Midlands whose profits are up, whose productivity and employment is 60 per cent up for a lacklustre Bedford organisation. That would be bad news in the West Midlands and almost impossible to explain. Margaret says that whatever her sympathies, we must decide – and so it was decided that the General Motors negotiations should end. It was a rather ill-tempered conclusion leaving no one very satisfied.

Having finished social security questions in the afternoon I stay on for Prime Minister's Questions and for Paul's statement. This is welcomed by the opposition (whose pressure has had no effect on our decision whatsoever) and by the Midlands members but condemned by a range of others on our side, including those around Luton. Throughout the exchanges Margaret Thatcher, who is sitting almost next to me, keeps up a running commentary. 'The next time,' she says, 'we will have some Luton members on the committee.' She follows this by 'you have won, Norman, but at what price to other constituencies?' I think that is a silly summing-up but I am not going to convince her in a hundred years. Thank goodness Easter is now on us.

TUESDAY 24 JUNE

I write to H committee advocating a new round of shorter advertisements on Aids. These would retain the risky-sex message and also venture into new territory on illegal drug taking. Research had shown that the public 'generally approve and are receptive to government action of

---

144   In the event we went ahead with the advertisements without much comment, although my obduracy did little to improve my relations with the Prime Minister.

this kind'.[145] I add that few appear to find the material offensive and there is strong support for the need for explicit language so that people understand the dangers. I suspect that if we have trouble, it will be on our advice to 'those who inject drugs and cannot give up'. This, of course, is some way from the usual language of the war against drugs.

FRIDAY 27 JUNE

The first attack on the advertisement comes from an entirely different direction. The draft says: 'Most people who have the Aids virus have caught it by having sex with an infected person'. This has provoked the ire of the Lord Chancellor, Quintin Hailsham. 'I am convinced that there must be some limit to vulgarity and illiteracy,' he writes.

> 'Sex' means that you are either male or female. It does *not* mean the same thing as sexual practice. Nor does 'having sex' mean anything at all. Could they not use the literate 'sexual intercourse'? If that is thought to be too narrow then why not 'sexual relations' or 'physical sexual practices', but not 'sex' or still worse 'having sex'!!!

Doubtless he is grammatically correct – although I seem to remember we used the phrase in the first campaign and frankly, unless there is pressure I do not intend to change.

AUGUST

I write round to say that we are now proposing a further step in our advertising campaign, and that is to send leaflets on the danger of Aids to all homes in the country. It is an obvious step. It means direct messages to something like twenty-three million homes.[146] Needless to say there are niggles. One is, who is to pay for it? Up to now the Treasury have refused to pay for anything extra. They know their strength. The Prime

---

145 Following the national advertising campaign placed in all the Sunday and daily papers in March and April, feedback found that public interest in Aids was considerable and few appeared to find the material offensive.

146 We had none of the digital campaign advantages available today.

Minister is not likely to back any bid from me, so to date I have provided the money out of the department's resources – the communications budget mainly but not exclusively, as one senior civil servant discovered when she made an involuntary contribution from her budget which had nothing to do with Aids.

THURSDAY 4 SEPTEMBER

Although preoccupied with the Aids campaign, I am obviously aware that a Cabinet reshuffle is coming up. In July I went to see Margaret. Her reaction was that she knew I wanted to move and she knew where I wanted to go. This was offered even before I had explained my case! She knows that the Department of Trade and Industry has been an ambition but I know that she is most unlikely to give it to me. She has not forgotten my position on Leyland. She regards me as representing Birmingham and an interventionist in the tradition (although perhaps not so developed) of Michael Heseltine and Peter Walker.

MONDAY 8 SEPTEMBER

Meeting with Wakeham who confirms that I am to stay where I am. I say if I am going to stay, I want my own team. I want Tony Newton as my Minister of Health and John Major as my Minister of State for Social Security. My choices for parliamentary secretaries are Edwina Currie and Nick Lyell. Edwina is not popular with her colleagues but she is a good ally and will get up in the morning to put the case. It may be a bumpy ride but a little bit of Edwina's push will be no bad thing. Nick comes highly recommended as the best lawyer in the House. Wakeham says he will see what can be done and rings later to say that Margaret has agreed to all my proposals.

TUESDAY 9 SEPTEMBER

The day of the shuffle. Some familiar names and good people are going. Tim Raison for example, has a first-class mind and personally I would put him in front of some of those staying. Ditto George Young while Chris Patten has a curious sideways move to the Foreign Office. I gather that she is not impressed with Chris and believes he failed to support Keith Joseph sufficiently. That seems a harsh judgement. I would have rated him very highly and indeed, he was my second choice for Minister of Health.

WEDNESDAY 10 SEPTEMBER

Our new team meets. We arrange the standard photo call. Normally, only the social services press come but this time every photographer for miles around turns up. They all want to photograph Edwina, who says rather plaintively that she is just part of the team.[147]

MONDAY 15 SEPTEMBER

The first formal meeting of all my ministers and the permanent secretaries. Tony Newton will become Chairman of the management board of the National Health Service. This will be a great challenge for Tony who is rather preoccupied with getting divorced and remarried. He is an outstanding minister but if he has one fault, it is that he will never say 'no'. The result is that he tends to disappear to speak to four men and a dog clustered around a gas fire in Writtle when I want him here. At the meeting the contrast in styles is apparent. Edwina talks a great deal – too much – but it is the sign of the enthusiast she is. John Major is not a great talker – although capable of it, as when he successfully took on the Prime Minister at one of the whips' dinners.

TUESDAY 23 SEPTEMBER

I propose to the Prime Minister that I take on Roy Griffiths as my adviser on management. Roy would prefer to be a minister in the Lords but this cannot be arranged. Willie Whitelaw wants a minister who will also 'muck in' and do the other jobs that Lords ministers have to do – speak on other subjects and vote. Margaret enthusiastically agrees to the suggestion that Roy Griffiths should sign up.

---

147   One photographer wanted a picture with just myself and Edwina. Her response was to the effect that she was not sure that her then husband would approve. In retrospect, given her relationship with my Minister of State for Social Security (at the time, totally unknown), this seems a bit rich.

THURSDAY 25 SEPTEMBER

Back at Alexander Fleming House, Roy is not keen on Ken Stowe joining us. It soon becomes clear why. He wants to be 'the Prime Minister's
adviser' on the health service. I say that this was not what was proposed
and I disagree. He was to advise me on how the health service could be
improved and he would have access to the Prime Minister. He says that
he needs the authority of the Prime Minister; otherwise he fears that he
will be neutered by the civil service. There is no way that I am going to
have an adviser in my department reporting to someone else. It is an
unhappy meeting and agreement now looks anything but certain.

By coincidence, it is a health day at No. 10 and in the evening Margaret has the regional chairmen to dinner. This goes quite well. Only
'quite' because she lectures the chairmen on getting out there and selling
the health service – which the best of them do already – and because
she complains about the regional allocation of resources, which she says
takes resources away from 'our people' and sends it to areas who are neither grateful nor will support us. The chairmen can hardly be expected
to share these political views and frankly, she has been much too influenced by one visit to Barrow where the consultants at a new hospital
simply grumbled about resources. No chairman came out in support of
her position and I, together with Edwina and Tony, argue against her.
You cannot defend a position where areas like Stoke have been deprived
of good hospital care for far too long. Afterwards we have a tense late-
night session on the Roy Griffiths position. I tell her what he wants and
her reaction is that this is what I must give. I say it is not acceptable. This
brings everyone up with a jolt. She believes that we need Roy Griffiths
on any terms: I don't. I think he would be good for us but only on terms
that are acceptable to me, who has responsibility for the health service. It
was an uneasy meeting and we ended after midnight.[148]

FRIDAY 26 SEPTEMBER

I go to the Isle of Wight to speak and leave Ken Stowe and Nigel Wicks

---

148   The later dispute between Nigel Lawson and Alan Walters shows how perilous such an appointment
      can be.

to negotiate with Roy Griffiths. Ken rings later to say that they have persuaded him to accept my terms. Good news.[149] Now, we all know where we are and where responsibility lies. There is no way that the health service could be run with an adviser responsible to No. 10 looking over the shoulder of the Secretary of State. I will seek to mend fences with Roy Griffiths.

MONDAY 6 OCTOBER

To Bournemouth and the party conference in style in Margaret Thatcher's Jaguar. She is visiting the new Bournemouth hospital. She tells me that she is terrified at the prospect of the speech – it has that effect on all of us, with the possible exception of Michael Heseltine. We are back on friendly terms after our row over Roy Griffiths. (She asks when Fiona will be coming down and says that 'DT' will be coming on Wednesday.) From time to time she looks out of the window to wave to passers-by in a rather regal way. The traffic in London is light and the police keep the roundabouts open. The result is that we get to the hospital site early. Fortunately, they are ready and we are met by the nation's cameramen. We do all the things you do on these occasions – dig holes, put on tin hats, and try to avoid falling over the camera crews. We have a good hospital building record and I hope to get this dramatised when I speak on Wednesday.

TUESDAY 7 OCTOBER

The party conference begins. My interest on the first day is in John Major's speech on social security. It is a difficult subject to get them enthused about but John does well.

WEDNESDAY 8 OCTOBER

The health debate goes like a dream. I have had standing ovations before at party conferences but none like this. The audience positively leap to their feet and stamp and cheer. I had the idea of setting our hospital

---

149   He became Deputy Chairman of the NHS management board (1986–89) and adviser to the government on the NHS (1986–94).

building programme on a computer print-out and this goes so well that when I flourish the list the audience breaks into cheers, which makes it impossible for me to continue. At the end, Margaret Thatcher and Norman Tebbit are beside me on the platform and after about ninety seconds of the ovation Margaret Thatcher says to me that the only way they will stop is if I sit down. We are seeking to relaunch the health ship and this has got us off to a good start. Later in the evening I meet Joe Haines of the *Daily Mirror* at a party. I had had some fun at his expense in my speech. He says that the *Mirror* would be doing the same for me the next day.

THURSDAY 9 OCTOBER
The *Mirror*'s attempt at humour is pretty feeble. They put my photo upside down on their front page to show the 'upside down view of Norman Fowler'. Jeffrey Archer says he would like to get on to the front page of the *Mirror* any way up.

FRIDAY 10 OCTOBER
The party conference ends with a good speech from Margaret Thatcher. It has been one of our best conferences. On the platform for the final session, John Wakeham says that I should have a word with Edwina who has apparently been on a breakfast television show marking the performance of ministers at the conference. She has given me an alpha, Ken Baker a beta, with a comment that he lacks experience in Cabinet, and Douglas Hurd a gamma, with the comment that the Home Office speech is difficult at party conferences. I gather that Ken and Douglas are not amused.

FRIDAY 24 OCTOBER
Back to Aids and a very important development inside government. A new Cabinet committee on Aids, HA, is to be set up under the chairmanship of Willie Whitelaw. We will put our case to them and bypass the main H committee, which has become a ludicrous way of doing business. Advertisements about Aids take weeks getting through because

they have to pass the critical test of ministers like Quintin Hailsham who are nowhere near the problem but have the strongest views on the language used. He is not a member of the new committee, neither is Norman Tebbit. Above all, the Prime Minister is not in the chair as she was for the social security review.[150]

The only other issue which takes my time today is the future of Richmond Yard, the new office building in Whitehall. To avoid a row between Geoffrey Howe and Margaret Thatcher, the No. 10 secretariat has persuaded Margaret Thatcher (against her own instincts) to say that Richmond Yard should go to the Overseas Development Agency. Civil servants who have never worked outside the comfortable environment of deepest Whitehall have decided that the poor old DHSS should stay out of sight at the Elephant and Castle. No. 10, in the form of Nigel Wicks, is most concerned that I should not try to overturn the decision or reopen the debate. I say 'no deal'. Next, I have Willie Whitelaw on the phone, also pleading that I do not provoke a great row between Margaret and Geoffrey. I won't win, he says. I say I accept that I won't win this one but I might win next time. He does not attempt to dispute my intent to send in a note.

TUESDAY 28 OCTOBER

Meeting with Sammy Harari on the Aids campaign. Up to now, our campaign has been low-key. We've made some of the public more aware of the dangers, but it's not yet a mass campaign. Our next task must be to get the message home. We are fortunate that Sammy, who has done valuable work on the drugs campaign, is now in charge of the agency where the Aids account is.

THURSDAY 30 OCTOBER

In the debate on Westland yesterday, Leon openly attacks Michael Heseltine for the first time on the entirely legitimate grounds that ministerial

---

150   The new committee was something of a triumph for Robert Armstrong, the Cabinet Secretary, who was a supporter of the campaign behind the scenes, and Ken Stowe, my Permanent Secretary, who knew only too well our frustration at the delays.

collective responsibility had been ignored. What should have happened was that Michael should have been fired, but Margaret could not bring herself to do that. She chose instead to fight the fight in a different way, using Leon to do her work. Westland remains a very sensitive spot for the government, and for the Prime Minister.

SUNDAY 9 NOVEMBER

In the *News of the World* Woodrow Wyatt claims that Aids could become 'the new black death.'[151] 'The start of Aids is homosexual love-making. Promiscuous women are vulnerable, making love to promiscuous bisexuals. They then pass Aids on to *normal men* (my italics). Labour councils give grants to homosexual centres. They encourage children to experiment with sex. This is murder.'

TUESDAY 11 NOVEMBER

The first meeting of the special Cabinet committee on Aids (HA). At the start, Willie makes it clear that he is giving no interviews on Aids, and that it is up to me to take the lead. Exceptionally, I would brief the press after this meeting. The first part of the meeting is spent in a sober discussion of the problem. Public education is seen as the first priority, but there is recognition that we will quickly have to decide on screening, research and drugs misuse. We go to my paper on public education. What is interesting is how opinion has changed. There is no longer a fear that we will offend the public. Now, the predominant view is that we must inform as directly and bluntly as possible. My proposals to step up the advertising in the press, to put up posters around the country and to mount a campaign aimed at young people are all endorsed. The next step will be radio and television. In his summing-up, Willie emphasises that the material should be hard-hitting and that there should be no inhibition on including explicit references to sexual practices where these were considered necessary. It was also agreed that I should get in touch

---

151   Woodrow Wyatt: The Voice of Reason, the *News of the World*, 9 November 1986, p. 8. Wyatt was a former Labour MP (1945–1970) who, in the late 1970s, became an admirer and confidant of Mrs Thatcher.

with the broadcasting organisations to see how they could help. The committee agreed to the idea of a leaflet drop to twenty-three million homes. In short, the committee give me everything I need.

The next step is to announce all this. The last thing I want at this stage is a full-scale press conference. Instead, I want an organised 'door-step': a minister caught just coming out of a meeting but able to get into his car when the questioning becomes more detailed than he wants. Romola Christopherson, my chief information officer, comes up with the idea of arranging it in Downing Street. It is given some drama, with TV lights amidst the evening gloom and the press gathered around. At the end of the kerb-side conference, one reporter asks me how people should conduct their sex lives. 'What would your advice be to the public?' I reply with the lines, 'stick to one partner, but if you can't, wear a condom; Don't use drugs, but if you do, don't inject'. It is, to put it mildly, strange advice for a politician to be giving on the doorstep of No. 10!

THURSDAY 13 NOVEMBER

A routine meeting of Cabinet and then on to see George Thomson, the chairman of the Independent Broadcasting Corporation, to seek his co-operation. This is forthcoming in minutes and he promises to do all in his power to help. He recognises the gravity of the position. From there to the House of Lords to see Willie Whitelaw. It is becoming clear just what an important ally Willie is. He is in the chair: his role is to get progress and that is what he will get. From my point of view, it means that at last decisions are being taken. We are way past the notices in public lavatories phase. We are also over the terminological hurdles of Quintin Hailsham. We are getting action, and action is what we need. The problem is unquestionably serious and if we act now, we can change behaviour and save lives.

FRIDAY 14 NOVEMBER

I have another successful meeting, this time with the BBC. Duke Hussey (Chairman) and Alasdair Milne (Director-General) are just as forthcoming as George Thomson was. They pledge their cooperation. Their attitude is very much 'how can we help?' Following the events of the week it is clearly sensible to have speech extracts for the Sunday papers. We labour over this at the Elephant and finally, I manage to get away to Sutton Coldfield at 4 o'clock. As soon as I step into my constituency role, the official support ends. I drive my own car away from the House of Commons and spend the next four and a half hours travelling to Sutton Coldfield. The traffic on the M1 could not be worse. Three lines of traffic on the newly opened M25 join three lines of traffic already on the M1. The result is chaos. I finally arrive two hours late for my meeting in Sutton Coldfield.

MONDAY 17 NOVEMBER

Work starts early to clear the wording of the Aids advertisement and the leaflet. The team is under some pressure. Donald Acheson is not present.[152] It is the funeral of his daughter; tragically killed in a car accident on the A1. Much of the burden is falling on his very able No. 2, Hilary Pickles, and we see now how short-staffed the team actually is. Sammy Harari is doing well on the advertising side, although there are some ads that Donald will want to see. He is particularly concerned about the message 'anyone can get Aids'. He has already pointed out that it is not a disease anyone can get in the sense of it being easily transmitted. It is still largely confined to a relatively small group made up of homosexuals and drug addicts, but it is also true that it can be spread by heterosexuals. In the evening I see Dick Marsh of the Newspaper Publishers' Association. He is much less forthcoming than the BBC and IBA. This is partly because the NPA do not speak with one voice. Marsh says that it is as much as they can do to agree the time of day. It is partially because Marsh is a natural trade union negotiator and he says that newspapers never give free advertising but his reaction is largely due to his underlying cynicism. He makes no secret of the fact that he regards newspapers with a distaste that borders on contempt and wants to be paid off by them with a golden handshake; every time he mentions this they put up his salary.

---

152 Donald was an invaluable help to me throughout the Aids crisis. He was a superb Chief Medical Officer from 1983–91.

The fact is that he cannot deliver anything, even if he wanted to. It is sad to see the ability that Dick Marsh undoubtedly has so underused.[153]

TUESDAY 18 NOVEMBER

A short meeting of the Aids committee but long enough to get them to agree to the leaflet and advertising campaign. And Sammy does a good presentation, including some very effective radio commercials.[154]

THURSDAY 20 NOVEMBER

We start with an 8.45 a.m. meeting of the Aids committee. For the first time we get down to the issues involved in screening. Mass screening is generally considered unacceptable and impractical. 'What do you do next?' asks George Younger. And that of course is the point. It is all very well testing the whole nation, but what do you do with the results? That is presupposing you can persuade the medical profession to carry out compulsory tests. Isolation for life is not practical even if it were remotely desirable.[155] It takes a deliberate act on the part of anyone to contract the virus; it is not spread through normal social contact. But there are issues of screening and testing which are less clear cut: overseas visitors, overseas students, recruits into the army, testing in prisons. We decide to give the discussion more time at our next meeting. Meanwhile, I must prepare for the first Commons debate on Aids tomorrow.

FRIDAY 21 NOVEMBER

The hours given to preparing the Aids speech are well spent. It goes well and appears to capture the mood of concern on both sides of the House. Both Michael Meacher and Archy Kirkwood for the Liberals make moderate responses and join in the broadly bipartisan approach

---

153 Richard Marsh was a former Labour MP and minister (1959–1971). He left Parliament to become Chairman of British Rail (1971–76). Later he became a Conservative supporter and later still, sat in the House of Lords as a crossbencher.

154 The excellent Paul Gambaccini was the main voice on radio and later, John Hurt did the voice-overs on the television advertisement.

155 A prominent opponent of my approach, Lord Monckton, proposed just that in the *American Spectator*.

I have suggested. I announce £20 million for public education. There is concern that there should be more resources for the health service for treatment and counselling, while David Crouch[156] makes a powerful plea for more money for research – which personally I think is our weakest ground. At midday, Tony Newton and I get away to a press conference and a presentation of our advertising campaign. The conference is over-flowing with cameramen and journalists. A journalist tells me that he thought it was very effective.

SATURDAY 22 NOVEMBER

There is massive coverage of the Aids campaign. In the main it seems fine, but there is some reaction. At a meeting of local Tories in Manchester, one questioner asks me if I wasn't simply encouraging safe promiscuity. Another woman said that she would burn any leaflet which came to her home to keep it away from her fifteen-year-old daughter. The audience was overwhelmingly on my side, but there will be other views put, particularly I fear, from my side of the House.

MONDAY 24 NOVEMBER

A meeting with Margaret Thatcher and the Health Policy Strategy Group (Nigel Lawson, Norman Tebbit, Roy Griffiths). I have put round a paper but it becomes clear that Margaret's mind is elsewhere. The meeting had been delayed because of the Peter Wright case in Australia. This appears to be going from bad to worse. Poor Robert Armstrong is not doing well and his bon mot about truth and its shades looks a certainty for any new book of quotations.[157] The opposition are beginning to press, and Margaret had an uncomfortable time in the House. It is the kind of issue which she does least well. She is a straightforward person. The world of the security service seems to require a public cunning which she doesn't

---

156 Conservative MP for Canterbury 1966–87.
157 The UK government tried to stop the publication of former MI5 member Peter Wright's memoir *Spycatcher*. The case was held in Australia and Robert Armstrong had to give evidence. He admitted in court that a letter he had written may have been 'economical with the truth'.

possess. The principle as she sees it is the unacceptability of an ex-secret service man revealing secrets which he has pledged to protect. We are fighting a battle over events which took place thirty or forty years ago. They have been trawled over continually ever since. In theory, Margaret is right, but the real question is whether it is worth the trouble.

FRIDAY 28 NOVEMBER

A very good meeting at the World Health Organization in Geneva. Their expert is an American called Jonathan Mann.[158] He gives a sober but frightening account of how he sees the Aids problem. He envisages that over the next five years, there will be up to three million deaths world-wide. Africa is most seriously affected, but the USA now faces a very serious problem. He endorses the plan on public education but raises other issues as well. One is sex tourism – people from the developed world going to the Third World (Africa, Asia) to find sexual partners (male or female). This kind of international prostitution is a certain way of spreading the disease. I get back to Heathrow in time to drive to Aylesbury to speak for Tim Raison. I am warned off not Aids but the rates system – the rates support grant settlement is hitting Buckinghamshire particularly hard.

WEDNESDAY 3 DECEMBER

The fifth meeting of the Aids committee. It is also the most difficult yet. The main issue is drugs. Should we give free needles to drug injectors so that they have clean needles rather than share them and spread the virus? My case is that shared needles is one of the chief ways in which the disease spreads – particularly among the heterosexual population. I see the difficulties – encouraging drug misuse etc. – but believe that provided such schemes are controlled then we should go ahead. I am not advocating free needles in every shop! Clean needles should be part of a series

---

158   Jonathan Mann, physician and advocate, was the first head of the WHO's Global Programme on Aids (1986–98). He was viewed as a pioneer in advocating a combination of public health, ethics and human rights. He died at the age of fifty-two in 1998, in the crash of Swissair Flight 111.

of measures aimed at reducing drug misuse. Douglas Hurd supports me but Malcolm Rifkind – who has the worst problem of all in Scotland – is very sceptical. Can we be sure it will do good? If it goes ahead it must be monitored. George Younger is totally opposed. He simply does not believe it can be right to recognise an illegal activity in this way. The other members of the committee are dubious. In situations like this the position of the chairman is vital. On the views expressed, Willie White-law would have been quite entitled to have ruled that the proposals were rejected. Instead, he asks me to work up proposals for pilot schemes. Willie is entirely invaluable.

MONDAY 8 AND TUESDAY 9 DECEMBER

In search of new ideas, I go to Berlin with its dividing wall and its eerie, floodlit no man's land between east and west. A gay-rights organisa-tion compliments me on our campaign (to the amazement of at least one British journalist here) and hopes that the German government will follow suit. My lasting impression, however, is of a consultant in charge of sexually transmitted diseases at the Rudolf Virchow Hospital. A gaunt man, he was obviously working under very considerable strain. He thought the position was already bad and was quite likely to become disastrous. He had lost twelve patients over the last two weeks – predom-inantly young men. In our emphasis on prevention we must never forget the compassion that is needed for those who are dying or the support that is needed for the staff working with Aids patients.

WEDNESDAY 10 DECEMBER

Today I see some of the action being taken in Amsterdam. They have a 'methadone bus', which goes direct to drug users and exchanges dirty needles for clean ones. It seems to work well here but that does not nec-essarily mean that it will work well in Edinburgh.

FRIDAY 12 DECEMBER

The chief constable of Manchester police, James Anderton, accuses homosexuals and drug addicts of 'swirling in a cesspit of their own making'. Apparently, he is a well-known Christian. Where, I wonder, does compassion come in his beliefs?[159]

SUNDAY 14 DECEMBER

Sir Alfred Sherman, who is a close supporter of the Prime Minister and another émigré from the left, writes to *The Times* saying that Aids was a problem of undesirable minorities: 'mainly sodomites and drug abusers together with numbers of women who voluntarily associate with the sexual underworld'.

TUESDAY 23 DECEMBER

Donald Acheson sends me an encouraging letter on the experience of the First World War: 'Does history repeat itself?' he asks. I thought that as we approach Christmas the Secretary of State might appreciate the following historical attempt to reduce the incidence of sexually transmittable disease. The British Expeditionary Force in France during World War I were distributed a leaflet advising sexual continence in the following terms:

'In this new experience you may find temptations both in wine and women. You must entirely resist both temptations, and while treating all women with perfect courtesy you should avoid any intimacy. Do your duty bravely, fear God, honour the King.'

Despite the message, 20 per cent of 5,000 troops on leave in Paris became infected in two months. The second approach was more successful. Men were issued prophylactic packs containing calomel ointment and treatment rooms were set up for soldiers to receive urethral irrigation within twenty-four hours of exposure. Subsequently, 300,000 troops visited Paris and only 3 per cent were infected.

---

159 *The Guardian*, 12 December 1986, 'Preacher Anderton thunders against the gays'. It was later revealed in declassified material that Margaret herself intervened to defend Anderton. In a message to the Home Secretary, she said it would be 'outrageous' if he was required to seek clearance for all his public-speaking engagements. Today (hopefully) he would be sacked.

TUESDAY 30 DECEMBER

TBWA, our advertising agency, showed us the advertisements they had created but the view was that they were too reminiscent of trailers for a horror film and to think again.[160] The Aids committee has approved our plan to have a ministerial broadcast but late in the afternoon the news comes through that the Prime Minister has vetoed the idea. She hasn't had a ministerial broadcast on any subject over the last seven years and does not intend to start now with Aids; she believes it would give an impression of panic and crisis. It is a great pity that we didn't know this before as we already have a crew lined up to produce it and I have approached Michael Meacher on the basis that this is not party political controversial. He has agreed that Labour don't want a right of reply.

WEDNESDAY 31 DECEMBER

My fear is that the story of the change will leak and the whole campaign will be dented on the basis that Margaret is distancing herself from it. I get Nigel Wicks to ring me. He is at his most bureaucratic and says that it is in the notes of procedure that the Prime Minister must be consulted before any official approach is made: the consent of a Cabinet committee is not enough. I growl at him that we are rather past that point now and that unless we are careful we will be embroiled in a public row on the cancellation. Wicks obviously feels 'and whose fault is that?' – but is tactful enough not to say so. More constructively, he suggests that the best approach to the PM is to point out that the ministerial broadcast is a public health message and not just a minister speaking straight to camera. I say the issue is urgent and I had better see her as soon as possible. The message comes back an hour later – come to No. 10 at 7 p.m.

---

160 Changes were made and what appeared on-screen was the now famous 'tombstone' advertisement. A drill carved out the word 'Aids' on a slab of rock: the sepulchral voice-over of John Hurt warning: 'There is now a danger that has become a threat to us all. It is a deadly disease and there is no known cure'. The advertisement ended with a bunch of white lilies on top of the gravestone and a picture of our leaflet. 'Read this leaflet when it arrives. If you ignore Aids it could be the death of you'. We followed this up with an advertisement showing the present problem as the tip of the iceberg: 'Unless we act now it's going to get much, much worse'. As these appeared on both TV channels, the agency ran campaigns for cinema and radio. The campaign was inevitably criticised by some as being over the top and altogether too Hollywood. My reply to that is that in all the comments that have been made to me over the following years, there is no doubt that it was the television advertisements which had the most impact and did the most to save lives.

It is a curious way to celebrate New Year's Eve but I go to No. 10 and up to her study where she offers me a whisky. She says that she is not doing anything in the evening – 'too much work to be done'. It becomes clear after one-minute flat that she will not change on the ministerial broadcast. She says that she has not had one on the Falklands, on the riots or on any other health issue. She thinks I will get quite enough publicity from news broadcasts and it is more effective. On some issues it is worth having an argument, but this is not one of them. There is no prospect of her changing her mind. I hate to admit it but we would have saved ourselves a lot of trouble had we discovered this before. This over, we then talk more widely. She was at her best – relaxed, intelligent, sympathetic. She has difficulties with her attitude to Aids. She recognises it as a profoundly serious health threat but another part of her would like to see us putting all our efforts into reducing waiting lists or giving further help in other disease areas. At one point, she says to me: 'you mustn't become known as just the minister for Aids'. Her (kind) point was that my party conference speech had gone exceptionally well and there were other frontiers in politics. True as this may be, I think I have a duty (if that doesn't sound too pompous) to inform the public of the dangers.[161] My fear would be that unless we do this, then in five years' time the judgement will be that the government 'didn't do enough'. I do not believe that can be said now but we must ensure that this remains the case.

At this point I thought that, as I had in other different areas of policy, I would see what the United States was doing. They had a much greater problem than us. It seemed to me that if any country had lessons to impart on how Aids should be tackled it was there. I was disappointed.

SUNDAY 18 JANUARY 1987

San Francisco has, by any standards, a major Aids crisis. The city – probably the most beautiful in the United States – became a centre for the

---

161   I fear that my diary interpretation of her words was too generous. She meant: 'Go and do something else'. Her aim was that by using charm and flattery she could move me on and away from Aids. I am unrepentant about my refusal to change direction.

gay population during the 1960s and '70s. The Consul General says 'they became respectable'. They were never accepted by everybody of course, and Aids has not only led to a backlash against them but confirmed the opposition of those who were always reluctant to accept them in the first place. Many of the health workers here compliment me as a minister taking a lead. This was seen as being in contrast to their own country. The Governor of California has pointedly not mentioned Aids in his state of the realm message and the mayor was similarly reticent. Nobody can remember President Reagan ever having said anything about Aids.

TUESDAY 20 JANUARY

Press and television interest hits a new high. It is not something we have sought. Indeed, my fear was that they would interrupt the briefing sessions. In fact, they have not intruded and if some of the messages we are receiving are transmitted back home then that would be very positive health education. The scale of the problem is coming through to the reporters and not all of them enjoy covering the subject. There is at least one writer who has asked his office not to put him on Aids again but without fail the press and television party are taking the visit seriously and are not attempting to score points.

Inevitably the highpoint for the media is my visit to San Francisco General Hospital – an early twentieth-century complex of red-brick buildings on what was once the edge of the city. I talk to the nurses who are working under stress but with enormous commitment. The nurse who has worked there longest – almost three years – is obviously going through something of a crisis herself. She has seen her patients die without being able to do anything to intervene. We will see what she does. My guess is that in spite of all the difficulties she will stay. On average, staff stay longer in the Aids unit than in other parts of the hospital. One of the patients has agreed to be televised. He is a young man in his thirties – the average age in San Francisco for Aids cases. He is remarkably cheerful and anxious to talk. He had been a shipping clerk but now there was no prospect of him working, although his employer was happy for him to come in for an hour or so a day. We talked for a few minutes. I was photographed shaking hands and I left to continue the tour. He was a brave man who would be dead in the next two or three months.

THURSDAY 22 JANUARY, WASHINGTON DC

We stay the night at the residence in Washington and Antony Acland, the British Ambassador to Washington, a rather aloof, withdrawn man, welcomes us. I do not get the impression that Aids is top of his list of interests and I suppose, inevitably, his mind is on American and particularly Washington politics. We have the biggest embassy of any in Washington, which always strikes me as showing an exaggerated view of our international importance. I suppose my real feeling is that the Foreign Office takes a rather superior view of Britain's domestic problems and regard themselves as a cut above everybody else in Whitehall – ministers included. Overnight, it has started snowing. The big Cadillac cannot make it down the drive to the residence and on the roads the traffic is slow-moving. We just about make it to Bethesda to talk research at the National Institute of Health. Our talks confirm a number of impressions. In particular, in spite of the unprecedented efforts being made to develop a vaccine and a cure, no one is optimistic about any immediate breakthrough. The other message is also clear: in Britain we may be doing a great deal on public education, but the Americans are devoting enormous resources to research. When we make our way back to downtown Washington, the road conditions are chaotic. Our driver tells us that government departments have been sent home because of the snow. However, we do manage to keep an appointment with Otis Bowen, the US Health Secretary. He is a doctor himself but is now over seventy. I had met him before, both in Washington and Geneva, and like him as a gentle and restrained man. What is clear however is that neither he nor the administration intend to take a lead on public education. 'That', says Bowen, 'is a matter for local decision'.

FRIDAY 23 JANUARY, NEW YORK

Washington airport is shut due to the snow so instead we take the Amtrak train up to New York. The problem in New York is drugs. The city health department paints a bleak picture of New York in 1987. They estimate that there are about 200,000 intravenous drug users. Some of them can be convinced not to share needles, but everybody believes that drug users are a more difficult group to influence than homosexuals. Many gays are well educated, middle class and certainly do not want to die from Aids. Some drug users are the same, but many are apathetic about their prospects. A third of HIV cases are drug addicts, but the numbers are increasing. Beneath the surface there are tales of pure tragedy. So far, 165 babies have been born with Aids: most have died within five years.

SATURDAY 24 JANUARY

We visit the Roman Catholic-run St Clare's Hospital. I speak to two women patients. One is twenty-three with a small baby; the other just over thirty with two children. They are both injecting drug users and they will both be dead in the next six months. Happily, the children are not infected, but what a waste. Both women are articulate and intelligent, eminently capable of being good mothers. In both cases, the children will be brought up by their grandparents.

SUNDAY 25 JANUARY

Back at Heathrow, Donald Acheson and I shake hands, although we will be seeing each other tomorrow. I think he realises that this trip has been both physically and emotionally gruelling for me.

MONDAY 26 JANUARY

Back to the department. A mountain of press cuttings on the American trip awaits me. The other ministers at the morning meeting tell me of the television coverage, which they say was both massive and good. I gather this feeling is not shared by either No. 10 or Central Office. A *Daily Mail* report says that Margaret Thatcher and Norman Tebbit are 'exasperated' by the education campaign. It is too late for them to intervene now. The campaign is launched and it cannot be reversed. Frankly, if they do not like it they can lump it.

MONDAY 9 FEBRUARY

An extraordinary meeting with the Chief Rabbi Sir Immanuel Jakobovits. His views on Aids are very similar to those of Margaret Thatcher. He hands me an aide memoire which, in passing, praises the 'urgency, boldness and effectiveness' of the campaign but then sets out in dramatic language a view held by many of the so-called 'moral majority'. Among his dozen objections to the advertising campaign, the Chief Rabbi says:

> Campaign breeds false sense of security, not to mention false values. In effect encourages promiscuity by advertising it. Introduces to many children and decent young people ideas of sex outside marriage entirely unknown to them.
>
> Tells people not what is right but how to do wrong and get away with it – like sending people into contaminated atmosphere but providing them with gas masks and protective clothing, or instructing thieves how to escape being caught.

The aide memoire ended: 'Say plainly: Aids consequence of marital infidelity, pre-marital adventures, sexual deviation, and social irresponsibility – putting pleasure before duty and discipline.'

It was stirring stuff but it went smack against all experience. We would lack credibility with the people we wanted to influence if we were thought to be preaching. Our internal research showed that among the people we needed to convince were gay men, who took an almost cavalier attitude to the disease, and drug users, who could be apathetic to their fate. Moreover, many heterosexuals regarded Aids as not relevant to them, in spite of the Chief Medical Officer's advice that the potential for its spread in the heterosexual community was real.

In January 1987, as the leaflets arrived in households throughout the country, our campaign became even more high profile. Posters were going up on billboards up and down the country, proclaiming 'Aids DON'T DIE OF IGNORANCE' and accompanied by the message: 'Gay or Straight. Male or Female. Anyone can get Aids from sexual intercourse. So the more partners, the greater the risk. Protect yourself. Use a condom'. To accompany the leaf-let-drop, we commissioned a television campaign.

COMMENT

The main decision for the government was how frank should a public health message be? My view (supported by the Chief Medical Officer, Donald Acheson) was that the message should not pull its punches. If we tried to dress it up it would be ineffective and invite ridicule. The trouble was that at the very top of the government the Prime Minister kept a semi-hostile distance to the campaign. She never saw it as a priority. Of course, her attitude had its effect on government, not least on the Treasury who resisted any pressure for an increase in resources. Looking back, I am frankly amazed at the progress we made.

So what was the result?

The independent British Market Research Bureau published a report in 1987 that found that knowledge of the causes of HIV and Aids had vastly increased, with follow-up research showing that 98 per cent of the public had become aware of how HIV is transmitted. It also showed that the vast major-ity of the country thought it was right to run such a campaign – in spite of fears that the material used was too explicit and would cause offence. Sum-ming-up, the authors concluded that 'the advertising campaign substantially achieved the objectives of educating the public and influencing the climate of opinion as a basis for behaviour modification'. They also disposed of one later criticism: 'No evidence has been found of a backlash against homosexuals as a result of the increased awareness and knowledge'.

I left the DHSS a few months later for the Department of Employment. The campaign had been an undoubted success with a significant fall in HIV transmission and other sexually transmitted infections like gonorrhoea. I sus-pect the new Secretary of State, John Moore, was under no pressure from the Prime Minister to proclaim the policy's success.

10

AFTER THE VICTORY

MARCH–DECEMBER 1987

Although successful, the 1987 election campaign was seriously divided, which in other times could have brought us to grief. Norman Tebbit, the Party Chairman (helped by Saatchi & Saatchi) was being second-guessed by a team put together by David Young, who was answering directly to Margaret Thatcher. The division came to a climax on 'wobbly Thursday' back at No. 10. According to Young's own account, he took Tebbit by the lapels and told him, 'We're about to lose this fucking election. You're going to go. I'm going to go. The whole thing is going to go'. In fact, opinion remained remarkably stable throughout the campaign. This did not prevent a massively expensive newspaper advertising campaign in the days immediately before the election, which had a minimal effect upon the outcome. The election was won first, on the government's overall record and the relative prosperity of the bulk (but by no means all) of the British public. Second, there was a mistrust of Labour; scepticism about their economic competency and of course a comparison with the new Labour leader, Neil Kinnock, who certainly did vastly better than Michael Foot but not well enough to cancel out Margaret Thatcher's authority; gained over eight years as Prime Minister.

WEDNESDAY 11 MARCH 1987

An amazing reversal for the Foreign Office in the battle for the office in Richmond Terrace. Following my outspoken minute after the 'decision' that the office should go to the ODA, Margaret Thatcher formed a committee on government accommodation. The result of the first meeting is that it has been decided that the DHSS should come in from the cold – that is in spite of the united opposition of the Cabinet Office, Robert Armstrong et al. Margaret gives robust views on the rich accommodation of the Foreign Office. She has been very good on this. My minute could have only reopened the issue with a sympathetic nod from the Prime Minister.

MONDAY 16 MARCH

Lunch with Ken Stowe. He has now left the DHSS to work with Robert Armstrong in the Cabinet Office until his retirement. Ken has been a tremendous prop. We have been through a number of serious wars together, the most testing, the perilous 1982 nurses' strike. The relationship between a Secretary of State and his Permanent Secretary is vital, particularly in a busy department. At the DHSS, we are the only two people who look over the whole department. Ken is a politician in his own right, no one knows his way around Whitehall better. I could always find out what Robert was thinking and usually the people at No. 11 as well. Ken had only to lift the phone and find out. I could not have had a better Permanent Secretary.

MONDAY 30 MARCH

Lunch with Max Hastings and his team at the *Daily Telegraph*. He's doing a good job at the *Telegraph*. After years of genteel decline, he has forced the paper into the 1980s. It is now a good read, but they have left their recovery perilously late. *The Times* and *Independent* are attracting new readers, and new young readers at that. I suspect the age profile of the *Telegraph* reader looks pretty grim. When we last met, he told me about his difficulty with Carol Thatcher. He had apparently become annoyed that she had written an article for another magazine without permission – and that was for the second time. He was also not a great admirer of Carol, so suggested that for everyone's sake paths should split. She refused and said that if he wanted to sack her, he should sack her and he would have to pay redundancy. Max says he was pretty horrified by the publicity all that would generate but said if she insisted then so be it. The parting did indeed receive publicity and in my view, the loser was Carol. According to Max, Carol was backed firmly by both Margaret and Denis Thatcher – and he now finds himself not the most popular man at No. 10.

THURSDAY 2 APRIL

Margaret reports to Cabinet on her trip to Moscow which has received rave reviews in the press. She talked for over thirty minutes without drawing breath and went through the whole visit. She is obviously delighted that Gorbachev made such very extensive preparations for the visit – including a special performance of the Bolshoi. The two leaders have obviously taken each other very seriously and had a series of combative meetings with each testing the other's views. Margaret has clearly done better than Reagan in this personal contest – if only she led the leading nation of the free West.

MONDAY 27 APRIL

A day of preparing for the election. Margaret wants six bullet points, three slogans and various special interest points like the number of hospitals going up in the West Midlands. Tony Newton is not available in the morning so we went on to social security with the ever-reliable John Major and Nick Lyell, who is developing very well although he takes a rather optimistic view of what the Treasury will add to our budget even in an election year. 'I would have thought that was half a billion pounds well spent,' he reacted to one proposal. There are two difficult areas. First is pensions. We will be outbid at the election on pensions by both Labour and the Alliance. The second major issue is the 'vote losers' from the social security reforms. Tony and I consistently argued for a cost-neutral reform; Margaret Thatcher and Nigel Lawson argued for substantial savings.

TUESDAY 28 APRIL

The issues in health are clearer. In spite of the public perception, the story is one of real progress, of record hospital building, record resources and a record number of patients treated. Labour's attack in their 'hidden manifesto' published today is that we are about to Americanise or privatise the National Health Service. It looks, and is, pretty silly stuff.

THURSDAY 30 APRIL

Tom King reports on the Northern Ireland situation which is going through one of its periodic crises of violence. There have been a number of terrorist incidents, including the murder of the Ulster judge, Maurice Gibson and his wife. Gibson, apparently quite openly, booked his holiday three months ago under his own name and using a travel agent. He also asked for special treatment on board the ferry, including a position which got him off the boat first. Unhappily, by all this he seems to have drawn attention to himself.

In the afternoon I go to Central Office to see Harvey Thomas,[162] our communications chief, for some television training. Some useful tips from Harvey and I even get the name of David Young's hairdresser. David Young is reckoned to have the best-cut head of hair in Cabinet. Nigel Lawson and I have both been given the hairdresser's name. 'What about Ken Clarke?' I think. The team are reasonably reassuring on my interview technique and advocate smiling even more often, so this will be the election in which I smile.

WEDNESDAY 6 MAY

To Geneva for the WHO's annual assembly. The real business is done in the corridors and lounges of the headquarters building which was once the headquarters of the League of Nations. The most interesting man I meet is the US Surgeon General, Everett Koop, whom I missed in

---

162   Harvey Thomas was a big man – 6ft 5in. tall and 18 stone with huge hands and size 17 shoes – and with a big personality. In the 1960s he worked for the American evangelist Billy Graham, organising all of his world tours and giant rallies. In 1978, he had walked into Central Office, offered his services and over the next decade he transformed the Tories' communications performance. He gave politicians media training and organised all of Margaret Thatcher's three winning general election campaigns, introducing big star-studded rallies with lots of American-style razzmatazz.

Washington. He is having an uphill fight in the United States on Aids. He is now the darling of the liberals and hated by the right: the exact opposite of how he started. He is in disputes with the White House and the Catholic education society and now has demonstrations against him when he attends meetings outside the capital. The great irony of all this is that his chosen field is medical ethics. He is not a man without moral beliefs, indeed he is a man with very strong moral beliefs. I am glad to say that his view and my view on how Aids should be tackled is identical. A good talk also with the Ugandan Minister of Health. He is one of the very few African ministers prepared to talk about Aids and admit that it is a problem.[163] Countries like Kenya still deny the problem. Why is it that children are being infected in Africa? One answer is simple: the lack of clean needles for inoculation. Children must be inoculated against measles but they are inoculated using needles that have been used many times before and are not sterilised. In the same way, blood used in transfusions is often infected. Thus, life-saving inoculations and transfusions can pass on Aids and give it to innocent children. How appalling this all is. We must be able to help.

THURSDAY 7 MAY

A swift Cabinet. Under European affairs, Michael Jopling (now Agriculture Minister) reports the outcome of the European fishing council. What a terrible job he must have. As far as I can judge he does it rather well. He says that sponges are now defined by the Commission as fish. Norman Tebbit grumbles that we have enough sponges in this country already.

Lunch with Ken Clarke at La Poule au Pot. It is very good to see him. I still regard him as the best man I have worked with in government. It is not long before the discussion gets on to what will happen after a victorious election. Who will be dropped and who will replace them? I say Ken must be favourite to succeed me at the DHSS, although he might be

---

163 Policy in Uganda changed radically over the following years and by 2023, practising homosexuals were being threatened with long imprisonment or even the death penalty.

regarded as part of the old gang. Ken obviously thinks that this is right. 'You and I have a lingering affection for the welfare state,' he says, 'that may not be required'.

FRIDAY 8 MAY

The local election results in the West Midlands have been the best of all. We have won five seats in Birmingham – although we have not done so well against the Alliance in Yardley and Hall Green, which bodes badly for the future. In Sutton Coldfield all our majorities have gone up. After an advice bureau, I go back to London to put my general election plans together (after the council results almost certain to be needed), leaving behind in Sutton a draft of my introductory leaflet. The difficult thing is finding new words. Each election tends to be 'vital', 'crucial' and the 'most important' since the last one.

MONDAY 11 MAY

At 9.30 I receive a summons that Cabinet is to be held at 11 o'clock. Press and television are out in force in Downing Street. Margaret speaks to the accompaniment of the Trooping the Colour rehearsal. She says that to end the uncertainty, she has decided that 11 June is the day and the dissolution will be next Monday. She will be going to the Palace at 12.30 and there will be an announcement at 2 o'clock. There will be a further Cabinet tomorrow at 9.30. Norman Tebbit gives a short description of how the press conferences will be organised. And then we are out into Downing Street again in front of all the cameramen. Everyone beams and it is quite clear that the election has been called. Frankly, it is a great relief. We all want to get it over.

TUESDAY 12 MAY

Cabinet. We go through the manifesto. The parts that take the time all belong to environment and Nick Ridley. Margaret Thatcher is obviously unimpressed but it goes deeper. I am not sure if we have it all worked out, particularly the number of losers from the new community charge. Health goes through without much comment and I have rewritten social security overnight. It is much better but not everyone has seen it and the Treasury are suspicious. Nigel Lawson tries to challenge the assumption that child benefit will continue to be paid 'tax free'. In the end, we agree that child benefit will be paid 'as now' but clearly there are going to be battles ahead.

WEDNESDAY 13 MAY

We win the battle on the social security 'losers'. John MacGregor and Nigel Lawson go down with a fight. Others would have supported them had Margaret shown much inclination for their arguments but she backs my election judgement, as does Norman Tebbit. In the end the social security review has turned out to be almost cost neutral. What a lot of trouble we would have been saved if we had agreed this at the beginning. Two years of battles could have been avoided.

TUESDAY 19 MAY

The campaign officially begins and the manifesto is launched at Conservative Central Office. Margaret believes that education and housing are the flagships of the manifesto. It means new policies. As far as my area is concerned, we have already reformed social security (although not implemented the changes) and new ideas in health are distrusted so are best discussed mid-term. In an election they can be dynamite. The manifesto is therefore designed to reassure. The point is picked up immediately at the press conference. Tony Bevins of *The Independent* asks why the government is so radical on education and housing and 'so wet' on health. Both the Prime Minister and I say that we are developing the health service and it is certainly not wet. Margaret is in good humour.

SUNDAY 24 MAY

The Sunday papers are full of the success of Labour's campaign. It is described as a well-packaged campaign. Kinnock has scored well, with good television appearances plus speeches to his own party. The substance is slight. 'We care', says Kinnock, 'the Tories don't'. But it is nevertheless an effective campaign. Health is proving to be – as we always knew – one of their major issues.

THURSDAY 28 MAY

The health press conference at Central Office. I had prepared a rather good map with lights of our hospital building programme and I take the press through it. Different coloured lights come on to indicate hospitals that have been completed, that are under construction or that are in the planning process. Then, surprise, surprise, there is spontaneous applause. The conference goes well and everyone is pleased.

TUESDAY 2 JUNE

I spend a few hours in Sutton Coldfield getting my campaign into shape. This includes organising the posters. We have a system in Sutton Coldfield that political posters can be hung on lamp posts, which is a gift for minority parties who may have no supporters but nevertheless a lot of lamp posts for their posters.

THURSDAY 4 JUNE ('WOBBLY THURSDAY')

Margaret is in a very tense mood at the 8.30 meeting. She says she needs to be on television more. She is shaking a lot of hands – too many – but she is not on television. One official is deputed to get her onto the David Frost show on Sunday morning. She tells Norman Tebbit that a message must go out to the entire party to talk about the country's economic strength. She also complains that she wants more young faces on television, like John Moore and Ken Clarke. She then turns to the press release, which is mine on social security. She tears into it. She pays me a half-compliment by saying that I could not have written it because it is so bad (she had previously taken the view that the DHSS part of the manifesto draft was the only well-written offering). Her view is clear: we are not getting the message over. We need more direct language; more of Maggie on TV; not ever more hands to shake.

Of course, the polls have changed and Labour are getting their act together in a way we have not. Norman Tebbit does his best to calm things down and says that it is better that she works out her frustrations on us in private. David Young acts as an anxious courtier ready to carry out her slightest command. Sadly however, she does not entirely succeed in working out her frustrations on us. She is like a greyhound who has been kept on the lead for too long. Her views come bubbling out. At the press conference she replies at enormous length. A question from Irish television receives a four-minute reply. More to the point however, is a question from Tony Bevins. He asks whether she can really be trusted with the NHS when she takes her own operations privately. Margaret launches a lengthy defence. The obvious response is a two-sentence one on the right to choose in a free society. No party wants to abolish private health. Instead, she gives a number of hostages including the thought that if she is really ill then she might at that stage go to the NHS.

FRIDAY 5 JUNE

Margaret Thatcher's performance at the press conference is not counted a success by the press or by the television viewers. She is regarded as coming over in an unsympathetic manner. Private health is still a very difficult, and sensitive, political issue. Many people, including Conservative voters, do not like the idea that you can 'jump the queue' by going private. The press conference has put health onto the front line of the campaign. It is just what we did not want.

SUNDAY 7 JUNE

In spite of our problems the opinion polls are all going our way. The remarkable thing is how little opinion has changed throughout the campaign. Labour has fought a good, professional (slightly disreputable) campaign but are not helped by their policies in areas like defence. Above all, their economic policies are not regarded as credible. The public fear is that if they were elected, we could return to the bad days of the 1970s. It is a version of the 1959 fear that Labour will threaten everyone's standard of living: the vast majority are in work, and perhaps for the first time, living in their own homes.

Health is quietening down but there is one problem. David Willetts has been rung at home by Nick Timmins of *The Independent*. Was it true, asked Timmins, that No. 10 and the Prime Minister had asked for an examination of the idea that the NHS should be turned into a commission? If it was turned into a commission would that not be a prelude to privatisation? David had sought to knock the story down but was not sure how well he had done. Nick True's view is that in the present sensitive position on health, this could be dynamite.

The truth of the story is rather complicated. It is not Margaret's view that the NHS should be made a commission: it is mine. I take the view that the NHS is not manageable in its present form with all lines coming into the DHSS. No one takes responsibility. If things do not go well, the centre can be blamed. I would like to see the NHS one stage removed from government with a chairman and a board responsible to the minister. There is no way that a service of over one million people can be run to maximum effect with the kind of organisation we have at present.

MONDAY 8 JUNE

The Independent runs its story. It is on page 2. Ironically, I have been saved by Victor Paige.[164] Victor obviously feels that a commission would be a good idea but does not expect there to be progress to that goal under '*this* secretary of state'. Victor's views plus David Willett's response have obviously done the trick. God bless Victor – he has managed to save a situation which could have been very difficult in the context of the 1987 election; the fact that he has got my views totally wrong is a separate issue.

Election day was Thursday 11 June. The Conservatives were returned to office with a majority of 102 MPs despite a revitalised Labour Party led by Neil Kinnock. I was home with an increased majority of 21,500. The final results were: Conservatives 376 seats, Labour 229, Liberal/SDP 22 and other parties 23 seats. The next step is the post-election reshuffle. After two major rows with the Prime Minister, my position was anything but certain.

SATURDAY 13 JUNE

The call comes in from No. 10 at 11 a.m. It is Nigel Wicks: Could I see the Prime Minister at 3.20 p.m. at No. 10? It doesn't give me much time

---

164 Victor became the first chairman of the NHS management board in January 1985 on a three-year contract. His appointment did not work out and he resigned in June 1986.

to get the whole family packed into the car and back to London. Nigel Wicks kindly guides me that 'it's all right' and if I can't make it the Prime Minister would doubtless speak to me on the phone. 'No,' I say, 'I will come down.' Having missed going into No. 10 in 1979, I have no intention of missing it again.

Fiona and I pack the children into the car, put our belongings together and make our way down the motorway to the accompaniment of a tape of 'Puff the Magic Dragon'. I pick up Ted at Hurlingham Road[165] and we get to No. 10 with a good ten minutes to spare. I go to the waiting room just off the hall outside the Cabinet room. To my surprise, there are already two others waiting – John Major and John Moore. I say to my surprise because when in 1981 I coincided with David Howell, who was taking over my job at transport, this was regarded as a breach of protocol – ministers were to be kept apart. But this is not to be all. Ken Clarke arrives next and he is followed by John MacGregor and finally, in comes Paul Channon. It is beginning to look like a doctor's waiting room. Paul mutters that he has already read in the press of his fate and that this is a 'ghastly' business. We collectively, and gently, point out that the sackings were this morning – John Biffen was one of the early visitors. We are the changes.

We have each been allocated five minutes. I have more experience of Cabinet shuffles than anyone else and put forward the theory – based on 1981 – that the man who goes in first gives his job to the man who comes next. John MacGregor is to hand over to John Major, but what I hadn't realised was that John Moore, and not Ken Clarke, was behind me. That is bad news because it means that Ken is not going to social services. Nor does John Moore think the prospect the best news he has ever heard. He protests that he is perfectly happy in transport, implying that the DHSS is not top of his promotion list.

Margaret is sitting in the study on the first floor of Downing Street. Nigel Wicks is the only other person there. We exchange some opening pleasantries. She says that I have done a 'superb' job at the DHSS and

---

165   Ted Johnson, my new government driver.

then says that she would like me to go to employment. This is a genuine surprise as I had believed, indeed I had been told by the man himself, that David Young was to stay there. But he is to move to DTI, with Ken Clarke in tow to be the Cabinet minister in the Commons. She has little to say about the job and we soon get on to other things. She says that John Biffen has gone as Leader of the House. She felt he was not active in promoting the government cause outside his job in the House. John Wakeham will become Leader of the House – 'we will have to teach him to speak.' She also adds that Norman Tebbit, 'my beloved Norman', has moved out of Cabinet and that will leave a big hole.

Downstairs, we compare notes. Cecil has indeed gone to energy – although he says it is not a department he is overwhelmingly interested in and which could disappear altogether after electricity privatisation. John Major is to become Chief Secretary. His primary concern is whether he can manage the brief. My view is that if he can manage social security he can certainly do the Chief Secretary job.

From Downing Street, we go in separate cars to the Palace. As I draw up in the inner court of the Palace, I see Peter Walker at the steps. He looks utterly dejected. My immediate assumption is that he is out. I open with a tentative 'How are you?' 'All right,' says Peter with the air of a man who has just been sacked. Others join us and it emerges that he is the new Secretary of State for Wales. He has obviously decided that he will take anything that is offered – and clearly did not relish a return to the back benches. It is difficult for him. He was promoted to Cabinet very young and has spent the last eight years falling slowly behind. He knows that Margaret will never give him any of the senior jobs like Home Secretary or even jobs like the ones I have had at the DHSS and transport but she cannot quite bring herself to sack him. She has a grudging respect for his political clout and does not want him roaming free with John Biffen on the back benches. But did she expect Peter to accept Wales? I rather doubt it.

We congregate in the waiting area outside the Queen's drawing room. It is a vast mansion of a room leading out onto a sweeping lawn. Most of us have been sworn in as privy counsellors before. We enter in order of seniority on the Privy Council, bow to the Queen and then take up a position to her right. John Major is sworn in for the first time as a privy counsellor as Chief Secretary. I am delighted with his promotion. I was not sure that his worth would be recognised so early but he was a first-class Minister of State and also a hardworking and reliable colleague during the election. I fear Tony Newton will feel a little peeved that he has not been promoted but it is his own fault.[166] After John is sworn in we go in turn to receive our seals of office from the Queen. The small red leather box would be rather impressive were it not for the plastic tag which simply says 'S of S employment'. We have all been invited back to Willie Whitelaw's mews cottage for a drink. Willie says he hopes that I am pleased with my move. He himself went to employment after his distinguished period of office in Northern Ireland.

MONDAY 15 JUNE

The first day at my new department.[167] I meet Michael Quinlan, my new Permanent Secretary, who has the reputation of being probably the brightest of permanent secretaries in Whitehall. Rumour also has it that he is not the most involved of permanent secretaries when it comes to the department's affairs. His heart really belongs to defence, where he made his reputation with a work setting out an ethical defence of nuclear weapons. As for my ministers, I am still in negotiation. At my request I have John Cope as my Minister of State but my parliamentary secretaries keep changing.[168] Lunching with John Moore at L'Amico when another call comes through from the Chief Whip, David Waddington. 'Would I take...' and he names a reasonably well-known backbencher. The answer is 'no.' I have nothing against him but I need someone a little stronger.

---

166 Tony refused to recognise his position as a national politician. During the election, he rang me to ask whether it was necessary for him to come to a morning press conference on health with the Prime Minister. He said that he had his agent and Chairman with him and they were concerned at the number of Liberal posters appearing. I was interested to see that his majority was 16,500. Nevertheless he was one of the best colleagues I served with in government.

167 The Department of Employment's building was everything that Alexander Fleming House was not. It was convenient to Westminster – 100 yards down Tothill Street which meant that you could make a diversion on foot if necessary – and it was a modern, spacious office in contrast to the tack of AFH.

168 John Cope – a government whip who joined me as Minister of State at the employment department. Invaluable.

Who do I suggest then? I suggest Virginia Bottomley. He says 'would Patrick Nicholls do'? I say 'yes' – although I don't know him well he is a lawyer, which will be useful for the industrial relations legislation lined up, and he is a good debater.

All these negotiations are going on in a public restaurant but fortunately, the only other politicians there are Roy Jenkins and Bill Rodgers who have problems of their own, both having lost their seats in the general election. My lunch with John Moore is inevitably disjointed but I try to give my frank assessment of the problems facing his department. John reminds me of an American businessman. There is a determination to keep to the point he wants to know. There are no jokes and absolutely no gossip.

TUESDAY 16 JUNE

Fascinating lunch with David Young. He marks my card on the Department of Employment and tells me whom he relied on and what his plans were. He reveals that he was asked by Margaret to go to the DHSS but after a sleepless night saw her on Friday morning and refused. Up to now all the publicity has been on the basis that John Moore has been specially selected for this crucial task of rebuilding our image. I assume that the rest of the plot would have been for John Moore to go to the DTI, which he would have preferred, and Ken Clarke to go with David Young to the DHSS. Fascinating. The trouble is that Margaret wants to have it both ways. She wants a more caring image and she wants further reductions in spending; particularly on social security. David Young sees the dilemma and wisely avoids the area; it is not in any event the kind of area in which he is likely to be good and he is sensible enough to realise that. There has not exactly been a rush for my old job. Most politicians appear to regard it as an undoubted bed of nails with no obvious upside.

THURSDAY 25 JUNE

I have my first meeting with the TUC. They all turn up to talk about industrial relations law – Norman Willis, Rodney Bickerstaffe (who gives me a friendly wink), Fred Jarvis. We have most difficulty on the proposal in the green paper that even when a vote goes for a strike the individual member should have the right to ignore it and work.[169] My position is that it is a pledge in the manifesto and defend it. By the end of the meeting, I am rather more convinced by the case than I was at the beginning.

TUESDAY 30 JUNE

My first debate on employment. This comes on a curious amendment put down by the opposition to the Queen's Speech entitled 'inequality of opportunity'. Douglas Hurd leads and makes a speech which is pretty tedious. He gives the impression that he has picked up a departmental script and not done very much, if any, work on it. He is a kind and rather gentle man, shy in personal dealings, and I suspect that he does not much like the public appearance side of politics. Looking back, it is extraordinary that Leon should have been moved to make way for him. Douglas is no fool but not in Leon's class. Above all, he does not have Leon's stamina and sheer application. Leon would not have made a 'lazy' speech of the kind Douglas gives. These Queen's Speech debates without a vote at the end are fairly calm affairs and this one is no exception. The main interest centres on John Biffen, who makes his first speech from the back benches. The speech is elegant and short – a quality much admired by colleagues waiting to make their own speeches. On the other side, Ken Livingstone sits there for a couple of hours and does not get called. John Prescott closes for the opposition. He is better than I expect. He is a difficult man to warm to as all too often he behaves like a political thug and has no sense of humour that I have ever been able to discern. Nevertheless, he is sincere and not to be discounted.

WEDNESDAY I JULY

I am now a member of the National Economic Development Council (NEDC) – a tripartite council where in theory, the government, the employers and the unions sit down to thrash out things with the common aim of improving economic and industrial performance. Having

---

169   *Trade Unions and their Members*, February 1987 – Cm 95.

endured five years of these meetings, Nigel Lawson is in no doubt about what should be done: the council should be abolished. Margaret won't let him do that so he has come up with a different solution. In future, meetings will be quarterly not monthly and he, the Chancellor, will only take the chair in the post-Budget session. The rest of us – myself, David Young and either Cecil Parkinson or Nick Ridley – will chair the other meetings. Being Nigel, he starts the meeting with the announcement that the government has 'decided' to reduce the number of meetings. As he reads on through his script the TUC representatives get more and more restless. Norman Willis intervenes to say that the announcement is 'outrageous' but he is persuaded to let the Chancellor finish. Norman then protests vigorously that it is tantamount to telling the TUC to 'get stuffed'. He says the TUC is entitled to be consulted before decisions of this kind are made. However, he begins to bluster and the more he blusters, the more he rambles and the more inarticulate he becomes. Bickerstaffe comes next. He asks (quite reasonably), 'is this the way that things should be done?' But then he veers off into a general denunciation of the government's non-caring ways. Next comes Edmonds, who says that the way it has been done is 'bloody insulting'. The TUC has, in effect, been told to like it or lump it; this is not a sensible way of handling affairs but in spite of all the protests the union men stay in their seats. The crisis is past and we go onto the day's agenda. The unions are put out, seriously put out, but they are reluctant to turn their backs on the system. They recognise their weakness. They have nowhere else to go. For now, Nigel's blunt frontal attack has been successful. As we leave, Cecil Parkinson says to me: 'Nigel gets away with murder.' He does.

SUNDAY 5 JULY

Sunday starts with a charity walk in Sutton Park. I do the first three miles and then hurry off to Oxfordshire for a cricket match – the Department of Employment versus the Labour correspondents. It is an idyllic setting. The ground is near a small village called Steeple Aston. The countryside is unspoiled and, I imagine, unchanged this century. I have not played cricket for twenty-five years but the technique comes back. I even take a wicket and would have taken a second with the next ball had one of my civil servants held a catch on the boundary. There is much hilarity at this and the poor chap is promised an interesting new career in our regional office in Sheffield.

MONDAY 6 JULY

In the evening Fiona and I have the employment ministers and wives for dinner. A pleasant evening and John Lee says it is the first time in four secretaries of state that he has served with, that this has happened to him.

THURSDAY 16 JULY

Cabinet photo of the new team. I find myself sitting down in the front row and not even outside right. I must be getting senior. Indeed, there are not many survivors from the 1979 Cabinet. We settle our attitude on MPs' pay, which is to give what is required but to do a little face saving with ministers' pay. We talk about Europe for a few minutes and Lord Cockfield's latest plans on VAT. Margaret, who brought Cockfield into the Cabinet and sent him to Europe, is obviously not best pleased but she observes 'at least he's there, not here'. Hilarity all round. Margaret rarely cracks jokes and Cockfield, with what Quintin Hailsham once called his undertaker's manner, is not the most popular of former colleagues.

TUESDAY 21 JULY

Education committee at No. 10. I will not attempt to describe the detail of it but the flavour is this. Margaret Thatcher knows exactly what she wants and deeply distrusts the Department of Education. When Ken Baker appears to be putting forward a departmental view, she cries out 'No, Ken, No'. Ken takes quite a hammering but as Margaret concedes always comes up smiling. The department is doing a lot of work quickly and this she recognises. At the end of the meeting she applauds Ken, rather like a teacher might a small pupil with a verbal pat on the head. It is a curious atmosphere in which to work. Margaret is tired and Ken does his best to handle her – which he broadly succeeds in doing. But the committee is a dialogue between Margaret and Ken with one or other of us coming in from time to time. In the afternoon, my first employment questions. Unbelievably, Michael Meacher has followed me over to employment, having done surprisingly well in the shadow Cabinet elections. I welcome him as my 'eternal shadow' and the questions go off without incident.

THURSDAY 23 JULY

Cabinet and public spending. It is a sign of how things have changed. There are no battles, no arguments. On the surface, everyone accepts that public spending will have to be restrained and there are 'tough decisions ahead'. As we leave John Major comes up. He tells me that John Moore is proposing the abolition of the social fund on the advice of the department.[170] John Major is furious. Apparently, the letter is worded in such a way that it raises questions about the political sense of moving in that direction and he sees it as a direct attack on his stewardship as Minister of State for Social Security. I say he shouldn't worry about that: it is much more likely that I will be blamed.

TUESDAY 28 JULY

I lunch with Michael Heseltine. His judgement on the leadership election has changed. He now thinks that Margaret Thatcher may go on for a full term. At the end of lunch Michael asks in a very tentative way whether I would support him. My answer to that is 'yes'. I will not conspire to bring down Margaret Thatcher. I think she is our best leader by quite a long way, but if things change and if there is a vacancy, I would support him. My only other candidate would be Ken Clarke but I doubt whether he could be a candidate in the short term.

AUGUST, SEAVIEW

My initial thoughts on my new department. The priorities are to reduce unemployment and to improve training – not just for young people but

---

170 Moore's proposal was rejected in Cabinet committee.

through life. The days are over when a person left school, took up a trade and stayed in the same trade and firm for the whole of their career. Unemployment is now down below three million but a number of issues need to be investigated further: the extent of real unemployment, the black economy, regional differences and other special factors such as housing, ethnicity and its relationship to social security. Long-term unemployment is the greatest challenge and a crucial key to future success is better training. The 20 per cent long-term unemployed are the target group.

WEDNESDAY 2 SEPTEMBER

Dinner with Leon and Diana. The BBC ran an immediate post-election story that he was coming back into government. It was not to be. Margaret does not want to know about Westland. It was the issue which almost brought her down. She was egging on Leon to fight back against Michael Heseltine's campaign. Margaret may not have known of the individual moves but she was as clear as crystal about the strategy. Margaret is not going to run the risk of the issue being raked up again. It is all deeply unsatisfactory for a man of Leon's abilities. Nevertheless, he is making a good fist of it and with Diana's encouragement his spirits are good.

MONDAY 7 SEPTEMBER

A two-hour public expenditure bilateral with John Major at the Treasury. This is the politest bilateral I have ever taken part in. I had big rows with Leon and Peter Rees and battles with John MacGregor. But John Major and I have worked together for the past three years, we have fought a number of battles together and I rate John highly. For our meeting we do no more than test each other's position.

WEDNESDAY 9 SEPTEMBER

Moving day for my mother. She has lived at 30 First Avenue, Chelmsford for over half a century. She lived through the war with a Morrison shelter in the dining room for when German bombs brought down the ceilings.

As the crow flies the house is only about ¾ mile from the Hoffman ball bearing company while Marconi's main factory was only a few hundred yards along the road. This was very convenient for my father who walked to work at Hoffmans (where he eventually became Sales Director) and indeed, walked back for lunch. But both Hoffmans and Marconi were favourite German targets. During the war, my mother went back to teaching at the local Kings Road infant school where I began my education. She had been trained as a teacher but with the heavy unemployment of the 1930s, married women were excluded from employment, a way of keeping the unemployment figures down. Since my father's death she has been living in the house alone. Although not a massive house, its large garden was too much for a lady in her mid-eighties.

TUESDAY 29 SEPTEMBER

I open a conference on tourism and am presented with a whole sheep as a reward. That sounds good. The bad news is that it is given to me by a hotel situated near Sellafield to demonstrate that the public have nothing to fear from the food there. Apparently, the proximity of Sellafield is a deterrent to some tourists. Ted is packed off to the Army and Navy store to get the sheep cut up and we prepare for a month of eating non-ticking Sellafield lamb.

FRIDAY 9 OCTOBER

Another war between Norman Tebbit and David Young is in progress. Norman is briefing heavily against David's attempt to be chairman of the party and head of the DTI. Apparently, the reports go that that line is being backed by Willie Whitelaw and John Wakeham – and I see, to my mild astonishment, myself. I am supposedly part of a 'gang of senior ministers' determined to stop David Young's bid to do both jobs. It is news to me and as far as I am concerned, David can attempt whatever he wishes. Why he should want to be chairman in the immediate aftermath of a victorious election when the only way you can go is down is another matter.[171]

---

171   I should have remembered this in 1992.

MONDAY 12 OCTOBER

Robert Armstrong came to see me just before the party conference to say that there were a number of important changes to settle resulting from his retirement at the end of the year. Robin Butler will succeed him and Clive Whitmore will move over to the Home Office. That leaves defence and Michael Quinlan is the obvious man for that. We both agree that it will make Michael Quinlan's year if not his decade. His heart is in defence. He has done employment loyally but it is not his natural area. Who then will replace him? Michael himself gives me a number of names and I choose Geoffrey Holland without hesitation.[172] He is an enthusiast, and employment and training are precisely what he wants to do.

THURSDAY 15 OCTOBER

Dinner at home with a number of pals including Nick Edwards, who today has been gazetted as a peer with a Welsh title (Lord Crickhowell) which will take me some time to remember. Some of the discussion is about David Young. Geoffrey Smith and Nick are united that he should not be allowed to do both jobs. As everyone leaves there appears to be a small gale blowing outside.

FRIDAY 16 OCTOBER

It is only when we wake up that the full scale of what has happened becomes clear. The radio reports trees are down and roads are blocked throughout southern England. Outside in Hurlingham Road a beautiful beech tree has fallen onto the road, blocking it entirely and crushing a builder's van underneath. I am supposed to be in Lichfield opening an office building but all the advice is to stay at home. Ted and I set out at about 10 o'clock but progress is painfully slow. The winds have calmed down but fallen trees are causing enormous traffic jams. It takes two hours to get as far as Heathrow and I eventually arrive in Sutton Coldfield well after the proposed opening ceremony. In the Midlands

---

172   He was the second Permanent Secretary in the department and now took over from Michael Quinlan. After retirement, he became Vice Chancellor of the University of Exeter.

there is no damage but London has suffered an environmental blitz. To lose all those magnificent trees is a disaster.

MONDAY 19 OCTOBER

After eight years in government, I have finally been selected to sit on the Star Chamber and listen to all the special pleading on public spending. No one has had better preparation for it, having consistently appeared in the dock for most of those eight years. It is a great example of poacher turning gamekeeper but there is one ironic snag: we may not have any prisoners to interrogate. According to Willie Whitelaw (once again the chairman) there are signs that everyone will settle with the possible exception of the Foreign Secretary who is concerned about overseas aid.

WEDNESDAY 18 NOVEMBER

I make a statement on a new training programme for the long-term unemployed.[173] It is met with unremitting hostility from the Labour side.

THURSDAY 19 NOVEMBER

Cabinet. Paul Channon reports on the terrible fire at King's Cross in which nineteen people have died. Paul is to set up an inquiry and make a statement in the afternoon. As always, the emergency services acted with great speed and effectiveness. Another piece of bad news is that John Moore has gone down with some illness, thought to be pneumonia. Needless to say, the press is critical on the grounds that he is staying in a private hospital.

SATURDAY 21–TUESDAY 24 NOVEMBER

To Sweden to study their employment measures. Two points about their experience are striking. First, they spend a lot of money on training and unemployment measures and second, they stand no nonsense about people refusing to take training. They do not call it compulsion, even less workfare, but they insist that the general feeling among the public is

---

173 The new programme would offer up to twelve months training for anyone who had been out of work for more than six months.

that people should train rather than sit at home. Another contrast is that young people regard the service industries like tourism, working in restaurants and hospitality, as desirable and glamorous jobs – and working assembling Volvos as dirty and not in the same league. How different to the UK, where we still have this sterile debate about whether tourism is a 'real' job or not.

THURSDAY 26 NOVEMBER

I report to Cabinet on industrial action being taken by some of my job centre and unemployment benefit office staff against YTS (Youth Training Scheme). It is appalling that action against youth training should be taken by the department responsible for it. Margaret Thatcher shares my anger and agrees with me that we should expand and not diminish YTS. I get a remit from Cabinet to do just this. Tom King reported on the Prime Minister's visit to Enniskillen, which was Margaret at her best. Standing symbolically defiant in driving rain in precisely the place where a terrorist bomb had killed so many at the Remembrance Parade a few weeks earlier. [174]

TUESDAY 1 DECEMBER

I spend the morning at the Employment Bill Committee.[175] The bill is controversial for only one point – clause 3, which gives union members the right to work in spite of a strike ballot and not be disciplined by their union. Christened the 'scabs charter' by the unions, it has aroused much opposition including, regrettably, from our own Conservative trade unionists. I sum up on the clause and we get it through without any votes against or abstentions on our side. The opposition looks at it entirely through the eyes of the unions. They don't give much for the rights

---

174 A Provisional IRA bomb exploded near the war memorial in Enniskillen during a Remembrance Sunday ceremony on 8 November 1987. Twelve were killed and sixty-eight injured.

175 The employment bill of 1987 gave new rights to trade union members concerning secret ballots, the right of a union member not to be disciplined by his union because he chose to work rather than take industrial action, postal votes and ended any legal protection of the closed shop. Part II dealt with training of the employed and unemployed. The Manpower Services Commission was renamed the Training Commission.

of the individual. Michael Meacher's case is that if the union member doesn't like it, he should leave the union. 'And what pray happens if closed shops still exist?' we ask. 'You are getting rid of closed shops', replies Meacher triumphantly. 'And you accept that?' we ask. 'And you assure us you will not bring them back if you are in government?' Silence from Michael. Provoked, he says we are debating Conservative plans not Labour's.

CHRISTMAS RECESS

There will be problems over the next few months and they will not be made easier by Willie Whitelaw's absence and possible retirement.[176] Among the issues which could blow up, the poll tax is the most serious. It has few friends. Looking back at Michael Howard's speech in the House, it is clear that there was no great enthusiasm on our side. Most of the party seem to be distancing themselves from the bill – polite interest but falling some way short of outright support. The matter is not helped by the fact that half the Cabinet have their reservations. Peter Walker (who was cruelly given the job of opening the debate on the second day) is totally opposed and in private you would not find much support from Nigel, Ken Baker or Geoffrey Howe. It is very much Margaret's own tax and this, of course, is the danger. She will be left in an exposed position if things in our own party should turn nasty.

---

176 Willie had a stroke during a carol concert at St Margaret's on 15 December. By chance, I was walking past and saw a stretcher being carried out of the church but had no idea who it was.

II

A RICH MAN'S BUDGET

JANUARY–DECEMBER 1988

WEDNESDAY 6 JANUARY 1988

The news programmes are all dominated by David Mellor's comments on Israel's strategy in the occupied territories and particularly in Gaza. He ticks off an officious Israeli colonel and condemns the conditions in the camp. David courts media coverage assiduously – and successfully. As it happens, I agree with him. Ever since standing on the banks of the Jordan in 1967 and seeing Israeli soldiers ushering Palestinians out and on one occasion, firing over their heads, I have had a rather sceptical view of Israeli policy in the occupied territories. In 1967 a Conservative politician would have been howled down for uttering the kind of views aired by David. The British saw it all in black and white then. I doubt if they do so today.

SUNDAY 10 JANUARY

The Sunday papers are full of the future of Willie Whitelaw. Predictions are that he will step down. Confirmation of this comes during the afternoon. This is very bad news. I can hardly conceive of the government without him. He has been very much the sheet anchor, a figure to whom not only Margaret but everyone else could turn. He is a consummate politician. He dominates any committee meeting or table in the smoking room. He could also inspire great loyalty, as in Northern Ireland where I first saw him in the early 1970s. A lovely man.

TUESDAY 12 JANUARY

A meeting at No. 10 on the dock work regulation scheme.[177] Paul Channon is proposing abolition but wrapped up in a big ports bill preceded by a white paper in April. We can't legislate until December or January at the earliest. I argue against this approach on the grounds that it simply gives the TGWU the maximum time to prepare. Margaret agrees. If we are to act then it should be by a short abolition bill. Officially, we have not yet decided on abolition and Nigel Lawson for one is anything but convinced we will ever act. One result of our new tactics is that I, not Paul Channon, will be responsible for the bill. The scheme, although not ports policy, is my responsibility.

MONDAY 18 JANUARY

John Moore says to me that Margaret thinks it would be a good idea if Ken Clarke and I were to be on the front bench for his speech to show the 'continuity' of policy. Continuity or not, he needs support. He has been the victim of a harsh press campaign. I do not know who is leading it but someone has put the knife in very deeply.

TUESDAY 19 JANUARY

Lunch with Charles Reiss of the *Evening Standard* and Philip Webster of *The Times* at Poule au Pot. They confirm the anti-Moore story. They do not name the minister responsible but give the impression that it was someone who did not like the post-election build-up of Moore. As promised, I sit on the bench for John Moore's speech. The debate is opened by Robin Cook[178] who is cogent and makes the kind of speech that Michael Meacher should have done. John appears to have lost his

---

177 The dock labour scheme dated back to the 1940s. Under the Attlee government's post-war legislation, every major port was included and it became an offence to employ anyone other than a registered dockworker. Following the 1972 national dock strike, the position became even worse. Port employers were required to retain any registered dockworker on basic pay even if there was no work. The only way to avoid this was to buy out the docker's rights. There were some non-scheme ports, such as Felixstowe, which had been too small to be registered but were now prospering and doing well. Inside the Conservative Party the abolition of the scheme was a long-advocated reform – although the Prime Minister feared it a would lead to a national dock strike.

178 Frontbench spokesman on health, later Foreign Secretary under Tony Blair. Exceptional debater.

voice and rather croaks. He only gets passionate when defending his own use of private health facilities. The speech is not a disaster but is not very inspiring. It will do but he needs to get a grip on the health service.

TUESDAY 26 JANUARY
A special dinner at the Carlton to mark Margaret Thatcher's record period of service as Prime Minister. The whole Cabinet is there, plus Willie Whitelaw, Peter Brooke and Robin Butler. Frankly, it is a rather disappointing occasion. It lacks warmth, not so much from the ministers but from Margaret herself. Here she is surrounded by her Cabinet, some of whom have been with her since 1975, let alone 1979, and she fails to give anything but a reasonable constituency speech, the kind of speech I might give at my annual dinner thanking the officers. Her main point was that there was no question of the government running out of steam. There were exciting new policies to implement. Above all, there was 'still more to do'. It was more like a pep talk to a board of managers. Of course, this is how Margaret Thatcher regards her Cabinet. They are hired to do particular jobs. A disappointing evening.

TUESDAY 2 FEBRUARY
Michael Meacher wishes me a happy birthday during employment questions and hopes I may take early retirement. I say I have only just begun. After questions I go home to pick up Fiona and the children. Nigel and Thérèse have leant us their drawing room at No. 11 to hold my fiftieth birthday party and the planning has taken considerable time and effort. All the guests need to bring their invitations to get through the security barrier and we have already presented a list of names so that they can be checked off. There is no question of people simply turning up on the doorstep in Downing Street these days. We get there half an hour beforehand to check the arrangements. Kate and Isobel in their party best join up with Emily Lawson and race together through the rooms of No. 11. Violet[179] has come to take charge of distributing the eats, and the

---

179 Violet Lynch, the Donalds' housekeeper for forty years.

drinks are in the hands of Nigel's staff. We bring together a mixture from politics, Cambridge and Fleet Street. Margaret comes, bringing a bottle from the Prime Minister's Reserve. She stays for almost an hour and I bring up a whole range of people to talk with her, like Tim Hart, Mark Weinberg and Gayle Hunnicutt. She relaxes and is (as usual) very good, none of those awkward pauses that characterised any social occasion when Ted Heath was on parade. Across the room are Michael Heseltine and Anne, and Leon Brittan and Diana. I don't think much conversation takes place between them. Everyone appears to enjoy themselves, feeling like it is a family occasion. None more so than my pals from Trinity Hall – Michael Roberts, Alan Howard, David Tetther and Simon Colllier, who leave last.

THURSDAY 4 FEBRUARY

Question Time is coming from Kirkby near Liverpool and it is immediately clear that it is not like any programme I have ever done before. Police are on the gates and the Special Branch take me in. It soon becomes apparent that the audience itself is predominantly and violently anti-government. There is a good sprinkling of Militant Tendency and Ann Clwyd is obviously regarded as a dangerous revisionist.[180] Derek Worlock, the Catholic bishop of Liverpool, plays along with the mood of the audience. Simon Hughes has unaccountably missed both plane and train, and therefore we are down to only three panellists. At one point, Robin Day asks the audience if there are 'any' Conservative supporters there. One or two hands sheepishly go up.

TUESDAY 9 FEBRUARY

The House vote on televising Parliament. I have supported this for many years. I think it is ludicrous that the major news media should be excluded from Parliament. Margaret has let it be very clearly known that this time she will be voting against. Having once toyed with the idea she is now very firmly against, mainly, I think, on the grounds that it will make

---

180 Respected Labour MP for Cynon Valley 1984–2019.

personal and libellous attacks more common. On going into the ayes lobby it is immediately clear that quite a number of the Cabinet are not following her advice. In the event we win by a mile. The Chamber will not be the same when television enters but that may not be a bad thing. The action could move back there. Debates could be well attended.

TUESDAY 16 FEBRUARY

The statement on the employment white paper goes well enough.[181] It is welcomed on our side almost without reserve, and the response from the opposition is muted. Of course the timing of a white paper advocating more and improved training for the unemployed could hardly be better. It is ridiculous that so many people are still unemployed. What prevents some from getting jobs is a lack of skills. This is the predominant complaint from employers.

THURSDAY 18 FEBRUARY

Cabinet. Margaret reports on the meeting of the NATO council. She had sought to persuade all the NATO countries that the alliance forces must be kept up to date with modern weapons, including nuclear weapons. There was a tendency in some countries, she says, to believe that the advent of Gorbachev in Moscow marked the end of the Soviet threat. We needed to recognise that Russia was continuing to modernise and upgrade its weaponry. She was scathing about the attitudes of some of the allies, including Genscher in West Germany, who practised 'followship not leadership'.[182] Lunch with Simon Jenkins at the Garrick. He believes that the poll tax is the biggest mistake we have made and that it will come back to haunt us.

---

181 I had promised a white paper following my statement on training last November. Existing programmes for the adult unemployed were to be combined into a single, unified training programme called Employment Training (ET). When fully operational, the programme would provide training for some 600,000 people a year. The Training Commission would oversee it. *Training for Employment*, white paper, 16 February 1988 – Cm 316.

182 Hans-Dietrich Genscher was Federal Minister for Foreign Affairs and Vice Chancellor of Germany from 1974–1992.

THURSDAY 25 FEBRUARY

Such are the wonders of modern travel that I am able to leave Cabinet at 11.30 a.m., travel to Heathrow to catch the 1 p.m. Concorde, and arrive in the United States for a full afternoon's work in Baltimore, followed by dinner at the Washington embassy. The aim of the trip is to take a brief look at some of the training ideas being pursued in the United States. The press is anxious for me to visit workfare schemes. They long to see the unemployed being compelled to work for their benefit and even more, to write pieces that I want to introduce the same in the United Kingdom. I, just as determinedly, want to prevent such stories. We certainly need to chase the people who refuse everything – jobs or training – but that does not mean publicly organised work schemes.

SATURDAY 27–SUNDAY 28 FEBRUARY

I fly to Los Angeles for the next part of the visit. We stay aboard the *Queen Mary*, now anchored permanently at Long Beach and used as a hotel. The enormous liner looms out of the darkness and is an impressive sight – on board it is less so. It is comfortable enough but there is a feeling of dowdiness. The old liner has not been kept in the immaculate condition that it once was. The best parts of it are the vast deck and the old pictures that remind one of its past, including a photo of the *Queen Mary* coming into New York with 12,000 returning United States servicemen in 1946. We are here to run an inward investment conference for American businessmen. We want them to invest in the United Kingdom, and preferably in areas like Scotland and the north east. Our bait for the meeting is that the conference is being held aboard the *Royal Yacht Britannia*, here in Los Angeles for the visit of the Duke and Duchess of York, and everybody (wives included) is offered a tour of *Britannia*.

MONDAY 29 FEBRUARY

We are on parade on *Britannia* just before 9 o'clock. The guests arrive up the gangplank fifteen minutes later. Coffee is served and Prince Andrew welcomes everyone. We then get down to work. I speak, followed by the ambassador, and there is an open session of questions. Many of the people on the yacht already have businesses in the United Kingdom and they have seen the change in the country. They see it as in their interests to invest. But it is not just the United Kingdom; it is also Margaret Thatcher. She has an unrivalled reputation. Britain and Thatcher are seen as synonymous in many American eyes. Lunch is served, with one of the *Britannia*'s naval officers taking the head of each table, and the day is rounded off with the tour of the yacht, which has just undergone an expensive refit. It is quite an operation, with something like 280 crew and comfortable, but not opulent, quarters and rooms. Of course the expense of *Britannia* is criticised, but to my mind it is part of having a royal family. What is significant is the way that it is now being used to support the national interest. We have some top men for the seminar – Ford, Pfizer, and many more – it cannot have harmed us to have *Britannia* as the venue. Philip Greening, the Master of the Household, asks that if I think this is a good use of the yacht, would I write to the Queen? He says, 'we tell her but it is better if it comes from someone like you.'

In the evening, we go down town to a reception for the Yorks in Los Angeles. There are about 600 guests and the Yorks work hard. They divide the room in two and work their way round. For some reason they don't receive a very good press at home. This is unfair. We expect a great deal of a couple still in their twenties. More to the point, they act as good ambassadors for the country overseas and certainly in the United States, they are going down very well. My Deputy Secretary was rather hoping for some glamorous film stars at the reception. We had to make do with Vincent Price, much more civilised but not quite what he had in mind. Just before leaving, we see Joan Collins cosying up to George Hamilton for the benefit of the photographers.

TUESDAY 15 MARCH

Budget Day. Nigel Lawson gives us his customary briefing in the morning before Cabinet. It is certainly radical, with both the basic rate down to 25 per cent and the top rate down to 40 per cent. It is this last proposal which will cause controversy. He has done very well for those in work and earning reasonably well but very little for the low paid: the incentive to go from unemployment to work is left largely unaffected. In his Budget speech he reveals another part of his strategy – to bring the basic rate down to 20 per cent. We can do without that target. It puts us in a straitjacket. We will not be able to do anything much for incentives for several years to come if the reduction of the basic rate is to be the only target. Inevitably, Labour object and mount a noisy demonstration while a Scottish Nationalist (Alex Salmond) deliberately gets himself suspended. So for the first time I can remember, the Budget debate itself is suspended for ten minutes to allow tempers to cool. It is all self-defeating, certainly for Labour, as Neil Kinnock makes a good speech attacking the Budget, but there is not much chance that it will be reported when competing with demonstrations on the floor of the House. I run into Margaret Thatcher after the debate has ended. 'We must avoid this being seen as a rich man's budget,' she says. That may be easier said than done with the social security changes coming in a few weeks' time. As a result of the public spending round, John Moore has taken money off both family credit and housing benefit in what was previously a cost-neutral package. The papers will be full of stories about the 'losers'.

SATURDAY 19 MARCH

Dreadful television film of two British soldiers in Belfast being lynched at the hands of a republican funeral procession. You can hardly believe that this is happening but it is there in front of your eyes: men being murdered by a crowd. I believe the pictures will have more impact than any event in Northern Ireland for many years. The British public will react very strongly to what is being done to the soldiers. I fear many will take the view that we should leave them to it. There is precious little sympathy on the mainland for what is happening in Northern Ireland.

MONDAY 21 MARCH

I open the Budget debate on the last day, but only after a very long statement on the Northern Ireland murders at the weekend. It is difficult to speak in the House just after a statement of that kind. The House's mind is elsewhere. I make the speech short – perhaps too short – but the main interest came in Ted Heath's offering. He takes so many side swipes at his 'colleagues' that he hardly has time to make any points of his own. Nigel Lawson looked 'too satisfied by half'. John Biffen (who was not there) had confirmed all Ted's views of him when he had said on Thursday that he had no training in economics. So it went on. The Labour benches very much enjoyed it. Ted now takes a perverse pleasure in attacking his own side entirely indiscriminately. The other notable feature of the debate is the assumption that Nigel Lawson is to go. Bryan Gould refers to the challenge for the 'next Chancellor'. Nigel just beams.

MONDAY 25 APRIL

I take Michael Heseltine to Brown's Hotel for lunch where we can have a quiet table in the corner. Michael wonders what his next cause should be. He thinks that the health service would be a good area but does not want to be regarded as an opportunist. I think this is precisely the kind of area that he should be in and I do not understand why he regards it as an opportunist issue. Disarmingly, Michael says, 'If the truth is known, I am an opportunist'. In fact, his views on the health service are exactly the views that should be expressed at this time. He believes that, irrespective of what happens in terms of financing health care, there must be no question that people are prevented from accessing health care because of their lack of means. We talk about the future and whether Margaret will go or stay. If she goes, Michael feels that his chief opposition will be Ken Baker – I agree. Fiona and I have just received our first invitation to dinner with him and although this may be partly because we are getting to know each other, it might just go deeper. It is difficult keeping up the kind of profile that Michael has managed on the back benches. He has made a good fist of it but he does not like it and would like to be back in government making decisions, influencing things and putting ideas into practice.

WEDNESDAY 27 APRIL

In the division lobby I meet Leon, who says he would like my advice. Of course I cannot resist the bait. Leon tells me that he has been offered the chance to go to Europe as one of our commissioners by Geoffrey Howe. The question is, should he take it or not? He says that he and Diana are going to and fro on whether to do so. We take a long walk down the corridor. Leon is obviously very tempted and it is a job which he is particularly well qualified to do. However, he also has the natural reservation that if he goes it will be the end of his Commons career. He also feels that it will be seen as Margaret getting him out of the way. I say that at first hearing, I am in favour of him taking the job, but I will think about it further.

THURSDAY 28 APRIL

I leave Cabinet with John Major. He says that there is no question that had he not been on a small group making social security concessions, a great deal of back stabbing would have taken place, the blame being apportioned between myself and him. John puts his finger on one of the aspects that is so disconcerting about John Moore. When you speak to him directly, butter could not melt in his mouth. However, it is known perfectly well that at the same time, he will be apportioning blame fairly freely. Even in politics, I have never experienced quite such a pronounced feeling that you need to watch your back.

MONDAY 2 MAY

We are making some progress on the black economy. For years, there has been anecdotal evidence that such an economy exists and that substantial numbers of people are working and claiming benefit at the same time. Our recent investigation into the taxi trade in the West Midlands has established beyond any conceivable doubt that there are appreciable numbers of taxi drivers or, to be more accurate, private hire car drivers who are both claiming benefit and working at the same time. Even more extraordinary is the result from Coventry. The prospect of a postal strike encouraged my ever vigilant staff to make strenuous efforts to get in touch with all claimants and ask them to collect their giro cheque personally at the local unemployment benefit office. Even with all the publicity that went with that, some 300 or 400 did not do so. They were then contacted by phone and in one or two cases, the wife at the other end of the line said that it was not possible to speak to Mr Brown because Mr Brown was out at work. In the evening, I have dinner with Leon. I think that he will take the job in Brussels. He intends to see Margaret and say that he would prefer to have a Cabinet job, but with no expectation that she will suddenly offer him one.

MONDAY 9 MAY

To No. 10 for one of the Prime Minister's Monday lunches with colleagues. Today, I find myself directly facing Margaret, in the chair that used to be occupied by Willie Whitelaw. I talk to Margaret for a few minutes about the employment position, but the conversation ranges wider. We face a challenge on the poll tax in the Lords. Margaret's view is that if the Lords changes the poll tax, she will change the Lords. She has never liked the House of Lords and particularly dislikes the way that former Conservative ministers transfer to the House of Lords and then take on a new independence. But changing the Lords might be easier said than done, even if they do seek to kick over the traces on the poll tax. We also have a revealing discussion on journalists and their qualities. It arises from the position of Jock Bruce-Gardyne, who no longer writes his weekly column for the *Sunday Telegraph*. Journalists, Margaret opines, are basically observers. Very few journalists, she says, combine the ability to be able to observe and the ability to act. Nigel Lawson, she says, is the outstanding exception to that rule. Then something triggers in her mind. She looks at me and says, 'of course you were a journalist'. I joke that having heard her remarks I was considering my future. To which she says, 'oh no, no, no' – she was thinking of John Biffen.[183]

WEDNESDAY 11 MAY

A debate on the P&O dispute. Michael Meacher leads for the opposition and makes a speech which is entirely dominated by the issue of safety. As

---

183 Of course John Biffen was not a journalist at all, but a city analyst who had been marked down at No. 10 as an unhelpful semi-detached member of the Cabinet. Among the journalists who might challenge the Thatcher theory that they were merely observers was her number one hero, Winston Churchill.

he nears the end of his speech, he says that the government's attitude is influenced by the fact that Jeffrey Sterling is Chairman of P&O and they are contributors to Conservative Party funds. I get up and ask him who the treasurer of the Labour Party is. Michael, being an honest chap, and not knowing any other way of answering this question but straight, replies that it is Sam McCluskie. This causes great amusement on our side of the House but Michael does not like being laughed at. He goes into orbit and says that the only reason that P&O have not been prosecuted for the Zeebrugge disaster is because of these financial links. This is a totally unsubstantiated claim and I ask Michael to repeat it outside. He bumbles and mumbles on and says that if he can be shown that he is wrong, then he will withdraw it.

I lunch with John Sharkey of Saatchis.[184] He gives me a fascinating insight into the 1987 general election. Wobbly Thursday was apparently a real nightmare. As far as David Young is concerned, Sharkey has no time for him. Apparently, after the election was all over, the newspapers were full of stories that David Young was to become the new chairman of the party. David Young himself rang up the agency and the Saatchi brothers to say that if that was the case he would like bygones to be bygones, and he would like Saatchis to continue with the account. Apparently, Saatchi put the phone down on him.

SATURDAY 14 MAY

The papers are full of stories about the conflict between Nigel and Margaret over exchange rate policy and the EMS.[185] On Thursday in the House, Margaret resisted Kinnock's call to declare her total agreement with the Chancellor on exchange policy. It is this that has fuelled the stories – together with Geoffrey Howe's speech at the Scottish party conference and

---

184 John was joint managing director of Saatchi & Saatchi UK, founded his own advertising company and in 2010 was appointed a Liberal Democrat life peer.

185 The European exchange rate mechanism (ERM) was set up in the late 1970s to stabilise currencies in preparation for economic and monetary union (EMU) and the introduction of a single currency. Countries seeking to replace their currency with the euro were required to keep the value of their currency within a specific range for several years. The UK joined the ERM in 1990 (and left in 1992) but the Chancellor, Nigel Lawson, had been secretly shadowing the Deutsche mark for some years before that.

his suggestion that we cannot delay for ever on EMS. The row is getting out of hand and we need to do something about it. We cannot allow it to get out of hand in the way that Westland did. The handling of the economy is our greatest claim and greatest achievement, anything that puts that at risk will do irreparable damage to the government.

MONDAY 16 MAY

Lunch with Robin Oakley whom I have not seen for some time.[186] Slightly surprisingly, I find that Robin is, if anything, rather more outspoken on the subject of Geoffrey than I am. He thinks that Margaret has treated Geoffrey very badly and that there comes a stage in her relations with nearly all her senior colleagues when things go wrong. I suppose this is right. She has no great personal following in the Cabinet based on affection and friendship. There are people like David Young who are elaborate courtiers and there would be courtiers under any reign. There is Nick Ridley who I think is a genuine friend but there are precious few others.

Geoffrey Howe is slightly down in the dumps after his Scottish speech and his apparently unintentional entry into the exchange rate row between the Prime Minister and Nigel. Geoffrey has seen a whole series of newspaper articles that have forecast his demise and takes the view that these articles could easily be stopped by No. 10 if that was their wish. His fear is that No. 10 are doing to him exactly what they did to John Biffen and Peter Rees in the past. Apparently, Geoffrey's case is that he made his remarks about the EMS at least seven times before. My sympathies are all with Geoffrey, but I do think that he might have foreseen what effect his comments would have at a gathering such as a party conference.

WEDNESDAY 25 MAY

I cancel a visit that I was due to make to Brighton to launch a tourist report and instead, stay in London to be on hand for the TUC decision on employment training. All of our information is that the result will be

---

186 Robin was a columnist and political editor for *The Times* 1986–1992, then political editor at the BBC from 1992–2000. After leaving the BBC, he became CNN's European Political Editor.

a close thing. With the changes that we have made, Geoffrey Holland and Roger Dawe[187] feel that there is now a chance that we will take the day. After lunch the news comes through that the TUC has given conditional support to the programme, and by the surprisingly high margin of 19–14. It is a great relief.

In the evening a freelance group of Dennis Skinner, Bob Cryer, the Scottish Nationalists and Ulster Unionists keep us voting on the firearms bill. After traipsing through the division lobby six or seven times, the Speaker invokes a procedural device which means that the House can vote by simply standing up in its place with four minutes between divisions. Through into the early hours of the morning, we all dutifully stand up every four or five minutes to register our votes. The result, needless to say, is always the same, a majority of 200 to 30. I get home at 5 a.m. It is a silly way of running the country, but nothing can be done to change it. The business managers on our side will take the conventional view that if we were in opposition, then we would want this kind of power as well. Oppositions have one serious weapon and that is the weapon now being used so effectively to delay government business and keep government ministers and supporters up for as long as they can. It does however fit very badly into not only normal business life, but also normal family life. In a week in which the Prime Minister and a number of others are preaching the virtues of the family, it is curious to see the heads of those families being made fit for nothing. I do not think that anyone has come to terms with the fact that the House of Commons has changed since the 1930s and that today, members do not have servants or chauffeurs and that some of us have to do everyday things like school runs.

TUESDAY 7 JUNE

I meet Michael Meacher in the corridor behind the Speaker's chair. He is very grateful for a telegram Fiona and I sent him on his wedding and goes on at some length about this. I ask him about his libel case against *The Observer*. He says his lawyers said it would be over in a week. It is

---

187 Civil servant, in charge of training.

now into the third week. They tell him he will probably win. I hope so because if he doesn't he will have a horrendous bill. I then get into a conversation with Douglas Hogg and Peter Viggers.[188] Douglas is emphatic. He hopes Michael Meacher loses. 'You have to be ruthless in politics.' Personally, I hope he wins.

MONDAY 13 JUNE

Dinner at Ken Baker's home in Pimlico is a jolly affair. The house shows every sign of Ken's addiction to collecting – prints and plates – and he and Mary are good hosts. Is he a future Prime Minister? I don't know. A Chancellor yes, but he doesn't seem to me to have quite the steel for it. This is not meant to be derogatory. The fact that he does not perhaps have the single-minded dedication to his own cause makes him a nicer man.

I get back to the Commons late and miss a vote. I run into Michael Meacher. He has lost his libel case and is very bitter. He believes that the judge's summing-up was biased, and that was crucial. He says it has affected his view of the law. He now wants to appeal. I have sympathy with Michael but his judgement is appalling. It may be unfair, but why risk a loss of £150,000 for an article by a malicious old journalist way past his best which no one had read in any case.

THURSDAY 16 JUNE

On my way to a reception in the House of Lords I run into Leon. I ask him how his recent meeting with Margaret went. He says exceptionally well. It was as if nothing had happened since they last met. The meeting lasted forty-five minutes and Leon said that although he was interested in the Brussels job he would prefer to go back into the Cabinet. He said he appreciated that this could not be at the level he left. Apparently, Margaret was very encouraging about the prospects and Leon thinks that a September shuffle is on the cards. They had ended up discussing who

---

188 Peter Viggers – another member of the Cambridge mafia. We shared rooms at Trinity Hall. Unjustly known for the 'duck house' incident. In fact, a very able and conscientious MP who served as industry minister for Northern Ireland from 1986–1989. During his national service he flew jets.

else could go. If Margaret intended to encourage him that he could go back into the Cabinet, then she has succeeded, but is that what she intends? Fiona thinks that he won't get back and thinks he should accept Europe. I would just put some money on him accepting Europe.

SUNDAY 10 JULY

Fiona and I go to Cambridge for Jeffrey Archer's party. A mixture of politicians, actors, journalists and sportsmen gather in less than summery conditions in Jeffrey's garden in Grantchester. I talk to Jeffrey about Michael Meacher's libel case. Jeffrey's view was that he was mad to bring it. He told a story about his own libel case against the *Star*. Victor Mishcon, his solicitor, asked him three questions. 'Did you sleep with this woman?' 'No sir' replied Jeffrey. 'Did you ever sleep with any prostitute?' 'No sir' replied Jeffrey. 'Do you want to continue with a political career?' 'Yes sir' said Jeffrey. Jeffrey says that it was only when he gave the third reply that Mishcon advised him to go ahead. Otherwise his advice would have been to forget about it.

TUESDAY 12 JULY

Visit of the head of state of Turkey. This brings London traffic to an absolute halt. Much to the amusement of my office, I set out with Ivor Manley, my Deputy Secretary, by Tube from St James's Park, abandoning the official car. It gets me through to Blackfriars and lunch at Unilever in ten minutes. I joke about this being the first time I have been on the Tube in nine years. It is an exaggeration, but only just.

THURSDAY 14 JULY

Leon has agreed to go to Brussels. Margaret has volunteered a splendid letter to his constituency association saying that he is the right man for the job (which he is) and that it is in the national interest. I will miss Leon very much in the House. It is a great shame that his talents cannot be used here. I doubt if he will return but his ability will ensure that he will not be lost to public life. It is a great tragedy that he should have been the victim of Westland.

SUNDAY 17 JULY

To Holme Pierrepont to support Oliver who is coxing the Eton Colts 8.
They are in the national final and if they win they will represent England
next week in a match against the French. They duly romp home and the
parents' supporters club celebrate with a tremendous feast of sandwiches
and champagne. I must admit that when I was at my grammar school I
hardly thought the day would come when I would be sitting on the back
of a lorry shouting out 'Come on Eton' as we travelled along the course.

FRIDAY 22 JULY

Lunch in John Stokes' constituency at Halesowen. John has a very pa-
trician view of his constituency. 'They are all NCOs here' he says, 'no
officers.'

TUESDAY 26 JULY

The papers are full of the reshuffle. There is a general welcome for the
splitting of the DHSS and for Ken's appointment as Secretary of State for
Health. He is seen as a consolidator and this appears to be celebrated by
the very same papers who were calling for radicalism only twelve months
ago. John Moore has been left with social security and the move is universally seen as a demotion. He will now find it very difficult to restore
his ministerial career. It is a cruel business. Twelve months ago, John was
the next Prime Minister with political correspondents hanging on his
every word. Now it is reckoned that he will be lucky to survive much
longer as a minister at all. There is speculation about the personalities
involved in some of the other moves, notably how Edwina and the new
No. 2 Health Minister David Mellor will get on together. Edwina will be
miffed that she is not the new Minister of State. Their personalities are
hardly compatible for a close working relationship. At Prime Minister's
Questions in the afternoon, Margaret is asked about the splitting of the
DHSS. She replies to the effect that it is a department that is too big for
any one man. Sitting two down from her I am not sure whether or not
I should regard this as a compliment. It is a notably false analysis. Whet
her the DHSS should be split up or not, the secretaries of state for social

services have, up to now, been a remarkably long-living breed – Keith Joseph did a whole parliament, I did almost six years, David Ennals did over three years and there were appreciable innings from Patrick Jenkin, Barbara Castle and Dick Crossman. The job has certainly not got easier as the years have gone by but Margaret would have done better to give some reason of principle for dividing the department.

SUNDAY 7 AUGUST, SEAVIEW

At lunch with the Bottomleys. Another guest was my old friend Peter Lloyd who is now in the Whips' Office. According to Peter, I am seen as a 'safe pair of hands'. I said that sounded a bit patronising. Not at all, said Peter, it is the highest praise that the Whips' Office can give. Be that as it may, it still leaves the substantial question of where next? The employment department has gone well and in retrospect my period at the DHSS has received some recognition. But I am not a crony and although the PM sees me running a good department, I don't see her promoting me to one of the more senior jobs unless there is a crisis of some sort to settle. I was amused to note that I was introduced as 'a very senior minister in the government' at the Saudi Arabian reception. It may be – no it will be – uncomfortable to leave the ministerial life but I have had a very good run and it can't go on forever. I would also like to see more of everybody in the family. There is not much chance of that with my present lifestyle and unless I am careful I will miss the children growing up. Final decisions over the next few months.

TUESDAY 6 SEPTEMBER

At the TUC conference in Bournemouth, Neil Kinnock has made a very surprising speech. He spent about a third of his time talking about employment training and urging the TUC to back the training programme, to fight from within and not to fight from without. This has of course infuriated the likes of Ron Todd but could help us. I only hope that he has some reason for believing that he can swing the debate. I can scarcely believe that Kinnock would be foolish enough to put his reputation on the line unless he has a sporting chance of winning, but in discussion it is pointed out that Kinnock has operated impetuously before and this may be the same characteristic coming out. Nevertheless, I am grateful for the support.

WEDNESDAY 7 SEPTEMBER

At 10.30 a.m. in the department, we all, ministers and officials alike, gather round the television. There are obviously mixed feelings about how we want the debate to go. In some ways it might be considerably easier to run things without this delicate and uncertain arrangement with the TUC. On the other hand, I think all of us in our heart of hearts want the conference to back it. Indeed in the debate itself, I think we unquestionably have the best of it. There are good speeches from Bill Jordan, Tony Christopher, Roy Grantham, John Ellis, and indeed from Norman Willis himself. The only really atrocious speech comes from Ron Todd. It is not an atrocious conference speech, it is just atrocious in the sense that he knows that what he is saying is untrue. He was one of the co-authors of the training programme itself, and for him to turn round and say that we are introducing workfare is too much. But you only have to listen to the applause to know that Todd probably represents the majority of the delegates and so it proves when the vote is taken. The TUC have turned their back on ET. I cannot see that we can continue with the present tripartite arrangement as far as the Training Commission is concerned.

THURSDAY 8 SEPTEMBER

The press is universally hostile to the TUC. The most outspoken leader is in *The Independent* which urges me to end the Training Commission arrangement and clearly has absolutely no patience at all with the TUC. I have already minuted Margaret on the result and we are now preparing another minute setting out the options. We will be proposing that we take the management of employment training back to the department, abolish the Training Commission and come forward with further proposals in a white paper.

FRIDAY 9 SEPTEMBER

In the evening I go to Nottingham and to Holme Pierrepont Hall to do an East Midlands fundraising event. It is nice to see some old friends from the Nottingham South days and after the dinner we go back to have a drink with Martin Suthers who lives nearby.[189] Ken and Gillian [Clarke] come. Ken regales us all with some splendidly funny stories about the press pursuing him on holiday in Spain. Apparently, the *Daily Mail* offered £10,000 to anyone who knew his address in Spain and their persuasive line was that it would be better for the *Daily Mail* to catch up with him first rather than the *People*.

WEDNESDAY 14 SEPTEMBER

Meeting on the Training Commission at No. 10. Margaret Thatcher is in the chair. The argument goes very swiftly my way. I say that we have no option but to take the action that I am proposing. That it would be an act of extraordinary weakness if we did not and would be interpreted as such. David Young comes in firmly on my side, as does the Chancellor. The decision is taken and I suggest that it should be announced tomorrow. Margaret readily agrees to this. I hear later that the Cabinet Office officials were very impressed by the presentation of the case.

THURSDAY 29 SEPTEMBER

One of the more interesting things that has happened over the last few weeks has been the way that the Prime Minister, in her Royal Society speech, raised the issue of the environment and its protection.[190] I am sure that this is right. Whether we will naturally be thought of as the protectors of the environment is another matter.

MONDAY 3 OCTOBER

At lunch I go to the Guildhall for the inaugural lunch of the National Aids Trust. The lunch has been entirely arranged and financed by Robert

---

189   Old friend from Cambridge, responsible for introducing me to Nottingham South.
190   Margaret Thatcher gave the speech on 27 September to the Royal Society where she had just been elected a fellow.

Maxwell. I sit next to Princess Diana and tell her what a great impact the TV pictures of her shaking hands with people with Aids had on the British public. I think it has, in many ways, changed attitudes. Sitting on my other side is Jonathan Mann from the World Health Organization and he makes an additional point, that the pictures are not just seen in Britain but around the world and they have had a great impact in the US as well as here. The Princess comes over as an exceptionally nice person, quite willing to talk about the problems of public life and of being constantly on parade. She says how impossible it is to relax and the constant fear that you say something more than you should. I think we all know that feeling. Maxwell is the chairman of the fundraising part of the trust. I actually find Maxwell a difficult man to dislike. He wears an expensive scruffy suit. In style, it is somewhere between Italy and Albania and he sports a luminous bow tie. 'Look at that bow tie!' says Princess Diana as he gets up to speak.

WEDNESDAY 12 OCTOBER

Proceedings at the party conference are fairly low-key. Training does not create the same passion that reforming trade union laws once had – and unemployment is now coming down. Margaret comes and sits on the platform next to me. I am told that it has been pretty calm up to now and so they were obviously waiting for a rather more spirited offering. At any rate, I get a good and instant standing ovation such as would satisfy even the most critical of political correspondents.

FRIDAY 14 OCTOBER

The end of the conference. The Prime Minister's speech is seen as slightly defensive. My guess is that we are in for a rough time over the next few months, with inflation going up and a perception that the economy is not as strong as we would like. It may also be that the Labour Party, in spite of all its public squabbling, is getting its act together and the younger members of the shadow team will give the party a much more cutting edge in the next few months.

From Brighton I go along to Seaview. Nick and Nicky Haywood of the Seaview Hotel have invited us to come to dinner to meet their friend, Michel Bourdin, the chef de cuisine at the Connaught. He is a great enthusiast about improving standards in the hotel business and in particular among chefs. In other words, getting chefs accepted as a professional group and getting British people to understand the opportunities that there are in the hotel business. He tells me that at the Connaught, which is the archetypal British hotel, there is not one single British waiter.

MONDAY 17 OCTOBER

Lunch with Geoffrey Goodman. He was one of the team around Harold Wilson and a longstanding member of the *Daily Mirror* staff. The most amazing thing he says about Wilson is not that he retired unexpectedly in 1976 but that he did not go earlier. There was no hidden scandal; he simply ran out of steam. This is a point which I remember Ken Stowe putting to me once, that it was sad to see a man of such stature and undoubted ability being unable to cope. He was tired out and by lunchtime would be completely exhausted. If you look back at Wilson's periods of office, it all now seems rather sleazy, although Geoffrey tells me that whatever took place between Lady Falkender and Wilson had ceased by the time he took office. Perhaps it is more that the sleaziness was a slickness: the deals, the beer and sandwiches compromises, the battles that were not joined like the battle on industrial relations – politically it was all very clever but there was no real heart to it. As a postscript, Geoffrey told me a story of meeting Wilson a few weeks ago at a reception at the Chinese Embassy. He was wandering around by himself, with no one in particular to talk to. He descended upon Geoffrey whom he recognised as a familiar face from the past. Geoffrey said that it was quite clear that he did not know his name and every time he went off to another discussion, he would always come back to Geoffrey: so they left together. He could not find his coat; he could not find his car; he did not know where it was. He had no idea about its general direction. Contrast that general picture of Wilson with the picture I remember from what must have been just before the 1974 general election when he was performing on the front bench. Ken Baker was viewing him with undisguised admiration, saying 'there is a real professional'.

FRIDAY 28 OCTOBER

To Oxford for a meeting with the university Conservative Association. A good meeting and extremely bright questions. One of the questions comes from an undergraduate whose style is so totally reminiscent of William Rees-Mogg that it could only be his son, Jacob, and so it proves to be when I meet him afterwards. He obviously does not give a fig that he is the only undergraduate in the hall wearing a double-breasted suit.

WEDNESDAY 2 NOVEMBER

Dinner with John Major's constituency association in the House of Commons. John is exceptionally kind and complimentary about me and says that there is still much to come in my distinguished career. It is very nice of him, but I always remember that when I go to Members' constituencies I have a standard piece. 'You know him as your constituency MP, I can only tell you what a great reputation he has at Westminster.' I confess that I have said this about some very unlikely people.

TUESDAY 8 NOVEMBER

In the evening, I go to a reception of Friends of the Elderly at the Mansion House. They run the Wimbledon home where my mother is and I am just about to disappear when I am introduced to Princess Margaret. She says that we haven't met previously and we have quite a long talk. She obviously thinks that the employment situation is going well and shows a remarkably detailed knowledge of the results of the fraud drive I announced some days ago in which £34 million was recovered. She knows the figure and believes that it is entirely good news. Back at Hurlingham Road the first forecasts for the '88 presidential campaign are now coming through. Judging from the midnight news it looks as though it is going to be a decisive victory for George Bush.[191] He would certainly be my choice. His experience puts him way above Dukakis and the undoubted friendship which exists between him and Margaret is going to be a considerable help for us.

191　The predictions proved to be correct and Bush won by a landslide.

THURSDAY 10 NOVEMBER

A meeting with a small group of ministers on the future of wages councils. I am proposing that we should abolish them. I think they have outlived their usefulness. We now have some wages councils which are faintly comic, like a wages council to determine wages in the coffin-making industry – all 200 of them. But more seriously, I think that this kind of pay determination is entirely against the kind of principles that we are setting out for pay.

In Cabinet, Margaret gives a fascinating report on her trip to Poland. She says that she was free to go anywhere she wanted to. Solidarity, she says, is much more than a trade union, it is the only form of political opposition there is in Poland. Just before she went, the Polish government had said that they were going to close the shipyard at Gdańsk. That was an entirely political decision and was to make things as awkward as possible for everyone concerned, but what depresses her is that Solidarity do not have an agenda. They do not have concrete proposals on what they want to do. She also says that the Polish view of Britain is not particularly good. They recognise that we came into the war in 1939 on their behalf but they also believe that we gave away parts of Poland in the Yalta negotiations. She has a number of vignettes from Gdańsk. She saw a banner with words to the effect of: 'Well done Maggie, you beat Arthur Scargill. We are against communists also.' Both Nigel and Geoffrey are very gloomy about the economic prospects for Poland. Recovery is going to take a very long time. Margaret was obviously impressed and rather moved by the visit and wants us to do what we can to help. She liked the way Warsaw has been restored, much of it an exact copy of what was there before. I certainly remember when I went to Warsaw in 1960 there were still large areas that had not been rebuilt and were just rubble left from the 1939–45 war.

In the early evening, I go to Birmingham to speak at a banquet of the British forging industry at the NEC. There are 800 people there and again, it demonstrates the great change of attitude that is taking place in British industry. The forging industry is the metal bashing industry and was one of the industries in the West Midlands worst hit by the recession. Today, order books are up and they are in much better heart than ever before. I must say that they were a magnificent audience. Ted collects me and drives me back to London and as we are entering London we hear the news that the Govan by-election has sprung a surprise and the SNP have won.[192] No one was really expecting that. It is going to reopen the whole issue of Scottish independence.

SUNDAY 13 NOVEMBER

The next few months will be quite hairy. The opposition will want to fight hard. The Scottish Labour Party will want to demonstrate that they are not as toothless as the SNP maintains. On Friday I met Robin Cook, looking tense and slightly overwrought, in the corridor and his view was that unless we got our act together then we would have an independent Scotland. It will be most surprising if that concern is not shared by Malcolm Rifkind. One of the things which the Scottish Nationalists have done is to talk about independence 'inside Europe'. That makes it a much more practical proposition as far as the public is concerned.

TUESDAY 15 NOVEMBER

Cabinet today as Margaret is off to Washington later. I report that we have won our case against Liverpool council. This is really quite a victory. I think it is the first time that a government minister has sought judicial review against a council. Normally, it is the other way round. But what Liverpool council was seeking to do was quite indefensible. Basically, they were threatening that anyone who cooperated with employment training would have any other grants or facilities taken away. It was pure blackmail. The judges upheld our case by three to nil.

WEDNESDAY 16 NOVEMBER

I have lunch at Pomegranates with Michael Dobbs. Michael is going to

---

192 Jim Sillars, previously a Labour MP, won the by-election for the SNP with a majority of 3,554 over Labour.

stay with Saatchi & Saatchi. He was thinking of moving out and starting his own business but what he has done instead is write a political novel and is now working on the second.[193] In the evening I go to the Hilton to present some English Tourist Board awards. Quite a genial evening and the tourist personality of the year is Peter de Savary.[194] I sit next to his wife during dinner and the de Savarys are rather good news. He does have the greatest difficulty in getting acceptance from what I suppose we call the Establishment. One of the runners-up is our dear friend, Tim Hart, for his new hotel in Rutland which has now been restored to great splendour. The best story that I have been told about Tim was when one of the guests looked out of the window and saw the proprietor cleaning the car windows. It is of course precisely because of this that he is such a successful host.

SUNDAY 4 DECEMBER

In the evening we have dinner at Michael Howard's to say goodbye to Leon. It is really a reunion of the Cambridge mafia plus wives. Geoffrey Howe makes an exceptionally good speech. He has obviously gone to a great deal of trouble to prepare and once again I am impressed by the conscientious and utterly reliable way that Geoffrey approaches all tasks whether big or in this case, entirely personal and small. I think that it is the best speech that I have heard him make. It is a very good evening.

MONDAY 5 DECEMBER

The publication of the white paper. My statement in the House of Commons is preceded by a private notice question to Ken Clarke about Edwina Currie's comments on eggs and salmonella poisoning. At the weekend, Edwina had suggested that most of the egg production in Britain is contaminated with salmonella. This has outraged the farmers

---

193 Author of many books but most famous for *House of Cards*. Conservative politician, now in the House of Lords.

194 Peter de Savary liked to describe himself as a swashbuckling entrepreneur, adventurer and sportsman. He came to fame in the 1980s and '90s for his unsuccessful attempts to win the America's Cup yacht race.

and has therefore also outraged many of our backbenchers. Hal Miller raises the private notice question and there is no doubt that they are out for Edwina's blood. Ken handles the private notice question very well and with great humour. Although half the House is outraged, the other half think the affair is something of a joke. For whatever reason, the House has half an hour of boisterous and lively debate preceding my statement. The result is altogether beneficial to me. The House of Commons is capable of exploding only once in an afternoon, and my proposals on training are regarded as a great anti-climax when compared to the major issue of cooking eggs. The result is that I announce the abolition of wages councils and the demise of the industrial training boards with hardly a demur from the other side of the House.[195]

WEDNESDAY 7 DECEMBER

Fit for Work Awards at Lancaster House. These are given to companies who have made some contribution towards employing disabled people over the past twelve months. Presenting the awards is the Princess Royal, Princess Anne. She makes an exceptionally good speech. I can see from where I am sat that the speech is written out in her own handwriting and when she comes to talk about the position of children, there is no question that she talks with enormous authority. She is the most intelligent and most perceptive member of the royal family that I have met. She went through a bad period a few years ago when the press was suggesting that she was rather unpopular but has emerged from that as a very formidable figure. She spent about two hours at Lancaster House. The only problem is that at lunchtime a small table has been reserved for us, so Princess Anne, Brian Wolfson, Head of the Training Taskforce, and I sit there. The butler asks us what we would like – beef stroganoff or seafood

---

195 The white paper looked at the operation of the pre-entry closed shop. It abolished the wages councils and industrial training boards and set out a new training framework. Following the TUC's decision not to cooperate, training and enterprise councils (TECs), independent, local and employer-led councils, were set up to take over responsibility for running the training and enterprise programmes previously organised by the department's training agency. *Employment for the 1990s*, white paper, December 1988 – Cm 540.

salad. She thinks and says that no, she would prefer just some cheese and biscuits. Brian and I do not feel that we can tuck into a big lunch so we also eat cheese and biscuits.

THURSDAY 8 DECEMBER

Cabinet. John MacGregor is away in Montreal but the egg row is continuing to rumble. Ken Clarke reports that basically, Edwina was cornered and that she did not quite have the experience to get out of the situation. He says that it is not the case that the majority of eggs are infected and that he intends to continue to put up the Chief Medical Officer to give advice on what the public should do. More worryingly, he says that there is a report from the public health laboratory which indicates that one egg in 750 is infected. If that is the case, that will not be good news. Gorbachev has postponed his visit to Britain because of an earthquake in Armenia where, as far as we know, tens of thousands of people are dead. There is no precise information but he is obviously going back. The Prime Minister herself was on the *Today* programme very early this morning and, as she said in her radio interview, the right place for a leader at such a time is with his people. It is altogether typical of her that she reacted so speedily. She heard a report at about 6.30 that there had been no government reaction to the postponement of the visit. She promptly contacted the BBC and did an impromptu interview.

Gorbachev's speech at the United Nations has been overtaken by the earthquake. Nevertheless, it was a significant speech. Margaret herself calls it fascinating and says that what he said on freedom of choice goes beyond anything that he has said before, but everyone is cautious about the detail. Nigel Lawson says that it is a triumph in packaging and George Younger points out that the USSR is still overwhelmingly superior in its troops, aircraft and tanks. The Prime Minister gets into some trouble with the opposition at Prime Minister's Questions for not giving a fulsome enough welcome to Gorbachev's speech. I think her reaction is entirely sensible. It is a significant speech, but no one should forget the enormous superiority that the Russians have in arms. It would be very foolish if we were to take everything at face value and believe that the threat from Russia has entirely come to an end.

WEDNESDAY 21 DECEMBER

A clearing-up day. We are not in bad shape. We have produced two important white papers and passed a potentially difficult employment bill while employment training is on the road. At the same time, unemployment has continued to come down steeply and at a much faster rate than elsewhere in Europe. There are however, still a number of important issues for the new year, like the future of the dock work regulation scheme. The day ends with a Christmas party – this time given by the private offices. Drinks, eats and music. Ministers should look in but should not linger.

THURSDAY 22 DECEMBER

After Cabinet I read the lesson at the Department of Employment's carol service at St Margaret's. For this service, the department past and present combine. Former permanent secretaries return, as do ex-messengers. We give them all mince pies and sherry in Steel House, just across the road from our main headquarters. One of the retired grandees makes a speech of thanks and says kindly that the department has been blessed with exceptionally genial secretaries of state over the last ten years. He makes no comment on their other abilities or lack of them.

FRIDAY 23 DECEMBER

The air tragedy over Lockerbie has knocked some of the stuffing out of Christmas.[196] You feel the atmosphere as you shop. The feeling is subdued; people talk quietly. In Hatchards, there is a low murmur of

---

196 In the evening of 21 December, Pan Am Flight 103 from London to New York exploded in mid-air over Lockerbie, Scotland, killing all 243 passengers and 16 crew members on board, as well as 11 residents of the town on the ground. A bomb had been planted on board and arrest warrants for two Libyan nationals were issued in November 1991. In 1999, after protracted negotiations and UN sanctions, Colonel Gaddafi handed over the two men for trial and in 2003, he accepted responsibility for the Lockerbie bombing and paid compensation to the victims' families.

conversation; there is no excitement. Somehow, we all feel that it would be disrespectful to show too much joy in the shadow of such an awful tragedy.

COMMENT

The victory of 1987 had been short-lived in its effect. Although we did not fully recognise it at the time, Margaret Thatcher was becoming more and more isolated. The loss of Whitelaw who, over the years, had patched up internal divisions was a heavy blow. The Chancellor together with his predecessor, Geoffrey Howe, was plainly unhappy about exchange rate policy while the number of supporters of the poll tax in the parliamentary party seemed to be decreasing rapidly.

12

TEN YEARS ON

JANUARY–JULY 1989

SUNDAY 1 JANUARY 1989

It is a time for decisions. No one can seriously complain that unemployment has not been brought down, that I have failed to develop training or for that matter, about my reception at the party conference. Nevertheless, I am in no doubt that the time has come to move on. I have spent some time contemplating the step but suddenly it hits you that you want to leave. I have broadly enjoyed the last ten years in government. There is no doubt that I have had a tremendous opportunity and I feel, quite genuinely, that it has been a great privilege. But you can only stay doing the same kind of job for so long – or at least I can. The prospect of yet another public spending round does not appeal. But above all, I want to try other things. For the next stage of my life I want to do things in the outside world of business or industry. The decision is taken: the only question is how I leave. This is not as easy as it might seem. In politics you are constantly in the middle of something. With any luck, the employment bill will be given its second reading in the first week we are back, and I have no intention whatsoever of going onto the committee, so that will be out of the way. That leaves the dock work bill – provided that Margaret agrees it. The bill cannot be introduced until early April and there is bound to be some strike action. How long and how big such a strike will be is anyone's guess. It is something I would dearly like to do – but I suppose that first I should see if Margaret agrees to go on the abolition course!

WEDNESDAY II JANUARY

Second reading debate of the employment bill. One of the main purposes of the bill is to sweep away some of the more archaic regulations governing the employment of young people between sixteen and eighteen. Some of the rules go back to the last century and many of them are plain daft. For example, young people working in factories have to clock in at the same time, have their breaks at the same time and go home at the same time, presumably to make it easier for the inspectors to check their whereabouts. Doubtless, this all made sense in pre-war days but it makes no sense today. Needless to say, Michael Meacher is implacably opposed to the abolition of these rules. Michael gets off to a bad start in the debate by missing its opening. There is a great cheer from our side when he arrives rather breathlessly and this enables quite a bit of fun throughout the speech along the lines of 'if I could bring the honourable gentleman up to date' and 'the story so far'. It is not a difficult debate and even old Frank Haynes cannot keep up his indignation at the prospect of women going down the mines. One of the bill's provisions lifts the restrictions on women working underground on the basis that it prevents them becoming surveyors and managers and geologists. Labour are split on the issue. Jo Richardson is in favour for impeccable anti-discrimination reasons; Michael won't express an opinion one way or the other; the mining MPs (not only Frank Haynes) are opposed to the whole notion on chauvinistic grounds, which are excused using the argument that there are no women's lavatories below ground.[197]

THURSDAY 12 JANUARY

Cabinet itself goes quickly. I have the chance of a quiet word with Nigel Lawson on the docks. Is he still in favour of abolition? I ask, '100 per cent' he replies. That now leaves only Margaret herself.

---

197   As well as getting rid of some archaic regulations concerning women and young people, the bill contained the training provisions from the December white paper.

THURSDAY 19 JANUARY

The day starts with the crucial meeting at No. 10 on the docks. I put the case for abolition and Margaret readily accepts it without any substantial discussion. The only questions are tactical. When shall we introduce the bill? How quickly can we get it through? The preparation has paid dividends. Both Wakeham, the Leader of the Commons, and Belstead, the Leader of the Lords, commit themselves to getting it through by July. Margaret makes it quite clear that, if necessary, she will expect them to act even more quickly. The next step is for instructions to go to counsel and for the contingency arrangements to be made. Nigel comes up afterwards to say well done. Indeed, it is quite a historic decision – although I am under no illusions that there are many problems ahead and the almost certain prospect of a major strike.

MONDAY 23 JANUARY

Lunch with Ken Clarke at L'Amico. He is in good form although not that pleased about the number of leaks there have been from his health white paper. The report is good – it says quite explicitly that it is building on what has gone before. A committee which included both the Prime Minister and the Chancellor has come up with proposals that are a long way from the idea of an entirely different service financed by private insurance. Ken says that he had some terrible rows in the committee. He concedes that they have not all been the PM's fault. I say that it is impossible to do any of the social policy jobs without having rows. Margaret is such an undisputed leader that the nature of normal political life has changed: what matters is getting the support of Margaret Thatcher.

MONDAY 30 JANUARY

A marvellous lunch at Lancaster House with a visiting delegation of Chinese Ministry of Labour officials. They have come a long way since I first made contact in my days at transport. They are much more sophisticated. I asked one of the women in the delegation – young and looking like butter wouldn't melt in her mouth – whether she regarded the International Labour Organisation as a helpful body. 'Frankly', she replied in excellent English, 'I think it's a complete waste of time'.

TUESDAY 31 JANUARY

To Kensington Palace for a meeting with Prince Charles on training. At dinner we talk mostly about the press. He is fascinated to learn that I was once on *The Times*. What comes through most clearly is his resentment at the way the press invades privacy today. He would like to see John Browne's Private Members' Bill on privacy succeed and is sceptical about my suggestion that the Press Council might take a stronger line. Like many in his position, he has adopted the policy of not reading all the newspapers and particularly not the tabloid press. He says, engagingly, that if he read all the things that the press wrote about him he would not dare show his face outside the Palace. It is clear that he feels both puzzled and hurt by the kind of attention he gets. Indeed, there is no reason why anyone should be followed by photographers on- and off-duty. Nor is there any excuse for the kind of rumour and innuendo directed at the Prince and above all, at his marriage.

THURSDAY 9 FEBRUARY

Cabinet. The great egg row rumbles on. The papers today are full of Edwina's appearance before the Select Committee on Agriculture. Most of the papers take the view that she slaughtered them and that is certainly Margaret Thatcher's view. It was a 'fantastic performance,' she says. What is more irritating is the way that the row seems to be mushrooming. From the outside, it looks as if the Department of Health and the Ministry of Agriculture have been unable to get their act together and at times they don't appear to be communicating with each other. From eggs, the attention is now going to soft cheese. Nick Ridley mournfully observes that raw eggs and soft cheese are about the only things he eats. Margaret, who is developing quite a sense of humour these days, responds that as he is not a pregnant woman he should survive. But under the banter there is irritation. The message is that the two departments must put this issue to bed – and the sooner the better.

SATURDAY 11 FEBRUARY

Young Conservatives conference at Southport. At breakfast I find Willie Whitelaw, who is going to stand in for Margaret. Her diary is in a dreadful state and the last thing she wants is another conference. The YCs are disappointed but have taken the news well. Willie is in very good form. He has been writing his autobiography and is in a reminiscent mood. He tells me that he was never quite a courtier. It is fascinating to hear even Willie using this term. There were some issues on which he suspended his own judgement in order to back Margaret, but that was inevitable in his position as Deputy Leader. There was no question that the issue that Margaret did not want to be reminded of was Westland. Willie had advocated Leon's return in 1987 but she would not hear of it. He said, enigmatically, that the real embarrassment in the Westland affair was the role of Bernard Ingham and Charles Powell. Later in the morning Willie was given a very warm reception and what came through was the inherent decency of the man. It was the kind of speech that no one else could make and included a line that we should be concerned at the way that some of the Labour front bench are developing – which is true, we should. I finally leave Southport at 11 p.m. in time to get the midnight sleeper from Liverpool and the weekend starts at 7 a.m. at Euston station.

MONDAY 13 FEBRUARY

Tomorrow, I am to take Margaret through our forward strategy. The work on the repeal of the dock labour scheme is going well. We now have a bill and the makings of a white paper. Training and enterprise councils are also going well and there is a great deal of enthusiasm throughout the country. Employment training is developing and we have over 140,000 on the programme – which given that we only began in September is some achievement. Perversely, one or two of the labour correspondents – notably the prickly lot on the *FT* – see it otherwise and wonder why we have not yet reached 250,000. This is always argued with the total assurance of people who have never organised anything more complicated than changing their typewriter ribbons or, to be fair, switching on their word processors.

TUESDAY 14 FEBRUARY

At Prime Minister's Questions, Neil Kinnock is in rather good form. He is trying much shorter questions and with some effect. He effectively exploits our difficulties and the confusion over eggs and food poisoning which shows no sign of calming down. Indeed, over the weekend, Ken Clarke and John MacGregor seem to have been saying different things. To some hilarity Neil Kinnock asks, 'John says one thing. Ken says another. What does Margaret say?' He then asks what she had for lunch apart from the Minister of Agriculture. It is rather unfair on John, who by any standards is an able and highly conscientious minister, but it is certainly doing him no good at the moment.

FRIDAY 17 FEBRUARY

Michael Portillo's annual dinner in Southgate. I have regarded Michael as a star ever since I first saw him on television in his by-election and I still do. There is a large and appreciative audience and it is clear that both Michael and his very bright wife Caroline are held in high affection.

MONDAY 20 FEBRUARY

To Richmond in Yorkshire for the by-election caused by Leon's resignation and move to Europe. It has been a beautiful sunny day and the views are breathtaking. I can quite see why Leon was reluctant to move. The new candidate is William Hague. He made his name at a Conservative Party conference over a decade ago when he was still a schoolboy. Since then, he went to Oxford, where he was not only president of the Union but got a first into the bargain, and now at the ripe old age of twenty-seven is the candidate in what should be a safe Conservative seat. Hague is a good candidate and the party officials say that although every newspaper man has come to Richmond with the idea of putting him down they have failed. Certainly, the two speeches I heard were good and his answer to a question on agriculture was far better than I could have managed. Perhaps that's not saying much given that in both the constituencies I have had there have been practically no farmers and no NFU. William is undoubtedly a future star.

TUESDAY 21 FEBRUARY

From the Richmond by-election to York where I meet one of our ET trainees working in the unlikely surroundings of the wax museum. After a brief tour I am comprehensively sandbagged by about half a dozen press photographers. As I leave, the wax model of Margaret Thatcher has been taken to the front door and at the request of the photographers her head has been taken off. The head is then presented to me and I am invited to put it back on the model. It is like one of those tests that we had thirty years ago at the War Office selection boards to see if you had the qualities judged sufficient to become an officer. Do I refuse to take the head on the grounds of 'disrespect' and have photographs of myself declining? Or do I accept and make a joke of it? I accept, grin my best grin, and inwardly curse the feather-brained information officer who has seen me set up in this way.

THURSDAY 23 FEBRUARY

Cabinet. We have been defeated in the Lords on football identity cards, leading Margaret to ask more or less rhetorically – 'what's happened to all those peers I have made?' and then add that we should consider making peers for a single parliament. Next, we moved to a new form of food threat – an unpronounceable disease called bovine spongiform encephalopathy or BSE. Normally, it would not have detained us for very long, if at all. These days everyone is so concerned about the presentation of these food issues that we rambled rather mournfully on for the best part of half an hour.

FRIDAY 24 FEBRUARY

I do a lunch for the CBI in Birmingham. On my return to the House I hear the result from Richmond. We have just squeaked in with a majority of about 2,500. There is no doubt that we are now in rough water with the public. The unpopularity that Margaret Thatcher had predicted for the autumn has come in the spring.

SUNDAY 26 FEBRUARY

To Wimbledon in the afternoon to see my mother. I get her talking about her own mother, my grandmother. She had a difficult and at times, hard, life. She was widowed very young when my grandfather died of consumption shortly before the First World War. He had managed a big wine and spirits business in Sale and with the job went a very spacious flat. My grandmother took on the business and at the same time brought up four small children. One day, the owners of the business came to see her and asked her to sign some papers, which in effect said that she was being paid at a rate above the rate she was receiving – the owners promised to make the difference up. But why sign the papers? According to my mother, there was some kind of regulation that had been passed. 'Wages councils?' I asked. 'That's it,' said my mother, 'wages councils.' I confessed that I was just abolishing what remained of the wages councils system. 'Well,' she said, 'I hope you know what you are doing.' I hope so too. I remember visiting my grandmother when she had moved to a small Lancashire town called Waterfoot and later, when she lived in retirement in Rawtenstall. She remained a very determined and very strong-willed lady until the end. I only hope that in the next world she will forgive me on wages councils.

WEDNESDAY 1 MARCH

A meeting at No. 10 on the repeal of the dock labour scheme. It goes well. We agree that the best figure for redundancy would be £35,000 – which is the most that has been paid so far in the ports industry.

FRIDAY 10 MARCH

A very early start. The plan today is to have a launch of training and enterprise councils which will take place simultaneously in Newcastle, London, Manchester and Plymouth. I have all my ministers in the different locations and the idea is that we should have what is in effect a televised press conference with questions coming to me in Newcastle from all the other centres. The technology is fairly complicated and at first, the producers want a rehearsal at 5.30 a.m. I say this is too early. There is no point in having the machinery working if the performing humans are too exhausted to put one intelligent word in front of another. We compromise on a 6.30 rehearsal and the event proper starts after breakfast, just before 8 a.m. Margaret arrives a little later and makes an impeccable speech – although she improvises on something to do with the guild companies, which is neither in the script nor is intended. She also remarks that this may seem an early start, but for some of us it is halfway through our normal day. The audience laugh politely, knowing it is true.

TUESDAY 14 MARCH
Nigel Lawson reveals the details of the Budget to us. The outstanding features are the reform of the National Insurance system – something which he refused to do when the social security review was taking place – and abolishing the earnings rule. Both of those measures were steps that I advocated, and both will have a beneficial effect on the labour market.

WEDNESDAY 15 MARCH
Michael Denison and Peter Plouviez from Equity come to see me. They are concerned by the reports that I am about to abolish the closed shop which would include Equity. They put their case in an altogether moderate way. The acting profession is chronically oversubscribed and chronically insecure. They believe that the end of the Equity closed shop will be disastrous for the profession and not only allow bad actors to be employed but bad managers to employ them. I see their concern – and I am sure that this is the first of many meetings of this kind – but I can't think what would be the grounds for making an exception for Equity.

THURSDAY 16 MARCH
To my old stamping ground in Nottingham in the evening for the dinner of the Chamber of Commerce. A capacity crowd of over 400 who respond well to the speech and even better to the jokes. I sit almost next

to Martin Suthers who is now Lord Mayor of the city. We go back a long way. Indeed, it was he who wrote to Leon and myself back in 1968 saying that the seat of Nottingham South was coming up and it might be worth our while applying for it, although Central Office were trying to land it for a promising young man called Nigel Lawson. In fact, the constituency did not even short-list Nigel and left it to Leon and myself to fight it out in the final. Martin told me that this was not the only independent action that Nottingham South took. They did not even grant an interview to one applicant, Norman Tebbit, and refused to see another, Sally Oppenheim, on the grounds that her introductory leaflet for the benefit of the selection committee was too glossy.

WEDNESDAY 29 MARCH

For the first time we have been invited to a family dinner with the Queen and the royal family at Windsor. Others there include David Windlesham, Michael Bishop of British Midlands Airways and the Belgian Ambassador. There are more of the royal family sitting down than we had expected – Philip, the Queen Mother, Margaret, Charles, Anne. I am placed between the Queen and Princess Margaret: not bad for a grammar school boy. Fiona is next to the Prince of Wales. Frankly, the food is a bit sparse – a little piece of fish, lamb and a chocolate mousse, which Margaret tells me on no account to eat.

MONDAY 3 APRIL

Back to the department. The number one priority is the repeal of the dock labour scheme. The white paper is now printed and the bill is ready to go. The plan is that the issue should go to Cabinet on Thursday and that I should make a statement the same day. The position is a little complicated by the visit of Gorbachev. He will arrive on Thursday and start talks with Margaret Thatcher at 10 a.m. She won't be there for the statement and we will have to have Cabinet at 8.30 a.m.

THURSDAY 6 APRIL

Cabinet. I briefly put the case for the end of the scheme. It is out of date; it provides a statutory monopoly in dock work in scheme ports; and it is unnecessary. It is unnecessary because there is no prospect of a return to casual working which was the scheme's original motive. There is virtually no casual working in non-scheme ports and no prospect of a return given that dockers today have to handle expensive equipment and are needed on a regular basis. A whole range of colleagues speak out in support. The issue is decided: the statement will be at 3.30 p.m. So far, the secrecy has been maintained – an almost unique achievement with a statement of this kind. The notice goes up on the screen at 1 p.m.that there will be a statement on the dock labour scheme.

In the afternoon the House is packed. John Wakeham is doing Prime Minister's Questions before me and brings the House down by explaining that Margaret Thatcher cannot be here because she is 'making herself available' to Mr Gorbachev. The laughter goes on and on. Just before I get up Michael Meacher tries a point of order but is slapped down by the Speaker and told to raise it later. My statement is given the loudest support that I have ever heard from our side. They cheer when I say that the scheme is to be abolished and when I say that the bill will be introduced tomorrow the reception is deafening. When I sit down there is an enormous cheer and the waving of order papers – the first time any of my statements have provoked quite that response! Michael Meacher gets off to a bad start. His initial response appears to be both hysterical and threatening and he gets a very rough reception on our side, and not a particularly good one on his. Our members rise one after another to welcome the news as does the official spokesman of the Liberal Democrats, William Wallace, although not the unofficial one, Simon Hughes. Labour attack but not with much force although Eric Heffer rambles on about the Tories being lower than vermin. Afterwards, I am told that the statement has gone down well, not just because of its contents but also because the secrecy had been so well preserved. It is a long time since the House had been taken so completely by surprise. But of course there are still many hurdles to overcome. The guess must be that there will be a strike and that we could be in for a very difficult time. Nonetheless, the move to abolition could not have got off to a better start.

FRIDAY 7 APRIL

The press is almost solid in favour of repeal. There are good leaders in *The Times* and the *Mail*. We hold the first of the regular monitoring meetings at 10 a.m. All the departments with an interest are represented but the handling of the strike will mainly fall to us and the transport department. So far, the reactions are as expected. There have been some stoppages, notably at Liverpool, Tilbury and Southampton but many ports are working normally and the non-scheme ports are working without interruption.

MONDAY 10 APRIL

Our worst scenario was that there would be widespread and instant industrial action but that is not how it is working out at all. Virtually all the ports are back at work today and the docks committee of the TGWU still has to decide whether to call for a ballot. There has never been a clearer example of the combined effect of our industrial relations law reform. The union is desperate not to get on the wrong side of the law, to lose their immunities and therefore to put their funds at risk. The issue that is worrying them is whether a strike would be a trade dispute which is covered by the law or a political conflict with the government which is not. The docks committee have met all today and adjourned without a decision. They are obviously taking the prospect that this might be held to be political action very seriously.

The papers are full of stories about Princess Anne's marriage. Some nice soul has leaked letters written to her by an equerry at the Palace. The assumption is that they are love letters, but for once *The Sun* sent the letters to the police without publishing them. They did of course make it known that they had carried out this public-spirited action. Rumours now abound and the unfortunate equerry has been revealed as a navy commander. I suspect there is quite a lot of truth in the suggestions – certainly Princess Anne and her husband live very separate lives. I have never seen them at the same event and I suppose much the same could be said about the Prince of Wales and Diana but I do not see why even royal people have to be hounded in this way over their private lives. It is not enough to say that they are a legitimate source of public interest. Sooner or later, we are going to have to try to draw up some form of working code. Meanwhile, the press get a dirtier and dirtier reputation.

TUESDAY 11 APRIL
We are now having daily meetings at the department on the docks position. The first stages have gone well and Margaret wonders in passing why we did not act earlier. It is a joke because we all know that the major obstacle was her own reluctance.

WEDNESDAY 12 APRIL
The phoney docks war continues. Much of the press comment is about the muddle inside the TGWU but this is only partly fair. The union has learnt the lessons of other disputes like the seamen's strike and is not going to put its funds at risk unnecessarily. There seems, however, no enthusiasm for a strike at Transport House itself and so far no other union has intervened.

FRIDAY 14 APRIL
The next scene in the slow-moving drama of the dock labour scheme will be an inconclusive meeting with the port employers. The port employers' tactics are to see the union but not to negotiate with them. There is also the battle of public opinion. It is important that the ports do not lose that – Nicholas Finney, the Director of the Employers, has done exceptionally well so far on radio and television. By train to Sutton Coldfield and I get to our house just after John Gummer, our speaker for the night. At the dinner John is in splendid form. He still looks much younger than any of his contemporaries and the audience greatly enjoys his speech. He is going to a meeting of church members in Cheltenham tomorrow, to campaign against the ordination of women. I tell him that I hope his speech does not go as well there.

SATURDAY 15 APRIL
An advice bureau and then we pack up to come back to London. As we

near London we tune into the radio to hear that there has been trouble at one of the football semi-finals. It soon becomes clear that it is the one at Sheffield and that apparently there are five people dead. Immediately, thoughts go back to Brussels and the deaths there. The assumption is that there has been a battle between rival supporters. Slowly, the picture emerges. By the time we are back at Hurlingham Road, the television news is reporting over fifty dead and the trouble seems to have been caused not by hooliganism but by overcrowding at one end of the ground. It is a major disaster with many young people and children among the dead and injured.

MONDAY 17 APRIL

The day of the second reading of the docks bill but all attention is on Hillsborough. Douglas makes a statement at 3.30 to a packed House. He is listened to in silence and all reactions are muted. Even so, it is clear that there will be pressure from both sides of the House to delay the members' card scheme which is due to come to the Commons soon. The most commonly held theory about the tragedy so far is that the crush was caused when a gate was opened, allowing hundreds of late arrivals to get into the ground and to push forward. The belief is that the identity card system could also cause a crush around the entrance gates for big matches. Members on both sides want the legislation delayed.

We do not get onto the docks bill until just before 6 p.m. I try to avoid the kind of attacking speech that I would have made on another day but this does not prevent there being a great deal of noise. Most of it comes when Michael Meacher challenges me to answer questions (which I do) and I challenge him to condemn industrial action and to say what his policy is on the restoration of the dock labour scheme. There is one superb moment of humour when Michael quotes, with great approval, a critical description of my white paper. 'Where does the quotation come from?' we shout Finally, he answers. He is quoting himself. The bill gets its second reading with a majority of over 100 and with many of the Liberal Democrats including David Steel in our lobby.

TUESDAY 18 APRIL

The shadow boxing on the docks continues. The TGWU led by Ron Todd go to see the employers today. The employers listen and refuse point blank to negotiate on a replacement dock labour scheme. Todd and his men leave saying that this makes it a trade dispute and a new meeting to decide on a ballot is scheduled for the end of the week.

THURSDAY 20 APRIL

News comes through that the TGWU have decided on a strike ballot on the docks bill.

SATURDAY 22 APRIL

The *Sunday Times* tell me that they have polled the ports and believe that there will be a 4–1 majority for a strike. Whether the majority will be that high I do not know, but I have never doubted that in a ballot there would be a majority. The ballot is expected to start next week but no result is expected until about 12 May – for Labour, nicely the other side of the Glamorgan by-election and the local elections. All the evidence is that Kinnock is not enthusiastic about strike action and if it is to come wants it as late as possible.

SUNDAY 23 APRIL

Lunch in Surrey with the Bottomleys. It is a great children's party to celebrate Adela's seventh birthday. At lunch, I sit next to Penelope Keith who is a next-door neighbour. She has reassuringly firm views on the Equity case that the end of the closed shop will mean the end of the acting profession. Virginia is settling down in the Department of the Environment and should go a long way. Peter, on the other hand, I fear may be shuffled. He does not deserve to be dropped: he has earned more coverage at transport for himself than the Secretary of State. But I suspect he is not considered sound on a number of issues. If the truth is known, we three – Virginia, Peter and myself – are all wildly unsound on what appears to be the official line at the moment that child benefit is a wasteful and extravagant benefit and should be abolished. It is the best way of providing help for low-income families and it would be an act of great eccentricity if the extra cost of children was not be recognised in either the tax or social security system.

MONDAY 24 APRIL

The day starts with our morning meeting on the docks. I deliver a lecture on the continued need for good security. This follows a DTI circular which, extraordinarily, sets out our contingency planning assumptions – including the expected length of a strike and the critical areas of shortage – and was then sent out to a whole army of people in an entirely unclassified form. Not surprisingly, the contents have leaked and the Socialist Workers have a copy of the entire document. They have not made as much of it as they could and the problem may pass but the action of the DTI defies belief.

WEDNESDAY 26 APRIL

A business conference at a country hotel in Surrey. There is an enormous turnout – over 1,000 people packed into what is usually the nightclub but also serves for major snooker matches. It is somewhere between addressing the party conference and giving a speech in a beer cellar. Jeffrey Archer has been on earlier in the day and John Cope tells me that he told a typical Archer joke. His bank had been in touch to ask if he would like one of the new cheque cards which allows you to draw £250 at a time rather than just £50. So he went into the bank and the cashier said there were one or two formalities. 'Do you make more than £10,000, Mr Archer?' he asked. To which Jeffrey replied, 'Some days I do – and some days I don't'.

THURSDAY 27 APRIL

A Cabinet photograph to mark ten years in office. The anniversary comes next Thursday. Looking back at the first 1979 photograph, there are few of us who have survived: Geoffrey Howe, Peter Walker, George Younger and myself. In all truth, that is a very large turnover. Margaret Thatcher may not like sacking people but she has done it consistently since being elected in 1975. It is an integral part of her approach to leading a political party. Looking around at the Cabinet in 1989 I can only marvel that we have so many good people left.

WEDNESDAY 3 MAY

The 1922 Committee lunch at The Savoy to mark Margaret Thatcher's ten years. There is a good turnout, including Ted Heath and virtually the whole Cabinet. Past members are also invited and Michael Jopling draws Edward du Cann as a next-door neighbour. Du Cann may have been Chairman of the 1922 for a long time but these days he is a much-disliked figure and seen as the puppet of the equally disliked Tiny Rowland.[198] I do much better. I have Peter Viggers on one side and two away is Peter Temple-Morris.[199] In my study I have a photograph showing the three of us as undergraduates thirty years earlier, talking to Rab Butler. Not only are we now all in the House but even more unlikely, we are all still friends. Going back to Westminster the traffic is terrible. I finally abandon the car and walk. It is a marvellously fine day. As I pass a line of stationary traffic, Max Hastings pops his head out of a car. He says he has been having lunch with Michael Heseltine. I had wondered if Michael was going to turn up for the lunch.

THURSDAY 4 MAY

Cabinet. Geoffrey Howe starts business with a very impressive tribute to Margaret Thatcher on the anniversary of her ten years in office. He says that during this period, the government's authority has been restored, the economy brought back to health and Britain's position in the world re-established. Margaret Thatcher thanks everyone, saying that some have been there since 1979. When we get down to business Margaret

---

198 'Tiny' Rowland was a maverick businessman, corporate raider and the chief executive of the Lonrho conglomerate from 1962 to 1993. He was dubbed 'the unacceptable face of capitalism' by Heath when he was Prime Minister, bought *The Observer* newspaper and became embroiled in a long-running battle with the Al-Fayed brothers over the takeover of Harrods.

199 Peter TM – another Cambridge mafia member and my Vice Chairman at the Cambridge University Conservative Association. A very good friend. Left-wing MP for Leominster. Later crossed to Labour but without causing any of the resentment that such changes often do. He became a Labour peer.

Thatcher asks that the decks be cleared by the summer recess. She wants to round off the first two sessions. She also, of course, wants to shuffle the Cabinet. I now have a problem. I cannot go in and resign while the docks dispute remains unresolved – even less so if there are other disputes going on at the same time.

In the evening, a dinner at No. 10 to celebrate the ten years. According to Margaret this is the first time in 250 years that Cabinet ministers and their spouses have collectively sat down together. It is a genial affair. The men are in dinner jackets; the wives in long dresses – Fiona looks super in a new dress that she has bought during the day. I sit between Elspeth Howe and Sheila Moore. Elspeth is very outspoken about Margaret's position on Europe. I gather from Geoffrey before dinner that he too is pretty fed up with her outright and blunt opposition to all things European. Geoffrey thinks that we would do better fighting our corner if we showed some sympathy for the European ideal. Geoffrey makes another good speech in thanking her, Nick Ridley presents her with a picture of Chequers and she responds. Margaret pays particular tribute to Denis – which goes down well with us. She jokes that if she is ever tempted to say something nice about the BBC, Denis soon dissuades her. I fear that is an accurate summing-up of the Thatcher family view of the BBC. As we leave, Denis says how well I am doing. That is exceptionally nice of him and contrasts with any view offered by Margaret herself. In my introspective moments I note that although virtually everyone in the parliamentary party has complimented me on the handling of the docks statement she has remained entirely silent. As Geoffrey Howe remarked some weeks ago, how much more she could have achieved with better man management.

FRIDAY 5 MAY

As I drive to Sutton Coldfield for a lunch, the news of the Glamorgan by-election comes through. We have lost by 6,000. By any standards this is a bad result and confirms the swing to Labour which was evident in the council elections (a swing of 12 per cent). I fear all this ten-year anniversary 'celebration' has been a mixed blessing. It has enabled every commentator to have a go. The very fact that we have been in power for ten years conspires to give an impression that we are dated and fighting yesterday's battles. There is now a substantial anti-Thatcher feeling. The public admire her courage but dislike her inflexibility and some of her gut views. Kinnock and Labour are beginning to make some progress. The red roses and the well-presented youngish men are changing the party's image for the better. If only they can keep the silly left out of the public eye and prevent people like Michael Meacher resurrecting foolish policies from the past they could have a chance.

SATURDAY 6 MAY–SUNDAY 7 MAY

A glorious weekend. The temperature is in the 70s and all the spring flowers are out. Hurlingham looks magnificent and I settle myself in a chair in the middle of the club and write a speech for Monday's debate. On Sunday I get a curious call from Jeffrey Archer via the No. 10 switchboard. How come he can use the No. 10 switchboard, which I had always thought was confined to ministers? Jeffrey says that he has been going round the country on the European elections. He has heard from a number of senior sources that I am to be the next chairman of the party. He wonders if we might have breakfast. Would an 8 o'clock breakfast at The Savoy suit? I mumble that there are always a lot of rumours in circulation and he should not take them too seriously, but if he would like to have breakfast I would be delighted. I can hardly tell him that I am about to stand down and that even if I was not I very much doubt if Margaret would make me Chairman. It just shows Jeffrey's enormous desire to get back into serious politics. Nor can I understand why he wants it when he is doing so well outside. Goodness knows he has not got very much from politics but it remains an obsession with him to succeed politically.

MONDAY 8 MAY

The Times carry a story that I am favourite to become the next Conservative Party chairman. Or at least that is what the headline says. In fact, Robin Oakley's story says that I am favourite among Conservative MPs. That is all very encouraging but sadly the chairmanship is not an elected post. It depends entirely on the Prime Minister. As with one or two other jobs, the crucial determinant is how well the individual gets on with the lady herself.

TUESDAY 9 MAY

In the evening I go to Grosvenor House and speak to an audience of 1,200 at the Road Haulage Association's annual dinner. It occurs to me that I am doing a farewell tour: Nottingham a few weeks ago and now my old transport area. One of the figures there from the past is Reggie Wilson, a former chairman of the NFC. As I come up to say good night he is confiding to a small group how much I have come on!

SATURDAY 13 MAY

I phone John Major. Tomorrow I am due to go to Paris to take part in a television programme on Europe, which is not boding well. Ted Heath is to be interviewed first and it is only after that that they will get onto my debate where I am debating with two prominent socialist spokesmen from France and Germany. What concerns me is the answer to the question: 'When will you join the currency mechanism of the EMS?' The standard answer to that is 'when the time is right'. This is all very well but leads to a number of other obvious questions like 'when *will* the time be right?' or 'what kind of conditions would you want to see in judging whether the time is right?' John's less than reassuring answer to all this is that there is no answer. The truth is that Margaret is not interested in joining this side of the millennium.

SUNDAY 14 MAY

Fiona and I fly to Paris on the same plane as Ted Heath. We are waved through the barrier at Paris and the only delay is when Ted has to rummage in his case to find his passport which fortunately he has. Ex-Prime Minister or not, documents are still required to get into France. We are then taken in separate cars to the Hôtel de Crillon where the BBC, at no small expense, have provided us with separate suites. For the opening shots of the programme, we all sit around the table. Ted confides to me that Margaret's views on Europe are disastrous and will split the party asunder. It is obviously going to be one of those programmes, and so it proves. Jonathan Dimbleby is only a few seconds into his interview when it becomes clear that Ted is really going to have a go. It has obviously been boiling up within him and out it comes. Margaret Thatcher was directly 'misleading' the country with her talk of Europe being a gigantic socialist state. Britain would just become a second-rate power, he says. The time had come to speak out. Ted's message could not have been clearer or more hostile to Margaret. Throughout this tirade I am sitting next to Karsten Voigt, the German Social Democrat foreign affairs spokesman, and frankly, what irritates me most is his great and obvious enjoyment of the attack. When it comes to my turn I insist on leaving the planned discussion to answer Ted's points. I accuse him of first going over the top in his attack which he quite obviously has. But I also argue that his view is out of date. We are in Europe. We are committed to Europe. But that does not prevent us arguing our case and fighting our corner on issues like the social dimension when we believe our interests are at stake. The debate then continues and it becomes very clear that neither of the other two have any idea what is going on in Britain. At the end a magnificent lunch has been prepared for us, but thankfully Ted has left to catch an earlier plane.

MONDAY 5 JUNE

The first full day back at the department after Whitsun. The docks case has still not finished.[200] All our predictions are that the employers will lose. This is on the basis that their case was comprehensively thrown out of court at the first instance. If that is indeed the result, then the chances are that we will be into an official strike either later this week or by the weekend at the latest.

---

200 Following the collapse of talks with the employers, the TGWU thought a strike could be considered industrial and called a national ballot on 20 April that resulted in a three to one vote for strike action. The port employers went to court arguing that the strike was political. As a consequence, the union's decision to take strike action was placed on hold while the courts deliberated over its legitimacy.

TUESDAY 6 JUNE

Back in Westminster there have been two statements on China and Hong Kong that have delayed the start of the debate. The murderous action of the Chinese troops in Beijing has outraged public opinion. There has scarcely been, in my memory, a more brutal suppression of a movement for democracy than the one we have witnessed over the last days. The nearest equivalent was Prague in 1956. The opposition now complain that they do not have time to debate the employment bill (which by any standards is uncontroversial) and ask for the debate to be put on another day. We refuse. They sulk, particularly because the opposition whips had forgotten to whip their party for later in the evening. The result is, that led by the remarkably surly Deputy Chief Whip Don Dixon, the Labour Party embark on a filibuster. For hour after hour the debate drones on. We finally finish at 5.35 in the morning and the third reading vote takes place in broad daylight. I finally go to bed at 6.00. It is an extremely odd way to run a country.

WEDNESDAY 7 JUNE

To everyone's surprise, the news comes in that the port employers have succeeded in winning an injunction against the dockers' leaders. Our woman at the court reports back that the grounds have nothing to do with the industrial relations laws we have passed since 1979 but everything to do with the original docks legislation passed in 1946, and particularly the scheme of 1967 which appears to place on dockers the statutory duty to work and not strike. The court has not held this to be the case, rather it has decided that there is sufficient doubt for there to be a full hearing on the issue. In the meantime the balance of advantage is that the injunction stays. Not surprisingly, the union is dismayed. One interpretation is that it means that every one of the many strikes they have had since 1967 has been unlawful. It is a bombshell for Ron Todd and it has also sent Michael Meacher into orbit. I go on television to point out that the decision results not from Thatcher's legislation but from the legislation of Attlee and Wilson.

THURSDAY 8 JUNE

At Cabinet, the first item is the televising of Parliament. Margaret asks if everyone accepts the report of the select committee under John Wakeham that has proposed a fairly restricted form of broadcasting. Malcolm Rifkind says that he for one is worried that it is so restrictive. Margaret will have none of it. Her message is that we must back the Lord President's report. She has a deep hostility to the broadcasting organisations, particularly the BBC who she quite obviously totally distrusts. She thinks that left to their own devices they will edit reports unfairly, as they do now with other reports. I have never heard her quite so openly outspoken on the broadcasting organisations.

Geoffrey Howe's report is dominated by the events in China. The *Daily Mail* is only one of the newspapers who are questioning the justice of leaving the 3.5 million British passport holders to their fate when China takes over, on present plans, in 1997. Margaret is very sympathetic to this case. She does not want an influx of new immigrants but she is not prepared to abandon her responsibilities. Her views become even clearer at the overseas committee directly after Cabinet. On the agenda is the problem of the Vietnamese boat people who are now flooding into Hong Kong. The latest figures seem to show this is at a rate of 10,000 a month. On this, Margaret is emphatic, it may be difficult but we have to find ways of stopping the inflow; that will include some form of compulsory repatriation. Her view is that we have a duty to the citizens of Hong Kong but we do not have the same responsibility to the people of Vietnam. Geoffrey Howe has a thoroughly miserable time. He tries to point out the difficulties of repatriation and the attention this will get from the press and television but his arguments get very short shrift. The Prime Minister and her Foreign Secretary do look a long way apart with Margaret showing little respect for Geoffrey's arguments.

SUNDAY II JUNE

Fly to Luxembourg for the social affairs council on the social charter.[201] Dinner is in a small hotel overlooking the Moselle. It is a fine night and

---

201 The social charter (not to be confused with the Social Chapter) is the popular name for the *Community Charter of the Fundamental Social Rights of Workers* signed by eleven of the twelve member states (the UK did not sign) in Strasbourg in December 1989. The charter had no legal force and was declaratory in nature. It describes a series of 'social' rights in rather general terms. It was intended to act as a stimulus for further activity in the social field.

the drink on the terrace beforehand makes the journey worthwhile. The hotel's owner says she knows all the British ministers like Sir Geoffrey Howe and what a pleasure it is to have me at her hotel *again*. It is very nice of her but to the best of my memory this is the first time I have been to the hotel.

MONDAY 12 JUNE

We get down to business slowly. For some reason, all council meetings start late and we are half an hour behind. It soon becomes apparent that the United Kingdom is in a minority. Commissioner Papandreou says that public opinion is demanding action in the social area. Others quickly come in behind her. I put my usual case against the charter: that these regulations will do nothing to create jobs and that we are being asked to sign a blank cheque. However, no one else seriously supports this root and branch opposition. These councils have a nasty habit of working through lunch. This means that there is the continual accompaniment of simultaneous translation and the clatter of cutlery, while the shining hour is not improved by the oppressive heat or by the fact that a good number of the ministers appear to be heavy smokers. Papandreou, in particular, is a chain smoker who smokes with the courses rather than just in-between. The next step is the European summit in Madrid at the end of the month.

WEDNESDAY 14 JUNE

A meeting at No. 10. Margaret is in a rather sunny mood. There is a great show of affection for Nigel. All the stories are that she and the Chancellor are at loggerheads over the European Monetary System and a range of economic policy issues. The stories have come from a weekend interview done by Nigel in which he was outspoken about Alan Walters and had the temerity to suggest that his own future is partly up to the Prime Minister and partly up to him. Good for Nigel. Margaret says that she is so fed up with the stance of the *Today* programme that she has given up listening to it and now works instead. Nick Ridley caps that by saying he has given up both listening to the radio and reading the newspapers. Margaret demurs at that. We still have some friends in the press, she says. Margaret calls on John Major to speak and playfully says that she sees he is destined for great things.

The day ends with a very close vote at 3 a.m. on, of all things, a dog registration scheme. Passions are running high on our side following some very nasty attacks by Rottweilers on children. Both the Home Secretary and Nick make statements during the day announcing new measures to allay the fears but the dog registration lobby refuse to be pacified. Cabinet ministers are literally dragged from their beds and we scrape home with a majority of thirteen.

THURSDAY 15 JUNE
Cabinet. I say that the unofficial action in the docks is crumbling and the major ports affected are, predictably, Liverpool and Tilbury. I warn that this does not mean that we are out of the woods yet but equally it is true that even the slowest company has had time to avoid action. There are only two ships locked in Liverpool – one from Russia and I can only imagine that the other one got lost.

After Cabinet the officials withdraw and Margaret warns that there will be all kinds of attempts to portray the party as divided after the European elections and the two by-elections taking place today. Her view is that all comment should be suspended until we know the official results on Sunday night. There will be the BBC exit poll but Margaret's view is that should be ignored. Not for the first time, Ken Clarke clings rather obstinately to a contrary view: namely that we would do better to prepare everyone for the disaster that he (and everyone else) expects to ensue. This outrages Margaret who believes it is unthinkable to concede defeat until the votes have been counted.

SUNDAY 18 JUNE
The European election results are bad although not quite as bad as the BBC exit poll predicted. Nevertheless, we have lost a clutch of seats that

we should have held.[202] I do an election results programme with Bryan Gould and David Steel. Halfway through our rather genial discussion Ted Heath comes onto the line – 'Ted from SW1'. Once again, he lays about him and once again attacks the Prime Minister for the lacklustre campaign. He points to the contrast with his own campaign which had taken him to every part of the country. My response to that is that it was not his energy that we were complaining about, it was the message that he gave when he arrived. We parry for a few minutes before the programme moves on but in truth the battles between Ted and Margaret have not done us any good whatsoever. Neither has the evident conflict between Margaret and Nigel Lawson over exchange policy.

MONDAY 19 JUNE

Back to Broadcasting House to do *Today* on the European elections. I have observed before that when we go down to defeat there is a shortage of volunteers to explain what has happened. Last night, after Geoffrey Howe and myself, the BBC had to turn to a parliamentary secretary, Eric Forth, to bat for the party having tried apparently every other member of the Cabinet. This morning I do five minutes with the BBC and go straight to an IRN radio car parked outside Broadcasting House. The interviews go well and John Redwood comes up later to say how 'professional' the performance was. In my book that is the highest form of praise.

In the evening Fiona and I go to the banquet given each year by the Foreign Secretary for the diplomatic corps. As the years have gone by the table has got better and better. When I was the most junior member of the Cabinet, I sat between the wives of two of the more obscure countries and struggled to make conversation with ladies who knew no English at all. Tonight, I head table two and sit between the wife of the Finn-ish Ambassador and Mary Soames. It was the first time that I had met Mary Soames properly, even though Christopher was in the Cabinet for the first couple of years that I was. Mary is good news. A daughter of

---

202 All told, the Conservatives lost fifteen seats although they maintained a third of the share of the vote, which was substantially better than in the next European elections when John Major was Prime Minister – and I was Party Chairman.

Winston Churchill, she is now Chairman of the National Theatre which she obviously enjoys greatly. I ask her about Jock Colville's diaries which I read a few months ago. She has no reservations about them whatsoever and thought that they showed Winston to good effect. Indeed, she thought that Winston knew that he was keeping such a record.[203]

WEDNESDAY 21 JUNE

In the evening I have dinner with Michael Heseltine. Michael is clearly interested in the stories about Ken Baker. I tell him that he will be in some trouble if his appointment as Party Chairman goes ahead and we then win the election. In those circumstances Ken will be the heir. Michael says that his support is building up in a way that has surprised even him and that the support extends to all parts of the party, including ministers. He is obviously working round the clock on his task. He is doing nothing else but politics. He is giving no time to his business. His speaking engagements are chosen on the basis of how useful they can be in his efforts to become Margaret Thatcher's successor. I tell him about my intention to leave, the only politician I have spoken to. Michael is entirely discreet and is under no obligation to report back to the whips as say, John Major may feel that he is. Michael is obviously surprised that I am considering leaving, most of the publicity over the last few weeks has been along the lines of taking a new job. He says first that I am highly regarded in the party and that he has not heard any criticism. He says it also depends whether I need the money or can struggle on and that clearly, I would be a 'highly marketable' person. He is also frank enough to say that from his point of view he would much prefer me to stay. His advice is to 'hang on'. Advice which he repeats as we leave.

THURSDAY 22 JUNE

A meeting of H committee where I report on the docks. The latest development is that the House of Lords (judicial) have lifted the injunction on the TGWU but not in time. They now need to have another ballot

---

203 Colville, Jock, *The Fringes of Power: 10 Downing Street Diaries 1939–1955*. Colville was a diplomat seconded to 10 Downing Street as private secretary to the Prime Minister.

if they are to mount an official strike (it is more than twenty-eight days since the last ballot). If all goes well the bill will be an act by the time any strike starts. There then follows a long discussion about the health service in which Ken Clarke is offered all kinds of dud advice on how he could get the case over better.

THURSDAY 29 JUNE

At Cabinet I report that the docks bill is now in its final stages in the House of Lords and that all being well it will have Royal Assent next Monday. The net effect will be that the scheme will have been abolished and that no strike will bring it back – but that will not prevent the TGWU from taking strike action from about 10 July.

SUNDAY 2 JULY

Margaret has given an interview to the *Sunday Express* in which she says we are looking at the position of strikes in essential services and the law. This has been hardened up very considerably by the paper to a story about introducing laws to ban strikes. I am in demand. I give what I hope will be the definitive interview to *The World This Weekend* in which I say we will review the position in a measured way and that a change in the law is not an instant solution: it takes time to get a bill through. The immediate solution lies in the unions calling off their strike and getting down to talks. Interviews of one kind or another take me though the day. It is a splendid way of spending the only day off in the week. Needless to say no one had told me previously about the Prime Minister's interview.

SUNDAY 9 JULY

To Oxfordshire for the traditional cricket match between the department and the press. I am run out by the news editor of *The Independent* – who later confesses that he was not holding the ball when he broke my wicket. I get my revenge by having him caught in the slips.

TUESDAY 11 JULY

As the morning goes on it becomes clear that the docks strike has not started as solidly as we expected. The big traditional scheme ports like Liverpool and Tilbury are out but about eighteen of the smaller ports are working normally – including ports like Sheerness and the South Wales ports.

FRIDAY 14 JULY
I bring in our labour attachés to talk to me about their experience of strikes in essential services in other European countries. Italy seems to have the worst record but France and Belgium also have problems. There is no neat hand-me-down European answer, but a number of countries insist that even where a strike takes place there must be a minimum level of service; a cooling-off period is another possible runner.

MONDAY 24 JULY
Everyone is waiting for the reshuffle. I go to the Ritz to have lunch with Simon Heffer. As we are waiting to order, who should come in but John Major with another *Telegraph* journalist, Godfrey Barker. John has not heard a word about his future, which surprises both of us. It is reported that John Gummer, Cecil Parkinson and Chris Patten had already been in to Downing Street. Prophetically, John says 'there is something missing in the reshuffle so far'.

Back in the office a call comes through from Andrew Turnbull from No. 10. My office look excited. It is only Andrew saying that I am staying where I am but that they would like to move John Cope to another Minister of State job. As long as John Cope is remaining within the government I have no objections to the move. It is confirmed that he is. Andrew suggests David Davis as a replacement. I say that would be fine but I would put Charles Wardle, my old PPS, as first choice and David Davis, who distinguished himself on the dock labour scheme, next. In the meantime, I warn John Cope about his imminent move and say that I will very much miss him. He has been a first-class Minister of State and from a weak initial position we have delivered a series of important changes in employment.

I call through to John Major but his office say that he has just been called to No. 10. They say they have their 'fingers crossed'. While all this is happening we are running a three-line whip on the electricity privatisation bill. In the first division I run into Cecil Parkinson who obviously wants to talk.

'She has given me transport', he says. 'What do you think of that?'

I say 'I am amazed', which is no less than the truth.

'Well', Cecil says, 'she says it is a vital political subject and she needs someone there with experience'.

'There's no question of that and if my experience is anything to go by you will enjoy it' I say. I hope this second response is more helpful to Cecil.

At the next division I meet John Gummer. John is making no secret of the fact that he is Minister of Agriculture – rightly so. He was badly treated as Chairman, and one thing you can say is that Margaret Thatcher remembers her debts. Mind you, it is all a bit surprising looking back to Cambridge when John was a very urban creature.

As we go down the stairs to the cars we see John Major in front of us. 'Now come on', says John, 'tell us what you have got'. John Major refuses politely and determinedly in spite of John's entreaties. John Gummer drives off and John Major comes over. 'I wasn't going to say it in front of everyone but I have been given the Foreign Office'. He appears in some shock – not surprisingly. 'I hope I can do it', he says. I remind him that that was exactly what he said when he was given the Chief Secretary's job. He nods. 'I will need all the help I can get from my friends' he says. It is a spectacular promotion for John. I am delighted. He is one of the good men in politics. Sound judgement and sound instincts. I suppose that means we agree on most things.

During the evening the rest of the news comes out. Most significant is that Geoffrey Howe is to become Leader of the House and Deputy Prime Minister. Stories are already circulating that Geoffrey is anything but pleased by the move. At yet another division he is surrounded by a group of well-wishers. I say I will ring him later.

When I get home I ring Geoffrey. He is very unhappy. According to Geoffrey, he was rung at nine in the morning to say that the Prime Minister wanted to see him. He had been assured as recently as Saturday by the Chief Whip that he was to stay where he was. David Waddington apparently knew that a change was in mind but felt that he could not break the secrecy. When they met, Margaret said that she would like him to become Leader of the House. If he wanted to he could, as an alternative, become Home Secretary but he hadn't shown any great enthusiasm for this in the past. Geoffrey had agreed about the Home Office and had asked for time to think about the Leader job. At this stage the Deputy Prime Minister had specifically not been offered. Several hours later, Geoffrey had returned – hence the delay for John Major – and said he would only take the job if he could be Deputy Prime Minister and Chairman of Committees. He wanted the position occupied by Willie Whitelaw. Margaret had said that no one could take that position but with bad grace accepted. Indeed, the guidance from No. 10 tonight appears to be that he is Deputy Prime Minister only in name.

Geoffrey is still concerned that he has made the wrong decision and whether he shouldn't have resigned: his daughter has rung to say he should. He was most concerned about what he regarded as the double dealing. For 'two pins' he says he would have resigned but that would have damaged the party. He had been part of the revolution for the last fifteen years. The last thing he wanted to do was to bring down the whole temple.

My advice is that he was right not to resign. The job he has now is one of great importance and could be developed, and I also say that there is a great deal of support and affection for him in the party. I leave him still a deeply unhappy man.

TUESDAY 25 JULY
The papers are full of the changes and in particular John Major's promotion. Geoffrey appeared on the *Today* programme and in response to sympathetic questioning by Brian Redhead said that this was an important job and he looked forward to the challenge. Nevertheless, I felt sufficiently concerned to ring up Leon in Brussels to check with him that I had given the right advice. Leon had been one of the people who had been consulted in the interim between the offer and the acceptance. Geoffrey had also rung him again last night. 'Should he resign?' but Leon's advice was the same. He had asked what Geoffrey would say to the question 'why are you resigning now

and not yesterday?' What indeed! Leon also tells me that Margaret Thatcher specifically didn't offer Geoffrey the deputy prime ministership although apparently she did say that he might have the job if in two or three months' time 'trust' had been re-established. The ridiculous thing is that had it been done differently it could have been successful. Had Geoffrey been offered the Deputy Prime Minister role at the time it could have been made into an attractive package. It is difficult to see how bridges can ever be entirely rebuilt. Margaret has had her way at the Foreign Office but she has paid a high price for it.

WEDNESDAY 26 JULY

The papers are full of the Geoffrey Howe switch which is recounted in great detail. No. 10 say that they have not leaked it. The assumption is that it comes from Geoffrey or his friends. It goes from embarrassment to embarrassment. It is reported that Douglas Hurd (with some justice) is miffed at the report that his job was being traded around and we also have stories about Geoffrey and Elspeth being moved out of Chevening and offered Dorneywood which has meant no home for the Chancellor. The whole reshuffle has become a disaster. Geoffrey is variously described as 'walking wounded' and the whole excitement of the changes has simply evaporated.

THURSDAY 27 JULY

Cabinet. Margaret tries to take the sting out of events. She says that 'barring accidents' this will be the team for the next election. I think about my own position. I can't go while the docks strike is on. Then? I am bound to say that the past two or three days have not persuaded me to stay. I will choose my time but the docks crisis must end first. In the afternoon I go to Prime Minister's Questions. The really significant event is the demonstration for Geoffrey that comes afterwards at Business Questions. He is greeted with an enormous cheer from our side. I notice Julian Critchley sitting on the front bench below the gangway waving an order paper frantically. Margaret Thatcher sits there in more than slight embarrassment.

13

GOODBYE TO ALL THAT

SEPTEMBER 1989–JANUARY 1990

After fifteen years in government and opposition with Margaret Thatcher I believed that the time had come to move out – or as I preferred to think of it, move on. But leaving voluntarily is not as easy as it might seem, particularly if you want to stay in the House of Commons which I loved and where I had been since 1970. Understandably, people want to know why and if you fail to give a convincing reply make up a reason for themselves. 'He was never really "one of us"'. 'He couldn't stand it (or her) any longer'. Or worst of all: 'You wait. There is some scandal about to explode'. As I struggled to set out my reasons I unconsciously hit upon a phrase which earned me a place in The Oxford Dictionary of Political Quotations *and which has been used ever since with varying degrees of truth by a range of figures in public life – a wish 'to spend more time with my family'.*

MONDAY 4 SEPTEMBER 1989

Lunch with Roy Griffiths. He says that Ken Clarke's National Health Service review was horrendous. The Prime Minister was forever intervening with her anecdotes. This of course is her characteristic approach on social issues – she would not remotely do this on the economy.

TUESDAY 5 SEPTEMBER

Lunch with Nick True. I tell him that I have decided to leave. In previous times he has argued against this course – not now. He thinks that over the last twelve months I have performed better than anyone. He does not see where the potential is in employment over the next year. The stage is too limited. He thinks the best time to go is between the old session and the new before I get involved in further legislation. I have a hankering for January 1990 – fifteen years to the month after I joined the first Thatcher shadow Cabinet.

SUNDAY 10 SEPTEMBER

To New York by Concorde. By far the best way to travel to the United States. The aim is to learn something about how the Americans tackle strikes in essential services. John Major is on the same plane. He is going to Washington on his first visit as Foreign Secretary. He tells me that he has had a difficult August reading himself into his new post. Norma is not overjoyed with the job because if it is done as Elspeth Howe did it, it requires many meetings and much entertaining. He too seems to have his mind on the next steps which are not political. He feels that he owes a lot to his wife and his family and the very least he can do is to ensure that they have enough to live on in retirement. Hence, he talks quite openly of going to the City. I suspect that the new job has heralded a moment of truth in his life. Like most of the Cabinet, he has no money and will certainly not earn any in government. Added to that, he has entered a way of life which obviously causes pressures at home. He is in the running for the leadership – not in front – but in the running behind Ken Baker and Michael Heseltine. In his present mood he will not pursue that. He tells me that there is only one job that he has ever wanted and that is Chancellor of the Exchequer.

THURSDAY 21 SEPTEMBER

A fascinating lunch with John Junor who has now left the *Sunday Express*. Since he has left he has been inundated with offers. The *Mail on Sunday* want him, the *Sunday Times* want him to write a column, and Murdoch wants him to write his memoirs for his Collins publishing house. Murdoch rang him up personally to put the proposition. 'Will people still be interested?' he asks. In my view they would be fascinated by his years with Beaverbrook. My guess is that he will sign up.

SATURDAY 23 SEPTEMBER–SUNDAY 24 SEPTEMBER

I confess to being depressed about the prospect of the next few weeks. There is the party conference and all the agony of preparing the conference speech. I think the real problem is what to say when I go. When Michael Heseltine left at least he had no problem of that kind. Equally, when John Nott and George Younger left there was little problem. They were leaving the government, leaving the House and had decided to pursue business careers. I want to stay in the House and campaign on some issues, including the position of women so that Kate and Isobel have exactly the same opportunities as any man. We cannot allow the waste of women's talent to continue. I suppose what I want is a change. I don't want to just hang on. There is everything to be said for going when you are in a relatively strong position but I still have not come up with a one-sentence reason why I am leaving. If I do not the newspapers will make it up for me.

WEDNESDAY 27 SEPTEMBER

An awful day. I had made the greatest effort to discover what the Prime Minister's views were on strikes in essential services. The Policy Unit had told me that there was no hint of disagreement but it was quite clear from the beginning of the meeting of the economic affairs committee that she was going to oppose. This is how she operates. Rather than allowing me to have the first word and introduce the paper, and then to get my colleagues' views, she marks everyone's card in advance. 'We have just had a meeting', she says (with whom we are not told). 'The proposals on industrial action are very good but I believe that the proposals on essential services will damage us.' No one can fail to get the message. I am then allowed to introduce my paper. My position with Margaret has been to take her head-on and not to retreat. If you retreat you are lost. I am under no illusion on the likely outcome. I put the case. She then comes on to the attack. Finally, she says this is 'ill prepared'. At that moment I snap. 'Look, you can say you don't agree', I say, 'You can't say it is ill prepared'. Colleagues have been looking on in silence. No one comes out against the proposal in principle. After about three quarters of an hour Margaret brings the meeting to an end. She says that the preponderance of opinion is against. I say that the committee is divided. With ill grace she says that a divided committee is not the basis for action. She may be right but where does she think that leaves the poll tax? What infuriates me is the lack of notice about it all. Who, I wonder, are the advisers she spoke with? Another reason to go.

FRIDAY 29 SEPTEMBER

Geoffrey Holland says that Robin Butler was horrified by the way the Prime Minister behaved. He said that I had handled myself with 'great dignity'. That is all very well but it means that we have lost the opportunity for the essential services legislation.

MONDAY 2 OCTOBER

Breakfast with John Wakeham who says that Geoffrey Howe had a major bust-up with Margaret Thatcher in Madrid and threatened to resign.

TUESDAY 10 OCTOBER

Party conference. The press is full of stories that the Chancellor could have a rough time. It's nonsense. As long as he provides a fighting speech the conference will cheer – but that will not cure the economy. In the employment debate, my map to show the fall in unemployment around the country half works. Everyone likes the idea but the background fails to flash out in total synchronisation. The real problem comes when the autocue runs out in the middle of a punchy piece about the Labour Party and then proceeds to play back the wrong ending. Fortunately, I have my speech with me and have kept it up to date page by page. I transfer to the written speech and come in strongly enough to get a two-minute standing ovation. Harvey Thomas is greatly embarrassed but I don't think the audience noticed.

WEDNESDAY 11 OCTOBER

The papers are still full of the fall of sterling and there are some absurd

pieces about Nigel. The man himself has left to write his speech in Leices-
tershire. Why not? The only trouble is that half the national press appear
to be camped outside his home demanding photographs and interviews.
There is one terrible piece in *Today* where the journalist – looking over
the fence – writes a piece along the lines of 'I watched the agony of the
Chancellor'. He then describes the normal process of a man writing his
speech. Dinner with Robin Day and Peter Jenkins. Robin does not look
at all well but makes an effort to be sociable and a good host. He is now
a rather sad and lonely figure with no particular role. It is a great pity
that it has worked out this way. He has obviously made enemies and had
tantrums, but above all, he is an honourable man with high and genuine
values. Peter talks about the leadership and says that if Michael Heseltine
was elected leader he would consider voting Conservative and so would
his wife, Polly Toynbee. The assumption is still that Margaret will lead us
into the next election but it is no longer regarded as automatic. She lacks
friends, certainly in Cabinet. She has shown fairly consistently that she
will not go to the stake for others. Not surprisingly, there are few who
would go to the stake for her. Even now her position tends to be that the
economic problems, or crisis as the press call them, belong to the Chancellor not to her. Peter Jenkins recounts what happened at the Madrid
meeting. He says that Margaret Thatcher actually barred her door to
Geoffrey. Geoffrey was insisting that a date should be given to join the
EMS and threatened to resign over it. If any of this is even half true one
can only wonder that Geoffrey was taken by surprise in the reshuffle.

TUESDAY 17 OCTOBER

The House is back and television has begun. The pictures won't be shown
to the public until the new session. The next month or so is to prepare
us. The Chamber is certainly brighter and big lights, like Chinese lan-
terns, have been suspended from the ceiling.

In the evening I speak at Michael Heseltine's constituency dinner in
the Commons. Afterwards we go to my room on the Cabinet floor. I tell
him that I am going to leave once the employment bill is through. He

says that the decision will come as a surprise. He did not think I would be accused of leaving a sinking ship but the presentation needed care. He advised going in to see Margaret, telling her of my decision and saying that although I would prefer to leave now I would not mind soldiering on until Christmas if it was convenient for her. We both recognise the irony implicit in Michael giving advice on how best to leave the Cabinet but as it happens, I think the advice is very sensible.

WEDNESDAY 18 OCTOBER

Lunch with Bill Deedes at The Savoy Grill.[204] I have not seen Bill for a long time. He was very good to me in the early stages of my political career and was the ideal ex-minister giving help and good advice. He is now well into his seventies but well preserved and still very acute. He is close to the Thatchers and particularly Denis, hence the 'Dear Bill Letters' of *Private Eye*. What is significant is that even Bill now talks of the end of the Thatcher years. Everyone now foresees it, although no one can predict how it will happen.

TUESDAY 24 OCTOBER

I get back to the House in time to listen to an exceptionally strong wind-up on the economic debate by Norman Lamont. I sit next to Nigel who is subdued. He had opened the debate and the one point that the 9 o'clock television news had headlined was his criticism of Alan Walters as a 'part-time adviser'. The row between Nigel and Walters on the issue of EMU and the ERM has been going full blast over the last week. I say that I hope that this is an end to it and there will be no more interventions from Walters. Nigel enthusiastically agrees.

THURSDAY 26 OCTOBER

I have invited Nick True to lunch and we look through my resignation letter. After lunch I go over to the House for Prime Minister's Questions.

---

204 Conservative MP from 1950 to October 1974, a Cabinet minister under Harold Macmillan and Sir Alec Douglas-Home in the early 1960s and the editor of the *Daily Telegraph* from 1974 to 1985.

Margaret is challenged on Walters but defends with some well-prepared formula that just falls short of whole-hearted support for Nigel Lawson or indeed, condemnation of Walters. 'Advisers advise; ministers decide'. But it seems to satisfy our side. At the department we go back to work on the social chapter. During a break at 6 o'clock, Graham Roberts, one of my deputy secretaries, comes in looking thunderstruck, saying 'the Chancellor has resigned'. And so he has. According to the news Nigel has gone over Alan Walters.

Our meeting is abandoned and I go over to the House. By the time I arrive it has been suspended and a statement promised. I meet Norman Tebbit. He has been asked by the whips to say something helpful. Do I have any ideas? Frankly, I do not. The resignation is a disaster. It is scarcely credible that we have lost the Chancellor of the Exchequer and on such an issue. The immediate criticism in the lobbies is of Margaret Thatcher. How can she have allowed the position to get to this point? It is quite ludicrous. Geoffrey Howe makes a short statement. The opposition of course can hardly believe their good fortune. It has the hallmarks of Westland all over again. Geoffrey Howe also announces the new shuffled team. Nigel's place is to be taken by John Major. I remember our conversation on Concorde that the chancellorship is the only job he has ever wanted. He will be delighted. The Foreign Office is not really for him. Douglas Hurd gets his just reward and goes to the Foreign Office and more surprisingly, David Waddington goes to the Home Office. This really must be the beginning of the end of the Thatcher years. She may hang on. She probably will, but she will never again have the affection that she once had. She has chosen to support her advisers and turn to her officials. She can hardly expect the friendship of her political colleagues. The question is not whether she will go but when.

FRIDAY 27 OCTOBER

Unusually for a Friday I am in the department. I have a dinner at the House of Commons tonight. At lunchtime I meet up with my PPS Peter Thurnham and we go off to the Members' dining room. Mark

Lennox- Boyd, Margaret's PPS, joins the table. His version is that Nigel, in effect, attempted to bounce the Prime Minister. He says she could not believe that Nigel wanted to make Walters a resignation issue. The crucial meeting was the 9 o'clock one before yesterday's Cabinet. Mark said that once the resignation had been offered Nigel felt there was no going back. Why didn't Margaret offer to get Walters to resign? I asked. The answer was that there was not enough time. It had all taken place in such a rush. It still seems to me incomprehensible that Margaret chose to protect her adviser and lose her Chancellor. The result is a full-scale crisis.

SATURDAY 28 OCTOBER

The Sun this morning wishes Nigel 'good riddance'. In the main however, I share the general reaction to his departure – sadness at the loss of a very good man and concern about how it has all happened. Later, I go to Sutton Coldfield and an evening party. They don't regard it as the end of the world but they clearly think that Margaret has damaged her reputation by appearing to have mishandled the situation and at the same time been too imperious.

TUESDAY 31 OCTOBER

Prime Minister's Questions and an economic debate to follow. Margaret responds robustly to Neil Kinnock. She continues to use her script from the Brian Walden interview and overuses the 'unassailability' of the Chancellor. But you can't help having respect for her toughness. She comes out fighting and you can see the disappointment on the faces of the Labour benches opposite that she doesn't just dissolve in front of them. She will never give them that satisfaction. Before the debate we have Nick Ridley announcing that 'the government' have decided to abandon the golden share in Jaguar.[205] In fact, quite a number of the government including the Party Chairman, Ken Baker, sitting beside

---

205   The share was established in 1984, when the government sold off the former state-owned car manufacturer. It was intended to give the government the opportunity to block any takeover of Jaguar.

me had no idea what the statement was going to say. There has been no collective discussion about this. Margaret obviously does not intend to risk the opposition she had from me and others during Leyland. So much for the return to collective government which the newspapers are talking about just now. In the economic debate John Major makes a decent debut. It is not brilliant but it is solid.

WEDNESDAY 1 NOVEMBER

I go to No. 10 for lunch with the Finnish Prime Minister. I am introduced to him as the conversation gets round to paper and newsprint. 'Now Norman', Margaret says, 'you used to be in newspapers. The *Manchester Guardian* wasn't it?' That says it all. She obviously regards me as someone from a highly undesirable background who may have made some progress but is emphatically not one of us.

THURSDAY 2 NOVEMBER

Michael Meacher has been moved from employment in the shadow Cabinet and transferred (again) to social security. I will miss him and not for the obvious reason that he is perhaps not the world's most effective opponent. He has been shadowing me for the best part of six years. In that time I have found him totally honest and a genuine believer in Tony Benn's alternative left-wing society. His successor is a lawyer called Tony Blair who, if my plans go right, I will not have the chance to get to know.

In the afternoon I meet Ken Clarke and break the news of my plan to leave. Bless him, he is rather shocked. 'Don't you think you will regret it? Why not take a week or so off and see how things seem then?' We have talked about the possibility in the past but it obviously comes as a shock that I am now serious and about to go. 'Your friends will miss you', he says. He also says that going at the present time might be seen as a further commentary on the views of senior Cabinet ministers about Margaret Thatcher. 'You might not mind that'. For the first time he discloses to me a conversation he had after the 1987 election with David Young. David told him that he had to persuade Margaret not to drop me after that election. Ken says that he believes a substantial part of what David told him, although not necessarily the key part played by David Young himself. My estimate was always that Willie Whitelaw stood up for me at the time and won. It confirms my view of Margaret Thatcher. In 1987 the worst thing that took place in the health debate was *her* press conference on wobbly Thursday. She turned health into a critical issue and all the evidence since is that she is simply not good, or at home with, social policy issues.

MONDAY 20 NOVEMBER

The day has come. I chair a routine ministers' meeting and go over to No. 10 shortly before 11.45. Margaret finishes her meeting in the Cabinet room and asks me to give her a minute before coming upstairs. Andrew Turnbull says he assumes that this is a private meeting and I tell him that it is. As we settle down it scarcely seems credible that it was really fifteen years since I first joined her shadow Cabinet, not least because she looks younger than her years. Her hair has been newly done and she has lost the tiredness which followed the Lawson resignation. I say that January will mark fifteen years with her and over ten years in her Cabinet. I have enjoyed it and I hope that in that time I have made a contribution – to which she vigorously assents. I feel now however that the time has come for a change and I would like to stand down. Obviously, I say, I will time my resignation for her convenience. I recognise that the next two weeks may not be the best, but when that is through I would like to go. I would like to see more of my family, my constituency, do some writing and develop my interests in industry. Why now? I now have the two bills of the last session on the statute book and I would like to go before becoming entangled with the next one.

Margaret's first response is, 'Norman, it is a blow. You're such a good communicator'. She goes on: 'I had hoped to be able to go on with the same team to the election'.

'You're not ill?' she asks. 'No', I say. 'Well, that is a relief. I thought you had come to say you were going into hospital for a period'.

'I have never felt fitter', I reply, taking in that she had given the meeting some thought. I suppose she must be a bit wary of private meetings with Cabinet ministers just now.

She asks me how old I am. 'Fifty-one,' I reply.

'Yes. I have seen it before. You have the chance of a fresh career and you want to take it. It was the same with Grey Gowrie and John Nott. You will be very successful'.

'I certainly want to do something in industry, but I want to stay in the Commons'.

'That's good', she said, thinking. 'Have you thought about when you want to go?'

'My view would be that we shouldn't do it when the House is sitting but wait until the Christmas recess. Ideally, I would like to go in early January'.

'It will be a blow', she repeats. 'You know I am now accused of having too many old Etonians in my Cabinet – there's Douglas and now Tim Renton (the new Chief Whip). I didn't know he went to Eton. It doesn't come into my reckoning but our Cabinet needs people like you who made it by your own ability. We both made it that way.'

Looking back, she says: 'It's rather ironical that it is only Geoffrey Howe and Peter Walker who have been there from the beginning.'

'Only Geoffrey', I replied. 'Because Peter of course wasn't in the shadow Cabinet'.

'Who can take your place?' she asks.

'Well, frankly there are a number of ministers of state who could do it but Michael Howard would be good on the industrial relations law. Tony Blair is a lawyer and he could certainly counter him.'

She doesn't respond to this. 'I know you said that you want to stay in the Commons. If you want to go to the Lords then that is entirely possible.'

'No', I say, 'I would like to stay in the Commons.'

Then another new tack. 'I think we should keep this between us. I will tell Andrew Turnbull but nobody else'.

For my part, I say there is only a handful of people who know and I don't intend to extend the circle. The discussion is coming to an end.

'You can go to the Lords if you change your mind.' I rise to leave. We need to go to the reception held for ministers on the eve of the Queen's Speech. She returns to my successor. 'You know I am not sure about Michael Howard. Michael Portillo might be a better choice. I know exactly where I am with him.'[206] I say that was her decision and wish her luck. I say that she should fight the next election. She thanks me for that and says she doesn't want to be thought of as clinging to power. Sometimes, Denis's view was that she should give up.

The meeting seems to have gone on for ever but in fact it only lasted twenty or twenty-five minutes. Margaret had behaved impeccably. It was clear that she had guessed why I was coming. The only time we mentioned my present job was when I said that frankly, I was rather under-employed. Her response to that was that I had done the 'creative work', which indeed is true. It was an entirely friendly divorce. We left together for the pre-session reception which was in the banqueting room of No. 10 and I listened with half an ear as Robin Butler read out the list of all the bills to be introduced this session – including my own employment bill. As soon as the reception, with short speeches by Margaret and the Speaker, was over, I slip away and pick up Fiona from Speaker's Court. You never know about a major new step until you have taken it. I have not the slightest tinge of regret. I do need a new challenge and simply marking time as a comfortable Cabinet minister is not enough.

WEDNESDAY 29 NOVEMBER

My first performance in the House since the introduction of television. The change is immense. The House is crowded. Interruptions in the opening speeches are much more frequent. Once you could expect four or five, now you get fifteen or twenty. I assume the incentive is a 'soundbite' (a dreadful word which is now in vogue) that can appear on the local or national news. The occasion is a three-hour scrutiny debate on the social chapter which for once is put down at prime time at just after 3.30 and not, as usual, after 10 p.m. . I suffer to the point that I

---

206 She did in fact appoint Michael Howard.

Margaret Thatcher's first Cabinet, 1979. Ten years later in 1989, only four of us had survived: George Younger, Geoffrey Howe, Peter Walker and myself. © KEYSTONE Pictures USA/Alamy Stock Photo.

Party conference ovation for my speech on health, Bournemouth, 1986. A rousing speech was needed every year.
© PA Images/Alamy Stock Photo.

Kate being vaccinated against whooping cough in the hope that other parents would follow our example, 1982.
© Anthony Marshall/Telegraph Media Group Limited.

With Kate and Isobel in Sutton Park, Sutton Coldfield, 1987. © *The Times*/News Licensing.

The DHSS team in 1986. From left to right: Tony Newton, Edwina Currie, myself, John Major, Jean Trumpington and Nick Lyell. © Eric Roberts/ Telegraph Media Group Limited

Pickets make way for Princess Diana as she visits the Department of Health during the strike of December 1982. © James Gray/ *Daily Mail*/Shutterstock.

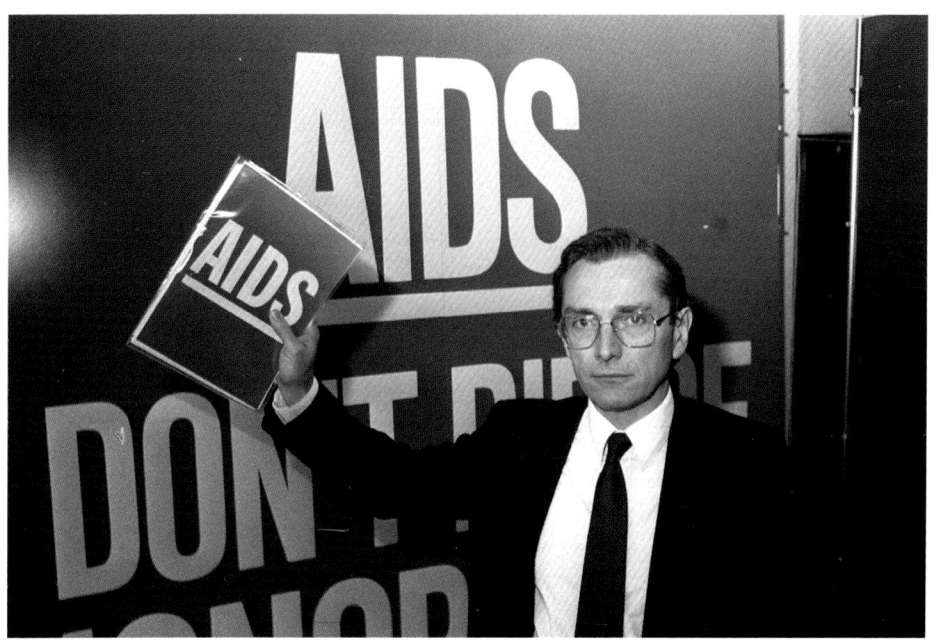

The start of the publicity campaign against HIV/Aids in 1986. I look tense, which I was. © PA Images/Alamy Stock Photo.

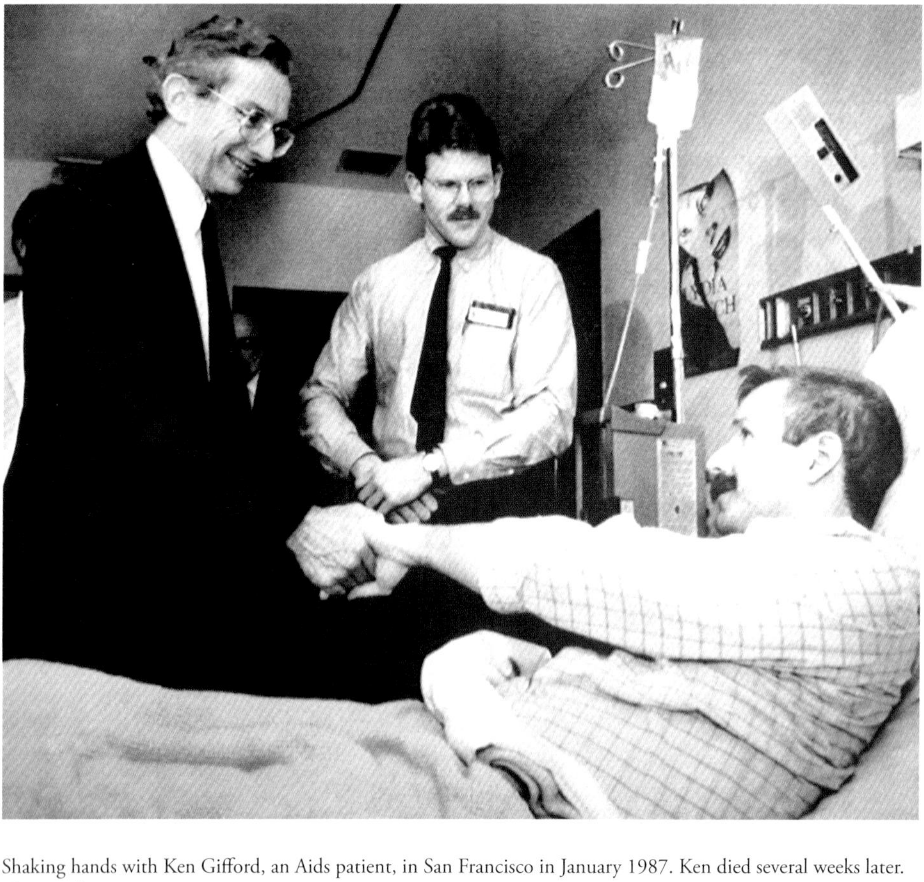

Shaking hands with Ken Gifford, an Aids patient, in San Francisco in January 1987. Ken died several weeks later. He was a brave man. © Associated Press/Alamy Stock Photo.

A trip to Yorkshire to launch a training programme in 1989. I was set up by the press as Margaret Thatcher is decapitated at the York Wax Museum. © Trinity Mirror/Mirrorpix/Alamy Stock Photo

Unemployment was on the way down in 1987. It wasn't always well reported when it was falling.

Photograph from author's personal collection.

Unveiling the latest training advertisement with help from Kate and Isobel, 1988.

Photograph from author's personal collection.

Resigning from government 'to spend more time with the family', 1990. © PA Images/Alamy Stock Photo

The children growing up – Oliver, Kate and Isobel, 1992. Photograph from author's personal collection

Margaret Thatcher with Denis on the steps of 10 Downing Street as she prepares to leave for Buckingham Palace to hand in her resignation to the Queen.

© PA Images/Alamy Stock Photo.

John Major after winning the 1992 election, a victory that few had predicted.

© Trinity Mirror/Mirrorpix/Alamy Stock Photo.

Douglas Hurd and John Major at Maastricht, 1991. The negotiations dominated the following years.

© Alain Nogues/Contributor.

Taking over as Party Chairman in 1992.

© Guardian News & Media Ltd 2023. Photographer: Sean Smith.

With John and Norma in Sutton Coldfield during the 1992 election campaign.
Photograph from author's personal collection.

The Cambridge mafia forty years on – we did not always agree! Left to right: Norman Lamont, Michael Howard, Ken Clarke (it was his sixtieth birthday), myself and John Gummer, 2000. Photograph from author's personal collection.

almost lose the thread of my speech. Tony Blair does no better. He is in full flow when Tim Raison points out that the social chapter will make the pre-entry closed shop illegal. Does he agree? Blair replies that he is not prepared to consider the question unless the government, as well as banning the closed shop, also bans any discrimination against union membership. In other words, everyone should have the right to join a union. I then ask that if the government gives that right will he back us in banning the closed shop? Blair blusters and loses the House. All told, it is quite a robust debate with honours about equal.

FRIDAY 1 DECEMBER

I have a series of routine meetings in the department but in the evening I go to the TUC headquarters – the first time I have been invited – to listen to an address from Lech Walesa. He is now a legendary figure in Britain and admired by left and right alike. Norman Willis greets me and leads me over to him. 'We didn't think you would come', he confides. Having affected a conventional introduction, Norman could not resist a dig. 'He is the minister who is persecuting us here', he says.

SATURDAY 2 DECEMBER

To Chequers for a lunch given by Margaret for Lech Walesa. Talks preceded the lunch and Walesa appeared to be bidding for British help, and in the short conversation I have with him he becomes animated on this theme. There is an undercurrent that although Britain is strong in words we are not impressive on actual help. As the most senior Cabinet minister, I am put directly opposite the Prime Minister in the place that Willie Whitelaw used to occupy. On my right I have a very impressive economics professor from Warsaw who says that he sees the economic future as developing small businesses and self-employment rather than the major industrial plans of yesteryear. An enormous amount needs to be done in Poland and they are ill-equipped to do it. According to my professor, even the economics lecturers are inadequate. They know little about economics and an enormous amount about Marxism. He tells me that a delegation from Solidarity had gone to Moscow for help – but found that the Russians were worse off than the Poles. As I leave, I wish Margaret Thatcher luck in the election against Anthony Meyer.[207] She says she will be glad when it is all over and she is not at all looking forward to Prime Minister's Questions on Tuesday – the day of the election.

TUESDAY 5 DECEMBER

Employment questions with Tony Blair in action. He goes on too long on his first question and loses the House. It is amazing how few on the Labour side realise that it is the short sharp question that is difficult to answer and does the damage. At about 3.10 Margaret Thatcher comes in to a great cheer from our side. Kinnock is wise enough not to challenge her on today's election. Straight afterwards I go upstairs to Committee Room 12 for the election. Outside in the corridor is the cream of Britain's political press – Robin Oakley, George Jones and Tony Bevins, as well as Simon Heffer who I assume is doing the sketch on what it is like to be outside the election room. Inside the room, Cranley Onslow, the chairman of the 1922 Committee, presides. A ballot form is handed over and the member is able to withdraw to any part of the large room and make his choice then deposit the paper in one of the two boxes. For the first time in three votes I vote for Margaret Thatcher – and not without some reservations. The only other voter there at the same time as me is Norman Tebbit. We leave together and tell the throng of journalists picketing outside that under our industrial relations law they should be limited to six. The result is due at 6.30 and minutes after that Clive Norris, my private secretary, hands me a note with the result:

Thatcher 314

Meyer 33

Abstentions 3

Spoilt papers 24

---

207   For the first time since she had become leader, Thatcher's position was challenged. Sir Anthony Meyer, a left-wing, pro-Europe Tory, courageously put himself forward as a 'stalking horse' candidate for the leadership. He was critical of the recently introduced community charge (which was seen by many as the key factor in the government's declining popularity), Thatcher's leadership style and her Euroscepticism.

The number of spoilt papers surprises me. As if to say if we were given a more serious candidate we would vote for him. As it is, Margaret has 75 per cent of the parliamentary party voting for her. It is not a bad result for her – but not a vote that she can easily ignore. The party has left a warning card. She is under notice that things must improve and they want no more accidents.

THURSDAY 14 DECEMBER

Cabinet. I report that unemployment is down again by 25,000 to 1.65 million, the lowest for over nine years. It means that I have been fortunate enough to report a drop in unemployment every month I have been at the department. Nick Ridley reports on the successful privatisation of water and says that the credit belongs to Michael Howard. William Waldegrave reports on Eastern Europe. The events there are quite extraordinary. The Iron Curtain is coming down and there is now the prospect of elections throughout the Communist Bloc. Elections are planned for next year in Czechoslovakia and in Bulgaria. Poland is now busily seeking aid to develop its economy while the Hungarian Prime Minister is here in London to attract investment. What is quite astonishing is the speed of change. It is as if all the Eastern European nations have suddenly woken up to the fact that the Russian emperor has no clothes. More sobering is the fact that the first group of fifty boat people have been returned from Hong Kong to Vietnam. At my end of the table with Chris Patten and John Gummer there is some amusement at William Waldegrave's Foreign Office description of them as 'involuntary returners'.

I go back to the department and Clive brings a message from Andrew Turnbull to say that the Prime Minister would like to see me before Cabinet on Tuesday 'to continue what we were talking about at our previous meeting'. I ring back and arrange to see Andrew at 6 p.m. Andrew and I settle down on opposite sides of the Cabinet table. I say my conclusion is that we should do it the week after the New Year and before the House returns. 'Ah', says Andrew. 'I think you will find that the Prime Minister will want to ask you to stay on to July. It would help her if you could stay on until the summer.' Andrew continues: 'when George Younger resigned there was no disturbance at all as it was all part of a general reshuffle. I think the Prime Minister would like to do it that way and make one or two other changes.'

Frankly, I am taken aback and had not been expecting this at all. I thought we were going to talk about the arrangements for January, not postpone them to July. My first feelings were mixed. There was the possible advantage that my resignation would not stand out or to put it another way my comfortable life would not be disturbed. But of course Andrew had argued the case based entirely on what suited her. His role was to work out a solution which, above all, helped the Prime Minister. His loyalty is to his boss. Ministers must work out their own interests which may not be the same.

MONDAY 18 DECEMBER

In the evening, Fiona and I drop into Geoffrey Holland's senior officers party. This is an occasion when all the senior officials and their wives come in for a drink at the department. The Department of Employment is probably the happiest and matiest department I have worked in. I will certainly miss people like Geoffrey and Roger and Clive Tucker who are all very good. Also, Brian Wolfson whom I meet as we are leaving. He is a real star.

TUESDAY 19 DECEMBER

The second meeting with Margaret. A Cabinet on Hong Kong has been put in for 10.30 so my appointment is brought forward. We meet in the room upstairs, which I regard as her study, again. Her desk is at one end and easy chairs are at the other. It is the almost invariable venue for private talks between the Prime Minister and any senior colleagues. 'Have we time for some coffee?' she asks the lady clearing the cups away. It is agreed we do. The coffee lady leaves, but on this occasion Andrew Turnbull stays, having cleared it with me. Margaret gets straight to the point. 'Norman', she says,

I have been giving a great deal of thought to our last conversation. I have spent a great deal of time thinking about it. I really have thought and thought about it. I wonder if you would stay on until July? There are many things to do. You have the industrial relations legislation and all the training. You are going to be so hard to replace. No one else has your combination of qualities. If you are not going to a job outside straight away it would very much help if you would stay on.

'Well', I reply. 'Andrew mentioned to me that you were thinking this. I would like to help but the fact is that now I have decided to go I think it would be bad to hang on with my mind not altogether committed to the job.'

'Norman, I don't want to see the government falling apart'. This is the first time in either of our discussions that she has expressed this fear but clearly this was uppermost. With Nigel's resignation, she is obviously most sensitive on this point. I reply, 'there is no question of the government falling apart. You have a supply of ministers of state who could go into the Cabinet'. 'But not with your qualities', Margaret says.

'I think it would be difficult and I do want to spend more time with my family and do other things. I don't think it would be a good idea to go on when I have decided to leave.'

At this point, the new supply of coffee came in and we changed the conversation but once the coffee lady had left, Margaret continued. 'Well, I can see that you have made up your mind. Tell me when you see the announcement.' I explained to her the advantage of going the week between the New Year and the House coming back. Once again, I mention 3 January. Andrew Turnbull, who to date, had not taken any part in the conversation, suggests that we might consider the Friday of that week. Friday being the classic day for getting a difficult announcement out. I say that I don't mind if that is preferable and mention to Margaret that my whole presentation will be to show that there is no dispute between us.

'There is no dispute,' Margaret insists. 'That is the true position'.

I agree, but say that it may be another matter to persuade the press of that. I suggest that Andrew and I stay close on the presentation. It is now time for Cabinet and Margaret must take the chair downstairs. She repeats that she is sorry about the decision but then says 'give me a minute or two. I don't want us to be seen coming downstairs together. That is how rumours start'. I stay behind with Andrew for a few moments. I reflect that when Nigel Lawson resigned what should have given the game away was Nigel arriving a minute or two late for Cabinet. I wonder if he was under the same instructions. I have a clear memory of her saying 'Missing the Chancellor' and a few seconds later Nigel taking his seat with 'Sorry I am late'. That afternoon he resigned.

When I get to the Cabinet room everyone is in their chairs. It is one of the few times I have been late over the last ten years. Peter Walker, sitting next to me on the left, mutters 'Good of you to come'. The discussion was on Hong Kong citizens. A small group consisting basically of Margaret, Douglas Hurd and David Waddington had agreed that we should offer 50,000 places. The theory, according to Douglas, is that this will give assurance to the leading citizens in Hong Kong and mean that they will stay. It is an insurance policy. The hope, like all insurance policies, is that we don't have to pay out and that thousands of people from Hong Kong don't come here. With dependents it could be as many as 250,000. Douglas is strongly in favour and so is Margaret. She believes that we have a strong moral duty. The man who is quite obviously unhappy is David Waddington. He looks very tense and says that he will abide by the collective decision but that every wrong decision on immigration has been justified on the grounds of 'moral duty'. Margaret feels that the comparison (in immigration terms) between the business community of Hong Kong and peasant families from Bangladesh is fatuous. It is, but it will be difficult to explain. We already know that Norman Tebbit is up in arms about the policy and intends to lead a major revolt. I met him in the lobby last night and he was incandescent.

A short meeting of EA follows but half of us have to get to the Palace for the Privy Council's Christmas meeting, where drinks follow the Queen approving various bills. We meet virtually the whole royal family, including the Queen Mother who comes up to say hello. A remarkable lady well into her eighties but sprightly and very alert. There is Fergie with her child (you have to think to remember that she is the Duchess of York) and Angus Ogilvy and the Gloucesters. This is the royal family's pre-Christmas lunch. I speed off to lunch with Michael White, Philip Webster and Elinor

Goodman (three of Fleet Street's finest) at Simply Nico – not perhaps the status but certainly the quality. In the evening I go to Anne Heseltine's party at Christie's. Obvious Heseltine supporters like Michael Mates and Peter Temple-Morris are there but I seem to be the only Cabinet minister.

WEDNESDAY 20 DECEMBER

Christmas lunch with the private office at L'Escargot. They have been a good team and I will miss them. When else will I have a graduate team of four special assistants to look after me, not to mention a secretary to look after my diary and another to look after correspondence. I leave just after 3 o'clock to go back to the Commons in time to hear Douglas Hurd's statement on Hong Kong. The notable feature is Norman Tebbit's response. Norman says that he agrees with Gerald Kaufman's position in opposing the proposals. He reminds Douglas that at the last election we were pledged to prevent any further mass immigration. How does this policy tie in with that pledge?

THURSDAY 21 DECEMBER

I introduce my new employment bill.[208] I have now dubbed it the 'abolition of the closed shop' bill following Tony Blair's dramatic conversion to our cause on this. Given that this was something the department advised against doing, the proposal has been spectacularly successful. The department didn't think that the problem of pre-entry closed shop was very large and were frankly surprised when surveys showed that there were at least 1.5 million people still covered. The Labour Party's acceptance of the proposal was justified on the grounds that this is required by the social chapter. It is something of a landmark. It means a decisive rejection of Labour's policies from the 1970s which were all about extending the closed shop. In narrow party political terms I suppose Labour's move is not so helpful although their conversion still has a long way to go. But in national terms it is important. With any luck there should be a consensus on the continuing need for at least a major part of our industrial relations legislation. After a series of interviews I hurry to the Banqueting House in

---

208   The bill covers the pre-entry closed shop, secondary industrial action and unofficial industrial action. It followed two green papers: *Removing Barriers to Employment* and *Unofficial Action and the Law*.

Whitehall to launch a project which has been on the stocks for some time – an academy of culinary arts. The idea is to improve the whole image of being a chef and to train young people who choose this career. We want to get Britain up to the standard of the French. An enormous turnout – five or six hundred and great enthusiasm. From there to reading the lesson at the Department of Employment carol service. I become the first Secretary of State for Employment to read three lessons in a row!

FRIDAY 22 DECEMBER

A message from No. 10. Would Fiona and I like to go to lunch at Chequers on New Year's Day? It's the first time that we have been invited to this and it is clear that we intend to part as old friends. In the evening I meet both Michael Heseltine and Geoffrey Howe at the *Telegraph* party. Michael says he will be in Barbados in the early part of the new year and wishes me luck. Geoffrey (who has now been told together with the Chief Whip) says that he is sad to hear the news and that we should talk on the phone. I also meet Jock Bruce-Gardyne. Poor Jock is unrecognisable from the former debonair figure that he was. He has had an operation for a brain tumour and the result is that he has no hair on the top of his head – although he has a well-developed beard. I read a very moving account of his transformation he wrote for *The Spectator*. Old friends really do not recognise him. He talks well and is still writing but I fear that the forecast for the future is not good.[209]

SATURDAY 30 DECEMBER

To Sutton Coldfield to break the news to some of the key figures in the association. I see my Chairman, John Holland, first and he entirely sees the point about the family and the only thing he wants to be assured of is that there is no row between myself and Margaret Thatcher. Next, I see Reg Hales, who also immediately recognises the point about the family. As far as Reg was concerned a new chapter in my life was about to open. Next, I see Michael Parr my agent. Again, there was immediate

---

209 Jock died on 15 April 1990.

understanding. Michael has seen my diary week by week and obviously marvelled how any sane individual could, or would, want to, carry it out. At the end he shook hands with me and wished me luck.

NEW YEAR'S DAY 1990

To Chequers and Margaret Thatcher's New Year lunch. It is much smaller than I expected. Just one table with about twenty guests. Of the politicians, those invited were Douglas Hurd, Ian Gow and Michael Portillo – who I imagine is to be my successor. From outside there are Marcus Sieff, Michael Richardson of Rothschilds and Charles Forte's daughter, Olga Polizzi. From the family, Denis and Mark but not Carol. Mark takes a host of photographs during lunch and the whole affair is a relaxed and happy family lunch. You can see where Margaret gets some of her strength. Denis stands by her through thick and thin. Mark could not be more supportive. As we leave the lunch, Denis takes me to one side. 'I am horrified to hear you are going', he says. 'You are the linchpin of the government'. I am a little taken aback by this. It is difficult to have a frank talk as people move round. I reply that I am not leaving Parliament and will still be supporting the government. He refuses to accept this. 'Yes, but you are leaving the government. You will be missed.' At this point we were shepherded out of the dining room to coffee next door where Ian Gow led an exposition of the stained glass windows which every Prime Minister is able to leave behind. Why no Edward Heath we ask? 'He thought he would be coming back,' Margaret Thatcher replies. A few more pleasantries and the party starts breaking up. Finally, when everyone has gone, Margaret Thatcher takes me into her small study. Mark comes charging in and then goes into full retreat as he sees we are in conference. I say that I am concerned that the letter does not really make it clear why I am leaving. I hate talking about my personal affairs in public but I feel that unless I see my children now I will miss them growing up. Like me, she dislikes talking about her personal affairs. She had read the draft letter. It looked fine – with one exception. At one point I had written 'The time has come to leave the government'. She says 'That sounds as though everyone should leave the government'. This is a point I hadn't considered! It is an entirely friendly discussion and as Fiona and I leave, Margaret says 'See you on Wednesday'. This is absolutely news to me. I had thought that this was my last meeting with her as a minister. Apparently not. It is intended that I go into No. 10 to formally say goodbye.

TUESDAY 2 JANUARY 1990

Into the office. There are very few senior staff there but Geoffrey Holland comes in during the afternoon. I had half assumed that some people like Geoffrey might have guessed that I was going. There seems to me to have been an enormous amount of comings and goings with No. 10 but Geoffrey hadn't guessed and was obviously taken aback. He said that he had thought that I might have decided to go at the next election but not this quickly. He then thought again. 'Congratulations,' he said. 'I think you have made the right decision'. We talked about the arrangements and the need for secrecy and Geoffrey says that he would not say anything except to ask Barry Sutcliffe, the head of the press office, to be back in the office the next day. In the evening I ring up a few friends and constituents whom I want to warn about the position. I find Peter Temple-Morris in Leominster and Michael Wilcox in Sutton Coldfield. All are surprised but not amazed. Perhaps there will be more understanding of the position than I thought. I also have letters to go out to people like Tony Newton and the Bottomleys saying what I am doing and why.

WEDNESDAY 3 JANUARY

Resignation day. With a great feeling of foreboding I come into the office. Nick True joins me and I spend the first part of the morning trying to find friends I have not spoken to previously. I find John Gummer and then talk to John Major. John Major is very interesting in his response. He says that he is surprised but fully understands. He says that he has missed out on a great deal of his children growing up and 'resents it'. The conversation has echoes of our discussion on Concorde. I seriously wonder how ambitious John is for further office beyond Chancellor. Next, I ring the political correspondents who happen to be in. It is after all the parliamentary recess and I invite them over to the department for the early afternoon so that I can brief them prior to the announcement. Andrew Turnbull then calls to say that he thinks the announcement should come forward from 5 p.m. He tells me that Ken Baker has rung up to say that he has heard that there is a rumour I am leaving.

The rest of the day is rather a blur. A press conference and innumerable photographs of Fiona and myself. There is no question that the message they are taking is that here is a minister who wants to spend more time with his family. The reaction includes the letter from Margaret praising my action on privatisation, personal pensions and social security reform but absolutely nothing about my campaign on Aids. As Douglas Hurd would say, 'hmm'!

THURSDAY 4 JANUARY

Photographers assemble in the park outside the house and take photographs of Kate and Isobel and a rather reluctant Oliver. I now have the opportunity to read what the press thinks of it all. George Jones in the *Telegraph* says 'Farewell to the quiet revolutionary'. *The Times* headline is 'Affable manner that disguised determination'. The *Financial Times* say 'Fowler's safe touch won grudging admiration' while *The Guardian* simply say 'Loyal toiler for Thatcher'. *The Sun,* with some exaggeration, say: 'He gets up at 6 to work through to 1 a.m.'

Frankly, they are not a bad collection of political obituaries as I start the next period of my life.

COMMENT

From a personal perspective, the most important decision I made was to leave the government of my own free will and under my own steam. In politics that is more important than in most occupations. Your departure as a politician is highly publicised, you have no nice redundancy payments to tide you over as you would have in business (or at least you didn't then). You need to hit the ground running. The trouble with so many political departures is that the politician simply hits the ground exhausted, depressed and often rejected. If I had any advice for a politician who wants any kind of decent future career, it would be to choose the moment when you go; try to take control of your life. If, on the other hand, you are content to end life as an elder statesman to whom people listen less and less, then by all means hand over your fate to the leader of your party and the Chief Whip.

Although the part of my resignation letter that received all the attention was the sentence where I said I wanted to spend more time with my family, I did set out some other aims. One of those was to enlarge my experience in industry. Within days of my resignation I was being approached by external companies. The first offer was from Jörgen Philip-Sörensen of Group 4 who in the first forty-eight hours had asked me to join his board. Peter Thompson of NFC (the company I had privatised at the beginning of the 1980s) was next to open negotiations and a week or two later, Peter Parker, the former chairman of British Rail and now the chairman of Aggregate Industries, took me for a drink at the Garrick and asked me to join his company. The formalities took several months to complete but it is these three companies I joined and stayed with over the next years. A number of others made offers but for one reason or another I declined. I refused an offer from a private health company for no other reason than I did not want to have commercial interests in private health as I would then be constrained from talking about the health service in the Commons. I also refused a role in a public relations company on the grounds that it could lead to a conflict of interest between my political role and the company's commercial interests.

So, spending more time with my family was only part of my reason for leaving the Cabinet but it was a very important part. I resented the way I had to put everything the family did last. If the choice was between Kate's sports day and some departmental event or a party visit, it was the politics that prevailed. As my diary says:

> I do not want to get back into that position. It must be the first priority to give the girls the support they may need and Oliver may also need a hand from time to time although he is now so independent. Above all, I must express my love for Fiona who has had such a good impact on my life.

My marriage was the event that transformed my life.

14

FALL OF A GIANT

JUNE-NOVEMBER 1990

We are now on the eve of the fall of a leader who was the most significant post-war Prime Minister since Clement Attlee. It is a good time to take a snapshot of the people around the Cabinet table (and one who was not) who are destined to play important roles in the dramatic events which were very soon to follow. There was Geoffrey Howe, deeply unhappy at being moved from the Foreign Office amid the clear signals that he had finally been side- lined by a Prime Minister who too often treated him with something just short of contempt. There was John Major who had only joined the Cabinet eighteen months earlier, who had been spectacularly promoted to Foreign Secretary, a job he had neither sought nor enjoyed. Now, as Chancellor of the Exchequer, he was in the job he had always wanted. There was Ken Clarke who was just like the description on the tin: good humoured, unruffled and the giver of straightforward, honest (but often unwelcome) advice. And finally there was Michael Heseltine, prowling outside the doors of Cabinet where he believed all real power resided, ready to pounce if ever the opportunity to lead came along. While of course, sitting in the centre of the green baize table with the picture of Sir Robert Walpole behind her, was Margaret Thatcher herself, fuelled by adrenaline and looking younger than her sixty-five years. She may have celebrated her tenth anniversary in power but she had absolutely no intention of standing down. There was still too much to do. Even more pressing, there was no one she considered a worthy successor.

WEDNESDAY 6 JUNE 1990

Breakfast with Jeffrey Archer who is not in his usual ebullient form. He has just finished his latest work for which he is being paid some astronomical sum. However, in politics, things have not gone so well. He has not been made Deputy Chairman of the party and he has not been sent to the Lords. He is very put out. He feels he is being used. The party are prepared to accept his offers of help but not to repay the debt. Margaret Thatcher still rings him from time to time to ask for his views on what the public are thinking, but he is getting nowhere in his ambition to get to the Lords. I advise him to keep going until the election – he has a number of debts to collect. Later to a very well-attended memorial service for Jock Bruce-Gardyne at St Margaret's and a fine address by Bill Deedes.

FRIDAY 8 JUNE

The first real signs of withdrawal since I left the government six months ago. My life is now very disjointed and I do not have the backup that I have been accustomed to for the last ten years – the secretaries, the office and to some extent, the driver. It is all a bit of a struggle. To cap it all, we now have a row about ex-Cabinet ministers' outside interests. It is directed at David Young who is taking over at Cable & Wireless but Labour are exploiting it as a general row. Gordon Brown says that there should be at least a two-year gap between a minister privatising a public company and joining the company's board. I point out to interviewers that there has been a nine-year gap between my involvement in privatising NFC and going on the board there. It is these personal attacks that hurt most in politics. You don't mind being attacked on your policies but it is a different matter if they go for your personal or professional life.

TUESDAY 19 JUNE

In the evening, Margaret Thatcher comes to the dinner for the 1970 intake of the House of Commons. About thirty survivors from the 1970 general election turn up, including Norman Tebbit and Ken Clarke. We have not done notably well in ministerial appointments but it is a genial group. There are very few you want to avoid. Toby Jessel has organised it and has asked everyone to draw numbers from a hat. Those who draw speakers' slips have to speak for two minutes. Winston Churchill's grandson does best. As for Margaret, she is in relaxed form. Before dinner she says to me: 'I hope you are making lots of money'. Her speech goes wide, but the point that interests me is her reference to televising Parliament. This, she pronounces a great success. She is right but can this be the Margaret who thought that television would be a disaster and completely ruin Parliament?

WEDNESDAY 20 JUNE

We ex-Cabinet ministers are being roundly attacked in the press over business interests. The awful Robert Harris of the *Sunday Times* refers to the 'scandal' of it all and then with weasel words says that of course he is not alleging anything improper. Save me from lectures from champagne socialists like Harris who take Murdoch's money and salve their conscience by weekly attacking the capitalist establishment. George Gale in the *Express* refers to 'politicians for hire'. I can hardly believe my eyes. Gale has worked for everyone on Fleet Street irrespective of the political stance of the paper. Everyone advises me not to react or to respond. They are not getting at you. I suppose they are right but it takes some self-control.

FRIDAY 29 JUNE

A day learning more about the NFC in Bedford. As I leave, one of the staff comes up to say how good it is to see a non-executive taking such a close interest. From Bedford up to Blaby to speak for Nigel Lawson. He is much more relaxed than he was some months ago. I suspect he is enjoying himself. He has just bought himself a Jaguar sports car but is not anxious that this should be too widely known. He has obviously had quite enough press coverage of his private life and who can blame him? I fear however that if you do buy a Jaguar sports car people will notice.

WEDNESDAY 18 JULY

Dinner with Geoffrey and Elspeth Howe. They have a new house next to the Tate Gallery. It is not as grand as Carlton Gardens but quite an expensive house all the same. I suppose they feel that they have come down in the world which, in a sense, they have. Geoffrey is not full of bounce – quietly unhappy. Elspeth is quite obviously disenchanted and seems to think that Geoffrey should spend some time thinking about where his pension will come from.[210] Where does Geoffrey go now? His public attitude is that he wants to see the revolution continue and succeed. With half an eye on me he says that too many ministers have just 'slipped away'. I cannot help feeling that he should have gone when he was moved from the Foreign Office.

MONDAY 30 JULY

Ghastly news. Going into the Cabinet Office to look at some papers for my book. I call in to hand some letters over to Caroline. 'Have you heard about Ian Gow?' she asks. 'He has been killed by a bomb'. Apparently, the news has just come through on the radio that a bomb under Ian's car killed him instantly. It is an absolute tragedy. Poor Jane. I remember back to Chequers at New Year when Ian was in such good spirits. Who do the IRA think they are persuading with these tactics? The overwhelming public reaction is one of revulsion towards the killers. You would not dream of letting them near power. As I park the car in the House of Commons car park it is given a very thorough search. The House is not sitting which is a pity. It prevents his old friends at least showing some collective sorrow for this great loss.

THURSDAY 2 AUGUST

The impossible has happened. Iraq has invaded Kuwait. Rather than rattling his sword, Saddam Hussein has invaded. The Middle East is in crisis. Where will he stop? Will the next stage be Saudi Arabia? It is a major test for Bush. He can hardly sit back and let it happen but the record of American intervention in the Middle East is not good. Personally, I am glad that Bush is there. In my view he is an underestimated

---

210   He gets a ministerial pension which would not be much greater than mine – under £10,000 a year. That for a man who has been both Chancellor and Foreign Secretary.

President. He is one of the most experienced politicians to reach the White House and he will need it all.

TUESDAY 7 AUGUST

Meet Peter Bottomley who has been removed from the government. I have already written but again express my sorrow and surprise. Peter has made a real impact. Far more than many other senior ministers. Perhaps she doesn't want two Bottomleys, Peter and Virginia, in the government at the same time. He tells me that the Chief Whip had warned him what was in store so he was not surprised when Margaret Thatcher saw him. Apparently, she said words to the effect: 'Peter, you are doing a really superb job – and incidentally you are fired'.

THURSDAY 16 AUGUST

Hallelujah. Oliver has passed his 'A'-levels. And how! Three As and an A1. It is a great tribute to his hard work. No one could have worked harder in the last year. It scarcely seems credible that his school career has ended and he is about to go to university.

THURSDAY 23 AUGUST

Fireworks in Seaview. 'Are you looking forward to the fireworks, Daddy?' asks Isobel solicitously. It is a perfect summer evening. The sea is calm. The lights from rockets illuminate the boats anchored off the shore. Earlier in the evening Kate collected her cup for winning the high jump and Oliver won a gallon of whisky in the raffle. By 7.30 the garage is full of young people making a start on the gigantic bottle.

THURSDAY 6 SEPTEMBER

Parliament is recalled today to debate the Gulf crisis. Margaret makes a speech of great authority and Neil Kinnock is also sensible. The only real dissent comes from Tony Benn but he is something of a spent force these days. The funniest speech comes from a mellow Denis Healey. When I leave at about 5.30 Michael Heseltine has still not been called. In a debate like this even Michael has to sidle up to the Speaker to press his claim to speak.

WEDNESDAY 19 SEPTEMBER

To Sky again.[211] The subject is Lord Young and his book. I fear we give him a rather hard time. I have to rescue him when he starts being brow-beaten by Austin Mitchell on Rover. What intrigues me are some of the details in the book. He says that he had been in to see Margaret to ask to become Secretary of State for Employment, irrespective of the feelings of the incumbent, Tom King. He says that he was very relieved not to be asked to go to the DHSS. Were you asked? 'Oh no', says David. Then why were you worried? 'I have a trouble-shooter reputation' he replies. His denial is flatly contrary to what he told me after the election. He then tries to have it both ways. He says there is nothing in the book which is not already in the public domain. I am sure that this is not going to be the line of his publisher and it also glides over one point. One reason why the 1987 election is in the public domain is because of a book by Rodney Tyler. And who is supposed to be Mr Tyler's best source? Well yes, David Young.

FRIDAY 19 OCTOBER

An extraordinary political setback. We have lost the Eastbourne by-election caused by Ian Gow's death. The Liberals are strong in Eastbourne, but even so we should have easily held a seat with a 17,000 majority. I fear the public is part bored, part discontented. We are thrashing around for direction and after fifteen years, Margaret Thatcher's own appeal is no longer a plus.

MONDAY 22 OCTOBER

Ian Gow's memorial service at St Margaret's. It is very crowded and Geoffrey Howe delivers a moving address. We have lost a genuinely good man.

---

211 Austin Mitchell and Norman Tebbit interview people in the news on the programme *Target* on Sky television twice a week. When Norman could not do the programme, I stood in for him.

MONDAY 29 OCTOBER

To Gravesend for a dinner for Jacques Arnold. I had always regarded Jacques as a super loyalist but going down to the constituency he tentatively raises the position of Margaret Thatcher. 'Do you think she is past her sell-by date?' I suspect quite a lot of Tory MPs in marginal or near-marginal seats are asking the same question. We are far behind in the opinion polls.

TUESDAY 30 OCTOBER

The House of Commons is packed to hear Margaret Thatcher on European monetary union. It is a formidable performance. She demolishes Kinnock. But the language she uses in her supplementary questions indicates that she is prepared to fight on the issue of sovereignty and keeping our own currency.[212] It cheers up Ridley and Teddy Taylor no end but it is a policy which will split the party. People like me will not sign up to this policy – so goodness knows where it leaves Ken Clarke and John Gummer, not to mention Douglas Hurd, Geoffrey Howe and John Major.

THURSDAY 1 NOVEMBER

Geoffrey Howe has resigned. I am having a drink with George Younger and Clifford Chetwood, Chairman of Wimpey, at The Savoy to assist in a charity to help the dire position of Romanian children when the news comes through. His reason for departure is policy on Europe and Margaret Thatcher's statement on Tuesday. It is a heavy blow and makes a slight nonsense of all the things he has been saying up to now: the need to stay on board to see the revolution through; no desire to bring down the whole edifice. He might just have achieved the removal of Margaret Thatcher. She is now desperately isolated. The phone has not stopped ringing as media company after media company ask for interviews. I

---

212   In her speech the PM said: 'The president of the Commission, Mr Delors, said at a press conference the other day that he wanted the European Parliament to be the democratic body of the Community, he wanted the Commission to be the executive and he wanted the Council of Ministers to be the Senate. No, No, No.'

finally agree to do *Newsnight* with Paddy Ashdown and John Smith. Frankly, I do not have much to say and try to suggest that it will not have too much effect on our electoral chances once the dust has settled. In truth, I am not so confident. To lose the number of ministers that Margaret Thatcher has lost is careless by any standards. There must now be a strong prospect that she will go. She will be a hero once her resignation is announced and everyone will regret the passing.

FRIDAY 2 NOVEMBER
Michael Heseltine rings. He says that he is sending a letter on Sunday to his constituency chairman on Cabinet collective responsibility. I say he should keep his head down and not give the impression that he is taking advantage of the situation. Fortunately, the next day he is going to Jordan.

SATURDAY 3 NOVEMBER
As I feared a storm is engulfing Heseltine. His letter looks totally opportunistic. Michael is far too impetuous. I know his past career – his mace swinging, the resignation – have established this but it still comes as a shock that he has not learned from the past. All he had to do was go to Jordan and say nothing. Instead he is becoming the issue.

MONDAY 5 NOVEMBER
In the evening I ring Ken Clarke. He is now Education Secretary. He says he resisted the move and would have preferred to have stayed at health. Margaret basically wanted to move John MacGregor. Ken made the mistake of saying 'well, if you insist Prime Minister'. 'That's settled then', she said. According to Ken she has no intention whatsoever of stepping down.

TUESDAY 6 NOVEMBER
I go into the Commons in the afternoon to clear some letters. The House is not sitting. We are in the period just before the Queen's Speech and everything opens tomorrow. The television lights are on in the

corridor between the Lords and the Commons and rehearsals are evident everywhere. Sitting in my office I get a call from Peter Morrison, now at Downing Street as Margaret's PPS. Could we meet privately for a talk? We go to his room in the Commons. 'This is a meeting which is not taking place', he starts. He is planning forward. He hopes no leadership election will take place. If it does he wants to be prepared. The plan is to open nominations this Thursday (much earlier than predicted) and for the whole thing to be over as quickly as possible. It gives possible contenders little time to consider their tactics. His idea is that Michael Jopling and I should be joint chairmen of her campaign. Margaret Thatcher would like this if we do. I say that subject to sleeping on it, it sounds OK. My assumption is that Michael Heseltine will not be standing. In my view he would be mad to do so. The Henley letter has done him a lot of damage. I cannot imagine Geoffrey Howe standing either. If he did he would get a bloody nose. My supposition therefore is that we are organising against another stalking horse. It is in no one's interest that such a candidate should do well. It is not so much loyalty to Margaret Thatcher as loyalty to the party.

THURSDAY 8 NOVEMBER

I start the day with an interview for *Today* on the state of the Conservative Party. My advice is that there should be no leadership election and I think that the two by-elections today will have little effect. When the results come they are bad. We have lost ground to both Labour and the Liberals. They are both northern seats – Bradford and Bootle – and confirm what I have always felt: that whenever the election comes, and whatever the result, there will be a majornorth–south division.

SATURDAY 10 NOVEMBER

The press is full of speculation that Michael Heseltine may indeed stand. I think that would be a mistake. He will not win, he will only wound. If he seriously wounds and Margaret is forced to stand down then he will not inherit. Douglas Hurd will. Even so, I would not be prepared to organise a campaign against Michael. I regret my too-casual agreement to help Margaret Thatcher's campaign. To be honest I have had my mind on other things, like the children in Romania. I will have to extricate myself.

SUNDAY 11 NOVEMBER

In Sutton Coldfield for the Remembrance Day service. I try to ring Leon Brittan and Geoffrey Howe on Sunday morning but can find neither. My agent, Michael Parr, arrives and tells me that my involvement with the Thatcher campaign is in the *Sunday Telegraph*. So much for the discussion that was 'not taking place'. After the service, I ring Michael Heseltine to see whether he is thinking of standing. He says he is. I give him my advice that it is a contest he cannot win and strongly advise him not to do so. He agrees with some of my arguments but says that even if he loses then his position is no weaker and arguably stronger. He has obviously been influenced by the argument in the press, notably the *Daily Mail*, that he does not have the courage to stand; 'Put up or shut up'. He says he would have no credibility left if he did not stand. He has been trying to get hold of me because of the *Sunday Telegraph* story. I say that if he is considering standing, which he obviously is, then I will not be part of a campaign against him and I will withdraw. I add however, that I will continue to argue as strongly as I can for no contest.

Tonight I am supposed to be dining with Peter Morrison – not to mention having lunch with Margaret tomorrow. We get hopelessly delayed going back to London and I am forced to ring Peter from a lay-by off the M40. I tell him that I have been giving further thought to the question of becoming a campaign manager. I had assumed a stalking horse. I am not prepared to run a campaign against Geoffrey or Michael. They are both friends. In the circumstances I will not come to dinner nor to lunch at No. 10 tomorrow. Peter is obviously taken aback but accepts it all quite well and is apologetic about the press story, which he knows nothing about. Later, I ring Geoffrey. He is very defensive at first and has obviously also read that I am Margaret's campaign manager. He perks up a bit when I tell him that is not so but it is an unsatisfactory conversation.

MONDAY 12 NOVEMBER

I write an article for the *Birmingham Post*, which sets out my position on the leadership and issue an appeal to both Geoffrey and Michael not to stand. Any remaining doubt that Michael might pull back is dispelled when Margaret makes a speech at the Mansion House in which she says that she will knock any hostile bowling all around the ground. She has thrown down the gauntlet. Michael will now pick it up. I assume she knows that. Perhaps the tactics were decided at the lunch I missed.

TUESDAY 13 NOVEMBER

Geoffrey makes his resignation statement in the afternoon and after that there is no way that a contest can be avoided. I am sitting just behind him. The television pictures show me sitting uneasily on the edge of my seat. The reason is that I came in wanting to wish him good luck but neither of the members sitting directly behind would make room. It was the 'doughnut' where publicity-conscious MPs crowd around a member who is in the news and who they believe will be in any pictures. I am afraid I rather mess up their plan. Geoffrey speaks from typed notes and it is obvious from the start that he has given it a great deal of thought. He puts in the knife. All the pent-up bitterness of fifteen years comes pouring out. He paints her as anti-European in thought and action. He attacks the background noise of Thatcher which means more than the substance of carefully worked-out statements. He says that we should have joined the ERM five years ago. He tells others to consider their position. The effect is devastating. It is difficult to exaggerate the impact on those listening to the attack. I come out of the Chamber feeling shell-shocked. Some make instant comments. I say nothing. There is nothing useful or helpful to say. Geoffrey has fired a number of torpedoes. They are well aimed and Margaret is now badly holed. She is not yet sunk but it is as nasty a position as I can remember in twenty years.

WEDNESDAY 14 NOVEMBER

To Birmingham to speak at an industrialists' lunch. As we go to the hotel I hear on the radio the announcement that Michael is standing.

My reaction to the press is that this is a great blow to the party and an unnecessary contest. That is also my private view but I am not so pessimistic as yesterday. I think that Margaret will win on the first ballot. As long as she does, the damage will have been limited. Nevertheless, we are in for a ghastly few days. Back in the House I run into John Major and go to his room to watch the seven o'clock news. An opinion poll on who would be the best Conservative leader shows John running behind Michael and Margaret. He is in front of Douglas. I say to John that that is good news for him. 'It's happened in one or two other polls', he replies. Let us not forget that John Major is the dark horse candidate in this contest. He is *very* ambitious and has been steadily building up his support both in and out of government. He has great influence with Margaret. His cautious approach to Europe appeals to the No Turning Back group. He is seen, unaccountably, as veering to the right. In fact, on social issues, he is a strong liberal. He is going into hospital to have his wisdom teeth out and tells Bernard Ingham, who rings, that he will therefore be unavailable for interviews to support Margaret over the weekend.[213] His only direct comment on the contest and his personal position is: 'I don't want Heseltine'.

THURSDAY 15 NOVEMBER

In the Commons there is feverish speculation. Michael's vote is now reckoned to be a hundred plus but I just wonder if his support is as strong as some suggest. His proposers are Neil Macfarlane (we shared a room in the Essex regiment in Germany back in the 1950s) and Peter Tapsell. He is backed by the perpetually disgruntled (the old wets), sacked ex-ministers (David Howell is the most distinguished), and those retiring at the next election (like Dennis Walters). The payroll vote will go with Margaret Thatcher and so too will many backbenchers. I still believe it is the wrong time for Michael to do it and I fear he may have done himself

---

213   I was in the room when Bernard Ingham rang up. Bernard took the news without any protest as far as I could judge and gave no hint, as later claimed, that Major was conveniently distancing himself from the Thatcher campaign. My memory is that Major's explanation was that he had been waiting a long time for the operation.

irreparable damage. I have to concede however that my view on leadership elections is not always very good. I felt that Ted Heath would see off Margaret Thatcher, so perhaps he has a better chance than I think. The press assume that I will support Margaret and indeed I will. I have many reservations but at this time I think that she is the best choice. I will write to Michael tomorrow to tell him that I will not be voting for him.

FRIDAY 16 NOVEMBER

I go into the Commons and write to Michael. I tell him that at this stage he will be getting many letters pledging support but that I am afraid I am withdrawing mine. I disagree with him that this is the time to challenge and I disagreed with his Henley speech. I then drive to Birmingham for a lunch in Edgbaston. Everyone is in a state of shock but my impression is that Margaret still has the majority support. When I arrive in the constituency office, John Holland my Chairman is waiting. He says that association members are solidly behind Margaret but adds that he is becoming aware that not all the Conservative voters in Sutton Coldfield feel the same. This is the first time I have heard John even express the possibility of doubt. In the evening, I go to South Staffordshire to speak for Patrick Cormack. He is backing Michael or to be more accurate, not backing Margaret as before he did not back Ted. I toy with doing a speech about the importance of party loyalty and Cormack is very concerned that I should not embarrass him. The temptation is almost overwhelming but I pull back. I am glad to see that the vast majority at dinner disagree with his stand.

SATURDAY 17 NOVEMBER

I ring Leon to thank him for the reading he has done on my book. Work has been in abeyance for the last few days until I know what the last chapter is going to be. By Tuesday I hope I will know whether I am writing an obituary or a commentary upon a serving leader. On the election, Leon thinks that it is quite likely that the beneficiary will be Douglas Hurd. Douglas has made it quite clear today that he will stand if Margaret is defeated. I ring Ken Clarke. He thinks there is no doubt that Michael Heseltine will get over 100 votes. He is to vote for Margaret. He says that he would feel a worm if having gone round saying that he will vote for the Prime Minister he secretly slinks away and votes for Michael. I agree exactly. Ken suggests that one or two of our colleagues might just do what we regard as wormish. What a thought!

SUNDAY 18 NOVEMBER

The leadership contest gets worse and worse. The Sunday papers are full of it, with opinion poll after opinion poll saying that Michael Heseltine will do best for the party in an election. In the afternoon the man himself rings up. He says my letter is a big blow. He then goes on to say how well his campaign is going. How it is certain that there will be a second ballot. How in that ballot he will win. The support is flooding in and he will be at No. 10. Of course what he is really saying is that if I have any further serious political ambitions then I should join up. I say to Michael that I am quite aware that what I am doing is totally against my personal interests but I still intend to do it. We talk on but it gets us nowhere. He ends up by saying 'well, I suppose at least you are being honest' but I get the impression that Michael does not put that quality highest on the scale just now. I imagine all kinds of people are saying to him that what they say in public has nothing to do with what they will do in the privacy of the ballot. I may not have handled my position very skilfully over the last few days but I am not prepared to do that.

The trouble with Michael is that he has many of the attitudes and qualities which naturally attract Conservatives like me. But there are two drawbacks. First, the naked ambition can be off-putting to those of us who like moderation in all things but that is probably another way of explaining why he may lead the party and I will not. Second, and much more serious, is the impulsiveness. He does not learn. He should not have written his Henley letter but he could not bear to be out of the action. If he gets the leadership we will be in for a very bumpy ride. His view that he could reunite the party in one or two days is in my view wildly optimistic.

MONDAY 19 NOVEMBER

We come back to Westminster from our constituencies with different messages. My own association of Sutton Coldfield is rock solid for Margaret Thatcher. In my view that is the overwhelming view of the constituencies in general but some say it is more mixed. My Chairman made this point and Fiona says that when I told the Conservative club dinner on Saturday that I was voting for Margaret Thatcher only half the audience applauded. I heard the enthusiasm of one table but behind that there was apparently a significant silence. The Conservative club is made up of general supporters of the party, not active workers. Over the weekend Edwina Currie has declared for Michael. Not a good performance from Edwina. Much wringing of hands and she had no greater supporter than Margaret. I meet Cyril Townsend who is also supporting Michael. He is now in serious trouble with his constituency who speak of deselection. No sensible work is being done. We are all gossiping in the tea room. How many votes does Margaret need to see off the challenge? I think she needs to win at the first ballot to do so. Some think that even that is not enough and if Michael polls say 130 or 140 votes and there are abstentions as well she should step down. What would be very difficult is if she is pushed through to a second ballot. She says she will fight on but at what price?

TUESDAY 20 NOVEMBER

I start with a range of television interviews and then go into the House of Commons. As I look around the tea room I see how big the vote against Margaret could be. Ex-ministers like Barney Hayhoe and old-fashioned wets like Jim Lester will not support her in a million years. I go to Committee Room 12 with Michael Howard to vote. We are both voting for Margaret but not without reservations. Inside the room there is a jolly atmosphere with Cranley Onslow presiding over the distribution of ballot papers. Outside, a scrum of reporters seek to keep a running total. The *Evening Standard* says that votes are going strongly for Thatcher. I am not so sure. I am sure that she will win but Heseltine will get a big vote.

In the corridors downstairs I run into Geoffrey Howe, who will go down in history as Margaret's assassin. I am not sure that he realises this will be his fate. He is in relaxed form but obviously conscious that he is not the revered elder statesman that he was a week or two ago. He looks at everyone for a friendly smile. Not all of them are prepared to play. I gather that Nick Fairbairn wrote him a very friendly letter after his resignation but then a ferocious attack following his speech, accusing him of treachery to the party. Fairbairn showed me the reply in which Geoffrey simply said that good advocates only resort to abuse when their case is weak. Fairbairn is an eccentric exception but feelings on the Howe speech run high.

The result comes through while I am sitting in front of ITN's cameras. It is bad news. Margaret Thatcher has a majority of fifty-two but that is four votes less than the majority required to put the issue beyond doubt.[214] There will be a second ballot. Alastair Burnet asks me whether Margaret will stand on the second ballot. I say she will. Will Douglas Hurd or John Major come in? Not as long as Margaret is standing I say. What will happen now? I say that it will be a straight contest between Margaret and Michael Heseltine and Margaret will win. In private, I am not so certain. I doubt whether the Thatcher vote will hold firm. It could be the end for Margaret. What a way to go. Why did she not stand down when she was ahead? Any leader – indeed any minister – must remember that their luck will not last for ever. Give yourself eight years as a Cabinet minister and anything above that is pure bonus. Do not hang on to the bitter end. It may be difficult standing down but it is not half as difficult as being rejected at an election or dismissed because you happen to be in the wrong position at the wrong time.

WEDNESDAY 21 NOVEMBER

The day starts with yet more broadcasts. *Breakfast Time* was not my favourite in government but I must admit that I quite enjoy it on the

---

214 To win in the first round, a candidate needed not just to win an absolute majority but also to have a lead over the runner-up of 15 per cent of the total electorate (not just those who voted). There were 372 Conservative MPs in November 1990, therefore a majority of at least 56 votes was required.

back benches. Perhaps it is because we are talking about politics not perpetually defending government policies. When I get home I find a message from Michael Howard to ring him. He had rung at 7 a.m. while I was doing my interviews. 'We are in a mess,' he says. 'Would you be prepared to be John Major's campaign manager?' He does not think that Margaret can hold on and believes that there will be an election in which Douglas Hurd and John Major will come in. If Douglas stands then so too will Norman Tebbit. I say that I will think about the position. It is a little late but I now apply my first lesson of political life: don't say 'yes,' say you will consider it.

When I get into the Commons there is widespread gloom. People who voted for Margaret Thatcher at the first ballot are now switching. Goodness knows what the logic of that is. How can you vote for Margaret one day and then against her five days later in a contest with the same alternative candidate? Sensible people like Michael Jopling, Francis Maude, Norman Lamont and Leon's successor, William Hague, think she is finished. I would not like to see her lose and be booted out. That would be a great tragedy. I would prefer her to stand down voluntarily in the cause of party unity.

Margaret makes a statement in the House on European security following her return from Paris. She gets a good reception and the statement goes well. I go out with Norman Tebbit and we talk for a few minutes. The men in grey suits have given an uncertain message. They do not know what to do. They say it is not lost but it could be close – which we have all worked out for ourselves. I meet Ken Clarke in the Members' lobby. He is obviously upset. He is seeing Margaret later in the evening and intends to tell her to go. She will not survive, he says, and if she stands it will prevent anyone from Cabinet standing as well.

Fiona and I slip off to the Coliseum to see *Così fan tutte* with friends but I do not have my mind on it. I make my excuses and go back early to the Commons. I go up to the Cabinet corridor in search of John Wakeham and run into him straightaway. He tells me the Cabinet have been asked one by one to give their views. The overwhelming advice is that she should stand down. Only one or two, like Cecil Parkinson and Peter Brooke, feel that she should fight on. The rest, to varying degrees, believe that she will be defeated or believe that the party should have a greater choice and that Douglas Hurd and John Major should be allowed to stand. At one stage she was on the brink of accepting this advice but then the 92 Group intervened and told her to fight on. [215] She is now not going to make a decision until the morning. John thinks that she will go but there is still some doubt. Some of the advice to the Prime Minister has been very emotional – John Gummer was in tears – but the consensus is clear.

As we leave his room we run into Ken Clarke, Chris Patten and Norman Lamont in the corridor. Ken says that if she does not stand down he will raise it at Cabinet in the morning. 'Perhaps this is the way we should have been acting ever since Nigel Lawson resigned'. [216]

Chris Patten is also determined to see her go so there is an atmosphere of deep crisis. It is not good seeing groups of Cabinet ministers standing in the corridor talking in this way. As I leave, Norman Lamont asks if he can have a word. He knows that Michael Howard has approached me to head John Major's campaign. What about it? I say I will need to review the commitments I have made. This election gets worse and worse. I only need Ken Clarke to throw his hat in the ring and every political friend I have will be competing with each other.

THURSDAY 22 NOVEMBER

My conclusion on waking is the same as last night. She will have to step down. There is no way that any campaign could now be successful. The news of the Cabinet's feeling will leak, and indeed there is even some hint of it in the press today. I only hope that she goes of her own accord and is not forced to move out after an argument in Cabinet. My guess is that she will tell Cabinet first thing. John Wakeham said last night that she had indicated that she would go and I can see no reason why she would change her mind.

---

215 A group of predominantly Eurosceptic Tory MPs

216 He meant that the Cabinet should have stood up to her more and not allowed her to get away with some of her statements on Europe.

Having dropped the children at school I go into the Commons just before 9 a.m. Shortly after 9.30 the first news of the resignation comes through. The Thatcher years are over. What a tragedy that it had to end this way. Why, why did she not have the sense to stop and step down gracefully after say, ten years? It would have been a much better way to end than being forced out in this unceremonious way. I set out to my office in Abbey Gardens but am waylaid by television cameramen. They are set out on the green like some medieval camp. You go from one tent to another. The BBC to ITN to Sky. As the morning goes on other cameras and microphones arrive. Interviews are conducted against a background of watching faces – the boys from Westminster School appear to have been given a half-day off. One interview merges into another. Interviewers ask how will I vote now? I say that this is the day that Margaret Thatcher resigned. It is her day. I have no intention whatsoever of announcing a decision on that yet.

In the afternoon her speech in the no confidence debate is the best I have ever heard her make. She goes with enormous style. Both John Major and Douglas Hurd have now announced their candidacy. John is already making some progress. He has the support of the right of the party. It is not that John is a right-winger. It is that he appears sturdier on the European issue than Douglas. He is seen as the natural successor to Margaret Thatcher and will be difficult to stop. In almost all other circumstances I would support him but I feel committed to Michael. But the day belongs to Margaret. Goodness knows there may have been some uncomfortable and infuriating times with her but she was a leader to be remembered. She changed Britain and she changed it for the better.

FRIDAY 23 NOVEMBER

The country wakes to the enormity of what has happened. There are pages and pages devoted to Margaret and what she achieved. Her performance in the House of Commons is rightly praised and perhaps for the first time in fifteen years she gets an overwhelmingly good press. There are also signs of the Major bandwagon gathering speed. I drive to Sutton Coldfield to talk with my Chairman, John Holland, and my agent, Michael Parr. They tell me that there is a lot of resentment against Heseltine and opinion is running strongly for John Major. John Holland says that it would be good if I would come to the executive meeting on Monday although he respects that the choice is mine.

COMMENT

Could Thatcher's defeat have been prevented? The answer is almost certainly 'yes' but that required her to fight back. The trouble was that she had become tired of these personal battles. Her failure to win the first vote with a conclusive majority – albeit by a mere four votes – was the obvious turning point. But it did not have to be like that. She could have won. Her obvious and glaring error was to go to Paris to take part in the jollifications which marked the end of the Cold War and not to continue campaigning. Margaret was always her own best advocate as anyone who came near her will confirm. A personal appeal by her to some of the doubters over the weekend would almost certainly have done the trick. If people like Ken Clarke stuck with her in the vote how many others could have been persuaded to follow suit?

Then comes the question of what difference it would have made. Surely, she would have fallen later? That is true and probably before the 1992 election. But crucially, it would have allowed her time to come to terms with her new position (which could never have been the same as it once was) and to construct her own narrative on the turn of events. The feeling that she had been betrayed and bundled ignominiously out of Downing Street explains much of her later reaction. It also haunted the next seven years and eventually led to disaster.

PART II

THE MAJOR INHERITANCE

15

THE NEW MAN

NOVEMBER 1990–DECEMBER 1991

In the leadership election that followed Margaret Thatcher's resignation there were three candidates – Michael Heseltine, John Major and Douglas Hurd. In winning, Major was supported by an unlikely coalition based on those MPs in the centre of the party, of Eurosceptics and of the 'anyone but Heseltine' group. The new Prime Minister had to establish that before the general election expected in 1991 or 1992 he could heal the divisions. He also had to persuade the public, not to mention his predecessor, that he was a worthy successor.

SATURDAY 24 NOVEMBER 1990

I ring up a number of people in Sutton Coldfield. There is no doubt that the tide is turning very strongly for John Major. Mid-morning Michael Heseltine rings. Will I declare for him? he asks. It is 'a moment of history'. I say moment of history or not, I am seeing my executive on Monday night and will not be saying anything before that. Michael argues that that will be too late to influence colleagues over the weekend. I reply that this contest was not my idea and that in my strong view everything that I forecast would happen is going to happen. The result of his challenge is that John Major will be elected Leader. I hope he realises the feelings in the party. Michael says that those will soon disappear as happened after Margaret Thatcher's defeat of Heath. I reply that this is not the case. The difference is that Margaret is popular with the party and Ted was not.

Back in London I receive a call from Downing Street. Could I take a call from Peter Morrison? Peter's message is clear. Margaret Thatcher has recovered formidably. What would make it 'alright' as far as she is concerned is if John Major was elected leader. I listen but cut him off when he threatens to develop on the theme of how terrible Michael Heseltine is. An hour later I receive a call from Warwick Lightfoot, my old special adviser. He also wants my support for John Major. He butters me up by saying how well I campaigned for Margaret Thatcher. Warwick is an engaging and likeable companion but I decline to tell him my views. My view is, in fact, very simple. Although I advised Michael not to do any of this, I still feel committed to him.

MONDAY 26 NOVEMBER

As I leave the house a lady in Wellington boots who has been exercising her dog comes up to me. She is Douglas Hurd's first wife, Tatiana. She hopes that Douglas will not be hurt by the developments. She cannot believe that he wants to be Prime Minister. I fear Douglas will come a distant third but will not be too upset. I suspect that he is only taking part because he is expected to.

In the library corridor of the House of Commons I meet Geoffrey Howe. Geoffrey thinks a decision for Major would be extraordinary. He does not have the experience, he says. 'He has never raised interest rates'. For Geoffrey, this is obviously the acid test of a Chancellor. He feels that it would be an enormous jump into the dark. At lunchtime, both Douglas and John appear in the tea room. Douglas and his supporters take one table and John and his team another. Symbolically, I am on a table between the two. After lunch I go to the library and write a letter to John. I have agonised yet I see no alternative but to stick to my course. I would feel an entire heel if I abandoned Heseltine's ship now – even given that it should not have been launched.

I travel to Sutton Coldfield for a crowded meeting of the association. I frankly set out for them what has happened. I point out that what brought Margaret Thatcher down was the overwhelming view of the Cabinet that she should stand down. I regret the election and the ejection of Margaret in this way. Nevertheless, decisions are now required. I say that the issues we need to consider are:

1) War looms in the Middle East. We therefore need a war leader.

2) We need someone who will win votes in the Midlands and the north.

3) We need a leader with experience.

The executive then talk. The deputy chairman very helpfully proposes a motion that we should give support to whoever is elected leader. The chairman, John Holland, makes it clear that we will not be taking a vote but there is no doubt that the majority back Major although there is more support for Michael than I expected. At the end I say it is a very difficult choice but I will vote for Michael. Everyone has had the opportunity to put forth their view and to question, and the executive has behaved magnificently. When I get back to London I ring Chris Moncrieff of the Press Association and issue a statement that I will be backing Michael.

TUESDAY 27 NOVEMBER

I do an interview with *Today* on my declaration and then another with *Breakfast Television*. I look into the House for a cup of coffee and run into Norman Lamont. He says 'You could have been campaign manager'. 'Well,' I say, 'I did indicate to you what the position was.' Norman says 'we spoke in code but the meaning was clear.' In the afternoon there are a variety of reactions. Most find my announcement surprising. One or two – Alistair Burt and Tony Marlow – call it 'brave'. We all know the outcome.

I hear the result in the Sky TV studio. Major, 185, Heseltine, 131, Hurd, 56. A few minutes later, Michael concedes defeat and the election is over. John is the youngest Prime Minister this century.[217] Michael will be in his Cabinet but it is the end for him. The party will take some time to recover but it is probably the right result. I doubt whether Michael could have reunited the party. John will do that and we will have a better chance of winning the election now than under Margaret. I remember putting the case for promoting John to John Wakeham, the Chief Whip.

---

217 Seven years later in 1997, Tony Blair became Prime Minister at the age of forty-three.

The first characteristic I put to Wakeham was that Major was 'ambitious'. It has been a spectacular climb.

WEDNESDAY 28 NOVEMBER

During the day the news comes through on the new appointments. Michael Heseltine is going to environment to sort out the community charge – a really poisoned chalice I fear. Norman Lamont is to become Chancellor. Ken Baker, Home Secretary. Chris Patten, Party Chairman. Good Cabinet building on John's part although I suspect one or two people like Ken Clarke will be slightly put out. I have not given too much thought to my own position but it is clear that any plans that I may have had to make a comeback after the election have been dealt a severe blow. The caravan has moved on and it will be difficult to join it again. As it is, I have not backed John and doubtless deeply offended Margaret into the bargain.

THURSDAY 29 NOVEMBER

John's first appearance as Prime Minister at the despatch box. It goes well enough. He is nervous. I am not surprised. Margaret Thatcher sits in the place I used to occupy on the fourth bench back. I now intend to take Michael's position on the front bench below the gangway. I am in a new position in the party. I am regarded as at least half a rebel. It is uncomfortable for a natural loyalist like me. I am still not attracted by the House of Lords. That leaves me with one way forward: to become a parliamentarian. I like the Commons. I believe I can have some influence. I will continue with industry but frankly, at present, it is a little bit tame compared to politics.

FRIDAY 30 NOVEMBER

I get back to Sutton Coldfield to find that the local paper has a big story about Conservative voters attacking my vote for Heseltine in the second ballot. I am suffering from a serious reaction to the events of the past two weeks. I am cast in some gloom about the future. My political future in terms of office is bleak. I need to get down to work again as a campaigning backbencher. The only thing that can be said is that I have wiped the slate clean. I don't owe anything to anybody.

SATURDAY 1 DECEMBER

Still cast in gloom I struggle through a charity event in Sutton Coldfield. In the evening I go to two Christmas parties run by the association. There is a slight atmosphere but only slight. Margaret Thatcher has of course now been transformed into a saint. There is a feeling of collective guilt and some anger that she should have been pushed out in the speedy and undignified way that it all happened. Some of my real Thatcher loyalists are very upset. We have had a few phone calls to the office saying that they will no longer support me. Michael Heseltine is seen as the chief assassin and anyone publicly associated with him is regarded as suspect. At both events I make a speech along the lines that the contest is now over and we must draw a line under it and work so that John Major can win the next election.

MONDAY 3 DECEMBER

I go into the House of Commons and meet Cyril Townsend who works in the library near me. Cyril is really down. He has supported Michael Heseltine from the start and is now paying the price. He faces a motion to deselect him in his constituency and is obviously not overconfident that he will win. Others are in similar difficulties. Michael Mates – Michael Heseltine's campaign manager – my friend Peter Temple-Morris, and Peter Tapsell, Julian Critchley and Peter Emery all face constituency battles. It is an indication of how deep passions go. Their offence is that they voted against Margaret Thatcher at the first ballot but there is now even a suggestion that my old PPS Charles Wardle, who supported Margaret Thatcher on the first ballot but voted for Michael Heseltine on the second, is also in trouble. I imagine that most will survive. It has to be admitted that for some associations the leadership election is simply seen as the last straw. Julian, for example, has given Aldershot plenty of reasons to take offence. Nevertheless, deselection moves belong to the old Labour Party and not to us. And it is to be profoundly hoped that none will be successful.[218]

TUESDAY 4 DECEMBER

John Major is presented to the party as the new leader at the Queen Elizabeth II Centre. It is his 'coronation'. I fear I miss it as I have been booked for weeks past to speak at the civil service college on the life of a Cabinet minister! Later in the tea room I hear that John Major's debut has gone well and again at Prime Minister's Questions he puts in a competent performance. He is scrupulously polite where Margaret Thatcher was aggressive. He is short where Margaret was wordy and long. His first week has gone well.

WEDNESDAY 5 DECEMBER

John Major's rise to leader has been spectacular but he is still largely unknown. There is something in what Geoffrey Howe said that we will be taking a tremendous chance with John as leader. But he has many talents. He is calm and unruffled in all situations. I never once saw him rattled at the DHSS. He is modest and never likely to overreach himself in the overconfident way of Margaret Thatcher. She went from one extreme to another. In the aftermath of victory, as in 1987 or in a successful overseas trip, she was beyond argument. She did not listen. In the midst of a crisis she would come up like a long-lost friend and expect support. We will not get those extremes with John. He is much steadier and the government will be much better for it. When John took over as Chief Secretary and then as Foreign Secretary, I remember that his only concern was whether he could do the job. He now has the most formidable challenge of all and my guess is that he will meet it successfully. I have two concerns. First, that the events of the next months which are beyond his control may make the next election very difficult. There is the very

---

218 All the MPs survived reasonably comfortably.

real prospect of war in the Gulf and who can forecast what the outcome will be? And there is the economy. We are in a recession. Sales are down and unemployment will rise. The only question is, how far? Second, I am concerned about John's own public image. Currently, he is doing rather better than Kinnock. Poor old Kinnock has had his favourite target taken away and he has no idea how to deal with John.

THURSDAY 6 DECEMBER

To a *Birmingham Post* Business of the Year lunch. I sit next to Graham Day.[219] He confirms the depths of the recession in the Midlands but says that Rover is coming through much better than at the start of the 1980s. Also at my table is the editor of the *Birmingham Mail*, Chris Oakley. We clashed when he was an editor in Liverpool but it is too early to say whether relations in Birmingham will be better.[220]

FRIDAY 28 DECEMBER

Leon and Diana Brittan come to supper. Leon says that Norman Lamont has had one and a half hours with Margaret Thatcher trying to persuade her that there was no kind of ministerial plot to get rid of her. Apparently, he failed. Margaret blames a number of Cabinet ministers, Norman Lamont included, for not rallying to the flag when she needed help. It is true that Norman Lamont and Michael Howard were quick off the mark in organising John's campaign – hence the approaches to me – but in all fairness they were only responding to events. John's wisdom teeth operation meant that he did not do very much in the leadership election. But frankly, nor did she. She went off to Paris at the crucial stage. Had she stayed then her direct influence would almost certainly have secured more votes. It was bad tactics to engineer an election and then be away from Westminster. Her other major mistake was to ask the Cabinet one by one what they felt. Once she had decided to do that she was finished.

---

219 CEO and Chairman of British Leyland, which he privatised in 1986 and renamed The Rover Group.
220 In fact Chris Oakley invited me to become a non-executive chairman of a successful management bid to buy the *Birmingham Post* newspaper group and relations could not have been better.

It was quite clear that some would advise her to go although the over-whelming number who gave her that advice was a surprise. What was beyond doubt was that once the advice had been given it would become public. She would have been finished – the weekend papers would have revealed her Cabinet was, at best, split. It is impossible not to feel sorry for her but there is no point in making scapegoats of ministers. They were asked their views and they gave them. There may have been a lack of enthusiasm for her leadership but that was hardly a massive plot against her.

SUNDAY 24 MARCH 1991

I am coming back to my diary after a layoff. The fact is that completing my book on the Thatcher years has taken all my energy.[221] Happily, it is now done. I have seen the proofs and Fiona and I have corrected those. There is now next to nothing left to do but to check a few outstanding points. I think it is going to be criticised on the basis that I am too kind to my colleagues. I am temperamentally averse to putting the knife into people that I have worked with for ten or fifteen years.

As far as the general political position is concerned, the Gulf War is over although the problems are anything but solved.[222] All political debate is now centred upon Europe and in particular, the forthcoming negotiations at Maastricht. We will probably get agreement to excluding the concept of a 'federal' Europe with all the loss of power that means but we will have much more difficulty with the social chapter.[223] There is also the poll tax and the government is in difficulty there.

The opinion polls are narrowing and we are running neck and neck.

---

221 *Ministers Decide* Chapmans 1991.

222 Iraq invaded neighbouring Kuwait in August 1990 and occupied it in two days. In January and February 1991 a United States-led coalition expelled the Iraqi military from Kuwait.

223 The creation of the European single market had led to demands to go further on the political front. The Maastricht Conference in December 1991 was to do this. It was proposed that the EC was to become the European Union and those who lived in it would be citizens of the EU as well as their own country. It introduced cooperation in the fields of justice and home affairs (the European Court of Justice), a move to a common foreign and security policy (improvements in the exchange of information) and included the possibility of a common currency. There were also the controversial social provisions that the UK was very much against.

Labour intends to mount a very personal campaign against John along the lines that he is a nice bloke but someone who finds decision-making difficult and who is not up to the job of being Prime Minister. It is a nasty little campaign and made nastier by the obvious enjoyment with which people like Roy Hattersley pursue it.

MONDAY 25 MARCH

Nigel Lawson launches a big attack on the government and on John Major in particular. Nigel apparently wants to abolish local authority taxation altogether. It would not have been too bad had he left it at that but he went on to say that the government was consulting too much – that's an entirely typical Nigel view of life – and was in danger of giving consultation a bad name. But the real knife stuff came right at the end when he quoted Pierre Mendès France, the late French Prime Minister, whose famous dictum was that to govern was to choose – the implication being that we weren't governing because we weren't choosing. I cannot imagine what has got into Nigel.

WEDNESDAY 27 MARCH

The opposition have put down a motion of no confidence but have confined the debate to the government's handling of the poll tax. The Speaker has ruled that any speeches which go beyond the poll tax will be considered out of order. That is bad news. I gather that half of John's speech is now of no use. I raise it as a point of order in a rather unaccustomed role as bovver boy before the big debate and John MacGregor comes in to support, but there is no change and we now have to have a debate on the poll tax and nothing else. Kinnock makes quite a decent speech. It could have been more effective but I think he has lost his nerve for these big censure debates. John makes a really good fighting speech. Ted Heath gives a surprisingly helpful speech as far as the government is concerned. I am called after him and attack Nigel, who I say has become demob happy having announced he is not standing again. I have discovered an interesting fact about Mendes France, whom

Nigel quoted with approval on decision-making. The biggest decision that Mendes France had to make when he was Premier was on German rearmament. He allowed a free vote in the French assembly with the government abstaining.

THURSDAY 4 APRIL

I go to Solihull for an Evered board meeting and travel with Peter Parker, the chairman. Peter looks much younger than his years and he is still extremely bright and lively. He tells me that after he left Oxford there was the expectation that he was going to marry Shirley Williams but in fact he had decided that Gill was to be his future wife. When this decision became known Shirley Williams' mother, the formidable Vera Brittain, arrived on the doorstep of the Parker parents to protest at his decision.

SUNDAY 7 APRIL

Fiona and I are invited to Chequers. I go with a certain amount of apprehension. I have not been in contact or spoken with John since the leadership election. I need not have worried. Relations were good from the start and the atmosphere at Chequers has changed out of all recognition. It is all much more relaxed than in the days of Margaret Thatcher. Perhaps it is simply the generational difference. Margaret was always the senior figure. She was a minister when I was starting my Fleet Street career and a Cabinet minister when I entered the House for the first time. It is not likely that I would ever have had a very relaxed relationship with her, nor did I. John on the other hand is entirely different. He worked with me in the DHSS. I managed to get him promoted from parliamentary secretary to Minister of State. Those sorts of relationships cannot be discarded. At times the lunch today seemed like a department reunion as others there included Ken Clarke and Nick True while John bustled about like a very good host.

I sit next to Norma. I have the longest conversation I have probably ever had with her. I did not know her very well when John was in the department. She is a good lunchtime companion. The Majors are sensitive about the press. In one or two instances this is well-merited. John took his sixteen-year-old son to a football match and his son brought along his sixteen-year-old girlfriend. Since then the press have been camped outside the girl's house trying to get photos and interviews. On other issues, however, John is being too sensitive. There is a great hooha going on at the moment about how many O-levels he has. It doesn't matter a damn how many O levels he has and the only thing which keeps the story running is the fact that he appears to be concerned by it.

John makes no secret that he is extremely irritated with Margaret Thatcher who, in an interview, has more or less accused the US and the British of standing by while Kurds are dying in Iraq. He is irritated on the entirely reasonable grounds that No. 10 had gone to the trouble of ringing her up to tell her exactly what was happening, namely that there was going to be an airlift of food and supplies to the refugees. It does not show Margaret up well but I wonder whether even at Chequers John should be so free in his condemnation of his predecessor. About the first thing John said to me when I arrived was that once the election was over I should come back into the Cabinet. I don't think that is very likely but it is a nice thought. I have to admit that the longer I am away the less I miss it.

TUESDAY 2 JULY

Margaret has announced her decision to go to the House of Lords. I see her in the division lobby and for the first time in months go up to her. I say that I am sorry to hear the news but I fear she is on autopilot. Rather than sorrow at leaving, all she expresses is her determination to continue fighting on the European issue. This is bad news politically but even sadder in personal terms. Her vision appears to be to keep as much British sovereignty as possible and create some kind of North Atlantic free trade area. NAFTA was where we were twenty or thirty years ago. The caravan has moved on. So far, I fear, Margaret has not handled her new position well. Rather than dignified, even aloof (like de Gaulle or Macmillan) she has appeared rather shrill, anxious to have her say, anxious not to be forgotten. She has not come to terms with her new role.

FRIDAY 12 JULY

A trip to Leominster to speak on behalf of Peter Temple-Morris. Peter had a lot of trouble during the leadership struggle when he came out in favour of Heseltine and not Thatcher. He survived a vote of confidence at a special meeting of about 800 – that is some meeting in local Conservative Party terms. Six months later, Peter's position looks totally secure. I remember Heseltine saying that things would blow over and he was right. There have been uncomfortable and bumpy rides for a range of individuals but they have all survived. The Conservative Party has settled down more slowly than when Ted Heath was ousted – but it has substantially settled down. If Margaret would go off the air then it would calm down absolutely.

WEDNESDAY 17 JULY

Lunch with Ken Clarke. We are both fairly gloomy about the immediate political future. John Major has done well in establishing his position but he has inherited an awful economic situation. Ken talks about the final Cabinet meeting when Margaret resigned. He says she broke down when reading her resignation statement to the Cabinet. It was all incredibly emotional and she was not the only one in tears.

SATURDAY 20 JULY

Jeffrey Archer's silver wedding and both Margaret Thatcher and John Major are there. Mary Archer steals the show with a number of songs like 'Who wants to be a name at Lloyd's?' Mary is on the Lloyd's council and Chairman of its hardship fund. The party is a star-studded affair – half the Cabinet, half the editors of Fleet Street plus a curious all-Japanese table who we assume have something to do with Jeffrey's latest book. I am talking to George Younger when Denis Thatcher comes up. There is the briefest hesitation before he shakes hands. You can almost see him thinking – is he (or rather was he) friend or foe? He is in good form and jokes that they have now moved into Eaton Square although no one has yet worked out how to pay for it. At dinner, Margaret Thatcher is on the next table with Cecil Parkinson. John Major comes about half an hour late and there is a ripple of applause as he enters. He walks slowly to his table and I can't help watching Margaret. She must find this part of life quite difficult to take – just another guest greeting the Prime Minister. The Thatchers go straight after dinner before the cabaret and long before the dancing where there is the most marvellous picture of Cecil dancing with a very frisky Lady Wyatt.

SUNDAY 21 JULY
Nick Ridley has written a successful and entertaining memoir but it is notably inaccurate. The chief villain is Nigel Lawson – his old friend – who has already objected that the book entirely mistakes the history of those years. It is amazing that such a disastrous politician should have risen so high. He apparently believes that one of the troubles with the Thatcher years was that we were not radical enough in the area of social policy. His idea of being radical would have had us out of power for a generation. Happily, he is going to the Lords at the next election.

WEDNESDAY 24 JULY
I listen to Michael Howard's statement on trade union reform. To the amusement of our side and the anger of Labour, he declares the union sponsorship of Labour MPs who rise to ask him questions. When I get called Labour call for me to declare my interests – meaning my director-ships. I declare my membership of the National Union of Journalists, which goes down well on our side.

FRIDAY 26 JULY
The day starts with a meeting at No. 10 with John Major and Chris Patten, the Party Chairman. They have the idea that I should help as a kind of super adviser during the general election. Both Judith Chaplin[224] and Graham Bright, John's PPS, have marginal seats to defend and I gather Chris in particular would be glad to have someone in the Prime Minister's team with experience of elections. John thinks that I should

---

224 Head of the Prime Minister's political office at Downing Street. She was elected MP for Newbury in 1992 and sadly died very young and most unexpectedly in February 1993.

travel with him so it seems that visits to Sutton Coldfield will be strictly rationed – that usually means my majority goes up. John is seriously fed up that he has Margaret looking over his shoulder all the time and second-guessing him. He breaks into a broad smile when I remind him that she will soon be in the House of Lords. Three interesting points to note. First, in conversation he quite clearly distances himself from the No Turning Back group[225] and 'ideologues' like Peter Lilley. Second, when I say words to the effect that I will back him after the election win or lose he says that he is not sure that he would want to go on if he lost. 'I have never gone back in my career'. I don't accept this but interesting that he should even mention it. Third, with enormous courtesy, John escorts me to the door of No. 10 – down the stairs and along the corridor. We pass Basil Feldman on the stairs who is obviously his next appointment.[226] Basil's eyes come out on stalks – 'something is up' is his unspoken reaction.

MONDAY 29 JULY–SATURDAY 3 AUGUST

We arrive in Seaview. Oliver has just arrived back from his tour of the Far East. He has obviously enjoyed every minute of it, teaching in Bangladesh and then travelling in China. He managed to keep up a constant stream of letters. He wrote one to me which I particularly valued. Being a stepfather is not the easiest role. You don't know how much you can interfere: you are conscious he is not your son. He wrote to say that he appreciated what I had done over the years of his childhood. I feel that I did all too little but it was good of him to write in that way. He is now very much an adult – mature and with a great ability to make friends wherever he goes – and about to go to Oxford. Kate and Isobel have settled into Seaview life as if they have never been away. Early morning trips to get the papers and swim in the sea. Kate is out each day learning to sail in a lovely little boat called an Optimist. They do things unsupervised here which we would never allow in London.

---

225 The group was formed in 1985 to defend Margaret Thatcher's right-wing policies and keep the flame of Thatcherism alive.

226 Basil had recently been elected Chairman of the National Union (now Convention). This is made up of the local associations' chairmen and officers and their role is to represent the views of the voluntary party to the leadership of the party. The chairman chairs the party conference.

FRIDAY 9 AUGUST

Over to Cowes with Jörgen Philip-Sörensen (Chairman of Group 4). Philip is sponsoring a yacht in the round the world race in which all the yachts are made of British steel. Chay Blyth who has sailed around the world against the prevailing tides and rowed across the Atlantic is in charge of the whole enterprise for British Steel. He is an engaging man with a fund of stories about his adventures. On one occasion he was in the water in an overturned boat for eighteen hours before being rescued. He now makes his living by organising such round the world events. 'It beats working,' he confides.

MONDAY 19 AUGUST

We wake up this morning to the news that Gorbachev has been removed from power in Russia. At first it is not clear who has been instrumental in doing this but the assumption is that it is the political old guard backed by the army high command. Seen from their point of view the last few years have been an erosion of their power and influence. The world holds its breath.

TUESDAY 20 AUGUST

The news from Russia continues to be grim. Gorbachev is under house arrest in Crimea cut off from all communications. There are television pictures of tanks on the streets of Moscow and reports of military intervention in Leningrad and the Baltic States. A great barricade has been erected in front of the Parliament building and there is increasing public opposition to what is happening. The only hope they can have is that the leaders of the coup lack the resolve to impose their will by force – or alternatively that the army refuses orders to fight Russian people. It seems a slender hope but just possibly on the cards.

WEDNESDAY 21 AUGUST

In the morning I am on the beach for the regatta sports – swimming and children's races along the sands in which Kate and Isobel are eager participants. Coming back to the house, Martin Levene from Sky rings to ask

THE BEST OF ENEMIES

me to do an episode of *Target* on the Russian 'coup' and tells me that it is all collapsing. Wonderful, incredible news. At 5 p.m. it is official that the coup has collapsed and Gorbachev will be returning to Moscow this very night. Now all of the questions are about what happens to Gorbachev, and of course Boris Yeltsin. Yeltsin is the undoubted hero and victor of the last sixty hours – his position is incredibly strong.[227] Twenty-four hours ago almost no one thought that he could defeat the army but he and above all the Russian people have done just that.

TUESDAY 27 AUGUST

Budapest with Philip Sörensen. The day starts early and we meet our partners in the Hungarian security firm who also happen to be the property-holding division of the government. This partnership has come about for a very practical reason. As the Russian troops left Hungary they vacated barracks all over the country. The result is that 1,800 guards are protecting them while the government seeks a purchaser. Sales, however, are slow to non-existent. There is no demand for barracks and not much just now for development land. At lunch our Swedish director tells me that his concern is that unemployment will grow and while the public like political freedom they will become impatient for economic prosperity. After lunch, I am driven to one of the old Russian barracks. Around the barracks there are still remnants of the old regime: a bust of Lenin; a picture of Gorbachev; a mural depicting workers and the army together. Elsewhere in Budapest, virtually all traces of the Russian regime have been removed. As I leave, the head of the guard unit offers me a Russian greatcoat. Regretfully, I refuse it.

WEDNESDAY 23 OCTOBER

A meeting with Chris Patten to talk about my role in the general election. The chairman has moved into new and more luxurious accommodation since I was last in Smith Square. If the rumours about the party's financial position are half-right, then it must rank as a pretty eccentric

---

227 Boris Yeltsin was President of the Russian Federation and was at the front of the barricade outside Parliament during the fighting in Moscow.

decision. Chris has become one of the undoubted heavyweights of the government. For the election he wants me to act as 'father confessor, friend and supporter' to John. I am not sure about the father confessor bit but the rest I am glad to promise. The plan for the election is to keep John to about five–six major rallies but to experiment with a new form of meeting. He will be televised in the middle of an audience and simply take questions. This is intended to play to his strengths as a natural communicator. I would like to see the recordings before pronouncing. I am sure John will be good at them but personally, I hope we do not drop the rallies. It will be important to give an impression of momentum. I would not want to see pictures on the evening news of Kinnock barnstorming through the country while John is shown having fireside chats. Margaret Thatcher complained that in 1987 she was forever being photographed shaking hands. The meeting idea is better than that, but they will be satirised if they are too tame and counterproductive if too dramatic. A good idea but we should be cautious.

Chris thinks the election will be in April 1992 (my guess too). It is difficult to go beyond the local and European elections in case we get a bloody nose. We are going to need all the time available for the economy to recover so it is difficult to see why it should be before. As I leave he says that one of the problems will be the loose cannons: Thatcher and Cecil Parkinson. Margaret has been very difficult on Yugoslavia, presumably thinking we should intervene in some way to stop the bloodshed. I sympathise with her view. The world does seem to be standing by, powerless to stop the killing. Chris thinks Margaret may be difficult on Europe and quite obviously does not trust Cecil one little bit. Cecil is 'nice to your face' but is suspected of being the author of a number of unspecified stories in the press that have done us no good. My view is that they will all behave provided they are given a useful task to do. Chris is the right chairman for this election. It will be closer than '87 but at the centre it will be a better-planned and happier campaign.

WEDNESDAY 30 OCTOBER
Peter Temple-Morris runs a group called the Lollards which is dedicated

to getting centre and left of centre candidates elected to party offices. Their great competitor is the 92 Group (the black hand gang) of George Gardiner who have had remarkable success in getting their 'right-wing' candidates elected. Peter believes that there will be a vacancy for the chairmanship of the 1922 Committee in the next parliament. The Lollards think it would be a good idea if I was to get onto the executive and then run when the vacancy comes. Alternatively, they would like me to run against Bill Cash for the chairmanship of the European Affairs Committee.[228] My first reaction is 'no' to both. I have no great ambition to be Chairman of the 1922 and on Europe I say I will think about it. There has already been a piece in one of the Sunday papers saying I will stand, which I have discounted to anyone who asked. It had not occurred to me to stand. However, I confess, when I think about it there are attractions. Europe is by any standards important. Bill Cash is a bad chairman of the committee. He (and all his officers for that matter) are anti-Europe and Bill is a great bore on the subject.

I talk about it in the evening with Fiona. She shares my views on the 1922 Committee but is enthusiastic about my becoming involved in the European Committee. If I want to get back into mainstream politics here is an opportunity. There is one point on which everyone is agreed: the chairman of the European Committee will have a lot to do on the media between now and the Maastricht conference at the beginning of December.[229] I seem to be alone in regarding this as something of a disadvantage. I will have to dance to the demands of the media. My nicely organised life will be wrecked. Nevertheless, the temptation is strong. I miss some of the involvement in politics, and some of the excitement as well. I have at least established to myself that I can look after myself in the world of business but in my heart of heart, politics is my first love.

---

228 William Cash, MP for Stafford. Strong Eurosceptic and a consistent opponent of the Major government.

229 As it was the turn of the Dutch to be president of the Council of the European Communities, the meeting was in the city of Maastricht in the Netherlands.

MONDAY 4 NOVEMBER

Pressure is building for me to stand for the European Committee. Peter obviously wants to know my decision as there is a campaign to be organised and candidates to be put forward for the other positions. We need to win the election. I am being pressed to stand by all sectors of the party. People like Nigel Forman, on the left, think it is a very good idea as (more surprisingly) do people like Tony Marlow. Bill Cash does not have much of a personal following but apparently the 92 Group are remaining loyal to him. The only advice I hear from Richard Ryder, now Chief Whip, is not to underestimate the opposition.

WEDNESDAY 6 NOVEMBER

I am at a business conference in Bishop's Stortford as messages start coming through from Peter Temple-Morris and others. I gather that the 'black hand gang' are now seriously worried about the election. They have heard that I might stand and they don't reckon Cash is a strong candidate. Norman Tebbit's name is being mentioned. That really would make it a high-profile contest. The election will be next week. Nominations are in by lunchtime on Tuesday and the election is the next day. That suits me. I do not want to have a long extended campaign in which colleagues ask my views on a range of European subjects.

THURSDAY 7 NOVEMBER

In the House for a vote I run into Norman Tebbit. A vintage Tebbit conversation ensues. In his best mafia style Norman says 'a word in your shell-like'. We go to the corridor behind the Speaker's chair. His message is clear. He has been under a lot of pressure to stand for the chair of the European Committee but he has resisted. In his view there shouldn't be an election at all. We should all wait until after Maastricht. He also believes that ex-Cabinet ministers should not stand for these committees. Nevertheless, he says menacingly that if he was to find another heavyweight standing then he would have to reconsider his position. 'Does that mean if I stand you will?' I ask. 'I would have to consider it', he replies. 'You will be seen as Major's man', he says, as if that is an insult inside the Conservative Party. 'Just think what would happen if I won', he smiles threateningly. So there we have it. If I stand Norman is threatening to throw his hat in the ring. His message is that the best way to retain party unity is for me not to stand.

FRIDAY 8 NOVEMBER

The tactics of the 92 Group are becoming clear. All kinds of people are being sent forth to try and persuade me not to stand. Their overtures are accompanied by high praise for my abilities, character and standing. Toby Jessel says how 'disappointed' he would be if I did. Teddy Taylor says he has far too high a regard for me to think I would want to stand. The only man I meet from the Whips' Office is David Lightbown who also advises me not to stand.

SATURDAY 9 NOVEMBER

I have decided to stand. I do not see why Tebbit should get away with his threats. I cannot believe that the majority of the party support his antagonism to the European Community and if they do then we are in a very shaky boat in any event. I will tell Richard Ryder what I am doing and if he feels that John would be embarrassed if I fail then I might reconsider, otherwise it's all stations go.

MONDAY 11 NOVEMBER

I meet Bob Hughes, the young MP for Harrow who used to be PPS to Ted Heath, who is to be my campaign manager together with Peter Temple-Morris. We have decided to go flat out to defeat all the Cashites and Peter himself is going to stand as one of the vice chairmen with Alistair Burt as the other. I have a high regard for Alistair who served Ken Baker very well as his PPS. The plan is that I should announce my candidature tomorrow when I am due to speak at a lunch in Notting-ham and let Tebbit do his worst.

TUESDAY 12 NOVEMBER

I arrive in my old stomping ground of Nottingham having left my nomination papers with Peter Temple-Morris to be handed in. I am interviewed by television and radio, make a declaration speech to a rather bemused audience of ladies who have not been following the European struggle inside the Tory Party and am driven back to the station by my old friend Martin Suthers. By phone I am told that Norman Tebbit is definitely not standing. It is a straight fight between myself and Cash. When it comes to it, Tebbit realises he does not have the troops that he claims support his views. Back in the Commons, I am descended on by the lobby. They say that Tebbit has referred to me as a 'recycled Cabinet minister' and that ex-Cabinet ministers shouldn't stand in these backbench elections. I say that unlike him I am continuing in the Commons and not retiring. As it happens, the press is not deceived. Norman Tebbit had publicly related his threat to me. Philip Stephens of the *Financial Times* says it leaves him a broken reed. Not really true – we should not underestimate his nuisance power.

Some nice people like Patrick Nicholls who would normally vote against me on Europe quietly tell me that they will support me. I notice however that Michael Grylls (whom I know well from the Isle of Wight) continues to organise against me while Bob Hughes asks 'what have you done to Geoffrey Finsberg? He won't vote for you under any circumstances'. I fear the only answer is I got him the sack from the DHSS. He was hopelessly misplaced and I did try to get him moved elsewhere – but I accept that there is no reason why he should support me.

WEDNESDAY 13 NOVEMBER

An extraordinary election. I have never seen so many backbenchers voting in such a confined space. Tebbit is very aggrieved to see both Ted Heath and Geoffrey Howe there. Why he thinks he has more right than they to vote, goodness knows. I gather that it's the first time in twenty-five years that Ted has voted at a backbench committee. Norman Tebbit quickly sees how the land lies. There is no chance that Cash will be elected on the size of this poll. Slowly everyone votes and the room empties as we wait for the result. In the meantime, Bill Cash invites in the visiting speaker, once again showing that he and his allies could not organise a fish and chips stall. You don't have a speaker and an election; you have speakers when there are no elections. Just as the unfortunate man has started, the whip comes through with the result and he has to withdraw. The result is that I have been elected. I thank Bill Cash for his efforts and we go back to a meeting which no one has their mind on. Bill Cash leaves to talk to the assembled press. I have to wait until the end of the meeting. I am then questioned about the result, which I interpret as a victory for the government's policies on Europe. I offer a comment on Labour and say that they must now explain their somersault on the issue. 'That's the first time for a long time we have heard the chairman of the European Committee talk about the Labour Party's policies', a reporter commented afterwards. That has been the trouble. Cash and company have led a debate on government policy along the lines that there are some issues in politics which are so crucial that party loyalty is not an issue. It is worth remembering that we are fighting an election in the next six months. The public may not understand all the issues of monetary union – who can blame them? – but they can smell a divided party.

THURSDAY 14 NOVEMBER

The election gets front-page coverage. The consensus is that this is good for Major and good for the government's position on Europe.

FRIDAY 15 NOVEMBER

A leader in *The Times* indicates that my election was all a massive plot on the part of the whips. It is a foolishly maverick leader article and has all the signs of being the work of the new editor, Simon Jenkins. I gather from Leon that Simon is, and has always been, 'bananas' on Europe and that his own reporting staff are dismayed at his stance. A moment's thought should indicate to him that if the whips had supported me there would have been a furious backbench reaction. I can imagine that Jenkins has the same conspiracy theory as Charles Moore in the *Telegraph*. According to Moore, the whips wanted to fix Cash even though he had been a loyal supporter of the government's position. If you believe Cash supported the government on Europe you will believe anything.

In the evening to Luton to speak for John Carlisle whom I have always regarded as a rather way-out right-winger with an obsession about South Africa. In fact, he reveals himself as rather a jolly man with a good sense of humour: with his constituency he needs it. The chairman finishes the evening by thanking me for my 'inspiring speech' and John for 'his usual offering'.

SATURDAY 16 NOVEMBER–SUNDAY 17 NOVEMBER
My major preoccupation is Europe. As the new chairman of the committee, I will have to speak in next week's two-day debate on Europe and I badly need to bring myself up to speed. I have never before been at the centre of domestic European politics and although I know something of the social chapter issues – which I handled at employment – the same is not true of all the others like the economic and agricultural issues. Of course, not everybody previously regarded me as a great Euro enthusiast. Tim Eggar, who argued with me at employment on the social issues, observed last week, 'my God, the party's come to a pretty pass when you are regarded as the leader of the moderates'.

WEDNESDAY 20 NOVEMBER
The start of the European debate. Kinnock makes a terrible speech – probably the worst I have ever heard from the leader of a major party. He is nervous and unsure, he is verbose and he is totally unable to deal with questions. In contrast, John's speech which opened the debate was masterly. It set out his position in very great detail and took the party with him. He will fight on the social chapter but he is not going to say that the idea of a single currency is so objectionable he won't even talk about it. The prospect is that we will be able to opt out – or opt in as he insists on calling it so it was a good, sound performance. But sadly, the star of the day is Margaret. She makes a typically robust speech but ends by calling for a referendum on the issue. She knows that will catch the press in the morning although she will be under some attack for her conversion to the idea of referenda. 'Let the people speak' she says. That was not the motto I felt was above our heads in the Cabinet room when she

was Prime Minister. Indeed, when people like John Biffen and Norman St John-Stevas spoke out they were immediately prepared for execution.

A meeting of the European Affairs Committee – the first that I have chaired. I meet Leon and take him upstairs. Leon injects his usual polished performance, setting out all the options in our negotiations at Maastricht. He is very interesting about Kohl. Kohl is from the generation who experienced and remembers the Hitler years. He passionately wants to see Germany firmly anchored in the community. Kohl's fear is that this would be less likely once his generation has gone and a new generation with no experience of those years takes over. My main concern as Chairman is to get all my colleagues' names right when I call them. The trouble with having been in government for so long is that I missed out on getting to know the three intakes since 1979 properly.

SUNDAY 8 DECEMBER

A ridiculously early 6 a.m. start to a Sunday. A BBC car takes me to Heathrow and I catch an aircraft with the *Guardian* journalist, Peter Jenkins to Brussels. We take a car from the airport to Maastricht along with an exceptionally pleasant Christian Democrat from Stuttgart who will be debating with me. We pass into Holland with no checks whatsoever. A few years ago there were both passport and customs checks. Today, it is just like going from one English county to another. The BBC has found a cafe in the main square and has taken over floors two and three. The only trouble is that on floor four an 'umpa umpa' band is rehearsing but they have promised to stop when the programme goes on air. It is a genial (I suspect rather dull) programme but there are one or two interesting points. In particular, a German journalist points out that only now is the German population getting round to debating the issues and many of them don't like what they see. In particular, one German paper reports that 96 per cent of its readers are opposed to giving up the Deutsche mark. After the programme I go into the square to give a few interviews. I am the only British politician in town. There is a pro-Delors, pro-federal Europe demonstration who give me a good-natured piece of barracking. 'Briton go home' and the like but when the television reporter asks them to be silent so that he can record his interview they are as quiet as mice. The health workers in Britain were never as considerate.

MONDAY 9 DECEMBER

The day begins early with interviews on Europe and continues that way throughout. The only trouble is that there is practically no information coming out of Maastricht. I am simply telling people what my views are rather than responding to events. I have lunch with Christopher Tugendhat in his smart office on the top floor of the Abbey National in Baker Street. Christopher is an old pal from army and Cambridge days but someone I have scarcely seen in the years since he left the House.[230] He is pessimistic about the election and thinks there's a mood for change and that one way or another we are on our way out. The only news out of Maastricht is that the 'federal' word in the treaty's aim has been dropped. We always thought it would be but nevertheless it is a good sign that things are going to plan. The big difficulty will be the social chapter.

TUESDAY 10 DECEMBER

The news from Maastricht is confusing. The *Evening Standard* begins with a headline saying John Major is on the brink of triumph but then changes the headline to say that it is all on the point of collapse. Tristan Garel-Jones (Minister for Europe) phones from Holland to say the Prime Minister wants guidance. If it all collapses on the social issues will that be acceptable to British opinion? Present at the No. 12 meeting are Chris Patten, John MacGregor, Francis Maude, John Wakeham and late to arrive, Michael Heseltine. Richard Ryder asks the question again. Chris says that he believes we would be in real difficulties if it all broke down on the social issues and Michael Heseltine puts it even more strongly,

---

230 On leaving Cambridge, Christopher became a journalist on the *Financial Times* from 1960–1970. In 1970 he was elected Conservative MP for the Cities of London and Westminster. He resigned in 1977 having accepted Roy Jenkins' invitation to go to Brussels as a commissioner.

saying we can defend retaining our immigration checks but we cannot stand out on issues like maternity rights and the disabled. I disagree. My view is that John Major has made a great deal of how unacceptable the social chapter is. I quote the unattributable briefing that he has given in Maastricht. I say it is essential that he should preserve his position. John MacGregor and Francis Maude nod in agreement.[231]

The discussion is interrupted by a call from Sarah Hogg on the line from Maastricht.[232] Chris Patten says that the view is somewhere between 'Michael's position and Norman's'. My only feeling on the subject is that there was no one there looking after John's position. Michael's advice was frankly bad and if John gives in on this issue the party will be all over the place.

Later in the evening, at about 11.00, the news comes through that John has stuck to his guns and appears to have won a great victory. The social issues will not now be included in the treaty. The other eleven will make their own agreement on these outside the treaty.[233]

WEDNESDAY 11 DECEMBER

The press acclaim John's negotiating as a great success – indeed a triumph. 'Game, set and match' says *The Times*. Indeed it is. He has achieved all his aims – options open on the single currency, exclusion of the social chapter and exclusion of the 'federal' concept.

In the Chamber John is given a hero's welcome on his return. 'Peace in our Time', shouts one Labour backbencher. The comparison with Chamberlain will not stand up. John has secured a deal which gets us through the election, which keeps us as a firm player in Europe and which has

---

231   In this context, 'social' means 'employment' more often than it means 'welfare'. The social chapter did not, of itself, contain any legislation or impose any new laws on any of the signatories. It set out broad social policy objectives, without details, on improving living and working conditions. The concern in the UK was that the treaty would transfer responsibility for aspects of employment and social policy from national governments to the Community. It was feared legislation could lead to increased industry costs and undermine competitiveness.

232   Sarah is an economist and was the head of the Prime Minister's Policy Unit under John Major. In 1995, she became a life peer and sits as a crossbencher.

233   The Social Policy Agreement, to use the correct term, or social chapter was not part of the main Maastricht Treaty but incorporated in the protocol attached to it. The UK's opt out meant that legislation passed under its procedures and agreed by the other member states did not apply to the UK.

not caused the kind of personal rancour that Margaret Thatcher always provoked. The lady herself sits more or less alone with a fixed smile on her face. She will find it difficult to vote against this and if she does then she will be isolated within the party. An impressive day's work for John.

COMMENT

Throughout the 1980s there was growing discontent within the Conservative Party on the direction that the European Community was taking and particularly the ever-increasing importance of the Commission in Brussels. But for most of the period there was none of the open warfare that was to characterise the 1990s. It was more a simmering fire. There were longstanding sceptics like Teddy Taylor, Richard Shepherd and Nick Budgen but in the main the doubters were prepared to give the Prime Minister the benefit of the doubt – even to the extent of approving the Single European Act in 1986 where majority voting was seen as the quid pro quo for the introduction of the single market. Following the 1987 election the position became more tense and her Bruges speech in September 1988 showed where Margaret Thatcher's heart really lay – 'We have not successfully rolled back the frontiers of the state in Britain, only to see them reimposed at a European level, with a European superstate exercising a new dominance from Brussels.'

Major managed the discussions with great skill. His triumph was the successful agreement on the social chapter where he managed to negotiate an opt out for Britain on some of the most damaging measures. His success as a negotiator was now coming to be publicly recognised but it was not enough to persuade Margaret Thatcher, who continued to harry him, calling for a referendum which she would never have agreed to when she was Prime Minister.

16

A VERY PERSONAL VICTORY

JANUARY–APRIL 1992

N*ear the end of the Thatcher years John Major had wondered aloud 'whoever has heard of a party winning four elections in a row?' Now at Downing Street, this became his task. For almost all of the 1992 election campaign, the opinion polls showed the Conservatives running behind with Labour on the verge of breaking through.*

WEDNESDAY 1 JANUARY 1992

The New Year begins with a lunch party at Chequers. The last time I went to Chequers for a New Year's Day party was just before I resigned. That was very much a family occasion with Margaret and Mark handing round plates of canapes and probably no more than twenty guests arranged on one long table. John and Norma's lunch is larger but more informal. Small tables but with everyone helping themselves from a gigantic buffet. Fiona and I are on John's table together with the Archbishop of Canterbury, George Carey, and his wife and John's next-door constituency neighbour, Brian Mawhinney. Others there include Tristan Garel-Jones, who has just been made a privy counsellor, Jeffrey Archer who I fear hasn't been made anything, and people like Tim Eggar who must be getting impatient to be made something more than a Minister of State. We give Bruce Anderson a lift to Chequers.[234] He says that Margaret Thatcher is still going round saying that the government has

---

234 Well-known columnist and formerly political editor at *The Spectator*.

no beliefs and has lost its way. She shows no signs of adjusting to her new life or finding herself a new role. Percy Craddock, who used to be our man in Beijing and now advises John, is also sitting at my table. I ask him about Margaret for the governorship of Hong Kong. He raises his eyes to the heavens in a way which I did not take as a declaration of support. I learnt later that he had asked Fiona if I would be interested in the job. She had replied that I was probably too wedded to the House of Commons. Quite right. It sounds to me like the last job in a career. On that basis, Geoffrey Howe seems the obvious choice but that would be a red rag to the Thatcher bull. David Wilson, the present Governor, it is confirmed, is leaving and will be going to the Lords. It has not been a comfortable time for him and I suspect he retires a rather sadder man. The English business community has apparently been very difficult.

MONDAY 6 JANUARY

A meeting at Central Office on planning the election, Chris Patten in the chair. This involves John Major's own programme. The idea is that he starts the day with a briefing, does his press conference at 8.30, gives a special interview to one newspaper a day and is then on his way. He will visit all parts of the country but the idea is that he will be back in Downing Street by the evening. The strategic decision is how many rallies he should have and how many of these new 'Ask John Major' meetings which Shaun Woodward, the head of communications at Central Office, is pressing strongly.

WEDNESDAY 8 JANUARY

To York for a trial of the 'Ask John Major' format. A small army of television technicians under Desmond Wilcox is assembled. We have chosen the Merchant Adventurers' Hall as a venue which is magnificent in appearance but woefully deficient in modern fittings like adequate power points. I do my introduction, John talks for about ten minutes and then the audience asks questions. The downside potential is quite high: if it goes well there is a danger of it being written off as a predictable party occasion. We should use it but not build our campaign around it.

FRIDAY 10 JANUARY

A 9 a.m. meeting at Central Office with John Major. Shortly after we begin there is an enormous bang from the direction of Whitehall. There is no doubt it is a bomb and John is on to Downing Street immediately. Sometime later they ring back to say it was an IRA bomb but that there are no injuries. The meeting continues and I again argue for rather fewer 'Ask John Major' meetings and one or two more rallies, including one in Birmingham, which is at present omitted. The only difficult moment comes on a role for Margaret Thatcher. Chris looks to me to open and I reply that we need her to declare her support early on otherwise it will become something of an issue. Chris suggests the candidates' conference at the end of the first week. The opposition comes from John. He says quite openly that she has chosen to snipe at him and to hold dinners where her comments on the inadequacies of his government find their way into the press. 'It was her choice to go that way', he says. 'It was not what I wanted. I am not inclined to give her a role'. I argue strongly against this. It seems to be my role (the only one there who isn't employed by the Prime Minister or a party functionary) to give independent advice. I say he must find some role for Margaret and above all they must appear together during the campaign; the same applies to Norman Tebbit. He says he 'supposes' I am right. I am sure of it. There are too many loose cannons in this election and we do not want Thatcher or Tebbit firing backwards into our troops. During the election campaign all must be sweetness and light – or as near as we can manage. There is no doubt how deep and genuine John's resentment is at the way Thatcher has behaved since leaving Downing Street.

THURSDAY 13 FEBRUARY

A dismal day for the government. Unemployment is up to 2.6 million and the figures are accelerating. Repossession of houses is rising at

70,000 a year. All very gloomy and Kinnock, for once, manages to exploit the position well in the Commons.

MONDAY 16 MARCH

Parliament dissolves for the election on 9 April. Caroline and I make a desperate effort to clear up all outstanding letters. Once dissolution has taken place the services of the House of Commons are withdrawn. There is no office, no phone, no fax, no free post and no car park in the middle of Westminster. We all cease to be MPs and become candidates. Peremptory notes from the Westminster authorities (saying: 'whatever happens to you we are here irrespective of the result') tells us that our secretaries are allowed access only to collect the post.

Fortunately, the withdrawal of facilities is not that serious a problem for me. I expect to be back – if I don't return defending a 21,000 majority and with 63 per cent of the poll our outlook is bleak to the point of extinction. The ever-reliable Caroline has done general elections before and is quite used to setting up her office at home. As for parking, Graham Bright has arranged a place behind Downing Street in Horse Guards.

TUESDAY 17 MARCH

The alarm goes at 5.45. I drive into Westminster in fifteen minutes and park in Horse Guards shortly before 7.00. From there I walk the back way into Downing Street showing my pass – a Central Office media pass – to the police on the approach to the rear gate. Inside No. 10 itself I am welcomed by cheerful 'good morning's.' I am sharing the office next to the Cabinet room with Jonathan Hill who has taken over from Judith Chaplin as political officer. He is a self-evidently bright and personable man in his early thirties who was once Ken Clarke's special adviser and then worked for the Tim Bell empire. At 7.15 I am in the lift to the Prime Minister's flat. There, I find Gus O'Donnell, his press officer,[235] and Ste-

---

235   Gus became Cabinet Secretary and head of the civil service from 2005 to 2011.

phen Wall from the Foreign Office.[236] John refuses all suggestions that he should eat some breakfast before doing the press conference.

John and I drive to Smith Square in his Jaguar, arriving in time for the briefing session at 7.30. John's chairmanship is much more relaxed than Margaret's. The trouble with a briefing meeting like this is that almost everyone in the room (and the cast must be fifteen or sixteen strong) has a potential contribution to make. In Margaret's time, people did not speak unless they were spoken to – the atmosphere was tense, not least because she was capable of flying around the ceiling at any moment. John is naturally much calmer and more patient. The downside is that there is an awful lot of talk. Ken Clarke bays on amusingly and we live in hope that some time before 8.30 his words may be distilled into a press release which can be distributed to the media assembling below. As it happens, the press is not that interested in education. They are more concerned about reactions to John Smith's shadow Budget. So far, he has managed most successfully to sell his line that his proposals make 80 per cent of the population better off.

Norma is waiting and after fifteen minutes (but still no breakfast for the Prime Minister) we set off to Northolt. This really is the way to travel. John and Norma are in front in the Jaguar, next is the police protection car and then two cars carrying the adviser entourage. We are flanked by police outriders. Traffic is halted. Short cuts are found through the middle of Hyde Park Corner and then by the banks of the Serpentine and the result is that we are at Northolt in twenty minutes. The only trouble is that the two coaches carrying our travelling press corps have only just arrived. They still have to be cleared by security. We sit waiting in the VIP hall for the best part of thirty minutes drinking coffee and getting more and more frustrated. Eventually, we are able to leave but now we are an hour behind schedule. John is on edge but not in the way Margaret was. Margaret took it out on everyone around her.

---

236   The Prime Minister's private secretary responsible for foreign policy and defence.

That is emphatically not John's attitude. His concern is that he should not let anyone down.

In Nottingham our first 'Ask John Major' meeting. All my old doubts about the format return. There is no excitement. John is surrounded by loyal supporters and the questions tend to be about how we can get our case over better rather than any serious questions on policy. They are good Sunday afternoon party events. Reactions on first day? We have a good travelling team. Shirley Stotter is in charge of the programme itself and John obviously likes and trusts her. Jonathan is a very effective operator, Tim Collins is a very good press officer and Edward Llewellyn a conscientious briefer. They regard me with a little suspicion. I am the outsider and they fear I may be too grand or want too much influence.

THURSDAY 19 MARCH

Another 5.45 start to the day and in with John to Central Office by 7.30. The aim today is to hit back at John Smith's shadow Budget but it soon becomes clear that Norman Lamont's advisers are not certain that the figures they have put into the press release are accurate. There follows an extraordinary fifteen minutes as the advisers now back away from the figures they have suggested. We are left with a vague statement that there will be 'millions' of losers rather than any specific numbers. I fear that Norman Lamont looks uncertain and unsure and he reads his statement from beginning to end without ever raising his head for TV or the photographers. Even in a couple of days I have picked up the fact that relations between No. 10 and No. 11 are not what they might be. Norman is not rated highly and judging from the display today I can see why.

We leave from Northolt and by the time we reach Blackpool we are only twenty minutes behind schedule. The unemployment figures come out at 11.30 and John gives an impromptu press conference. We are helped out today by an outside intervention – the Duke and Duchess of York are separating. Fergie's matrimonial position takes the lead in all the bulletins. Unemployment figures come lower. I suppose as a campaign manager my attitude should be that if it was to happen then it was the best day for it to be announced but frankly, it has to be said – a young couple, young children – could they not have sorted it out?

We arrive in Bolton about 4.15. It is immediately clear that we are in the middle of a demonstration, the crowds throng around as the coach draws up. Most are on our side but there is a determined and vociferous minority who most certainly are not. Carrying Labour posters they chant, jostle, push and shout. Peter Thurnham (defending one of the tiniest majorities in the country) is at the bottom of the steps to greet us as is Tom Sackville, our other Bolton candidate. We then set out on what is euphemistically called a walkabout. It is, in fact, more like pushing through a football crowd going the opposite way. John is surrounded by police and Special Branch. Those of us just behind, including Norma, are not so fortunate. She is a real hero. She never loses her cool and frankly, is pushed and shoved rather more than John. The police know who the Prime Minister is, they are not quite so sure about the identity of his wife. I try to stay near to Norma but we are simply taken over by the crowd. The idea is to walk around the square and speaking personally, I have never had a more difficult time. Even the health service demonstrations were not as bad as this.

John is now in a fighting mood for his speech. Bolton has made him angry: it reminds him, he says, of what we are fighting against. An elaborate stage has been constructed in an air hanger for the rally. A special overture based on Purcell has been composed by Andrew Lloyd Webber and the composer has flown north for the occasion. It is a tremendous build-up for the speech and John does his stuff. It is excellent and the crowd love it. There is enormous enthusiasm. The advice from Central Office was that he wasn't much good at rally speeches and hence it would be better for him to concentrate on what he did well – meeting people and answering questions. It was bad advice. We return to London in a very cheerful mood.

FRIDAY 20 MARCH

We are now getting into our stride. The morning press conference goes well and Norman Lamont publishes a document on Labour's shadow

Budget. This shows that although Labour claim that eight out of ten people will gain, nine million families will gain only 2–4 pence per week and another two million only 34 pence per week. So much for the 'gainers'. The pity is that we couldn't have had this rebuttal out earlier. The feeling is that this story is going off the boil and there is also a feeling, I fear, that John Smith has got away with it.

SUNDAY 22 MARCH

Back to London for the first candidates' conference I have ever been to. My reaction in the past has been that I was better employed in my constituency. This time however, it is important – and particularly important that John's speech goes well compared with Margaret's. I go over to the Queen Elizabeth Conference Centre with Ronnie Millar[237] and we perch at the back of the hall next to Norman Tebbit. Margaret makes a vintage fighting speech. We could not have asked her to be more supportive. Perhaps it is only my suspicious nature that sees Margaret carving out her position for the future when she says that the 1987 manifesto was hers and the 1992 one belongs to John. We won on the 1987 manifesto and well, we shall see. We are now at the end of the first week. We are still behind (but only just) in the opinion polls. Labour have not broken through but they are reckoned to have had the best of the first week's campaign.

MONDAY 23 MARCH

Michael Heseltine is at the press conference briefing this morning. He is obviously enjoying every minute of the election. He is a natural campaigner – it is one of the reasons I voted for him for leader. I have to admit, however, that there would have been no way that he could have held the party together over Maastricht. Had he been leader I fear we could have been torn asunder.

We travel by helicopter to a lovely house in North Derbyshire where we work on the speech for the rally in Sheffield this evening. The speech is good but we are getting it out to the press far too late. Again, John is

---

237 Well-known playwright who wrote speeches for Margaret Thatcher and later helped John Major.

reading it through for the first time as we leave for Sheffield. My night is made by one of the guests here, a cricketing giant from the past, Brian Close. He was put into the English team before he was twenty but never quite fulfilled all his potential. Nevertheless, he was a cricket god. Rather sad to find that he is a normal, middle-class Yorkshireman.

TUESDAY 24 MARCH

To Edinburgh by air. I had forgotten just what a magnificent city Edinburgh is with its wonderful terraces. *Newsnight* have flown in the ever-arrogant Mr Paxman to interview the Prime Minister and have said that the interview would cover the economy, how the campaign is going and public services. We get a message that they now want to interview John on the health service, having just seen Labour's party political broadcast on health to be screened tonight. This gives us no time to analyse it and brings to a head John's frustration with the BBC. He feels that from the first the BBC have not reported on him well and have also failed to report any of the 'gaffes' being made by Labour. The *Newsnight* change of plan is the last straw. He says point blank that he will not do the interview and *Newsnight* can collectively jump in a lake. It is left to me – already seen as the apologist for the BBC after an earlier defence of John Simpson – to persuade him out of it. I agree there is no question of responding to a party political but on the day that Labour are starting their health offensive the Prime Minister cannot refuse to answer questions on health. We will go back and say that of course he will answer questions on health but we want an interview on the terms previously agreed. John grumbles but concedes. The number one requirement of this campaign is that there should be no outbursts of temper and nothing, nothing like Margaret's wobbly Thursday in 1987.

WEDNESDAY 25 MARCH

There is a great deal of coverage in the morning's papers of Labour's party political on health. None of us have seen it but apparently it portrays two little girls waiting for operations – the one who goes private is operated on at once. The other waits in pain. The scene is played out by child actors – although the cases are allegedly real. I notice that the operation is for grommets which Isobel had to wait only a short time for at Charing Cross but what I really note is the piece in *The Independent*. They have found the consultant who handled the little girl's case and he is obviously indignant that the Labour Party are exploiting it. He says that Labour have got their facts wrong and the only reason for the wait was an administrative error not underfunding of the health service. Over breakfast it is clear that John is still furious about the BBC. He warns me that I won't be able to restrain him for ever. I reply that he can do what he likes after 9 April. In pursuit of our policy of helping the photographers we take John to Scottish Central Office fifteen minutes before the press conference so that he can be photographed watching the cricket final on television. John is unimpressed with our efforts. As he settles down to watch, Botham is immediately given out.

THURSDAY 26 MARCH

A new and rather more disturbing story reaches us. William Waldegrave has had a shambolic press conference at Central Office about who revealed the identity of the small girl, Jennifer. William has admitted that Central Office advised the consultant in charge of the case to contact the press after he had approached them. It also appears that we had tipped off the *Daily Express* about the consultant. William has defended the position but not with notable success. It is all very muddy and Robin Cook, who had been having a terrible time over the case, is now demanding William's resignation.

SUNDAY 29 MARCH

When I reach Downing Street I find a cheerful team. Jonathan Hill says that the Prime Minister was very taken with the way that the soapbox went in Luton yesterday and it will be on the bus tomorrow when we go to Cheltenham. It looks like becoming a regular feature of the campaign.[238]

---

238 The introduction of the soapbox was entirely Major's idea and part of his aim of getting closer to the electorate. It was much criticised by some Tory grandees as not 'prime ministerial' but proved to be a total success.

It is best that John does what he is most comfortable with. He has been hankering for direct meetings with the public ever since the start of the campaign. I fear the security men will have a fit but it demonstrates the contrast with Kinnock who is being carefully kept from the public.

MONDAY 30 MARCH

The morning press conference is on the economy. John promises progress 'year by year' to a 20 pence basic rate for all. We get under way on time and from Northolt make a spectacularly bumpy landing at Staverton airport – it is certainly the worst landing I can remember since travelling on Polish Airlines in 1960. We survive and John makes an impromptu speech from the soapbox to several hundred people in the centre of Cheltenham. The speech is made by the occasional heckler who the Prime Minister relishes. The soapbox is with us to stay.

As we make our way to a country hotel for lunch we receive news that Norman Lamont is being interpreted as distancing himself from the Prime Minister on tax cuts. Norman is much more cautious about the scope for manoeuvre. John is furious with the reported conflict. 'If Norman screws this one up I will get a new Chancellor.' He complains that he has the greatest difficulty getting a half-decent political Budget out of Norman. Jonathan is told to get hold of Sarah so that it can be sorted out. She is left the ticklish job of communicating these feelings to the Treasury.

TUESDAY 31 MARCH

After the press conference on housing at Central Office, John beckons me to join a small meeting he is having with Chris Patten and our polls expert, Keith Britto. John cannot understand the division between the magnificent reception he is receiving and the polls. It is not just the national polls but the local ones as well. The marginal seats look as if they are swinging against us. Understandably, Keith Britto can offer no explanation beyond that the polls have got it wrong and the local polls (often conducted by untried companies) are likely to get it more wrong than anyone. I repeat my by now well-known line about the first election I fought in 1970 when the opinion polls showed us 12 per cent behind on the weekend before polling day and we won five days later with a comfortable overall majority. Then, as now, the feeling on the ground was much better than the polls. When we arrive at Chester the strange dichotomy of this campaign is shown once more. There must be 2,000 people out on the streets to greet John. They rush around the battle bus and cram the windows. We couldn't ask for a better reception. It is only when we get to Manchester airport and onto the aircraft that the news begins to seep through of a disastrous opinion poll. Labour are shown as 6 per cent ahead. If this is true then they are getting the breakthrough they have been seeking. We smile and laugh off questions but the fact is that this is the worst night of the campaign so far.

WEDNESDAY 1 APRIL

The west country. For the first time in the campaign John mentions the prospect of defeat. Up to now he has not even spoken privately of the prospect but the polls have cast us in some gloom. We have not had a bad day. A lively soapbox speech in a small town called Thornbury in John Cope's constituency; a pleasant if subdued buffet lunch with local candidates near Bristol; and a boisterous visit to Bath where John is hit by an egg and the coach by two others. Doubtless the eggs will get the publicity but he received a tremendous welcome in Bath which, after all, is one of our most marginal constituencies. We then drive to a country house in a nearby village to prepare for the evening rally. Inevitably, the speech is our main preoccupation but we make good progress. Jonathan goes off to the battle bus to get it typed up and John and I are left alone.

'What do I do, Norman, if we lose this election?' he asks.

'You stay on and fight and win the next one,' I reply.

He thinks on that for a moment. 'You know I don't want to spend the next five years in opposition working to get a job I don't particularly like.'

I say 'this is not a decision to be taken now when you're feeling down.'

He nods in a rather resigned way. 'I suppose you are right.'

A short time later, John returns rather obliquely to the subject. We are eating and there are one or two others there. 'You know,' he says, 'I never sought the job of Prime Minister. My friends persuaded me to stand.'

'But just remember this,' I say. 'No one else, no one, could have kept the party together on Europe.'

'Yes,' he agrees, 'that is true. That is one thing I did which no one else could have achieved.'

The subject is then closed and we do not return to the prospect of defeat again.

Our period of rural introspection ends in the late afternoon. This is when we get wind of the opinion polls for that night. Our information is that tonight's crop put us neck and neck. Labour have held a large rally in Sheffield tonight. Apparently, they have marched 10,000 supporters plus the whole of the shadow Cabinet to the city to applaud Mr Kinnock. I remain to be convinced that it is wise. It is just too 'over the top'. It may encourage his own troops, but badly scares the voters.

THURSDAY 2 APRIL

Lunch with John in the flat and I explain that I am going to get him a good business-type setting for photos tomorrow. Our political theme is recovery from recession. We need photographs to illustrate it. All we have tomorrow is a visit to some pleasure park. Someone from the Policy Unit has suggested the Medway Port, a brilliant suggestion. It has everything. A recently privatised port following the abolition of the dock labour scheme. I get on the phone and bless him, the head of Medway says that of course he will do it. Sarah and I are delighted with the news. Sarah is not everyone's cup of tea. There are some who find her too bossy by half and no one would claim that she suffers fools gladly or is particularly patient with arguments where she disagrees. But she is by any standards outstandingly bright and as far as I can judge, straight. She is not a plotter. You know perfectly well where you stand with her. Above all, she is trusted absolutely by the Prime Minister. The only faintly comic touch is when we receive faxes from her in the battle bus that are signed 'piglet'.

FRIDAY 3 APRIL

To the Medway Port. John arrives by helicopter and is photographed with cars and then with tractors for export. As we go round the port the reporters hear about the advantages of privatisation: the port will ultimately be owned by the managers and the dockers. What a fantastic change this is from the position a few years ago when the TGWU ruled the docks. The photographers get endless opportunities for good photos in good industrial settings. If I had my way we would miss out the leisure park but for fear of offending our hosts the visit has survived. We tour some fake historic coast house and then awfulness of awfulness – John is asked to put on a big glove; a couple of barn owls circle round and come back to him. Which photographs will now make the television and the press? The odds are on the dreaded barn owls.

In the evening I debate with Roy Hattersley at Central Television. We are in front of an audience from Edwina Currie's seat in Derbyshire and, although we are only due to continue for twelve minutes, we go on for thirty-two. It is a ding-dong contest with honours split evenly. I had a difficult time with Edwina's comment on John a few days earlier when she said that the Prime Minister was behaving more like a Leader of the Opposition by resorting to the soapbox whereas Kinnock was behaving like a Prime Minister. That went down like a lead balloon with John. He was furious. Edwina is like Jeffrey Archer. She has no concept of the damage that her words do. She is totally unable to control her tongue and will be damn lucky if she is offered a parliamentary secretary job if we win the election. Ironically, John has always been an Edwina fan and there was a chance – I put it no more – that she could have gone really high.[239]

So, I had to survive Edwina and Roy had to survive the party's policy on proportional representation. Everyone knows he doesn't believe in it and he made a remarkably poor job of defending it. Nevertheless, it takes more than a poor case to get Roy down. As he leaves the hospitality room after the show (for that is what it was) he beckons to me

---

239 I should make it clear that at this point I knew nothing about John Major's affair with Edwina and indeed, did not learn about it until the publication of Edwina's diaries in 2002.

and half-smiling, half-smirking says, 'you shouldn't take this so personally you know.' The 'this' in question is our forthcoming defeat in the
election. He is obviously confident that his long exile from ministerial
office is about to end and believes that by the weekend he will be Home
Secretary.

SATURDAY 4 APRIL

A day canvassing in Sutton Coldfield. We finish the day with a not very
well-attended and rather cold meeting in a school. Afterwards, we repair
to the local pub simply to be seen and regrettably I am, by a very ample,
very drunk, peroxide blonde.

'Are you Norman Fowler?'

'Yes,' I reply.

'I don't know what to say,' she replies. 'Can I sit on your knee?'

I escape with difficulty and take the view that canvassing is over for
the day.

SUNDAY 5 APRIL

The last Sunday of the election. According to the polls, we are losing.
No Sunday paper poll puts us ahead – the best is Gallup which shows
us level pegging. Our deficit in the other polls ranges from 2 per cent
to 6 per cent. However, Labour's best understood policies are those to
increase tax and their campaigns on health and education have failed to
take off as positive issues. Above all, Kinnock still trails John in the polls.
For some reason that I don't entirely understand, the public don't like
Kinnock. He may have transformed Labour into an electable party but
he has never achieved general popularity with the public. The likeliest
result is that we will lose our overall majority, probably the next parliament will be hung with the awful prospect of another election in the
autumn.

TUESDAY 7 APRIL

The Independent's headlines say it all: 'Major warns against hung Parliament, but regional polls suggest outright Labour victory'. 'Labour

surge in marginals'. The biggest poll is one done for the Press Association which shows a 7 per cent swing to Labour overall. No poll puts us ahead and the best makes us 1 per cent down.

I arrive in Downing Street just after 7 for the last time in this election and make my way up the steps to No. 10. In spite of all the forecasts of doom I have never enjoyed an election more. The receptions around the country have been exhilarating and the adrenaline has continued pumping throughout the long days. John has been a really good man to work with throughout the campaign. There have been none of those displays of temper and nerve that so disfigured Margaret Thatcher's campaigns. He has only once shown any gloom and then only privately. Above all, he has kept his nerve throughout and the result is that everyone else on his campaign and at the centre has done the same. It would have been so easy for the campaign to have collapsed in a 1987-type shambles with everyone blaming everyone else. Norma has been a great support and has cheered up the travelling team with her good humour; both of them have responded magnificently. So much for all those Labour predictions before the election that John would collapse under pressure. He has never shown any sign of collapsing. Whatever happens on Thursday the Majors could not have done more.

We move over to Central Office. A tape of *Aida* or some other rousing opera plays quietly in the front of the car – John sees this as a way of hyping himself up for the day. At the briefing meeting there is some talk of the polls and one interesting fact comes out. The big poll for the Press Association covered so many people, about 10,000, that the field work took place last week. It is thus out of date.

To Northolt on my last journey with the campaign team. I will miss the outriders, the traffic being held up and the short cuts. Travelling in London will never be the same. When we arrive at Birmingham International it is pouring with rain and a number of drenched candidates, including John Taylor from Solihull, join us. This is the visit nearest to my own constituency and ironically under sod's law it is the most shambolic of the tour. It is still pouring with rain so the outdoor walkabout in the heartlands redevelopment area is changed to an indoor visit. Eventually we leave, wave to the bedraggled and drenched crowd, which includes some of my own supporters and both Oliver and David Mathew[240] and we retreat to the airport. It is still raining steadily.

The Wembley rally. John's last big speech. John is tired but he has got reserves of stamina. My old friend, the head of Wembley, Brian Wolfson asks John if there is anything he would like. 'Fish and chips' replies John. 'Right,' replies Brian quite unperturbed and fifteen minutes later, fish and chips arrives as Jonathan, John and I work on the speech. It is strong – a little too strong – but we don't have the time to cut it down. But at least this time we are able to go through it from beginning to end and John is familiar with it by the time he reaches the podium. John delivers the speech with enjoyment and force. Once again, he demonstrates his ability as a speaker and the audience give him a tumultuous reception.

For me this is the end of the national campaign. I say goodbye to Norma, whom I have come to know much better during the campaign and like immensely, and then to John. He says that 'no one could have done more.' In truth, that sums up his contribution – win or lose no one could have done more than John during this election. I wave as the entourage sets off for central London and then I find my own car and drive up the M40 to Birmingham.

THURSDAY 9 APRIL. ELECTION NIGHT.
The first interview is with Brian Redhead on Radio 4 at 10 p.m. just as the polls have closed. Brian solemnly intones that the result of the BBC exit poll is that it is a hung parliament. Labour will be making gains but the swing is not enough to give them overall control. Bryan Gould for Labour, Alan Beith for the Liberal Democrats and myself are to give instant reactions. We all make cautious noises about exit polls and I remind the audience of how they got it wrong in 1987. Bryan Gould says it is already clear that the Conservatives have lost the authority to govern but you can sense the disappointment in his voice.

I have another radio interview and make my way to the indoor arena

240 Faithful friend who helped in two elections.

where all the Birmingham seats (including my own) are being counted. It is a faintly clinical atmosphere. The advantage is that all the media are there together; the disadvantage is that the arena is so big that we are all rather lost in the expanse. Constituencies are divided into separate cubicles and as the evening progresses, news comes through that 'Selly Oak looks bad.' 'It is very close in Yardley.'

All the time we are getting news from the television about what is happening in the rest of the country. By far the most significant piece of information is that we have held Basildon. If Labour could win Basildon then they could win this election. The prospect by midnight is still of a hung parliament but everyone agrees that we will be the largest party. There have been some sad losses for us but generally we are doing much better than the polls indicated – and it is already being seen as a defeat for the pollsters.

My result does not come until after 2 a.m. and it is extraordinary. I have increased my majority to 26,000 and have a 3 per cent swing to the Conservatives from the Liberals. In my speech I praise John Major and Oliver as my workers all cheer. It is (on the information I have) too early to claim that we are going to have an overall majority but it is now the prospect. A tremendous personal victory for John.

More interviews and by the time we are home, it is clear that we have an overall majority. Not very big but an overall majority all the same. And indeed it seems to be creeping up. It could be twenty. It takes some time to sink in that we have won. In spite of the opinion polls, in spite of the experts, in spite of those biased television interviewers we have won. It really was like 1970.

FRIDAY 10 APRIL

To bed at 4.15 a.m. and up again two hours later to go into Pebble Mill for *Breakfast News*, the *Today* programme, West Midlands radio and later, *The Jimmy Young Show*. The victory is acknowledged but I am asked if John Major really was confident. Obviously, my presence with John on his travels around the country has been noted on television. I am credited with much more influence than I had. The overall campaign was entirely the responsibility, and to the credit, of Chris Patten. All I managed to do was to be a friend at court for John and to intervene when others found it difficult (because of youth) to do so. I notice another question now entering the list: would you be prepared to take over as the next chairman of the party? I evade the question and praise Chris who certainly deserves it. It is a cruel irony that he has won the election but lost his own seat in Bath.[241]

SATURDAY 11 APRIL

Now comes the big question for me. Will I be offered anything I want to accept or indeed, will I be offered anything at all? Fiona and I have already discussed what is at stake. As she predicted after four weeks total immersion in politics it is politics that has taken over my life again. I think John has the chairmanship in mind for me. He has never said as much. He has told me what a tough job needs to be done. He has told me that Jeffrey Archer has no chance of having it. (He illustrated Jeffrey's chances with an 'O' formed by his thumb and index finger.) There has been no promise although Sarah Hogg talks confidently about me taking over Central Office.

As the hours go by the phone remains conspicuously quiet. I try not to listen for it and decide it would be better if we were back in London. Chris, having lost Bath, is no longer an MP and cannot take over as Chancellor – which otherwise I believe would have been the case. Indeed, the only job he can do is Chairman of the party. He does not need to be an MP for that. Thus, I assume that Chris will stay on – perhaps not indefinitely but certainly for some time. The eventual announcement does not specify what Chris will be doing but there are some good appointments. Virginia Bottomley to health is excellent and Michael Howard to environment is a notable example. But John has not been a butcher. Norman Lamont survives as does Peter Lilley.

Fiona and I walk over to the Hurlingham Club to have a quiet drink. Just as we are starting our second glass of wine a breathless Oliver

---

241 The result was Conservatives 336 seats, Labour 271, Lib Dems 20 and other parties 24, giving the Conservatives a majority of 21.

appears. No. 10 has been on the phone and want me to call back. I put a call through to Downing Street. We exchange greetings and John says how much he enjoyed the travelling campaign part of the election. He then comes to the point of the call. He says that Chris is going to think about his future over the next few days. He has not accepted a place in the House of Lords and there are a range of alternatives he wishes to consider. He will remain Chairman for the time being but then wants to step down. He feels he has been harshly criticised over the campaign and should move on. John wonders if I would be interested in taking over the job. I say that I would and that this has always been one of the jobs I have wanted to do. We then talk about how it could be done. John gives me the impression that it is up to me. I can attend Cabinet if I want to – or I might prefer to do it outside government altogether. I say that we can talk about that but one of the requisites is that the Prime Minister and the chairman get on. 'We shouldn't have any difficulty there,' laughs John – and nor should we.

'What about timing?' I ask. John replies that very few people know of his call and we must keep it secret. But for my information, he adds, the change will take place 'in weeks not months.'

COMMENT

No one could quite believe Major's election victory. The pollsters were covered in embarrassment and the political correspondents generally fared no better. Virtually no one predicted a new Conservative government with an overall majority – albeit a slim one of only twenty-one. So why did we win? Basically, the fear of Labour was greater than any resentment towards us regarding the recession. Labour's plan for extra taxation was finally understood. Wavering voters came back to us believing that a Labour victory would lead to a possible economic crisis and the near certainty of increased taxes. Labour did not help themselves by their triumphalist campaign. The Sheffield rally was a mistake and so too was their 'taking it for granted' manner in the final days of the campaign. Most of all, Kinnock was not seen as a popular national leader. He had done a vast amount to make the Labour Party a contender again but the public seemed to regard him as not quite up to handling the economy.

The government was fortunate in one respect. European policy was the issue that was shortly to transform British politics but in 1992, the official policies of the three main parties were not that far apart and the Tories had been careful to kick many of the controversies of Maastricht to the other side of the election.

Major's approach to the election was in marked contrast to that of Margaret Thatcher. Major had one aim which set him apart from her and the traditionalists in the party. He wanted as close contact as possible with the electorate – an approach symbolised by the use of the soapbox. In the 1987 election, setbacks such as wobbly Thursday could lead to near-panic around the leader. Whatever grumbles Major might have had were usually in private to his personal team. John Major was exactly the right man at the right time. A middle-of-the-road Tory who promised a more sympathetic approach than his predecessor.

17

THE PARTY IS BUST

APRIL–AUGUST 1992

Inside Conservative Central Office I inherited one of the most unaccountable and divided organisations known to man. Fundraising was in the hands of two party treasurers. They were appointed by the Prime Minister and answerable only to him. Thus, any scandal involving fundraising was a matter for him, not the Party Chairman who was only responsible for spending the money. So, he could authorise a new office for himself or authorise spending several million pounds on a press advertising campaign without any consultation. The whole organisation badly needed reform.

MONDAY 13 APRIL 1992

I go to a publishing party for Michael Dobbs' latest book. Meet Philip Stephens of the *Financial Times* who is doubtless seriously fed up with being taken to task for the paper's leader which invited all their stockbroker readers to vote Labour. Bruce Anderson tells me that the McAlpine election party, where Margaret Thatcher was the chief guest, broke into applause when it was announced that Chris Patten had lost his seat. What an appalling group. The kind that makes you vote Labour. It has been McAlpine and his kind who have been sniping at us throughout the election. They have not had the guts to come out against John; instead they have criticised the campaign. Margaret was a great Prime Minister but she is now surrounded by a pathetic group of hangers-on. It is about time everyone concerned came to terms with the reality that the political caravan has moved on.

TUESDAY 14 APRIL

The junior appointments to the government have not caused many surprises. The major hiccup has been Edwina Currie's refusal to take the Minister of State job at the Home Office to look after prisons. She is very lucky to have been offered anything after her comments during the election and her refusal must mark the end of her ministerial career. Quite mad. In John she had a committed supporter. She will never get an opportunity like that again.

WEDNESDAY 15 APRIL

I gather Chris is considering becoming Governor of Hong Kong. If true it sounds an odd move to me. I cannot see what the upside is, nor why he wants to remove himself from politics for five years. Richard Ryder also leaves no doubt that Edwina's career as a minister is over. 'That's it' he says with feeling. 'That's it.' I am still no clearer why she refused. She apparently does not like working with Ken Clarke and was anxious to have a European post, whatever that means. As it happens she might have done prisons well. Goodness knows there is enough to do.

FRIDAY 17–MONDAY 20 APRIL, EASTER

The first days off since the election. The children race about on the beach with their friends. Fiona and I enjoy the fresh air and get to bed by 10 o'clock each night. Virginia Bottomley comes in to talk about her new job as Health Secretary. Peter Bottomley canvasses my support for Peter Brooke in the speakership election. I say that if it was left to me I would vote for Betty Boothroyd but if we are determined to have a contest I agree that Peter Brooke is the strongest candidate.

TUESDAY 21 APRIL

Back to London in the afternoon to find a number of messages on the answerphone asking me to comment on Margaret Thatcher's latest outburst. This is an article for *Newsweek* where she says that John is 'not his own man' and that 'there is no such thing as "Majorism" although

"Thatcherism" will live long after Thatcher has died.'[242] I have no intention of commenting. It is irritating but frankly irrelevant. It all sounds faintly potty in any event. Obviously, we should not write her off but at this moment she lacks clout. Things could change – particularly on Europe – but by her decision to go to the Lords she has removed herself from the only chamber where she could have real influence.

THURSDAY 23 APRIL

To Sutton Coldfield where someone has thrown a brick and a bottle through the front window of our house. It is always said that if you put up a political poster a brick is the inevitable result. According to the police the damage was done by three very drunk youths – the room smells like a brewery. The police are a little sheepish given that they are supposed to provide a mobile check every hour. It all goes to show that if assailants are really determined (or just lucky) they will penetrate any security precautions. By the time I return from my advice bureau, the boarding is down and the window replaced.

FRIDAY 24 APRIL

A call from John who tells me that later this morning Chris Patten is to be announced as Governor of Hong Kong. Chris would like to stay on for the local elections and then go. Later, I meet Chris himself. He is about to give a press conference about his new job but gives a potted summary of the Central Office organisation: the party is in debt to the tune of between £11 and £15 million pounds; the treasurers' department operates as an independent fiefdom within the organisation and needs a thorough overhaul; the area organisation needs abolishing and the communications department is a total shambles and is still not right.

MONDAY 27 APRIL

Lunch with Maurice Saatchi at his request. He is obviously keen to keep

---

242 *Newsweek*, April 1992, 'Don't Undo our Work'.

the Conservative account and as he points out, the agency has more experience of the Conservative Party than any other agency. It is not remotely a
heavy sell for his agency. Rather, he is concerned that the party had so few
friends during the election that Labour outspent us on press and poster
advertising by four to one. What concerns Maurice was that even when we
did match Labour's spending, as in the last weekend of press advertising, it
was with money we did not have. We simply added to the overdraft.

Betty Boothroyd wins the speakership by a mile. Peter Brooke speaks
well and polls respectably but Betty receives over 50 per cent of the votes
on the first ballot. There is no other challenger and we elect our first
woman Speaker.

TUESDAY 5 MAY

Lunch at the Ritz with Simon Heffer. He tells me that his *Evening Standard* column is all about what a good chairman I would make (I see it
later and it is indeed what actors would call a very good notice). I will try
and get him together with John but I may fail as John has no high regard
for the school of journalism to which Simon belongs – Charles Moore,
Christopher Monckton, Frank Johnson et al. In the evening a rare visit
to the theatre to see *Death and the Maiden* – tremendously powerful.

THURSDAY 7 MAY

The nitty-gritty of making the changes in my team at Central Office.
Richard Ryder agrees that I am the man to both hire and fire. Gerry
Malone (Deputy Chairman) is over the moon – gobsmacked – and Tim
Smith is equally delighted to be Vice Chairman. Andrew Mitchell is
concerned that it may be a consolation prize. It might bar him from promotion to the Whips' Office. He will agree however. I confess I would
have preferred more initial enthusiasm but I cannot really complain. He
wants to make progress in the party and fears Central Office may be seen
as a political graveyard – my point exactly to John.

SUNDAY 10 MAY

Fiona and I drive to Huntingdon to announce my move to Party

Chairman. Just before we leave, John comes on the phone. I assume it is some urgent matter of state, not a bit. He wants to know if Chicken Kiev will be alright for lunch. I cannot imagine Margaret checking whether we had any dietary foible. John's house is fronted by an impenetrable security gate. For a moment I am not sure how to gain entry but eventually a policeman appears and inside, I find some of the familiar special protection team whom I got to know during the election. The house is a country house built, I would say, in the 1920s or 1930s. Not extravagant but stylishly furnished, I imagine, by Norma. It is surrounded by a garden of one or two acres and the photographers want John and I to walk among the trees – under the branches of a cherry blossom tree. I can see why. Now that all the papers have the capacity for colour, the pink of the blossom makes an obvious background. My only fear is that the whole picture will turn out to be more like the announcement of an engagement than a political picture.

We are only four at lunch and talk widely. I wonder whether I can attempt any bridge building with the Thatcherites in exile, particularly Margaret herself. 'It would be a waste of time' replies John bleakly. Apparently, Margaret did her interview with *Newsweek* in which she said John was not his own man after a good lunch and a few drinks. There are stories that she is now drinking much more than when she was in government. She had the opportunity to correct the script before publication but failed to do so. I ask if John wants to meet Simon Heffer who is one of Thatcher's leading courtiers. 'Definitely not', he says. 'You have not seen the things he has written about me.' John does not forgive personal attacks.

MONDAY 11 MAY

Chris Patten is waiting on the steps of Central Office. We go inside to find all the staff waiting in the conference room. Chris makes his valedictory speech and then I follow, thanking Chris, but also giving a rather complicated message, namely gratitude to the staff for their efforts but emphasising the need for change. We all go out into the square to wave off the former chairman. I spend the rest of the day meeting my new staff. Shirley Oxenbury[243] and John Gardiner look after my office,[244] and Shirley in particular has great experience going back to Norman Tebbit, Peter Brooke, Ken Baker, John Gummer, and many before. By reciting that list I make one obvious point: Central Office has suffered from too many chairmen in the last few years. There is no continuity. There is no central management. I mischievously think of asking to be taken to the executive in charge. The fact is that there is no one in charge – apart, that is, from myself as Chairman.

TUESDAY 12 MAY

I spend the day going from one department to another and introducing myself. There is a mood of understandable apprehension. They are not sure that they will all have jobs in a few weeks' time: nor frankly am I.

MONDAY 18 MAY

Back to the old meetings routine which appears to be a requirement of modern government. At 9 o'clock the regular No. 12 committee meet, headed by the Chief Whip, Richard Ryder, together with Leader of the House, Tony Newton, the Leader of the House of Lords, John Wakeham, advisers Sarah Hogg and Jonathan Hill and Downing Street press officer, Gus O'Donnell. Our job is to think of the banana skins and problems ahead. From No. 12 to No. 10 for meetings with John on the week ahead and parliamentary business, together with my own issues. From No. 10 back to Central Office for a meeting with the departments and vice chairmen. This is now to be my Monday morning routine.

TUESDAY 19 MAY

In the evening I look in at a party of the Conservative Way Forward. I see Margaret Thatcher in the distance where she is so surrounded by admirers that there is no chance of having a quiet word. Then to The

---

243   Ran the office of successive party chairmen, later became Dame Shirley.
244   John was later made a Conservative peer and became Deputy Senior Speaker.

Savoy for a dinner of the Conservative Women. I get a good cheer when I go in and John and Norma are received rapturously. John is in particularly good form, both funny and forceful. It seems an age ago that Shaun Woodward was explaining to me how the Prime Minister was not much of a big occasion speaker.

THURSDAY 21 MAY

Lunch with David Poole who is seeking tips on his new position in the No. 10 Policy Unit. Sooner or later, the gossip diaries will work out that both Oliver's father and stepfather are working fairly directly for John Major, and that Oliver is the grandson of one of the most effective former chairmen of the Conservative Party. In the Commons we easily win a vote on the Maastricht bill. There are only twenty-two abstentions but that understates the strength of the Eurosceptics in the parliamentary party.

SATURDAY 23 MAY–WEDNESDAY 27 MAY

I have been mulling over my plans for the party. We need a Chief Executive. Thanks to the generosity of Philip Harris we now have the money to afford one. Their duties should not only include management but also liaising with advertising and the newspaper proprietors. That leaves the job of Communications Director more clearly focused on media relations, together perhaps, with responsibility for party political broadcasts. Tim Collins has agreed to do the job – a big break for him – but I fear this leaves Shaun Woodward without a role.

SUNDAY 31 MAY

Really sad news. My old friend Alan Howard has died from leukaemia at the ludicrously early age of fifty-four. For two years Alan and I shared a room at Trinity Hall in Cambridge. He was a very good man – kind, dependable, a rock on whom you could rely. He was genuinely concerned with the welfare of others – his family, his friends and many others whom he knew far less well. As he fought his illness in his hospital room, he was concerned about knowing what was happening to other mutual friends and national figures. When I last visited him he told me that he was now reconciled to death if it came. His first reaction had been that it was unfair – 'why me?' – but that had passed. He would fight against death to the end but if it came, he was prepared: a very courageous man. I phone a number of friends and we plan that his Cambridge group be represented at the funeral tomorrow.

MONDAY 1 JUNE

Jewish funerals follow very quickly after death. David Tether, another friend from our Cambridge days, and I drive out to the cemetery in Edgware where the congregation of about 200 has gathered. It is a simple ceremony but with a moving tribute by Alan's rabbi. Afterwards we meet Angela, the children, Ken, his brother, and Alan's mother whom I first met in Cambridge over thirty years before. They are all incredibly brave. Perhaps the large number of mourners helps. The reality of the final loss strikes home at the end of the funeral. A small excavator has dug a pit. There is a mound of turf and thick clay. The coffin is lowered and the mourners throw in earth. It is that image of the actual burial that remains with me.

TUESDAY 2 JUNE

It is as if a steam roller has hit me. Everyone in the party wants to see me. My diary has suddenly transformed into wall-to-wall engagements. Max Beaverbrook, one of the treasurers, brings the unwelcome news that the poster sites for the local elections that we had thought were free are in fact going to cost us several hundred thousand pounds. No one now admits to doing the poster deal but Beaverbrook says that James Hanson is insistent on being paid. The only alternative would be for it to appear as an extra contribution from him which he will not do.[245] The Danes have rejected the Maastricht Treaty by the tiniest of margins (50.7 per cent to 49. 3 per cent).[246] Inevitably, there is a call from the sceptics

---

245 Had Mrs Thatcher still been leader would he have refused?
246 A second referendum was held on 18 May 1993. This approved the treaty by 56.7 per cent.

for a 'new start' to the British government's negotiations. Ominously, a motion calling for such a start is signed by ninety Tory backbenchers.

MONDAY 8 JUNE

John agrees my plans for a Chief Executive at Central Office. Being Chairman to John Major, and not to Margaret Thatcher, has one vast advantage. I could not conceive of the easy relations which I have with John being possible with Margaret. She was basically not interested in strengthening the party organisation. Some say she feared that it could be used as an alternative power base. At the end she succeeded in leaving the party in a very un-Thatcherite state – heavily in debt and overspending. Just the position she warned all other companies – public and private – not to contemplate.

WEDNESDAY 10 JUNE

Strasbourg to see the Conservative MEPs. Christopher Prout[247] looks after me and takes me to lunch with Giscard D'Estaing. I am very impressed. I remember all the stories about the grandeur which contributed to his defeat as President. That seems to have vanished and he appears as a civilised and cultured man. All the discussions in Strasbourg are dominated by the Danish referendum.

MONDAY 29 JUNE

A rumour has reached me that Lord Beaverbrook is in substantial debt to the Royal Bank of Scotland. They have been trying to get the matter resolved for months but without success. They now feel they have no alternative but to get their lawyers to tell him that unless he pays immediately, they will petition for his bankruptcy. John has sent a letter to both Hector Laing and Beaverbrook telling them that in the future they will be reporting to me which gives me the opportunity of reshuffling the pack and getting rid of Beaverbrook. I am not prepared for a treasurer

---

247   MEP from 1979–1994, who in 1987 became leader of the Conservative group in the European Parliament.

of the Conservative Party to be declared bankrupt. If he is no longer in office the damage will be less.

Both treasurers were Thatcher appointments. One is too grand by half, and the other looks as though he is going to end up in Carey Street. A marvellous duo for raising money in hard times but raise money we must, for the other part of the Thatcher legacy is a whacking great overdraft.

TUESDAY 30 JUNE

During the afternoon I drive to the House to meet the author Jack Higgins. He wants to see the terrace of the House of Commons. He cannot believe how easy it would be to climb up from the Thames, thus avoiding all the security at the official entrances to the palace. I imagine that this will all feature in his next book. Back at Central Office, Hector Laing asks to see me. He says that he is far too old to be offended by anything but then goes on to demonstrate that he is very seriously miffed. He is prepared to report to me provided no one knows and it is not made public. He says that otherwise such an arrangement would destroy his team's morale. They would see their role as being diminished. This is all, of course, the greatest nonsense but confirms my view that Hector, feeling bruised and unloved, might well decide to call it a day if his companion treasurer was asked to stand down.

WEDNESDAY I JULY

Europe continues to rumble on as the political issue of the moment. The Conservative Party is badly split, very badly split. We have total irreconcilables like Cash, Taylor, Budgen and Shepherd who we will never persuade, plus a much greater number who are biding their time but cannot be relied on. Inside the party there are similar divisions, all of which bodes ill for the party conference in October. John has decided on a policy of strongly defending Maastricht. He knows that this policy has its risks but he tells me that he is prepared to be beaten and to resign on the issue. He feels that he cannot renege on the deal that he made. He is allowing Margaret to seriously rile him. Relations are now non-existent. I hear him say again that he did not seek the leadership and if he is defeated on Maastricht then there are other things that he would like to do with his life. We should all remind ourselves that it is July. We are all tired. Tempers are getting frayed. The sooner the House is down the better.

THURSDAY 2 JULY

John makes a strong speech on Europe to the 1922 which helps to counter Thatcher's maiden speech in the Lords in which she again calls for a referendum. She really has a hell of a nerve. She would not contemplate a referendum when she was Prime Minister, nor do I recall the emblem 'let the people speak' emblazoned on the Cabinet wall.

SUNDAY 12 JULY

To Cliveden for John Lewis's birthday.[248] The Profumo affair was set here. Perhaps his guard was brought down by the atmosphere of the place, its luxury and a slight feeling of decadence. Cliveden was in the news again last week when Margaret made an attack on the government's economic policy at what was supposedly a private dinner. Needless to say, it was lovingly relayed to the *Evening Standard* by one or two of the guests there.

TUESDAY 14 JULY

The first political Cabinet since the election. There is a welcoming cheer (a rumble of hear, hears) as I take my place to the right of John. Michael Heseltine gestures to me. He is sitting in exactly the same seat from where he walked out on Thatcher. He points to the chair next to him where I used to sit in those days. That is about the liveliest part of the meeting. I have never seen twenty-two more exhausted figures: their tiredness is tangible. Jonathan Hill tells me later that last week two of them actually

---

248 A generous friend, businessman, solicitor and charity executive. He was Chairman of Cliveden between 1984 and 2002 and on the British Tourist Authority in the 1990s.

went to sleep in Cabinet. They have had quite a bashing with no real break since the election. They need a holiday and I feel rather guilty about my message that departments must be manned during August.

Lunch with David Stevens, Chairman of the *Daily Express*. Just the two of us. I like David but I cannot understand why he is in newspapers. He does not like journalists and cannot understand his own paper's pre-occupation with all things royal and particularly the state of the Prince and Princess of Wales's marriage.

SATURDAY 18 JULY

John Smith and Margaret Beckett are elected leader and deputy leader of the Labour Party. A safe choice. I suspect they would have done better to miss a generation and go for Tony Blair. Smith is too similar to John Major. I am not sure how he is going to illustrate the new thrusting party ready to lead the country out of recession. I got to know Margaret Beckett in the 1970s when we both attended the Republican convention in Kansas City. I like her but she is a genuine left-wing socialist. I condemn them both for the benefit of television and radio. During the evening Tim Collins rings me to say that the *Sunday People* are running a story that David Mellor is having an affair with an actress. It hardly comes as a surprise that Mellor is having an affair. I picked up that piece of information during the election and if I know I assume it is a fairly open secret.

SUNDAY 19 JULY

A family christening party in Wiltshire. Kate and Isobel both look very pretty in their different ways and spend their time wheeling the young baby around the large green lawn. In the kitchen I find the *Sunday People*. They have used an extraordinary ploy to excuse their intrusion into the Mellors' lives. They allege that Mellor's extramarital activities have made him too exhausted to carry out some functions of his ministerial life, like properly preparing his speeches. It is reassuring to know that we have such a guardian of the public interest.

MONDAY 20 JULY

No. 12 meeting with Richard Ryder and Tony Newton. We discuss the Mellor case. My view is that he will need help. I volunteer to issue a statement of support and do the inevitable interviews which follow. I check with Mellor himself. After some delay we get through to him on his car phone. I tell him what we could do. The message would be a) private lives are private lives and b) let's get back to politics. Mellor is not convinced that it is necessary and obviously feels that the 'let's get back to politics' point is too defensive. He feels that the major villains of the piece are the *Sunday People* who used scurrilous methods like phone tapping to get their piece. I am sure the *People* should be blamed but I cannot help feeling that he will need to show some regret if he is to get any sympathy from the public. He gives the impression that all this fuss is a total irrelevance; he has nothing to explain and needs no help. I think he is wrong but it is up to him. Nevertheless, I prefer that a minister should not be forced to resign because of a press story about his private life.

TUESDAY 21 JULY

A new problem. Kelvin MacKenzie, editor of *The Sun*, has alleged that during the election an unknown Cabinet minister rang him with the names, addresses and telephone numbers of a number of women who have had affairs with Paddy Ashdown. This piece of information was intended to show the hypocrisy of a government which is intent upon introducing a law of privacy. *The Sun* story is running very strongly. It is potentially more serious than Mellor, raising the prospect of a dirty tricks campaign being organised by 'a prominent Cabinet minister' near to the heart of the election campaign. The press is giving the impression that Central Office are carrying out an investigation to check and indeed it is difficult to see how we can issue a statement without some inquiry.

Richard Ryder thinks that I should ring the Cabinet one by one. The major suspect is John Wakeham because he was the man most in touch with the press during the election but he denies the story. He spoke to

Kelvin MacKenzie during the election but not to give him names and addresses. Hardly anyone else can remember ever talking to the editor of *The Sun*, including Chris Patten whom I spoke to in Hong Kong. 'Perhaps it is a commentary upon me as Chairman but I didn't speak to him.' The whole process of making the calls takes about two hours. The most bizarre call I make is to John Gummer who takes it on a mobile phone in a field at the Eastern Counties Showground. The result of all the calls is clear: absolute denials. Gus suggests that we tell Kelvin MacKenzie about the statement we are issuing. Tim Collins rings him and MacKenzie responds with a gale of laughter. He also makes it clear that what really motivates him is not opposition generally but a deep antagonism to the prospect of privacy laws, which he believes we are likely to introduce. This happens to be wrong and we are being attacked for something we do not intend to do. At the end of my round of phone calls I jokingly grumble about the embarrassment of ringing up all of the Cabinet, asking them when they last spoke to the editor of *The Sun*. 'Welcome to the Gestapo,' Richard responds.[249]

WEDNESDAY 22 JULY

The press is full of our denial and it looks as if it may have ended the story. There are rumbles that one Cabinet minister is not telling the truth but there is no proof. However, the Mellor affair is continuing to bang along on all cylinders. There is pressure on him to resign and I get the distinct impression that there is a touch of panic in the air in David Mellor's Putney constituency. The press is camped out down there and there is a growing belief that he will have to go. Inside Central Office, life goes on. We decide motions and the order of play for the party conference. There are going to be big and difficult debates on Europe and the economy but fortunately no motion which can be balloted separately to provide a vote on a referendum.

---

249 I have always been dissatisfied with our verdict in this case. My investigation (if such it can be called) amounted to no more than one or two questions on whether ministers had spoken to the journalist. Frankly, it was not a matter for the Party Chairman but for the whips. As the months went by, I became convinced that *The Sun*'s report was correct. What made the matter worse was that it undermined any government policy that there should be some check on intrusion into the private lives of politicians.

THURSDAY 23 JULY

The press on Mellor is horrendous. The *Mirror* is of course having a field day but even the *Daily Mail* is baying for his blood. Gus rings me at home to see what I think. He is obviously concerned that the position is becoming difficult to maintain, even untenable. My advice is that we cannot be seen to be running scared of the press. My concern is that something else may emerge out of the woodwork. If it does then Mellor would have to go but if it does not then I think we should hang on. A great deal depends on the weekend. During the day, John's personal support for Mellor is again made clear. There is no question that Mellor is now very concerned about whether he can survive. Richard Ryder and he had a long dinner. Mellor then woke him up at one in the morning with further thoughts on the position, then at six in the early morning having heard the press he was receiving.

FRIDAY 24 JULY

Breakfast with Jeffrey Archer. He has not yet been introduced into the House of Lords. There is such a long line of ex-ministers in front of him in the queue – Thatcher, Howe, Parkinson, Tebbit and more. He tells me that he still wants to be Chairman of the party. Mellor used to be his personal assistant and Jeffrey says that he had warned him previously about running girlfriends on the side.

MONDAY 27 JULY

The usual Monday morning meeting with John. We talk briefly about Mellor. I say that I hope he realises that he owes his survival entirely to him. 'He does' says John. 'I have talked with him.' It is a clearing of the decks meeting before the August holiday. Top of John's list of concerns is the ERM.[250] We are now under daily bombardment on high interest rates. A whole range of the great and the good from Margaret Thatcher downwards advocate either devaluation or leaving the mechanism altogether. John wants a letter to *The Times* signed by businessmen who actually support the policy and want us to retain our influence in Europe.

---

250 The UK had entered the ERM in October 1990.

I fear it is easier said than done. An attempt last week to organise such a letter met with failure; the businessmen we approached were simply unwilling to sign such a letter.

The afternoon is spent almost entirely on the management review of the party. I am now confident that we can produce a radical improvement. In essence, it will mean Central Office being more accountable to the party and the constituency parties being more accountable to Central Office. A good old-fashioned board of directors would mean that in future if the chairman of the party wanted to spend £4 million on refurbishing the building, he would have to take the proposition to the board. They might ask where the money is going to come from.

SATURDAY 1–SUNDAY 2 AUGUST

The weekend press is full of gloom about the recession. The *Sunday Times* says that although they oppose Norman Lamont's 'do nothing' policies they are declaring a truce until the end of the year. No more attacks on the Chancellor for five months but their fury will be vast if there is no improvement by the New Year – which is quite likely. It is a time for us to don tin hats as with the public spending rounds to come things can only get worse.

SATURDAY 8–SUNDAY 9 AUGUST

The press is dominated by the position in the old Yugoslavia. The Serbs are being roundly condemned for their assault on Bosnia and for their callous disregard for women and children. There are now new accusations that they are running what are in effect concentration camps where prisoners are ill-treated and kept on starvation rations. Up to now the conventional wisdom has been that the west cannot intervene, but this is now being challenged. Above all there is public outrage and a feeling that something must be done.[251]

---

251 In March 1992, the government of Bosnia-Herzegovina declared its independence from Yugoslavia. Bosnian-Serb forces, with the backing of the Serb-dominated Yugoslav army, set out to 'ethnically cleanse' Bosnian territory by systematically removing all Bosnian Muslims, known as 'Bosniaks'. They perpetrated atrocious crimes, resulting in the deaths of some 100,000 people (80 per cent of them Bosniak), over two million people being forcibly displaced and between 20,000–40,000 women systematically raped, all due to their ethnic and religious identity.

WEDNESDAY 12 AUGUST

I go to London for a meeting with Tony Newton and Gus. Gus reports on the preoccupations of the moment. In his mind the economy is of primary concern, with more bad unemployment news tomorrow. We agree that Stephen Dorrell, the Financial Secretary, has done well in the last few days defending the government's policy. This, apparently, is contrary to the Chancellor's view. He evidently feels that we would be better to stay off the air. In his restrained way, Gus is obviously deeply frustrated by Norman Lamont's attitude. And he is right to be so. Our friends in business and industry (and politics) need a lead. If the Chancellor does not give it then the slide in morale will continue.

THURSDAY 13 AUGUST

Peter and Virginia Bottomley walk round from Priory Bay for coffee. Virginia is concerned about the public spending round. The Treasury has asked her to consider abolishing exemptions from prescription charges for retired people. A revealing postscript on the Mellor affair. Virginia inherited her initial health job from David Mellor, and also his office. She could not understand why her office went into convulsions of laughter when she put a two-hour slot for 'shopping' in her diary. It was revealed to her that this was the code that David Mellor used when he wanted to visit a girlfriend. I still have this sneaking feeling that there is more to come on the Mellor affair.

WEDNESDAY 26 AUGUST

In the world outside Seaview we are in the middle of a sterling crisis. German policy is keeping their interest rates up when the general need in Europe is for them to come down. The pound has been under a great deal of pressure. Norman Lamont has returned from holiday and made a rather remarkable three-sentence statement for the benefit of the television before scurrying back into the Treasury. His message is that we will do everything necessary, including increasing interest rates, to defend the pound. So far he has been successful but everyone is holding their breath. The latest opinion polls suggest that the French referendum on Maastricht could go the wrong way. The result is great nervousness; the dreaded uncertainty which is the bane of the markets. We are going to need a great deal of luck to get through the next month unscathed by interest rate rises and the subsequent wrath of British industry.

CHAPTER 18

BLACK AUTUMN

SEPTEMBER 1992

The ejection of Britain from the Exchange Rate Mechanism in the autumn of 1992 was the most serious political and economic setback since the devaluation of the pound in 1967. Newspapers commented on the similarities between the two events but in truth the differences were more striking. In 1967 a shell-shocked Chancellor, Jim Callaghan (as I remember from my days covering these issues for The Times) was shifted to the Home Office as Roy Jenkins smoothly took his place in the Treasury. The most extraordinary feature of the 1992 crisis was that no such exchange of ministers – Heseltine or Clarke for Lamont – was seriously considered at the time. Instead, ministers (and the chairman) immediately rallied around the Chancellor. There were, of course, good reasons for the government's inaction. The first was that although Lamont was on the bridge when the ship went down, he was not responsible for the decision to join the ERM. That was the decision of the then Chancellor, John Major, two years earlier. The argument from the growing band of Eurosceptics (including Norman Tebbit) was that if Lamont went, so too must the Prime Minister.

FRIDAY 4 SEPTEMBER 1992

To Watford to speak for Tristan Garel-Jones who is as happy as a sand-boy in his European role at the FO. Ken Baker has revealed himself as an enemy of Maastricht and Tristan is scathing. He says that Ken was on the committee that agreed the negotiating hand and was the minister who led the cheers around the Cabinet table when the Prime Minister returned from Maastricht.

SUNDAY 6 SEPTEMBER

Chequers. John is irritated with life and particularly with Tory back-benchers who are playing up on Europe and the economy. I talk about Margaret Thatcher and the party conference. 'We should think about what arrangements we make for her' I suggest. 'I don't want any special arrangements made after all she has done,' he replies. 'Do I take that as a steer?' I say, attempting a joke. He looks at me for a moment and then smiles. He is sounding off and he knows he is sounding off.

MONDAY 7 SEPTEMBER

Lunch with Sue Tinson of ITN. She is responsible for a programme on the royal family shown last night. It mainly consisted of the observations of well-paid royal watchers but it was certainly effective in painting a picture of an isolated Diana. We gossip about David Mellor who has most recently been portrayed as making love to his actress friend while wearing a Chelsea football club kit.[252] The conventional wisdom now is that Mellor is in danger of being laughed out of court. On politics, Sue says that she is no longer close to Margaret and is perceived as having sold out to Major. I say that if I have any criticism of John it is that he takes the press too seriously and reads too much of it but Sue sees it as a good fault. It prevents him falling out of touch in the way that Thatcher did. She only read what Bernard Ingham thought was fit for her.

At 5.30 I go to see John Major, but not at No. 10 which is crawling with builders renovating the house and putting in security windows which will withstand attack, even mortar attack. Instead, we meet at John's temporary flat in Admiralty House. John is not at his best. He is totally preoccupied with the coverage of his speech to European ministers in London. He watches the 5.40 news and complains bitterly that they have done no justice to the speech. Gus gets orders that he should point out to the television companies the error of their ways, and a great deal of nervous energy is used trying to correct the report.

---

252 A totally untrue made up story.

TUESDAY 8 SEPTEMBER

In the evening I go to a party thrown by Rupert Murdoch in his magnificent flat in St James's. Half the world is there, including Peter Stoddart, the new editor of *The Times*, and Alastair Burnet who, since leaving ITN, has been leading a very retiring life as if no one wants his views now that he no longer has the position he once had.[253] Untrue, but he believes it.

FRIDAY 11–SUNDAY 13 SEPTEMBER

The weekend at a villa on Lake Como which was once the home of Konrad Adenauer and is now run by the foundation which exists to improve Anglo–German relations. A magnificent setting in green gardens overlooking the lake itself and with mountains encircling the water. The autumn sun shines through the mist. The problems of London seem far away. A very genial group from Britain. British ministers include Virginia and Peter Bottomley and David Hunt. One impression comes through with tremendous force: the problems of reunification in Germany. There are a few there from the old East Germany and they speak at length of the disillusion that has set in there. Unemployment is high and for some the change has not been beneficial. The civil servants who staffed the old communist regime in Berlin have been radically reduced. They now face a bleak future with no prospect of work. The old Communist Party has polled well in Berlin, partly because of this. One point is clear to us in Britain. We are preoccupied by the recession and high interest rates. There seems little chance of substantial help from Germany. The Germans are bound up with their own problems. Their concern is the process and cost of reunification, not the recession.

MONDAY 14 SEPTEMBER

The 6.30 a.m. news tells us that German interest rates are to be reduced. On the face of it this is dramatically good and unexpected news. It could allow other interest rates to fall and would certainly take the pressure off sterling, now at the bottom of the ERM league since the devaluation of the Italian lira. At the No. 12 meeting there is optimism and Gus O'Donnell

---

253 Alastair Burnet, journalist and broadcaster, with a long career at ITN as chief presenter of the *News at Ten*. He retired in 1991 and died in 2012 after some years of ill health.

says that the Bundesbank will reduce by half a per cent. That is not dramatic perhaps, but it is a step in the right direction. However, when I get back to Central Office the news of the exact cut has come through: a cut of a mere quarter of a per cent. There is a feeling of complete anti-climax. There will be no rejoicing in the boardrooms at the size of that reduction.

WEDNESDAY 16 SEPTEMBER

An extraordinary day. I have a sudden free morning. The No. 12 meeting with Richard and the meeting with John have been postponed until tomorrow. Tim Collins and I sit down to work on my conference speeches, which are not getting the attention they deserve. We are interrupted by the news that interest rates have been increased by 2 per cent. That is bad but there is worse to come. It rapidly becomes clear that the interest rate increase is having no effect. It has not lifted sterling at all. It has hit the stock market like a sledgehammer and the poor construction industry is now almost down and out. The news is coming through that the Chancellor, in defence of the currency, is to raise interest rates to 15 per cent from tomorrow morning. We are getting into catastrophe territory. A message comes that John would like to see me at 5 p.m.

My driver has taken the afternoon off and cannot be found so Tim Smith drives me to Admiralty House through a vast swarm of photographers grouped around the gates. I meet Jonathan Hill in the hall and we walk into a big stateroom on the ground floor. Jonathan looks and sounds a trifle shell-shocked. I soon see why. There is a small meeting of ministers going on but the prospect is that we will suspend membership of the ERM. The only briefing I have with me for my meeting goes into great detail on the benefits of the ERM and the folly of devaluation. Jonathan retreats back into the meeting saying that he hopes I will show suitable surprise when the PM tells me the decision. A few minutes later Stephen Wall appears and takes a call from either the German Bundesbank or the German government. 'The decision is inevitable', he says. 'The government has been left no option.' The tone is icy.

About twenty minutes later I am called into the room which proves to be the Admiralty House dining room. I had come expecting a one-to-one meeting with the Prime Minister. It proves to be the inner Cabinet. The Prime Minister is in the middle of the table and facing him are Douglas Hurd, Kenneth Clarke and Michael Heseltine. Richard Ryder is on John's side of the table as are one or two advisers like Sarah Hogg. I take a place in the centre facing John, which I imagine had been occupied by the Chancellor. Douglas, Ken and Michael give a 'hear, hear' growl of ironic approval when I appear. The reason soon becomes clear. I am to go on television and radio to explain the government's decision. The reason for this is that for our suspension to be 'official' we have first to inform and meet the monetary committee.[254] It is meeting in Brussels tonight. The theory is that until they have formally waved us goodbye no minister can really comment. Hmm. Well, maybe. It does seem just a little curious to have the government's case presented by someone who has not heard the argument or been party to the decision. Whatever the formal rules, this was an obvious job for the Chancellor of the Exchequer. The theory became then, that as the Chancellor would not appear to take questions, the ban also applied to all other government ministers. My position as Party Chairman but outside the government was seen as a godsend.

John is very calm and runs through the history of the day for my benefit. There has been a 'tidal wave' of selling sterling, he says. The pressure has come partly because of the uncertainty caused by the French referendum. But John blames the Bundesbank and their president, Helmut Schlesinger, most of all. His comments last night to the effect that there should be a realignment – that is a devaluation – of sterling have been the immediate cause of the pressures, but these comments are obviously seen by John and the others as just one item in a long list of complaints against the Germans.

Taking up the story again, John says that interest rates were raised by 2 per cent this morning but with no effect on the value of sterling. The promise of another 3 per cent rise had also done nothing to improve the position. A hefty whack of the reserves has already been committed. Faced with this situation the government had four theoretical options: borrow, devalue alone, seek a general realignment of the ERM currency,

---

254 The monetary committee, as the name suggests, oversees European monetary policy.

or temporarily leave the ERM. Leaving the ERM and floating the pound was the only realistic option. Borrowing more was not an option: devaluing meant a new battle to sustain that value with the certainty that there would be very high interest rates and general realignment was not in their power to deliver. So, Cabinet would meet tomorrow at 9.30 to be told the decision – the decision had been taken only by those in the room. Parliament would be recalled next Thursday.

The Chancellor intends to announce the decision very briefly on the steps of the Treasury but take no questions. I can do nothing until the Chancellor has made the announcement and John asks me to come up to the flat to see Marcus Fox whom he has invited over.[255] Marcus takes a gulp as John gives him the news but loyally offers to defend it in the media. We now wait for the Chancellor's announcement. I take Jonathan to a corner and we work on a possible presentation. It seems to us that our best argument is that the only alternative policy would have been ever increasing interest rates – anathema to industry.

When the news comes through that the Chancellor has made the initial announcement I prepare to leave.[256] Up to now the Prime Minister has been remarkably cheerful. He tells Jonathan to ensure that there is a full note of the meeting that made the decision. Good or bad it has been a 'historic day'. He thinks Margaret should be informed and asks me whether he should do it personally. My emphatic advice is yes. He now wants the room to himself so that he can talk to her. She will find it very difficult to suppress her glee, although it has to be remembered that she was the prime minister who took us into the ERM.

When I leave Admiralty House the cameramen have moved on to the Treasury to record Norman Lamont's brief statement. I return to Central Office and Tim Collins rings both the BBC and ITN. The result is live appearances on both the news at 9 p.m. and the news at 10 p.m. Curiously, although there has been no decision like this since Wilson and Callaghan

---

255 Chairman of the backbench Conservative 1922 Committee 1992–1997, MP for Shipley 1970–97 when he lost his seat.

256 The Chancellor made a very brief statement of only a couple of sentences to the effect that it had been a 'difficult and turbulent day' and that 'massive speculative flows continue to disrupt the functioning of the ERM', leading to the decision to leave.

devalued the pound back in 1967, I am not put under any real pressure. This is because the programmes are still grappling with the implications of what has happened. It is a genuine shock. The well-prepared hostile questions have not yet been refined. hen there is Labour's position. They urged our entry into the ERM and Gordon Brown is reduced to calling for a plan of national reconstruction with more emphasis on training: very worthy but he is entirely silent as to what Labour would have done in the circumstances. At 11.35 I eventually get to Liz and Mike Goold's twenty-fifth wedding anniversary party in Highgate – four hours late and very hungry.[257]

THURSDAY 17 SEPTEMBER

The morning press is dire. It is a humiliating defeat for the government and the Chancellor and leaves our economic policy in tatters. One or two commentators say that it is the best thing that has happened in years and will help recovery, but their voices are drowned out in the general condemnation of the government. It is devaluation and therefore a political disaster.

SUNDAY 20 SEPTEMBER

The French government win their referendum on the Maastricht Treaty, but only just. It could not be closer – a mere 2 per cent: 51 per cent to 49. It is certainly better that they have won than lost, but in truth it does not really help our position. The sceptics will simply point to a divided Europe.

TUESDAY 22 SEPTEMBER

I am called to Admiralty House. The Prime Minister is still with the whips and I talk with Jonathan Hill as we wait in what is now becoming the familiar flat at the top of the building. Jonathan says that the PM and everyone were very downcast on Sunday night after the French referendum but are much more chipper today. When John arrives, this is anything but my impression. He seems tired and dispirited. He still smiles but he is obviously still depressed about the position. We talk about the Mellor affair first. John tells me that a libel case concerning a Palestinian lady whom he

---

257   Two of Fiona's closest friends from university.

stayed with in Spain has just ended in farce. John thinks that we will have trouble with Mellor having accepted free air tickets which is against all the guidance in the ministerial rules. For the first time I get the impression that time may be running out for David Mellor.

But the more important part of our meeting is Europe. John asks for my thoughts. I say that we cannot be seen as rudderless and we need a new initiative. For my money, the best plan would be to try and put some flesh on the subsidiarity bones.[258] He listens and says that something of that sort is what he intends for his Thursday speech when the House is called back. It will doubtless be stormy but perhaps not so stormy given that the House will be coming to the debate cold without any parliamentary questions to crank them up.

As I leave, John comes with me to the lift. 'I am very concerned,' he says. 'I won't have any credibility with the other European leaders. I wonder if the negotiations should not be done by someone else.'

'You mean a new leader?'

'Yes' he says bleakly.

'That would be absurd', I reply. 'There is no one else who could do it remotely as well. The party, the country and Westminster would think it extraordinary.'

'That's what the others say', John says, unconvinced.

We go on talking at the lift head. His concern is that his two achievements – entry into the ERM and the Maastricht negotiation – have collapsed. He does not see how he can go back to his European colleagues with whom a few months ago he agreed and seek a new deal. I argue that he is the only man who can hold the party together on the European issue. He sees the issue as a matter of 'my integrity'.

Thinking back on the conversation (and I record this only an hour later) my feeling is that John is speaking in the middle of the kind of blackish depression that I encountered once or twice during the election. I only hope I have encouraged him to fight through this admittedly grizzly period.

---

258   In the context of the EU, subsidiarity rules out intervention when an issue can be dealt with effectively by a member state itself.

WEDNESDAY 23 SEPTEMBER

An extraordinary farce of a meeting at No. 12. Builders drill and hammer throughout. It is difficult to hear what is being said or make oneself heard. Gus bravely persists with his analysis of the morning's press. What this amounts to is that yesterday's 1 per cent interest cut has been overshadowed in much of the press by the latest episode in the Mellor affair.[259] I arrive home in time to catch the last part of *Newsnight* where David Mellor is putting up a stout defence against the irritating interruptions of Jeremy Paxman. David appears to be saying that he has no intention of resigning.

THURSDAY 24 SEPTEMBER

I arrive early at Central Office but am interrupted almost immediately by a call from Richard Ryder. He is concerned about David Mellor's position but is much more anxious about the voting position in the special debate for which Parliament has been recalled this afternoon. He fears that we may have as many as eight voting against or abstaining. Added to this, the Cabinet is all over the place on policy towards the ERM and Maastricht. Richard believes that the government's capacity to continue in its present form is now in question. He says that he is meeting with the whips at 9.45 and would like myself and Marcus Fox to meet with him first and then come to the whips' meeting.

We meet for ten minutes in Richard's office in the Commons. It is a confused discussion with two crises – Mellor and the vote – intermingling with each other. Our minds are concentrated however, when David Mellor himself comes on the phone. Richard wants both Marcus and myself to speak to David and tell him where he stands. This is, to put it mildly, a bounce and I am certainly not prepared to have such a conversation over the phone. Marcus does speak to him. He does not quite say 'you must go' but leaves David in no doubt that his support on the back benches is running out. I tell David that I would like to see

---

259 A libel case brought by Mona Bauwens against *The People* revealed that Mellor had accepted a gift of a month long holiday in Marbella for his family. This had not been registered and was an embarrassment as Bauwens was the daughter of Jaweed al-Ghussein, finance director of the Palestine Liberation Organization (PLO).

him. We arrange to meet at No. 12 after the morning Cabinet. 'Shall I go to Cabinet?' David asks. My view is that he should but I am not the Chief Whip. Richard agrees. We then all go through to a meeting of the whips next door. Richard asks for views on the Mellor affair. It soon becomes abundantly clear that David's position is untenable. There is a recognition that it has all slipped away. The reasons hardly matter any-more. David has lost the support of the parliamentary party or at least that is the collective judgement of the whips.

We move on to the economic debate. Richard says that as he predic-ted, Michael Spicer (a leading Eurosceptic) is planning to see him later that morning to ask for reassurances on the future direction of economic policy. Following the PM's instructions, he is going to listen but not nego-tiate. The whips then go through the possible doubters with the accompa-niment of hostile comments – 'he is mad' – and various succinct epithets. Quite right too. To all intents and purposes, this is a vote of confidence.

Two hours back at Central Office and then to No. 12 again. Entering by Whitehall and avoiding the squads of photographers in Downing Street, I settle in Richard Ryder's office and a few minutes later, David Mellor appears. He is in remarkably good shape for a man who has gone through so much. The only trace of pressure is when he asks for some cigarettes. He starts by saying that he has decided to go and that it is all rubbing off on the government. What do I feel, he asks? I say that my concern is the meeting of the 1922 executive. I do not want to see him forced out. 'If you have to go it must be you deciding. You must not be forced out either by the 1922 or the press.' David agrees and then says that he has been immensely grateful for my support. 'As it happens we have never come into contact much in our political careers nor got to know each other but no one could have done more.'

For the first time in this whole sorry affair, I am beginning to see some of the attractive side behind David's brash exterior. He is facing his fate with outward resignation and good humour. The resignation is decided; the only issue now is the timing. We agree that there is no alternative but to announce today. He should see John after his speech, with an announcement made in the early evening.

All the whips' predictions that the start of the debate on the economy will be seriously delayed by Labour backbenchers prove false. I am still at Smith Square as John begins his speech. I arrive in the Chamber after he has been speaking for about seven or eight minutes. The Chamber is packed. John's speech is workmanlike but not brilliant. Given what has been happening over the last few days I am amazed that he has had time to prepare anything but the damage is done not by the speech, but by the succession of interruptions from our own side by people like Teddy Taylor and Nick Budgen. As I stand at the House bar it is abundantly clear that we have a major problem of dissent on our benches. They may not all interrupt but they are not convinced and are not prepared to be convinced. Bad trouble ahead I fear. Richard Ryder is definitely right about that.

In contrast, John Smith makes the most of his opportunity. It is a very polished Commons performance. I cannot help noticing the saddest face in the Chamber. Neil Kinnock is sitting, squashed up in the middle of the third row, behind John Smith. A backbencher with no particular role looking at what might have been.

When John Major comes out of the Chamber, I report to him on my conversation with David Mellor. I return to Central Office with Jonathan Hill, who remarks that the Chief Whip has been searching for someone to tell David that he should go for a long time. The announcement makes the early evening news programmes. Once more, I am busy not so much defending David but defending John. The criticism is that the PM should have acted earlier. In other words, he should have thrown David Mellor to the wolves without any attempt at defence.

Back in the Commons I catch the two wind-ups. Gordon Brown is his usual mixture of humour and oratory, but the real surprise was Norman Lamont's performance. Fluent and forceful and in much better form than I have ever heard him. Perhaps his possible imminent execution has concentrated his mind or perhaps, as some papers now suggest, he is just happier with the policy outside the ERM (he is reported these days to be singing in his bath!). For whatever reason it is a considerable Commons triumph and brings the debate to a good end for us. In spite of all the Chief Whip's misgivings we win the votes very comfortably. Only one

Tory votes against us – Richard Shepherd – in spite of a long discussion I have with him myself. He cannot accept that the vote is tantamount to a vote of no confidence. I wonder what he thinks we would have done if we had lost.

FRIDAY 25 SEPTEMBER

Birmingham is over the moon that the European leaders are to meet there in mid-October and I am credited with the achievement of getting the European Council here. In the evening, Jeffrey Archer comes to our Sutton Coldfield annual dinner. It is a sell-out but Jeffrey is simply not my style of speaker. His jokes are quite good but the serious politics is thin to lamentable. He does, however, have a nose for what Conservative audiences want to hear. Just now, they like to hear the Germans being blamed for our economic difficulties and what really sticks in their throat is that the Germans are now giving the French the kind of help to defend the franc which we felt we needed to defend the pound.

SATURDAY 26 SEPTEMBER

The government in general, and John in particular, have a universally bad press. The general message is that we do not know where we are going, that there is a policy vacuum and that John should get a grip on events. When I reach Hurlingham Road there is a message to ring him. He is very down. He fears that he is 'damaged to the point of not being able to recover'. He adds, 'I am not going to take all this without answering back. The press all say they want action without having the first idea what the action should be.' Slowly, he cools down. Two points really irritate him: the first is the poor reception his Thursday speech received, the second is that he does not know what the Chancellor is up to. Norman is now basking in the praise of the Eurosceptics. I suggest it is to preserve his position. It is, after all, only a few days ago that everyone was saying he should resign. John is in no mood to be cheered up. Did I know that William Hill were giving odds of 13 to 8 that he would not be Prime Minister by the Budget? Telling this to Fiona later, she tells me that the same bookmaker is giving 14 to 1 that I will be the next PM. It is all comic opera. There is no chance of persuading John of that just now.

SUNDAY, 27 SEPTEMBER

I ring Richard Ryder and spend an hour on the phone with him. He is very pessimistic about the prospects of getting any Maastricht bill through.[260] There are three options, he says. The first is to go ahead. The trouble is that a very significant proportion of the parliamentary party are now opposed to ratification – a hundred he estimates. The second option is to 'play it long' and wait for the Danes. The trouble is that the Danes will probably not have their referendum until next summer. The third option is to say that circumstances have changed since we left the ERM. The argument would be 'we can only govern with consent. We have not got that consent so we will abandon Maastricht.' The certain result of that course would be ministerial resignations.[261]

Richard Ryder says that as a business manager he would prefer to play it long but he concedes it is not his reputation. I say that we need to preserve the Prime Minister's position over the next week and we need to ensure that he does well at the party conference. He needs to restore his authority. 'How?' asks Richard. I reply that what is doing the damage is the different statements coming from ministers. Ministers should be told to toe the line or go. That order should be publicly relayed to the press. Richard's alternative, or perhaps complementary, strategy is that John should see the Cabinet one by one to see where they stand. 'That's fine', I say. 'But on Thursday he should lay down the law at Cabinet.' 'But they will all argue that they have kept inside the policy', says Richard. 'Do what Margaret did and take along the newspapers and quote them', I suggest.

---

260 The treaty was signed on 7 February 1992 but had to be ratified 'by the High Contracting Parties in accordance with their respective constitutional requirements'. In the UK, Parliament had to approve the ratification, hence the bill to amend the European Communities Act. In Denmark, France and Ireland a referendum was required.

261 The most prominent pro-Maastricht Cabinet ministers were Heseltine, Clarke, Hunt, Waldegrave and Gummer. The sceptics were Howard, Lilley and Portillo.

A few minutes later, I hear the news that the cavalry have arrived to help us. At the start of the Labour Party conference, Bryan Gould has resigned from the shadow Cabinet because of Labour's European policy which supports Maastricht and opposes a referendum.[262] Tomorrow's headlines should be about Labour. Just what we wanted; just in the nick of time.

COMMENT

September 1992 ended any idea of a coalition on Europe inside the Conservative Party. Up to then there had been zealots on both sides of the argument: those who were opposed to the whole concept of the European Union and those who argued that Britain should accept the idea of the union together with the rules and regulations which went with it. My own position (and I believe the position of many others) was to accept membership and the undoubted advantages, like the single market, that went with it, but to 'fight from within' to preserve essential national interests. I also wanted Europe to be a power in the world looking outwards and not a bureaucratic rule-maker along the lines of 'fortress Europe'. It was that kind of Europe I had argued for in the Commons during the debate on entry in 1972. September marked the start of the decisive parting of the ways. It was a division powerfully aided by Mrs Thatcher. Her public support for a referendum on Maastricht gave an enormous fillip to the campaign against the treaty. Even her most dedicated supporters found it difficult to deny that her very public jibes had undermined the new Prime Minister's position.

---

262 Resigned from Smith's shadow Cabinet in protest against Labour's support for the ERM. In May 1994 resigned his parliamentary seat and returned to New Zealand.

19

DISUNITED WE STAND

OCTOBER 1992–APRIL 1993

All the press predictions were that the October party conference would be very difficult. Ken Clarke, quite an expert on party history, thought it could potentially be the most difficult for twenty years. I was more optimistic than that. We had not done well as a government in explaining the benefits of the Maastricht Treaty. The usual explanation was in terms of what we had avoided, like the social chapter and the single currency. There was little about any positive benefits. As it happened, a few days after the conference closed, Central Office was deluged with letters and emails, not about the ERM but about the pit closures policy.

SUNDAY 4 OCTOBER 1992

Brighton is bathed in bright sunshine. I conduct a television press conference on the seafront, almost dazzled by the sun. From there I go to the Grand Hotel and am shown up to an enormous suite of two rooms, which to my alarm, I see will cost £450 a day. I must check with John Gardiner who is to pay this bill. I do not mind being an unpaid chairman but there is a limit to my generosity. I have an early dinner with Tim Collins and Andrew Lansley who have become my speech writing team.[263] Both have their regular jobs to do and are filling the gap left by the absence of any special adviser. During the evening, news comes in that a Boeing cargo plane has crashed into a block of flats in Amsterdam with many feared dead. The evening news programmes say that there is

---

263 Tim and Andrew both became Members of Parliament in 1997.

no evidence of terrorism, which at least distinguishes it from the 1984 Grand Hotel bomb.

MONDAY 5 OCTOBER

John and Norma arrive in the evening. He is in good form but irritated at the way Tory MPs are queuing up to present the anti-Maastricht case on television. He feels personally betrayed by some of the Eurosceptics. He regards the old, established sceptics like Taylor, Cash, Budgen and Shepherd as irredeemable and sometimes plain batty. His chief scorn is preserved for people like Baker whose new position can be traced to the moment he was sacked from the government, while the biggest villain of all is Margaret Thatcher. Having selected John as her heir apparent she has done everything in her power to undermine his authority. I can see the justice in John's resentment. Margaret holds court on the inadequacies of the government in general, and John Major in particular. I wholeheartedly share John's sentiments but I do not think there is much to be gained by 'Major attacks Thatcher' headlines on the first day of the conference. John agrees and delivers a well-received and uncontroversial speech to the agents' dinner.

TUESDAY 6 OCTOBER

A day of high drama in the European debate. The tactic of Basil Feldman, the chairman of the National Union, is to call for an amendment on the very general foreign affairs motion. The amendment sounds fairly ferocious in its opposition to a federal Europe but is in fact quite acceptable having had Garel-Jones's help in drafting it. Basil proposes a general exclusion of speeches from the floor by MPs, peers and MEPs – none are to be called. This all sounds fine and I go to rehearse my speech which will close the morning. This thirty-minute speech has taken weeks to prepare and it is important to my position as Party Chairman that it goes reasonably well. I would also like to demonstrate to my staff at Central Office that even after a two-year layoff I can still make good speeches. When I get to my feet my nervousness goes almost immediately, I know the words so well. I actually enjoy delivering them. The conference like the jokes and applaud the attacking lines. The message is an undisguised plea for unity. 'We must all stand together and that includes our Members of Parliament at Westminster.' John, by my right side, applauds enthusiastically throughout and at the end the conference rises to their feet.

My joy is short-lived. When I get back to the National Union room after the lunch I find Basil in a great panic. He says that Norman Tebbit has put in a slip to speak. He and the conference chairman, John Mason, do not think they can refuse to call him. They fear he will cause a disturbance if he is refused. I say that this is a 'total reversal' of the policy that he suggested a few hours previously. Basil agrees somewhat sheepishly that neither he nor John have the stomach for a fight with the conference on the calling of one of the all-time conference darlings. I ask Douglas Hurd who agrees that Tebbit should be called, as does Douglas Hogg who is with him. So there it is.

Right from the start it is clear that this debate is going to be unlike any other we have had at a party conference. Any criticism of European things is greeted with cheers and thunderous applause from a section of the audience. Any defence of Maastricht meets with catcalls. All the noise (which is substantial) is coming from a comparatively small part of the conference. As the debate goes on the noise increases and I try to identify the shouters. In the main they are young, in T-shirts, aggressively self-confident and their only reactions are moronic cheers or hisses. The kind of people who tried to interrupt my speech on Aids at the YC conference in 1986: the lager louts of our party.

When Tebbit is called they erupt in joy. He receives a standing ovation as he makes his way to the rostrum. There then follows five minutes of pure venom in which he knifes John and suggests that if the Chancellor were to go on the issue of the ERM defeat, then the Prime Minister would have to go as well. He finishes with a number of rhetorical questions along the lines of 'Do you want a United States of Europe?' With a malicious backwards glance at the platform he makes his way back to his seat. To thunderous applause from the lager louts, Tebbit makes his real mistake. He stands Mussolini-like, arms outstretched, accepting the plaudits of the crowd. It is the very nastiest display I have seen by a senior Conservative politician.

A few more speeches to the accompaniment of further catcalls then Douglas is called. He begins as he told me he would: 'I could try to smooth my way to a standing ovation or give it to you straight'. He proceeds to give it to the conference straight and very good. There is some barracking but the conference rallies. Strong applause begins to punctuate Douglas's speech. He stands before them as an elder states- man. He appeals to their patriotism. He warns them not to split the party. If they do, we will be out of power for a decade. The conference rise spontaneously to their feet and at the end, the vote sees the lager louts easily defeated. Douglas has won the day.

We have survived but the debate leaves a nasty taste in the mouth. There was a moment in the debate, even before Tebbit, when I wondered what I was doing in such a party. We have a fight on our hands – not just on Europe but to preserve the party from a takeover which would be both unacceptable to people like me, but would also make us totally unelectable.

WEDNESDAY 7 OCTOBER

This is a rollercoaster of a party conference. There are ups of great ela- tion and downs of enormous gloom when you wonder whether the Conservative Party really wants to stay in power at all. The day starts with excitement. Michael Heseltine on top form takes the Eurosceptics head-on and wins triumphantly. Michael sets out the case for Europe without compromise and knocks the hecklers down with contempt. He is rewarded with a standing ovation in the middle of his speech which eclipses the reception for Tebbit yesterday. Michael's performance is much better than his usual conference triumph. All the conventional advice would be for him to keep out of the European debate and not to raise the temperature. Michael has ignored the safe course and taken a very substantial risk. It is an act of great courage.

I go to lunch feeling much better but am soon brought back down to earth. The news comes through that Margaret has launched an attack on

Maastricht in a newspaper article – in of all newspapers, *The European*. It has been carefully timed and it has the intended effect. Michael's bravura performance is knocked off the top spot of the news. The new lead story is Margaret Thatcher's attack on the government.

THURSDAY 8 OCTOBER

The press is again horrendous, with Thatcher's attack dominating every front page. We should all be waiting for Lamont's speech. In fact, we are more concerned about Thatcher. The plan for Margaret's arrival is this: she will arrive about ten and I will take her onto the platform. Our hope is that she will keep to her intention and not speak.

Margaret arrives on time and we give her coffee in the ministerial waiting room upstairs. She is dressed in a rather severe apparently black suit which she insists is dark blue. She is certainly not dressed to kill and I cannot help thinking that Edwina would have given her better advice on what to wear. I ask her twice whether she wants to say anything. She repeats twice that she does not – 'It would be quite inappropriate' – and she repeats it to the chairman of the conference. As we enter the conference hall it seems to me that Margaret is receiving a tremendous ovation but as I leave her and go to my chair it becomes apparent that this is not quite the case. I suggest she motions to the audience to sit which she does and thirty seconds later the audience are all back in their chairs and the conference can commence.

The debate is on the environment and I listen with half an ear to a rather good speech by Michael Howard before going out to complete the rest of the Thatcher manoeuvre – getting her and the Prime Minister together. We join in a crocodile with the Chancellor and his team. John mutters about whether he should kiss her or not. Norma makes it quite clear that nothing is further from her mind. The crocodile advances. The reaction to John's entrance is at least as good, and arguably better, than that for Margaret. He goes up to her and does kiss her to the joy of the photographers. The audience then settle back and we begin on what is the main political issue – the future of the economy. By some marvel, Basil has managed to call a long line of speakers opposed to the government's economic policy – which is bad enough – but they are also speakers of a very high quality. They lay into the Chancellor's policies with gusto and the women are particularly outstanding. Norman does not match this spirit but nevertheless it is a speech that will do.

MONDAY 12 OCTOBER

Back to Westminster and a No. 12 meeting. The mood is gloomy. Even apart from the forthcoming problems related to Maastricht there are a long list of difficulties ahead. The day has already started with announcements of job losses at Lucas and a big lost order for Vickers from Kuwait. The latest, not good, unemployment figures come on Thursday and tomorrow we have an announcement on coal. Neither Richard Ryder nor John Wakeham elaborates on this.

TUESDAY 13 OCTOBER

The pit closures announcement comes like a thunderclap. It emerges that half the country's pits are to be closed with thousands of miners instantly declared unemployed, albeit with generous redundancy. The immediate reaction is shock. No one was prepared for the scale of this announcement. It has been utterly inept. At Central Office we are without briefing or explanation. No government or party can have entered a major political battle caught so off guard. We have survived the conference, even enjoyed something of a victory, only to fall flat on our face a couple of days later. The government is in serious trouble. I will be amazed if we get the support of either the public or the party.

The case for further closures is strong. We cannot go on stockpiling coal that we do not need. Apparently, we are paying out £100 million a month to produce coal we don't need but I only learn this from Michael Heseltine's announcement.[264] Doubtless, energy experts realise it only too well but the general public know next to nothing of these

---

264 Heseltine announced the closure of thirty-one collieries, many within six months, some within weeks. Generous redundancy pay-offs for 30,000 miners costing 'up to a billion' were included, but the main concern was the lack of alternative employment opportunities in the areas affected.

arguments. We have failed lamentably to prepare the ground. Michael Heseltine must take most of the blame.

WEDNESDAY 14 OCTOBER

A horrendous press. We are condemned without exception. At the No. 12 meeting, Richard Ryder asks me to lead the discussion. I say that this is the worst day's press ever and that the government's position is serious. The public have not been readied for this announcement. We are still waiting for the promised DTI briefing. There has been no sensible explanation of why this closure programme could not be phased. More to the point, I say to Richard I see no point in having a No. 12 committee if we are not to have any part in an announcement of this kind. It is a complete waste of time.

There is an embarrassed silence when I finish. We all remember the guarded, almost secretive, way that the coal announcement was dealt with at our Monday meeting. It was Wakeham who broke the silence. 'Well, I agree with what Norman says,' John started, ' I have to say that however it was announced it would not have been popular'. True, but if we took that view about political life we would not spend a penny on press officers, advertising or advice.

THURSDAY 15 OCTOBER

To Birmingham for a board meeting. One advantage of getting away from Central Office is that I can get some sense of how industry view the developments over the last few days. Leaving Peter Parker aside, all the other members of the Aggregates board are Tory voters. They think we have taken leave of our senses but there is something else, and that is a sense of shame. No one wants to be identified with a government that is perceived as having taken this draconian action against mining communities, including the Nottinghamshire miners who supported us against Scargill. The chief executive, Peter Tom, tells me a story that illustrates the unhappiness. He is a member of a committee consisting of some of the best-known companies in the construction industry, Tarmac and the rest. He tells me that on Wednesday the committee seriously considered giving industry the day off and marching on London: a march organised not by the unions but by the bosses. All the danger signals are flashing bright red.

SATURDAY 17 OCTOBER

Throughout the day I talk with some of the main players in the pits drama. First to ring is Richard Ryder. He confirms that it is the whips' view that the government cannot win the debate on Wednesday without a change of policy. That change should include a new development board headed by a well-known figure like Peter Walker and the staging of closures. I say that it should also include the cancellation of some of the closures. We must ensure that what will inevitably be seen as a U-turn actually succeeds. Richard agrees. He says that Michael's performance at Cabinet on Thursday was very strange. He appeared to be out of touch with public opinion and genuinely surprised that his proposals were causing such a reaction. He did, however, recognise in conversation privately that if the Wednesday vote was lost he would have to resign.

During the afternoon I speak to Michael and tell him about the reaction in the party and the country and that we need a change of direction. Michael says he understands but what change of direction is possible? He has no market for 25 million tonnes of coal and feels that he is being forced into this position by pressure from the Treasury to make savings as quickly as possible. It is an unsatisfactory conversation. Michael is on autopilot, addressing an audience not talking with a colleague.

Half an hour later, John Major comes on the line. I tell him my summing-up: incompetent presentation, no support in the country and precious little in the party. The area agents say it is 'the worst reaction for 20 years'.[265] John says that he has read the reports and believes that it would be a good idea if Norman Lamont also sees them. It becomes clear that

---

265 Central Office reported that the hostile reaction from the party on the ground went far beyond that on the ERM. Members who had loyally supported the government in the 'fight' against Scargill found the ground cut from beneath them. Totally unprepared, they had been pitched into another battle on the coal mines but this time it seemed they were being asked to turn on the very people they had supported like the Nottinghamshire miners.

John not only wants to announce a package on the mines but a bigger package for industrial recovery. The difficulty is of course the Chancellor. Hence his desire that the Chancellor should see the reports from our agents. John needs to persuade the Chancellor; his concern is that if he pushes too hard the Chancellor will resign. Personally, I do not regard that as the greatest threat to the government but I can see the PM's problem: he faces a possible conflict with his Chancellor and the prospect of Michael's resignation if he is forced to backtrack too much. Later in the evening, Jonathan Hill comes round to collect my party reports and take them off to the Chancellor. He says that John is keen to go on television and present a recovery package to the nation. This is fine I say, but it must have the content: it can't just be words.

MONDAY 19 OCTOBER
Richard Ryder rings early to say that the evening meeting with Michael Heseltine went reasonably well. At first, Michael wished to defend his existing position but was persuaded off this course. The question now is how far he is prepared to go in changing policy. John wants to have a political Cabinet after the official Cabinet business has ended. I walk past the forest of cameramen and the incredible shambles of building works in No. 10 to the bunker Cabinet room in the Cabinet Office. What effect, I wonder, has the chaotic working conditions had on decisions made over the last two months?

To my surprise, John really wants to talk about the government's position rather than the specific coal dispute. He is concerned not only about the present position but about the impression that the government has lost its way. Withdrawal from the ERM was a catastrophic blow. The decision on the pits was another big blow. He wants to make a statement – with substance – that puts us back on course. John looks drawn but is obviously determined to take the fight to the enemy – including some of our own backbenchers.

In the discussion that follows there is a profound split on the way forward. John wants an industrial recovery package. He is backed, as far as I can tell, by the majority of the Cabinet. Ken Clarke, in particular, argues for no cuts in the capital programmes and observes that 'we have no economic policy'. John Gummer, Virginia Bottomley and Malcolm Rifkind support this argument but the Chancellor does not. He speaks like a Treasury mandarin not a minister. He recognises that there may be some political difficulties, but he suggests that we are ignoring, and the press is not reporting, the encouraging signs. His message is that we should persist and he 'must make his position clear'. I would have judged his contribution as a clear warning against the government changing course with the additional threat that if the government ignores his advice then he would have to consider his own position. It is not a dramatic banging of the table but the threat is there for anyone who listens.

At 3.30 Michael makes his statement on the collieries and lists the concessions he is now prepared to make. He avoids using the word 'review' and it is clear that a number of Tory rebels are pacified, not all however. People like Winston Spencer-Churchill still say it is not enough but I think we are at least out of the immediate parliamentary problems on coal.

TUESDAY 20 OCTOBER

Fiona and I go to a Foreign Office party thrown by Mark Lennox-Boyd. As we enter I see Ken and we meet later in his room. I confide my view that we need a new Chancellor. Typically, Ken does not beat about the bush. 'I agree', he says. 'Norman is an old mate of mine. I have defended him. But I think he should go'. He then adds some reasons of his own. Last Friday there was a meeting of the public spending committee which ended with most of the members saying that there was no prospect of getting through the kind of cuts the Treasury was contemplating. Norman became so rattled that he brought the meeting to an end by walking out and threatening that there would be no further meetings. Ken believes that he is frozen in immobility, like a rabbit caught in the headlights.

WEDNESDAY 21 OCTOBER

A No. 12 committee meeting. The most revealing part of the discussion takes place before the meeting begins. Richard has invited Michael Heseltine to attend. Michael arrives a few minutes early. Michael, John Wakeham and I go over the position while we wait for Richard. Suddenly, John Wakeham observes that in his judgement we were ill-advised to press ahead with the plan to close thirty-one pits. 'How can you say that?' asks Michael indignantly. 'You were on the committee that agreed the policy.' John begins to bluster. 'I can see why you say that', he begins lamely but the sentence trails away into incoherence. Richard joins the conversation, the meeting begins and a potential stand-up row is avoided. John cares passionately about his reputation as a good adviser and hence for sound judgement. He has no intention of standing by a policy which has become discredited and no intention of being associated with its failure.

Later in the morning, I am called over to see John Major in his House of Commons office to talk about honours. The only peerage is likely to be Shirley Williams. John is in good form after his success yesterday. I tell him my belief that the government and he as PM would be better served by a new Chancellor. John listens very carefully to what I say. It then becomes clear that he agrees. The difficulty is how do we get rid of him. John says that frankly, he would have expected Norman to have resigned by now but he doubts if he will go of his own accord unless it is on an issue like public spending. He also feels obligated to him as his campaign manager for the leadership.

The discussion is brought to an end by the move to the Chamber to hear the coal debate. In the lobby I run straight into Michael Heseltine who is still seething over John Wakeham's comment that morning. The debate that follows is pure farce. Labour MPs jump up to interrupt Michael's speech. At first, their tactics seem to be succeeding. There is continual uproar and Michael seems to be losing control of the debate. After thirty minutes of shouting points of order and cries to resign, Michael abandons his script and rounds on Labour and says that they are not interested in debating the issues and invites the government benches to unite against such tactics. A brilliant piece of opportunism – he rescues his speech from disaster and unites all but the most hardline Tory critics.

Five hours later, we win the Commons vote with a majority of thirteen. Far too close for comfort but much better than seemed possible a few days ago. The government has been damaged, Michael Heseltine has been damaged, but neither has been damaged irretrievably.

SATURDAY 28 NOVEMBER

The unusual weekend calm is broken at 7 p.m. by a call from the *Sunday Telegraph*. The journalist says that newspapers are running a story that back in June 1991, Norman Lamont had his legal bills for expelling an unwanted tenant from the basement of his Notting Hill house paid for by the Treasury and Central Office. The Treasury has evidently agreed that it did pay. The question is what did we do? Fortunately, Fiona takes the call. I have not the first idea about the position. It was before my time. Of course, I remember the lodger to whom the Lamonts let their basement and my memory is that she turned out to be a sex therapist, who the press christened 'Miss Whiplash'. I also remember that she was eventually expelled. How she was given her marching orders and who paid the legal fees is totally unknown to me.[266]

SUNDAY 29 NOVEMBER

The day is a story of one phone call after another. Tim Collins rings to say that the press is in full pursuit. Their main question is can the Chancellor survive? Their concern is the use of public funds. Richard Ryder rings. He knew about the payments and remembers that Chris Patten was not at all pleased about taking receipt of them. Chris Patten returns my call from Hong Kong. He says that he was 'pretty unhappy about it' but did not want an unhappy Chancellor on his hands just before what could have been a general election. John Pearson, who deals with accounts at CCO, confirms that a payment of about £18,000 was made by him but because of the crazy way that Central Office finances were organised has no note on whether a special payment was made into our accounts – that would be a matter for the treasurers!

---

266 The Chancellor was provided with a flat in Downing Street and had the use of Dorneywood in the country. The rules allowed him to let out his own home quite legitimately.

MONDAY 30 NOVEMBER

Breakfast with the PM in his flat at Downing Street where he is living again. Sarah Hogg and Jonathan Hill join us. We turn to the issue of the Chancellor's legal bill. Sarah says that there was a great clash in the Treasury on whether public funds should be used. Apparently, Peter Middleton, the outgoing Permanent Secretary, thought it should be paid, not just in part but all of it, but Terry Burns, his successor, took a very different view. It was Burns who reduced the Treasury cost to £4,000, thus leaving us with the balance.[267]

TUESDAY 1 DECEMBER

During the afternoon I see the Chancellor himself. He is in remarkably good shape and argues his version of events very strongly, and he has no doubt that he took the right course. He had had early warning that the *News of the World* would run a story on him. The first rumour was that it was a 'sex scandal'. Eventually, his private secretary brought him what he described as the bad news, that the tenant in his basement was rather more than she appeared. By this time, Norman was extremely jumpy and his immediate reaction was to bring in the solicitors, Carter Ruck (had he no idea that Carter Ruck would need to be paid?). His purpose was to stop any allegations that might come, like that he was living on immoral earnings.

Looking back, it is easy to see that he overreacted. Frankly, a three-line statement threatening legal action if any paper made such a preposterous allegation would have sufficed. Nevertheless, it is not difficult to see how this intrinsically trivial affair was blown up into an affair of state. There is no doubt that Norman believed the bill had been picked up by an anonymous party contributor. What all this reveals is the ludicrously casual way that Central Office has been regarded as a place to shuffle off embarrassing obligations.

WEDNESDAY 9 DECEMBER

I go to the House of Commons for a coffee in the tea room. Coming

---

267 Later Terry Burns was appointed to the House of Lords and became Chairman of my committee proposing ways to reduce the number of peers.

away, I see a notice in the Members' lobby that the PM is to make a statement at 3.30. What statement is this? No one had mentioned it at the No. 12 meeting. When I arrive back at Central Office, I ask Shirley whether she knows anything about the statement. According to Sky, she says, the Prince of Wales and Diana are to separate. I am afraid I do not have the heart to return to the Commons to hear John's statement. Separation is bad enough without it being the subject of a parliamentary statement. I remember the great elation at their wedding on that bright morning in July 1981. It is sad that those high expectations should have been defeated. But given the frosty relations which now only too obviously exist it is best to bite the bullet. The marriage has self-evidently been going wrong for several years. I remember when I was Secretary of State for Employment sitting next to the Prince of Wales and his clear fascination that I had been divorced and was now married for a second time. He clearly felt some time ago that he had made a mistake. Ironically, Charles's sister Anne has just announced that she is to remarry. On the one occasion that I sat next to the Queen at dinner she had gestured to Anne, 'She is the strong one', meaning that although Anne has had her difficulties, she has handled them impeccably.

SATURDAY 12–SUNDAY 13 DECEMBER

John has done it again. In spite of all the predictions the Edinburgh European Council is a success for him. He gets what he wants on the Budget rebate, on the Danish position and on subsidiarity. Even the sceptics have to concede that he has handled negotiations well. He really excels in the negotiating chamber. It gives us a much-needed fillip at the end of a grisly six months.

MONDAY 14 DECEMBER

Andrew Mitchell asks to see me. He has received warning that he is being considered for a vacancy in the Whips' Office, Tim Boswell having just been promoted. Andrew's message is that he does not want to move. He would like to be a whip but not until he has finished his job as Vice Chairman for candidates. I listen to what he has to say and

– given Andrew's slight reluctance to come to Central Office – am rather touched by what he says. Nevertheless, my reply to him is that he must go. Andrew is rather taken aback by this advice but I say that a move of this sort would be good for him and good for us too. It would demonstrate that Central Office is a step up and not a step out.

THURSDAY 17 DECEMBER

Dinner with Leon and Diana. Leon is now as happy as a sandboy at Brussels and is looking forward to having one part of a divided foreign affairs portfolio. He will look after the non-Community countries and will be responsible for GATT (General Agreement on Tariffs and Trade). On British politics, neither he nor Diana are in the slightest doubt that Norman Lamont should go.

WEDNESDAY 23 DECEMBER

The party's bank manager wants to see me. His message is that they will not let us increase our overdraft limit. Paul Judge, our new director general, and Martin Saunders, the finance director, come in to discuss the position. They say that the manager has been overturned at board level. The bank is not happy with our predictions of income although they appear to accept that our cost-reduction programme is reasonable. The man who is really cheerful, however, is Martin Saunders. He is like a dog with a bone. 'This is what being a finance director is all about', he grins happily. Thank goodness we have recruited him. I confess that I share some of Martin's cheerfulness. We are in a mess but that gives me the power to change. No one can maintain that change is unnecessary. It also allows me to insist that there will be no further monetary deals based on the false assumption that Central Office has a bottomless purse.

FRIDAY 1 JANUARY 1993

The party's financial position is dire. To rescue it from bankruptcy must be my first aim. Over the next twelve months we must reduce the deficit. I suspect one of the real difficulties is going to be persuading the Cabinet and MPs of the acuteness of the financial crisis but the fact is, that to all intents and purposes, we are bust. If we were a company we would be going into liquidation.

THURSDAY 7 JANUARY

Martin Saunders comes in very worried. The Inland Revenue are asking for payment of the PAYE bill. At the moment we are not in a position to pay that. It shows how deep the financial crisis has become. We now urgently require a loan of £1 million simply to keep going and pay the staff.

FRIDAY 8 JANUARY

I go to Nottinghamshire to see the position on the coal pits for myself. I can understand why the issue is so emotive. If you go to the pits near Mansfield they are separate, isolated communities. There is no other development of any size. It is no wonder that there is concern that if the pits close there will be nothing to replace those jobs. One piece of good news comes in. Paul Judge rings me to say that they have raised a loan of £1 million at normal commercial rates until September. This at least enables the tax bill to be paid.

MONDAY 25 JANUARY

In the evening I see Philip Harris about the treasurers. Philip is very anxious to help and I have designated him as Appeals Chairman. In effect, this means that he will be chief executive to Charles Hambro as Chairman of the Board. I am sure there are going to be a number of alarms along the way but I think we are now putting together a really good board of fundraisers. There is no greater priority than to fundraise our way out of our present debts.

I have dinner at the Carlton Club with Toby Aldington who must now be over eighty. He very much has all of his faculties and I am bound to say that I hope that I am as well preserved at that age as he obviously is. He reminisces a bit about the past as he was once Deputy Chairman of the Conservative Party but he fell out with Macmillan when he told the Prime Minister that what the press was saying about Jack Profumo was correct. He was told not to talk such nonsense.

TUESDAY 26 JANUARY
In the evening Fiona and I go to dinner with the American Ambassador, Raymond Seitz. There is great speculation about whether he is going to continue under the new President. As we wait to shake hands we spy a children's teddy bear with a notice round its neck saying: 'Don't ask me'. There is an amazing story in the *Daily Mail* this morning which says that I am the 'safe' choice as the next Chancellor of the Exchequer. I am not sure who has been briefing and doubtless, suspicion will fall upon me. It is the obvious conclusion; the write-up is so extraordinarily good. I do have to say that it has nothing whatsoever to do with me but few will believe that.

MONDAY 1 FEBRUARY
Meeting with John at No. 10. Right at the end, as an afterthought, John says that at 9 p.m. he is talking with the Chief Whip and others about the handling of the redistribution of European constituencies. Why, he suggests tentatively, don't I come too. I duly turn up. It soon becomes clear that he has a serious problem. Progress on the Maastricht bill depends on a very fragile majority and we rely on the Liberal Democrats to get through some of the votes.[268] Paddy Ashdown has now written to John to say that the party are not prepared to do this without some kind of return deal by us. The return deal that they want is predictably enough proportional representation as far as the six extra European seats are concerned. The general view around the table is that we should submit to this threat. I find myself entirely alone in saying that we should not deal. It seems to me that the issue of proportional representation is a major one as far as the party is concerned. Unless we are careful, we will be giving the Cashs, the Shepherds, the Thatchers and the Tebbits something with which they can rally the middle of the party. One thing that

---

268 Unless we can close down the debates on a group of amendments there is no reason why they cannot go on and on for ever. Without the support of the Liberal Democrats the whips feared that we would be unable to do this and would therefore lose control of the bill. Up to now, the Liberal Democrats had supported us on the procedural motions.

John made absolutely clear during the last election is that he would have no truck with such proposals.

TUESDAY 2 FEBRUARY

My 55th birthday. Subdued celebrations. Fiona and I had planned to go to a party in Oxford but that had to be cancelled because of the three-line business in the House. The Railways Bill requires all our support. It is the bill I am least enthusiastic about in the whole of the government's programme so I feel doubly offended. Richard Ryder rings to suggest I join a meeting in the House of Lords with Wakeham and co. to continue the business of last night. I go prepared for another dustup with the business managers but I find that the mood has now changed. And that trying to call Paddy Ashdown's bluff, what is now referred to as the 'Fowler option', is now seen as the practical course of action.

WEDNESDAY 3 FEBRUARY

Lunch with Stewart Steven, the editor of the *Evening Standard*. Politically, I find myself much more at home with Stewart than with some of our more vigorous right-wing supporters. He tells me that he has got rid of Alan Walters who was writing a column which is extremely good news. He has been a pain in the neck since leaving his post as an adviser to Margaret Thatcher. He has given the new government no support and no credit. I think he is intellectually and personally arrogant, qualities which make him peculiarly unqualified to be a political adviser.

THURSDAY 4 FEBRUARY

St Mary Abbots Church in Kensington for Oliver Poole's funeral. He had a distinguished life. The sadness is that the last eighteen or nineteen years were spent in a kind of twilight after his stroke. It made it very difficult for him to communicate and for most of the time he was more or less bedridden. The other sadness is that most of his political friends are now dead and those who are alive, like Quintin Hailsham, have been out of touch for a long time. It is a rather sad funeral. Low-key, downbeat.

Oliver has apparently made one request in his will and that is that there should be no memorial service so that's the end of the matter. David is now the new Lord Poole and our Oliver is his heir.

FRIDAY 5 FEBRUARY

The time has come to present to the staff and to the world at large the reorganisation plans for Conservative Central Office. At the centre is the idea of a new board of directors of the Conservative Party which will hold Central Office to account but will also progressively hold the party to account. We have already appointed our new director general, Paul Judge, and with him and Martin Saunders as director of finance that part of the operation is going well. We are planning to have more women on the list of candidates but also more people with business experience. We want to end the position where people over forty feel barred from becoming Conservative candidates. Of course, as far as the staff and the press is concerned, one issue is uppermost and that is the issue of redundancies. I had to break the news to my driver yesterday that his post was redundant. We cannot possibly justify a situation where we are paying over £20,000 to provide the chairman with a driver. Frankly, you have to take a lot of taxis to run up that kind of bill.

MONDAY 22 FEBRUARY

We begin with the meeting at No. 12. There is no doubt that the issue of the moment is crime. The public is outraged by the murder of a two-year-old child in Liverpool, apparently by children probably no older than ten or eleven. But this murder has only crystallised and underlined concern. In spite of how we have prioritised the police, crime continues to increase remorselessly.

WEDNESDAY 24 FEBRUARY

The Archbishop of Canterbury, George Carey, asks me to Lambeth Palace for a cup of coffee. It is a getting-to-know-you meeting but our conversation ranges very wide. He asked me how I saw the position of Prince Charles whom he is seeing next week. What would my advice be?

My advice, which I am not sure is in line with Church thinking, is that Charles and Diana cannot live separate lives as ordinary people. It would be much better if they made a clean break of it. To my surprise, I think the Archbishop agrees with me. He discusses how Charles could be remarried in the Church, south side of the border. Princess Anne 'bounced him' by going north of the border to Scotland for her remarriage. He believes that apparently remarriage could take place south of the border, in England, by a suffragan bishop.

THURSDAY 25 FEBRUARY

I go to the House of Commons to see Douglas Hurd. He is concerned. We agree that the government gives the impression that it has lost its way, that it lacks authority and that the Prime Minister is looking weak. John was elected as a young Prime Minister, approachable, the opposite of Margaret Thatcher, and that served us unbelievably well during the general election and the period leading up to it but we need more than that now. We both feel that he is involved far too much in the detail of too many policies. He needs more time to stand back. He also needs more life of his own. I think that No. 10 is beginning to grind him down. He is losing his zest for life. Douglas also thinks there are far too many briefings taking place.

FRIDAY 26 FEBRUARY

Good news this morning. Kate has got into St Paul's.

SATURDAY 6 MARCH

John's speech at the Central Council goes well. Again, there is a call for unity. The delegates respond well and he is given a long standing ovation. There is no question that the people who have come to Harrogate go away feeling better. It has improved morale and that after all is one of the things that the conferences should be about. I travel back to London with Michael Howard. He made a good speech this morning at the end of the environment debate. He is a cool player. A number of us were complaining slightly about having to make speeches weekend after weekend. His response was that none of us were conscripted into our jobs. His attitude to programmes like *Question Time* is that he doesn't much like them but it is part of the job. It reminds me of what Margaret Thatcher used to say about party conferences. It is the price we have to pay. There have been stories in the press about the rivalry to succeed Norman Lamont. The contrast in style between the two frontrunners is very distinct. I went to a breakfast meeting with Ken this morning when we were briefing the press. He was expansive, genial, perhaps indiscreet about the effect that Maastricht was having on the rest of the government's legislative programme. It is for all of these reasons that someone like John Major takes the view that Ken is no longer very interested in detail but has become a rather broad-brush politician. Michael [Howard] on the other hand is very hard-working, conscientious and I suspect, much more in line with what the Prime Minister sees as the personality of a Chancellor of the Exchequer. It is a bit of a toss-up but although they may not know it, I think John would temperamentally get on better with Ken and they are certainly closer in their political outlook on issues like Europe.

WEDNESDAY 10 MARCH

After the No. 12 committee I go over to the House of Commons library. Tristan Garel-Jones comes up and says that he has been having a stand-up row in the tea room with Nick Budgen. Budgen is apparently going around complaining that I and the party in general are trying to get him deselected in Wolverhampton. This is complete nonsense. I would not do that. I would not want to do that. Budgen himself then enters the library. I go up to him with the intention of having a calming talk. That is entirely impossible. Budgen is hysterical. He believes that the party is out to get him. He really does expect to be able to vote against the government and then for everyone to come round and pat him on the back and say what a good chap he is.

FRIDAY 19–SATURDAY 20 MARCH

A horrendous weekend. On Friday the aim is to get to Cumbria where

I have agreed to do an *Any Questions*. Everything goes well in the morning. I get myself briefed and prepare to catch the train north. With about an hour to go a desperate message comes through from the BBC that there has been an accident on the line and the result is that trains are subject to long delays of two or three hours. They suggest that I instead fly to Glasgow where a car will pick me up and take me south to Cumbria. The BBC car fails to turn up remotely on time. It takes the most idiotically slow route to Heathrow with the result that I miss the 3.15 plane and have to catch the 4.15. I arrive in Glasgow and no sooner am I off the plane than there is a fire alert at the airport. None of us can move. After about fifteen minutes the fire alarm stops and I eventually find my driver to go south. We make spectacularly quick progress south out of Glasgow but then we come to roadworks. The next period is pure nightmare. The traffic has built up so much that we travel about three miles in over one hour. By this stage there is no way that I am going to get anywhere near the venue for *Any Questions* and I ring the BBC to tell them. Next on the line is Jonathan Dimbleby who tells me that Howard Davies of the CBI who did get the 3.15 is in a very similar position. He is slightly ahead of me in the traffic jam but not much. Neither of us is going to make the *Any Questions* session. The only thing that Jonathan can suggest is that we do it over our mobile telephones with the messages being sent through their London control: and so it is. I sit in a lay-by with lorries trundling past, shaking the car and take part in an *Any Questions* with Jack Cunningham and Charles Kennedy comfortably and securely seated in the school hall where we are all meant to be. I imagine that I get a number of sympathy points but it is only the beginning of my problems. When the programme ends, the next problem is how I am going to continue my journey.

I am supposed to be in Newbury for Judith Chaplin's memorial service, so the poor driver who has brought me from Glasgow is asked whether he minds doing the detour and driving south to Newbury. It slowly dawns on him just how far that is but he says he is prepared to do it. We stop at a motorway cafe to have some supper and he rings his wife. His wife patently doesn't believe a word he is saying. It sounds so ludicrous that her only response is that he is obviously taking time out with another woman. Nevertheless, off we go again and after a long, long drive south we arrive at Newbury at 3 a.m. The poor driver has a couple of hours' sleep and then goes back to Scotland. He has a football match to play at two o'clock Saturday afternoon. I stay for Judith's memorial service, which is a good occasion and the only part of the weekend that is worth the effort. The service is made by the choir from Downe House.[269] Girls of Kate's age and older dressed in wonderful scarlet robes.

SATURDAY 3 APRIL–SUNDAY 11 APRIL

The Easter break at last. The whole family, with the exception of Oliver, decamp to Florida and Disney World. It is another world of rides, parades, shows and fireworks. Dolphins jump incredible heights, children scream in delighted terror on rollercoasters, waiters serve pancakes and syrup. Kate and Isobel love it and so do we, even a fifty-five-year-old like me.

COMMENT

This period was dominated by the pit closure policy. Central Office reported that the hostile reaction from the party on the ground went far beyond that on the ERM. Members who had loyally supported the government in the 'fight' against Scargill found the ground cut from beneath them. Totally unprepared, they had been pitched into another battle on the coal mines but this time it seemed that they were being asked to turn on the very people they had supported like the Nottinghamshire miners. Heseltine's bravura performance in the Commons had secured victory but it did not carry the country – nor very many Tory MPs, who had held their noses as they reluctantly moved through the division lobby.

Politically, an important development was the hardening of views on European policy. The battle lines were being set on moving to an inflexible

---

269 The school that Isobel later attended and where she had a very happy time.

Eurosceptic course. Hurd and Major's policy to stand by Maastricht was creating fresh divisions which went well beyond the usual suspects and included Cabinet ministers. All the signs of our future disintegration were now becoming evident, not least the stance of the deposed leader who put the fight on Europe above mere issues of party politics and the survival of John Major's premiership.

20

THE FALL OF THE
CHANCELLOR

APRIL–MAY 1993

WEDNESDAY 14 APRIL 1993

Blanket coverage for Margaret Thatcher after an outspoken interview on Bosnia. It is seen as an attack on the government and particularly on John. The difficulty is that Margaret has correctly detected the mood of the British public. They hate what is going on – the slaughter of civilians and children by the Serbs. There is a clear wish that 'something should be done'. What? Margaret's solution to arming the Muslims is not regarded as the way ahead.

MONDAY 19 APRIL

Meeting with the Prime Minister. I fear that much of the good of the break has been undone. Margaret's activities have put him under pressure on Bosnia, a terrible issue on which we are all divided, heart and head. Instinctively, people like me would like to see intervention and the Serbs stopped and prevented from their murderous activities but it would not be a quick in and out campaign. It is a civil war and the danger is that we are left in the middle – as in Northern Ireland and Cyprus. Margaret, of course, gives the impression not of doubt but of certainty. Analogies are dangerous but I remember Eden coming under pressure 'to do something' over Suez. He did and it was a disaster.

In the evening I run into the Chancellor. I tell him that I am running 'economic recovery' as the major theme in the county council elections.

'Oh don't talk about recovery', says Norman. 'Encouraging signs but not recovery'. I say that it is far too late, I have used the phrase about a dozen times in the last two days. 'Perhaps soon we will be able to talk about recovery', he says. 'We do have elections, Norman,' I remind him. He is not convinced.

SUNDAY 2 MAY

A bad poll in the *Mail on Sunday* puts the Liberals a long way ahead in Newbury. We cannot hold it. We have fought a good campaign and have even persuaded some writers that we could do it but the public is too fed up to forgive the government that quickly. The only question is how badly we lose.

THURSDAY 6 MAY

This was always going to be a difficult day but none of us predicted how disastrous the elections would be. We were reconciled to losses in the county councils and to the loss of Newbury but as soon as the results start to come in, it becomes clear that it is a rout. Massive swings against us. Enormous gains by the Liberals. Labour not doing spectacularly but well enough. By the end of the night we are down to controlling one county council – Buckinghamshire. We have done particularly badly in the south of England where the recession has bitten hardest and, ominously, in the west country. I go on television to say that the results are obviously 'disappointing'. There is some resistance at Central Office to even using that word on the grounds that it concedes too much – but the public are not fools. They are not going to be taken in by platitudes about mid-term blues. The results are actually disastrous rather than disappointing. I make what I can by comparing them with 1985 – a particularly bad year for us – when we polled 32 per cent. Our poll tonight is 31 per cent. My point is that the results are not unprecedented. That is my public stance but even this gets blown sky high when the result from Newbury comes through. Fortunately, the BBC has closed down their election night programme by the time that result is announced. As a consequence I have taken the opportunity of an hour's sleep. The phone rings just after 4 a.m. It is Tim who tells me that our people in Newbury have rung to say that the Liberals have a majority of over 20,000 and so it proves. It is an awful night. A swing of almost 30 per cent to the Liberals.

FRIDAY 7 MAY

At 6.15 I ring John from Central Office. He is in Huntingdon and has only just woken up to the result. He remains calm. None of Margaret's histrionics. He agrees that the only way to respond is to admit the size of the defeat, and in effect, say that we will learn from our mistakes. By 6.45 I am into a round of a dozen radio and television interviews. Curiously, they are not as bad as I feared. Even the interviewers don't hit a man too hard when he is down. My most convincing line is that the public were voting on the history of the past twelve months of recession. The recovery is under way but they have not seen it. That is certainly part of the explanation. The other part is that a government embattled over Maastricht gives the impression of weakness.

I ring John again just after 8.30. His mood is now more belligerent. He is particularly incensed by Carlisle's and Gardiner's remarks that the government has lost its sense of direction. Whoever else can make the charge it is not those two who have spent most of the last months trying to push the government off course. Why not attack the sceptics, John asks. My response to that is that one of the aims must now be to bring the party together. John reluctantly accepts this advice and goes on his constituency tour. Later, I see him on TV at his reasonable best saying that we have received a 'bloody nose' and he has no excuses. Exactly right on the immediate response – now we need a strategy to take us forward.

SATURDAY 8 MAY

The press is dominated by stories about the Chancellor and speculation about his demise. It is now only a matter of time before he is moved but the delay in bowing to the obvious has had an effect that could have been avoided. It was the case that the public would have settled for his transfer to, say, the Home Office. Now, I am not so sure. If he had the slightest political sense he would have insisted on going after the ERM debacle. Resignation would have been in his political interest. He would have had respect.

SUNDAY 9 MAY

A horrendous press. Attacks on the government abound. In précis the right-wing press is saying to John, act now or get out. In the afternoon, John says that the worst criticism is that it is an 'incompetent' government. He also believes that the 'drift and decay' argument is off beam. Richard Ryder says there is no great support for the Chancellor and that there is a list of issues of complaint coming from MPs of which VAT on fuel is number one. We are in for a hairy few days.

MONDAY 10 MAY

The important meeting takes place between John and me in the afternoon. I insist that no one but Jonathan should be there, and probably should have insisted on a one-to-one. The third person means that there is an audience. There is a question of keeping face. The Prime Minister cannot entirely let his defences down. Nevertheless, for all that, it is by any standards a frank meeting.

I start by saying that the comments about him and his government have come from his friends. The party like him and he has broad personal support but at present his leadership and the government do not inspire confidence. The public need to understand the strategy. Where is the government going? What does it want to achieve? There is also a personal agenda. How do you, as Prime Minister, want to be seen? There must be a reshuffle and at the first suitable opportunity Lamont must go. He must not go to the Home Office where we need a strong minister in a politically crucial area.

John intervenes to say that he sees the case for that. He would put Ken Clarke in the Treasury and make Michael Howard Home Secretary. Norman Lamont would be given environment if he would accept.

I enthuse about John's solution although frankly, I doubt Norman will accept environment.

We move on to the press. I say that he takes the press too much to heart. The press knows it, as does the Labour Party. Max Hastings reports that they believe they can wear him down. He also courts the editors too much. They regard it as a sign of weakness not strength. John does not accept the criticism. The reason that he is sensitive, he says, is that all too often he is left undefended. Margaret had Willie and Norman Tebbit looking after her interests. There are no Majorites putting the positive case for him and the government. In essence, he feels himself exposed to criticism without anyone coming to his aid. I don't agree with his analysis and say so. He has never had the kind of problems that Margaret Thatcher had with her Cabinet nor do I think he would have enjoyed Norman Tebbit being his Chairman. There is a unity around him that frankly, Margaret Thatcher never had. Nevertheless, I take the message. If the Prime Minister feels he is undefended then we must do more.

On policy, I say that the best course is to pick three or four themes – the economy, law and order, industrial recovery, Europe, better public services – and concentrate on those. Our approach is too scattergun at the moment. We need more specifics in areas like industry policy.

'Such as?' he asks.

'Well, we are getting over the message to industry that we want a new partnership. We now need to dramatise that. For example, you send out instructions to all embassies telling them that they are trade posts and we expect them to help British industry.'

'Good idea', he says. 'That is a specific thing we can do.'

'It is a specific', I reply. 'But the others require action as well.'

The last point I raise is that he is in danger of losing his zest for his job. 'No', says John. 'I have lost my zest for the job. I saw my mother -in-law at the weekend. "Why do you do it?" she asked?' He has taken a terrible pounding over the past twelve months. The result is that at times he is tired to the point of exhaustion. He does not have the energy to take on new policies and new ideas. All the more reason, I say, why you need to get out of this place more. 'You have an excellent team but you need some life away from No. 10.' In his heart he agrees with me. It is a great pity that none of us these days have grand houses, servants, and the money, to organise a social life for the Prime Minister.

THURSDAY 13 MAY

I am rung up early to be told that poor Robert Adley has died. Of course there will now be a difficult by-election in Christchurch. But that is to-morrow's problem. It is a sad loss. Robert spoke out on the issues he cared deeply about like railways and Europe. He managed however to keep any malice out of his opposition to government policy. He played it straight. Sadly, his death is not unexpected. He has never recovered consciousness since a major heart attack two weeks ago.

In the evening I go over to see Norman Lamont. By mistake I go to No. 11 first rather than the Treasury. Worse than that, because I am driving myself these days, I carry out an inexpert three-point turn in Downing Street and end up hopelessly entangled with the Prime Minister's Jaguar. His Jaguar is armour-plated and strengthened. My Rover is not. The result is that I half pull off my front bumper, the second bash in two weeks.

At No. 11 I met Rosemary Lamont. She is very wound up about the attacks on Norman. Who wouldn't be? He was not responsible for the recession, she says. Nor was he responsible for policy on the ERM. 'If no one else will say that I will go out and say it myself' she ends.

Norman is in embattled mood. What can be done, he asks. We run through the editors who could come to his aid and his problems immediately become clear. He has a series of implacable Fleet Street opponents – Andrew Neil of the *Sunday Times*, Max Hastings of the *Telegraph*, Kelvin MacKenzie of *The Sun*, who is running a countdown to the dumping of Norman. With the best will in the world it is mission impossible. No amount of persuasion will convert Fleet Street. As for radio and TV, Norman has consistently been reluctant to appear. He says this is the case with all Chancellors but I wonder. Would Kenneth Clarke or Michael Heseltine be so defensive? I doubt it very much. We agree rather lamely that his special adviser, David Cameron, will come over to Central Office and we will try to see what can be done.[270]

FRIDAY 14 MAY

A day in Sutton Coldfield. In the afternoon an excellent speech from Edwina Currie on Europe – positive, enthusiastic. Just how the case should be put. It remains a great pity that Edwina has set all her ambitions on the European Parliament. She will be a great loss to Westminster.

SATURDAY 15–SUNDAY 16 MAY

A weekend in London. As Ken Clarke observed to the world we are in 'a dreadful hole'. We have twelve months to recover before the European elections and the next local elections in 1994. We face deep disillusionment with the government, the Liberals are poised to make further gains in the south west; we need to fight back and to start that fight now. There needs to be urgency in our response. The Cabinet reshuffle needs to be at Whitsun. It needs to be more extensive than previously thought. The double whammy of Ken Clarke and Michael Howard is only the centrepiece. We must become identified with the recovery in the public mind. We need to have some credit for it and not just for reducing inflation. The party needs to come together. We give an impression of disunity. In the background are Margaret Thatcher and Norman Tebbit who could not have been more unhelpful over the past months. It is going to take superhuman efforts to achieve political recovery in twelve months but evidence of such a recovery is vital. Without that we could well lose another Prime Minister.

MONDAY 17 MAY

No. 12. Before the meeting begins there is a discussion about Alan Clark's just-published diaries. John Wakeham says that Clark came into

---

270 At the time David Cameron was special Adviser to the Chancellor. He was elected MP for Witney in 2001, party leader in 2007 and Prime Minister in 2010, leading Britain's first coalition government since the Churchill caretaker ministry. He resigned in June 2016 when Britain voted to leave the EU.

the government for one reason. Following the massive 1983 election victory he wrote to a few like-minded souls and invited them to Brookes to discuss how there could be an effective Conservative opposition to the government. Wakeham, hearing of this potential trouble, immediately recruited him to the government and what is more kept him there in spite of his incompetence as a minister, his disloyalty and his appalling gaffes, which were legion. I am not sure who comes out of this story worst – Clark or Wakeham.

This is going to be a crucial week. The Danish referendum on Tuesday.[271] The third reading of the Maastricht bill on Thursday. Unemployment figures on Thursday and then the RPI on Friday. Richard Ryder thinks the main issue at the weekend will be railway privatisation.

TUESDAY 18 MAY

An early start to No. 12 for a meeting with Transport Secretary John MacGregor. He tells us what he is planning over the next six weeks. It shows only too clearly one of the problems facing the government. There is no politics and no votes in any of the measures, only argument and more argument. First on the list of political horrors is railway privatisation which goes from bad to worse. Having rejected the regional companies idea[272] we have the second best – a railway track authority together with franchised companies. It is complex and a solution without friends. We could well be defeated on this next week. Following soon afterwards on the transport list we have motorway tolls (no applause there), widening the M25 and increasing night flights to Heathrow. 'What is the good news,' I ask. 'The roadbuilding programme', John replies.

MONDAY 24 MAY

Richard Ryder wants the dismissal of John Wakeham. He has been responsible for a number of leaks from the committees he chairs and has

---

271 The Danes said 'no' to the Maastricht Treaty in June 1992 but they now said 'yes' in reply to a new referendum in May 1993. The result was approved by 56.7 per cent of voters on an 86.5 per cent turnout.

272 To divide the railways into regional companies, Southern Railways, the Great Western and the rest, and make agreements for taking the trains over their boundaries.

won the enmity of ministers like John Patten and Michael Heseltine. Richard also thinks that his chairmanship of committees is one of the reasons for the government's lack of direction – he will not make up his mind. I fear that John Wakeham has had it coming for a long time although I question the tactics of changing the Leader of the Lords just as we are starting the Maastricht debate. What surprises me – perhaps horrifies is the better word – is that the Prime Minister and Richard have come up with Geoffrey Howe as the replacement leader in the Lords. I say this would cause 'civil war' in the party. It would be seen by the right as the 'return of the assassin'. It would be viewed by Margaret Thatcher and her supporters as a declaration of war. I should make it clear that I am not opposed to Geoffrey as a person. My view is that he made an outstanding contribution throughout the 1980s. Most of the things he believes in I believe in too. My objection is purely on the grounds that it would widen splits in the party at a time when we want unity. Richard says that he would make a superb chairman of committees. I agree, but we cannot ignore his part in the fall of Thatcher.

TUESDAY 25 MAY

A talk with Ken. I tell him the changes we have in mind in the government. I know perfectly well that it will stay between us. In all these years nothing has ever leaked from one of our conversations and in that time we have had a number of very sensitive ones. I am still not convinced just when the changes will take place and it is important that Ken keeps off the air and plays safe until the announcement is made. Neither of us have any animosity against the Chancellor but the fact is that his credibility has been destroyed. Ken's reaction to the news that he is to take Norman's place is a typical 'That's very good'. And a beaming smile. There is no question that he is delighted and will relish the challenge.

'Are you going to take my place?' he asks.

'No, Michael is' I reply. 'John wants me to stay as Chairman'.

'Michael will be good', Ken replies. 'But you would be better than either of us at that job. Why are you holding back?'

I shrug. I suppose that really was my last chance at the Home Office.

'I have always wanted two jobs, the other one is the job I am in. By any standards the next twelve months will be crucial to the party.'

WEDNESDAY 26 MAY

There are a scattering of stories on the reshuffle but rather more on railway privatisation and Bosnia. In the afternoon David Cameron comes over to Central Office for a prearranged meeting on Norman Lamont's public relations. He asks me whether he could have a private word. He says that he is embarrassed to raise this but that the Chancellor feels that I have been telling the press that he should go. This is a bit thick considering that since the ERM debacle I have been consistently defending his position. Whatever my private views, I have not been seeking to undermine him. David seems embarrassed to be the messenger and confides that not much work is being done at the Treasury amid all the rumours. I tell him I will ring Norman myself, which I do almost immediately.

THURSDAY 27 MAY

The day of the changes. I go in to see Richard Ryder at No. 12, avoiding the cameras by entering from the Cabinet Office entrance on Whitehall and walking through No. 10 and No 11. Richard hands me a list. The main changes are as expected but John has had his way on one or two of the others in the event that Norman Lamont refuses to serve. In particular, he has moved John Gummer to environment and Gillian Shephard to agriculture. John deserves a move, goodness knows.

In Richard's room the phone calls continue. I notice that *The Sun* is blaming me for Norman's demise – a bit rich for a paper which has been running a twelve-month campaign 'to dump Norm'. At around 10 o'clock the news comes through from No. 10 that Norman Lamont has refused another job and thus John Gummer will inherit environment. The word is that the meeting was 'dignified' and that Norman was very calm. Outside in Downing Street, ministers are coming and going. We agree that it would be silly for Ken to do *Question Time*. Tony Newton will do that and I will do *Newsnight* and the news interviews.

Opposite me in the *Newsnight* studio are Norman Tebbit, Max Hastings and Anthony Howard. Norman Tebbit barracks as I say it is a pity that Norman Lamont did not accept environment. That does not matter but his hostile attitude to the government, and to John Major personally, does. If John falls then Tebbit will have a lot to answer for, as too will Margaret. Neither of them has given the Prime Minister any support. Having pleaded to have him elected as leader, they not only abandoned him but they attacked him both publicly and privately. I for one will never forgive them for that. Anthony Howard makes the charge that John is just like Eden. He will soon fall and he has just promoted his successor, Ken Clarke – as Eden promoted Macmillan.

It is clear that we are not going to get a wonderful press for the changes. Norman Tebbit is scathing and others will be too. But in my view, the initial reaction is not crucial. What we have achieved is getting the right people into the right jobs. Ken and Michael Howard are correctly positioned. So too are Douglas Hurd and John Gummer. The right team at the top – that is what the shuffle has achieved. The effect may not be instant but with this team we *can* recover.

COMMENT

After Britain's ejection from the ERM the question became who was to blame? Who should take responsibility? Inside government, Ken Clarke's immediate response that it was the failure of the German government to help held sway for a while but as the days went by other explanations were offered. A popular explanation among Brexiteers was that it was the responsibility of the Prime Minister. He had negotiated the policy for entry. If anyone was to blame it was Major but most in the party were unhappy with such a conclusion. Few wanted to lose another Prime Minister so soon after the last. That left the Chancellor of the Exchequer, the man on the bridge when the ship went down. There were ample precedents for the senior minister taking the blame, the most recent being the resignation of Peter Carrington and his team for failing to spot Argentina's intention to go to war over the Falklands. In Lamont's case, the press's complaints against him multiplied and became a general argument against his handling of the economy.

21

'IN OFFICE BUT NOT IN POWER'

MAY–OCTOBER 1993

SATURDAY 29 MAY 1993

I feel exhausted, drained. The events of the last week or so have kept me going but now the reshuffle is over there is a reaction. John rings in the late morning. Jonathan Hill has suggested that the Prime Minister should do a barnstorming tour of the country. Open meetings, taking the message to the people in the footsteps of Gladstone. John has refined the idea. How about arranging question and answer meetings with local associations throughout the country. I am enthusiastic. It is what the party would want. On timing I would wait until after Christchurch – it could then be a rallying series of meetings win or lose.

A number of Sunday journalists ring up. I have become classed as the power broker behind the reshuffle. According to the reports it was Richard Ryder and I who insisted the Chancellor went. I am intrigued where these stories have come from. My suspicion is that they have been put around by the old Treasury team. Personally, I do not mind taking my share of responsibility for advising that the Chancellor should go but I cannot accept that the feeling was confined to the Party Chairman and the Chief Whip!

MONDAY 31 MAY–WEDNESDAY 2 JUNE

To the Isle of Wight. I slowly, very slowly recover. The highlight is a long walk that we all take along the beach at St Helens and then round to the yacht club on the causeway leading to Bembridge. As I catch up with them there is this wonderful picture of three figures on a virtually empty beach. In the middle Fiona, the lynchpin of the family, on the right Kate, now almost as tall as Fiona, bouncing up and down as she walks. On the left, the smaller delicate figure of Isobel, long red hair streaming in the wind. For me, a memorable interlude. An exceptionally low tide makes it possible. Wet sand and mud and marvellous pieces of memorabilia. Some old wooden railway coaches now serve as bathing huts. Old vessels which look like remnants from the Second World War lie gently rusting away. A pill box which certainly is a remnant of the last war stands with its slits now bricked in.

WEDNESDAY 9 JUNE

At the end of a short business trip to the United States I fly back overnight from Boston to Heathrow. It is as comfortable as American Airlines can make their first-class compartment but I am fairly shattered when I arrive. I would have travelled back later but the whips want me back to vote in a debate on the economy that Smith is leading for the opposition and John is being asked to respond. I have not had more than three or four hours' sleep for the last three nights. A driver takes me to Sutton Coldfield for the funeral of one of my long-serving councillors then back to London. My intention is to go home and sleep off the jet lag. Halfway down the M40 I learn that Norman Lamont is to make a personal statement of resignation. Thus, all Lamont's signals that he did not intend to make such a statement and that he would maintain a dignified silence are proving to be false. He knows only too well that he could not have chosen a more embarrassing time. An opposition supply day – the Leader of the Opposition leading the attack; the Prime Minister already on a very difficult wicket.

I see no point in going into Westminster to hear Lamont's statement but instead watch it on television. He seeks to defend his decision not to resign after withdrawal from the ERM on the grounds that other Chancellors and other finance ministers in Europe have refused to resign in similar disasters. He rests his argument on a letter which he alleges was sent to him by John urging him not to resign. He has a side swipe at party managers, by which he means Richard and me, and goes on to mount a full-scale attack on the short-termism of the government. He portrays the government as not looking any further forward than thirty-six hours – a government in office but not in power.

Why then didn't he resign from it? If he felt that all along why not just go? They were not of course questions that John Smith was going to ask. He had been presented with as wonderful an opportunity of demolishing the government as he is ever likely to receive. The result was an amusingly stylish speech but not a devastating one. John's response as it came over on television seemed in the circumstances good enough, not notable but given the circumstances adequate. That was my impression from television which concentrates on the man speaking rather than the response to the speech. I soon find that is not the reaction in the House of Commons.

Gerry Malone had rung after the Lamont statement saying that Central Office is being pressed for a response. My reply had been that the debate was still continuing. I had no intention of responding at this stage. When Gerry next rings, he has Tim Collins with him. Their joint message from the Commons is that the Prime Minister's speech has gone down very badly – that it was listened to almost in silence on our side. I said I would do the breakfast programmes tomorrow and in the meantime we would rely on Ken Clarke to respond in his wind-up. He does this brilliantly. He demonstrated in one speech why he and not Lamont should be Chancellor. Our benches cheered him to the echo but it will not be enough to save us from a ferocious press tomorrow.

THURSDAY 10 JUNE

The worst headlines. The message is: 'it's not whether John goes, it is when'. *The Sun* sets out his obituary. The so-called 'qualities' are hardly less restrained. The Prime Minister, the Chief Whip, the deputy chairman all agree with my inclinations that I should have a go and I do. I roundly attack Lamont's speech which has brought down this torrent of criticism on our heads. I variously call the speech dud and nasty, and I come close to losing my temper. I am angry. There is no disguising that. All I need is a question or two to trigger me off.

The public reaction does not come until an hour or two later. My office gets a scattering of calls that I have overdone it. Gerry Malone rings to say that of all people, Budgen has raised it at the 1922. Ken Baker (again of all people) has called for 'unity' in the party. By the time I get to Llandrindod Wells, for the Welsh party conference, it is obvious that I am in the middle of a full-scale row. The complaint is that I have gone way over the top in my attack on Lamont. Our very good press officer, Vanessa Ford, plays back the press comment. Was it, she wonders, a deliberate strategy – this display of temper? I remain unrepentant. The strategy of having a go was deliberate. The aim was to cut down the Prime Minister's critic. If I have overdone it, then that is too bad. It is difficult to finely tune such attacks but given the headlines and the general response it was imperative that Lamont's speech was undermined.

FRIDAY 11 JUNE

I deliberately refuse to read the papers. It is clear from what Tim says that I have had a bad press. My inclination when under attack from the press is to turn the other way. You cannot entirely ignore it but no need to wallow in it. John and the Prime Minister's entourage arrive an hour or so later. John is quite amused by the furore over my remarks – 'Ah, Norman the Knife', he says as I go in to see him. As Jonathan observes later, my defence has taken the pressure off the Prime Minister and that is the point. It is part of what being Chairman is all about. Forty-eight hours ago the battle was Norman Lamont versus the Prime Minister. Today, it is the much less dangerous Norman versus Norman.

MONDAY 14 JUNE

John asks for a private word. He fears that his advisers at No. 10 have not been frank. He believes that his slump in popularity may have gone too far to be possible to recover from. He has said this to me before but what he says next is entirely new.

'Your job', he says 'is to advise me if the position becomes irrecoverable. It is not just a question of defending me. If I went we would be able to turn over a new page. Even the blood lust of the press would be satisfied.'

John speaks quietly and with total command. His message is quite clear. He is prepared to go if it is in the interests of the government and the nation. If the government cannot recover without such a change, then the economy will not recover either. I do not believe we are at that point. No one but a fool would claim that the last twelve months have been other than very bad but it is my view that we can recover. The criticism was not that we moved Lamont but that we had taken so long.

TUESDAY 15 JUNE

A day devoted to preparing for the select committee on party funding. I wonder if select committees know just how much work goes into an appearance. New allegations about the source of Tory funds are being made by the day. A magazine called *Business Age,* which sounds respectable but is in fact totally daft, fuels the fire. It charges that we have a few hundred million pounds slush fund hidden away for emergencies. If only we did!

A genuine concern centres on Mr Asil Nadir, now a fugitive in North Cyprus. His companies, Polly Peck and Uni Peck, gave some £440,000 to the Conservative Party between 1985 and March 1990. They did not declare those donations which as far as British law is concerned is what they are required to do. Nadir has fled. The demand is made therefore that we should repay the money. My answer to this is that we will examine what the administrators, Touche Ross, say but so far our letter to them from October 1991 has received no response. Touche Ross staff have talked to the press but they have not talked to us. I am not going to be bounced by a press campaign to repay the money which has long since been spent. If it is established to have been stolen, then we will return it. I pass over the practical problem of finding the £440,000 in a party that already owes £19 million.

WEDNESDAY 16 JUNE

The preparation for the select committee pays off. I am master of my brief and the Labour members fail to land a severe punch. They are an unimpressive group. Barbara Roche simply looks flummoxed when I ask her a question and an intense young man called O'Brien reads out a long carefully prepared statement rather than asking short questions.[273]

MONDAY 21 JUNE

Dreadful news. Michael Heseltine has had a heart attack. Dreadful for Michael, dreadful for the government. He has been smitten down in Venice, where in 1979 Fiona and I met him as we started our honeymoon. The surprise and shock is enormous. Of all people Michael would appear the unlikeliest candidate for a heart attack. Bad, bad news.

The party funding row is now going full tilt. At the centre is Asil Nadir. We are under great pressure to repay his contribution. Labour will be after me in the debate and so will some of my own side. Ever since Lamont's dismissal and my subsequent interview I have been something of a hate figure for the right. They would love me to fall flat on my face.

TUESDAY 22 JUNE

The debate on funding has all the subtlety of a slanging match in a public bar just before closing time. Margaret Beckett is dreadful – Labour makes a tactical mistake in not opening with Cook – and David Hunt for our side is much better. I speak just after the openers. The speech goes very well; the whole party get behind me. It is just like the old days. We are fighting the other side. Labour made a big mistake. They sought to play up a report in *The Guardian* that we were given £7 million by the Saudi royal family just before the 1992 election. It is total nonsense. We have not received any money from the Saudi Arabian government – or any Saudi individual as far as I can see. The Saudi member of the royal family alleged to have contributed is their ambassador in the US and

---

273   Barbara Roche, Labour MP for Hornsey and Wood Green, 1992–2005. Mike O'Brien, Labour MP for North Warwickshire, 1992–2010.

he is threatening legal proceedings. We challenge Labour to disassociate themselves, which they refuse to do.

After my speech I go to No. 10 to see John and stay for supper. John wonders whether there is some way we can make ourselves more open, more obviously accountable. Curiously, the debate has had a good effect on us. It has brought us together. The other major issue has become what to do about Michael Mates.[274] His gift of a watch to Asil Nadir was not very bright but as John says it is scarcely a hanging offence.

THURSDAY 24 JUNE

Our luck does not last. The *Daily Mail* publish a letter from Michael Mates to the Attorney General pleading Asil Nadir's case. The heat is now really on Michael and at 3.15 the Prime Minister announces that he has resigned. Sad but by this stage, right. Unlike Mellor and Lamont I have played no part in the Mates resignation. I am sad to see him go. The most that can be said is that he has been a chump.

FRIDAY 25 JUNE

Much criticism of John Major. All the old enemies take the field. The charge is that he has shown delay and indecision in the Mates affair. It is the greatest nonsense. As I understand it, he was quite rightly dealt with by the Chief Whip and offered the silver revolver. It is absurd to believe that it could have been any quicker. The night at Belvoir Castle and a speech to the East Midlands Industry Council to raise funds. The castle is rather less comfortable than Hurlingham Road in spite of all the magnificent paintings. The duke is in good form but the duchess seems nervily tense to the point of rudeness. She smokes incessantly and is in great contrast to the young beauty I remember from the early 1970s when I was Member for Nottingham.

MONDAY 28 JUNE

For once we are off the front pages. The Americans' attack on Baghdad has seen to that. Great debate ranges over whether Clinton's action was

---

274 Michael Mates's troubles began when it emerged he had given a watch to Asil Nadir bearing the inscription, 'Don't let the buggers get you down'.

justified. Downing Street ring shortly after eight and it is John on the phone. 'Could I come in to see him fifteen minutes early?' He rings off leaving me no wiser. My guess is that it will be about the weekend's press concerning him and the Mates affair.

And so it is in part. He is sitting at the Cabinet table with his jacket off, outwardly calm and composed, inwardly he is seething. In effect, he tells me: 'I can't take much more of this. I can't take it and I am not prepared to see my family take it.' He resents the criticism of the handling of the Mates resignation. Quite right too. The future of a Minister of State is a matter for the Chief Whip and not for the Prime Minister engaged in a European summit. But what has really distressed and angered him is an interview given by the editor of *The Times*, Peter Stothard. In it, he boasts of introducing 'American-style' journalism in which leaders' mental capacity to lead can be questioned. Thus, he defends Simon Jenkins's nasty and untrue allegation that the Prime Minister had some kind of 'wobble' on the day that we withdrew from the ERM and even the notoriously inaccurate later piece 'John lived an isolated and cut off life in Downing Street.' John says that all of this is 'flatly untrue' but who has denied it? 'I for one', I reply. But John feels that there are others who should have gone to his defence. We need a 'proactive' set of Cabinet supporters. I tell him that I will organise this and only the storm over party funding has prevented it so far. Howard, Bottomley, MacGregor, Newton and Dorrell are the agreed five.

TUESDAY 29 JUNE

Lunch with Charles Hambro and Conrad Black. I have not talked in depth with Black before. We have passed but not talked. I am impressed. He talks well, and perceptively, about the political position. He makes one point clear. He is not a member of the 'dump Major' club. As long as John is a candidate (and doesn't just give up) he will support him. He is a newspaper proprietor and obviously the support will not be uncritical, but he wants him to succeed as Prime Minister. He has told Charles Moore that that is the policy. He has not tried to give the same message to *The Spectator*. They appear to have total editorial freedom – which has produced an admittedly much more readable magazine.

THURSDAY 1 JULY

John Major is not the only man under fire. I am now under constant bombardment, mostly from the right of the Conservative Party. They hold me personally responsible for getting rid of Lamont and promoting the left-wing figures of Ken Clarke and David Hunt, while the Eurosceptics believe that I have not been sympathetic enough to them in their efforts to destroy the party. There is now a significant 'dump Fowler' movement. There is real malice behind this campaign from the likes of Budgen and Gardiner, while in the Lords there are friendly figures like Tebbit and Parkinson, never at a loss for a usually anonymous quote or steer. In the press I am described as 'embattled'. It is precisely what I am.

MONDAY 5 JULY

We are having difficulty in our working peers list. We would dearly like Charles Hambro but given the present mood on finance and party contributions, it is impossible. My other leading candidate is Christopher Tugendhat. He should have gone to the Lords years ago and would have done so had it not been for the opposition of Margaret Thatcher who never forgave him for becoming a European commissioner over her head. Wakeham's preferred candidate is Peter Morrison who he says is underemployed. There are other names being considered. The trouble is that the Lords whips want new peers who will turn up and candidates who promise the most are also the most undistinguished. I think however I have won on Christopher.

WEDNESDAY 7 JULY

Meeting at No 12. John Major is doing well in Tokyo with the GATT talks. At the end I raise the issue of the press digest which goes to us and to the PM. It goes into incredible detail on the morning's press including the diary stories. It records that Nesta Wyn Ellis has added a chapter to her book on John saying that he is indecisive etc. Do we really need to summarise this kind of rubbish, I ask. Jonathan Haslam nods his head sadly. He agrees but is taken to task by the boss if pieces mentioning him get missed out.

MONDAY 19 JULY

Breakfast with the Prime Minister. The motion on Maastricht and the social chapter is set for Thursday.[275] In John's view there is no doubt that we are going to lose. Remembering the conversation with Richard Ryder, I ask about giving a pledge on not rejoining the ERM. John's reply is emphatic. 'I am not prepared to do a deal with those bastards'. In any event he adds there is no guarantee that such an assurance would buy anything. Robin Butler's advice is that if we lose we should put it to a confidence vote or call an election. We are in no position to fight a general election but nor are any of the other options attractive. John makes it clear that he would rather resign than return to Europe to negotiate on the social chapter so it is stalemate all round.

THURSDAY 22 JULY

I go over to No. 12 before Cabinet. Tony Newton briefs me on the result of yesterday's meeting. In the end, there were three options put forward in the likely event of defeat but only one is realistic: a vote of confidence but including the social chapter. If we lose there will be a general election.

The afternoon debate could not go better. A crowded House. Every seat taken, members in the gangway. John makes the speech of his life – forceful, authoritative – and is greeted by a white mass of waving order papers. Smith is not on form. An insubstantial speech better delivered at a university debating society. John follows up the speech on the floor with an equally impressive display upstairs in the 1922. So much better than twelve months ago. The real authority of the Prime Minister. A tumultuous reception. Hammering of fists on the table greet his pleas for unity. A display meant to intimidate the rebels like Budgen and co.

In spite of John's two performances we lose the vote. Labour's amendment is tied but the second vote results in a decisive government defeat. An enormous cheer from Labour and John announces during the noise

---

275 We had no choice but to have the debate. During the proceedings of the European Communities (Amendment) Bill (the Maastricht bill) the government had accepted a new clause from the Labour front bench, which required an explicit vote by both Houses of Parliament on a government motion 'considering the question of adopting the Protocol on Social Policy' before the Act could be implemented.

that a vote of confidence approving the government's policy on the social chapter will be debated tomorrow.

FRIDAY 23 JULY

Four hours sleep and back to Central Office. We have a simple message to send out to the constituencies. We want to settle the Maastricht debate. If we lose the vote of confidence there will be an election. In the House John makes an adequate speech, not as good as the two yesterday, and Smith does much better but the signs of forthcoming government victory are unmistakable. Budgen has already made it quite clear that he will support the government and although the rebels meet after the opening speeches they know that they have nowhere to go but into our lobby. The alternative would be the withdrawal of the whip.

Richard Ryder calls to ask me to a meeting with Michael Spicer. Michael goes on at some length about how difficult it is to prevent his colleagues voting against the government. He wants something in Douglas's speech and something from me. We all know he is overstating his difficulties getting his group to vote with the government. Nevertheless, it is also my dearest wish to get the party together. I tell him I am writing a letter to all constituency chairmen. I would certainly be willing to put in a passage on the need to draw a line under the events of last year. Michael is very keen on having a word about the 'honourable fight' the rebels have put up. I will try something of that kind. What is indisputable is that peace has broken out. The vote is almost an anti-climax. No Tory votes against us and only one absentee – Rupert Allason who has remained missing and is presumed to be in Bermuda. It is a racing certainty that the whip will be withdrawn. I end the day on *Newsnight*, fending off Ted Heath who wants vengeance on the rebels. It has been a good forty-eight hours for John Major and if there is any justice should be seen that way tomorrow.

SATURDAY 24 JULY

A bad press. John is given no credit. He is attacked for using the nuclear deterrent of a confidence motion to drive the party into line. The sympathy is with the rebels although that is not the prevailing view of the back benches where there is some resentment that the rebels are treated with such deference. Ted Heath speaks for much of the parliamentary party here. I do two television interviews and then try to settle down to catch up with the mountain of work now piling up on my desk. No chance. By teatime we are in the foothills of another row. According to Tim and Jonathan, the recording equipment at No. 10 was left on after an interview with Michael Brunson of ITN. Not knowing that he was on the air, John lashed out at his opponents, including some 'bastards' in the government. *The Observer* has the story courtesy of some mole and will be using it tomorrow.[276]

SUNDAY 25 JULY

The Prime Minister's comments are the lead story everywhere. I have an hour to work out some line before appearing on the Frost breakfast show. The obvious counter is to deplore the manner in which a private conversation has been leaked, as well as denying that the Cabinet was split on the social chapter.

WEDNESDAY 28 JULY

The closing press conference at Christchurch. Good humoured because they know we are going to lose the by-election. Following the press conference, I travel round all the committee rooms in the constituency and ask them what the public feel. In the words of one very bright helper who had interviewed 700 voters, 'They are fed up. They are fed up with the government.' He is right. The public are fed up. They believe what they read and are told. They believe that there is drift. Uncertainty. Weakness. They criticise the Prime Minister for not being decisive. They criticise the government for being remote and not caring. There have been other issues – like VAT on fuel, the leaks on prescription charges – but at the heart of it the public are not confident that they are being

---

276 After the interview had ended, Michael Brunson asked Major why he did not simply sack the rebels. He could easily find three new Cabinet members. Major replies, 'But where do you think most of this poison is coming from? From the dispossessed and the never-possessed. You can think of ex-ministers who are going around causing all sorts of trouble. We don't want another three more of the bastards out there.'

well governed or that the government knows where it is going. Another reason (probably the greatest) is the disunity in the party. Four fifths of the population now see us as a divided party.

THURSDAY 29 JULY

The Christchurch result comes through in the early hours of the morning. A Liberal majority of 16,000 – a 35 per cent swing from us to the Liberals. Labour lose their deposit. A ghastly result.

On TV with David Dimbleby and Jack Straw. I argue that the result can be explained by the effects of recession and the disunity of the party, which is now hopefully behind us. I defend John but the interviewers make no bones about it. If they cannot have the Prime Minister's head, would I mind offering my own?

SUNDAY 1 AUGUST, SEAVIEW

An old acquaintance comes up as I am pulling dinghies in and out of the sea. 'That was a good cartoon of you in the *Sunday Telegraph*', he says, and adds quickly, 'Of course I did not read the article'. The bait is placed. When I get back I find, slightly hidden, in the impenetrable print of the *Sunday Telegraph,* a profile or more accurately, a hatchet job. It is crude, undergraduate journalism and I can picture Charles Moore sitting there giggling over his paper's handiwork. It is also filled with inaccuracies. For example, it is based on the premise that I was appointed to the chairmanship as a reward for my support of John Major during the leadership contest when even the most superficial student of this period knows that I backed Michael Heseltine. It is also a bit rich for Charles Moore of all people to blame me for any loss of Tory support given the efforts he has made to undermine the government. The Euro rebels are out to get their own back. There is not much I can do but grin and bear it, says Fiona and Tim Collins agrees. I do however, vow that when I come to write an account of this period, it will include the role of papers like the *Sunday Telegraph* and editors like Moore. The conventional wisdom is that you do not attack the press. It would be impossible to write about this period and leave out their part – so often discreditable.

WEDNESDAY 4 AUGUST

I am exhausted after the longest twelve months I can remember and depressed at the indiscriminate attacks being directed at the Prime Minister, the government and of course, myself. On the seafront launching Isobel's Optimist, I meet Peter Bottomley, 'relax', he says, 'and remember you are the lightning conductor'.

SUNDAY 15 AUGUST

Ring John in Huntingdon. We both sound the same. Low, exhausted, in need of rejuvenation. His initiative of flying injured children out of Sarajevo this week has received public acclaim but not the full-hearted support of the press. Foremost among the critics is of course the *Sunday Telegraph*. 'Had I read it?' 'No', I reply, not adding that I do not have his masochistic desire to know what this second-rate bunch of journalists think. John does not believe that the press will allow him to recover, not until they have more blood. They will want to see him out and then, and only then, will they offer us support. The plot is to bring down Major, change the leader and then support the government – in time for the next general election.

FRIDAY 20 AUGUST

An article by Cecil Parkinson is being widely quoted. He criticises the government as 'disunited'. This is a bit much on two counts. First, he has been one of those disuniting the Conservative Party on the European issue. Second, and more important, he is a former chairman of the party and knows the score. He knows he has provided precisely the kind of attack that the party can do without just now.

SUNDAY 29 AUGUST

Ken Baker's memoirs are in the *Sunday Times*. He claims that John Major remained silent in Margaret Thatcher's hour of need when she was being challenged for the leadership.

WEDNESDAY I SEPTEMBER

In the evening Charles Hambro and Philip Harris ask to see me. Both are very concerned about the financial position. Charles says there is a real danger of the party being 'broke' by Christmas. Firms are not giving. Philip agrees, 'it is very, very difficult out there'. They both believe that we should make further cuts in spending, which Paul Judge is reluctant to do. I agree to have all the main financial players around the table next week. We cannot have separate meetings with Paul Judge and then me with the treasurers. That will take us back to the bad old days.

THURSDAY 2 – SATURDAY 4 SEPTEMBER

To Manchester, Liverpool, Brighouse, Sheffield, Derby, Coventry and Bury St Edmonds. In three days I meet a quarter of the local chairmen. My overall reaction is that it is not a demoralised party. They are deeply disappointed, but they are not demanding the Prime Minister's head. They like him, they want him to do better. They hope that the ex-Chairmen might help and the parliamentary party come together. Above all, they want certainty, direction. They are not always good at defining how this can be achieved. They detect however when it is absent.[277]

FRIDAY 10 SEPTEMBER

At noon I go to see Margaret at her home in Chesham Place. With the police, the security protection, the photographs of her Cabinets from 1979, it is more of an office than a home, reminiscent of No. 10. In appearance and style she seems hardly to have changed since her days as Prime Minister. Still smart, alert, courteous on small things like the coffee, outspoken on big things like the economy. We start our talk with the financial position of the party. She deplores the action of the select committee in raising the whole issue and defends with total certainty the right of every individual to give to a political party and not to make their gift public. It is that kind of total certainty which was reassuring when we were under attack.

'Will you do a couple of fundraising dinners for us?' I ask.

She does not hesitate. 'Of course I will, Norman, of course I will' she

---

277   Later in the month I also met the local chairmen in the west country and Wales.

pauses. 'I would prefer them to be in the New Year but yes, you organise them.'

She explains that she is just off to the United States – among other things to make a presentation to George Bush – and from mid-October will be heavily committed to her book.

So far so good. We then turn to the economy. She basically regards what is being said about public spending as 'dishonest'. The government is not reducing public spending. It is merely keeping to the previously agreed increase. She makes no attempt to disguise the fact that she believes the management of both the economy and the government to be shambolic. 'How have we got into this position', she asks rhetorically. I let her speak without interrupting. And then ask, 'Have you put this to John? Do you see him?'

I think (I cannot be sure) I detect a flicker of sadness in her face. 'No, we don't meet at all these days'.

'Would you like me to get such meetings arranged?'

'No', she says quickly. 'He doesn't want people peering over his shoulder.'

'What about Ken?' I persist.

'No Norman. I am happy to see you but...' she leaves the sentence half finished. 'I am not sure that Ken wants advice. He doesn't lack confidence.'

Clearly, Margaret regards Ken as rather cocky – I am not at all sure she didn't use that word. 'I think you would have done better putting in Michael Howard as Chancellor and leaving him to finish off the job he started with the police'.

As for Norman Lamont, she does not begin to question the decision to move him. 'I think the only place you could have put him was Leader of the House'. She obviously felt her swap of Geoffrey Howe from Foreign Office to Leader of the House was the model transfer.[278]

---

278 There are at least two objections to this proposal. First, the united view of those involved in the original discussion on the position of Norman Lamont was that he should remain as Chancellor. Second, it was always highly unlikely that Major would move out Tony Newton, then Lord President, given that he was one of the best and most loyal members of his Cabinet.

On the question of leadership she said that there must be no question of that being raised again. 'We cannot have a fresh leadership election, that would be ridiculous. There is no obvious successor: the Prime Minister must be supported'. My guess would be that she believes that there is only one proper heir and that is Michael Portillo. He needs time so no challenge yet.

The old magic is still there but a coming together of the two leaders looks as far away as ever. Margaret does not for a moment believe that the Maastricht issue is over. Nevertheless, some form of outward unity between Margaret and John is necessary if this party is to come together. They do not have to like each other but there must at least be a facade of unity. We cannot go on forever refighting the battles of the past. Margaret's agreement to do a couple of dinners is a modest but useful start.

SUNDAY 12 SEPTEMBER

Back in London I ring Michael Heseltine who sounds in very good spirits. He says that he goes up and down. He has periods of strong recovery followed by lapses. He is obviously not yet 100 per cent. Anne is passionately opposed to him speaking at the party conference and although his instincts are to speak, he sees the sense of what she is saying.

'You and I know the nervous energy which is expended before a big speech. You cannot just throw it off.'

I say that the party conference should not be his chief concern. His chief concern should be recovery and getting back to his government job. He obviously wishes to do that. 'It has been my life', he says. 'I seem to remember advising you not to leave the government. You did and then you came back. It is in the blood.' He says that he will concentrate on getting back to work if everyone can be patient. If he does not recover quickly enough then he would have to do the 'honourable' thing and resign.

My reply to that is that he should have as much time as he likes. The important thing is that he comes back into the government. We cannot afford to lose Michael. As he says, his absence from Westminster has made the press heart grow fonder. The *Daily Mail* apparently gave him an enormously good write-up on Saturday.

WEDNESDAY 15 SEPTEMBER

A drink with John just before dinner. Apparently, Lamont is again threatening to launch a torpedo against the Prime Minister and threatens to 'reveal all' about what happened on the day we left the ERM. In my view there is nothing to reveal, certainly about John's demeanour which, as I remember, was amazingly and notably calm. John is not so laid-back. 'If he wants a fight he can have one. I will tell them about the times he went missing and not even his driver knew where he was.'

I tell him of our plans for the party conference including the handling of Margaret Thatcher. In essence, my aim is to normalise relations, welcome her, give her dinner, treat her with the respect that is proper for a leader of her success. We need to move away from the position where Margaret is smuggled in and out of the conference with embarrassment all round. John listens to what I say. He doesn't dissent but simply observes: 'Do that by yourself'.

THURSDAY 16 SEPTEMBER

We are too late for Lamont. He has already struck in articles for *The Times* and *The Sun*. His message is that withdrawal from the ERM (of which today is the anniversary) was a humiliation for him, but also for the Prime Minister. He adds that the country now needs strong leadership, implying that the Prime Minister is not providing it. As I travel down to Cardiff, continuing my tour of constituencies, I study the press. In my view his articles are the musings of a disappointed and bitter man. My advice is that we keep out of it. Reacting will only give the attack more publicity.

FRIDAY 17 SEPTEMBER

Lamont has now done a U-turn. The press all report his admittedly less than fulsome statement of support for John – and I gather that on *Question Time* he was taken apart, limb by limb, by Roy Jenkins. Entirely satisfactory but evidently not satisfactory enough for the Prime Minister. Jonathan rings me in Sutton Coldfield. The Prime Minister is off to Tokyo but not before he has given Jonathan and co. a very rough time.

Among his main targets is me. Among his complaints is that no one is out there defending him. 'It is not sustainable like this. If it goes on it is not worth carrying on', he apparently said. 'We will end up with a Labour government as the party pulls itself apart. No one is prepared to put his head over the parapet.'

All this has been provoked by Lamont but Lamont is simply the occasion of the complaint. What John resents so deeply are all the attacks on him from our benches. I agree. After all, I am a fellow victim, but we are politicians. The real question is how do you react? My all-out attack against Lamont after his resignation speech may have pleased John at the time but it did us no long-term good. It did not strengthen our position. If anything, it gave some quite unjustified sympathy to Lamont.

SUNDAY 19 SEPTEMBER

A new leadership row has developed. There is Sunday paper talk of a challenge to John. The people who appear to be behind it are towering figures like Teresa Gorman and Richard Body. It is derisory but what is keeping it going are John's comments from Tokyo. His irritation at being pursued on this issue while he is supposed to be leading a trade mission is palpable. According to one report he is dismissing his critics as 'barmy',[279] thus ensuring a new instalment of the depressing story. Graham Bright rings to say what I already know, that the Prime Minister was in a ferocious mood when he left on Friday; blaming everyone in sight including myself. He was 'critical of us all', Graham says. 'He feels no one supports him'. The real problem remains the Prime Minister reacting to the press stories. It is his reaction which is keeping the ferment going.

MONDAY 20 SEPTEMBER

John is reacting all over the place. He is attacking his backbench critics but worst of all he is attacking his supporters. The *Daily Express* report

---

279 The comments were taped and later leaked to the press. He said he had a hit list of eight rebel Tory members of Parliament he would like to punish for their criticism of the administration. 'I could name eight people,' he said. 'Half of them are barmy.' Later, the *Daily Telegraph* alleged that the 'barmy' lawmakers were Carlisle, Gorman, Marlow and Body.

his view that he has been deserted by his friends specifically, including myself and Ken Clarke. As I arrive at No. 12 Gus is on the phone from Tokyo. He has been asked to tell both myself and the Chancellor that the *Express* story is untrue. I listen politely to what Gus has to say and then point out that if that is the Prime Minister's view then he better correct the story to the press out there. Of course I know that John has said what is reported or something very near it. He may not have said it to the press directly but he said it to someone on the trip who has kindly passed it on. The problem is that he feels it. At times of strain he has this tendency to blame those around him. Sarah Hogg has obviously suffered this way. I leave No. 12 in a thoroughly bad temper and go into a meeting at Central Office with my vice chairmen and directors where I pick a row with the unfortunate Eric Pickles who suggests I might meet local government leaders, as well as constituency chairmen, as I move around the country. 'That's your job', I say unreasonably. In the last week I have travelled 2,500 miles and seen 300 chairmen. The meeting shuffles uncomfortably and I pull back. My irritation is not with Eric – it is with John and the No. 10 machine. What the hell? I am working around the clock in an unpaid job. I am continually being attacked, particularly from behind by the so-called Tory press and now I am being publicly blamed by the man I am often carrying the can for. For the first time Fiona also expresses her frustration – a result of being with me through a grisly August and September. I cannot just walk away, however tempting the prospect may appear today, but one thing I do say is that if we go on like this we are lost.

TUESDAY 21 SEPTEMBER

I go to Wapping for the first time to see Kelvin MacKenzie. It is another world, somewhere between a barracks complete with guardhouse and Roald Dahl's chocolate factory. MacKenzie is a lively, intelligent man who knows exactly what he wants. His message is:

> We will support the Conservative cause. And Rupert Murdoch will support the Conservative cause.

We report what we hear. We are a newspaper. It is not personal.

Provided John Major survives we will back him. We will be there at the next election.

Tell the Prime Minister not to read the newspapers.

Don't punish us with VAT on newspapers and the law on privacy.

Baker is the most dangerous of the rebels.

Meetings between him and the Prime Minister are not a good idea. They are never likely to have a meeting of minds.

Tell the Prime Minister not to be rude to my staff.

He was genuinely outraged that after some article or other John Major turned his back on Trevor Kavanagh (sensitive lot these journalists). Of all the messages, the 'don't punish us' is the most important. *The Sun* has dropped its price and is losing a lot of money. VAT would be a hammer blow.

FRIDAY 24 SEPTEMBER
Lunch with Bill Deedes. Still in wonderful form although now eighty. He tells me a good story about Norman Lamont. Peter Palumbo invited both Lamont and Max Hastings to a dinner. Worst of all, he put them almost next door to each other. After a little while Lamont could take it no longer and verbally attacked Hastings to which Hastings responded in kind. The result was that a deathly hush fell over the dinner party.

THURSDAY 30 SEPTEMBER
I know exactly what I want from the party conference. I want a conference unity based on reconciliation. What Downing Street do not seem to understand is that the party is puzzled as to how to respond to the Thatcher years. They hear the rumble of battle between John and Margaret and note the embarrassed way that Thatcher is smuggled in and out of the party conference but they also remember the triumphs of the Thatcher years.

All this changes if we can only normalise relations between John and Margaret. They don't have to like each other, just behave in public with proper respect and preferably some small show of affection. If we can achieve that then we can outmanoeuvre our critics. John has not vetoed my plans but he has made his position quite clear. 'You are on your own', he says. He burns with resentment at the way that she has undermined him. For her part, Margaret has still not come to terms with her overthrow and does not regard John as a worthy successor.

We have a short political Cabinet. My message is that our first aim is to send the conference away enthused. We need to set out Conservative values: law and order; strong defences; the minimum of state intervention. We need to set out the differences between the parties and not allow the Liberals to portray themselves as 'soft Tories'. We need to remind them that the journey begun in 1979 still continues. We do not want fringe meetings overshadowing the conference and we need ministers to exude confidence. After political Cabinet, George Jones[280] comes in and I tell him my plans for Margaret Thatcher, the fundraising dinner, the way she will be received. The *Telegraph* is exactly the paper I need to set out the message of reconciliation.

FRIDAY 1 OCTOBER

The *Telegraph* do us proud. The story about Margaret Thatcher leads the paper. The signal has been given to the potential rebels that if they do their worst, it is without her support. The party wants unity, not a fresh bout of division. I give the same message to the Sunday lobby who show a deep interest in just who is coming to the dinner party at Blackpool.

TUESDAY 5 OCTOBER

Blackpool. The day opens with the front pages dominated by the attempt to overthrow Yeltsin in Moscow – with one exception. The *Mirror* claims to have a copy of the Thatcher memoirs, memoirs which it says are highly critical of John Major. The charge is that she regards the Prime Minister as a lightweight. The press is very excited by the story but inside the conference hall it hardly causes a ripple. As I suspected,

---

280 The very best of the political reporters.

calls for unity are loudly applauded and there is a wish for reconciliation between Major and Thatcher. I make the point, 'for years I was called a Thatcherite. Now I am called a Majorite and I wear both labels with pride.' That is greeted with prolonged applause and at the end I receive a long standing ovation. So much for the stories that I would be heckled in my opening speech!

The mood established in the morning continues. The European debate has none of the cheers and counter-cheers of 1992. The lager louts in their T-shirts do not seem to have made it to Blackpool. It is not that the EEC or Maastricht has suddenly become popular. It is that no one wants to rock the boat this year.

In the evening a dinner with John and the National Union. He is very edgy about Margaret Thatcher's visit. He sees no advantage in even the appearance of reconciliation. Apparently, he is happy for the current standoff to continue indefinitely. He refuses point blank to kiss her on the cheek and threatens to ignore her altogether. The dinner itself goes well enough until the last fifteen minutes. John then discovers that *The Times* are holding a party in the hotel and that a number of Cabinet ministers are likely to attend. How can Cabinet colleagues attend a reception given by *The Times* after all they have done, he asks. I suggest politicians will turn up for receptions given by newspapers. It is the name of the game. That does not mollify him one bit. He even threatens to raise it at Cabinet. The officers of the National Union watch on with bemused expressions. He has taken the press criticism far too much to heart. It is getting in the way of his judgement but he still will not stop reading the papers. He encourages the very process which hurts him so much. Because the editors and writers know only too well about his legendary sensitivity, they see a target and they jab away at it. They have a Prime Minister who really deeply cares about what they say.

WEDNESDAY 6 OCTOBER

Again the conference goes well. Michael Howard makes one of the meatiest speeches ever given by any minister at a party conference. It will be criticised as electioneering on crime but what too many of the comfortable middle-class experts fail to understand is just how seriously ordinary people in the country take it. The rest of my day is dominated by managing Margaret. She arrives shortly before 6 p.m. I take her into the hotel through a thick scrum of photographers. She ignores all questions about her book and we go up to her suite. No sooner have we arrived than we are joined by Alistair McAlpine, Tim Bell and Gordon Reece. The old court in exile although Gordon at least would like to be a member of the new court too. Downstairs, she visits the women's reception. The response is fascinating. There is not an instant burst of applause as she enters. They are glad to see her but she is not seen as a god. She goes to another reception and I receive a message asking me to see the Prime Minister. There is still an hour to go before Margaret is due for dinner in my suite.

I find John in a mood of black depression. He has obviously already sounded off to his staff and Sarah and the rest melt away, leaving us alone. John's message is that it 'won't do'. He doesn't agree with how I am handling Margaret. He doesn't feel that she should have been welcomed, he doesn't feel that she should have been asked to fundraise and (quite clearly but not explicitly expressed) he doesn't feel that she should have been asked to dinner.

His complaint here is that he was going to take his staff to a fish and chip dinner tonight. That is now impossible. Why? Because it would lead to stories that the poor old Prime Minister could find no one else to have dinner with but his staff while the chairman was entertaining his predecessor at a slap-up dinner.

My reply to all this is that he does not seem to understand that the conference is going well – much better than we might have hoped, that the party is coming together and that part of the reason for this success is the silencing of the rebels because of the way we are handling Margaret. Well, he says, he is not going anywhere near her on the platform. My reply to that is that he should at least go past her and pat her on the shoulder or shake hands. A friendly peck is quite obviously a bridge too far! Eventually, he thaws and gives me his speech to look through (late as usual), which is coming on fine. I leave him ordering a meal from room service, having refused Norma's sensible suggestion that they should all bring the fish and chips to him.

John may be difficult at times but my dinner with Margaret establishes just how impossible she has now become. The other guests are John and Penny Gummer, Alison Wakeham (John is speaking at a meeting), Charles Hambro, Maurice Saatchi, Michael Bishop and Paul Judge and his wife. It is not that she deliberately intends to be disloyal, at least I think that is the case. It is rather that it all comes pouring out. Touch a button and you will get the frank response. No one quite knows what will come next.

I start cautiously on the progress of her book launch. She tells me that she is spending two and a half hours a day simply signing her name. These are for special plates that will be stuck in the books. But the book doesn't satisfy her. She quite deliberately turns the conversation to current politics. We are talking one-to-one and not to the table at large. 'Kenneth Clarke', she says, 'is behaving disgracefully. He is undermining the Prime Minister. He is running for his job.' She will take no contradiction. She is totally determined in her view that Ken is simply making an unscrupulous play for the succession.

John Gummer then comes into the conversation and steers it towards foreign affairs. A big mistake. We do well enough on Russia but then there is a short trip to Bosnia. Margaret says it is disgraceful that the Muslims have been deprived of arms. John reasonably asks how the further arming of the Muslims would have helped stop the bloodshed. The dispute escalates upwards. John begins to look agitated and finally, Margaret brings it to an end. 'John', she says, 'you are wrong. I am not going to continue arguing it. Just understand you are wrong.'

Eventually I have to slip away to join up with the Prime Minister's party at the Young Conservatives Ball. Fiona is left in charge and both Maurice and Michael Bishop tell me she does splendidly.

Margaret has not mellowed. She has still not come to terms with the loss of office. She feels passionately that no Prime Minister should have to endure what she did. She no longer has the discipline of the No. 10 machine and is thus a loose cannon. But for the public, she remains

THE BEST OF ENEMIES

a towering figure. Probably the greatest political figure since Churchill. That means, in spite of all the difficulties, we have to live with her. John's way will simply not do. I do not claim that finding a modus vivendi will be easy. Almost certainly there will be crises and upsets along the way but it is a better course forward than any other. We cannot afford the conflict to continue.

THURSDAY 7 OCTOBER

Margaret's appearance at the conference goes like a dream. I take her onto the platform in the middle of the employment debate. She gets a good reception at the conference but it is not overwhelming. It is nothing like the reception she received in 1991, nor as prolonged as the one last year when I had to bring it to an end. Most of the conference take my view of the grand old lady. They respect her achievements but now want to move on. When I bring John Major onto the platform, the reception is deafening, and deliberately longer.

FRIDAY 8 OCTOBER

The last day of the conference. My second speech goes well which is a nice end. More to the point, John's speech goes much better than last year. The ovation goes on for over ten minutes and we make our way out through a still cheering audience. For John it is a successful end to a gruelling week. And most significant of all, the party have come together. It has been a very successful conference, I tell John. 'I am afraid you have not had much help from me', he observes wryly.

22

BACK TO BASICS

OCTOBER 1993–FEBRUARY 1994

Even today, 'Back to Basics' is reported as a moral campaign mounted by Major which swiftly and disastrously blew up in the Prime Minister's face. The truth is different. Major used the fateful phrase in his speech at the very end of the Conservative Party conference in October 1993. His actual words deserve to be repeated. 'We must go back to basics', he said. We want our children to be taught the best; our British industry to be the best. And the Conservative Party will lead the country back to these basics right across the board: sound money; free trade; traditional teaching; respect for the family and the law. And above all, lead a new campaign to defeat the cancer that is crime.'

THURSDAY 14 OCTOBER–WEDNESDAY 20 OCTOBER 1993

Almost a week in the United States. Fiona and I stay in a house near the waterfront at Alexandria just outside Washington. The occasion of the visit is a housing conference but I take the opportunity to meet the ambassador, Christopher Meyer, who is to be the new head of information at No. 10. My advice to Christopher is that he must wean the Prime Minister away from his minute study of the British press. If John continues in the way he has over the last twelve months it will destroy him. He takes his judgements on himself from the press. I was surprised how starkly I put this point but it is the most important.

THURSDAY 21 OCTOBER

To the *Birmingham Post* Literary Dinner for Margaret Thatcher. Her book sales are going incredibly well. Her reception at Birmingham

467

shows why. We could have sold the tickets for the dinner three times over.[281] The audience are not particularly interested in reading the 900-page book. They want to see a living legend. They want to hear her speak. They want her signature. A little piece of history. The Lord Mayor turns up and the bookselling dinner is transformed into a great public occasion, somewhere between a royal visit and a farewell tour by some much-loved opera singer. From the beginning she has the audience eating out of her hand – 'I can see I am among friends' – and at the end the audience rise to applaud her before forming an orderly queue for her book. What do I notice about the speech? The entire speech is couched in what 'I' achieved. Very rarely 'We'. At no stage does she refer to her successor as Prime Minister. At one point, when describing the Cabinet's decision to send forces to the Falklands, she looks at me. She is describing how the Cabinet were at one in confirming her decision to send the task force. Of course, as she well remembers, they were not. John Biffen argued against but as Chairman of the party I have no complaint. As Elizabeth Buchanan, the star lady who handles her press relations, says, she is trying very hard to behave.

MONDAY 15 NOVEMBER

No. 12 meeting. I argue that the Back to Basics theme is being hijacked for attacks on single families. I assume we are not opposed to deserted mothers, the divorced and widows. That leaves teenage pregnancies, so what is our line? An awkward pause. There is no real reply. Finally, it is agreed that Tony Newton should do his best to put together a case starting with the proposition that it is the interests of the children which come first. We all agree that we want to get off single families and onto law and order, education and the economy.

TUESDAY 16 NOVEMBER

John Major's remarks on the Irish question dominate the headlines. He

---

281 The *Birmingham Post* was the best-known title in the Midland Independent Newspapers group of which I was Chairman.

has decided to show his willingness to seek a fresh solution. Entirely right. The Irish government want this, so does British public opinion. We should not be over-optimistic but the attempt is well worth making.

MONDAY 22 NOVEMBER

A meeting with the MEPs. According to Christopher Prout, relations have been immensely helped by their move to Central Office. 'It's so different from 1989', he says. The MEPs have particularly sour memories of the European elections then. I have no doubt that we will fight a better campaign but how can we do better unless we can improve our position in the opinion polls?

MONDAY 13 DECEMBER

Charles Hambro is concerned that the message he is receiving from the Prime Minister is that he does not want Margaret Thatcher to be given a fundraising role. I take this head on with John and receive the same bleak reply. He resents 'what she goes around saying about me' but says that 'it is up to you. You know what I feel. I don't want to discuss it.' It is all very well but the fact remains that Margaret Thatcher will be around for a long time to come. There is no way that they are capable of becoming friends but it is sensible politics to hide their enmity.

WEDNESDAY 15 DECEMBER

To the Commons in the afternoon to hear John Major make his statement on Northern Ireland. He speaks with authority and has the support of virtually everyone in the House. Predictably, one of the few to attack him is Ian Paisley but John puts him down conclusively. We will be lucky to succeed in our goal. The chances must be that the IRA are now so steeped in evil that they will refuse to lay down their arms and talk. Nevertheless, it is an attempt well worth making. The public mood demands some such action. It is important that the British public continue to support our policies in Northern Ireland. It will be all too easy for them to wash their hands of the whole issue. This, after all, is what the IRA aim to achieve.

TUESDAY 21 DECEMBER

A long lunch with Shirley, John and Caroline. My office at Central Office represents all that is good about the organisation: hard work and loyalty. In spite of all the criticisms, Central Office is the jewel in the crown of the party. Give me them rather than the parliamentary party any time. As for Caroline, I simply could not do without her. If she left my whole life would change. She runs my office impeccably. She has now been with me for fifteen years. Irreplaceable.

WEDNESDAY 22 DECEMBER

The last meeting of the No. 12 committee for the year. At the end of the meeting, Richard Ryder asks me to come next door where I find John Gummer. The meeting is about the future of Tim Yeo who Richard has already told me has been having an affair and is now the father of a child. Richard thinks that the birth of a child outside marriage makes the government's position on the family look ridiculous and that Yeo should go. John disagrees. The mother is able to look after the child. She is a professional woman who is not looking for any publicity and is not going to have to rely on social security. I am asked to decide. Without hesitation I back Yeo. It is a private matter and does not remotely affect his job in the environment department. In my view, we would look ridiculous if we sacked Yeo just because the *News of the World* was about to run a story on him and the child.

THURSDAY 30 DECEMBER

End of year report. Outside, the rain is lashing against the skylights of my attic study. The last two months have seen one dreary wet day after another. In spite of this there are at long last signs of the public mood lifting. The stock market is at a record high. The post-Christmas sales are doing a roaring trade. Unemployment is coming down. Inflation is down, interest rates are low. Above all, individual ministers have shone. Ken Clarke and Michael Howard have been two ministerial stars, an entire justification of the reshuffle. It should mean that the political mood is also improving but so far there has been little sign of this. We continue to lose council by-elections, mainly to the Liberals, and the opinion polls show little signs of improvement.

The longer I remain in this job at Central Office, the more sceptical I am of some of our MPs. Some are just bloody awkward and frequently disloyal. They will fill half a column with anonymous comments, usually about colleagues or their policies. 'One senior backbencher said', etc. In truth they are not always backbenchers. The maverick, the sour, the disgruntled, the frustrated are a powerful alliance and it becomes stronger as the years of government extend. Perhaps the prospect of losing their own seats will concentrate their minds.

So where does this leave me? I have virtually completed the job of turning round the party organisation. The next chairman can let the organisation run itself. I have no wish to return to Cabinet. I want to stay in the Commons but not as a member of the government.

FRIDAY 31 DECEMBER

I am attacked by the *Daily Mail* and doubtless other papers for sticking up for Yeo. How dare I suggest that this is a private matter for Yeo and his family and the lady involved. It is a matter of public interest although no one can say how it can affect Yeo's job in the environment department.

TUESDAY 4 JANUARY 1994

The wolves are closing in around Tim Yeo. All depends on the meeting with his association this evening. The usual assumption is that the local association will rally to support their member but not this association.

WEDNESDAY 5 JANUARY

The phone rings at 7.15 with Tony Garrett reporting on last night's meeting. They intend to issue a statement later in the morning but the most it does in supporting Tim is to 'acknowledge' his parliamentary service. It then goes on to rehearse the concern and widespread disappointment and criticism being expressed in the constituency. The sting in the tail comes when the officers urge Tim to 'reflect on the views expressed'. In other words, do the decent thing and resign.

The Chief Whip and I then see Tim. Tim is entirely dignified. He obviously feels that he has done nothing that he needs to apologise for. He agrees in minutes that he will go from the government and that the resignation should come from him. He is concerned above all that the press should stop pursuing his wife and the other woman. As with David Mellor we are losing a good minister.

We leave him to draft his statement and I talk to John, who is most concerned that the affair should not damage the Back to Basics message. He never set it out as a message of personal morality but I fear that is how it is being seen. We will have difficulty rewriting the script at this stage.

THURSDAY 6 JANUARY

The Prime Minister is right. The Back to Basics policy lies in tatters according to the press. The Prime Minister is blamed, and I am blamed. The dreadful (William) Rees-Mogg cannot contain his glee at the turn of events and calls for me to go. The reaction is all wildly over the top and Philip Webster of *The Times*, whom I meet by chance in the Commons, says 'it is not up to you to sack ministers'. Let them think what they like. I would prefer to be attacked for standing by a colleague rather than stabbing him in the back. In my view we were right to defend him when the *News of the World* story appeared. The press talks about moral principles although God knows how many of the editors and leader writers are adulterers. I had always regarded understanding and forgiveness to be principles too.

FRIDAY 7 JANUARY

It is going from bad to worse. The latest story concerns a backbencher, David Ashby. The charge is that he has left his wife and set up house with a bloke. The *Sunday Times* (can this be the kind of story a quality newspaper reports?) is onto the story. Ashby is seeking an injunction and in the meantime I am being attacked by all and sundry. Paul Johnson and the *Mail* pretend to speak for Tory constituency opinion. Surely it cannot be the same Johnson who was a far-left activist and editor of the *New Statesman*. David Evans, a not very bright new member of right-wing beliefs, has another go at me and to cap it so does the Chief Whip's constituency chairman. He apparently believes that the whips report to me and then I sack ministers. I toy with the idea of sending him a telegram telling him to take up the issue with his own MP.

To round off the day, Richard Ryder rings me to say that the press has a story on another of our backbenchers, Alan Duncan, who is also PPS to the Health Minister. It involves using the right to buy policy for council houses to finance the purchase of a house next to him in Gayfere Street. There is nothing illegal in what he has done so we are advised, but it is alleged to be sharp practice. The press is now in full cry.

SATURDAY 8 JANUARY

Another dreadful day with the papers still dominated by Back to Basics. Richard rings early to say that Duncan is prepared to go from his position as a PPS. Do we say yes? If he does not resign then the Prime Minister will be attacked at the first Question Time when the House resumes. 'Is this what the government mean by their right to buy policy?' Full marks to Duncan for doing the right thing quickly.

Shortly after I return home, the phone rings. It is Tim Yeo. He wants me to know that he has a second illegitimate child. It was twenty-seven years ago at university and the child was adopted. There have been no repercussions and everything has gone smoothly until this week. The press has been digging and have found the story. Why Tim did not tell us before goodness only knows. We can defend one child but two?

The next news is even more ghastly. Richard Ryder rings to say that Malcolm Caithness's wife has shot herself. The suspicion is that Malcolm has been having an affair. It could not be worse. Yeo could be written off as pantomime but this is the suicide of a mother leaving two children. He says the news is not known yet but is bound to become public in the next twenty-four hours.

SUNDAY 9 JANUARY

The Sunday press is terrible. Yeo's second child is the main interest, followed by Alan Duncan and the Westminster Council house story, followed by a piece about Ashby. It could not be a worse prelude to the television interviews that both the Prime Minister and I are doing.

I watch John on the Frost programme and then drive to No. 10. He is worried that he was low-key. Not surprising, given the circumstances, but he did not put a foot wrong. It may not have been inspiring but it didn't deepen the crisis. Similarly, my interview with Peter Allen went perfectly well, as did the news interviews afterwards. Challenged on my support for Yeo I replied that it would be extraordinary if the chairman of the party did not defend a government minister. So it would be. Had I gone the other way I would have precipitated his resignation and doubtless would also be blamed for that. In the evening the Prime Minister rings up to say that Malcolm Caithness has resigned and the story of his wife's suicide is now out.

MONDAY 10 JANUARY

No sensible work is being done. The events of last week wrecked the three days put aside for election preparation and today is no better. The tragedy of Caithness's wife is now all over the press. Michael Howard has a torrid time on *Today* and refuses to define the government's attitude to adultery. The debate is getting out of hand with the BBC playing as gleeful a part as any tabloid newspaper. The 'respectable' reason for raising it all is Back to Basics. It is just like Marcus Lipton raising Profumo as a 'security' issue years ago. The truth is that the media (the BBC very much included) are fascinated by the scandal and the sex.

Richard Ryder warns that there is worse to come with a report by the district auditor on the tangled affairs of Westminster Council on Thursday. Shirley Porter, the former council leader and the great protégée of Margaret Thatcher, is the main culprit. One touch of farce during the afternoon. Ashby, for reasons totally unknown, decides to give an interview to the Press Association. He admits that he shared a bed with a man but says that he had often done this in the past and anyone who jumped to conclusions simply had 'a dirty mind.' General hilarity in Central Office.

More sinister are the activities of the press. It is believed that the alleged 'other woman' in the Caithness case has a name very similar to Michael Ancram's wife's maiden name. The result is that they are besieging Michael's home. They have the wrong woman. A little later, a statement comes over to Central Office from Michael Ancram: 'My wife, Jane Ancram, has met Lord Caithness only once or twice in the mid-1980s at public functions and otherwise does not know him. I would be grateful if you would now leave our premises. We do not intend to answer further questions or issue further statements.' We shall see if the press report their own stupidity.

TUESDAY 11 JANUARY

An early start with the *Today* programme. Predictably, I am asked my attitude to adultery. My reply is that I do not approve of adultery but that is not the question. The question is whether adultery means that a minister cannot do his job and must resign and the answer to that depends on the circumstances. In other words, it must be considered case by case. The interview goes well but the *Evening Standard* reward it with a report which says that there is still a place in the government for adulterers. John is still in Brussels and Prime Minister's Questions are taken by Tony Newton. Our side looks demoralised although the whips say the spirit is better than they had imagined.

WEDNESDAY 12 JANUARY

We are now preoccupied with the next row. Westminster Council. The only thing I insist upon at No. 12 is that this time we should make every effort to know what the actual position is. In particular, we must know whether Peter Brooke and John Wheeler knew what was happening.[282]

---

282 This was a genuine issue of public concern. The district auditor was told he could not publish the findings of his four-year inquiry into alleged gerrymandering by the Conservative-run Westminster Council. The row involved Dame Shirley Porter, the former council leader, and Barry Legg, a Tory MP. He also looked into allegations that Sir John Wheeler, Minister of State for Northern Ireland, and Peter Brooke, Secretary of State for National Heritage, MPs for the two Westminster constituencies, were involved in the early planning of the 'designated sales' policy.

THURSDAY 13 JANUARY

The Westminster Council announcement will come later this morning. I am shown the answers that Peter Brooke will give. Frankly, they are not very convincing. John Wakeham takes a different view. 'They must be improved', he says, entirely missing the point about what the true position is.

Inside the House the affair goes off without incident. Outside the House the press can hardly fail to have a field day. We cannot complain. Corruption is a matter of public concern. It is frankly a rather sleazy leftover from the Thatcher years but I fear that is not a defence.

The meeting of the 1922 goes off without incident and in the evening I dine in the Members' dining room. I even buy a bottle of champagne to celebrate the birth of Gerry Malone's baby son, born very much in wedlock. Michael Ancram is also there. He says that no fewer than thirty-five journalists and cameramen including the BBC turned up at his home. The rat pack chasing the wrong victim.

FRIDAY 14 JANUARY

The press on Westminster Council is dreadful and it is difficult to see how to counter-attack. 'No rush to judgement' is one line; attack the process of the district auditor is another: neither will convince the public. Nor will we get very far by saying Labour are equally bad, however true that may be. Westminster puts Yeo into context. Yeo is sexual verging on pantomime with a new baby appearing from the wings at each new act. Westminster is corruption.

Back in London the phone rings twice. First, the good news that the special meeting in Suffolk have backed Yeo as their MP. The second, from Graham Bright, is the bad news. The Prime Minister is being quoted in the press as having launched a savage attack on the right of his Cabinet at a private dinner along the lines of 'I'll crucify the bastards for hijacking Back to Basics.'

SATURDAY 15 JANUARY

For once I buy *The Sun*. 'Government Crisis' it exclaims. And then, a lurid account of the Prime Minister's alleged conversation. I notice it is by Simon Walters and Trevor Kavanagh. Simon Walters was the number two political correspondent and as I remember well, an imaginative reporter. When I resigned from the government, he invented a whole nineteen-hour day for me. It was not hostile, quite kind, but largely fictitious. Gus tells me that there is no truth in the piece and suspects Michael Brunson of being the source of it. When I ring John I find him in a very low mood. I say he should laugh the story off. We must not increase its importance. John says that is also Bernard Ingham's advice.

SUNDAY 16 JANUARY

Gus's efforts to downplay the story have been unsuccessful. Most of the press leads with the Downing Street dinner. The BBC continues to pump the allegation out every hour. There is such an atmosphere of crisis around the government that anything sticks. The trivial is inflated into the serious substance of politics, added to which the media can smell blood. The ideological (Moore and Stoddard) combine with the mischievous (Kelvin MacKenzie) and the opportunistic (English and Dacre). For their different reasons they love the drama. They acquired a taste for it in the events leading up to the fall of Thatcher. Normal political life is dull in comparison. Just as war correspondents find difficulty in adjusting to peace, so too do the editors. In the real world the stock market is booming and the economy recovering but the headlines of the last two weeks have been dominated by the trivial and the unimportant.

WEDNESDAY 19 JANUARY

Danger signals all round. The Prime Minister wants us to hit back at John Smith and his campaign of smear and character assassination. The result is that Tim Collins, Andrew and I spend a couple of hours considering a challenge to Smith. As it happens, our efforts are overtaken by a Labour backbencher, the maverick George Galloway, who is reported as praising Saddam Hussein in glowing terms on a visit to Iraq. At once, the media turn on Labour and Smith is forced to disown his supporter while Galloway himself sets out a number of unconvincing defences on why he has been misunderstood.

MONDAY 24 JANUARY

Brian Redhead has died aged sixty-four. The *Today* programme is full of tributes. I remember him as above all a fair reporter, not an interviewer intent upon talking down his subject. During the National Health Service strike I actually won an apology from him. Unknown to me the BBC had sent a reporter to my house in the very early morning. There had been a ring at the bell and Fiona had told the caller that it was far too early and to get in touch with the press office. Brian had announced on radio that 'Fowler is refusing to come out of his house so I will interview Rodney Bickerstaffe.' I had been blithely unaware of it all including the door bell ringer and when this was pointed out, Brian had apologised on air. The one and only time I have ever won a correction from the BBC.

THURSDAY 27 JANUARY

Jeffrey Archer gives an interview to the BBC in which he puts in a public application for the job of Party Chairman. What a chump. Does he really think that this is the way to get the job? I am cheered up by a headhunter I sit next to during an industrial dinner. 'Would I be interested in taking on any other companies as well as Midland Newspapers?' 'Not before June', I reply.

FRIDAY 28 JANUARY

A day in Birmingham. Douglas Hurd at both lunch and dinner. He is a success at the Chamber of Commerce. He explains in simple terms just why it is good that the Foreign Office know about business as well as politics. He defends aid with commercial strings and is listened to attentively by an audience who in the past have been less than enthusiastic about Conservative policy. He is a genuine elder statesman who talks with absolute authority. The evening event is marred by reports from Tim Collins of an interview that Norman Lamont has given to *The Times*. In it he calls the Prime Minister 'weak and hopeless' and makes various other complaints about John. It looks very black but it then transpires that Lamont is denying that he said it. 'Out of context and off the record' is his less than convincing defence. Let Lamont and *The Times* fight it out.

SATURDAY 29 JANUARY

The other newspapers have fallen on the interview with glee. The BBC solemnly report that even if not a true account of what is said, it could have been. So much for the standards of Lord Reith.

MONDAY 31 JANUARY

Rover is to be bought by BMW. The news comes over the radio as I drive into Downing Street. Sadly, a sale of this kind or something like it was inevitable. No manufacturer the size of Rover could hope to survive indefinitely. The only choice was the bride. In the West Midlands I suspect they would have preferred Honda. Curiously, the Japanese are rated higher as owners or partners than the Germans.

At No. 10 I find John in a very grim mood, not about Rover but about the events of the weekend. He sets out a plan. It is basically to go to the 1922 Committee this Thursday and confront the parliamentary party. He would say 'we are letting down the party and the country. We need to end the factionalism. I will lead but if you cannot follow under these terms then you should find another leader.' In other words, 'back me or sack me'.

As the day goes on I consider John's plan. At first hearing it sounds extreme, even reckless, but then what have we to lose? By the evening meeting with Jonathan and Christopher Meyer, I am running in support. The other two also support. As Christopher says, the Prime Minister's reputation is in spiralling decline. The new element that has been added during the day is that rather than 'back me or sack me' the cry will be 'I am taking our cause to the country. I am going out from Whitehall. Unite and follow me.' Better. Having slept on it John might have other ideas by tomorrow. I hope not. His basic political instincts are normally good.

TUESDAY I FEBRUARY

John is meeting George Gardiner and his group this afternoon. They have heavily leaked their visit and he intends to throw them out. During the afternoon, the news comes through that he has done just that. The meeting lasted less than two minutes. The news that Gardiner has been thrown out spreads quickly through the lobbies, much to the delight of most of the parliamentary party. The general view is that 'it couldn't have happened to a nicer bloke' but we need more than the head of Gardiner. John still needs to go to the 1922.

WEDNESDAY 2 FEBRUARY

At No. 12 there are chuckles all round on John's well-reported action in throwing out Gardiner. New jokes are already being offered.

'I have a spare thirty seconds. Could I see the Prime Minister?'

'The open door has become the revolving door.'

Less amusement over Gerry Adams's visit to the US which is evidently a public relations triumph. It doesn't say much for the American media. They have allowed him to get away with the IRA case. In the evening, Fiona and I have dinner with Peter and Taheré Temple-Morris. After weeks of hesitation I first invited Fiona out to our joint 40th birthday party in 1978 in Hampstead. A real turning point for me. I hope Fiona still feels the same. I am not sure she bargained for the kind of politics that now fills the paper day after day.

THURSDAY 3 FEBRUARY

The Prime Minister does go to the 1922 and it is magnificent. I have never heard him speak better. The message is blunt. Unless the party comes together we will go into opposition. 'Unite and fight' is his message and they all get to their feet and applaud. True, I notice some like Powell and Cash getting to their feet slowly but even they manage it. I hurry away to brief the lobby in their upstairs lobby room and take them through his speech. No awkward questions. We have taken them by surprise. Their deadlines press. The party is delighted, the loyalists purr, we have the initiative.

FRIDAY 4 FEBRUARY

The press fully report John's triumph but it is too good to last. As the old team, Tim, Andrew and myself, pore over my speech to the Young Conservatives' conference tomorrow at Southport, we receive Jeffrey Archer's speech for the same conference. It is a terrible pastiche of a company chairman reporting to shareholders. It contains one passage of undoubted danger when he tells disloyal ministers to resign,[283] just the message that we don't want this weekend. We want to put our fire on Labour. Jonathan is embarrassed as Archer has shown his speech to the Prime Minister who has ticked it through as approved. This is intolerable. I send through a message that I need to see the Prime Minister urgently. Twenty minutes later the message comes back that the Prime Minister now agrees with me. Archer will be told to alter the speech. Needless to say, Archer has released his speech already. The next chairman of the party!

MONDAY 7 FEBRUARY

During the afternoon I find myself with no meetings and untypically drift into Shirley's room, put my feet up and watch Sky news. The predictions are that the increase in US interest rates will lead to a crash in the stock market. As I watch I become aware that Shirley is at the receiving end of what is obviously becoming a very emotional telephone call. 'Please don't cry', I hear her say. Eventually she ends having taken the number. Shirley is obviously shaken and explains the identity of the caller.

'She says she is Stephen Milligan's secretary. She has just found him dead and is now at Hammersmith police station.'

We check the Commons directory and sure enough she is shown as Stephen's secretary. Our initial disbelief is giving way to the dawning realisation that we are in the middle of a ghastly tragedy. I ring back and speak to a very distraught woman when a detective constable intervenes to say that we shouldn't speak over the phone in case it is tapped.

---

283   The obvious challenge is who are these disloyal ministers?

Would you like me to come down? I ask. She would.

So far, the conversation has been about the body she found in Stephen Milligan's house. 'Can you just confirm one point?' I ask, 'is there any doubt about the identification?'

The voice breaks at the other end of the line. 'I can't', she says. 'It's impossible.'

'God what has happened?' I think. Has he been murdered? The face smashed?

A phone call to the whips. Richard Ryder is not around but I speak to Greg Knight, his deputy. They are also getting first reports of the death via the police at the Palace of Westminster. Thirty minutes later Gerry and I are at Hammersmith police station. A television crew is already there. How? So much for a private visit. So much for not speaking over the phone. Gerry and I wait in line with various clients. A man on a bench strums a guitar bringing down curses on 'the pinstripes', '*The Times*' and the 'SDP' (obviously a 1980s hippy). A man with an official badge, a probation officer, responds to a call from the police desk as to whether anyone has any crimes to report. 'The crime against the British people in 1992' he shouts before disappearing into the station.

Eventually, a detective sergeant comes and escorts us to a CID office. Slowly over the next hours the story emerges. It clearly is Stephen Milligan's body and according to the superintendent in charge of the case there seem to be all kinds of bizarre features. A naked body wearing women's black stockings with a plastic bag over his head. The plastic bag explains why he could not be identified.

The police we speak to are at pains to say that they cannot yet confirm identity, let alone any other aspects of the case. Investigations are still taking place at Stephen's home. I of course accept this although when I ring Tim at Central Office he says that the lobby is full of stories about Stephen's death and all its lurid details. What is not known yet is whether it is suicide, murder, or most likely, some act of his own.

His secretary tells us that she went to Stephen's house when he did not turn up at Westminster. She found the key to the house and then the body in the kitchen. She wants to go back to Westminster but I advise her very firmly against that. She would be set upon by the press and eventually she agrees to go home in a police car and not to return until we have contacted her in the morning.

As I leave there is a battery of TV cameras. I report the line that Gerry and I have agreed: 'No identification has taken place but obviously there are fears that it is Stephen Milligan. If it is, then it is a great personal tragedy and loss to politics'.

We return to Central Office and none of us have the heart to go to the winter ball where we are due. We end the day eating pizzas and watching the news programmes, which seem remarkably well-informed. Fiona comes in from the ball soon after 11 p.m. and we return to Hurlingham Road shattered and depressed. What a way for a man of such ability to go. Sad and tragic. Apparently he had nothing to do that weekend. No meetings, no friends to see. A lonely man drawn in on himself.

TUESDAY 8 FEBRUARY

The papers give blanket and detailed coverage of Stephen Milligan's death. One exception is the BBC. When I am interviewed on *Today*, Peter Hobday exhibits a restraint which is unique among the media. Doubtless they will be roundly criticised for it. It does need to be remembered that so far the cause of death has not been discovered. The mood on our side of the House is gloomy and depressed. The party has been sent reeling. Most of my colleagues consider the Milligan case above all sad. Not all. One comes up to say we should not praise his political skills. Another, Peter Tapsell, says we should keep people 'like him' off the candidates' list. Just how, pray, does he think Central Office can vet the private habits of candidates?

WEDNESDAY 9 FEBRUARY

The Stephen Milligan case is still the headline but there has now become a new line. A number of colleagues are saying that the police leaked the details and that Milligan's parents only discovered the news through a television broadcast. It is undoubtedly true that the news about the death was leaking all over the place. The details of his death almost certainly came through the police. Not the senior policeman I was talking to but down the line. Who leaked my visit to Hammersmith police station? But for all that we will not win a battle of this kind with the police. The police will say, quite accurately, that much of the information emanated from Westminster. It was the political correspondents not the crime correspondents who knew most.

THURSDAY 10 FEBRUARY

A new revelation in *The Sun* and the *Mail*. Apparently during my time at Hammersmith police station I had a 'stand-up' row with Superintendent Edwards, the officer in charge of the Milligan case. Not only did I not have such a row but to my knowledge I have never met Superintendent Edwards. I issue a correcting statement but even so the *Evening Standard* are condemning me in the leader columns of their first and second editions. We manage to get it out by the last edition. Another example of the 'too good to check' story. The national press bleat about their rights and campaign against the law of privacy but their standards are at times lamentable. It is nothing to do with their rights, it is everything to do with their professionalism. Accuracy must be the minimum standard required of any journalist on any paper.

FRIDAY 11 FEBRUARY

The Sun still persists with their untrue story. They refuse to publish a correction so what now? Sue or let it go? The question that everyone treated unfairly by the press has to ask. We should not be so concerned about press invasions of privacy but much more about the press ignoring the demand for accuracy and their refusal to make amends when they have got it wrong.

SATURDAY 12 FEBRUARY

Incredibly, there is a new scandal. Hartley Booth, Margaret's successor in Finchley, has been discovered having an 'affair' with some 22-year-old woman student who worked for him. In normal times it would hardly raise a mention. These days it is front page news. He is a senior Tory we are told. In fact, he is the PPS to a Minister of State, a pretty lowly bag carrier. Nevertheless, the formalities have to be gone through. He has told everyone that he is going to resign but incredibly, his minister, Douglas Hogg, is refusing to accept it. When I ring Douglas he is emphatic. 'There is a McCarthy-like atmosphere. Someone must make a stand.' Normally Richard and I are attacked for defending. This time the attack is on the opposite flank. When I ring him again having spoken to Alex Allan,[284] Richard Ryder and Tim Collins who has intelligence on the *Sunday Mirror* report, it is my turn to be emphatic. 'He has already announced he is offering his resignation.' It is not like Yeo. Yeo did not offer his resignation. It would be untenable to refuse Booth's resignation. Finally, Douglas accepts the case and his resignation is made official. An all too familiar Saturday evening spent phoning round the country trying to firefight and handle yet another little local difficulty.

SUNDAY 13 FEBRUARY

The Sunday papers are all about Booth. Methodist lay preacher and the nude model is about as extreme as the headlines get. In the local newsagents I am looking for a Valentine's card so hear the comments of the public as they buy their papers. 'I don't believe it. Not another one.' 'They are all the same these bloody MPs'.

MONDAY 21 FEBRUARY

To the Commons to vote on the homosexual age of consent. In the debate the age of sixteen has by far the strongest advocates. In the vote the decision is eighteen. The House, me included, does not feel brave enough to go from twenty-one to sixteen. The age of majority of eighteen is a sensible compromise. The House of Commons is surrounded by hundreds of gay demonstrators with candles. When the vote becomes known some become rough. They do not make any new friends tonight

---

284 Principal private secretary to John Major 1992–1997 and to Tony Blair at the beginning of his premiership. Later became British High Commissioner to Australia and Chair of the Joint Intelligence Committee. He resigned as Boris Johnson's Independent Adviser on Ministers' Interests in November 2020.

though I suspect that we have not heard the last of this issue. Sooner or later the age will come down to sixteen.

COMMENT

Considering the words that Major actually said at the end of the party conference, it seems almost incredible that the speech should have been interpreted as some kind of crusade about personal morality. The trouble was that like so many announcements from No. 10 it was released at the last minute without the press office being properly briefed. Major consistently protested that he had no intention of trying to tell people how they should lead their private lives. With the benefit of the later revelations about Major's affair with Edwina Currie we can see how crass the moral interpretation was. Major was not a fool. He was hardly likely to start a campaign which could end up with him as the chief victim. The real reason is that the speech gave some of the media a bogus justification to do what they wanted to do in any event. David Mellor was pursued relentlessly way before the 'Back to Basics' speech. Major's speech was useful fuel for a fresh foray into the private lives of Conservative politicians.

23

THE DEATH OF JOHN SMITH

FEBRUARY–JULY 1994

MONDAY 7 FEBRUARY 1994

A day dominated by the prospect of privacy legislation. It starts at
No. 12 when it is revealed that Peter Brooke intends to make a
statement in the House and introduce a white paper next week. This is
precisely the kind of announcement we don't want in the run up to the
local elections. A surer way of alienating the public, not to mention the
press, is difficult to imagine. The most remarkable conversation takes
place. It becomes clear that all three of the politicians present agree but
despite that, they have allowed it to get to this stage. Richard Ryder has
always been against it and obviously welcomes my intervention. Tony
Newton concedes he has his doubts and that he fears ministers are split
on the subject. Most extraordinarily of all, John Wakeham now says that
it is always dangerous to bring in legislation where ministers are split.
Well, so it is. But who is the chairman of the committee that decides
which legislation should go forward? He turns to me to explain: 'This
has been driven by the Prime Minister'. Well so it has. We all know that.
But one of an adviser's functions is to tell the Prime Minister when he
has got it wrong. We are politicians not courtiers.

Only Sarah Hogg has a good word to say for the plans. Her strongest
argument is that the press know that it is coming. How do we explain
the delay? My reply to that is typically truculent. I am an admirer of
Sarah. 'Give me two or three minutes and I will work one out but as I
have not been involved you cannot expect me to have instant answers

to every problem'. Sarah wonders if the answer is to make the white paper 'greener'. That does not meet the point, I reply. We will still be launching the debate. Given the series of personal affairs of the past months – Yeo et al – it will be seen as self-serving. Sarah apart, no one raises a single argument in favour of going ahead. Quite the contrary. Greg Knight argues passionately that we should abandon our plans on the grounds that we are at serious risk of not getting them through Parliament!

The meeting moves next door to No. 10. We take the issue to the Cabinet business meeting and for the first time I remain. The Prime Minister knows my newspaper interests but it is my judgement that this will not only be unpopular with the press but with the public too. They will regard it as a response to the recent cases. I add that what has become clear during the morning is that ministers are split on the issue. John smiles and looks around the table. 'Well, if we had not gone ahead with proposals when ministers were split then we would not have introduced very much.' 'Some might say that we would have been better advised not to have done so in those circumstances', I reply.

I do not like having a public dispute with the Prime Minister. But there is no option. There is now no doubt that John is isolated. John Wakeham has become an almost passionate advocate for abandoning the white paper. Richard and Tony agree. John does not explicitly surrender. He asks that we find out how long the white paper can be delayed and that reasons for the delay should be worked up. Now, it will not be published before June and there is a substantial chance that the plans will be abandoned. My interest as a party manager ends after the election but if the government have the slightest sense they will abandon their plans altogether. It is a recipe for one row after another. I concede that there is a perfectly respectable case for privacy legislation although personally, I am more concerned with ensuring press accuracy than protecting privacy. But as a political exercise it is legislation for a government with a large majority, governing in calm and prosperous times. It is not legislation for an administration struggling to survive.

THURSDAY 10 MARCH

Lunch with Trevor Kavanagh of *The Sun*. He explains the alienation of his paper in these terms. *The Sun* lost its circulation because of its support through thick and thin for Margaret Thatcher so whoever Margaret Thatcher's successor had been there was never any prospect of the same slavish adherence. *The Sun* reckoned that had they been more independent in those years they would have gone through the five million circulation barrier. It follows that they intend to make the most of their independence.

A further talk with the PM alone. In brief, my message is that I am not a candidate for any job in government after the elections. John says that he fears that he has dragged me into 'a terrible mess'. I reply that that is not remotely my view. I have enjoyed the job and I have enjoyed working with him – which I have. I am not sure that he believes me. No, I am certain he does not. He looks exhausted and certainly is not enjoying the premiership one little bit at the moment. I doubt if he can imagine anyone else enjoying the process either.

MONDAY 14 MARCH

The headlines are dominated by the IRA mortar attack on Heathrow and the resignation of the Chief of the Defence Staff, Peter Harding. Harding has gone because of an affair with Tony Buck's ex-wife. A silly way to go. The woman had trouble stamped all over her in capital letters. She apparently set the general up for a *News of the World* exposé. And she had led poor old Tony a merry dance before abandoning him once he ceased to be an MP. At least Harding has done the sensible thing and resigned straight away. Government ministers please note. No waiting around for questions in the House. Labour are already muttering about the 'defence implications' of the affair although they know perfectly well that there are no defence implications. A quick resignation also has one other effect. It shifts the attention. The press is now fascinated to know how much the unappetising Lady Buck received for her story.

Leadership speculation continues. At No. 10 John says one way forward is for him to offer himself for election immediately after the European elections are over. The assumption is that the results will be bad. It is a perilous course. Even a maverick candidate can do damage. What happens if such a candidate wins forty or fifty votes? Much better there is no contest. There are beginning to be uncanny comparisons with the last days of Ted Heath. Ted eventually agreed to an election after losing two general elections. We are firmly in 'back me or sack me' country.

TUESDAY 15 MARCH

A long lunch with Charles Hambro. He remains very concerned about the financial position. There could hardly be a worse time to raise money. I think we have done wonders. We will have a current account surplus this year – the first since 1988. If we can achieve this in the kind of political climate we have experienced over the last twelve months, how much easier it would have been in years past. The irresponsible way the party has been run still makes me very angry. Even now, there is a feeling in Central Office that money will be provided automatically for the higher political task. Raising money, spending wisely, managing efficiently are not the natural goals of a political party but the truth is that sensible rules of that kind are essential for any organisation. We are paying a political price today because we have ignored them in the past. Our budget for forthcoming and crucial elections is much more limited than we would like.

WEDNESDAY 16 MARCH

A new row is developing in Europe on the unappealingly named subject of qualified majority voting.[285] With enlargement of the Community most of Europe want to increase the number of votes which will block

---

285 The European Council acts, in some areas, by a qualified majority vote (QMV). The votes of each member state are set roughly according to their population. For example, the UK had ten, the same as France, Germany and Italy. At the time, fifty-four votes out a total of seventy-six possible votes were required to pass a proposal from the Commission, so twenty-three were needed to block it. The problems arose over the inclusion of four new states. The UK wanted the block to remain at twenty-three, whereas most of the rest of Europe wanted to increase it to twenty-seven in line with the increased number of votes.

agreement to twenty-seven. We want to stay on twenty-three. There are difficulties all ways for us. We have been passionate advocates of enlargement and so it is assumed we go along with the consequences. On the other hand, it will be more difficult for us to stop proposals where we disagree and in the parliamentary party there is a feeling of 'Europe strikes again'. So far, only Spain supports our stand. Better news on the domestic front. Unemployment is down by 38,000, job vacancies are up. Will anyone take any notice of these good figures?

THURSDAY 24 MARCH

At Central Office we toil over my speech to the party's central council in Plymouth. I break off to watch Prime Minister's Questions. John is in a belligerent mood. The issue, again, is majority voting. He reads out an obviously prepared piece about John Smith, 'Monsieur Oui – the poodle of Brussels'. Much liked by our side and it makes a strong point. Smith would not even negotiate to improve our position.

SATURDAY 26 MARCH

At Plymouth, Douglas goes first as he needs to catch a plane to Greece for a meeting of foreign ministers. I have a few minutes with him when he comes off the platform. He says the weekend meeting will be very tough, he expects Spain to give way and we will then be isolated. My speech is, in all probability, my last from the Tory Party platform. They need cheering and I respond. I am bound to say that I now quite enjoy the process. It depends first upon having a good script and making time for it. You can then enjoy the performance! This after all is rally-speaking not debating. A beauty parade of would-be leaders, plus a real one. The result is utterly predictable. Michael Heseltine is lively, oratorical, the complete conference performer. Ken Clarke is ill-prepared and therefore dull and disappointing. John Major is sound but still needs a script writer. The best part of his speech is on Europe, and that he wrote himself. He gets a good reception. The majority of the party want to see him succeed rather than believe that he is succeeding.

MONDAY 28 MARCH

'Another great triumph' mutters John Wakeham at No. 12 – a comment which doubtless he will repeat. The subject is of course qualified majority voting.[286] Today's press is baleful. 'Surrender' is the flavour of the headlines. Only last week John Major was jeering at Smith as 'Monsieur Oui' and now he appears to have capitulated after the briefest of engagements. At No. 10 John is in a ragged mood. He is becoming more and more sceptical about Europe but his most heartfelt comment is that his whole premiership has been dominated by the impossible task of keeping the Tory Party together on Europe. He talks of retirement – peaceful and preferably rich – but for all his grumbles John is a determined man. Unless the elections are a total catastrophe, I believe he will fight to continue.

TUESDAY 29 MARCH

John announces the 'compromise' settlement on majority voting in the Commons in the afternoon. He is greeted with delighted derision from the opposition benches. Much more ominous is the reaction of our own side. They remain disapprovingly silent. I can remember only one similar scene and that was the response that followed Ted Heath's second defeat in 1974 only a month or two before his fall. Curiously, the one intervention that most helped us was from Tony Marlow who called on the Prime Minister to stand down. Marlow is rightly regarded as a buffoon but his question is seen by the middle of the party as an act of treachery. Ironically, he manages to rally the troops but the conversation in the corridors leaves no doubt that John is in serious trouble.

WEDNESDAY 30 MARCH

A bloody crisis. The press is appalling with calls for the Prime Minister to stand down. *The Times* gloats and on radio Charles Moore calls him a truly 'hopeless' leader. This from a man who has plotted to bring down Major, hounded him at every stage, attacked him and stabbed him in the

---

286　EC foreign ministers finally agreed that the threshold for QMV would rise to sixty-four votes, with the effect that twenty-seven votes would be required to block.

back. If John falls, people like Moore will say it backs their judgement when the fact is that they have done everything to secure this outcome.

SUNDAY 3 APRIL

The *Mail on Sunday* lead with the Prime Minister's statement that he is determined to continue as PM. The position has been secured for this week but let us not deceive ourselves. We are in desperate trouble. We are living from day to day – and we still have the local elections, a by-election, and above all, the Euro elections to come.

MONDAY 4 APRIL

Reading *The Observer* I recognise the mood of the party. The party has tired of being led by an 'ordinary' person – hitherto John Major's great strength – and now want an 'extraordinary' person. Good news for Michael Heseltine, bad news for Ken.

TUESDAY 5 APRIL

A press conference at Central Office. Stephen Dorrell defends the tax rises coming into effect tomorrow. He does it well but it is rather extraordinary that neither the No. 1 nor the No. 2 at the Treasury are available this week. Both Ken and Michael Portillo are holidaying abroad as the biggest Tory tax increases for a decade are brought in. We need a decision on our European slogan. Tim Collins, a not-so-secret sceptic, backs 'Putting Britain first in Europe' as does the rest of Central Office. The research backs 'A strong Britain in a strong Europe' as having wider appeal. That is also the passionate view of Christopher Prout who makes the entirely fair point that 'putting Britain first' has a rather curious ring to it after the qualified majority voting fiasco. Douglas Hurd and I both support Christopher. The very last thing I need is European candidates as unhappy about the slogan as they were in 1989.

WEDNESDAY 6 APRIL

I launch the local government campaign with John Gummer. What part will the Prime Minister play I am asked? The reality is that some of our leading councils, like Wandsworth, have told us in no uncertain terms that they don't want any government minister associated with them – Prime Minister or anybody else. They don't want the government's unpopularity rubbing off on them. Not a good story. Potential stories that 'Tories cold shoulder Major' etc. and alternatively, if the PM plays no part the story will be 'Major retreats into bunker'. I reply that these elections are not a referendum on the PM and that the PM would take a 'leading part' in the local elections and a 'very leading' part in the European elections.

FRIDAY 8 APRIL

A long day on trains to and from Birmingham and then down to the Isle of Wight. I am fairly knocked out. Another holiday week has come and gone without a break. My mood is not made better by the growing realisation that virtually the entire Cabinet are abroad. And yet we are at the start of a campaign which could well determine the future of the Prime Minister. We exhibit all the signs of a government that has been in power too long. Tired, jaded and without the energy to fight politically. My mood is not improved by the *Telegraph*'s Gallup poll. Forget that we are polling only 25 or 26 per cent or that Labour are over twenty points in front. Just remember that we are trailing behind on every policy handling issue but one. Only on defence do the public believe we do it better than Labour – and then only by the slenderest of margins. In all other areas we are behind. The public even believe that Labour would run the economy better. We have lost our reputation for ministerial competence and until we regain that we are doomed to thump along the bottom.

SATURDAY 9 APRIL

The second anniversary of the general election. Most of the papers are scathing – although the *Financial Times* says that if the Prime Minister's performance has been lacklustre John Smith's record is dismal. There is no doubt that the Prime Minister is being written off. It is not 'if' but 'when' say the leader writers almost in unison. And yet for all the government's errors, the economy is recovering, we have come out of recession, we have the longest period of low inflation I can remember. Ditto interest rates. Unemployment is tumbling. There is growth in the economy. If John was to fall tomorrow, he would hand over a magnificent legacy to his successor.

TUESDAY 12 APRIL

I see John, as we need to decide what he will do following the local election results. If the results are bad he will have to act quickly. His plan would be to ask Marcus Fox to arrange an early leadership election. In other words his plan remains as before. He would ask for a vote of confidence from the party and then go on to a major reconstruction of the government. I point out the obvious disadvantage.

'Say a paper candidate gets seventy votes in the election, what then?'

'If he gets that then I go', John replies. 'I can lose fifty votes but no more'.

'The other option is to tough it out', I suggest.

'My fear is that I would not have the authority to carry out the reshuffle'.

I say I will think about it more. John nods. 'I will take some persuading off it', he warns. 'There are family reasons also'. He doesn't specify. But I imagine that this means that Norma and the children are at the end of their tether. Remorseless attack after attack. Half the press want him out. They want blood. John then puts forward a proposal which could be of immense significance. Europe has split the Conservative Party wide open. It is why we have lost our reputation for unity. Thus, he believes that any decision taken at the Intergovernmental Conference in 1996 should be subject to a referendum.[287] Personally, I am sympathetic to this. Ted Heath won't like it but the party is genuinely split. We need

---

287   The IGC convened for 1996 was triggered by the Maastricht Treaty to review some of its provisions. Qualified majority voting and Commission membership, a greater involvement of national Parliaments in the activities of the Union and a review of the common foreign and security policy were all mentioned as areas for discussion.

to find some modus vivendi and I can think of none better. It allows everyone to state their views but still retain their membership. My suggestion to John is that if he is set on this course then he should announce the policy prior to the local elections. It should not be seen as a panic response to bad local election results and a fear of what will happen in the European elections.

WEDNESDAY 13 APRIL

At Stephen Milligan's memorial service, I represent the Prime Minister. I sit next to Ted Heath. The service is well supported by the parliamentary party but noticeably short of Cabinet ministers although William Waldegrave, Peter Brooke and Michael Portillo are present. When you listen to Stephen's career you realise just what a loss his death represented.

SATURDAY 16–SUNDAY 17 APRIL

In Sutton Coldfield for a weekend of constituency engagements. We now seem to be in difficulty over the celebrations for the anniversary of D-Day in June. We appear not to have consulted the British Legion and are accused of trivialising and politicising the event.

TUESDAY 19 APRIL

To Rotherham to launch our by-election campaign. It is a decidedly low-key affair. The only question is whether we come second or third. I am reminded of the Rotherham by-election of 1963, one of the first I ever reported on for *The Times*. Nothing changes. There was a leadership crisis. Would Macmillan survive? The Conservative candidate was asked his view. 'I stand four square behind Mr Macmillan' he replied. 'As long as he remains Prime Minister and leader of the party'.

THURSDAY 21 APRIL

At No. 12 'the D-Day fiasco' as Christopher Mayer calls it eclipses all else. The good economic news is relegated to the inside pages. Richard Ryder is particularly irritated. 'Who is in charge?' he asks, not unreasonably. The position seems to be that responsibility is shared between the

Department of Defence and the Department of Heritage, with a committee of whom Lord Cranborne (currently in the Far East) is Chairman and his deputy is the publicity-conscious Iain Sproat. He was meant to have seen the British Legion about the event in Hyde Park but apparently has not done so. The net result is that we now have the British Legion, Vera Lynn and most of the national press against us. Yet again, it is the competence of the government that is brought into question. The public have decided and their verdict is that it is a cock-up.

SATURDAY 23 APRIL

Returning to London from Sutton Coldfield I tune into the BBC news. To my surprise I am the second item just behind the crisis in Bosnia. One of my interviews on Thursday is taken as a strong hint that I am standing down soon and will want to go to the back benches and not into government. That is exactly my position but I confess that I thought it was so well known that it hardly merited the full news treatment. Nevertheless the BBC keep running the story throughout the day on both radio and television using my admittedly frank replies. Not to be outdone, ITN also arrive unannounced on the doorstep and are told by me (politely) and by Fiona (less politely) that I am giving no interviews.

SUNDAY 24 APRIL

Lunch at Chequers with John Major and the National Union. John and I settle on the sofa after coffee. He is obviously depressed. 'Churchill had black days', he explains and 'this is one of mine'.[288] His concern is the elections and he fears we could do catastrophically badly in the European elections. 'Have you ever considered the possibility of ending with no seats?' he asks. 'It is more or less what happened in Canada'.

MONDAY 2 MAY

Visits to our campaigns in Birmingham and Wolverhampton. A leader

---

288 Churchill had dark moods during several periods of his life. His term for these episodes was the 'Black Dog', a common description used by Victorian nannies.

in Wolverhampton looks over my shoulder to where Nick Budgen is standing and says: 'Just keep the MPs off the air'. That is also the view of Bernard Zissman in Birmingham. The parliamentary party is deeply unpopular with the party in the country and blamed for much of what has gone wrong. Any hopes that MPs may be biting their tongues are soon comprehensively dashed. As I drive back to Central Office the radio news tells me that David Evans has called for the sacking of a third of the Cabinet, myself and the advisers at No. 10. Hours to go before polling day and this lunatic gives a long radio interview attacking his own side.

WEDNESDAY 4 MAY

A final press conference for the local government campaign with John Gummer. I am asked who is to blame if the results are bad and give the only answer possible. 'I take responsibility. The buck stops with the Party Chairman.' There is an ironic grumble of protest led by Michael White who obviously believes that it may not be the organisation which is letting the party down just now.

At lunchtime, Prince Charles talks to the Newspaper Society on the theme that Britain's achievements are being underplayed. The speech is delivered in the curiously hesitant half-apologetic manner which is his wont. The content however is first class. The kind of speech we should be making.

THURSDAY 5 MAY

Election day and a meeting of the political Cabinet to approve the European manifesto. The manifesto is approved without a hitch. There are no arguments, no disputes. Portillo and Lilley say nothing and Redwood and Howard both congratulate the Foreign Secretary on it. At the end I warn the Cabinet that there will be a difficult week to get through. Just how difficult that task is becomes clear when the results start coming through. Labour are making gains although not as many as they would like. We are losing seats around the country although we have hung on to Wandsworth and Trafford. The real victors of the night are the

Liberals. Their local government campaign has been imperceptible but they are the repository of disillusioned Tory voters.

FRIDAY 6 MAY

The inquest. These are the worst results for us in twenty years although not as bad as the 1968 council results for Labour. We have lost around 516 seats. Given what has happened over the last two years, I am slightly amazed that our support still stands at 27 per cent.

SATURDAY 7 MAY

The usual Saturday. I ring John who is depressed about the results and like me he has heard the *Sunday Times* leader will call for him to be replaced. Then in the afternoon an all-too-familiar problem. The *News of the World* has a story about a government whip, Michael Brown, who they have revealed holidaying in Barbados with a twenty-year-old man. The age of consent is still twenty-one although the law is in the process of being changed. Eventually, at 11 p.m. we have Brown's resignation after it is clear that the *News of the World* are indeed leading with the story. What angers me is the sheer lack of common sense displayed. Brown is a whip. More than anyone he should know how the press have us under surveillance. Heterosexual or homosexual, this is not the time to indulge in careless affairs.

SUNDAY 8 MAY

The story about Michael Brown duly appears but it is a commentary upon the political times that by the end of the day is of mere passing interest. A new political debate has broken out. On the radio, Ken Clarke has ruled out the use of a referendum while on television, John Redwood has kept our options open. What is our policy? John Major previously favoured the move as the only way of keeping the parliamentary party together. But John's initiative was shot somewhere along the way. I suspect by the Policy Unit and the Foreign Office. John says the line should now be that the question of a referendum does not arise.

THE BEST OF ENEMIES

MONDAY 9 MAY

The referendum issue dominates the morning news programmes. All kinds of people are coming out of the woodwork. Lamont pronounces his support, as does Lord Young. The maverick John Nott also makes a guest appearance, helpfully confiding to the public that the Tories need a period in opposition. John asks me to find out where members of the Cabinet stand. I do this over the next hours to find, unsurprisingly, that they are all over the place. John promises that he will try to keep the door open but as we are having dinner a message comes through from Jonathan Hill. He warns me that the guidance against a referendum has hardened up. A great mistake. We need the referendum option.

TUESDAY 10 MAY

In the tea room, Dennis Skinner comes over to me and says we must get onto the attack against the Liberals. It is not that he dislikes the Liberals, it is more that he has intense contempt for a party that stands for nothing and is all things to all men. In the afternoon a masterful performance by the Prime Minister. Attacked by John Smith on our policy on the referendum, John manages to defuse the position entirely. He is 'sceptical' about a referendum but he avoids slamming the door shut entirely. Lamont and Baker sitting next to each other nod approvingly while Ted, sitting three rows in front, also nods in agreement. John has managed to send both sides away satisfied.

THURSDAY 12 MAY

Grim news. The death of John Smith. Unusually, I was away from Central Office. The first warning I received was when I was called out of an NFC board meeting to be told by Gerry Malone that John Smith had been taken to hospital with a heart attack, believed to be 'very serious'. Over the next hour the interruptions became more frequent until the terrible news came that he had died. I make my excuses and return to Westminster. What can you say at such a moment? Like everybody else I am stunned, shocked. I came into the House with John Smith in 1970.

I did not know him well but what I knew I liked. He was of course a great debater, an entertaining speaker in the Commons, a good intellect and a unifier as leader of the Labour Party. But there was also a certain mischief. He would sit down after a telling attack on our front bench and look around with a satisfied glint in his eye as if expecting us, his opponents, to approve. His attacks had none of the grim intensity of Kinnock. You felt that John at least felt his opponents were human. They had strayed and mistakenly joined the wrong party but even now could be convinced of the error of their ways.

None of this is to say that he did not fiercely believe in his cause. He obviously had strong and genuine principles. He also had courage, as he showed when he returned after his first heart attack. In the Commons the tributes are heartfelt. When the Prime Minister gets up you could hear a pin drop. Every member concentrating on his words. John's tribute is excellent. Equally, Margaret Beckett is outstanding. The only exception is Ashdown who is wooden as if he has said it all in the television and radio soundbites that both he and I have been doing at the Millbank centre.

We have immediate decisions to make. Our Scottish conference is suspended, as is all other political activity. We have the Scottish conference tomorrow and the Welsh rally on Saturday. They will continue but on the understanding that political attacks on our opponents are forbidden. At Central Office I go through my speech for Inverness with a red pencil. It is early days to talk about the political consequences but two results are clear. The pressure on John Major is reduced – there will be no stomach for two leadership elections. Equally, Michael Heseltine's chances of success have been dealt a severe blow. His own heart problems have assumed a much greater importance. The political world – on both sides of the divide – has changed.

FRIDAY 13 MAY

To Inverness for the Scottish conference. Already, the speculation is that Tony Blair will succeed John Smith as leader of the Labour Party. It is an amazing change. Only a day or so ago all the forecasts were that John Major would go following the European elections. Now no one feels that. Indeed, John Major is beginning to appear as the great survivor.

The Prime Minister and Norma arrive in Inverness in the late afternoon. He makes another excellent speech. It is serious. It sets out his beliefs. It is the kind of speech that he has been waiting for months to make. He is not a natural party conference performer. He does not enjoy the theatre and knockabout like Michael Heseltine, or for that matter Fowler, but on an occasion like today he comes into his own. There is prolonged applause when he says the job is only half-done and he intends to stay on and finish it. Afterwards at dinner, he is relaxed in a way I haven't seen him for many weeks. For the time being the pressure is off.

We are entering a very curious election campaign. John Smith's funeral is to take place next Friday. John and I have decided that there will be no national campaigning until after the funeral – the manifesto launch is put back, the party political broadcasts and the posters are postponed. The campaign will in effect be a little longer than a fortnight.

SATURDAY 14 MAY

The mood is already changing. There is agreement that the Prime Minister is in no danger in the short term but even now his enemies are questioning his long-term position. But the real spotlight remains on Labour. Blair, a youthful forty-one, is the clear frontrunner. He could be a difficult opponent: young, presentable, middle class. Should we be more worried about him or the Liberals? I confess that one minor element in my decision to stand down in 1990 was being given Blair as an opponent at employment. I had been around for fifteen years, and as long as I had Meacher that was not a concern. But Blair presented a different challenge. As it happened, I never found Blair particularly formidable. He was like a highly strung racehorse. Talented, but easily upset. What I do not know is whether Blair is tough enough for the job. We have not seen him under pressure. He may be excellent but at this point no one knows. If he is elected leader (which looks certain) then John will face a difficult autumn. Blair will have triumphal appearances at the TUC and Labour conferences and then will come our own conference. Grumbling inside the Conservative Party is so deep in the soul I wonder if we are capable of mending our ways.

WEDNESDAY 18 MAY

Lunch with Linda. I ring her after reading a piece in one of the magazines where an unsuspecting ex-Tory MP called Summerson started to lecture her on the need to replace the chairman of the party and was sent away by Linda with a flea in his ear. She has remained remarkably loyal to me over the years.[289]

FRIDAY 20 MAY

To John Smith's funeral in Edinburgh. It is an impressive yet simple service. Three addresses, all excellent, particularly Donald Dewar whom I have never heard speak better. Two lessons read by Margaret Beckett and by Lord McCluskey, reading particularly well. At the reception afterwards I meet Elizabeth Smith whose eyes light up when I recall the mischievous way John used to look at our side after a particularly good foray against our front bench. I have to admit there is one political feature I notice about the service. In Scotland, Labour have the support of the middle class. They appear, at any rate to an outsider like me, to be the natural establishment. Well turned out, bright, with natural authority. A long way from the wild left we lovingly paint from Central Office and which still exists in many southern cities. If the Scottish habit catches on then we are in real trouble.

MONDAY 23 MAY

Normal politics have resumed. The manifesto launch goes off without a hitch. The Prime Minister takes virtually all the questions. The layout of

---

289 I met Linda (Christmas) when we both worked on *The Times* and we were married for five years. She is a talented writer. She was a feature writer for *The Guardian* from 1971–1982 and senior lecturer at the City University's Department of Journalism from 1989–2005. She is the author of *The Ribbon and the Ragged Square: An Australian Journey* (1986) and *Chopping Down the Cherry Trees: A Portrait of Britain in the Eighties* (1989). I am pleased we are still friends and we try to meet regularly for lunch.

Church House for the event helps considerably. There is not the cheerful mateyness of our Central Office conferences where, too often, the conference becomes a debate between the reporters and the speaker. This is impossible in Church House. To ask a question, the reporter has to rise in their pew, wait for the green light of the microphone, and once the question is delivered the microphone is switched off. No supplementary question is possible. Why did the party spend so much money trying to improve the facilities at Central Office when it would have been infinitely cheaper to have hired a room at Church House every time we needed a big press conference?

TUESDAY 24 MAY

The trouble with this election is clear. The single currency, the veto, the ERM, reform of the common agricultural policy, leave most of the British public cold. Most do not know who their MEP is or what the European Parliament does. Unhappily, what the public do understand is that they have an opportunity to pass judgement on the government and the Prime Minister. Every interviewer is interested, above all, in one question. What will happen to John Major if these elections go badly?

WEDNESDAY 25 MAY

The Eastleigh campaign (Stephen Milligan's old seat) would like Margaret Thatcher to visit them, so back in London I phone her. I also ask if she will warn the public against voting Liberal in the Euro elections. Nothing doing. Margaret is perfectly friendly but says she is keeping 'a low profile'. Her view is that most of our MEPs are the worst kinds of federalists. 'I see your problems Norman, and I don't envy you your job,' she adds cheerfully. She ends the conversation with the encouraging words 'I shall be voting, dear, and so will Denis.'

SUNDAY 29 MAY

The *Sunday Telegraph* are in effect advising their readers to abstain from the elections. The *Sunday Times* enthuses over the prospect of Blair.

THURSDAY 2 JUNE

The election rally in Nottingham could hardly have gone better. Introducing the Prime Minister I remind the audience of when I was a Nottingham member in 1970. The issue was whether we should go into Europe. That is no longer the case. The issue now is what kind of Europe we want. John then spells out his vision for Europe with the maximum left to the nation state. He speaks for ten minutes too long but it is another powerful speech. The audience reacts with real enthusiasm. The Midlands is not as naturally enthusiastic as say Lancashire, which makes John's reception more notable. Sadly, the mood lasts only as long as it takes us to leave the cheering crowd in the hall and arrive back at our private room.

Tim Collins is on the phone. The news is the Gallup survey being published in the *Telegraph* tomorrow. The results are devastating. Labour, 54 per cent. Liberal, 21.5 per cent. Conservatives, 21 per cent. Tim says it is the lowest ever Tory showing and the biggest ever Labour lead – although Labour were above 54 per cent support at the height of the community charge row. John says there is a further piece of bad news I should know about – the crash of a Chinook helicopter in Scotland. Thirty people have been killed and even worse, they are our top security people in Northern Ireland.[290]

MONDAY 6 JUNE

D-Day celebrations dominate everything. I watch the TV coverage from Shirley's office at Central Office. How can you fail to be moved by the sight of hundreds of veterans marching past on the wet sands of Normandy. The crowds sing Second World War songs – even the Queen joins in. It is magnificent.

---

290 The Boeing Chinook mk2 helicopter had taken off from Belfast, heading for Fort George near Inverness. On board were twenty-five passengers, almost all of them involved in the police and intelligence services plus a crew of four. They were to attend a secret high-level meeting on the peace process. Seventeen minutes into the flight and enveloped in thick fog, the Chinook ploughed into a hillside on the Mull of Kintyre. The helicopter caught fire and everyone was killed instantly.

WEDNESDAY 8 JUNE

The final press conference at Church House. John plus Douglas and Ken. No great passion, just friendly parrying of questions on how we are going to do. Everyone knows that we are going to do badly. I am prepared for the worst. If we get fifteen seats I will be well satisfied. John's position will be secure. The nightmare remains single figures. It is impossible to call.

THURSDAY 9 JUNE

In the afternoon I try out some lines to take for the by-election results with Tim. Although the European results will not be announced until Sunday, we have the four by-elections tonight. Three safe Labour seats and Eastleigh, which was held by Stephen Milligan, where we will certainly lose. The results prove to be just as awful as we expected. In Eastleigh we are knocked into third place and in the others we are unable to get our vote even to the 20 per cent point. There was one piece of luck with the David Dimbleby election programme. There is an industrial dispute at the BBC and the Labour leadership refuse to cross the picket lines. The big victor tonight is Labour. Marvellous that their hang-ups about the unions should prevent them taking credit for their victories.

FRIDAY 10 JUNE

Christopher Prout comes in to say that it was a good European campaign and light years away from 1989. You run 'a tight ship', he says. Christopher has been a very good man to work with and I only hope that he manages to hold on in Shropshire. At lunchtime I ask all the staff at Central Office to come to the meeting room for a drink. I thank them for their work and above all, loyalty. It ends up as something of a valedictory speech. I do not say in clear terms I will be standing down but the message is easily read between the lines.

SATURDAY 11 JUNE

A few hours' sleep and back at 7 a.m. to Downing Street. John has just returned from Huntingdon and Norma is in the flat with Jonathan. John leans back in his chair. 'Are you all sitting comfortably?' he asks with a smile. 'Prepared for any kind of shock?'

We nod assent.

'Well, back in Huntingdon I have had the chance to think', he says. 'If they want my job they will have to prise me out.'

'Good for you,' says Norma. 'Excellent news,' says Jonathan. 'Good. We all know where we are,' I say. 'We will fight for you. Just remember it will be a fight. The Sunday press will continue to go for you.'

John replies that the Sunday press is one of the reasons he is determined to stay. 'I couldn't bear those people on the *Sunday Telegraph* to win.'

SATURDAY 11 JUNE

My 'farewell' speech at Central Office makes the front page of *The Times*. Not surprisingly, some bright chap noticed that I thanked the staff for all their help but made no reference to future campaigns.

SUNDAY 12 JUNE

All eyes are on the European election results and I hear the first results in the invariable TV studio. It appears that Labour are doing well but the Liberal Democrats are not doing as well in the local elections. A crucial early result is the Isle of Wight. The Liberals should take this but just fail. The same pattern emerges elsewhere. We are going to get about 27 per cent of the poll. Labour about 43 per cent but the Liberals right down at 17 to 18 per cent. The Liberals have not had their breakthrough. We are going to get at least a dozen seats, probably more. The single figure disaster has been avoided. So too has the crisis for John. By any objective standard these results are bad but the press has helped us. By so freely predicting wipe out they have made the results look much better than they are. I issue a statement expressing disappointment but adding that the Liberal Democrats must be the really disappointed party.

MONDAY 13 JUNE

The Times, for once, accurately sets it out. There has been no meltdown and John has won himself 'breathing space'. We have ended up with eighteen seats and 28 per cent of the vote. But frankly, the margin between success and failure was very thin. A few thousand votes going other ways would have reduced us to single figures and even to under five seats. We have lost some really good MEPs, like Christopher Prout and Bill Newton Dunn, but nevertheless the reaction of the bulk of the party is that it could have been worse and we have had a lucky escape.

TUESDAY 14 JUNE

The papers are full of reshuffle speculation, including my own position. It is widely accepted that I want to leave and the press favourites to succeed me are Michael Heseltine and David Hunt. As for me, I want my position made clear. I intend to leave this voluntary job which has taken up most of my waking hours for the last two years. It is a beautiful evening when I drive over to No. 10. John is in the garden and it is there that I join him. We talk for a few moments about the European elections. John moves his hand across his neck in mock relief. He has escaped the executioner but, as he recognises, only 'just'.

I then move on to my own position. He has guessed that this is my official visit to tell him of my intentions. He says that he is disappointed but that I had already made my position clear to him. 'You will stay to the reshuffle?'

'I will stay but I would like my position announced in the next few days.'

'When?' he asks in some surprise.

'I would like to do it on Thursday. I am on *Any Questions* on Friday and I think it would be in no one's interest that we should have weeks of speculation.'

John's fear is that my announcement will put pressure on him to bring the reshuffle forward. My concern is that uncertainty undermines my position as Chairman and is not what I want. I think I allay his fears. We leave the garden and walk to the door of No. 10 in just the same way as I saw him first before the 1992 election. The typical gesture of a courteous and kind man who also has that touch of steel which has enabled him to withstand the unprecedented barrage he has been subjected to over the last two years. 'No one knows what a debt I owe you,' he says as I leave.

WEDNESDAY 15 JUNE
During the day I brief the ever-resilient Tim Collins that I will be announcing my resignation the next day and we prepare our inevitable questions and answers. I cannot believe that there will be overwhelming interest. It has been well trailed – and I have, of course, done it once before!

THURSDAY 16 JUNE
The announcement comes after Prime Minister's Questions and there is an overwhelming feeling for me of déjà vu. The exchange of letters with the Prime Minister; the interviews with the press; the photographs and the TV. Not as much drama as in 1990 although I still manage to achieve some surprise. The lobby was not expecting me to act independently or so quickly. Sky give me a bottle of champagne and I take Fiona, Gerry and Tim off to Simply Nico. Ironically, my sense of déjà vu is complete when I find Geoffrey Holland (my Permanent Secretary at employment when I left) dining at the next table.

FRIDAY 17 JUNE
I cannot bear to read the press. I am the exact opposite of John Major on this. If I know there is going to be flack I don't read it. I quickly skim the two papers we have delivered at home, *The Times* and *Daily Mail*, and know I am right. *The Times* is fine but the *Mail* has a notably bitchy piece by David Hughes, doubtless ordered by his editor. I go to Somerset for *Any Questions*. At dinner we are joined not only by Paddy Ashdown but his wife who is quite a character who apparently, Paddy frequently defers to. The programme itself is in shirt sleeves in a stifling village hall. I put in an adequate performance but land one punch on Jonathan Dimbleby. The current joke is that I am leaving to spend more

time with my business interests. Dimbleby intervenes that I am going off to make a lot of money. 'Not as much as you, Jonathan', I reply which earns a laugh from the audience but does not go down at all well with Mr Dimbleby.

MONDAY 20 JUNE

Tired and washed out. A reaction to the last two years and even more to the last six months. I can hardly bear to read the papers and when I do I concentrate on the city pages and the sport. To make matters worse we start our house move today – moving out of the house which has served us so well for the last fifteen years and is virtually the only home the children have known. I toy with the idea of jettisoning all my usual Monday morning meetings, including the ones with the Prime Minister, but decide that re-entry will be no better if delayed. The right decision. The discipline of the meetings brings me out of my introspection.

John wants a written report on my Deputy Chairman and Vice Chairman. It is not difficult. Gerry Malone has been a star and should be promoted. Eric Pickles has been excellent and Patrick Nicholls ditto but underused. Joan Seccombe is a good and loyal worker. Geoffrey Pattie should be retired.

THURSDAY 23 JUNE

Charles Hambro comes in to make his farewells. Charles has been a hero. He has helped us avert bankruptcy, and my hope (and expectation) is that he will be one of the new working peers this summer. In the evening to Birmingham and the NEC for a concert by Pavarotti. Over 10,000 people wildly enthusiastic. The atmosphere is more like a party conference than Covent Garden. Great entertainment in spite of the stifling heat. Pavarotti is staying at the smartest hotel in Sutton Coldfield. It is said that they have had to spend £4,000 to provide ground-floor accommodation for the great man to prevent him having to go to the trouble of walking up a flight of stairs to the first floor. Still, with 10,000 people paying on average £50 or £75 a head there should be a little change left over.

SUNDAY 26 JUNE

Back in London we have now moved temporarily to a flat in Rivermead Court. Seventh floor with a panoramic view over the Thames and Putney Bridge. The Hurlingham Club is just around the corner and I think the girls believe they have been taken on holiday early.

MONDAY 27 JUNE

At the business managers' meeting the discussion turns on when the House should go down. Richard Ryder and I are strongly of the view that it should end on 21 July, preventing Blair from having a coronation week in the Commons. The Prime Minister is concerned about being accused of silencing Blair or even of running scared. My view is that the overwhelming political argument is for Blair's election to be an anti-climax. At the moment we have the political initiative and we should move heaven and earth to keep it. In the House, John receives an almost ecstatic reception from our side and Margaret Beckett is demolished.

THURSDAY 30 JUNE

The ever changing Rees-Mogg now believes that John will lead the Tory Party into the next election. This is seriously bad news since on most political issues Rees-Mogg is unerringly wrong. A supper party at No. 11 with Ken and Gillian. A genial gathering of the Cambridge mafia. Sitting on the stairs or on whatever chair can be found, red or white wine. This may be No. 11 but life has not changed much. Ken has just made it clear in a speech that he does not intend to go along with the Eurosceptic tide. I suspect that the last few days are a lull in the battle for the heart of the Tory Party rather than an end to hostilities.

FRIDAY I JULY

An article in the *Mail* asks 'Is Clarke a socialist?' It is accompanied by a picture putting Ken in Harold Wilson's clothes plus pipe. The article is only half in jest. We can expect a campaign to put down the 'Tory deceivers' and to praise and build up the 'true believers' like Portillo, Lilley and Redwood from Dacre's *Mail*. To the opera in the English countryside to see *The Barber of Seville*: a warm night; champagne by the lake; a spirited performance with a roll of actual thunder coinciding with the opera storm. We go with David Mathew and among a bevy of pals there are Leon and Diana. Leon was far and away the best candidate for the European presidency but had the disqualification of being British. He will stay on and become the power behind the throne.

FRIDAY 8 JULY

The news is dominated by Jeffrey Archer. The DTI have confirmed an investigation is taking place into insider trading in Anglia shares. Why it has decided to reveal Jeffrey's name is not clear. I am opening a housing development in Basingstoke and am not back until shortly before 5 p.m. The story is, if anything, running harder. It is desperately bad news for Jeffrey. He was never going to be Chairman of the party but had a very good prospect of a Minister of State job. Now all that is at risk although he has not been charged with anything, let alone convicted. I ring Jeffrey at his London flat. Apparently, his flat is surrounded by press and TV cameramen. I ask if there is anything I can do to help. Jeffrey's answer is immediate. He believes the inquiry will clear him and he wants a DTI statement that no action is being taken as soon as possible, i.e. next week before the reshuffle.

He believes the leak has come from a DTI official and the reason the DTI have named him is that otherwise Michael Heseltine would be accused of a 'political cover-up'. I say I will issue a short statement, which I do. 'The public should not rush to judgement', I say. 'The only point that has been confirmed is that an investigation is taking place. That does not imply guilt.' Whatever the facts of the allegation of insider trading it is difficult to resist the conclusion that Jeffrey has been badly treated. Even we politicians have some rights. One is not to be presumed guilty of an offence even before it has been decided whether there is going to be a trial.

SATURDAY 9–SUNDAY 10 JULY

An echo of the bad old times. Gerry Malone rings me on Saturday to tell me that the *Sunday Times* have a story on two PPSs – Graham Riddick and David Tredinnick – who have accepted £1,000 payments to put down parliamentary questions. If true it is an act of utter folly – no, worse than folly, just wrong. The *Sunday Times* Insight team has set them up but so what? Members of Parliament should not accept payments of this kind. I tell Gerry that we at Central Office have no responsibility for MPs in Parliament. That is a matter for the Chief Whip and he should also tell Downing Street. The story duly appears and Richard Ryder suspends the two PPSs. But that will not be an end to it. An investigation by the Committee of Privileges is certain and also a fresh debate about Members' interests generally. Personally, I have always felt that the 'consultancy/adviser' area is an area to be avoided. My aim in outside interests has been to go onto boards of PLCs where my experience might be of use to them. The non-executive director is by definition an independent voice exercising judgement on behalf of the shareholders. He is not a parliamentary adviser lobbying at Westminster and putting down questions. In 1990 Peter Gummer of Shandwick (a man whom I admire and like) offered me a place on the board of his public relations company. I declined. Too many clients. Who knows whom you would be asked to advise. Your first responsibility is to represent your constituents and you should ensure that nothing you do conflicts with that.

MONDAY 11 JULY

The £1,000 questions dominate the press. Labour have honed in on the issue and are making a case against outside interests generally. At our regular Monday meeting I tell John of my conversation with Jeffrey Archer. Wisely, he is keeping entirely out of the case – it is a matter for Michael Heseltine – but does not see how he can put Jeffrey into the government with the allegation of insider trading hanging over him. As far as the chairmanship is concerned, John has ruled out Jonathan Aitken on the grounds that the press would dig into his past. It is now down to Jeremy Hanley, Gillian Shephard and David Hunt.

THURSDAY 14 JULY

In the evening to the Blue Ball where the Prime Minister pays me a long and generous tribute. We have had a few downs in our working relationship over the last two years but in the main it has been excellent – given the times we have lived through, exceptional. I sit next to Sandra Howard, one of the nicest of the Cabinet wives. She confesses an ambition to write a book – a tale of passion with lots of sex – perhaps after Michael ceases to be Home Secretary.

SUNDAY 17 JULY

A day of two parties. Jeffrey Archer's in Grantchester is a sit-down buffet in a marquee: a gathering of the famous and the good. Jeffrey draws me to one side to say that there is now no chance that the DTI inquiry will be announced in time for the reshuffle, but what the Prime Minister could do is to leave a gap in the team to be filled later in the summer. What strikes me most at lunchtime is not Jeffrey's position but Mary's. Mary is meant to be the rock in the Archer household, helping Jeffrey out of scrape after scrape but in this case she is a central player. After all, it is she who is the non-executive director of Anglia. Her reputation is also threatened. For a moment or two the mask slips. She tells me that it is much worse for her than Jeffrey and for a moment I think she is on the verge of tears but then her self-control reasserts itself and she glides off to perform the role of the perfect hostess. Her concern is easy to understand. Over the last few years Mary has established an independent public role for herself. She is a personality in her own right. She is self-evidently a professional and skilled woman, an obvious attribute to any board of directors; now all that has been challenged by the inquiry. Yet again, her independent life would have been brought crashing down because of her husband.

In the evening a party with no internal tensions. Peter Bottomley's fiftieth birthday party. Virginia has asked me to propose the toast and I am delighted to do it. Peter is a great character – entirely a one-off, a good friend. I try to ensure that my speech does not sound like a friendly obituary. Peter is one of the few friends who may still be around in fifty years' time and still saying, 'I've got this great idea.'

TUESDAY 19 JULY

I make one last attempt to persuade John on the chairmanship. I put Jeremy ahead on skill with the media; appeal to the constituencies; and appearance and interest as a character (he is the son of Dinah Sheridan and Jimmy Hanley). There would be no doubt about Jeremy's loyalty and the only question mark is his experience. John should back his own instincts. It was he who first thought of Hanley. His instincts are usually right.

WEDNESDAY 20 JULY

Jeremy Hanley is to be the new chairman. The Prime Minister is seeing him at 9.40 and would like me to meet Jeremy in his flat at No. 10 straight afterwards. Jeremy is a trifle shell-shocked. It is quite a jump from a comfortable Minister of State job to Party Chairman. He is now right in the firing line. There is no Secretary of State to provide friend-ly shelter. We arrange a handover at Central Office at four o'clock that afternoon.

Before leaving the No. 10 flat I say goodbye to Norma. She has grown into the role she never sought as Prime Minister's wife. Back in 1990 she froze when she saw that bank of cameramen outside No. 10. Even during the general election she was reserved and retiring. Today, she is assured, poised and relaxed – as well as being a thoroughly nice woman.

At 4 p.m. Jeremy Hanley arrives at Central Office. There is a tremen-dous turnout of cameramen and we then move inside where both Jeremy and I talk to the staff. Jeremy is excellent, telling the staff that he is above all an 'enthusiast'. I am then seen off by the staff who form a line out to my car and clap me away. Central Office do the farewells extremely well. I will miss the friendly atmosphere of the office and the quality of many of the people there. Yet, mixed with those emotions as I drive to the Commons there is the feeling that once again, I am a free man.

24

'BACK ME OR SACK ME'

OCTOBER 1994–DECEMBER 1995

F or some time I laid my diary aside. After two years as Party Chairman I
needed a break from day-to-day politics. When I returned, the divisions
inside the Conservative Party continued as before and our electoral position
continued to look grim. The comforting theory that it would be much better
on the day of the general election was about to be disproved.

1994

THURSDAY 20 OCTOBER

Northern Ireland is going well[291] but the morning papers are dominated
by a story in *The Guardian* that Tim Smith and Neil Hamilton accepted
money for putting down questions for Mr Al-Fayed, the owner of Harrods. Hearing the story was by David Hencke, I was half-optimistic that
the piece would prove to be untrue. Unfortunately not the case. Tim
Smith, one of the nicest men I know in politics, resigned his government
post. Hamilton is staying on to sue but his hold is precarious.

FRIDAY 28 OCTOBER

In Birmingham for the motor show and then on to the *Post and Mail*

---

291 The most significant event of the last two months had been John Major's success in getting a cease-
fire in Northern Ireland. It seems incredible that I went there as a young reporter in 1968 and 1969
at the start of the 'Troubles' and they continued with increasing ferocity throughout the next twenty-four years. John's achievement was thus immense although, as usual, he received little credit for it.

where I meet Kelvin MacKenzie. He refers back to the 1992 election campaign when he says he was rung by a government minister and given a list of women who were alleged to have had affairs with Paddy Ashdown. He put all his reporting staff on the story but all he received was a shoal of solicitors' letters.[292]

MONDAY 5 DECEMBER

My first proper speech in the Commons since standing down as Chairman. I am called after the opening speeches and advocate for a new pension credit for low-income pensioners. The basic pension is a general pension which is the same for everyone. It will never be increased to a point that will satisfy poorer pensioners. It is absurd to give the same pension increase to Arnold Weinstock as you do to an elderly widow totally dependent on the basic pension. You need to target your resources towards those who need them. Gordon Brown's Labour Party committee was on the same point. The speech was well received but the general position of pensioners is too difficult a problem for the newspapers. Most politicians do much better to concentrate on VAT on petrol and ignore the old people shivering at home.

WEDNESDAY 14 DECEMBER

I am interviewed by Roy Hattersley. Extraordinarily, he is doing a 400-word profile of the Prime Minister for the *Mail on Sunday*. Hattersley says that he has heard such outright criticism of John Major from Tory backbenchers that he must do something to balance it.

THURSDAY 15 DECEMBER

We are slaughtered at the Dudley by-election. The Labour majority is over 20,000 and the swing against us is the biggest since the war. There is next to nothing for our comfort.

SUNDAY 18 DECEMBER

As I wait to do an all too early television interview, I read a piece by

---

292   See p 385 when first reported.

Alistair McAlpine in the *Mail on Sunday*. What a malicious spiteful creature he is. His piece consists of nothing more than an outspoken attack on Jeremy Hanley. Does McAlpine seriously think that Jeremy could have prevented the Dudley defeat? McAlpine is a man who the Tory Party has rescued from obscurity and made a peer of the realm. He repays his debt by knifing the Party Chairman in the back. What a toad.

MONDAY 19 DECEMBER

In the evening to a reception given by Jeremy Hanley at Central Office. John Major arrives a few minutes later and comes over, taking me aside for a private word. He knows I have seen Hattersley – doubtless No. 10 suggested my name – and his first question is how it went. I shrug. The man is a former deputy leader of the Labour Party, I reply. But John is anything but philosophical about the profile. I tell him the Hattersley theory that class explains much of the personal opposition to him and my reply that the party has long since washed that out of our system as shown by their election of grammar school products like Heath and Thatcher. To my surprise, John does not agree. He thinks class explains a great deal.

1995

MONDAY 16 JANUARY

Lunch à deux with David Stevens on the top of the *Express* building with a magnificent view up the Thames to Blackfriars Bridge. He confirms one point. There was an undoubted conspiracy during the 1992 election to discredit Paddy Ashdown. The charge being made was that he had affairs with other women apart from the one that became public in the months before the election. The aim was to get a newspaper to publish the women's names. Stevens had been approached by an intermediary who said that he had been 'deputed' to ask Stevens to follow up a story that Ashdown had flown to the United States in pursuit of extra-marital sex. Yet more confirmation that there was a plot to expose Ashdown's personal life.

WEDNESDAY 18 JANUARY

A cup of tea with Nicholas Soames who, beneath the outrageously nine-teenth-century exterior he chooses to adopt, is a shrewd observer. He tells two wonderful stories about Alan Clark and his much-wronged wife, Jane. On one occasion when she rightly suspected he was leaving home early on a Sunday afternoon to pursue an affair in London she asked him to choose her a good bottle of wine from the wine cellar for her solitary supper. Once Clark descended into the cellar she promptly locked the door and left him there all night. On another occasion, she suggested he hid from demonstrators around his front gate by hiding in the boot of their car. Thus, he did and was left there for six hours. Nicholas affects to be surprised that I regard Clark as a shit. He then confesses his mother can't stand him and his father couldn't be in the same room. It seems to me I am not in bad company.

WEDNESDAY 25 JANUARY

Lunch with Maurice Saatchi. A 'new' Saatchi company is about to rise and Maurice seems cheerful and full of optimism. He tells me that one lesson he has learned from politicians like me is how to withstand a press barrage. In the old days he used to go through articles about himself with a toothcomb and take umbrage at even the smallest criticism in otherwise favourable pieces. Now, he lets it bounce off him. Maurice says he was at a meeting at Central Office when the Ashdown plot had been revealed as the secret weapon for the election. I am still intrigued to know how high the conspiracy went.

MONDAY 30 JANUARY

Geoffrey Howe delivers a broadside against John Major on Europe. The Prime Minister, he says, should have formed a cross-party coalition to force through Maastricht against the Conservative opposition. He seems oblivious to the fact that it would have split the Tory Party down the middle. Geoffrey has crossed over the water. Europe comes way above petty things like party politics and the survival of a Conservative government.

FRIDAY 3 FEBRUARY

Lunch with Linda. (I am lunching with 'all my exes' this month says Fiona!) She is looking very well but her husband John sounds poorly.[293] He has given up work on *The Times* but is able to write reviews and obituaries from home. She was putting together a biography of Michael Heseltine but the publishers lost interest when John Major won the leadership.

FRIDAY 10 FEBRUARY

I travel to Harrogate to speak to a business dinner and stay at the Old Swan where Agatha Christie went missing for a week or two in the 1930s. The only people I find there are a group from the trade union of my old foe Rodney Bickerstaffe. For some reason, one or two wished to be photographed with me. I fear I am remembered for the health strike of 1982.

WEDNESDAY 22 FEBRUARY

Major makes his Northern Ireland statement. It is very strong and almost all of the other parties support him. Predictably, the rumbles come from the Unionists. Nevertheless, by any standards, the PM's achievement has been immense. He has achieved six months of peace in Northern Ireland and has cleared the first hurdles of the negotiation process.

WEDNESDAY 1 MARCH

The day of the opposition's debate of no confidence in the government's policy on Europe. The debate itself goes well enough. Many colleagues think John Major speaks well but personally, I think Blair has the better of the exchanges. Norman Lamont interrupts both the PM and Douglas Hurd's wind-up. Douglas puts him down magisterially and points out that the position is the same as the one he helped to negotiate at Maastricht. Lamont, who has squeezed onto the front bench two down from me, continues to protest and I offer him the first words of advice I have directed to him since his fall – 'for goodness sake, calm down'. He does

---

293 John Higgins, journalist and opera critic, arts editor of the *Financial Times* 1962–70 and then of *The Times* 1970–88.

not respond. He is more concerned about the precariousness of his perch. James Hill, the substantial member for Southampton, has returned and is not amused to find the ex-Chancellor in his seat. Lamont is now sitting on the very edge of the bench and is in danger of being edged onto the floor. 'Look, if you want me to go and sit on the Labour benches I will' he protests petulantly. He is allowed an inch or two more of backside room but when the vote comes it is clear that we should not have bothered. Alone among the Tory Party he votes against the government.

THURSDAY 2 MARCH

There is a fierce press reaction to Lamont's vote. The consensus view appears to be that he has committed political suicide. I am not so optimistic. Leon's view on Lamont is that there is an irreconcilable conflict of aims: he could aim to bring down the Prime Minister; he can aim to return to the Cabinet; he can aim to find another seat. To pursue all three aims simultaneously presents problems. In the Commons, Labour members stick a notice on an empty place on the opposition benches spelling out one word: 'Lamont'.

FRIDAY 10 MARCH

Farewell lunch for Jonathan Hill at No. 10. I meet Norma at the door. She says that it has been a ghastly period and the press has hounded her family. To say the Majors dislike the press is a substantial understatement. Their attitude is a mixture of hatred and contempt. Left to his own devices, John Major would not hesitate to introduce a law on privacy. In the evening to the Birmingham Chamber of Commerce annual dinner with Michael Heseltine. He speaks well – very well – and looks in top-class condition. If John falls now then Michael is the successor.[294] Ken is entirely out of fashion. He is under attack from the right for his European stance. He is portrayed as a hopeless European enthusiast. Being a transparently honest man, Ken is not prepared to deny his position and robustly – probably too robustly – defends himself. Michael,

---

294 This may have been optimistic. He was still fiercely opposed by many inside the parliamentary party.

on the other hand, has learnt discretion. His views on Europe are no different to Ken's – but he steers clear of issues like the single currency. He has set his mind on establishing his credentials as Industry Secretary; making steady progress while the rest of the government falters.

THURSDAY 27 APRIL

A meeting with the PM at my request. Basically, I want to know what I can do to help after the local election results on the assumption (generally held) that they will be awful. John is anything but cheerful. He says that if there is a demand for a leadership election after the local elections that is what he will give them. Not in November when the annual opportunity comes, but now. He can resign as party leader but remain as Prime Minister while the election is arranged. He is not prepared for this to drag on into the autumn – 'left dangling in the wind'. He has not put his plan to anyone else but he's not going on for another six months being attacked by his own party. He has had three and a half years of it and it is enough. Frankly, I am horrified by his plan. 'What would be victory?' I ask. John says that if the number voting against him and abstaining exceeds eighty then he will certainly have to stand down. The more I think about it the more I am opposed to it. I reply, 'you will be fighting an election at what could be your weakest moment'. I cannot imagine that the Chancellor will welcome this move, I add, uncertainty is just what he doesn't want now. John says that he expects others will argue against it too but he will take some persuading.

MONDAY 12 JUNE

Margaret strikes again. Promoting her book on her early life she gives a series of interviews which are widely seen as attacks on the government in general, and John Major in particular. Having demolished every policy in sight, she says that she would not favour a change of leadership. She even adds the incredibly patronising comment that John Major is now 'coming on' and 'becoming more Conservative everyday'. Even today, Margaret appears to have no concept of the harm that she has done her successor. She believes that she was overthrown because she said 'No,

No, No' to Europe – when the truth is that she was overthrown for a variety of reasons of which Europe was only one. The more important reasons were that the party felt she had been leader long enough, they had tired of her style, and the opinion polls suggested that policies like the poll tax were leading us to defeat. Her legacy is likely to be that the Conservative Party goes into opposition for a decade but she will never admit any personal responsibility if that is the outcome. A great Prime Minister but a catastrophic ex-Prime Minister.

FRIDAY 16 JUNE

The papers are full of stories of a fresh leadership crisis. The usual cast including myself deny that a change in leadership will solve anything but in truth, John's position is weaker than it has been at any stage in the last five years. There is now a vast gulf in the party: the Eurosceptics appear to believe that all will be solved if only the Prime Minister comes off the fence and proclaims his opposition to a single currency and a range of other federalist measures. They have no concept that a move of that kind would cause the most terrible rift with the other side of the party.

TUESDAY 20 JUNE

To a Foyles luncheon at midday for Margaret Thatcher's book. Her critics say that she looks old these days and over the top. Not so today: she looks very good, smart, impeccable, speaks well for over half an hour without a note. As she looks down the table at Willie Whitelaw, Hailsham, Parkinson, Tebbit, Baker and myself she says it reminds her of a 'revivalist meeting'. What comes through is her love affair with the United States – 'that great nation'. In her ideal world we would have a North Atlantic Free Trade Area. The trouble is that she is a quarter of a century too late.

Willie tells me that at one stage Margaret seriously considered putting Alan Clark into her Cabinet. Willie told her that if she did that he would resign and Margaret never raised the issue again. He also confirmed that following the 1987 general election I was a potential name for the transfer list. 'You needed a little help', he agrees to my question.

THURSDAY 22 JUNE

A day of high drama. Just after lunch I receive a message from Ian Lang to ring him.[295] Can we meet straight after PMQs in his room? The Prime Minister has asked him to see me, he explains. John has decided to bring the uncertainty to an end and rather than waiting for November he will call a leadership election now, today. Ian, who was told only this morning, is to be one of his campaign managers with Brian Mawhinney. They would like me to use the contacts I have with the political editors to further the campaign.

Ian looks at me quizzically. 'What do you think about the plan?' he asks. 'Frankly' I say, and not to be repeated back to John, a mistake. I am worried, not about those voting against, but that his position will be undermined if there are a large number of abstentions – and there are too many people with motives for abstaining. But the decision is taken and obviously I will do everything I can to help. John has taken virtually everybody by surprise, including his own supporters.

The announcement is still over an hour away but the rumours are already beginning in the lobby. A press conference has been called for 4.30 in the Rose Garden at No. 10. I watch the announcement with Tom King in the TV room at the Commons. A simple, dignified statement, no questions taken and John retreats inside. I get to the 1922 Committee meeting while it is still considering next week's business. Marcus Fox then reads the letter the Prime Minister has sent. This is greeted with prolonged banging of tables in support of John. I watch Lamont mechanically going through the same process and wonder just how many others are hiding their true feelings. Down in the lobby I am taken away to Millbank and an endless succession of interviews.

FRIDAY 23 JUNE

The press headlines vary from 'Major throws down gauntlet' to the less helpful 'Major's great gamble' in the *Mail* and the hostile 'Major's suicide

---

295 Government whip, later Secretary of State for Scotland and one of the good men in politics.

note' in *The Sun*. In the constituency the reaction to John's move is supportive. They are all rather taken aback by the speed of events but his call to see the issue of leadership settled is strongly supported. In the afternoon I put through a message to John that I would like to speak to him sometime in the next twenty-four hours. He comes back less than thirty minutes later. He is in fighting form and obviously much more cheerful now the decision is taken. His concern is not Lamont but John Redwood. Redwood is the only Cabinet member not to have pledged his support for the Prime Minister and he is not planning to say anything until Monday. 'What do you think he's playing at?' John asks. Clearly the prospect of a challenge from within the Cabinet had not been contemplated.

I explain to John that Norman Tebbit had taken me to one side and given me a message which he obviously expected I would relay to him. In short, it was that if he underlined his Eurosceptic credentials then all he would need to worry about was David Currie or Hugh Dykes standing against him. But what did this mean? Was the pledge of a referendum on the single currency enough? 'No', said Norman, 'he would have to declare against it'. My reply to that was that I did not see how John could do that given his position up to now was that he was keeping his options open. John's reaction is surprising. I had expected him to agree with my interpretation of his position. Instead, he sets out his position on the single currency: he is against it, not least because of its constitutional implications, but he has to keep the Cabinet together. In other words, he wishes he could make such a pledge but he would lose Ken and Michael as well as, I would estimate, people like John Gummer, Douglas Hurd and David Hunt. Frankly, if that is his position he should have pledged a referendum weeks ago but this is not the moment to reopen a general discussion. We only have ten days.

SATURDAY 24 JUNE

The slightly euphoric atmosphere of the last twenty-four hours is changing. There is a growing recognition of just what a risk Major is taking. The press is now giving pages of coverage to likely contenders. During the day I ring Jonathan Holborow of the *Mail on Sunday*. He says they are receiving very strong reports that John Redwood intends to stand. A 'bombshell announcement' is expected on Monday. He pledges editorial support for John Major. I ring Ian Lang with the news. He says that they have been trying to get through to Redwood but he has left his fax machine on, blocking incoming telephone calls.

MONDAY 26 JUNE

At 7.00 I ring the *Evening Standard* with an all-situations-covered article defending John Major. Three hours later, I hear the news that Redwood has resigned from the Cabinet and is holding a press conference a little later when he will announce his candidature. My first reaction is that this is spectacular disloyalty from a man who has served in John's Cabinet for the last five years and accepted the policies of that government including the European ones. I rewrite my *Evening Standard* piece in the Commons library and phone it in by 11.30. It is a good job I still have some pretensions to be a journalist. In the Commons there is some feeling that Redwood has scuppered Portillo. Evidently there is no love lost between the two men. Redwood resents the 'personality' cult that has built up around Portillo. My knowledge of Redwood is slight. I knew him as one of Thatcher's policy advisers in the 1980s. He is bright. There is no doubt about that but he is a cold fish. He is convinced of the rightness of any case he espouses or any decision he makes. He is a modern-day Enoch Powell, brighter than Portillo but not as appealing, but nevertheless a formidable opponent. It is bad news for John. He will still win but the question will be by how many, has he the authority to govern?

TUESDAY 27 JUNE

John is in Cannes for the European summit but unlike Margaret Thatcher intends to hurry home tonight. Tony Newton stands in at Prime Minister's Questions, which is boisterous and very noisy. Total hilarity when a Tory backbencher praises the government's policy of 'choice and diversity'. That he was referring to education did nothing to reduce the gales of delighted laughter. I'm sitting next to Ted Heath. 'What do you think of it all?' I ask. He thinks for a moment: 'a bit of a mess', he says eventually. We talk on for a few seconds. 'They are a nasty lot', he observes of the parliamentary party. Well he has his own experiences of leadership elections and he's obviously scarred by them. Nevertheless, there is truth in his observation. The party is demonstrating once more how tricky it can be. More to the point, it *is* a bit of a mess.

WEDNESDAY 28 JUNE

A robust intervention on *Today* from Michael Heseltine promising total support for John. It is very good – as much as we could hope Michael to do. He says that at one point he was consulted before the step was taken. We are all back to the media-driven timetable of early mornings and late nights.

TUESDAY 4 JULY

Election day. The *Mail* print a front page leader urging MPs to ditch Major. *The Sun* is also totally hostile. All the Murdoch newspapers have come out against the Prime Minister. We have been so foolish to allow the media to be dominated in this way. When all this is over we should revisit. Murdoch doesn't give a stuff who is in control as long as his companies prosper. His view of John Major is that he is a 'loser' and his papers and columnists parrot his views. I'm gloomy about the outcome. I meet Alastair Goodlad, the Chief Whip, who urges me to get a message to the PM saying, in effect, that victory is victory. The rules lay down what is required. I relay the message through to No. 10 and then by chance, have the opportunity of giving it to John in person. I meet him in the corridor on his way to vote. He listens to my advice, which he has obviously heard from others. 'Fine', he says, 'but if you want me to do that you must all take on those newspapers'.

As at the time of Margaret Thatcher's leadership election I am in a television studio for the declaration. David Davis has provided me with figures that prove that anything over 165 votes is a victory. To my mind, anything above 200 is enough. I'm prepared to defend any victory figure but we are in obvious difficulties below 190. My fear is that John's vote will be somewhere in the grey to black area of 180 to 199. My forebodings are all demolished when the declaration takes place. John has polled 218, two thirds of the vote. Immediately, I tell David Dimbleby this is a decisive victory. Robin Oakley agrees that 218 is enough and there is no question of the Prime Minister resigning. We have won. John has again confounded his critics.

WEDNESDAY 5 JULY

The various newspapers who have loudly proclaimed their opposition to Major come to terms with his victory in different ways. Some like the *Telegraph* do it graciously; others like *The Sun* simply lick their wounds; the Murdoch press has not succeeded in having its way but it will try again. All eyes are now on the reshuffle. The Cabinet is announced just after lunch. The most important appointment is Michael Heseltine as Deputy Prime Minister; at last the necessary man to chair the Cabinet committees and head the government's presentation effort. It has taken us three years to get to this point but at least we are there now. It is desperately late but if anyone can make it work, Heseltine can. I meet Jeremy Hanley in the lobby. He has been sacked as Chairman to make way for Brian Mawhinney. He has accepted a Minister of State post and tells me he will loyally 'go on smiling' although obviously he is disappointed not to have been moved sideways in the Cabinet. Malcolm Rifkind is Foreign Secretary and William Hague goes into the Cabinet as Welsh Secretary. David Hunt, surprisingly, goes out and John Redwood, unsurprisingly, is not invited to rejoin.

THURSDAY 6 JULY

At PMQs John Major receives a loud welcome from our side and does well enough. John Redwood wisely intervenes straight away to offer congratulations. I met him by chance in the tea room yesterday. Cheerful, relaxed, he gives the impression that his greatest contest is with Michael Portillo not John Major.

TUESDAY 26 SEPTEMBER

John Major is holding a seventieth birthday party for Margaret Thatcher at No. 10. The list has been vetted by Margaret and we are on the list. I meet the Brussels train at Waterloo and looking very smart and fresh in a black dress, Fiona comes through the barrier. We arrive late and Margaret, resplendent in a ball gown, is in full flow. It is a strange rambling speech. She then looks around the room where many of the team from 1979 are assembled. 'We were more than friends', she says, 'we were allies'. The Second World War analogy continues but it is an interesting rationalisation of her position. Politically, the most significant change is that at last Thatcher and Major seem to be prepared to get on with each other. There are a great many references to the 'Prime Minister' in her speech and she awards John with what she must feel is the ultimate accolade: 'You were one of the team', she says. So peace has at last broken out. I do not wish to be unduly cynical but John has just won a leadership election. His next challenge will be the general election. We will probably lose it but Margaret does not want to be blamed. She will behave herself for the next eighteen months and hope everyone forgets the last four years.

SUNDAY 22 OCTOBER

A dash of cold water on our hopes of recovery. An opinion poll shows us still thirty points behind, languishing at 26 per cent support. Even more ominously, we are viewed as having ceded the political centre ground to Tony Blair's Labour Party.

WEDNESDAY 25 OCTOBER

Peter Temple-Morris says there has been a meeting of the MacLeod Group, a centre-left group of Tory MPs. They would like me to stand for the chairmanship of the 1922 Committee. Peter laughs apologetically, 'We have been round this course before'. Indeed we have and my reaction to this latest offer is an emphatic 'no thanks'.

FRIDAY 27 OCTOBER

The *Financial Times* duly report the MacLeod Group's approach under the headline 'Left wing aims to capture 1922 post'. Have I become a leading left-winger? That does say something about the press perception of the present state of the Tory Party.

SUNDAY 10 DECEMBER

We return after a weekend of constituency parties in Sutton Coldfield to receive a telephone message from the nursing wing. My mother has relapsed. When I get to Wimbledon, she is sleeping peacefully but cannot be woken. The nursing staff are obviously concerned.

MONDAY 11 DECEMBER

My mother dies. She never woke up and simply stopped breathing. It could not be more peaceful. She has lived for ninety-three years and she has not had a serious illness in all that time. If I live to ninety-three and die in the same way, I will be satisfied. Nevertheless, her death is a great blow. I regret that in her last years we could not talk of her younger days and of her life in teaching. Her memory was so short in the end she could not remember her fifty years in Essex.

So what do I remember? First, I remember the war. I remember a daylight attack on the local works, just 800 yards away. A fighter swooped low over our garden in First Avenue with its guns blazing. My four-year-old friend from next door and I sheltered under the stairs inside the house but my mother could not find us and ran through the garden searching for us. She was lucky not to be killed. I remember another time, a little later, when a bomb fell nearby, causing the ceiling to come tumbling down on the Morrison shelter in the back room. There was an immense crash. My father was away from the house on his air raid duties, my mother was convinced that half the house had been destroyed and indeed it sounded like that. I remember travelling up to London with her to see the Festival of Britain. In those days it was quite a journey with steam trains and ninety minutes to reach Liverpool Street. I remember when my father died at the beginning of the 1960s. My mother told the neighbours it was 'God's will' and slowly adjusted her life. She went back to teaching and worked the last few years necessary to gain her pension. She was a good woman. There were no sins that need to be forgiven. If there is a heaven, she will go straight there.

FRIDAY 15 DECEMBER
The funeral is at Putney Vale. The vicar speaks well and wisely does not pretend he has known her for years. In my turn, I say that the trouble with living to ninety-three is that you have outlived most of your contemporaries. Personally, if it were left to me, I would prefer a long life to a well-attended funeral.

A few days later our mood changes.

MONDAY 18 DECEMBER
Fiona's fiftieth birthday party. Ken and Gillian kindly say we can use No. 11. I have had a great deal of trouble persuading Fiona that this is an anniversary that should be celebrated but now it has arrived, she enjoys it. In part it is the release of emotion from last week. In part a successful mix: Fiona's Oxford friends, my Cambridge ones, Fulham and politics. The Cambridge mafia are there in force, Heseltine looks in and Major arrives late but is almost the last to leave. Ken and I try to persuade him to come out to dinner. He would obviously like to do so but a solitary curry has been prepared for him upstairs in his flat. To change arrangements would mean all kinds of security precautions and new orders to his staff. Impromptu decisions about dinner are impossible for Prime Ministers. They are prisoners of their own protection force. It is not a problem for Chancellors of the Exchequer and Ken comes with a dozen or so of us to dinner round the corner and is in great form.

25

FROM GOVERNMENT
TO IRRELEVANCE

FEBRUARY 1996 – MAY 1997

THURSDAY 22 FEBRUARY 1996

John Major is pressed again on the *Scott Report* at Prime Minister's Questions. Labour have their tails up. They smell blood. They could easily beat us and if they do, then William Waldegrave and Nick Lyell could well be forced out.[296] In the division lobby I run into Virginia who has been sitting on the selection committee for the Millennium Exhibition. She doesn't exactly tell me who has won but the signs are clear enough. Heseltine has used every bit of influence he has to get the exhibition to Greenwich. To complete a grim day, Peter Thurnham announces he is resigning the whip. I cannot find it in my heart to condemn him but it is, I fear, a decision he will come to regret. Not all his old friends will be as charitable as me.

MONDAY 26 FEBRUARY

The debate on the *Scott Report*. 'Are you speaking?' I ask Ted Heath as he slumps into his corner seat on the front bench below the gangway. 'It's not my mess', he grunts. He then adds with a twinkle, 'my people used to resign'. In the debate John gives a long, detailed speech

---

296 The *Scott Report* on the export of defence equipment to Iraq was a judicial inquiry commissioned in 1992. It followed the prosecution of three directors of the machine tools company, Matrix Churchill, for breaching export controls. In fact, it had permission although the government denied it following a change of policy. Waldegrave and Lyell had both been mentioned as being involved.

in which his purpose is to show the waverers on our side that we really are taking the report seriously and acting upon it. The triumphalism of last week has entirely disappeared. He ends with a good piece of abuse directed at Robin Cook but it is not a convincing performance. If anything, it reminds me of Hattersley defending Labour in the last days of the Callaghan government. The same grim faces on the government back benches and mocking laughter from the opposition. Robin Cook makes the most of his opportunity and tears into the government's case. It is a remarkably effective Commons performance. We look doomed to defeat. The Ulster Unionists have apparently decided to vote against us but then the cavalry arrives in the unlikely shape of Rupert Allason. Having roundly condemned us in his speech he nevertheless turns up in our lobby. The result is that we win by one. In all truth however, it is not a good day. The odds on an election in 1996 have shortened.

SUNDAY 3 MARCH

An extraordinary fiftieth birthday party of Michael Ashcroft. Five or six hundred friends sit down in the Great Room of Grosvenor House. There is a funfair in the gallery; bucking broncos; try your strength hammers and fortune tellers. Paul Anka plus full orchestra is flown over from Los Angeles to sing songs from the '50s and '60s, 'Diana' to 'My Way'. Midnight is brought in by the band of the Royal Marines and hundreds of balloons fall onto the dance floor. Politicians abound.

THURSDAY 7 MARCH

John is back from Hong Kong and in reasonably good form at PMQs. He gives apparent encouragement for a referendum on the single currency. But why don't we just get on and announce it? Extraordinarily, there are still those in Cabinet – including Ken I fear – who are opposed. By the time we get around to announcing it we will have lost all political advantage.

SATURDAY 9 MARCH

To Aston Villa and who should turn up but the Chancellor accompanied by Terry Burns who is a confirmed QPR supporter. Sitting next to Terry at lunch we chat about the time we left the ERM. He says Lamont very much wanted to stay and that explained his refusal to resign or swap with Ken Clarke at the Home Office. He muses had Lamont swapped then the fire would have been centred on Major.

TUESDAY 2 JULY

Lunch with Jonathan Hill who suggests that Major is more isolated than ever. He is not sure who his real friends are anymore. Of course, all his staff loyally support him but are they 'mates' in the way that Sarah and Jonathan were? Special pleading perhaps but I suspect a huge element of truth. John's real soulmate now appears to be the Chief Whip Alastair Goodlad.

THURSDAY 11–TUESDAY 16 JULY

A break in the sun in Majorca with Tim and Stefa. Another guest is Charlie Gregson who is on the main board of United. A good break. There is only one moment of anxiety when Kate and the boys jump 50 foot from some cliff into the sea. Fortunately it *was* sea. The alternative doesn't bear contemplating.

SUNDAY 21 JULY

Press stories coming through that Heathcoat-Amory is to resign on the single currency issue. There are no denials from Heathcoat-Amory and therefore the stories are assumed to be true. The resignation could scarcely be at a worse time, coming a few days after Major's passionate pleas to the 1992 Committee for unity. HA is a former Deputy Chief Whip and knows the score. He also knows that if we were to come out absolutely against the single currency at this stage the party would split. We would lose the Chancellor and the Deputy PM from the Cabinet and render ourselves unelectable. Who would support a party that nine months before an election splits in this way? This, of course, is not how the sceptics see it. Outright opposition to the single currency is an issue which would sweep the country and bring the Tory Party back to power. The internal party debate on Europe is now a dialogue of the deaf.

MONDAY 22 JULY

Heathcoat-Amory duly resigns. Were it not for the occasion of his departure it would hardly deserve comment. Grey, aloof, uninspiring. He was a Minister of State and few if any thought he would rise higher – perhaps a Chief Whip in a lean year. On one charge however, he can be acquitted. His opposition to the single currency and all things European is not new ground. He has been a consistent sceptic. The crisis in the Tory Party is gathering pace. The sceptics make it clear that they want no compromise. They spurn the idea of a political party being a coalition, trying to find policies that can bind the different strands together. John has given the pledge of a referendum on the single currency but the sceptics will settle for nothing less than 'no single currency in the course of the next parliament'. In my mind, Major's pledge is superior in all ways. It leaves us at the negotiating table able to influence the outcome. While the pledge of a referendum has infinitely more public appeal than the limited pledge of the sceptics.

TUESDAY 23 JULY

For the first time in many years we go to a royal garden party at Buckingham Palace. MPs are automatically asked each year with the inevitable result that you become rather blasé about it all. This year, Fiona thinks it would be a good idea to take Oliver. The policy for garden parties has changed. Whereas once, MPs could only take unmarried daughters over eighteen, now we can take unmarried sons – even stepsons – up to twenty-five. A minor victory in the battle against sexual discrimination. So off we went, myself in morning dress, Fiona very smart in a green suit and a wide brimmed black hat, and Oliver wearing his one well-cut suit. We need hardly have bothered. No sooner had we arrived at the Palace than the heavens opened: torrential rain; explosions of thunder; jagged cuts of lightning. There was a stampede for cover. Tea tents burst to overflowing, the band stands were rapidly occupied while many guests could find no other shelter but the trees. This proved to be a great mistake. On the far side of the vast garden an ambulance with its blue lights flashing was making its way down one of the paths. Two guests sheltering under a tree had been struck by lightning, not killed, but injured and taken to hospital.

For Tory MPs a garden party is followed by drinks at No. 10. I confess to thinking that this might be the last occasion for some years that we receive such an invitation. A 7 p.m. vote interrupts the drinks and in the lobby there is a scene which sums up the state of the Conservative Party. David Heathcoat-Amory is surrounded by a small group who are congratulating him as if he has just been promoted in government. Quite openly among the group is a Cabinet minister – Peter Lilley.

The European battle inside the Conservative Party becomes fiercer. There are signs of the disintegration of the party. There is no sign that Tory MPs generally have the will to come together and try to make things better – although everyone with a majority of less than 10,000 is in danger. In the meantime Tony Blair establishes himself as a credible alternative leader of the country.

WEDNESDAY 11 DECEMBER

The start of a two-day debate on Europe. Ken Clarke battles through a barrage of heckles from, of course, the Conservative side. Mavericks like Marlow and Tapsell join Lamont and Redwood in trying to put the boot into the Chancellor. They don't quite succeed but that is because Ken is such a resilient performer. Gordon Brown has an open goal and the sceptics retreat from the battlefield having made the election of the Labour Party, who stand for all they abhor on Europe, that much more certain.

THURSDAY 12 DECEMBER

I speak in the European debate. I have never been an enthusiast but I was prepared to go along with the conventional wisdom. My lurch against has far less to do with the single currency than with the European social policy now being forced on Britain. For three years I argued against the social chapter and measures like the 48-hour week. But the Commission has won. They have entirely ignored our opt out and pushed through the working hours directive as a health and safety issue. So we now have to fall into line despite the fact that our opposition was the policy of the elected government of the UK. I remember only too well the kind of people who looked after these affairs at the Commission when I was Secretary of State. The awful Papandreou may have given way to an Irishman called Flynn but to judge from his public utterances he is no improvement. The bureaucrats continue their relentless pressure to bring us into line and defeat the democratically elected government.

MONDAY 16 DECEMBER
Speak at a lunch in Michael Heseltine's constituency. Anne is also there and we have perhaps the longest conversation we have ever had. She is no fan of Heath. During our years of opposition, she organised a number of dinner parties for the great man. Never once did he send a note of thanks. She also revealed a hitherto unknown part of her early life to me. For six months she had worked for the *Birmingham Evening Mail* in London as a jack-of-all-trades including part-time theatre critic.

FRIDAY 20 DECEMBER
John Major comes to Birmingham for the annual Chamber of Commerce dinner. He says the speech he has been dished up is unusable. What do I think about an off-the-cuff speech on the economy and Europe? I agree and he duly gives one of the best speeches I have heard him deliver. A page of notes and he speaks without pause for a good forty minutes. What is fascinating is the way he sets out his views on Europe. We are a truly international trading nation, he says. He wants membership of the European Community but not an arrangement which leads either to political centralisation or one that excludes the rest of the world, in particular the United States. Afterwards I congratulate him on the speech and say that he should develop the theme. John agrees but says there are problems – not least our mutual friend. Our mutual friend is Ken and it appears that the newspaper stories about the rift between them on Europe have real substance.

1997

SATURDAY 25 JANUARY

I hear on the radio that Alan Clark – the 68-year-old adulterer and the man who came out of the Scott Inquiry smelling of cabbages – has been selected for Kensington and Chelsea. An incredibly bad choice. The safest Tory seat in the land and they throw it away on Clark. His selection gets full coverage but the press is fickle and inconsistent. In the main they welcome the selection of 'a character'. It will lighten the grey ranks of the Commons they say!

SUNDAY 9 FEBRUARY

I am rung by David Mathew who has been seeking a seat to fight for the election. He tells me that as a resident of Kensington and Chelsea he was canvassed by a highly placed supporter of Alan Clark. 'We thought that as you both went to Eton you would support him'. To which David, a mild-mannered and scrupulously polite man, untypically replied, 'having been to Eton it enables you to detect a shit at a hundred paces'.

FRIDAY 14 FEBRUARY

Terrible news. John (Fiona's father) dies suddenly during the night. Eileen rings soon after seven and Fiona speeds to her flat. I am a few minutes behind. There is no doubt: no chance of recovery as there was in 1978. Eileen is bearing up bravely but suddenly she looks frail and old. Fiona and James are suppressing their grief in the organisation which goes with death: undertakers; registrars; doctors. Kate and Isobel both break into tears as I break the news. A dear and devoted grandfather is gone.

MONDAY 17 FEBRUARY

The death notice is in *The Times*. A rather good one which manages to set out the sadness of all the generations. Oliver is flying back from Hong Kong for the funeral. I still cannot quite appreciate that John is gone. I half expect that voice on the phone 'Oh, Norman, John here'. Everyone says how good it was that he went so quickly and without pain and to some extent that is right but it did mean that no one was able to say goodbye and above all how much we had appreciated him in life. For me he was quite simply a good and very loyal friend. He supported me in some pretty black moments in government and always had time to listen and advise.

MONDAY 24 FEBRUARY

John's funeral. The greatest praise I can give it is that John would have thought it magnificent. It is organised, of course, by Fiona. John was deliberately unreligious. He had carefully considered the question and had come to the conclusion that he did not believe. Our first inclination had nevertheless been to ask a vicar to officiate. That is after all what happens at funerals but Fiona decided that John would have preferred it if the family carried out the service so James gave the address, Stephi read a Shakespeare sonnet, I read a wonderful piece from Bertrand Russell's autobiography and Kate did magnificently with a piece from Joyce Grenfell. But above all it was Fiona who controlled proceedings. With tremendous poise she settled the crowded congregation, explained what was happening and put them at their ease. She then took the service in its entirety: the welcome; the period of reflection and eventually pressing the button that took John's coffin through for cremation. My abiding memory of the funeral will be of Fiona smiling at the gathering of John's old friends and colleagues and leading them gently in their remembrances.

THURSDAY 27 FEBRUARY

The BBC ask me if I would do an interview on Norman Tebbit's article on Michael Heseltine. What article? I am pointed to *The Spectator* and a book review by Tebbit which describes the Deputy Prime Minister as 'tacky' and accuses him of killing off our greatest peacetime Prime Minister. It is a predictable Tebbit rant, only made notable by its crass timing in an election campaign, and the depth of his hatred for Heseltine. At one point in the article is a phrase about how he put personal ambition to one side in the cause of defeating Heseltine. This is his 'official' excuse for backing Major in the second round of the leadership campaign. The only man who could beat Heseltine.

FRIDAY 28 FEBRUARY

A depressing day. We lose the Wirral by-election by a mile – a 17 per cent swing against us. Why do we think this is all going to change by the time of the general election? Why do we assume the conventional political wisdom that it will be 'much closer than you think'?

TUESDAY 4 MARCH

Michael Howard goes a long way to losing my support in the post-election leadership contest. Until today I had assumed a vote for Ken Clarke on the first round and one for Michael when, as I fear is inevitable, Ken is knocked out of the contest. Now I am anything but sure. My doubts come after a meeting in the smoking room. I gently upbraid Michael for the Home Office action in leaking all his crime proposals in advance. I am old-fashioned enough to believe that statements should be made to the Commons first and not leaked to the *Mail* or trailed on *Today*. Slightly to my surprise, Michael makes no pretence that he is doing anything other than leaking. Everyone does, he says. He then goes on to speak with an unattractive religious fervour along the lines of 'I am involved in a deadly struggle. I want to fundamentally change the criminal law system. Some are on my side. Others oppose me. You would expect me to go to my friends'. Well actually, I would not expect the Home Secretary to leak.

THURSDAY 6 MARCH

Sitting on the front bench below the gangway, I move along to make room for Ted Heath who these days is quite a bulk. 'Don't worry', he says jocularly, 'you are not as big as you think'. At PMQs one of our backbenchers brings down the House by congratulating the government on the success of its economic policy 'compared with the last eighteen years'.

WEDNESDAY 12 MARCH
A newspaper story that Margaret Thatcher is backing Portillo for the leadership. This is strenuously denied by the lady herself and she is putting in a complaint to the Press Council.

THURSDAY 13 MARCH
A new story about Margaret Thatcher. This time that she has praised Tony Blair. There is no comment on this and no complaint to the press council.

WEDNESDAY 19 MARCH
The election is finally called. John Major comes to the 1922. It is crowded and he speaks well enough. At the end he receives a massive reception which has more to do with the affection in which he is held than the rousing nature of his speech. His plea for a united campaign receives loud table-banging applause. Paul Marland standing in front of me turns on Cash – 'Do you hear that Bill?' he asks, 'do you hear that?' The interesting part of his speech is when he proclaims his belief in the welfare state – a decidedly unfashionable Tory view these days.

THURSDAY 20 MARCH
A deeply unpleasant Prime Minister's Questions as John swaps insults with Blair on sleaze. Blair concludes the events have left a 'stain' on the government but John responds ferociously accusing Blair of being in the pockets of the unions and flying free on Concorde without declaring it. The noise is massive. Most of our side seem to think we have won. Personally, the whole exchange leaves me with a nasty taste in my mouth.

FRIDAY 21 MARCH
More on the Hamilton front. *The Guardian* publish page after page of

the evidence given to Downey.[297] Five Tory MPs are seriously implicated, including Hamilton and Tim, and the charges range from accepting gifts to the non-declaration of payments to either Parliament or the tax man. There could hardly be a worse way of starting an election campaign. It puts the old sleaze stories back on the agenda.

WEDNESDAY 26 MARCH

Poor Tim Smith resigns his seat. He has done the honourable thing although he has been more a chump than anything else. There is no sign of Hamilton following suit.

TUESDAY I APRIL

With the public suitably distracted, Blair's people announce that there will be no television debate with Major. There is a lot of hot air about impossible Tory conditions but we all know the true reason. Blair is miles ahead. Why on earth should he risk a television debate with the Prime Minister?

MONDAY 7 APRIL

Martin Bell is to stand as the anti-sleaze candidate against Neil Hamilton. Everyone is over-excited by the news. I think it will marginalise the sleaze issue; the issue will be fought out in Knutsford, not nationally. Whatever persuaded Bell to take such a step is beyond me, he is a reporter – and a very good one – not a politician.

TUESDAY 8 APRIL

In the evening, my adoption meeting in Sutton Coldfield. I am duly confirmed as candidate by a surprisingly well-attended and genial meeting. Some of the members there were with me when I began back in

---

297 Sir Gordon Downey began his inquiry into the so-called 'cash for questions' affairs in early 1997 but the general election was called before he could publish his report. The report was eventually published in early July and found that Neil Hamilton and several other MPs had concealed payments from Parliament.

1974. Whatever others may say about their constituents, I could not have had a more loyal bunch, almost without exception, they have been magnificent.

WEDNESDAY 9 APRIL

I am fighting this election as a traditional constituency campaign – no ministerial duties, no Party Chairman role, not even a special travelling assistant to the Prime Minister. The last time I fought the election on the doorsteps was 1974 and I enjoyed it. I intend to enjoy myself again. I've swapped my shoes for trainers and we spend the day happily racing from house to house. The reception is friendly. I know I have been here for a quarter of a century but I am amazed by the number of people who say I have helped them in this case or that.

THURSDAY 10 APRIL

To Uttoxeter, to John Major's Midlands rally. Jeffrey Archer has asked me to introduce the Prime Minister, which I duly do. During the three hours I am there, I meet most of the old travelling gang. It all sounds very much like last time: press releases of speeches still late, the travelling press corps mildly dissatisfied but John making good speeches and impressing everyone whom he meets face to face. Jeffrey warms up the rally admirably and organises the whole show – for that is what it is – with real style. Full marks to him.

WEDNESDAY 16 APRIL

The European issue is now a full-scale crisis. Two junior ministers, John Horam and James Paice, have explicitly come out against the single currency. Horam, a refugee from both Labour and the SDP, is particularly unconvincing in his later declaration of support for the government line. *The Times* reveals that a whole range of other ministers like Michael Forsyth and Eric Forth are taking a different route to express their single currency doubts. In their printed material they keep to the government line but the advice from their constituency offices is that they are opposed. Not surprisingly the opposition is now in full cry. A divided party, they cry. That cannot be denied. Weak leadership, they chant. That is not true. On Europe we have two factions fighting for control. That cannot be denied. John takes the issue head-on. At his morning press conference he appeals to the party not to wreck his policy on Europe and in the evening, instead of the planned party political, he delivers a hard-hitting statement straight to camera. He stresses the referendum; he stresses his opposition to a federal centralised Europe; he stresses (rightly) his negotiating skills. It is a remarkably effective performance, but, but … I cannot remember another occasion when in the middle of an election campaign with two weeks to go until polling, a party leader has been forced to appeal to his own party for their loyalty.

SATURDAY 19 APRIL

Canvassing in the Sutton shopping centres today I meet one observer of the political scene who put forward a startling theory. 'Tell me privately', he said, 'are you really trying to lose this election so that Labour can inherit all the problems that there are?' As far as I could judge he was a Conservative voter, absolutely serious, convinced that there was some rational explanation for our behaviour. If only that was true.

SUNDAY 20 APRIL

The polls suggest that Labour could have a majority of 100 plus. That is also becoming my view. Even as I write, a new row on Europe is breaking out between Michael Howard and Ken Clarke. In the evening I ring John Major as promised. 'Is there anything that I can do to help?' I open. 'You can ring Ken', the Prime Minister replies. There is no doubt that John places the blame for the divisions over the last few days on the shoulders of Ken. Evidently, Central Office have been tearing their hair out in despair at his utterances. Many of his colleagues are blaming Ken for the chaotic way the campaign on Europe is going. 'It used to be Bill Cash. It is now Ken Clarke' is the summary of John's message.

FRIDAY 25 APRIL

An IRA bomb warning causes chaos in Birmingham. Their tactic of targeting the motorways continues and the police warn the public to stay at home. I have to get into Birmingham and drive along almost empty roads. I do a television discussion with Clare Short where the IRA tactics come up. Clare Short shows just why Blair and the spin doctors hold their breath whenever she gives public utterance. Rather than the safe denunciation of the IRA, tactics uttered earlier by Blair himself, Clare goes on a path all alone. She talks of the goal of a united Ireland and comes within a hair's breadth of backing it. She is an endearing character but not I fear a long-term player on the Labour front bench.

SATURDAY 26 APRIL

The last weekend in the shopping centres of Sutton Coldfield. During the election the campaign team and I have covered at least five miles a day on foot. As a result, I am certainly much fitter at the end of this election than the beginning. Less reassuring is that I have yet to meet any voter who voted Labour or Liberal Democrat in 1992 who is now going to switch to us. Not one. On the other hand I have met plenty who voted Conservative in 1992 and are now switching away.

SUNDAY 27 APRIL

We are losing. The only question is how badly. We, the parliamentary party, have thrown this election away, aided by such figures as Margaret Thatcher, Norman Tebbit and a host of editors, columnists and newspaper proprietors from Charles Moore to Rupert Murdoch. We will not be wiped out as in Canada. Even I do not believe that we will lose Sutton Coldfield. In the press a Tory defeat is taken for granted and all the speculation is about who will be the next Tory leader. Portillo v. Heseltine seems the likeliest choice.

THURSDAY 1 MAY

I go through the usual rituals of election day but it is only filling in time. Minds are now made up and we are just waiting for the polls to close. The first exit poll at 10 p.m. predicts that we will lose by over 150 seats. By the time I get into the radio studio at Pebble Mill the forecast is down to 100 and it seems that the worse disaster might be avoided but when I arrive at the indoor arena in Birmingham it is clear that we are being slaughtered. From around the country come reports of the rout. Rifkind out in Edinburgh, Budgen out in Wolverhampton, Currie defeated in Derby. Just a few of the tales of defeat brought to me as our count drags on. Birmingham Council have decided to count the marginal seats first. The effect is that my result is declared last and way past 3 a.m. My majority comes down to just under 15,000 with about 53 per cent of the vote. The share of the vote figure is the lowest I have ever received but among Conservative candidates I will be regarded with great envy. Blair has a majority of around 180. We are reduced to a pathetic figure somewhere between 160 and 170. Portillo has lost his seat so all bets on the next leader are off. My assumption is that John Major will immediately step down and the next event will be the Tory leadership election.

FRIDAY 2 MAY

A television programme in the morning raking over our defeat. My verdict on John Major is that he was a leader who never received the support he deserved. Much of the blame goes to Thatcher. She had the power to make or break him. She backed Major as the only man who could beat Heseltine and then withdrew her support once that purpose had been served. She should be thoroughly ashamed of her role but of course it will not even cross her mind that she bears any responsibility. As for John himself, he never received the credit for his achievements – the victory in 1992, the opt outs at Maastricht and above all, the strongest economy since the war. All this was obscured by the antics of a hopelessly divided parliamentary party where a low majority invested the rebellious, the sour and the straightforward nuts with an importance that they never deserved.

My interview over, I settle down for the first time to examine the list of defeated candidates. Poor Tony Newton defeated in Braintree. Andrew Mitchell in Nottinghamshire. Cabinet ministers like Roger Freeman and William Waldegrave rejected. Extraordinary results like the loss of Wimbledon and Surbiton to the Liberals. Later in the afternoon

I hear news of the Winchester result. My old Deputy Chairman, Gerry Malone, defeated by two votes – two votes!

SATURDAY 3 MAY

More very bad news. Michael Heseltine has been admitted to hospital and is no longer a candidate for the Tory leadership. Ironically, he probably had the party leadership within his grasp. The constituencies would have gone for him and among Tory MPs he had more broad appeal than any other candidate. He was acceptable to many on the right in a way that I fear Ken is not. How cruel that he should be denied at this stage. Both Portillo and Heseltine (one defeated, the other with a heart attack) are now out of the race. The beneficiary is probably Michael Howard who rings me at home. He wants my support but I say that I am still considering my position – which I very much am. My natural inclination is to vote for Ken but I do not share his enthusiasm for all things European. On Europe I am not hostile but sceptical – in the true meaning of the word.

SUNDAY 4 MAY

Ken rings me. He too wants my backing and appears to want me to run his campaign. I repeat that I have not yet decided. I say that as a friend I would vote for him but I am concerned about Europe and whether he could unite the party. Ken mutters unconvincingly about votes on issues like the single currency. I say I will come back to him which I fear is not the reaction he was expecting. To be frank, there is a high degree of frustration in my response. I pressed for Ken to be Chancellor and overcame the opposition of Richard Ryder and the reservations of John Major himself. From that point onwards, Ken could have been heir apparent but he gave not an inch on Europe and in the end succeeded in alienating John himself. Ken will doubtless say he was being true to his beliefs and so he was but he fails to recognise that the majority of the party are marching the other way. Those who really want to lead have to do a little more than pronounce that they are absolutely right and everyone else is absolutely wrong. Even Margaret Thatcher never did that. Months ago, I approached Ken with a view to getting something organised if and when Major stepped down. Not a group plotting against John Major – that would have been unthinkable – but setting out his political position so that he could attract as wide support as possible. Ken listened, I thought he agreed, but he never acted. His phone call to me today is the response but it is all desperately late. If he loses he has only himself to blame.

TUESDAY 6 MAY

Leadership canvassing is in full force. Sitting at home having a late lunch I am interrupted twice. First is William Hague who talks of a fresh start. I say to him that my advice is that he should leave it for five years or so and gain experience as say, shadow Chancellor. He says that others have voiced the same thought. Immediately following is John Redwood who points out that he left the unsuccessful Major government. Why he should think that this kind of argument would persuade me is entirely beyond me. I tell him that he cannot rely on my support.

WEDNESDAY 7 MAY

The House resumes for the formality of electing the Speaker. Everyone knows that Betty Boothroyd will be re-elected and she does not display even a touch of reluctance as she is 'dragged' from her seat. The interest is in the makeup of the new House. A solid mass of Labour MPs fill the government benches and overflow onto the side benches. They seem much younger than Old Labour, many more women and much more polite. As Betty Boothroyd enters they clap delightedly rather than giving the kind of welcoming growl that we would offer. But it is not only Labour which has grown. The Liberal Democrats are now forty-five in strength and have immediately occupied the front bench below the gangway, expelling the likes of me. We are being physically marginalised – confined largely to one section behind the opposition front bench. Nothing better shows the scale of our defeat. It is not like 1974 when we were so obviously still the alternative government. We are now the biggest of the opposition parties – but dwarfed by Labour and challenged by the Liberals.

MONDAY 12 MAY

Michael and Sandra Howard come to supper. Michael is at present caught up in a bizarre row with his former Minister of State Ann Widdecombe. It is all about the sacking of a man called Derek Lewis who was the head of the prison service. Widdecombe was evidently passionately opposed to this but not so passionately that she resigned. She has waited to take her revenge and now pronounces Howard unfit to be leader in an extraordinarily unattractive way.[298] I fear that the row is doing Michael great damage. For some reason, his public appeal is not as great as it should be. In the constituencies they say he doesn't come over on television. The Widdecombe affair is adding to the doubts. Sandra says that Widdecombe is 'obsessed' but although they both laugh off the attack I fear that it is not so easily cast aside.

WEDNESDAY 14 MAY

The state opening of the new parliament which I watch half in the Commons and half in a BBC TV studio. In the Commons Blair is greeted ecstatically by the massed ranks of Labour luvvies. John is given a warm cheer on our side and listened to with some sympathy by the government front bench. There is one scene which sets out the difference between the last parliament and the new one. At one point in his speech, Blair says 'I now turn to Europe'. Immediately up spring two of the leading Tory sceptics, Bill Cash and Michael Spicer, as if triggered automatons. In the last parliament they would have been cheered by Labour while most of us on our side would have watched in embarrassment. But they forget that it is not Major out there as Prime Minister but Blair. Labour don't cheer. They laugh uproariously at these two irrelevant opposition backbenchers continuing their battle even though the ship has sunk. Blair then completes the coup de grâce by thanking them for the contribution they have made to the election of his government.

---

298 She described Michael as 'dangerous stuff', saying that there was 'something of the night' in his personality to deliberately harm his prospects of becoming party leader.

KEY PLAYERS

PADDY ASHDOWN   Leader of the Liberal Democrats 1988–99.

KENNETH BAKER   Education Secretary 1986–89, Conservative Party Chairman 1989–90, Home Secretary 1990–92. Emerged as Eurosceptic after 1992.

JOHN BIFFEN   Chief Secretary to the Treasury 1979–81, Trade Secretary 1981–82, Leader of the House of Commons 1982–87 until sacked by Margaret Thatcher.

TONY BLAIR   Leader of the Opposition 1994–97, Prime Minister 1997–2007.

LEON BRITTAN   Chief Secretary to the Treasury 1981–83, Home Secretary 1983–85, Trade and Industry Secretary 1985–86. Carried the can for PM's failure on Westland policy.

GORDON BROWN   Shadow Chancellor of the Exchequer 1992–97, Chancellor of the Exchequer 1997–2007, Prime Minister 2007–2010.

JAMES CALLAGHAN   Prime Minister 1976–79, Leader of the Opposition 1979–80.

PETER CARRINGTON   Leader of the House of Lords 1963–64, Defence Secretary 1970–74 under Ted Heath, Foreign Secretary 1979–82. Resigned over Argentine invasion of the Falklands.

PAUL CHANNON   Trade and Industry Secretary 1986–87, Transport Secretary 1987–89.

KENNETH CLARKE   Paymaster General (Commons Spokesman on
Employment and Trade and Industry) 1985–
88, Health Secretary 1988–90, Education
Secretary 1990–92, Home Secretary 1992–93,
Chancellor of the Exchequer 1993–97. Should
have been party leader.

NICHOLAS EDWARDS   Welsh Secretary 1979–87. Strong independent
voice.

MICHAEL FOOT   Leader of the Opposition 1980–83.

JOHN GUMMER   Chairman of the Party 1983–85, Minister of
Agriculture 1989–93, Environment Secretary
1993–97. One of the best speakers in the
Commons.

QUINTIN HAILSHAM   Renounced hereditary peerage 1963 to re-
enter Commons as Quintin Hogg and contest
party leadership. Took life peerage 1970, Lord
Chancellor 1970–74 and 1979–87.

MICHAEL HESELTINE   Environment Secretary 1979–83, Defence
Secretary 1983–86. Walked out of Cabinet in
1986 and in 1990 unsuccessfully challenged
Margaret Thatcher for the party leadership.
Environment Secretary 1990–92, Trade and
Industry Secretary 1992–95, Deputy Prime
Minister 1995–97. Unlucky to miss out on
top job.

JONATHAN HILL   Downing Street Policy Unit 1991–92, Political
Secretary to John Major 1992–94. Unruffled
aide to PM.

SARAH HOGG   Economics journalist, head of John Major's
Policy Unit 1990–95.

MICHAEL HOWARD   Employment Secretary 1990–92,
Environment Secretary 1992–93, Home
Secretary 1993–97. Later Leader of the
Opposition 2003–05 in difficult years.

GEOFFREY HOWE — Chancellor of the Exchequer 1979–83, Foreign Secretary 1989–90. Resigned from government in dispute over European policy. Totally undervalued by Mrs Thatcher.

DAVID HOWELL — Energy Secretary 1979–81, Transport Secretary 1981–83. One of the brightest men in Thatcher's first Cabinet.

DOUGLAS HURD — Northern Ireland Secretary 1984–85, Home Secretary 1985–89, Foreign Secretary 1989–95. Unsuccessfully contested party leadership 1990. Consistent help to both Prime Ministers.

BERNARD INGHAM — Started career as journalist on the *Yorkshire Post*. Effective Chief Press Secretary to Margaret Thatcher 1979–1990.

MICHAEL JOPLING — Respected Chief Whip 1979–83, Minister of Agriculture 1983–87.

KEITH JOSEPH — Social Services Secretary 1970–74. Stood aside to allow Margaret Thatcher to successfully challenge for the leadership in 1975. Industry Secretary 1979–81, Education Secretary 1981–86. Influential figure in the development of policy for the new Conservative government.

NEIL KINNOCK — Leader of the Opposition 1983–92. Resigned after the party's defeat in 1992.

NORMAN LAMONT — Chief Secretary to the Treasury 1989–90. Campaign manager for John Major in 1990 leadership election. Chancellor of the Exchequer 1991–93, including when Britain left the ERM in 1992. Became prominent critic of the government.

NIGEL LAWSON — Energy Secretary 1981–83, Chancellor of the Exchequer 1983–89. Resigned unnecessarily in a dispute over the economic adviser to the

Prime Minister, Alan Walters.

PETER LILLEY   Trade and Industry Secretary 1990–92, Social
                  Security Secretary 1992–97.

JOHN MAJOR   Chief Secretary to the Treasury 1987–89,
                  Foreign Secretary 1989, Chancellor of the
                  Exchequer 1989–90. In 1990 defeated
                  Michael Heseltine for the Conservative Party
                  leadership after Margaret Thatcher withdrew.
                  Prime Minister 1990–97. Resigned after the
                  government's defeat in 1997 general election.

MICHAEL MEACHER   Shadow of author in both health and
                  employment. Absolutely straight.

JOHN MOORE   Transport Secretary 1986–87, Social Services
                  Secretary 1987–89. Regarded as future leader
                  but moved out of government in 1989.

TONY NEWTON   Trade Minister 1988–89, Social Security
                  Secretary 1989–92, Leader of the House of
                  Commons 1992–97. Very able minister who
                  could have been Chancellor.

JOHN NOTT   Trade Secretary 1979–81, Defence Secretary
                  1981–83.

GUS O'DONNELL   Patient Press Secretary to John Major as Prime
                  Minister 1990–94. Later Cabinet Secretary
                  and head of the civil service.

CECIL PARKINSON   Conservative Party Chairman 1981–83, Trade
                  and Industry Secretary 1983. Forced to resign
                  after an affair became public. Would have
                  been Foreign Secretary. Energy Secretary 1987
                  –89, Transport Secretary 1989–90

CHRIS PATTEN   Environment Secretary 1989–90, Party
                  Chairman 1990–92. Lost his seat in the 1992
                  election. Governor of Hong Kong 1992–97,
                  European Commissioner 1999–2004.

CHARLES POWELL   Diplomat who became Private Secretary to

Margaret Thatcher 1983–90. Kept ministers at a distance.

JAMES PRIOR
Employment Secretary 1979–81, Northern Ireland Secretary 1981–84. Consistently unhappy about direction of government policy.

FRANCIS PYM
Defence Secretary 1979–81, Leader of the Commons 1981–82, Foreign Secretary 1982–83. The most dangerous of Thatcher's critics inside first Cabinet. Sacked after 1983 general election.

JOHN REDWOOD
Welsh Secretary 1993–95. Unsuccessfully challenged Major for party leadership in 1995. In 1997 again stood for Party Leader and again defeated.

RICHARD RYDER
Chief Whip 1990–95. Took government through most difficult of times, including handling the Maastricht legislation. Received less credit than he deserved.

NORMAN ST JOHN-STEVAS
Leader of the House of Commons, promoted the select committee system, Arts Minister 1979–81. Regarded as 'wet' on economic policy.

JOHN SMITH
Leader of the Opposition 1992–94 when he died suddenly of a heart attack.

CHRISTOPHER SOAMES
Son-in-law of Winston Churchill. Leader of the House of Lords and Lord President of the Council 1979–81.

DAVID STEEL
Leader of the Liberals 1976–88. Established an electoral alliance with the SDP and in 1988 the two parties officially merged to become the Liberal Democrats.

NORMAN TEBBIT
Employment Secretary 1981–83, Trade and Industry Secretary 1983–85, Party Chairman 1985–87. Seriously injured by the IRA bomb at the Grand Hotel and his wife, Margaret, even

more grievously. Strong supporter of Margaret Thatcher and persistent critic of John Major.

MARGARET THATCHER — Education Secretary 1970–74. Successfully stood against Ted Heath for party leadership in 1975. Prime Minister 1979–90. Exceptional Prime Minister; disastrous ex-Prime Minister.

JOHN WAKEHAM — Chief Whip 1983–87, Leader of House of Commons 1987–89. Entered House of Lords 1992, Leader of Lords 1992–94.

PETER WALKER — Minister of Agriculture 1979–83, Energy Secretary 1983–87, Welsh Secretary 1987–90.

WILLIAM WHITELAW — Leader of Commons, Northern Ireland Secretary, Employment Secretary under Ted Heath. Home Secretary 1979–83, Leader of the Lords 1983–88. Indispensable minister for both Ted Heath and Margaret Thatcher.

DAVID YOUNG — Minister without Portfolio 1984–85, Employment Secretary 1985–87, Trade and Industry Secretary 1987–89.

GEORGE YOUNGER — Scottish Secretary 1979–86, Defence Secretary 1986–89. Liked by all.

ACKNOWLEDGEMENTS

In editing this book I acknowledge the great help of: Nigel Fletcher, George Young, Martin Redfern and Fiona Fowler, who did heroic work in helping to reduce the original text to its present size. From Biteback, I particularly thank for their assistance and professionalism: James Stephens, Lisa Goodrum, Olivia Beattie, Suzanne Sangster and her team. I also acknowledge the contributions of the many players in the drama of those years – without whom the book would not have been possible.

INDEX

1922 Committee 159, 162, 444, 476, 525
Chairman 261, 290, 340, 530–31
John Major 383, 450, 479, 480, 542

abortion 6
ACAS (Advisory, Conciliation and Arbitration
    Service) 84, 102
Acheson, Donald 178, 183, 188, 190
Aids 163, 164, 299
    advertising 166, 167–70, 174, 175–80, 184,
        184n, 190
    Africa 195
    attitudes to 176, 183, 185, 189
    committee 174, 176, 177, 179, 181, 184
    Commons debate 179
    ministerial broadcast 184, 185
    National Aids Trust 235
    needles 181, 182, 195
    United States 185, 186, 187, 188, 195
    World Health Organization 181n
Allan, Alex 485
Amery, Julian 82
Anderton, James 182, 183, 183n
Anne, Princess, the Princess Royal 241, 242,
    256, 424
Archer, Jeffrey 149, 174, 260, 302, 351, 387, 478,
    481, 512, 514
Argentina 71, 72, 75, 76, 78, 81, 83, 439
Armstrong, Robert 61, 132, 143, 158, 162, 180,
    192, 211
Ashby, David 473, 474, 475
Ashdown, Paddy 308, 385, 422, 501, 509, 518,
    520–21
Atkins, Humphrey 20, 32, 36, 37, 44, 70, 73
Atlantic Conveyor 83

Baker, Kenneth 154, 174, 214, 223, 229, 237,
    271, 378, 444

Conservative Party Chairman 271, 284
    Education Secretary 122, 207
    Europe 391, 500
    Home Secretary 326
    leadership prospects 278
    memoirs 454
Baldwin, Peter 24, 44, 51, 56
Bank of England 48
Beckett, Margaret 384, 446, 501, 503, 511
Berry, Anthony 129
Bevins, Tony 197, 199, 290
Bickerstaffe, Rodney 90, 91, 204, 206, 478, 521
Biffen, John 5, 14, 24, 42, 71, 119, 123, 227, 468
    back benches 202, 205
    Leader of the House 56, 74, 201, 202
Black, Conrad 448
Blair, Tony 287, 384, 543, 545, 550
    election as Prime Minister 546, 547
    Labour leader/Leader of the Opposition
        511, 521, 530, 542
    praise from Thatcher 542
    prospective leader 502, 505, 537
    shadow Employment Secretary 285,
        288–90, 502, 503
Booth, Albert 7, 10
Booth, Hartley 485
Boothroyd, Betty 374, 376, 550
Bottomley, Peter 232, 259, 298, 305, 374, 389,
    393, 454, 515
Bottomley, Virginia 204, 232, 259, 298, 305,
    369, 374, 389, 414, 515
Bourdin, Michel 236
Bowe, Colette 162
Bowen, Otis 187
Boyson, Rhodes 108, 117, 121
Braine, Bernard 72, 82
Bramall, Field Marshal 69
Brighton 18, 95, 105, 124, 125, 136, 228, 238, 405

Brighton bomb 126–9
British Leyland 28, 164, 165, 168, 170, 285
British Rail 3, 8, 9, 12
    Camp, Will 19
    electrification 29, 34, 35, 39–41, 88
    Faulkner, Richard 19
    hotels 37, 38
    Margaret Thatcher's views on 87, 138, 138n
    Parker, Peter (Chairman) 9, 16, 19, 30,
        40–41, 43–4, 300, 332, 411
    privatisation 8, 16, 26, 37, 38
    public relations 19
    subsidiaries 8, 16, 17, 26, 37
Brittan, Leon 24, 39, 150, 157, 165, 175, 176,
    240, 275, 313, 329, 512
    Chief Secretary to the Treasury 24, 54, 58,
        61, 62
    European Commissioner 224, 225, 230, 231,
        345, 419
    Home Secretary 108, 148
    Industry Secretary 148, 149, 151–9, 162
    resignation 159, 160
Brixton riots 42, 43
Brown, Gordon 145n, 147, 302, 397,401, 518,
    538
Brown, Michael 499
Bruce-Gardyne, Jock 126, 225, 296, 302
Brussels 22, 225, 230, 231, 346, 349, 475
BSE (bovine spongiform encephalopathy) 251
Buchan, Norman 57
Budget, the 25, 31, 32, 138, 139, 206, 222, 223,
    253, 403, 418
Bush, George 238, 304, 305, 456
By-election(s) 53, 250, 269, 309, 471, 493, 506
    Chesterfield 118
    Christchurch 434, 441, 452
    Crosby 63
    Dudley 518
    Eastbourne 306
    Glamorgan 259, 262
    Govan 239
    Hillhead 66
    Richmond 250, 261
    Rotherham 496
    Warrington 43
    Wirral 541

Cabinet
    economic 38
    first as Secretary of State 25
    government 30–31
    Office 23, 58, 153, 192, 234, 304, 413

public spending 20, 21
    reshuffle 23, 48–51, 121, 148, 170, 200–202,
        231, 273–6, 435, 438, 508
    shadow 208, 278, 285, 286, 363, 404, 438
    splits 19, 21
Caithness, Malcolm 474, 475
Callaghan, Jim 9, 17, 18, 54, 156, 391, 396, 535
Cambridge University 19, 37, 91, 102, 218, 274,
    347, 380, 532
Cameron, David 435, 438
Carrington, Peter 5, 13, 14, 39, 73, 74, 439
Casablanca 23, 49
Cash, Bill 340, 341–4, 382, 406, 481, 542, 545,
    550
cash for questions 517, 533, 542, 542n, 543
Central Policy Review Staff (CPRS) 35, 35n, 94,
    95, 97, 98
Channel Tunnel 9, 10, 157
Channon, Paul 168, 201, 212, 216
Chapman, Sydney 5
Charles, Prince 248, 254, 256, 418, 424, 498
Chequers 80, 149, 262, 289, 296–7, 304, 332–3,
    351–2, 392, 497
child benefit 58, 73, 124, 141, 197, 259
China 10–12, 265, 267, 336
Churchill, Winston 270, 303, 466, 497
civil service 13, 19, 54, 146, 166, 172, 328
Clarke, Kenneth 24, 92–3, 159, 195, 208, 241–2,
    269, 285, 303, 320, 326, 414, 541
    Chancellor of the Exchequer 432, 433, 443
    Department of Employment 148, 149
    Department of Trade and Industry 202
    DHSS 108, 121
    Education Secretary 308
    European referendum debate 500, 537, 545
Clay, Trevor 96
Clinton Davis, Stanley 17
closed shops 214, 253, 259, 289, 295
coal 29, 30
coal dispute 122–4, 132, 150, 413
Cockfield, Lord Arthur 74, 207
Collins, Joan 222
Colville, Jock 270
commercial surrogacy 135, 136, 141
Common Market 14, 22, 106
community charge (poll tax) 86, 154, 196, 214,
    220, 225, 244, 280, 326, 330, 331, 505, 524
Conservative Central Office 46, 194, 197, 373,
    423
Conservative Party Chairman 47, 210, 263, 373,
    478, 498, 544
    Baker, Kenneth 271, 284

Fowler, Norman 377, 391, 395, 407, 442, 517
Hanley, Jeremy 515, 519
Patten, Chris 326, 335
Tebbit, Norman 124, 191
Thorneycroft, Peter 46
Conservative Party conference
    1980 18, 19
    1982 98
    1983 116
    1984 124–9
    1986 173–4, 185
    1987 211, 235, 236
    1989 279, 280
    1992 405, 407, 408
    1993 461, 463, 467, 486
Constantine, Theo 135, 136
Cook, Robin 217, 239, 360, 446, 534
Cope, John 203, 260, 273, 362
Craddock, Percy 12, 352
Crossman, Richard (Dick) 27, 54, 232
Crouch, David 180
Currie, Edwina 170, 241, 315, 364, 374, 435,
    486, 546

Daily Telegraph 92, 192, 282, 459
Dalyell, Tam 76
Day, Robin 218, 281
de Rothschild, Philippe 22
death grant 112, 118, 142, 145
defence spending 21, 72
Department of Defence 151, 155, 497
Department of Education 207
    Department of Employment 190, 191, 202,
    203, 204, 208, 243, 292, 296
Department of Health and Social Services
    (DHSS) 51, 54, 65, 114, 192, 195, 200–202,
    343
    budget 114, 139
    expenditure 55n
    John Major 328
    spending 95
    split 231, 232
Department of Trade and Industry (DTI) 148,
    152, 155, 158, 170, 202, 204, 210, 260, 411
    Jeffrey Archer investigation 512, 514
Dewar, Donald 503
Diana, Princess of Wales 47, 235, 256, 384, 392,
    418, 424
Dimbleby, David 160, 453, 506, 529
Dimbleby, Jonathan 264, 426, 510
Dixon, Don 266
Dobbs, Michael 240, 373

docks 257, 258, 260, 262, 265, 364
    1946 legislation 266
    British Rail subsidiaries 16
    committee 256, 271
    dispute 261, 269, 272, 276
    Dock Work bill 246, 258, 259, 271
    dock work regulation scheme 216, 216n, 243,
        245, 249, 252, 254, 255, 257, 258, 273, 363
    privatisation 16, 17, 363
    strike 272
dog registration 268, 269
Donald, John (father-in-law) 59, 116, 539–40
Dorrell, Stephen 389
drink driving 14, 15, 26
du Cann, Edward 72, 261
Duke and Duchess of York 220, 221, 294, 356
Duncan, Alan 473, 474
Dunwoody, Gwyneth 84, 99

early leavers 113
earnings rule 112, 253
Eastern Europe 291
electrification 29, 34, 35, 39–41, 88
employment 31, 133, 148, 225, 237, 273, 278, 345
    Beveridge 112
    bill 213, 243, 245, 246, 266, 282, 288, 295
    compulsory occupational scheme 134, 137
    debate 205, 280, 288, 289, 466
    questions 208, 217, 290
    self-employment 289
    Sweden 212, 213
    training 219n, 228, 233, 234, 240, 243, 249
    United States visits 220–222, 278
    white paper 219
essential services 272, 273, 278, 279, 280
European Affairs Committee 340, 346
European elections 120, 263, 270, 339, 469,
    494, 496, 498, 508
European Monetary System (EMS) 227, 228,
    264, 268, 281
Evening Standard 91, 216, 315, 347, 376, 422,
    475, 484, 528
exchange rate 44, 227, 228, 244, 391
Ezra, Derek 30

Falkland Islands 69–86
    Atlantic Conveyor 83
    Commons debate 75, 82
    cost of conflict 74
    exclusion zone 75, 79, 80
    Galtieri, General 76, 78
    General Belgrano 81, 82

Falkland Islands *cont.*
  Goose Green 84
  HMS Coventry 83
  HMS Sheffield 82
  intelligence 70, 73, 76, 439
  Margaret Thatcher and 69, 86, 87
  Nott, John 72, 73, 75, 78, 81
  Operation Journeyman 77n
  Peter Carrington 73, 439
  Port Stanley 70, 83–5
  press 71, 73
  reclaiming of 85
  Sir Galahad 84
  South Georgia 78, 79, 80
  task force 78, 468
  Woodward, Admiral Sandy 80
Fanshawe, Nigel 37
father 113n, 210, 531
Field, Frank 119, 147
Fields, Terry 132
fiftieth birthday party 217, 218
Financial Times 18, 104, 299, 343, 373, 495, 530
Finsberg, Geoffrey 50, 108, 343
firearms bill 228
Fisher, Nigel 72
Foot, Michael 28, 32, 71, 76, 77, 81–5, 95, 105, 107, 191
Fowler, Fiona (neé Donald, wife) 6, 11, 33, 59–61, 94, 116, 120–21, 125, 201, 262, 264, 296–8, 539–40
Fowler, Isobel Geraldine (daughter) 121, 218, 279, 299, 305, 336–7, 360, 384, 427, 442, 454, 539
Fowler, Kate Genevieve (daughter) 59–61, 63, 89, 92, 94, 121, 218, 299, 300, 305, 336–7, 384, 424, 427, 442, 539–40
Frost, David 198, 452, 474

Gandhi, Indira 132
Gandhi, Rajiv 48, 132
Gardiner, John 378, 470
General Belgrano 81, 82
General Election 35, 39, 97, 424, 450, 454, 515, 530, 541
  1983 105, 106, 107
  1987 191, 196, 197, 198, 199, 200, 226
  1992 335, 338, 354, 367–9, 525
  1997 541, 542, 543, 545, 546, 547
Gibson, Maurice 194
Gilmour, Ian 5
Godber, Steve 134, 142
Goodman, Elinor 295

Goodman, Geoffrey 236, 237
Gorbachev, Mikhail 193, 219, 242, 243, 254, 255, 337–8
Government accommodation 175, 192
Gow, Ian 46, 297, 304
great storm of 1987 211
Griffiths, Roy 171, 172, 173, 180, 277
Guardian, The 18, 93, 99, 106, 111, 115, 132, 144, 285, 299, 446, 517, 543
Gummer, John 24, 91, 257, 273–4, 291, 307, 438–9, 465, 494, 498

Hague, William 250, 251, 317, 530, 550
Haig, Alexander 75, 76, 77, 78, 81, 86
Hailsham, Quintin 42, 47, 70, 135, 169, 177, 207, 423, 524
Haines, Joe 174
Hales, Reg 296
Hambro, Charles 420, 448, 449, 454, 465, 469, 490, 510
Harari, Sammy 175, 178, 179
Harding, Peter 489
Haslam, Jonathan 449
Hastings, Max 192, 193, 261, 433, 434, 439, 461
Hastings, Stephen 82
Hattersley, Roy 27, 43, 331, 364, 518, 519, 534
Hauff, Volker 22
Havilland, Julian 40
Haynes, Frank 246
Healey, Denis 75, 77, 305
health dispute 83, 84, 87, 89, 94, 95, 98
Health Policy Strategy Group 180
Health Services Committee (TUC) 96, 100, 104
Heath, Edward (Ted) 218, 261, 269–70, 331, 343, 451, 490, 496, 519, 528, 534, 538, 541
  Euro elections 120
  Falklands 82
  leadership elections 313, 324, 334
  Paris 264–5
Heffer, Eric 132, 355
Heffer, Simon 37, 273, 290, 376, 377
Heseltine, Michael 10, 40, 46, 94, 110, 119, 170, 173, 208, 279, 334, 416, 522, 546
  campaign against 155, 161, 166, 209
  Deputy Prime Minister 529
  Environment Secretary 326
  Europe 408
  heart attack and recovery 446, 457, 547, 548
  housing 6
  leadership efforts 271, 278, 301, 309, 310, 314–16, 323, 325, 501, 547

Liverpool 43, 44, 45, 102
Maastricht Treaty 347, 358
Moscow Olympics 10
pit closures 410, 411, 415
resignation 153, 154, 155, 160
support for Major 528
Tebbit article 540
view on health service 223
Westland 151–60, 175, 209
Hillsborough tragedy 257, 258
HMS Coventry 83
HMS Sheffield 82
Hogg, Douglas 229, 407, 485
Hogg, Sarah 348, 369, 378, 395, 417, 460, 488
Holland, Geoffrey 211, 228, 280, 292, 298, 509
Holland, John 296, 313, 319, 325
Hong Kong 265, 267, 291, 292, 294, 295, 352, 374–5, 386, 416, 524
hospital building 173, 174, 193, 194, 198
Howard, Alan 380
Howard, Michael 214, 317, 439, 471, 541, 545, 548, 549
  Employment Secretary 287, 288, 335
  Environment Secretary 369, 409, 425
  Home Secretary 433, 463, 474, 514
  leadership elections 315, 318, 329
  privatisation of water 291
Howe, Geoffrey 13, 165, 175, 214, 227, 240, 244, 261, 270, 328, 521
  Chancellor of the Exchequer 20, 24, 25, 324
  Deputy Prime Minister 274, 275
  Foreign Secretary 108, 131, 154, 224, 267
  Leader of the House 274
  public spending 94
  resignation 307, 316
  treatment by Margaret Thatcher 33, 85, 262, 280, 301
Howell, David 16, 17, 29, 30, 47, 50, 51, 109, 201, 312
Humphreys, John 90
Hurd, Douglas 78, 148, 174, 182, 205, 276, 307, 407, 424
  Foreign Secretary 283, 294, 295, 428, 478, 521
  leadership 309, 313, 316, 317, 318, 319, 324, 325
Hurlingham Road 47, 93, 95, 121, 201, 211, 237, 258, 263, 402, 447, 483
Hussey, Marmaduke 177

Independent, The 192, 197, 199, 200, 233, 272, 360, 365
Independent Broadcasting Corporation 177
inflation 20, 44, 45, 106, 236
  decreased 21, 38, 91, 435, 471
  high 13
  inflation-proof pensions 26, 27, 45, 124
  low 495
Ingham, Bernard 95, 144, 161, 249, 312, 392, 477
IRA 37, 46n, 129, 304, 353, 470, 480, 489, 545–6
Israel 215

Jacques, Peter 93, 95, 96
Jakobovits, Chief Rabbi Sir Immanuel 189
Jenkin, Bernard 19
Jenkin, Patrick 19, 20, 50, 51, 58, 59, 111, 119, 127, 141, 232
Jenkins, Peter 281, 346
Jenkins, Roy 43, 66, 156, 204, 391, 458
Jopling, Michael 15, 23, 127, 195, 261, 309, 317
Joseph, Keith 6, 7, 17, 21, 28, 30, 31, 38, 62, 126–7, 138, 142
Junor, John 278

Keith, Penelope 259
King, Tom 148, 153, 194, 213, 306
King's Cross fire 212
Kinnock, Neil 43, 191, 197, 200, 250, 259, 263, 284, 290, 329, 339, 354, 401, 501
  General Election defeat 361, 363, 364, 365, 370
  speeches 156, 160, 222, 226, 232, 233, 305, 331, 345
Kirkwood, Archy 179
Koop, Everett 194–5

Labour Party conference (1981) 27, 28
Lamont, Norman 282, 329, 416, 438, 445, 447, 459, 479, 521, 522, 526, 535, 537
  Chancellor of the Exchequer 326, 356, 388, 390, 401, 409
  Exchange Rate Mechanism (ERM) 391, 458
  resignation 442–4, 446
  tax cuts 361
Lancet, The 91
Law, Frank 23, 38
Lawson, Nigel 38, 50, 51, 56, 57, 62, 109, 110, 127, 243, 303, 331, 335
  Chancellor of the Exchequer 105, 108, 150, 223, 253
  coal dispute 122
  compulsory occupational scheme 134, 137
  dock work regulation scheme 216, 247
  exchange policy 270

Lawson, Nigel *cont.*
   Health Policy Strategy Group 180
   resignation 283, 294, 318
   SERPS 142, 143, 144
   social security 124, 131, 139, 193, 197
Leach, Sir Henry 69
leadership election 208, 313, 323, 328–9, 332,
   495, 523, 525, 530, 547
Lever, Harold 22
Leyland 28, 164, 165, 168, 170, 285
limited list of drugs 134, 135
Livingstone, Ken 205
local elections 106, 196, 259, 375, 435, 487,
   493–6, 507, 523
Lockerbie bombing 243, 244, 244n
Luce, Richard 73

Maastricht 330, 341, 346–8, 358, 371, 404, 410,
   450, 522
   bill 379, 391, 403, 421, 436
   conference 330n, 340
   debate 437, 451
   John Major's policy on 383, 398, 428, 547
   opponents 391, 397, 403n, 406
   Thatcher's position 404, 409
   Treaty 348n, 381, 397, 405, 436n, 496n
MacGregor, Ian 22, 30, 122, 123
MacGregor, John 197, 201, 209, 242, 250, 308,
   331, 347, 348, 436
Maclean, Muriel 129
MacLeod Group 530
Major, John
   1992 General Election 365–71
   1997 General Election 542, 546
   'Ask John Major' 352, 353, 356
   Back to Basics 467, 472, 474, 486
   Chancellor of the Exchequer 278, 283,
      285, 301
   Chief Secretary to the Treasury 202, 203, 209
   criticism of 447, 462, 520
   dislike of press 332, 522
   Exchange Rate Mechanism 439
   Foreign Secretary 274, 275, 278
   leadership election 312, 316, 317, 318, 319,
      323–5, 501, 526, 529
   leadership style 328
   Minister of State 170
   Northern Ireland 469, 521
   parliamentary under-secretary 148, 149, 150
   policy on Maastricht 383, 398, 428, 547
   Prime Minister 325
   social services 173, 193, 208

Thatcher's treatment of 349, 375, 406, 462,
   523, 547
Malone, Gerry 376, 443, 444, 476, 501, 510,
   513, 549
manifesto
   Conservative 111, 196, 197, 198, 205, 358,
      499, 502, 504
   Labour 106, 194
Mann, Jonathan 181, 235
manpower 33, 85, 88, 101, 115
manpower policy 116
Margaret, Princess 237, 254
Marsh, Dick 178, 179
Mates, Michael 295, 327, 447, 448
Maude, Angus 17
Maude, Francis 317, 347, 348
Maxwell, Robert 215, 235
Mayer, Anthony 23, 24, 49, 51
Mayhew, Sir Patrick 158n, 161
Maze Prison 20
Meacher, Michael 147, 184, 208, 214, 226, 246,
   258, 263, 266, 285
   libel case 229, 230
Mellor, David 232, 385, 387, 392, 400, 401, 472
   affair 384, 385
   comments on Israel 215
   press 387
   pressure to resign 386, 387, 398, 399, 400
Meyer, Anthony 290, 290n
Meyer, Christopher 467, 479
Milligan, Stephen 482, 483, 484, 496, 506
Milne, Alasdair 177
Misc. 111 (Cabinet committee on social security
   proposals) 136–42
Mitterrand, President François 47, 157
Moore, Jeremy 85
Moore, John 190, 198, 201, 203–4, 208, 212,
   216–17, 222, 224, 231
Morrison, Peter 309, 310, 324, 449
mother 113n, 118, 128, 209–10, 237, 252, 531
Murray, Len 99

Nadir, Asil 447
National Coal Board 30
National Economic Development Council
   (NEDC) 205
National Freight Corporation (NFC) 3, 4, 38,
   56, 264, 300, 302, 303, 501
National Health Service (NHS) 51, 58, 61, 65,
   79, 109, 171, 194
   commission 199, 200
   dispute 87–104

manpower policy 116
pay 83, 84, 85, 88
privatisation 199, 200
review 277
strikes 83, 84, 86, 89
Thatcher's views on 87, 113, 199
National Insurance Contributions Bill 62
National Union of Mineworkers (NUM) 29
National Union of Public Employees (NUPE) 90, 102, 103
nationalisation 3, 7, 26, 106
NATO 75n, 219
Nellist, Dave 132, 133, 156
News at Ten 155
Newspaper Publishers' Association 178
Newton, Tony 125, 139, 146, 155, 180, 389, 438, 468
Chairman of NHS management board 171
DHSS 65, 73, 108, 117
election defeat 547
Leader of the House 378
Minister of Health 170
Minister of State 121
privacy legislation 487
social security reform 133
Northern Ireland 8, 20, 37, 41, 44, 48, 121, 129, 148, 194, 203, 215, 222, 429, 469–70, 505, 517, 521
Nott, John 13, 14, 16, 39, 44, 75, 94, 500
Falklands 69, 70, 78, 80–84
Nottingham South constituency 234, 254
Nurses and Midwives Council 89
nurses' pay dispute 65–6, 85, 88–9, 93, 95, 101–4, 192

Observer, The 96, 228, 452, 493
Oldfield, Maurice 8
Onslow, Cranley 290, 315
Otton, Geoffrey 54, 133
Owen, David 16, 17, 28, 28n, 43, 43n, 72, 76, 77n, 83, 85, 105
Oxenbury, Shirley 378, 418

P&O dispute 226
Paige, Victor 200
Paisley, Ian 469
Papandreou, Commissioner Vasso 268, 538
Parker, Peter 8, 16, 19, 30, 40–41, 43–4, 300, 332, 411
Parkinson, Cecil 46, 63, 82, 111, 117, 202, 206, 273–4, 317, 334, 335, 339, 449, 454, 524
Parr, Michael 296, 310, 320

Patten, Chris 170, 272, 291, 318, 326, 335, 338, 348, 369, 373
Governor of Hong Kong 375, 386, 416
Patten, John 101, 141, 437
pensions 51, 95, 113, 119, 137, 142, 146, 193
conference 113
improvements 133
inflation-proof 26, 27, 45, 124
occupational 67
personal 152, 299
pledge 55, 56
portable 113
private 143, 144, 146n
review 117, 118, 123, 131
SERPS 137, 146n
Pickles, Eric 460, 510
Pickles, Hilary 178
poll tax (community charge) 86, 154, 196, 214, 220, 225, 244, 280, 326, 330, 331, 505, 524
Poole, David 379
Poole, Oliver (stepson) 13, 33, 36, 48, 92, 103, 231, 299, 305, 379, 423, 427
Port Stanley 70, 83–5
Porter, Dame Shirley 475
Portillo, Michael 250, 288, 457, 493, 496, 512, 527, 542, 547–8
Powell, Charles 161, 162, 249, 481
Powell, Enoch 26
Prescott, John 7, 26, 205
prescription charge 58, 61, 141, 389, 452
Price, Vincent 221
Prime Minister's Questions 30, 82, 98, 114, 146, 168, 232, 243, 250, 276, 283–4, 328, 491, 533, 542
Prior, Jim 13, 16, 18, 19, 21, 31, 39, 45, 48, 50, 94
private health 95, 102, 199, 217, 300
privatisation 19, 38, 41, 299, 363
British Leyland 329n
British Rail 16, 436, 438
British Rail subsidiaries 8, 16, 17
docks 17, 364
electricity 202, 273
Gleneagles 38
National Freight Corporation (NFC) 4n, 23n, 38, 56, 300, 302
NHS 194, 199, 200
policies 9
water 291
Privy Council 26, 203, 294
public sector borrowing requirement (PSBR) 31, 45
public spending 6, 456

public spending *cont.*
　　bill 118
　　Cabinet meeting on 20, 21
　　committee 414
　　control 44
　　cuts 13, 63, 122, 222
　　debate 5, 212
　　DHSS 55–7, 61, 67, 114, 117, 123, 208, 222
　　Labour manifesto plans 106
　　long-term options 94
Pym, Francis 3, 19, 21, 39, 74, 78, 82, 108, 109

Queen Mary 220
Queen's Speech debate 205
Question Time 218, 425, 438, 458, 473
Quinlan, Michael 203, 211

rail unions 28, 38, 41
Raison, Tim 170, 181, 289
Raphael, Adam 48
Reagan, Ronald 4, 75n, 186, 193
recession 13, 21, 239, 329, 363, 370, 384, 388,
　　393, 430–31, 434, 453, 495
Redwood, John 123, 133, 270, 499, 500, 526–7,
　　529, 537, 549
Rees, Peter 110, 113, 114, 123, 137, 139, 144, 209,
　　228
Rees-Mogg, Jacob 237
Rees-Mogg, William, 237, 472, 511
Reiss, Charles 216
resignation from Cabinet (Norman Fowler)
　　286–8, 291–300
Riddick, Graham 513
Rifkind, Malcolm 154, 182, 239, 266, 414, 529,
　　546
road safety 15, 26
Roberts, Graham 283
Rodgers, Bill 28, 43n, 204
Rooker–Wise amendment 31
Ross, Stephen 16
Rossi, Hugh 108
Rowland, Tiny 261
Royal College of Nursing (RCN) 89, 90, 93,
　　94, 96, 97, 99, 101, 103, 104
Royal wedding 47–8
Royal Yacht Britannia 220, 221
Ryder, Richard 347, 376, 401, 402, 410, 475,
　　487, 511, 548
　　Alan Duncan 473
　　cash for questions 513
　　Chief Whip 341, 378
　　coal 411, 412, 413

David Mellor 385–7, 399, 400
Edwina Currie 374
John Wakeham 436
Malcolm Caithness 474
Norman Lamont 416, 432
Tim Yeo 470
views on Maastricht bill 403

Saatchi & Saatchi 226, 240, 376, 520
Saatchi, Maurice 376, 465, 520
St John-Stevas, Norman 3, 5, 15, 18, 24, 25,
　　157, 346
Sands, Bobby 36
Scargill, Arthur 122, 123, 133, 150, 238, 411, 428
Scarman, Lord 43
Scott Report 26, 27, 533
Scottish independence 239
Scottish National Party (SNP) 16, 228, 239
seat belts 15, 16, 26, 38
Sellafield 210
SERPS (State Earnings-Related Pension
　　Scheme) 117n, 124, 134, 137, 140, 142, 143–5,
　　146n
Sharkey, John 226
Shattock, Jeanne 129
Shephard, Gillian 438, 514
Sherman, Sir Alfred 183
Shore, Peter 16, 17
Short, Clare 545–6
Skinner, Dennis 38, 228, 500
Smith, John 308, 358, 401, 443, 478, 491, 495
　　death 487, 500–502
　　elected Labour leader 384
　　funeral 502, 503
　　shadow Budget 355, 356
Soames, Christopher 15, 22, 25, 39
Soames, Mary 270
Soames, Nicholas 520
social chapter 283, 288, 289, 295, 323, 330, 345,
　　347–9, 405, 450–52, 537
social charter 267, 267n, 268
Social Democratic Party (SDP) 16n, 28n, 43,
　　43n, 56, 63, 66, 72, 107, 119, 482, 544
social security
　　bill 156, 157, 161
　　budget 58, 115, 131
　　inquiry 114
　　reforms 133, 139, 151, 193, 299
　　review 117, 131, 133–46, 149, 175, 197, 253
social spending 110, 111
Solidarity 238, 289
Spanswick, Albert 93, 93n, 96, 97, 102, 103

Spencer-Churchill, Winston 414
Spicer, Michael 400, 451, 551
St Thomas' Hospital, Lambeth 89, 120
steel 25, 30, 336, 337, 509
Steel, David 77, 85, 258, 269
Steven, Stewart 422
Stevens, David 384, 519, 520
Stewart, Donald 16
Stokes, John 28, 231
Stowe, Ken 54, 74, 95, 133, 140, 143, 172, 192
Sunday People 384, 385
supplementary benefit 56, 58, 62, 67, 111, 124,
    132, 134, 137, 139, 142
Suthers, Martin 234, 254, 342

taxation 44, 110, 111, 131, 139, 331, 370
Taylor, Eric 129
Taylor, Jock 115
Taylor, Neville 80
TBWA advertising agency 184
Tebbit, Norman 22, 46, 56, 57, 102, 108, 116,
    191, 194, 196–7, 254, 283, 290, 341–3, 358,
    378, 387,433, 435, 439, 449, 525, 527, 547
    Brighton bomb 127, 128, 129, 136
    coal dispute 123
    Conservative Party Chairman 124, 191, 198
    David Young 191, 210
    Europe 341–3, 391, 407–8
    Falklands 70
    films bill 119
    Health Policy Strategy Group 180
    Heseltine article 541
    House of Lords 449
    immigration 195, 294, 295
    leadership prospect 317, 341
    leaves Cabinet 202
    Margaret (wife) 128, 129, 131
    speeches 123, 126
televising Parliament 219, 303
Temple-Morris, Peter 261, 295, 298, 327, 333,
    339, 341–2, 480, 531
Thatcher, Margaret
    10 years in office 260, 261, 262
    1983 General Election 105
    1997 General Election 546, 547
    Aids/Aids advertising views 163, 166, 167,
    189
    anti-Thatcher feeling 262, 306, 315
    as ex-Prime Minister 333, 334, 348, 349, 353,
    375, 406, 409, 420, 429
    Carol (daughter) 192, 193
    coal dispute 122

    Denis (husband) 33, 193, 262, 282, 288,
    297, 334
    distrust of Department of Education 207
    economic policy 18, 47
    EEC Budget settlement 14
    Falkland Islands 69–87, 105
    first Cabinet 3, 5–6
    force and conviction 21
    Fowler's resignation 286–8, 292, 293
    House of Lords 383, 387
    isolation 244, 307
    leadership challenge 290, 309, 310, 316, 454
    leadership defeat 320
    leadership style 166, 217, 260, 328
    Mark (son) 297
    memoirs 462, 468, 524
    Ministry of Pensions 67
    Poland visit 238, 239
    position on Maastricht 404, 409
    praise for Tony Blair 542
    resignation 319
    resignation of Geoffrey Howe 307
    resignation of Nigel Lawson 283
    resignations of Heseltine and Brittan
    153–62
    seventieth birthday party 530
    social policy issues 277, 286
    social security 67
    stamina 42
    treatment of Geoffrey Howe 33, 85, 262,
    275, 280, 281, 301
    USA 4, 221
    views on British Rail 87, 138, 138n
    views on broadcasters 262, 267
    views on House of Lords 225
    views on NHS 87, 88, 113, 199
    views on transport 27, 29, 33, 35, 39
    Westland 151
Thomas, Harvey 194, 281
Thomson, George 177
Thorneycroft, Peter 46
Timmins, Nick 199
Today programme 89–90, 91, 97, 149, 242, 268,
    270, 275, 309, 325, 368, 474, 475, 478, 483,
    529, 542
Tory rebels 414, 450, 451, 452, 453, 462, 464
Toxteth riots 41
trade unions 28, 66, 96, 102, 178, 235, 238, 335,
    521
training and enterprise councils 241n, 249, 252
transport
    bills 4, 14, 26, 36, 45

transport *cont.*
  compulsory seat belts 15, 16, 26, 38, 45, 46
  drink driving 14, 15, 26
  road safety 15, 26
  Transport Act 1980 18
  Transport Bill Committee 7
  Transport Council 22
  Transport Select Committee 5
Transport and General Workers Union
  (TGWU) 216, 256–9, 265,271, 272, 364
Tredinnick, David 513
Trident 65–7, 72
True, Nick 116, 125, 200, 277, 282, 298, 332
TUC 99, 101, 204, 206, 233–4
  Bournemouth conference 233
  Brighton conference 93, 95
  Health Services Committee 96, 100, 104
  on training 228
Tucker, Clive 292

unemployment 21, 25, 39, 44, 91, 329, 338, 389
  benefit 58, 62, 112, 138, 213, 224
  debate 16
  figures 18, 25, 39, 106, 209, 210, 354, 356,
    410, 436, 491
  high 111, 393
  reduction 209, 235, 243, 245, 291, 471, 495
  solutions 39
  training 212
  youth 41

Vietnam 267, 291
Viggers, Peter 229, 261

Waddington, David 203, 274, 283, 294
wages councils 238, 241, 252
Wakeham, John 136, 160, 170, 174, 266, 317,
  386, 415
  Brighton bomb 127–9
  Chief Whip 121, 326
  dismissal 436–7
  Leader of the House 202, 247
  PMQs 255
  televising Parliament 256
Wakeham, Roberta 125, 128, 129
Waldegrave, William 291, 360, 496, 533, 547
Walden, Brian 160, 284
Walesa, Lech 289
Walker, Peter 39, 47, 79, 122, 124, 164–5, 202,
  214, 412
Walters, Alan 34, 35, 268, 282–3, 422
Weatherill, Jack 109

Webster, Philip 216, 295, 472
Weinberg, Mark 123, 133, 218
welfare state 100, 138, 196, 543
Wells, John 82
Wenham, Brian 126
West Midlands 107, 120, 165, 166, 168, 193, 196,
  224, 239, 368, 479
Westland 151–61, 165, 166, 175, 176, 209, 227,
  231, 249, 283
'Wets' 32, 72, 312, 315
White, Michael 19, 99, 294, 498
Whitelaw, Willie 15, 20, 21, 35, 42, 45, 128, 137,
  142, 149, 158–9, 171, 225, 249, 286, 289
  Aids crisis 166, 174, 177, 182
  Deputy Prime Minster 275
  Falklands 76
  government buildings 175
  legislative programme 119
  public spending 212
  retirement 214, 215, 244
  Star Chamber 58, 212
  stroke 214
Whitley council, the 66, 88, 104
Whitmore, Clive 49, 50, 61, 211
Whitney, Ray 72, 121, 149
Wicks, Nigel 166–7, 172, 175, 184
Widdecombe, Ann 549–50
Willetts, David 133, 199
Williams, Shirley 43, 63, 105, 332, 415
Willis, Norman 204, 206, 233, 289
Wilson, Harold 54, 236, 237, 512
Wilson, Reggie 264
'wobbly Thursday' 191, 198, 199, 226, 286, 359,
  371
Wolfson, Brian 242, 292, 367
Woodward, Admiral Sandy 80
World Health Organization 181, 235
World in Action 90, 91
Wright, Peter 180
Wyatt, Woodrow 176

Yeltsin, Boris 338, 462
Yeo, Tim 470, 471, 473, 474, 476, 477, 485, 488
Young, David 148, 159, 194, 202, 204, 206, 210,
  211, 226–7, 234, 285–6, 302
Young, George 50, 170
Younger, George 35, 39, 58, 69, 128, 153–4, 179,
  182, 242, 260, 279, 292, 307, 334
Youth Training Scheme (YTS) 213